ALWAYS GOOD SHIPS
by William A. Fox

William A. Fox

This is number **1443**
of a Limited Edition of 1,500.

ALWAYS GOOD SHIPS

GOOD

SHIPS

HISTORIES OF NEWPORT NEWS SHIPS

THE BATTLESHIP USS INDIANA

ALWAYS GOOD SHIPS

HISTORIES OF NEWPORT NEWS SHIPS

USS NEWPORT NEWS, 1949

by William A. Fox

Foreword by Alexander Crosby Brown
Designed by Sharon Varner Moyer

THE
DONNING COMPANY
PUBLISHERS
NORFOLK/VIRGINIA BEACH

The Donning Company/Publishers
5659 Virginia Beach Boulevard
Norfolk, Virginia 23502

Library of Congress Cataloging-in-Publication Data

Fox, William A., 1943-
 Always good ships.

 Bibliography: p.
 Includes index.
 1. Newport News Shipbuilding and Drydock Company—
History. 2. Shipbuilding—Virginia—Newport News—
History. 3. Ships—Virginia-Newport News—History.
4. Newport News (Va.)—History, Naval. I. Title.
VM301.N79F69   1986   338.4′76238′09755416   86-16511
ISBN 0-89865-500-5 Limited Edition
ISBN 0-89865-498-X Trade Edition

Printed in the United States of America

CONTENTS

S.S. UNITED STATES, 1952

Photo by Bill Radcliffe

FOREWORD

Newport News native William A. Fox, born in 1943 some years after local promoters proclaimed to the world that this was the "World's Greatest Harbor," expectedly came naturally on his all-consuming enthusiasm for the sea and ships. Not only is his profession now maritime-related, but as a hobby he has dedicated himself to marine research and the production of scholarly articles on various facets of shipping and shipbuilding. Indeed, for most people who read the papers hereabouts, he needs no further introduction for he has been contributing chapters of this book piecemeal to the Sunday *Daily Press* every week. They present biographical sketches of the some 500 ships built here over the past century.

In its various publications, Newport News Shipbuilding has already presented listings of the various vessels which began their careers in the waters of the James River. What happened to them since is another matter, however. Naval architect Bill Fox's perserverence has contrived to reveal all facets of their subsequent careers—where they went, what they did, and how long they survived. For the most part, their illustrious records serve to point out that his title for the book, *Always Good Ships*, is no misnomer.

When Collis P. Huntington elected to build a shipyard in 1886 to serve the world's greatest harbor, he determined that it should be known the world over for the quality of its products. In 1916 this business philosophy was distilled by then shipyard president Homer L. Ferguson for the so-called Shipyard Monument, now reposing by the entrance to the Mariners' Museum here. This specified for his ship builders in no uncertain terms that there should be no scrimping on the product—profit or loss should be minor considerations as long as Good Ships were the result.

Bill Fox tells this exceptionally well.

ALEXANDER CROSBY BROWN

DOROTHY, APRIL 1891

PREFACE

During the past century, some of the world's greatest and most historic ships were built at Newport News. This, while not the first book on the subject, is a comprehensive work on the careers of approximately 500 merchant and naval vessels built at the shipyard since its founding in 1886. Following my involvement with the restoration of tug DOROTHY (Newport News Hull No. 1) in 1976, I continued with research into the stories of first, the tugs, then others, until the total reached 500 ships. This total generally includes self-propelled vessels only and not the 140-or-so barges, dry dock gates, caissons, and other structures which were once given hull numbers. I now have the great pleasure and satisfaction of sharing these stories with readers interested in Newport News ships and shipbuilders and in their contributions to maritime history.

This book begins with a brief general history of the shipyard which describes its rise from construction of tugs DOROTHY and EL TORO in 1891 to the awesome NIMITZ-class aircraft carriers and LOS ANGELES-class submarines of the 1980s. Vessel histories and photographs follow, with merchant ships first, then naval types. Entries are arranged in order of hull number by type of ship, except where several sister ships are grouped together or where required for efficient design of the book. The photographs are of special interest since virtually all are from shipyard archives, and many have never before been published. Appendices include a References listing and a Hull List by type of ship. The Ship Name Index concludes the book.

Data given in the detailed histories and in the Hull List are generally based on "Particulars of Ships Built at the Newport News Shipbuilding and Dry Dock Co.," an unpublished tabular listing maintained for years by the shipyard's Hull Technical Department. Physical data describe the particulars of each vessel at the time of its delivery or commissioning and, especially for naval ships, may not be the same as operating or ultimate characteristics. Each ship's name and classification is that at the time of delivery or commissioning and subsequent names and classifications are given in the text. Dimensions given in feet are length overall, maximum beam, and depth to main deck; and displacement in long tons is that as measured at the shipyard. It was not possible to determine the deadweight tonnage (DWT) for every tanker, so only full load displacement is given in some cases. Armament for naval vessels is generally main battery only, as commissioned, but may be more detailed for smaller ships. Horsepower and speed are usually design values at time of completion, not trial results or maximum attained, and submerged speeds for submarines are given in parentheses. Propulsion is single-screw unless otherwise indicated.

Sources for the data and histories presented here are listed in the References appendix or are apparent from the Acknowledgments. Major sources for merchant ships include news articles and histories from shipyard publications, U.S. Coast Guard official documents and vessel listings, Lloyd's Register of Shipping publications, the splendid Eldredge Collection at the Mariners' Museum, and a number of published histories. For naval vessels, the Dictionary of American Naval Fighting Ships; shipyard publications; Jane's Fighting Ships; ships' histories at the Naval Historical Center; and published histories were primarily used. Much of the work in writing this book consisted of either sorting through dozens of sources for consistent information on the important ships or locating even a single reliable source for the less important ones. I hope that the result has been a concise and accurate career history for each Newport News ship.

Extensive research and correspondence over the past five years have yielded the almost-complete record of subsequent names and ultimate dispositions of Newport News ships which appear in the text. Dispositions of a few have eluded me, and it has been necessary to give their last known service or location instead of their ultimate fate. I would greatly appreciate hearing from readers who can fill in the gaps so that the listing can be completed. In a work of this magnitude, using many often-conflicting sources, errors creep in which no amount of research can reveal. I would, therefore, also be grateful to hear from readers regarding any apparent error, as long as the source of their information is identified, so that correc- tions can be made for any future editions.

I sincerely hope that after a few pages the reader will share my enthusiasm for the stories of Newport News ships and that this book will be read, referred to, and enjoyed by shipbuilders and others for years to come.

William A. Fox

1892

ACKNOWLEDGMENTS

Here at last is my opportunity to thank properly the many individuals and organizations who gave help and encouragement so that this book could become a reality. This is a formidable task as this book represents the collective contributions of a number of authors, photographers, institutions and organizations, companies, and individuals, both contemporary and historical.

The many authors who contributed are acknowledged by their inclusion in the References section of this book, but I owe a special debt to Howard J. Balison; Alexander C. Brown; Elwin M. Eldredge; Robert B. Hopkins; George C. Mason; and Edward O. Smith. These men were writing about Newport News ships before I learned to write at all. Photographers include Lloyd Everton; E.P. Griffith; B.J. Nixon; and William T. Radcliffe; as well as the shipyard's current staff, headed by Stuart F. Gilman, who took many and printed all of the fine illustrations used in this book.

Kenneth R. Hall of the National Archives was patient with my requests for official documents for hundreds of merchant vessels, while Robert J. Cressman and Raymond A. Mann at the Naval Historical Center allowed me to work for days with the Ships Histories Branch files on naval ships. My research work was greatly facilitiated by Katherine B. Braig, Roger T. Crew, Paul B. Hensley, Ardie L. Kelly and Charlotte B. Valentine of the Mariners' Museum Library. Steamship Historical Society of America members William A. Clark, Harry Cotterell, Jr., Rev. Raymond M. Donahue, Peter T. Eisele, Capt. William Frappier, Alan Frazer, Prof. John H. Kemble, Charles Luffbary, Jim Murray, Edward A. Mueller, John H. Shaum, Jr., James L. Shaw, James Stewart, James Wilson and Graham T. Wilson provided me with a wealth of vessel information themselves and led me to many other sources. Paul V. Ackerman, Robert A. Bryan, George L. Clark, and the late Charles W. Schumacher of the Maritime Administration provided statistics and data cards on both merchant and military ships in the reserve fleets. Dr. Robert Scheina, Historian of the Coast Guard, sent histories of seven cutters from his files; Branch Chief Eleanor P. Fischer provided information on dispositions of nine vessels; Lt. Martha Maurer-Jennis of MSO Hampton Roads helped by providing vessel data from Coast Guard files. Martin K. Gordon of the Army Corps of Engineers' Historical Division shared his files on dredges and tugs and Philip F. Baumgardner of Jacksonville District helped with information on the elusive Hull 13. Others to whom I am indebted are Dorothy Becker and Jean Hood of Lloyd's Register of Shipping; Vladimir S. Bortsov of the USSR Ministry of Merchant Marine; Cdr. W.G.M.H. Canisus, RNN; Mr. Julio Chanson of the Government of Panama; Capt. Enrique G. Lonzieme of Museo Naval at Buenos Aires; Mr. Kaoru Saito of the Museum of Maritime Science at Tokyo; and to all those who, whether they had information or not, took my calls and answered my letters.

At Newport News Shipbuilding Phyllis Kyle Stephenson provided photographs and encouragement throughout this project, as she did for my work for DOROTHY ten years ago, while Dalton Barham, Deborah Chapman, and Emma Pittman helped with archival information and photographs. Other corporate assistance came from John W. Halpin and D.V. Reardon of American President Lines, Bill Condon and Bill Cahill of Bisso Towboat Co., D. Kaparis of Chandris Line, Jim Stewart of El Paso Marine, Lars Swanberg of Svenska Esso A.B., Bonnie L. Rodney of Exxon Corp., Robert X. Caldwell and Dwight W. Koops of Exxon Shipping Co., Capt. Edgar F. Carpenter of Harbor Towing & Docking Co., J. Argitis and Capt. Nicolaos Xagoraris of Hellenic Telecommunications Organization, David L. Schrock of Interocean Management Corp., Ho Moon Yoo of Korea Dredging Corp., Bill Withers of Sabine Towing & Transportation Co., Anita McGurn of Texaco, Messrs. Utanc and Zergecit of Turkish Maritime Lines, and J.T. Strempek of United States Lines. All were most helpful in relating their operating experiences with Newport News ships and in providing information from their files.

A great many individuals helped, both directly and indirectly, and these include Alexander C. Brown, Robert H. Burgess, and John L. Lochhead who have taught, encouraged, and advised me for many years. Among the many others who offered information and assistance were Dewitt D. Barlow, Jr., Bernard L. Denny, W.J. Harahan, Steven Lang, Ben Livermon, Fraser M. McKee, Col. William C. Rogers, Capt. Jesse Simpkins, Zinovy Slonimsky, George Vickery, and Paul Wilkins. Special thanks go to Barbara Evans, who patiently typed most of the manuscript from handwritten drafts and made many corrections without a whimper of complaint. Thanks also to Connie Jarvis, Jane Gray, and Connie Hayden who typed, advised, and processed thousands of words for me. My friend Susan Pongratz worked against an impossible deadline to copy edit this book and deserves credit for making it more readable. Ten years late, thanks to Andrea DiNoto for giving me encouragement and my start as a writer.

Without the patience of Mary and Chris, dear wife and stepson, this book would not have been completed. They helped and advised with the text and put up with my moods and late-night noise for almost five years to make it possible.

Finally, I dedicate this book to my parents, Katherine and Erwin Fox, who gave me their love of ships and history and encouraged me to share it with others.

1960

INTRODUCTION

Founded by Collis Potter Huntington in 1886, the Newport News Shipbuilding and Dry Dock Co. quickly became a major builder of ships for the Navy and for commercial customers. The village of Newport News had previously been chosen by Huntington as the eastern terminus of his Chesapeake and Ohio Railway, and he had the vision to realize that a large shipyard would be an asset to business in the port. The new enterprise was granted a charter as the Chesapeake Dry Dock and Construction Co. by the Virginia General Assembly on January 28, 1886, and opened its first dry dock to the monitor PURITAN on April 24, 1889.

Gaining experience with the reconstruction of the wrecked steamer KIMBERLEY in 1890, Newport News shipbuilders were awarded their first construction contract, for the tug DOROTHY, on April 25 of that year. Also in 1890 the shipyard's name was changed to its present one, and in July, contracts for a second tug and for two large cargo steamers were signed. Named EL SUD and EL NORTE, the two 7,400-ton steamers were delivered to the Morgan Line in 1892, and their success helped establish the reputation of the yard for building good ships. The second tug, named EL TORO, was also built for the Morgan Line and went on to serve for more than 50 years in the Navy. Two more cargo steamers were delivered in 1893 and, with their two previous sisters, saw naval service as auxiliary cruisers in the Spanish-American War.

In January 1894 Newport News was awarded its first naval contracts; for gunboats NASHVILLE (PG-7), WILMINGTON (PG-8), and HELENA (PG-9). By the end of 1900, the yard had completed battleships KEARSARGE (BB-5) and KENTUCKY (BB-6) and had established itself as a major naval shipbuilder. More battleships followed, and six of the sixteen in the Great White Fleet of 1909 were Newport News-built. Eight submarines were built for Simon Lake between 1904 and 1912: six were sold to Russia, and the last two joined the Navy as G-1 (SS-19-½) and G-2 (SS-27). By 1920 Newport News had built 11 battleships, five cruisers, the two submarines, 30 destroyers, three gunboats, a monitor, eight oilers, and two colliers for the Navy, representing over 20 percent of its total tonnage. During the early years, Newport News also built a number of outstanding merchant ships, including giant liners KOREA and SIBERIA of 1902; tankers CHARLES PRATT and five of her class from 1916 to 1918; and a large fleet of cargo ships, auxiliaries, and service craft which brought hull numbers up to 250 before 1920.

After the burst of activity brought on by World War I, business slowed at the shipyard to the point that its survival was in doubt. Guided through the lean years by president Homer L. Ferguson, the yard survived the Naval Holiday with a greatly reduced work force which contented itself with rebuilding the liner LEVIATHAN and building new coastal liners, yachts, industrial products, and even railroad cars. Manufacture of hydraulic turbines and other heavy industrial equipment during this period helped diversify the company into other fields which remain as a large portion of its business today.

Giant liners CALIFORNIA, VIRGINIA, PENNSYLVANIA, PRESIDENT HOOVER, and PRESIDENT COOLIDGE brought the lean 1920s to a close and ushered in the 1930s with the promise of new naval shipbuilding. Cruisers HOUSTON (CA-30) and AUGUSTA (CA-31) and aircraft carrier RANGER (CV-4) were the first naval newbuildings at the yard in almost ten years. Before Pearl Harbor, Newport News had delivered three more carriers, two more cruisers, and two destroyers to the Navy.

In 1940 the shipyard was sold by the Huntington family and stock was offered to the public; while in that same year a major plant expansion was begun in anticipation of war production, and the famous liner AMERICA was completed.

During World War II, employment at Newport

News rose to over 31,000 and a subsidiary, North Carolina Shipbuilding Co., employed 21,000 more and produced 243 merchant ships. The shipyard itself concentrated on naval work and built 47 fighting ships including nine ESSEX-class carriers, battleship INDIANA (BB-58), eight cruisers, 11 LSDs, and 16 LSTs. Fully 185 Newport News ships served during the war, including 89 naval ships, and they carried such famous names as YORKTOWN, ENTERPRISE, HORNET, ESSEX, INTREPID, FRANKLIN, and HOUSTON into battle for the Allied cause.

After the war, MIDWAY (CV-41), CORAL SEA (CV-43), and NEWPORT NEWS (CA-148) were completed, but many naval contracts were cancelled and the shipyard occupied itself with postwar conversions and repairs. A huge boom in tanker construction began in 1949 and continued for 15 years, during which 45 ships were delivered to commercial customers.

One of Newport News shipbuilders' proudest products, superliner UNITED STATES, was completed in 1952 and, joining AMERICA on the North Atlantic, set new speed records on that route which still stand. The shipyard designed and built the Navy's first postwar aircraft carrier FORRESTAL (CV-59) and delivered her sisters RANGER (CV-61), AMERICA (CV-66), and JOHN F. KENNEDY (CV-67) during the 1950s and 1960s.

Newport News began nuclear shipbuilding with Fleet Ballistic Missile submarine ROBERT E. LEE (SSBN-601), delivered in 1961, and continued with SHARK (SSN-591) and the superlative carrier ENTERPRISE (CVAN-65). During the 1960s, 14 FBM submarines and seven attack submarines were delivered to the Navy, and 14 modern cargo liners were completed for merchant owners.

Independent since its founding in 1886, the shipyard was purchased in 1968 by Tenneco, Inc., a multiindustry corporation based in Houston. In subsequent years the new owner was to effect significant plant improvements and bring increased profitability to the yard's operations. In the 1970s Newport News designed and produced five LOS ANGELES (SSN-688)-class attack submarines and nuclear carriers NIMITZ (CVN-68) and DWIGHT D. EISENHOWER (CVN-69). A major plant expansion in this decade added a huge 900-ton gantry crane and a 1300-ft graving dock which were intended for an expected tanker-building boom. Five large merchant ships including three EL PASO SOUTHERN-class LNG carriers and two 397,140 DWT U.S.T. ATLANTIC-class tankers were constructed before the expected boom fizzled, and the new facility was dedicated to carrier construction in the early 1980s.

Nuclear carrier CARL VINSON (CVN-70) was delivered in 1982, and production of SSN-688-class submarines continued until the total completed or under contract reached 21 in 1985. A contract was awarded for THEODORE ROOSEVELT (CVN-71) in September 1980, and on December 27, 1982, the largest shipbuilding contract in history, for carriers ABRAHAM LINCOLN (CVN-72) and GEORGE WASHINGTON (CVN-73), was obtained.

In anticipation of their centennial in 1986, yard workers laid the keel for attack submarine NEWPORT NEWS (SSN-750) in 1984 as their numbers grew to World War II levels. The unoffical yard slogan "Always Good Ships," attributed to its founder, endured as they accepted the challenge of their huge backlog and continued to produce ships as worthy as those built by four generations before them.

1979

PASSENGER SHIPS
LA GRANDE DUCHESSE
1899

LA GRANDE DUCHESSE

Hull No: 15
Owner: Plant Investment Co.
Launched: January 30, 1896
Delivered: April 9, 1899
Dimensions: 404 x 47.67 x 36.5 ft
Gross Tonnage: 5,017
Displacement: 5,780 tons
Machinery: Quadruple Expansion Engines,
    4 Boilers, Twin Screw
Horsepower/Speed: 6,820/17 knots
Fate: War Loss, 1918

LA GRANDE DUCHESSE was the first passenger vessel constructed by the shipyard and she had a number of birthing pains. Through difficulties in getting her owners to accept her at completion, the yard lost $536,000: more than her contract price. Her owner was Henry B. Plant of the Plant Investment Co., which also ordered SOMMERS N. SMITH and MARGARET. Mr. Plant sowed the seeds of disaster when he insisted on water-tube boilers for LA GRANDE DUCHESSE instead of the more conventional fire-tube type.

The graceful new ship with the lovely name was christened by Miss Nellie S. Eldridge of Boston on January 30, 1896. After completion and three local trial trips, the new ship sailed for New York on November 28, 1896, but was refused by the Plant Co. and returned to the yard in May 1897. After adjustments, she again sailed in September 1897 but was returned in the spring of 1898 to have her boilers replaced with fire-tube boilers built at the yard.

After successful trials in June 1898, she was chartered by the government for transport service in the Spanish-American War. After the war her owners still would not accept her until April 9, 1899, over three years after her launch!

In November 1901 she passed to the Ocean Steamship Co. and was renamed CITY OF SAVANNAH. She was in coastal service between New York and Charleston, SC, with occasional trips to the West Indies.

In January 1906 she was sold to the New York and Porto Rico Steamship Co. and was renamed CAROLINA. She was extensively remodeled at Newport News in 1914 as Hull 172 (q.v.) and re-entered service as a single screw vessel on March 1, 1914. After four more years of service she was torpedoed by a German submarine on June 2, 1918, off the mouth of Delaware Bay. Of 333 on board, only 13 persons were lost.

CREOLE
1896

CREOLE

Hull No: 16
Owner: Cromwell Steamship Co.
Launched: August 8, 1896
Delivered: December 5, 1896
Dimensions: 375 x 44 x 32.5 ft
Gross Tonnage: 3,801
Displacement: 6,000 tons
Machinery: Triple Expansion Engine,
    3 Boilers
Horsepower/Speed: 3,228/15 knots
Fate: Scrapped, 1930

CREOLE was the shipyard's second passenger ship, and she was the first of three ships built for the Cromwell Steamship Co. CREOLE was christened by Miss Edith Fitzgerald, daughter of the general inspector for the Plant Investment Co. ships. The new ship entered service with Cromwell late in 1896, making regular runs between New York and New Orleans.

In April 1898 she was sold to the Navy, converted to a hospital ship in 16 days at the shipyard, and renamed SOLACE (AH-2). She was the first U.S. ship to fly the Geneva Red Cross Flag, and her white hull and the red cross on her stack were distinctive. She saw extensive service during the Spanish-American War, returning wounded troops from Cuba to East Coast ports. She brought 400 wounded Spanish prisoners to Norfolk after the Battle of Santiago, and after the war she served the Navy in worldwide service.

In 1909 her superstructure was considerably enlarged and this, coupled with her narrow beam, made her prone to rolling in heavy seas. Around 1913, it was rumored that 200 Civil War cannons embedded in concrete were placed in her hold to counteract this roll making her the "most heavily gunned ship in the Navy."

After World War I service with the Atlantic Fleet, SOLACE was decommissioned and laid up at the Philadelphia Navy Yard on July 20, 1921. She was stricken from the Navy list on August 6, 1930, and sold for scrap.

COMUS
1900

COMUS

Hull No: 28
Owner: Cromwell Steamship Co.
Launched: November 9, 1899
Delivered: April 28, 1900
Dimensions: 405.75 x 48 x 33.75 ft
Gross Tonnage: 4,828
Displacement: 7,360 tons
Machinery: Triple Expansion Engine,
   3 Boilers
Horsepower/Speed: 3,800/15 knots
Fate: Scrapped, 1934

COMUS was the shipyard's third passenger vessel, and she was built for the Cromwell Steamship Co. about three years after CREOLE. COMUS was larger than CREOLE and was similar to the 12 Morgan Line cargo steamers built at the yard at that time.

She was christened by Miss Josephine A. Rohrer, daughter of the executive officer of the battleship KENTUCKY, then being built at the yard. COMUS was delivered on April 28, 1900, and took up service with Cromwell between New York and New Orleans. In 1902 she was sold to the Southern Pacific Co. but kept her name. Her career was routine, except that she rammed and sank a coal barge off Atlantic Highlands, NJ, in July 1916 while en route from New York to New Orleans.

In December 1929 she was sold to the North American Fruit and Steamship Co. and was renamed WESTERN OCEAN. In August 1930 she passed to the Midland Steamship Corp. of New York. In June 1934 her papers were surrendered at New York and she was sold and scrapped at Baltimore.

PROTEUS
1900

PROTEUS

Hull No: 29
Owner: Cromwell Steamship Co.
Launched: December 16, 1899
Delivered: June 6, 1900
Dimensions: 405.75 x 48 x 33.75 ft
Gross Tonnage: 4,836
Displacement: 7,360 tons
Machinery: Triple Expansion Engine,
    3 Boilers
Horsepower/Speed: 3,800/15 knots
Fate: Collision, 1918

Not to be confused with the naval collier of the same name delivered by the yard in 1913, PROTEUS was built for the Cromwell Steamship Co. and was the sister ship of COMUS. PROTEUS was christened on December 16, 1899, by Miss Pauline Antoinette Rearick, daughter of the Navy's senior inspector of machinery at the yard.

The new ship was quickly fitted out since she was also similar to the Morgan Line ships built at the yard, and she entered Cromwell's New York to New Orleans service in the spring of 1900. With her sister, she was sold to the Southern Pacific Co. in 1902, retaining her name.

In October 1914 she lost her propeller in the Gulf of Mexico, beginning a series of mishaps which were to lead to her early demise. In January 1916 she collided with the British steamer BRABRANT in New York harbor and apparently was not heavily damaged. She ran aground near the mouth of the Mississippi in November 1917 but again was not heavily damaged. Her luck ran out 30 miles south of Diamond Shoals, NC, on August 18, 1918, when she collided with the steamer CUSHING and subsequently sank. CUSHING was not seriously damaged and stood by to save all but one of the 95 persons who had been aboard PROTEUS.

KOREA
1902

KOREA

Hull No: 31
Owner: Pacific Mail Steamship Co.
Launched: March 23, 1901
Delivered: June 17, 1902
Dimensions: 571.42 x 63 x 40 ft
Gross Tonnage: 11,276
Displacement: 18,360 tons
Machinery: Quadruple Expansion Engines,
    8 Boilers, Twin Screw
Horsepower/Speed: 1,800/18 knots
Fate: Scrapped, 1934

KOREA was the first of two fine large passenger ships built for the Pacific Mail Steamship Co. in 1901-1902, and she and sister SIBERIA were the largest ships built in the United States up to that time. KOREA had extremely powerful engines for her day which propelled her at a fast 18 knots.

KOREA was christened by Miss Katherine Winthrop Tweed, daughter of the shipyard's New York counsel, and the launch drew a sizeable crowd befitting the largest ship ever launched in America.

During outfitting, KOREA was fitted with two enormous funnels, each measuring an extraordinary 108 feet from grate to top. Her passenger accommodations were fitted out in fine style, incorporating all the improvements in fireproofing known at the time. Most notably, she had an ornately molded main staircase of solid bronze and a minimum of wood trim.

KOREA left the yard on June 18, 1902, bound for San Francisco via Cape Horn with coaling stops at Montevideo and Valparaiso. She arrived 54 days later and took up service between San Francisco and Hong Kong with intermediate stops.

She continued in routine service with Pacific Mail and later with Atlantic Transport Co. without incident until being damaged in a collision with the German steamer SOPHIA off the English coast in December 1915. She was repaired but in July 1916 was sold to Toyo Kisen Kaisha of Yokohama, transferred to Japanese flag, and renamed KOREA MARU. She served T.K.K. until 1926, then passed to the ownership of Nippon Yusen Kaisha, continuing to sail under this name until being broken up for scrap in 1934.

SIBERIA
1902

SIBERIA

Hull No: 32
Owner: Pacific Mail Steamship Co.
Launched: October 19, 1901
Delivered: November 19, 1902
Dimensions: 571.42 x 63 x 40 ft
Gross Tonnage: 11,284
Displacement: 17,940 tons
Machinery: Quadruple Expansion Engines,
    8 Boilers, Twin Screw
Horsepower/Speed: 1,800/18 knots
Fate: Scrapped, 1934

Sister ship to KOREA, SIBERIA was christened on October 19, 1901, by Miss Belle Norwood Tyler, daughter of the governor of Virginia. SIBERIA and her sister were considered among the finest steamships afloat when she was delivered in November 1902. Fireproofing was extensive and included iron beds, slate and rubber tile deck coverings and, like KOREA, a solid bronze stairway. The tradition of heavy carved panels and molding was maintained by the use of fireproof composition panels which closely resembled wood, and elegant decoration was thus achieved.

The completed SIBERIA set sail for San Francisco from New York on December 18, 1902. She entered service between San Francisco and Hong Kong with stops at Hawaii and other Pacific ports. Sailing with Pacific Mail and, after 1915, with Atlantic Transport Co., she was never known to have suffered a serious casualty during her worldwide service.

With KOREA, she was sold to Toyo Kisen Kaisha in 1916 and transferred to Japanese ownership. She served this owner and later Nippon Ysen Kaisha under the name SIBERIA MARU before being broken up for scrap in 1934.

MONROE
1903

MONROE

Hull No: 42
Owner: Old Dominion Steamship Co.
Launched: October 18, 1902
Delivered: April 3, 1903
Dimensions: 366 x 46 x 37 ft
Gross Tonnage: 4,704
Displacement: 5,375 tons
Machinery: Triple Expansion Engine,
   6 Boilers
Horsepower/Speed: 4,500/15.5 knots
Fate: Collision, 1914

The next passenger ship delivered after the large twins KOREA and SIBERIA was the much smaller MONROE, built for the Old Dominion Steamship Co. of New York for service between that city and Hampton Roads. The MONROE was a slender and graceful vessel with accommodations for 144 cabin passengers, 78 in steerage, 57 deck passengers, and 81 officers and crew.

She was christened on October 18, 1902, by Mrs. Andrew Jackson Montague, wife of the governor of Virginia. MONROE was the largest and most luxurious vessel in her owner's fleet when delivered in April 1903. She entered routine service between New York and Hampton Roads ports, providing convenient and comfortable service on that route.

In December 1906 she collided with the Newport News-built battleship VIRGINIA in Hampton Roads. Though found at fault, she was not seriously damaged and continued her routine service. She was not so lucky, however, when she collided in dense fog with the steamer NANTUCKET on January 30, 1914, about 25 miles southeast of Hog Island, VA. Heavily damaged, she sank taking 41 of her 138 passengers and crew with her.

BRAZOS
1907

BRAZOS

Hull No: 65
Owner: New York and Texas Steamship Co.
Launched: June 29, 1907
Delivered: November 6, 1907
Dimensions: 416.5 x 54 x 37 ft
Gross Tonnage: 6,399
Displacement: 9,200 tons
Machinery: Quadruple Expansion Engines,
    8 Boilers, Twin Screw
Horsepower/Speed: 6,250/15.5 knots
Fate: Scrapped, 1934

Passenger and cargo ship BRAZOS was built for the New York and Texas Steamship Co. (Mallory Line) for service between New York and Galveston. BRAZOS was christened by Miss Hally B. Bryan, great-granddaughter of Moses Austin who pioneered the settlement of Texas by Americans.

The new ship was of medium size by 1907 standards, but her interiors were little short of lavish. She featured a grand staircase of traditional style, which featured an elaborate carved clock at its middle landing. Her dining saloon was furnished with heavy wooden swivel chairs with velvet padding and had dark wood paneling and shutters over the portholes. Her smoking room was done with heavy wooden pillars and railings with heavy furniture in the style of a tavern parlor.

Delivered on November 6, 1907, she made her maiden voyage from New York to Galveston shortly thereafter. In 1916 she was involved in two incidents: the first when she collided with the steamer SUFFOLK off Barnegat, NJ, and was forced to return to New York and the other when she had a hold fire in her cargo of hay off New York. Neither of these incidents was serious, but BRAZOS was sold to the New York and Porto Rico Steamship Co. the next year and was renamed SAN LORENZO. After over 16 years of routine service with this owner, she was sold to an Italian breaker and was scrapped in 1934.

LURLINE
1908

LURLINE

Hull No: 81
Owner: Matson Navigation Co.
Launched: January 11, 1908
Delivered: March 18, 1908
Dimensions: 437 x 53 x 33.5 ft
Gross Tonnage: 5,929
Displacement: 12,100 tons
Machinery: Triple Expansion Engine,
    4 Boilers
Horsepower/Speed: 3,500/14.5 knots
Fate: Scrapped, 1953

Cargo and passenger steamer LURLINE was the first of four such ships of different designs built at Newport News for the Matson Navigation Co. between 1908 and 1913. The shipyard also built the cargo vessels HAWAIIAN PLANTER and HAWAIIAN PACKER for Matson in 1941 and extensively remodeled their liner MATSONIA in 1957.

LURLINE was a passenger vessel of medium size and was the first steamer built for the Matson line.

She was christened on January 11, 1908, by her namesake, Miss Lurline Matson, daughter of Captain William Matson who was the line's founder and president. LURLINE was built to carry a considerable amount of cargo and had modest accommodations for 84 passengers.

The new ship entered service between San Francisco and Hawaii in the summer of 1908 and remained there for over twenty years. She had an apparently spotless record, except for being damaged by grounding off Makapuu Point, Hawaii, in October 1916.

Taken over by the U.S. Shipping Board during World War I, she made nine trips to Honolulu and three to Manila before being returned to Matson in January 1919. In 1928 she was sold to the Alaska Packers Associates, renamed CHIRIKOF, and placed in the fishery trade supporting canneries and carrying passengers and cargo.

In the late 1930s she was again in the passenger and freight trade where she stayed until after Army transport service in World War II. She was sold to Yugoslavian owners in 1947, was renamed RADNICK, and served in Mediterranean waters until being scrapped in 1953.

WILHELMINA
1909

WILHELMINA

Hull No: 121
Owner: Matson Navigation Co.
Launched: September 18, 1909
Delivered: December 7, 1909
Dimensions: 451 x 54 x 33.5 ft
Gross Tonnage: 6,974
Displacement: 11,350 tons
Machinery: Quadruple Expansion Engine,
    6 Boilers
Horsepower/Speed: 5,500/16.5 knots
Fate: War Loss, 1940

Passenger and cargo ship WILHELMINA was the second vessel built by the yard for Matson, and she had cabins for 147 first class passengers, considerably more than LURLINE. She was christened by her namesake, Miss Wilhelmina Tenney, daughter of Matson's vice president, on September 18, 1909. WILHELMINA was built for the San Francisco-Hawaii route, and, like LURLINE, her appearance was distinctive since her machinery and single stack were installed well aft.

She served Matson without incident until she was taken over by the Navy in 1918 and placed into war transport service. She was considered one of the busiest transports of World War I, and she survived the war intact after carrying over 22,000 troops to and from Europe.

She was returned to Matson in August 1919 and continued between San Francisco and Hawaii. Laid up in March 1932, she was sold to Lockinver Ltd. of Glasgow in May 1940. In convoy service bound for Halifax, Nova Scotia, she was torpedoed and sunk by the German submarine U-94 in the North Atlantic off Iceland on December 2, 1940.

BEAR
1910

BEAR

Hull No: 125
Owner: Union Pacific Railroad Co.
Launched: October 16, 1909
Delivered: January 23, 1910
Dimensions: 380 x 47 x 34 ft
Gross Tonnage: 4,507
Displacement: 5,970 tons
Machinery: Triple Expansion Engine,
   6 Boilers
Horsepower/Speed: 4,000/15 knots
Fate: Stranded, 1916

BEAR and BEAVER were two identical passenger and cargo ships of medium size built for the Union Pacific Railroad in 1910. They were handsome vessels with a long superstructure and a single large funnel amidships, and they had accommodations for 273 first class and 300 second class passengers and 79 crew. BEAR was christened by Miss Allene Wiley Willet of Newport News on October 16, 1909, and was delivered on January 23, 1910.

The career of this fine new ship was to be short-lived. She was placed in coastal service between San Francisco and Portland early in 1910 and was operated by the San Francisco and Portland Steamship Co. BEAR's service was without incident until, on June 14, 1911, she stranded in fog near the mouth of the Bear River, Humboldt County, CA, and was wrecked. Of her 212 San Francisco-bound passengers and crew, five were lost. Attempts to salvage her were futile except that one of her boilers was recovered and then sold and shipped to Shanghai.

BEAVER
1910

BEAVER

Hull No: 126
Owner: Union Pacific Railroad Co.
Launched: November 27, 1909
Delivered: February 13, 1910
Dimensions: 380 x 47 x 34 ft
Gross Tonnage: 4,507
Displacement: 5,970 tons
Machinery: Triple Expansion Engine,
    6 Boilers
Horsepower/Speed: 4,000/15 knots
Fate: Scrapped, 1952

Delivered only a few weeks after BEAR, BEAVER was to enjoy a much longer and more varied career than her sister ship. BEAVER was christened by Miss Anna Barret Manville of Newport News on November 27, 1909, and was quickly completed by mid-February 1910. She sailed from New York for Portland and stopped at Montevideo and Coronel for coal, arriving after 55 days on April 29.

She entered service with the San Francisco and Portland Steamship Co. and served without major incident, except for a collision with the steamer NECANICUM off the California coast in November 1913. Repaired, she continued until sold to the Navy in 1918 and converted to a submarine tender (AS-5). She served on the Pacific coast until 1921 when she became flagship for Submarine Flotilla 3 based at Portsmouth, NH.

In late 1921 and 1922, she operated on Asiatic Station, then operated in U.S. waters until 1925. She returned to the Far East and served in the Philippines and China until 1932. After spending the rest of the thirties at Pearl Harbor, she was modernized and joined the Atlantic fleet in 1940. She served at New London, CT, until October 1942 and then spent nine months on duty at Roseneath, Scotland. She returned to the Pacific in late 1943 and helped establish the submarine base at Attu Island, Alaska.

She sailed to San Diego in February 1944 and stayed until converted to an internal combustion engine repairship (ARG-19). She served with the U.S. Occupation Force in Japan until decommissioned on July 17, 1946. The tired old ship was transferred to the War Shipping Administration on August 5 and was laid up until she was sold for scrap in 1952.

CITY OF ST. LOUIS
1910

CITY OF ST. LOUIS

Hull No: 128
Owner: Ocean Steamship Co.
Launched: March 30, 1910
Delivered: June 15, 1910
Dimensions: 397.5 x 49.5 x 35 ft
Gross Tonnage: 5,425
Displacement: 6,815 tons
Machinery: Triple Expansion Engine,
    4 Boilers
Horsepower/Speed: 2,300/12 knots
Fate: Scrapped, 1946

CITY OF ST. LOUIS was the sister ship of CITY OF MONTGOMERY, and she was christened by Miss Louise Neugent of St. Louis on March 30, 1910, in the presence of a large crowd of spectators. Contemporary marine publications praised the arrival of the two handsome new steamers with their graceful sheer, long deckhouses, tall masts, and single tall funnels.

CITY OF ST. LOUIS apparently had a less accident-prone career than her sister, but she served on the same New York, Boston, and Savannah run until also being sold to the War Shipping Administration in May 1942 and converted to a freighter. She served in cargo service during the war and escaped torpedoing only to be scrapped at Pittsburg in 1946.

CITY OF MONTGOMERY
1910

CITY OF MONTGOMERY

Hull No: 127
Owner: Ocean Steamship Co.
Launched: February 28, 1910
Delivered: May 25, 1910
Dimensions: 397.5 x 49.5 x 35 ft
Gross Tonnage: 5,425
Displacement: 6,815 tons
Machinery: Triple Expansion Engine,
    4 Boilers
Horsepower/Speed: 2,300/12 knots
Fate: Scrapped, 1947

CITY OF MONTGOMERY was the first of two identical passenger and freight steamers built for the Ocean Steamship Co. (later Savannah Line) for service between New York, Boston, and Savannah. She was of moderate size for a coastal steamer and featured a dining saloon in the forward end of her superstructure which afforded diners a fine view of the ocean. The new ship was sponsored by Miss Helen C. Steiner of Montgomery, AL, CITY OF MONTGOMERY's namesake city.

The vessel was completed and left the yard in May 1910, beginning a long and varied career in which she was involved in several collisions, a fire, and a grounding. She collided with the schooner PERRY SETZER in a gale off Cape Hatteras in 1911 and with an Army dredge at New York in 1931.

In 1934 a fire broke out in her hold halfway between Savannah and Boston, but she raced to her destination before it got out of control. She ran aground at Boston in 1935 but was freed.

In October 1942 she was sold to the War Shipping Administration and was cut down for use as a cargo ship. She served as a freighter during World War II, then was sold for scrap in September 1947.

MADISON
1911

MADISON

Hull No: 136
Owner: Old Dominion Steamship Co.
Launched: October 8, 1910
Delivered: January 31, 1911
Dimensions: 373.58 x 42 x 35.5 ft
Gross Tonnage: 3,734
Displacement: 4,480 tons
Machinery: Triple Expansion Engine,
  4 Boilers
Horsepower/Speed: 3,600/15.75 knots
Fate: Scrapped, 1947

MADISON was built for the Old Dominion Steamship Co. for service between New York, Old Point Comfort, and Norfolk. She was slightly smaller than MONROE, Hull 42, which was built for Old Dominion in 1903. MADISON had a long superstructure, single mast, and one tall stack amidships. Her accommodations were roomy and comfortable. She was christened by Miss Fannie B. Landon, daughter of the Old Dominion Line agent in Newport News, and entered

MADISON was to enjoy a long and varied career but one marred by several accidents. In February 1912, after only a year in service, she collided with the steamer HIPPOLYTE DUMOIS off Norfolk and sank, but was raised and was repaired at the shipyard. In June 1920 she was sold to the Holland-America Line and sailed under Dutch flag with the name WARSZAWA. She returned to American ownership in 1926 with Eastern Steamship Lines and regained the name MADISON. She remained in routine coastal service, sailed for a while with the Gulf and Southern Steamship Co., then returned to Eastern Steamship Lines. She was damaged in the great hurricane of 1933 but was repaired.

Due to changing regulations regarding subdivision, she was removed from passenger service after the summer of 1936 and entered freight service. She was the smallest Newport News-built ship to be placed in troop carrying service during World War II, and she was one of 16 "Inter-Island Troop Transports" in Army service. After the war she returned to Eastern but her days were numbered and she was abandoned, then was scrapped in 1947.

LENAPE *1913*

LENAPE

Hull No: 157
Owner: Clyde Steamship Co.
Launched: August 17, 1912
Delivered: January 18, 1913
Dimensions: 399 x 50 x 30 ft
Gross Tonnage: 5,179
Displacement: 6,230 tons
Machinery: Triple Expansion Engine,
    4 Boilers
Horsepower/Speed: 3,500/14 knots
Fate: Burned, 1925

LENAPE was the first and smallest of seven passenger and cargo ships built for the Clyde Line of New York between 1912 and 1926. She had a crew of 90 and accommodations for 350 passengers, and she was built for service on the New York-Jacksonville run. Named after an Indian tribe like her Clyde sisters, LENAPE was christened by Miss Margaret Stone, daughter of Galen L. Stone, who was a director of the steamship line (and for whom the yard built the yacht ARCADIA in 1926).

Early in her career LENAPE had at least two accidents which preceded her early tragic demise. In November 1915 she ran aground ten miles below Jacksonville, and in June 1916 she collided with the steamer C.W. MORSE in the Hudson River; apparently neither of these incidents was serious. During World War I she served as a transport with both the Army and the Navy, and she made at least three trips to France with troops and equipment.

She returned to her former service with Clyde after the Armistice and sailed routinely between New York, Charleston, and Jacksonville until the night of November 18, 1925. On that chilly evening she caught fire during a trip from New York to Charleston and was totally destroyed three miles off the Delaware breakwater. Of 104 passengers aboard, only one was lost. LENAPE was later broken up for scrap.

MATSONIA
1913

MATSONIA

Hull No: 166
Owner: Matson Navigation Co.
Launched: August 16, 1913
Delivered: November 6, 1913
Dimensions: 501 x 58 x 44.75 ft
Gross Tonnage: 9,729
Displacement: 13,500 tons
Machinery: Triple Expansion Engine,
    9 Boilers
Horsepower/Speed: 8,500/16 knots
Fate: Scrapped, 1957

Largest of the four passenger ships built at the shipyard for Matson, MATSONIA featured the long superstructure and aft-located machinery and stack, which made their fleet distinctive. MATSONIA had accommodations for 242 passengers and 132 crew and was christened by Miss Lurline Matson, who had christened LURLINE at Newport News in 1908.

After serving Matson in the Pacific, MATSONIA served as a troop transport in World War I, designated SP-1589, and made a total of 14 Atlantic round trips carrying over 36,000 passengers. She was returned to Matson in September 1919 and, refitted at Newport News, continued her Pacific service between San Francisco and Hawaii. She was laid up in 1932, was placed in Matson cargo service in 1936, then was sold to the Alaska Packers Associates in 1937, and was renamed ETOLIN.

She remained in cargo service until chartered for Army transport service in 1940. She was requisitioned for war in September 1942 and saw extensive war transport service in the Pacific until being laid up in the James River in 1946. Her working days over, she was ultimately scrapped at Baltimore in 1957.

MANOA
1913

MANOA

Hull No: 168
Owner: Matson Navigation Co.
Launched: November 1, 1913
Delivered: December 13, 1913
Dimensions: 446.18 x 54 x 33.5 ft
Gross Tonnage: 6,805
Displacement: 11,990 tons
Machinery: Quadruple Expansion Engine,
    6 Boilers
Horsepower/Speed: 4,000/13 knots
Fate: Repair Ship, 1967

MANOA was the last of four passenger and cargo ships built for Matson by the shipyard and she was christened by Mrs. C. Montague Cook, wife of a Matson director, on November 1, 1913. MANOA had comfortable accommodations for 90 first class passengers and 49 crew and featured three masts and a single slender funnel situated well aft. She served Matson out of San Francisco until 1933 when, with declining passenger trade, she was put into cargo service.

She was requisitioned by the War Shipping Administration in December 1942 at Seattle and shortly thereafter was loaned to the U.S.S.R. under lend-lease. She was renamed BALHASH and remained under Russian ownership after the war, homeported in Vladivostok. Outfitted to carry 667 passengers, she engaged in passenger and cargo service to Southern Sakhalin and the Kuril Islands. During the 1950s BALHASH operated in express passenger-cargo service from Vladivostok to the Sakhalin and Kuril Islands and to Kamachatka.

By 1965 she was showing her age and was converted at Vladivostok for use as a repair ship. Moored there in 1967, she continued service as the Main Unit for Fleet Technical Maintenance of the Far Eastern Shipping Co. into the mid-1980s.

HENRY R. MALLORY
1916

HENRY R. MALLORY

Hull No: 193
Owner: Mallory Steamship Co.
Launched: August 19, 1916
Delivered: October 21, 1916
Dimensions: 440.18 x 54.25 x 33.75 ft
Gross Tonnage: 6,063
Displacement: 9,890 tons
Machinery: Triple Expansion Engine,
    4 Boilers
Horsepower/Speed: 4,100/14 knots
Fate: War Loss, 1943

HENRY R. MALLORY was similar to freighters NECHES and MEDINA built at Newport News for Mallory in 1913, but she was provided with 35 small cabins for 75 passengers and quarters for 57 crew. She was named for the owner of the line who later became chairman of the famous AGWI Line, and was christened by Mrs. Henry R. Mallory on August 19, 1916. The new ship had a fine dining saloon with leather chairs and carved columns and a comfortable panelled smoking room divided into semi-private compartments.

She was placed in New York-to-Florida service with occasional trips to Gulf ports, and in 1918 was acquired by the Navy, designated ID-1280, and placed in transport service. She was equipped to carry up to 2,200 troops and transported about ten times this number to and from Europe during World War I. She was returned to Mallory in 1919 and resumed coastal service.

She passed to Clyde-Mallory then Agwilines ownership in the thirties with her fleetmates, and then was requisitioned for more wartime service by the War Shipping Administration in 1942. On several trips she carried troops and equipment to England, Iceland, and Canada. She left New York on January 24, 1943, with almost 500 troops and crew aboard as part of convoy SC-118 bound for Iceland and scheduled to be detached for Ireland. Before dawn on February 7, 1943, HENRY R. MALLORY was torpedoed and sunk in mid-Atlantic. Her loss was a tragic one as about 300 of those aboard either went down with her or died in the rough chilly water.

GOLDEN STATE
1921

GOLDEN STATE

Hull No: 256
Owner: Emergency Fleet Corp.
Launched: July 17, 1920
Delivered: February 1, 1921
Dimensions: 535 x 72 x 50 ft
Gross Tonnage: 14,123
Displacement: 21,280 tons
Machinery: Geared Turbines,
    8 Boilers, Twin Screw
Horsepower/Speed: 12,000/18 knots
Fate: War Loss, 1942

GOLDEN STATE and sister SILVER STATE, started as army troopships but completed and delivered as merchant ships to the Emergency Fleet Corporation in 1921, were the largest passenger ships built by the shipyard since the 18,000-ton KOREA and SIBERIA of 1902. Fourteen similar ships of this "535" class were built for the U.S. Shipping Board in other shipyards and they differed from the Newport News ships mainly in interior decoration.

GOLDEN STATE was christened by Mrs. Joseph T. Martin, wife of the local Shipping Board manager, on July 17, 1920. The new ship was the first passenger ship built at Newport News to be powered with steam turbines and her machinery was designed and built at the shipyard. GOLDEN STATE, named for the state of California, was outfitted for 265 first class passengers, 300 third class, and 196 crew. Her decorations, largely done by local firms, were attractive and equalled those in fine hotels ashore. Five pairs of kingposts gave her a somewhat cluttered appearance and she was provided with nine cargo hatches.

The new ship was placed in Pacific service from San Francisco to Hawaii, Japan, and China. She was renamed PRESIDENT CLEVELAND in 1922 and served with the Dollar Line and later the American President Lines. She was chartered by the Army in 1941, renamed TASKER H. BLISS, and made five voyages to the Pacific with troops.

In August 1942 she was transferred to the Navy and after conversion loaded troops and equipment for the "Operation Torch" invasion of North Africa. She arrived off Fedhala, Morocco, on November 8, 1942; then on November 12, she and two other transports were torpedoed by the German submarine U-130. Attacked in the evening, TASKER H. BLISS burned until 2:30 A.M. on November 13; then, abandoned, she sank at anchor with 34 of her crew. She had received one battle star for her World War II service.

SILVER STATE
1921

SILVER STATE

Hull No: 257
Owner: Emergency Fleet Corp.
Launched: December 11, 1920
Delivered: May 16, 1921
Dimensions: 535 x 72 x 50 ft
Gross Tonnage: 14,123
Displacement: 21,280 tons
Machinery: Geared Turbines,
    8 Boilers, Twin Screw
Horsepower/Speed: 12,000/18 knots
Fate: Scrapped, 1948

Passenger and cargo ship SILVER STATE was the sister ship of GOLDEN STATE, and she was the last of ten merchant ships built for the government by the shipyard during the war emergency. SILVER STATE was christened by Mrs. Carlton W. Betts, wife of the U.S. Shipping Board commissioner, on December 11, 1920. Like her sister, SILVER STATE had a wide glass enclosed first class promenade and canvas swimming pool which was supported by spars. Both these ships had Newport News as their homeport when delivered, but they were shortly transferred to San Francisco after entering service.

SILVER STATE, named for the state of Nevada, served with the Pacific Steamship Co. for the Admiral Orient Mail Line, Dollar Line, and American Mail Line in West Coast to Far East trade through the twenties and thirties under the name PRESIDENT JACKSON given to her in 1922.

Transferred to American President Lines in 1938, she was acquired by the Navy in July 1940 and was converted to the attack transport ZEILIN (AP-9, later APA-3), named for the Marine Corps' first general officer. She was placed in Pacific service in the thick of the fighting and survived heavy bombing attacks in November 1942 at Guadalcanal and in January 1945 near Luzon. She took heavy damage from both attacks, especially from a suicide plane during the 1945 episode. In both cases she stayed with her convoy and, in spite of the damage, continued her duty.

At the end of the war, she carried occupation troops to Korea, made several voyages along the West Coast, and then was transferred to the East Coast for decommissioning. Winner of eight battle stars for her World War II service, ZEILIN was decommissioned in April 1946, was renamed PRESIDENT JACKSON, and was ultimately sold for scrap in May 1948.

CITY OF CHATTANOOGA
1923

CITY OF CHATTANOOGA

Hull No: 266
Owner: Ocean Steamship Co.
Launched: July 28, 1923
Delivered: September 28, 1923
Dimensions: 401 x 52 x 35 ft
Gross Tonnage: 5,861
Displacement: 7,180 tons
Machinery: Triple Expansion Engine,
    4 Boilers
Horsepower/Speed: 2,700/12.5 knots
Fate: Scrapped, 1948

CITY OF CHATTANOOGA and sister CITY OF BIRMINGHAM, delivered to the Ocean Steamship Co. in 1923, were only slightly larger than CITY OF MONTGOMERY and CITY OF ST. LOUIS, delivered to this line (also known as the Savannah Line) in 1910.

These ships were among the first liners built for coastal service after World War I and each had accommodations for 204 passengers.

CITY OF CHATTANOOGA was christened by Miss Dorothy Patten of Chattanooga on July 28, 1923. The new ship featured an open top deck which offered a fine unobstructed view of the sea.

She entered the New York-Savannah run where she stayed in routine service but for a few incidents. In February 1926 she struck a barge on a trip from Boston, without major damage. In May 1932 she struck and sank the steamer GRECIAN off Block Island, with a loss of four lives aboard GRECIAN. In 1940 she collided with the French liner SAN FRANCISCO but damage was minor.

She is said to have served as an Army barracks ship, and in April 1943 she was sold to the government and became the merchant marine training ship AMERICAN NAVIGATOR. She served in this capacity until sold for scrap in 1948 to Kaiser Co. of Richmond, CA.

CITY OF BIRMINGHAM
1923

CITY OF BIRMINGHAM

Hull No: 267
Owner: Ocean Steamship Co.
Launched: August 30, 1923
Delivered: November 3, 1923
Dimensions: 401 x 52 x 35 ft
Gross Tonnage: 5,861
Displacement: 7,180 tons
Machinery: Triple Expansion Engine,
    4 Boilers
Horsepower/Speed: 2,700/12.5 knots
Fate: War Loss, 1942

CITY OF BIRMINGHAM was the fourth and last passenger and cargo vessel built by the shipyard for the Savannah Line. Hull 267 was christened by Miss Rose Duncan Smith of Birmingham, AL, on August 30, 1923, and was smoothly launched into the James River from Shipway 4. The new ship entered coastwise service in November 1923, serving between Savannah, Charleston, New York, and Boston.

Her career was uneventful except for one grounding in March 1928 from which she was freed without serious damage. In November 1934 she went on a "football cruise," offering a round trip from New York to Boston for the Harvard-Yale game for only $12 including meals!

CITY OF BIRMINGHAM remained in routine coastal service with Ocean Steamship Company for almost twenty years before her luck ran out. On a voyage from Savannah to New York, she was torpedoed and sunk on June 30, 1942, about 300 miles off Cape Hatteras. Her end was swift since, holed amidships by two torpedoes, she reportedly went down in three minutes.

CHEROKEE
1925

CHEROKEE

Hull No: 274
Owner: Clyde Steamship Co.
Launched: February 10, 1925
Delivered: June 17, 1925
Dimensions: 402.18 x 54 x 31.5 ft
Gross Tonnage: 5,896
Displacement: 7,220 tons
Machinery: Geared Turbines,
    4 Boilers
Horsepower/Speed: 4,200/15 knots
Fate: War Loss, 1942

CHEROKEE was the second of seven passenger and cargo liners built for the Clyde Steamship Co., and she was slightly larger than LENAPE which had been delivered in 1913. All of the Clyde liners carried the name of Indian tribes, and they were among the most well known and popular coastal steamers of their day. CHEROKEE was to have an interesting career which came to a violent wartime end.

The new Clyde ship was christened by Mrs. Richard F. Hoyt on February 10, 1925, and the launching from Shipway 2 was delayed for over an hour due to dense fog. After four months at the outfitting pier, CHEROKEE was ready to enter service. She was provided with accommodations for 367 passengers and 80 crew and her public rooms were luxuriously appointed. The new ship had steam turbine propulsion and large refrigerated cargo holds for oranges.

CHEROKEE became one of the most popular ships on the New York-Jacksonville run and became known as "Little Cherokee." Her career proceeded without incident except for one minor collision. In 1925 her owner became known as the Cherokee-Seminole Steamship Co. and in 1941 she passed to Agwilines with some of her fleetmates. She was chartered to the New York and Porto Rico Line in the early 1940s, sailing from New York to Puerto Rico and the Dominican Republic.

In 1942 the War Shipping Administration took over the former Clyde fleet. CHEROKEE made three more trips to Puerto Rico, then in March 1942 was converted for Navy service at New York. She was sent to Iceland with passengers and naval stores in May and arrived at Reykjavik without incident. On her return trip to Halifax, her luck ran out, and she was hit under her bridge by a torpedo on June 15 and sank in less than seven minutes, carrying half of her 169 passengers and crew with her.

SEMINOLE
1925

SEMINOLE

Hull No: 275
Owner: Clyde Steamship Co.
Launched: April 14, 1925
Delivered: August 19, 1925
Dimensions: 402.18 x 54 x 31.5 ft
Gross Tonnage: 5,896
Displacement: 7,220 tons
Machinery: Geared Turbines,
    4 Boilers
Horsepower/Speed: 4,200/15 knots
Fate: Scrapped, 1952

SEMINOLE was the sister ship of CHEROKEE, and she enjoyed a varied career as a popular passenger steamer in peacetime and as a troopship and hospital ship in wartime. SEMINOLE was christened by Miss Barbara Stone, youngest daughter of Galen L. Stone, on April 14, 1925, and was launched from Shipway 5.

The new ship completed trials and was delivered to Clyde in August 1925. She was placed on Clyde's run from New York to Galveston with an intermediate stop at Miami and became very popular, especially with her Texan passengers.

In 1941 Agwilines Inc. became her owner, and in 1942 she was requisitioned for use as a troopship. She was not greatly modified for this service and spent about a year ferrying troops to Europe from New York and making voyages to Iceland and Brazil.

In May 1943 she was converted for use as a hospital ship at Brooklyn. With her home port as Charleston, SC, she made many trips back and forth to the Mediterranean bringing wounded troops home from the war.

After this hard service she was decommissioned at Norfolk in December 1945 and laid up in the James River Reserve Fleet. Her service in war and peace at an end, she was withdrawn from the fleet and sold for scrap in February 1952.

ALGONQUIN
1926

ALGONQUIN

Hull No: 317
Owner: Clyde Steamship Co.
Launched: September 9, 1926
Delivered: December 10, 1926
Dimensions: 402.17 x 55 x 31.5 ft
Gross Tonnage: 5,945
Displacement: 7,250 tons
Machinery: Geared Turbines, 4 Boilers
Horsepower/Speed: 4,200/15 knots
Fate: Scrapped, 1956

Last of seven passenger and cargo ships built by the shipyard for the Clyde Line, ALGONQUIN was similar to CHEROKEE, SEMINOLE, and MOHAWK but measured one foot greater in beam. ALGONQUIN was christened by Mrs. Nellie D. Raymond, widow of a former Clyde Line vice president, on September 9, 1926. Outfitting and trials were completed, and the new ship was delivered the following December.

She served with SEMINOLE on the New York to Galveston run for years, stopping and meeting her at Miami each week. The two ships were very popular and provided dependable and comfortable coastal service.

In 1929 ALGONQUIN collided with and sank the British steamer FORT VICTORIA without loss of life or major damage to herself. In 1941 she passed with her sisters to Agwilines, and in January 1942 she was chartered for troopship service in the Caribbean area.

During the second half of 1943, she was converted at Mobile for hospital ship service, subsequently making a number of voyages to and from the Mediterranean, caring for and repatriating wounded servicemen. Her hospital service ended in December 1945, and she was placed back into troopship duty making at least two more trips to Europe and one to Bermuda.

Surprisingly, her career closely paralleled that of her sister SEMINOLE and at the end of their wartime duties, both were laid up together in the James River. Out of documentation by 1950, old ALGONQUIN was finally scrapped at Baltimore in 1956.

MOHAWK
1926

MOHAWK

Hull No: 287
Owner: Clyde Steamship Co.
Launched: October 21, 1925
Delivered: February 1, 1926
Dimensions: 402.18 x 54 x 31.5 ft
Gross Tonnage: 5,896
Displacement: 7,220 tons
Machinery: Geared Turbines, 4 Boilers
Horsepower/Speed: 4,200/15 knots
Fate: Collision, 1935

MOHAWK, a sistership of CHEROKEE and SEMINOLE, was launched and delivered to the Clyde Steamship Co. just a few months behind her sisters. MOHAWK was christened by Miss Margaret A. Denison, daughter of the vice president of Clyde, and was launched from Shipway 4 into the James River on October 21, 1925. Delivered just over three months after her launch, MOHAWK offered her passengers the same luxurious public rooms, glassed promenades, and comfortable accommodations as her sisters.

She entered the Jacksonville-New York trade early in 1926 and began her career unaware that she would have the shortest life and meet one of the most tragic ends of all the Clyde liners. Her service was routine except that she collided with O.D. JEFFERSON in 1928 but was repaired and returned to service. She passed with her owners to the Clyde-Mallory Lines in 1932, then to Agwilines in 1935.

Under charter to the New York & Porto Rico Line in service to Cuba and Mexico, she met a tragic end on the bitter cold night of January 24, 1935. Off Sea Girt, NJ, her steering gear had frozen and she was being steered by her aft-facing emergency wheel on her stern. As she approached the Norweigan steamer TALISMAN in clear weather, a command was misunderstood by the helmsman and MOHAWK crashed into the other ship. An hour later MOHAWK was beached four and a half miles off the coast and she later turned over and sank. The freak accident claimed 30 of her passengers and 15 of her crew and the ship, now known as "Mohawk Reef," still lies sunk off Sea Girt.

GEORGE WASHINGTON
1924

GEORGE WASHINGTON

Hull No: 276
Owner: Old Dominion Line
Launched: August 20, 1924
Delivered: November 16, 1924
Dimensions: 390 x 53.75 x 29.75 ft
Gross Tonnage: 5,185
Displacement: 6,520 tons
Machinery: Geared Turbines,
    4 Boilers
Horsepower/Speed: 4,750/16 knots
Fate: Scrapped, 1955

GEORGE WASHINGTON was the first of a pair of cargo and passenger steamers delivered to the Old Dominion Line of New York in 1924 and 1925. These ships were originally intended for service between New York and Hampton Roads but were both destined for more far-flung careers.

GEORGE WASHINGTON was christened by Miss Patty W. Washington, a descendent of George Washington's brother, John Augustine Washington, on August 20, 1924. The new ship, with accommodations for over 600 passengers, had the simple but functional interior which characterized coastal steamers of the 1920s. She was less ornamented than earlier ships but did feature richly molded furniture and hardwood paneling in her staterooms.

GEORGE WASHINGTON's first winter was spent under charter to the Clyde Line for the New York to Florida run. She began her regular service the following spring but under the ownership of Eastern Steamship Lines which had bought Old Dominion. She was chartered for New York-Boston service in the winter of 1927-1928 and served Clyde in charter often during the 1930s.

She was placed under the War Shipping Administration and made many trips between New York and Caribbean ports and Bermuda during the war. Nicknamed the "little" GEORGE WASHINGTON, she was once confused with the much larger ex-German liner of the same name when an unsuccessful attempt was made to load 4,000 troops intended for the larger ship aboard her at Trinidad.

She was operated by Alcoa Steamship Co. during and after the war and was sold to the Alaska Transportation Co. in February 1948. She was later sold to the French Line in 1948 and, renamed GASCOGNE, sailed between France and the West Indies. Later operated by Messageries Maritimes, she was eventually sold to Hong Kong shipbreakers in 1955.

ROBERT E. LEE
1925

ROBERT E. LEE

Hull No: 277
Owner: Old Dominion Line
Launched: October 16, 1924
Delivered: January 17, 1925
Dimensions: 390 x 53.75 x 29.75 ft
Gross Tonnage: 5,185
Displacement: 6,520 tons
Machinery: Geared Turbines, 4 Boilers
Horsepower/Speed: 4,750/16 knots
Fate: War Loss, 1942

Sister ship of GEORGE WASHINGTON, ROBERT E. LEE also had a sponsor who was a direct descendent of her famous namesake. ROBERT E. LEE was christened on October 16, 1924, by Miss Mary Custis Lee, granddaughter of General Robert E. Lee. The new ship entered service in January 1925, chartered to the Clyde Line with her sister for Florida service.

Several incidents during her early years preceded her tragic wartime loss to an enemy torpedo. She ran aground at Miami in January 1926 and again in March 1928 but was refloated both times. She suffered a fire once while under charter to the Ward Line; then in late 1929, engine trouble caused her to put back to Boston and send her passengers to New York by train. Her official owner during her first 12 years was the Robert E. Lee Steamship Co., a subsidiary of Eastern.

During the war, like her sister, she was operated by Alcoa for the War Shipping Administration. Not as lucky as GEORGE WASHINGTON, she was torpedoed and sunk on July 30, 1942, off the mouth of the Mississippi River in the Gulf of Mexico. She had sailed from Trinidad on July 17 with 425 on board including 200 survivors of torpedoed ships. The torpedo hit the starboard side near the stern and she went down quickly with 106 men who died with her.

CARACAS
1927

CARACAS

Hull No: 319
Owner: Red "D" Line
Launched: June 30, 1927
Delivered: August 27, 1927
Dimensions: 336.33 x 51 x 22 ft
Gross Tonnage: 3,365
Displacement: 6,480 tons
Machinery: Geared Turbines, 2 Boilers,
   Twin Screw
Horsepower/Speed: 3,500/13 knots
Fate: Scrapped, 1961

CARACAS was a relatively small passenger and cargo ship built for the Atlantic and Caribbean Steam Navigation Co. (Red "D" Line) and delivered in 1927. She was christened by Mrs. Elizabeth A. Dallett and was launched from Shipway 5 on June 30, 1927. The new liner was designed by Theodore E. Ferris and featured comfortable accommodations for 137 passengers and 87 crew.

CARACAS was delivered only two short months after her launch and began what was to be a long career under several names and owners. She served along the eastern seaboard and in the Caribbean until changing owners in 1937.

Passing briefly to the ownership of Grace Line in that year, she was sold to the Alaska Steamship Co. in 1938 and was renamed DENALI. During World War II she was operated as an Army troopship by this company and she served between Seattle and Alaskan ports for the duration. In 1942 she was rebuilt and had one deck added, increasing her gross tonnage to 4,302. After many voyages for the Army, she was returned to her former service in April 1946.

In 1954 she was sold to the Peninsular and Occidental Steamship Co. of New Haven and was renamed CUBA. She served this owner but briefly and was sold to the White Steamship Co. in September 1955, transferred to Liberian registry, and was renamed SOUTHERN CROSS. After a few more useful years with this owner, the weary old veteran was sold for scrap in 1961.

COAMO
1925

COAMO

Hull No: 280
Owner: N.Y. & Porto Rico Co.
Launched: July 22, 1925
Delivered: December 22, 1925
Dimensions: 429.18 x 59.5 x 35 ft
Gross Tonnage: 7,057
Displacement: 11,040 tons
Machinery: Geared Turbines, 5 Boilers
Horsepower/Speed: 6,000/15.5 knots
Fate: War Loss, 1942

COAMO was a 7,057 gross ton passenger and cargo ship built for the New York & Porto Rico Steamship Co. in 1925. She carried 325 passengers in a single class and had steam turbine propulsion, by now the standard for her type. COAMO was christened by Mrs. Franklin D. Mooney, wife of the owner's president, and was launched from Shipway 3 on July 22, 1925. The luxurious and handsome ship was delivered in December 1925 to a subsidiary of her owner known as the Coamo Steamship Co.

She was very popular on the New York to Caribbean run, and in September 1930 she survived a severe hurricane which made her popular with shipyard publicists as well. She came through the monstrous storm without injury to crew or passengers prompting her Chief Engineer to state to the press, "Don't praise me. Praise the shipbuilding company. They made a fine ship when they made this one." Her Captain further confirmed, "No other ship could have done it."

Early in 1942 she was converted for use as a troopship and chartered to the Army. After several trips to the Ascension Islands, Brazil, Argentina, and Sierra Leone, she left New York in convoy for Liverpool in October 1942. She carried troops from Liverpool to the invasion of North Africa. Then, in convoy from Gibraltar, she was ordered to break off and proceed unescorted. This sealed her fate as she was sunk by enemy action on December 9, 1942, about 150 miles west of Ireland en route to New York, taking her merchant crew of 16 with her.

CHATHAM
1926

CHATHAM

Hull No: 288
Owner: Merchants & Miners Transportation Co.
Launched: February 3, 1926
Delivered: May 17, 1926
Dimensions: 368 x 52 x 36 ft
Gross Tonnage: 5,649
Displacement: 6,950 tons
Machinery: Triple Expansion Engine,
    4 Boilers
Horsepower/Speed: 2,700/12 knots
Fate: War Loss, 1942

CHATHAM was the first of a trio of passenger and cargo ships built in 1926 for the Merchants and Miners Transportation Co. of Baltimore. These steamers were built for the booming trade between Florida and northern ports, and they were designed by A.D. Stebbins, president of Merchants and Miners, and other officers of the company. A contemporary publication noted that they had accommodations designed for the luxurious comfort of the Florida traveler and complete in every detail as found in the finest hotel.

CHATHAM was sponsored by Mrs. A.D. Stebbins and was launched from Shipway 5 on February 3, 1926. The new ship completed trials and was delivered just over three months later.

She enjoyed years of routine service on the Florida run before being requisitioned for Army transport service in the spring of 1942. She kept her name and crew and made two uneventful round trips to Newfoundland and Greenland from New York and Boston before her luck ran out. She left Sydney, Cape Breton, on August 25, 1942, in convoy and was torpedoed and sunk in the Belle Isle Straits on August 27. Fortunately, help from her escorts was close at hand, and of 569 aboard only 26 were lost.

DORCHESTER
1926

DORCHESTER

Hull No: 289
Owner: Merchants and Miners
    Transportation Co.
Launched: March 20, 1926
Delivered: July 17, 1926
Dimensions: 368 x 52 x 36 ft
Gross Tonnage: 5,649
Displacement: 6,950 tons
Machinery: Triple Expansion Engine,
    4 Boilers
Horsepower/Speed: 2,700/12 knots
Fate: War Loss, 1943

DORCHESTER was the second of the three Merchants and Miners ships delivered in 1925, and she was to have both a spectacular beginning and a heroic end. Christened by Miss Louise Cromwell Brooks, DORCHESTER was the largest vessel launched on March 20, 1926, a day which saw nine launchings and three keels laid before a crowd of many thousands.

Like the other Merchants and Miners ships built at the shipyard, DORCHESTER was modern in having oil fuel but traditional in retaining a triple expansion engine for power. Like her sisters, she had comfortable accommodations and spacious public rooms for 314 passengers, and she enjoyed routine service between Miami, Jacksonville, Baltimore, Philadelphia and New York until called for war service in March 1942.

Armed and converted for troop transport service, she made regular trips between Boston and Newfoundland and Greenland until the end of 1942.

In convoy with two other steamers and escorted by Coast Guard cutter TAMPA and two others, she sailed from St. John's to Greenland on her last trip on January 29, 1943. Early in the morning of February 3, DORCHESTER was torpedoed and sank quickly. Notwithstanding heroic efforts by the Coast Guardsmen, 605 were lost of the 904 on board in the icy North Atlantic water. Among her passengers who died were four Army chaplains: a Methodist minister, a Catholic priest, a Reform minister and a Jewish rabbi. In one of the most famous acts of heroism of the war they "led those on board the vessel in prayer, and gave their own life jackets to others, creating a saga of faith and heroism that will long remain an inspiration to all those who believe in God and love their country."

FAIRFAX
1926

FAIRFAX

Hull No: 290
Owner: Merchants & Miners Transportation Co.
Launched: June 12, 1926
Delivered: September 4, 1926
Dimensions: 368 x 52 x 36 ft
Gross Tonnage: 5,649
Displacement: 6,950 tons
Machinery: Triple Expansion Engine,
    4 Boilers
Horsepower/Speed: 2,700/12 knots
Fate: Scrapped, 1957

Last of the Merchants and Miners ships to be delivered in 1926, FAIRFAX was the only one of the three to enjoy a long and varied career. She was christened by Mrs. Walter R. Abell on June 12, 1926, and was delivered just over three months later.

According to official documents, she served between Boston, Providence, Philadelphia, Baltimore, Norfolk, Savannah, Jacksonville, and Miami, and in addition to cabins for 314 passengers, she accommodated 90 crew. She entered war service in October 1941 and made many trips along the East Coast early in the war and several later on to the Pacific.

After a trip to the Philippines, she returned to the U.S. early in 1945 and, as her owning company was dissolved, she was sold to the Chung Hsing Mining Co. of Shanghai, China. Renamed CHUNG HSING, she was repaired at the shipyard before sailing on August 30, 1946, to become her new owner's flagship.

She was placed in Chinese coastal service until 1950 when she was sold to the Far Eastern and Panama Transport Co. and renamed PACIFIC STAR. She remained under Panamanian flag for only a year until being sold to the Indonesian Navigation Co. of Jakarta and renamed BINGTANG SAMUDRA. After a few years of uneventful service in Indonesian waters, the tired old veteran was broken up for scrap in 1957.

IROQUOIS
1927

IROQUOIS

Hull No: 306
Owner: Clyde Steamship Co.
Launched: December 11, 1926
Delivered: April 18, 1927
Dimensions: 409.33 x 62 x 30.5 ft
Gross Tonnage: 6,209
Displacement: 8,650 tons
Machinery: Geared Turbines,
       6 Boilers, Twin Screw
Horsepower/Speed: 8,500/18 knots
Fate: Scrapped, 1981

The most historic and long-lived of the Clyde liners, IROQUOIS was to become one of the most famous Newport News-built ships. IROQUOIS and her sister SHAWNEE were also the largest of the seven Clyde ships built at the yard. Her keel was laid on that gala day March 20, 1926, which saw nine launchings and three keels laid. She was christened by Miss Marion Shutts of Miami and was launched from Shipway 8 on December 11, 1926.

Delivered at the opening of the summer season of 1927, IROQUOIS saw East Coast service in her first few years but was laid up or tried out in alternative services on both coasts during the early 1930s. In July 1927 she went aground at the entrance to Halifax harbor.

When MORRO CASTLE burned in 1934, IROQUOIS was handy and substituted for her for a while. She was generally underutilized during the depression years when trade in general was slow, and her owners were doubtlessly pleased when she was purchased by the Navy in July 1940.

She was extensively converted to a hospital ship, called the "newest and most completely equipped in the world," and then renamed SOLACE (AH-5). The morning of December 7, 1941, found her as the only hospital ship at Pearl Harbor, and she received the Navy Unit Commendation for her gallant service there. In tribute to her stout construction, she steamed over 170,000 miles during the war without major repair and treated over 25,000 patients.

After the war with seven battle stars to her credit, she was laid up. In April 1948 she was sold to Turkish Maritime Lines and returned to Newport News for conversion to the passenger liner ANKARA (Hull 487, q.v.). She re-entered passenger service in April 1949 and was an immediate success in Mediterranean waters often carrying pilgrims to Mecca. Old IROQUOIS was finally laid up in 1977 and, 54 years old, was scrapped in 1981.

SHAWNEE
1927

SHAWNEE

Hull No: 307
Owner: Clyde Steamship Co.
Launched: April 18, 1927
Delivered: July 14, 1927
Dimensions: 409.33 x 62 x 30.5 ft
Gross Tonnage: 6,209
Displacement: 8,650 tons
Machinery: Geared Turbines,
    6 Boilers, Twin Screw
Horsepower/Speed: 8,500/18 knots
Fate: Burned, 1949

SHAWNEE was the sixth Clyde liner built by the shipyard. She was christened by Miss Eleanor Hoyt of New York on April 18, 1927, and was delivered two months later. SHAWNEE, sister ship of IROQUOIS, became the Clyde Line's flagship and was extremely popular on the New York to Florida run. The new ships each featured a spacious dining room with a view forward and were said to be the largest liners ever built for coastal service.

After a maiden cruise to Canada, SHAWNEE settled in to the routine of coastal trade. She repeated Canadian cruises during the summer months of the 1930s.

In 1940 her ownership passed to Agwilines, and in 1941 she was chartered to the government. Quickly converted for service as a troopship at New Orleans, she made four trips from there to the Canal Zone, cruised in Caribbean and South American waters, and then served in the Atlantic and Mediterranean. In 1944 she was in the Pacific where she remained until the end of the war.

She was returned to Agwilines in March 1946, but a year later she was sold to a Portugese owner, placed under Panamanian flag, and renamed CITY OF LISBON. She served between Lisbon and Rio de Janiero briefly, then was sold to Yugoslavian owners and renamed PARTIZANKA (partisan girl). She operated between Yugoslavia and Australia and South America for a short time but, while in a Split shipyard for repairs, she caught fire and was destroyed in September 1949.

PENNSYLVANIA
1929

PENNSYLVANIA

Hull No: 329
Owner: International Mercantile Marine
Launched: July 10, 1929
Delivered: October 10, 1929
Dimensions: 613.08 x 80 x 52 ft
Gross Tonnage: 20,526
Displacement: 30,924 tons
Machinery: Turbo-Electric, 8 Boilers,
    Twin Screw
Horsepower/Speed: 13,500/18 knots
Fate: Scrapped, 1964

The third and last of the famous IMM liners built by the shipyard was PENNSYLVANIA, christened by Miss Eleanor Jane McCarthy in the presence of Virginia Governor Harry F. Byrd on July 10, 1929. Like the previous two IMM ships, PENNSYLVANIA was fitted with twin turbo-electric main engines developing a total of 13,500 SHP.

After outfitting late in 1929, she entered the Panama Pacific Line trade where she stayed until 1938. In that year she joined Moore-McCormack's "Good Neighbor Fleet" with her sisters as ARGENTINA after a conversion similar to that done to them. As ARGENTINA, she was probably the best known of the three ships. She saw a preview of war in December 1939 when she entered Montevideo harbor on the day that the German battleship GRAF SPEE was scuttled and abandoned by her crew.

ARGENTINA later became one of the most active troopships of the war. She served in both oceans and was the first large liner to be placed in "bride ship" service. Her first trip from England saw 456 brides and 170 babies aboard, and she made a total of three such trips. After reconversion to merchant service ARGENTINA was the first of the "Good Neighbor" ships to resume peacetime trade, sailing for South America in July 1947.

After serving her owners faithfully during the 1950s, she was replaced by a new ARGENTINA and was laid up in the James River in 1958. Inevitably, she was withdrawn and scrapped with her sisters in 1964.

CALIFORNIA
1928

CALIFORNIA

Hull No: 315
Owner: International Mercantile Marine
Launched: October 1, 1927
Delivered: January 13, 1928
Dimensions: 601.08 x 80 x 52 ft
Gross Tonnage: 20,325
Displacement: 30,260 tons
Machinery: Turbo-Electric,
 12 Boilers, Twin Screw
Horsepower/Speed: 13,500/18 knots
Fate: Scrapped, 1964

CALIFORNIA was the first of three similar passenger ships built for the International Mercantile Marine by the shipyard in the late 1920s. Hull 315 and sisters VIRGINIA and PENNSYLVANIA were the largest American merchant ships built to that time, and they were ordered for Panama-Pacific Line service between New York and the West Coast. These ships were also the first liners constructed in the United States to employ turbo-electric machinery and were among the earliest to feature air conditioning, added in 1933.

CALIFORNIA was christened by Mrs. Roland Palmedo, daughter of the IMM's president, on October 1, 1927, and was launched from Shipway 8 into the James. The new ship was outfitted quickly and entered service the following January.

After ten years of routine service, CALIFORNIA was rebuilt at the shipyard in 1938 as Hull 377 (q.v.), and her forward and dummy after stacks were replaced by a single streamlined funnel. Renamed URUGUAY, she served Moore-McCormack Lines as part of the popular "Good Neighbor Fleet" sailing to South American ports.

In January 1942 URUGUAY was allocated as an Army troopship and made a great number of voyages in worldwide service. On February 13, 1943, URUGUAY collided with the Navy oiler SALAMONIE (Hull 372) near Bermuda and 13 people were killed. URUGUAY was repaired at the shipyard, where a body was found and removed while the ship was in drydock.

After the war she was returned to Moore-McCormack and resumed South American and Caribbean cruise service. Thirty years old in 1957, URUGUAY was withdrawn from service and placed in the James River Reserve Fleet. This turned into permanent retirement, as she was removed and scrapped early in 1964.

VIRGINIA
1928

VIRGINIA

Hull No: 326
Owner: International Mercantile Marine
Launched: August 18, 1928
Delivered: November 26, 1928
Dimensions: 613.08 x 80 x 52 ft
Gross Tonnage: 20,773
Displacement: 30,924 tons
Machinery: Turbo-Electric, 8 Boilers,
   Twin Screw
Horsepower/Speed: 13,500/18 knots
Fate: Scrapped, 1964

VIRGINIA was the second of three liners built at Newport News for the IMM, and she stole the "largest ever built in the country" title from sister CALIFORNIA by virtue of being 12 feet longer. Her launching was a matter of considerable pride with Virginians and was attended by a large crowd on a hot August 18, 1928. She was christened by little Miss Anne Thomas, daughter of the vice president of the IMM, and the tiny girl charmed everyone who attended.

VIRGINIA was completed and delivered in November 1928 and, with her sisters, was considered the most modern ship of her time. Her interiors were spacious and her public rooms included a skylighted first class lounge which converted to a ballroom and a paneled smoking room. Also built for the New York-Panama-San Francisco run, VIRGINIA featured accommodations for 850 passengers and 377 crew.

She also passed to Moore-McCormack in 1938 and, after modernization, joined the "Good Neighbor Fleet" with the name BRAZIL and with one stack in place of her original two. From early 1942 to 1946 BRAZIL, converted to carry 5,155 passengers, made over 30 voyages as a troopship in both the Atlantic and Pacific.

She was one of the busiest troopers of the war and in mid-1946 was placed in "bride ship" service, bringing British brides and children to American servicemen across the Atlantic.

After this she was returned to her owners and was converted back to a peacetime liner with accommodations for 515 passengers. Serving for ten more years with Moore-McCormack, BRAZIL was laid up in the James River Fleet on December 27, 1957. After a few years of rest, she was sold for scrap in 1964.

MORRO CASTLE
1930

MORRO CASTLE

Hull No: 337
Owner: Ward Line
Launched: March 5, 1930
Delivered: August 15, 1930
Dimensions: 508 x 70.75 x 39 ft
Gross Tonnage: 11,520
Displacement: 16,113 tons
Machinery: Turbo-Electric, 8 Boilers,
    Twin Screw
Horsepower/Speed: 14,000/18.5 knots
Fate: Burned, 1934

The dubious title of the most infamous ship ever built at Newport News would probably have to go to MORRO CASTLE, built in 1930 for the Ward Line's New York to Havana service. MORRO CASTLE and sister ORIENTE were a pair of handsome medium-sized liners with accommodations for 437 first class passengers, 95 others, and 237 crew. MORRO CASTLE was sponsored by Miss Ruth Eleanor Mooney, daughter of the Ward Line's president, and was launched on March 5, 1930.

Designed by Theodore E. Ferris, MORRO CASTLE and her sister were praised as the most ornately decorated liners ever built in America. Ship interiors had become almost bland in the early 1920s after decades of heavy ornamentation, but ten years later the trend was back to more elaborate decorations and the inevitable use of flammable decorative materials.

This trend was to seal MORRO CASTLE's fate, for on the night of September 8, 1934, she caught fire off Sea Girt, NJ, and was destroyed. She was on a return trip from Havana and of 549 persons on board, 134 lost their lives. The cause of the fire was never officially established, but the great loss of life was attributed to inexperience of the crew and to the fact that the ship was driven into the wind, fanning the flames to an inferno.

The MORRO CASTLE later stranded at Asbury Park and was subsequently removed and scrapped. Her demise, tragic as it was, marked a turning point which led to stringent standards of fireproofing and fire control required by the Merchant Marine Safety Act of 1936.

ORIENTE
1930

ORIENTE

Hull No: 338
Owner: Ward Line
Launched: May 15, 1930
Delivered: November 21, 1930
Dimensions: 508 x 70.75 x 39 ft
Gross Tonnage: 11,520
Displacement: 16,113 tons
Machinery: Turbo-Electric, 6 Boilers,
    Twin Screw
Horsepower/Speed: 14,000/18.5 knots
Fate: Scrapped, 1957

Sister ship of the ill-fated MORRO CASTLE, Ward liner ORIENTE enjoyed a safe if busy career in both peace and war. ORIENTE was christened by Miss Virginia Hoyt, who was a granddaughter of Galen L. Stone, on May 15, 1930. The new ship completed outfitting and trials of her turbo-electric machinery and was delivered on November 21, 1930. She was operated by the Ward Line, an Agwilines subsidiary, on the New York-Havana run during the 1930s and was very popular, notwithstanding the fate of her sister.

In 1937 her ownership passed to the New York and Cuba Mail Steamship Co. In June 1941 she was sold to the War Department and was converted to a troopship with accommodation for 3,600 passengers, a great number for her size. She proved durable and, renamed THOMAS H. BARRY, made 70 voyages including trips with the first and last troop convoys of the war. She served in both oceans and was designated AP-45. THOMAS H. BARRY had an almost perfect safety record, except for a collision with a fishing trawler off Nantucket in October 1945, which sank the trawler and took the lives of seven of her crew.

In January 1946 she was hastily converted for war bride service and later became a transport for Army dependents. She was decommissioned on January 22, 1950, and was laid up in the James River Reserve Fleet. In 1957 the old veteran of 1,000,000 miles of merchant service and 500,000 miles of Army service was withdrawn from the fleet and scrapped.

PRESIDENT COOLIDGE
1931

PRESIDENT COOLIDGE

Hull No: 340
Owner: Dollar Line
Launched: February 21, 1931
Delivered: October 1, 1931
Dimensions: 654.25 x 81 x 52 ft
Gross Tonnage: 21,936
Displacement: 31,441 tons
Machinery: Turbo-Electric, 12 Boilers,
    Twin Screw
Horsepower/Speed: 22,000/20 knots
Fate: War Loss, 1942

PRESIDENT COOLIDGE was the second of the Dollar liners with the distinctive funnel markings built at the shipyard, and she was christened by Mrs. Calvin Coolidge on February 21, 1931, with the traditional champagne. The new ship was fitted with turbo-electric propulsion machinery and, like PRESI-DENT HOOVER, she had luxurious interiors. As a large amount of decorative glass was required for the two ships, an art glass shop was set up in the shipyard to manufacture, among other things, main lounge domes containing over 3,000 pieces of glass.

PRESIDENT COOLIDGE entered trans-Pacific service with her sister and steamed uneventfully until she began evacuating refugees from the Orient in 1940. She was taken over by the Army in July 1941 and made several trips to Honolulu and Manila. In 1942 she was converted to carry 3,486 troops and began service between San Francisco and the Southwest Pacific.

She was apparently never attacked, but on October 25, 1942, she ran into an American mine at the entrance to the channel at the island of Espiritu Santo and she sank in twenty fathoms of water. Almost 5,000 persons were aboard but only two were lost since the captain ran her in to within 200 yards from shore. This prudent decision enabled the men to climb down the side of the ship and get ashore safely, and a great disaster was averted.

PRESIDENT HOOVER
1931

PRESIDENT HOOVER

Hull No: 339
Owner: Dollar Line
Launched: December 9, 1930
Delivered: July 11, 1931
Dimensions: 654.25 x 81 x 52 ft
Gross Tonnage: 21,936
Displacement: 31,441
Machinery: Turbo-Electric 12 Boilers,
    Twin Screw
Horsepower/Speed: 22,000/20 knots
Fate: Stranded, 1937

PRESIDENT HOOVER was the first of a pair of large passenger and cargo liners delivered to the Dollar Line in 1931. Both were to have short careers and come to untimely ends. The two liners were the largest built in America to that time and featured bulbous bows and twin screw turbo-electric propulsion.

PRESIDENT HOOVER was christened on December 9, 1930, by Mrs. Herbert Hoover. In deference to Prohibition and since she was the President's wife, Mrs. Hoover christened the new ship with waters blended "from the Seven Seas" in lieu of the traditional champagne.

PRESIDENT HOOVER was outfitted and was tried and tested before her delivery in July 1931. As her construction predated the MORRO CASTLE disaster, her interiors were paneled in rare woods and wooden furniture was used extensively. She offered accommodations for 330 first class, 140 tourist class, and 800 steerage class passengers as well as for 314 crew.

Her home port was San Francisco and her trade was widespread. Official documents indicate that her normal trade was New York, Havana, Cristobal, Balboa, Los Angeles, San Francisco, Honolulu, Yokohama, Kobe, Shanghai, Hong Kong, Manila, and then return via each port. PRESIDENT HOOVER entered routine service, marred only once by being accidentally bombed by Chinese planes near Shanghai in August 1937. Damage was slight and she was able to continue service carrying passengers and evacuating refugees.

The big ship was not so lucky three months later when she ran aground on Hoishoto Island near Formosa on December 10. There was no loss of life, but heavy seas broke PRESIDENT HOOVER's back in a few days and she was declared a total loss. Speculation that Japanese ship-breakers had intentionally moved lights on shore to lead the ship onto the rocks for salvage was never proved.

FLORIDA
1931

FLORIDA

Hull No: 342
Owner: Peninsular & Occidental Steamship Co.
Launched: March 7, 1931
Delivered: May 20, 1931
Dimensions: 387.67 x 56.5 x 28.5 ft
Gross Tonnage: 4,923
Displacement: 5,886 tons
Machinery: Geared Turbines, 4 Boilers,
   Twin Screw
Horsepower/Speed: 8,500/19.5 knots
Fate: Scrapped, 1969

FLORIDA was a relatively small passenger and cargo ship built for the P & O Steamship Co. and delivered in 1931, intended for the Florida to Havana trade. FLORIDA was christened by Miss Leile Delano on March 7, 1931, and was launched into the James River from Shipway 2. The designer and supervising architect for the new ship was Carroll S. Smith. FLORIDA was designed as a pleasure craft and combined the virtues of an ocean liner with those of an excursion ship.

She was very popular on the Havana run and sailed routinely and uneventfully until being chartered by the Army in 1942. She served mainly in the Caribbean due to her limited range and made 48 voyages during the war. Her original accommodations for 742 were expanded and on one trip she carried 1,387 troops. She was considered a lucky ship since enemy torpedoes struck her on at least two occasions and failed to explode. At war's end FLORIDA was used to return war brides and children from South America.

In July 1946 she returned to Newport News and was converted back to merchant service. Her staterooms and public rooms were refurbished, and her machinery was given a much-needed overhaul.

After conversion, she returned to the Miami-Havana route and remained there until 1955. In that year, she was transferred to the Liberian flag and, still with P & O, took up trade between Miami and Nassau. In 1959 she passed to the Blue Steamship Co. and served them in the Caribbean until the late 1960s.

She served as a hotel ship in the late 1960s during Montreal's "Expo." FLORIDA was transferred to Panamanian registry in 1968 but in 1969 was taken out of service and subsequently scrapped abroad after almost 40 years of service in peace and war.

TALAMANCA
1931

TALAMANCA

Hull No: 344
Owner: United Fruit Co.
Launched: August 15, 1931
Delivered: December 12, 1931
Dimensions: 446.75 x 60 x 34.75 ft
Gross Tonnage: 6,963
Displacement: 10,930 tons
Machinery: Turbo-Electric, 4 Boilers,
   Twin Screw
Horsepower/Speed: 10,500/17.5 knots
Fate: Scrapped, 1965

TALAMANCA was the first of a trio of combination passenger and fruit cargo ships built for the United Fruit Co. (United Mail Steamship Co.) and delivered in 1931 and 1932. These ships were designed for passenger service between the U.S. and Central America and were fitted with extensive refrigeration equipment for carrying fruit cargo.

TALMANCA and a sister ship were both launched on August 15, 1931, by Mrs. Herbert Hoover. This very popular First Lady and sponsor of four Newport News ships christened the ship with blended waters of eight rivers bordering on the Caribbean.

TALAMANCA joined the "Great White Fleet" in December 1931 and served uneventfully on both coasts until taken over by the Navy as an auxiliary stores ship (AF-15) in December 1941. She was quickly converted at Baltimore and sailed for New Zealand on February 13, 1942. She spent the duration of the war in the Pacific, making numerous voyages to supply American bases and to transport personnel.

In late 1945 she was returned to the United Fruit Co. and after reconversion resumed her former trade. She was converted to a freighter in 1953 and continued until August 1958 when she was sold to Elders and Fyffes of London and transferred to the British flag. She was renamed SULACO and served this owner until being scrapped in 1965.

SEGOVIA

—

SEGOVIA

Hull No: 345
Owner: United Fruit Co.
Launched: August 15, 1931
Delivered: —
Dimensions: 446.75 x 60 x 34.75 ft
Gross Tonnage: 6,963
Displacement: 10,930 tons
Machinery: Turbo-Electric, 4 Boilers,
 Twin Screw
Horsepower/Speed: 10,500/17.5 knots
Fate: Burned, 1931

SEGOVIA was the second of the United Fruit Co. liners built at Newport News and was to have the shortest "history" of any ship built at the yard. She was christened by Mrs. Herbert Hoover just an hour after TALAMANCA on August 15, 1931, and waters from several rivers in Central America were used for the ceremony instead of the traditional champagne.

SEGOVIA was alongside Pier 1 nearing completion on December 20, 1931, when fire broke out onboard and threatened to destroy her. Heroic efforts were made to extinguish the fire and such a great amount of water was used that she became unstable and capsized. All of the shipyard's engineering expertise was put to the task of righting her, and on March 3, 1932, using a complex arrangement of blocks, falls, and pontoons, she was righted.

On May 27 a contract was signed for the reconditioning and completion of the ship, which was assigned Hull No. 354 and was later renamed PETEN (q.v.).

PETEN
1933

PETEN

Hull No: 354
Owner: United Fruit Co.
Launched: August 15, 1931
Delivered: February 24, 1933
Dimensions: 446.75 x 60 x 34.75 ft
Gross Tonnage: 6,968
Displacement: 10,930 tons
Machinery: Turbo-Electric, 4 Boilers,
  Twin Screw
Horsepower/Speed: 10,500/17.5 knots
Fate: Scrapped, 1969

Originally built as SEGOVIA, Hull 345 (q.v.), and gutted by fire at her outfitting berth, this third United Fruit Co. ship was given Hull No. 354, reconstructed, and delivered in 1933 as PETEN. Under this name and later the name JAMAICA after 1937, she served her owner without incident.

She was acquired by the Navy in March 1942 and converted for service as the naval supply ship ARIEL (AF-22). She made one voyage to the Mediterranean and one to Iceland but served chiefly in familiar Caribbean and East Coast waters until April 1944. At that time, she crossed the Atlantic to support the Normandy invasion, afterwards returning to her usual service.

She reverted to the United Fruit Co. in June 1946, was renamed JAMAICA, and took up her prewar trade. In 1957 she was sold to Union-Partenreederi of Bremen, transferred to the German flag, and renamed BLUMENTHAL. After serving this owner for 14 years, she was sold for scrap in 1969 and was replaced by a new ship of the same name.

CHIRIQUI
1931

CHIRIQUI
Hull No: 346
Owner: United Fruit Co.
Launched: November 14, 1931
Delivered: March 18, 1932
Dimensions: 446.75 x 60 x 34.75 ft
Gross Tonnage: 6,964
Displacement: 10,930 tons
Machinery: Turbo-Electric, 4 Boilers, Twin Screw
Horsepower/Speed: 10,500/17.5 knots
Fate: Scrapped, 1971

CHIRIQUI was the last of three passenger and fruit cargo ships ordered by the United Fruit Co. in 1930, but she was delivered almost a year ahead of PETEN (ex-SEGOVIA), which had burned at pierside.

CHIRIQUI was launched three months after the twin launching of her two sister ships. She was christened by Mrs. H. Harris Robson, wife of the owner's general manager. As with the other ships, waters from South American rivers were used for the christening.

With cargo capacity for 60,000 bunches of bananas, CHIRIQUI entered the "Great White Fleet" in March 1932. In June 1941 she was acquired by the Navy, converted to a stores ship, and renamed TARAZED (AF-13). She served in the Atlantic and Mediterranean areas during the war, receiving one battle star for her service.

Her wartime service was uneventful, and she was returned to her owner at New Orleans in January 1946 and again took the name CHIRIQUI. She stayed in her former service until August 1958 when she was sold to Union-Partenreederi of Bremen, transferred to German flag, and renamed BLEXEN. After 13 years with this owner, she was removed from service and sold for scrap in 1971.

HAITI
1932

HAITI
Hull No: 348
Owner: Colombian Mail Steamship Corp.
Launched: September 17, 1932
Delivered: December 15, 1932
Dimensions: 404.42 x 57.5 x 31.5 ft
Gross Tonnage: 6,185
Displacement: 9,560 tons
Machinery: Geared Turbines, 4 Boilers
Horsepower/Speed: 6,500/16 knots
Fate: Scrapped, 1968

HAITI, a sister ship to COLOMBIA, was launched by Miss Margaret Stone Hardwick of Boston on September 17, 1932. Both of the ships were designed by Theodore E. Ferris, who designed many others built at the shipyard. Hull No. 349 was set aside for a third ship for the Colombian Mail Steamship Corp., but no contract for it was obtained.

HAITI was delivered on December 15, 1932, and, with COLOMBIA and another ship, enabled her owner to offer weekly service from New York to Haiti, Jamaica, and Colombia. A letter to the shipyard from Colombian Mail's president praised the new ships as perfect in every detail and lauded their arrangement and finish.

After six years of uneventful service, HAITI passed to the Puerto Rico Navigation Co. in 1938 and was renamed PUERTO RICO. In 1939 she went to the New York and Cuba Mail Steamship Co. with her sister and was renamed MONTEREY.

She was converted to an Army troopship with accommodations for 1,055 passengers in March 1942, made a voyage to India, then assisted during the invasion of North Africa. From February 1943 to February 1946 she served in the Caribbean area and made one voyage to Egypt in June 1945. She collided with a tanker near New Orleans in early 1946 but was not heavily damaged.

In 1948 she, like her sister, was sold to Turkish owners and was renamed ADANA. After ten more years of service she was withdrawn and scrapped in 1968.

COLOMBIA
1932

COLOMBIA

Hull No: 347
Owner: Colombian Mail Steamship Corp.
Launched: August 6, 1932
Delivered: November 17, 1932
Dimensions: 404.42 x 57.5 x 31.5 ft
Gross Tonnage: 5,236
Displacement: 9,560 tons
Machinery: Geared Turbines, 4 Boilers
Horsepower/Speed: 6,500/16 knots
Fate: Scrapped, 1967

COLOMBIA was the first of two handsome passenger and cargo vessels ordered in 1931 by the Colombian Mail Steamship Corp. These ships were slightly smaller than the United Fruit Co. steamers, but they were similar in appearance and were also designed for tropical service. COLOMBIA was launched by Mrs. C.H.C. Persall, wife of the owners'

vice president, on August 6, 1932, and the new ship completed trials and was delivered on November 17.

With accommodations for 144 passengers and a refrigerated cargo volume of 70,000 cubic feet, COLOMBIA entered the South American and West Indies trade, her maiden sailing being from New York on November 24, 1932. In 1937 her owner became known as the Colombian Steamship Co., and in December 1938 she was sold to the New York and Cuba Mail Steamship Co. and renamed MEXICO.

Placed in Army service in April 1942, she made 13 voyages in both the Atlantic and Pacific Oceans until July 1944 when she was placed in Southwest Pacific local service for ten months. Near the war's end she made several more long Pacific trips, then returned to New York for extensive repairs in February 1946.

In May 1947 she was sold to Turkish owners and was renamed ISTANBUL. She served faithfully in Turkish and Mediterranean waters until being broken up in 1967.

SAINT JOHN
1932

SAINT JOHN

Hull No: 350
Owner: Eastern Steamship Lines
Launched: January 9, 1932
Delivered: April 22, 1932
Dimensions: 403 x 61 x 29.75 ft
Gross Tonnage: 6,185
Displacement: 6,811 tons
Machinery: Geared Turbines, 4 Boilers,
   Twin Screw
Horsepower/Speed: 11,400/20 knots
Fate: Scrapped, 1959

SAINT JOHN and ACADIA were two fast coastal liners built for the Eastern Steamship Lines for service between Canada's maritime provinces and the northeastern United States. Designed by Theodore E. Ferris, they offered accommodations for 745 passengers and 178 crew and had spacious decks and expansive public rooms for their size.

SAINT JOHN was christened by Mrs. Robert G. Stone of Boston on a dreary January 9, 1932, with water from the famous Reversible Falls of Saint John, New Brunswick, and entered service with the Eastern fleet the following April. In a letter to the shipyard, her designer praised her as "just a wonderful ship" and noted that she received a grand welcome upon arriving at Boston on April 25.

The sleek SAINT JOHN enjoyed a routine career and was a popular ship during the 1930s. After almost ten years with Eastern, she was sold to the Navy in March 1941, converted for use as a submarine tender, and renamed ANTAEUS (AS-21). She remained in the submarine service until August 1942 when she was converted for transport service between Newfoundland, the Caribbean, and the Canal Zone.

During the winter of 1944-45 she was again converted, this time for hospital service, and renamed RESCUE (AH-18). She served off Okinawa in June 1945 and supported Third Fleet action against Japan in July and August. After entering Tokyo Bay with Halsey's fleet, she returned to San Francisco in September 1945.

She was decommissioned in April 1946 and, having won two battle stars for her war service, was transferred to the Maritime Commission and laid up. She remained inactive until 1958 when she was withdrawn from the Marad lay-up fleet and scrapped.

ACADIA
1932

ACADIA

Hull No: 351
Owner: Eastern Steamship Lines
Launched: February 13, 1932
Delivered: June 7, 1932
Dimensions: 403 x 61 x 29.75 ft
Gross Tonnage: 6,185
Displacement: 6,811 tons
Machinery: Geared Turbines, 4 Boilers,
    Twin Screw
Horsepower/Speed: 11,400/20 knots
Fate: Scrapped, 1955

ACADIA was the second of two fast coastal liners built for the Eastern Steamship Lines for service between Canadian and American Ports. Hull number 352 was reserved for a third ship but a contract for it was never signed. ACADIA was christened by Mrs. Calvin D. Austin of Boston on February 13, 1932, and, like SAINT JOHN, water from the Reversible Falls was used.

The new ship completed sea trials and was delivered on June 7, 1932. Fitted with side ports and elevators for autos, ACADIA served between New York and Yarmouth during the summer and between New York and Boston in the winter. In 1938 she entered the Bermuda-Cuba-Nassau trade; then, the following year she went to work returning stranded Americans from Europe.

In 1939 after surviving a hurricane in the North Atlantic, she served as a transport and supply vessel to American bases. She made headlines in her evasion of enemy submarines which, it was said, were hunting her on orders from Hitler himself. Shortly after Pearl Harbor she was converted at New York to carry 513 officers and 1,122 troops.

She operated in Caribbean waters until ordered in June 1942 to be converted to a "hospital transport." She made three trips to and from North Africa in this service and in June 1943 was converted to a true hospital ship—the first ship of the war so designated under Hague convention rules. Outfitted to care for 738 patients, she made many trips to North Africa and Europe before being transferred to the Pacific in mid-1945.

On her second trip to Manila she reverted back to transport service and her distinctive markings were removed. In May 1952 she was again converted to carry troops and dependents but shortly thereafter, was inactivated and laid up in the James River Fleet. In September 1955 the old veteran was withdrawn from retirement and sold for scrapping in Belgium.

AMERICA
1940

AMERICA

Hull No: 369
Owner: United States Lines
Launched: August 31, 1939
Delivered: July 2, 1940
Dimensions: 723 x 93.25 x 45.5 ft
Gross Tonnage: 26,455
Displacement: 35,440 tons
Machinery: Geared Turbines, 6 Boilers,
    Twin Screw
Horsepower/Speed: 37,400/23 knots
Fate: Laid up, 1982

Few ships built by any shipyard ever earned the fame or lived the history of a ship like AMERICA, delivered in 1940. Her contract cost was $17 million, and she was the largest passenger ship built in America up to that time. She was designed by Gibbs and Cox and her keel was laid by Emory S. Land on August 22, 1938. AMERICA was launched from Shipway 8 on August 31, 1939, being christened by Mrs. Franklin D. Roosevelt.

When completed and delivered in July 1940, AMERICA was the queen of the American merchant fleet. She had accommodations for 1,219 passengers and 639 crew and featured great advances in fire resistance and watertight subdivision. AMERICA enjoyed a tumultuous welcome in New York Harbor on July 29, 1940. Her maiden voyage began from New York on August 10 and was a 12 day cruise to the Caribbean.

Her early service was restricted due to the war in Europe, and she was requisitioned for troop service in mid-1941. She was extensively converted for this service at Newport News and sailed as WEST POINT on July 11, 1941. She had an incredible wartime service making 151 voyages totalling almost a half million miles.

She returned to Newport News on February 28, 1946, and was reconverted for merchant service as Hull 461 (q.v.). Her maiden postwar voyage from New York to Europe began on November 14, 1946, and she served U.S. Lines alone on this route until joined by the new UNITED STATES in 1952.

In 1964 with decreasing passenger volume, she was sold to Chandris Lines and transferred to Greek flag under the name AUSTRALIS. An unsuccessful attempt was made in 1978 to return her to American ownership and her original name; however, she was again sold and renamed ITALIS.

After overhaul and removal of her forward stack, she was sold to a Swiss firm and renamed NOGA. She remained laid up in Perama Bay, Greece, with plans for her to become a hotel ship, and in 1984 was sold to Silvermoon Ferries of Piraeus and renamed ALFERDOSS.

PRESIDENT JACKSON
1940

PRESIDENT JACKSON

Hull No: 379
Owner: American President Lines
Launched: June 7, 1940
Delivered: October 25, 1940
Dimensions: 491.75 x 69.5 x 42.5 ft
Gross Tonnage: 9,256
Displacement: 16,175 tons
Machinery: Geared Turbines, 2 Boilers
Horsepower/Speed: 8,500/16.5 knots
Fate: Scrapped, 1973

PRESIDENT JACKSON was the first of seven C-3 passenger and cargo ships built for American President Lines in 1940 and 1941. These ships were delivered for merchant service but were destined to be called for the war effort. They were of distinctive modern design and featured accommodations for 97 passengers and 76 crew. PRESIDENT JACKSON was sponsored by Mrs. William Gibbs McAdoo, wife of the owners' chairman, on a sunny June 7, 1940. The new ship completed trials successfully and was delivered to the Maritime Administration, then to American President Lines, successor to the Dollar Line, on October 25, 1940.

PRESIDENT JACKSON and her sisters were intended for round-the-world and trans-Pacific service, but the war intervened. She made two such trips from New York before being acquired by the Navy in June 1941.

Outfitted to carry 1,388 troops, she kept her name and was designated AP-37. After an intensive training period, she served faithfully in the South Pacific until the end of the war when she was placed in "Magic Carpet" service. During the war she was hit by a 550-pound bomb which did not explode, and in February 1945 she was shelled and suffered minor damage.

She operated with the Pacific Fleet until 1949 and served in China and Japan. She saw service in the Korean War and participated in the assault on Inchon in September 1950. After her Korean service she continued duty as a Navy transport moving personnel, dependents, and supplies between West Coast ports and Pacific bases.

Winner of eight battle stars for World War II service and three for Korean War service, PRESIDENT JACKSON was placed out of commission in reserve in July 1955 at San Francisco. In December 1958 she was transferred to the Maritime Commission and was laid up in Suisun Bay; then, in 1973 she was withdrawn and sold for scrapping in Taiwan.

PRESIDENT MONROE
1940

PRESIDENT MONROE
Hull No: 380
Owner: American President Lines
Launched: August 7, 1940
Delivered: December 19, 1940
Dimensions: 491.75 x 69.5 x 42.5 ft
Gross Tonnage: 9,256
Displacement: 16,175 tons
Machinery: Geared Turbines, 2 Boilers
Horsepower/Speed: 8,500/16.5 knots
Fate: Scrapped, 1970

PRESIDENT MONROE was the second of seven C-3 passenger and cargo ships built under Maritime Commission contract for American President Lines service. Like the other ships, Hull 380 was of the shelter-deck type with raked stem, cruiser stern, and two continuous decks. In addition to having accommodations for 97 passengers and 76 crew, the ships had a total cargo volume of 147,660 cubic feet.

PRESIDENT MONROE was christened by Mrs. Thomas G. Corcoran, wife of the special counsel for the Reconstruction Finance Corp., and was launched from Shipway 2 on August 7, 1940. As there was a great amount of Navy work underway in the yard, the launching was not open to the public.

The new ship was outfitted very quickly, completed trials, and was delivered on December 19, 1940. She entered round-the-world service with her owner and was clearing San Francisco Bay when word was flashed to her to return as the Japanese had attacked Pearl Harbor.

Like her sisters, she was taken by the WSA for service as a troopship. She was converted for the carriage of 2,043 passengers and was designated AP-104, retaining her name. She earned five battle stars for her World War II service and steamed across the Pacific and to Alaska on many voyages.

In January 1946 she was decommissioned and returned to American President Lines which she served until 1966. In that year, she was sold to the White Star Shipping and Trade Corp. of Athens, transferred to Panamanian flag, and renamed MARI-ANNA V. She served this owner for a few years before being scrapped in 1970.

PRESIDENT ADAMS
1941

PRESIDENT ADAMS
Hull No: 383
Owner: American President Lines
Launched: January 31, 1941
Delivered: November 19, 1941
Dimensions: 491.75 x 69.5 x 42.5 ft
Gross Tonnage: 9,261
Displacement: 16,175 tons
Machinery: Geared Turbines, 2 Boilers
Horsepower/Speed: 8,500/16.5 knots
Fate: Scrapped, 1973

PRESIDENT ADAMS was one of the so-called "unholy three" C-3 troopships of World War II fame. Originally ordered under a Maritime Commission contract, she was delivered directly to the Navy after some delay due to her conversion for naval service. PRESIDENT ADAMS was christened by Mrs. Robert H. Jackson, wife of the Attorney General of the United States, on January 13, 1941.

After her commissioning on November 19, 1941, PRESIDENT ADAMS soon saw action when she fired her guns at an enemy submarine on Christmas Day 1941. She was designated AP-38 (later APA-19) and supported the marines at Guadalcanal and later at Iwo Jima. She served with distinction in the Pacific war with her sister ships ferrying troops, supplies, and casualties and winning nine battle stars for her efforts.

After the war she moved occupation troops to the Far East and returned tired veterans to the West Coast. She later carried dependents and supplies to Navy bases in Japan, China, and the Philippines. In March 1947 she was transferred to Norfolk and was engaged in passenger and supply runs to the Caribbean until January 1950.

Designated for inactivation, she arrived at San Francisco and was placed in the Pacific Reserve Fleet in June 1950. In October 1958 she was struck from the Navy List and transferred to the Maritime Administration fleet at Suisun Bay where she remained until she was scrapped in 1973.

PRESIDENT HAYES
1941

PRESIDENT HAYES

Hull No: 381
Owner: American President Lines
Launched: October 4, 1940
Delivered: February 20, 1941
Dimensions: 491.75 x 69.5 x 42.5 ft
Gross Tonnage: 9,256
Displacement: 16,175 tons
Machinery: Geared Turbines, 2 Boilers
Horsepower/Speed: 8,500/16.5 knots
Fate: War Loss, 1942

The third C-3 passenger and cargo ship built at Newport News was PRESIDENT HAYES, Hull 381. This ship along with PRESIDENT JACKSON and PRESIDENT ADAMS, which followed, served together in the Pacific war and became known as the "unholy three." They were among the best known ships in the Pacific and their huge single stacks were distinctive.

PRESIDENT HAYES was launched by Mrs. Cordell Hull, wife of the Secretary of State, on October 4, 1940. As with the other ships, security restrictions related to the large amount of naval construction in the yard made the launching a quiet non-public event.

The new ship, when delivered on February 20, 1941, had large American flags painted on her sides and stern to identify her as a neutral. She did not stay in that status long, for on July 7, 1941, she was acquired by the Navy, outfitted for troop service, and designated AP-39.

She served faithfully during the Pacific war moving vital supplies and reinforcements and received 7 battle stars for her labors. While participating in the Rendova landings in June 1943 as APA-20, her gunners shot down seven enemy planes in that action.

PRESIDENT HAYES made several voyages in "Magic Carpet" service returning troops home after the war, then served with the Pacific Fleet until being decommissioned in 1949. She was placed in the Pacific Reserve Fleet at Stockton, CA, in February 1950 where she stayed until being transferred to the Maritime Commission in October 1958. She was laid up at Suisun Bay and remained there until June 2, 1975, when she was withdrawn for scrapping at Richmond, CA.

PRESIDENT VAN BUREN
1941

PRESIDENT VAN BUREN

Hull No: 384
Owner: American President Lines
Launched: May 1, 1941
Delivered: September 11, 1941
Dimensions: 491.75 x 69.5 x 42.5 ft
Gross Tonnage: 9,261
Displacement: 16,175 tons
Machinery: Geared Turbines, 2 Boilers
Horsepower/Speed: 8,500/16.5 knots
Fate: Scrapped, 1975

PRESIDENT VAN BUREN was the sixth of seven passenger and cargo liners built for American President Lines between 1940 and 1941, and she was the only one to be lost to enemy action during the war. PRESIDENT VAN BUREN was christened by Mrs. Alben W. Barkley, wife of the Senate Majority Leader (and later the 35th Vice President) on May 1, 1941. The new ship was delivered to American President Lines in September 1941 but was commissioned as a naval vessel and renamed THOMAS STONE (AP-59, later APA-29) in May 1942.

Converted for use as a war transport, the still-new ship saw a short and unlucky Navy career. She participated in exercises in British waters in October 1942, then loaded troops and equipment for the "Operation Torch" invasion of North Africa the following month. In the Mediterranean nearing Algiers, she was torpedoed on the morning of November 7 and her propeller, shafting, and rudder were damaged. Despite bad weather, salvage crews towed her into Algiers. On November 19, while at anchor awaiting repairs in Algiers harbor, she was hit by a bomb which exploded beneath her. On November 25 her fate was sealed as gale winds and heavy seas drove her aground and further damaged her hull.

Efforts to salvage her continued for over a year, but these were unsuccessful and she was placed out of commission in April 1944. Sold for scrapping, she was abandoned by her purchasers and was destroyed by the U.S. Government in July 1945.

PRESIDENT GARFIELD
1941

PRESIDENT GARFIELD
Hull No: 382
Owner: American President Lines
Launched: November 20, 1940
Delivered: March 26, 1941
Dimensions: 491.75 x 69.5 x 42.5 ft
Gross Tonnage: 9,261
Displacement: 16,175 tons
Machinery: Geared Turbines, 2 Boilers
Horsepower/Speed: 8,500/16.5 knots
Fate: Scrapped, 1973

PRESIDENT GARFIELD was the fourth of the Newport News built C-3 passenger ships which saw service in World War II. Hull 382 was launched from Shipway 5 at noon on Wednesday, November 20, 1940, by Miss Eugenia Merrill. The new ship completed trials and entered the service of American President Lines in March 1941.

PRESIDENT GARFIELD was on time charter on December 7, 1941, and, having left San Francisco on December 6, received word of the Pearl Harbor attack and turned back on December 8. Later she made three round trips to Honolulu before being acquired by the Navy in May 1942, converted to a troop transport at the shipyard, and renamed THOMAS JEFFERSON (AP-60, later APA-30).

She was commissioned on August 31, 1942, and shortly thereafter was one of four transports loaded with invasion troops bound for Fedhala, Morocco. On November 7, 1942, 16 of her 33 boats landed on a rocky beach instead of the intended invasion area and were lost. During November she rescued survivors of several torpedoed ships including those of TASKER H. BLISS (ex-GOLDEN STATE, Hull 256). After brief service in the Pacific, THOMAS JEFFERSON participated in the invasion of Italy and shuttled men and supplies throughout the Mediterranean.

In December 1944 she was transferred to the Pacific war and supported the Allied move into Okinawa. In September 1945 she carried occupation troops and supplies into Sasebo, Japan then was assigned to "Magic Carpet" duty returning servicemen to the United States.

After the war she stayed with the Navy and saw extensive Korean War service, earning four battle stars to add to the six she had earned in World War II. In 1955 she was placed in reserve; then, in 1958 she passed to the Maritime Administration fleet at Suisun Bay. In 1973 the old veteran was removed and sold for scrap.

PRESIDENT POLK
1941

PRESIDENT POLK
Hull No: 386
Owner: American President Lines
Launched: June 28, 1941
Delivered: November 6, 1941
Dimensions: 491.75 x 69.5 x 42.5 ft
Gross Tonnage: 9,261
Displacement: 16,175 tons
Machinery: Geared Turbines, 2 Boilers
Horsepower/Speed: 8,500/16.5 knots
Fate: Scrapped, 1970

Hull 386 was the seventh and last of the C-3 passenger and cargo ships with active wartime service records built at Newport News. PRESIDENT POLK was christened by Miss Patricia Kennedy, who was accompanied by her mother Mrs. Rose Kennedy and brother and sister Edward and Jean.

The new ship was acquired by the Navy in September 1943 after having been bareboat chartered since just after her delivery. Under charter she made one trip completely around the world and then served between West Coast ports and Alaska and Pacific islands.

PRESIDENT POLK was commissioned at San Diego in October 1943 and was designated AP-103. She served during the invasion of Tarawa, saw some duty as an emergency hospital ship, and won six battle stars. She stayed in the Pacific theater and at war's end was placed briefly in "Magic Carpet" service.

In January 1946 she was released from Navy service and was returned to the American President Lines. PRESIDENT POLK was operated by her original owner until being sold in 1965 to Ganaderos del Mar, S.A., and transferred to Liberian registry. She served this owner first as GAUCHO MARTIN FIERRO and then as MINOTAUROS until being sold for scrapping in Taiwan in 1970.

UNITED STATES
1952

Photo by Bill Radcliffe

UNITED STATES

Hull No: 488
Owner: United States Lines
Launched: June 23, 1951
Delivered: June 20, 1952
Dimensions: 990 x 101.5 x 74.83 ft
Gross Tonnage: 53,329
Displacement: 53,300 tons
Machinery: Geared Turbines, 8 Boilers,
    Quadruple Screw
Horsepower/Speed: 240,000/38.32 knots
Fate: Laid up, 1969

Only superlatives can be used to describe the fastest and most famous merchant ship ever built at Newport News, UNITED STATES. She was called an "engineering marvel," "a miracle in steel and aluminum," and she was the masterpiece of naval architect William Francis Gibbs. The UNITED STATES was designed to be the ultimate in ocean liners for 2,000 passengers and 1,000 crew, but was also intended for use in wartime to carry up to 14,000 troops.

UNITED STATES was christened by Mrs. Tom Connally, wife of the senator from Texas, on June 23, 1951, and was floated and pulled out of Shipway 10. Legend has it that proud shipyard workers had unoffically "christened" her the night before with Carolina corn whiskey smuggled into the yard for the purpose.

Over 2,000 tons of aluminum were used in the construction of the new liner and her huge stacks, the world's largest, were in place at launch. Her completion and modern decoration took until June 1952 and she went on highly successful trials on June 9-10.

She was delivered on June 20 and left the yard on June 22 for New York. She received a thunderous welcome in New York and sailed for LeHavre and Southampton on July 3, 1952. To no one's suprise, she easily won the Blue Riband from QUEEN MARY, making the voyage from Ambrose Light to Bishop Rock in three days, ten hours, and 40 minutes at an average speed of 35.59 knots.

The UNITED STATES joined AMERICA on the North Atlantic route and immediately became successful. During her first ten years of service, she sailed more than 1.6 million miles without a major breakdown and carried 653,638 passengers with an average load factor of 88.5 percent.

Her success was not to last, however, since competition from jet airliners, increasing operating losses, and continuing labor problems plagued her in the 1960s, eventually leading to withdrawal from service on November 14, 1969. She was at the shipyard where she had faithfully returned for every annual overhaul when the announcement was made. She remained at the yard until June 19, 1970, when she was moved to a permanent layup berth in Norfolk. She was purchased in 1981 by Richard H. Hadley of Seattle for $5 million with hopes of putting her back in service but she remained idle at her pier into the mid-1980s.

SANTA ROSA
1958

SANTA ROSA

Hull No: 521
Owner: Grace Line, Inc.
Launched: August 28, 1957
Delivered: June 12, 1958
Dimensions: 583.58 x 84 x 42.75 ft
Gross Tonnage: 15,367
Displacement: 19,238 tons
Machinery: Geared Turbines, 3 Boilers,
    Twin Screw
Horsepower/Speed: 20,000/20 knots
Fate: Laid up, 1975

SANTA ROSA was the first of two medium-sized liners of Gibbs and Cox design built for Grace Line and delivered in 1958. These were the last passenger ships built by the shipyard, and they had brief careers typical of liners built after the war. The compact single-stack design was somewhat reminiscent of UNITED STATES and AMERICA and featured an unusually large amount of space for 300 passengers.

SANTA ROSA was christened by Mrs. J. Peter Grace, wife of the president of Grace Line, on August 28, 1957, and was slip-launched from Shipway 5 into the James. Outfitting took just over nine months and interior decoration, was extensive. A Latin American motif was used in the decoration and SANTA ROSA's promenade deck was entirely devoted to public spaces. Her suites and passenger staterooms were roomy and handsome and the suites were given names associated with the countries along her route.

Sea trials were held in bad weather on May 26-28, 1958, and SANTA ROSA was delivered to Grace Line on June 12. Replacing an older SANTA ROSA, she was operated by Grace Line (later Prudential Grace Line) with moderate success into the early 1970s.

In March 1959, SANTA ROSA was involved in a collision with the tanker VACHEM off the New Jersey coast, and a new 50-ton bow was built and fitted to her at the shipyard in just under three weeks. Taken out of service by Prudential Grace in 1974, she was sold to Vintero Corp. of New York, who planned to put her in the Caribbean cruise trade. She was removed to Baltimore for renovation, but financial problems and a shipyard strike in Baltimore thwarted these plans, and SANTA ROSA remained in layup into the mid-1980s.

SANTA PAULA
1958

<table>
<tr><td colspan="2">SANTA PAULA</td></tr>
<tr><td>Hull No:</td><td>522</td></tr>
<tr><td>Owner:</td><td>Grace Line, Inc.</td></tr>
<tr><td>Launched:</td><td>January 9, 1958</td></tr>
<tr><td>Delivered:</td><td>October 9, 1958</td></tr>
<tr><td>Dimensions:</td><td>583.58 x 84 x 42.75 ft</td></tr>
<tr><td>Gross Tonnage:</td><td>15,367</td></tr>
<tr><td>Displacement:</td><td>19,238 tons</td></tr>
<tr><td>Machinery:</td><td>Geared Turbines, 3 Boilers, Twin Screw</td></tr>
<tr><td>Horsepower/Speed:</td><td>20,000/20 knots</td></tr>
<tr><td>Fate:</td><td>Converted, 1978</td></tr>
</table>

Twin sister of SANTA ROSA, SANTA PAULA was the last of 63 passenger ships built by Newport News Shipbuilding. She had the clean functional lines of her sister and, likewise, her public rooms were spacious and luxurious. The extensive safety precautions of fireproofing and a high degree of watertight subdivision which had been so innovative on UNITED STATES less than ten years before were commonplace by the time of the construction of the Grace Line ships. Like her sister, SANTA PAULA was fitted with Gyrofin stabilizers to reduce rolling in heavy seas and insure passenger comfort.

SANTA PAULA was launched from Shipway 7 on January 9, 1958, being christened by Mrs. Patricia Nixon, who was assisted by her daughters. The bottle was stubborn and would not break after two blows, but, as the ship got away from Mrs. Nixon, a shipyard worker hoisted it aboard and broke it on the bow.

After outfitting, the new ship completed 30 hours of sea trials and was delivered on October 9, 1958. Before entering the Caribbean trade, alternating with SANTA ROSA on sailings from New York, SANTA PAULA made a voyage up the Hudson to Albany, the largest ship ever to do so.

With passenger accommodations for 300, all in first class, and 418,000 cubic feet of cargo space, the new ships enjoyed success during their early years in service. They carried on the "Good Neighbor" tradition that Grace had established a century earlier but were eventually overcome, like most liners of their time, by increased operating expenses and declining passenger revenues.

In 1972 SANTA PAULA was withdrawn from service and, after a brief layup, was sold to Oceanic Sun Line Special Shipping of Greece and renamed STELLA POLARIS. The still relatively new ship was operated by this owner until 1978 when she was sold to National Hotels and Tourism Co. and transferred to the Liberian flag. Also in 1978 she was converted for use as a floating hotel and opened at Kuwait in February 1979 as the Kuwait Marriott Marina Hotel.

CARGO SHIPS
EL SUD
1892

EL SUD

Hull No: 3
Owner: Pacific Improvement Co.
Launched: March 16, 1892
Delivered: July 27, 1892
Dimensions: 405.75 x 48 x 33.75 ft
Gross Tonnage: 4,659
Displacement: 7,360 tons
Machinery: Triple Expansion Engine, 3 Boilers
Horsepower/Speed: 3,800/15 knots
Fate: Foundered, 1900

EL SUD (The South) was the first large ship built at Newport News and also was the first of a veritable fleet of 12 cargo vessels built for the Morgan Line between 1892 and 1902. In fact, these were the first 12 cargo ships built at the shipyard, and their fine construction and good speed did much to establish the yard's reputation in the early years and lead to profitable naval contracts.

The new steamer was successfully launched amid great celebration on March 16, 1892, and her launching was the only one at the shipyard ever attended by founder C.P. Huntington. EL SUD was christened by Miss Louise Armstrong, daughter of General S.C. Armstrong of Hampton.

Outfitting of the new ship was completed quickly and EL SUD was delivered to the Morgan Line on July 27, 1892, and started a brief but spectacular career. She entered the New Orleans to New York service after delivery and, with her sisters, quickly became known for her speed and efficiency.

After six years of routine merchant service, she was sold to the Navy for Spanish-American War service. Two of her four masts had been removed in 1896, and for naval service she was converted to an auxiliary cruiser at the shipyard and was renamed YOSEMITE. She was placed in Cuban blockade duty in June 1898, and soon after her arrival in Cuban waters, she bravely intercepted the Spanish steamer ANTONIO LOPEZ and practically destroyed her, despite enemy fire from shore batteries and gunboats.

After the war she remained on the Atlantic Coast until May 1899 when she left New York for the Far East via Suez. She arrived at Guam on August 7 and took up station there. On November 13, 1900, she was blown ashore and then out to sea by a violent typhoon. After two days of effort by her crew to save her, she sank about sixty miles from Guam on November 15, 1900.

EL NORTE
1892

EL NORTE
Hull No: 4
Owner: Pacific Improvement Co.
Launched: June 14, 1892
Delivered: September 15, 1892
Dimensions: 405.75 x 48 x 33.75 ft
Gross Tonnage: 4,659
Displacement: 7,360 tons
Machinery: Triple Expansion Engine, 3 Boilers
Horsepower/Speed: 3,800/15 knots
Fate: Stranded, 1908

The second Morgan liner built at the shipyard was EL NORTE (The North), whose keel was laid just one day after that of EL SUD. Like Hull 3 her construction was delayed by construction of the yard, and she was not launched until June 14, 1892. EL NORTE was christened by Miss Mary W. Orcutt, daughter of shipyard president C.B. Orcutt. A large crowd attended the launch of this large ship destined for New York, New Orleans, and Galveston service.

EL NORTE successfully completed trials on September 6, 1892, and was delivered just over a week later. With EL SUD, she saw routine coastal service during the 1890s and had two of her four masts and her auxiliary sailing rig removed while under Morgan Line ownership.

In May 1898 her official documents were surrendered and she was sold to the Navy, converted to an auxiliary cruiser, and renamed YANKEE. She was heavily armed, having eight 5″ guns mounted in hull casemates and two on deck in addition to six 6-pounders and two machine guns. She served with distinction during the Cuban blockade; then, after peace came she stayed on the Atlantic Coast and in the Caribbean. She was reclassified as a transport but was taken out of commission in September 1906 and was laid up at Portsmouth, NH.

Two years later YANKEE was recommissioned at Boston and took up training duty. During a training exercise in September 1908, she ran aground on Spindle Rock near Hens and Chickens Lightship, New Bedford, MA. She was refloated on December 4, 1908, but subsequently sank in Buzzard's Bay while being towed to New Bedford.

EL RIO
1893

EL RIO
Hull No: 5
Owner: Pacific Improvement Co.
Launched: October 26, 1892
Delivered: February 9, 1893
Dimensions 405.75 x 48 x 33.75 ft
Gross Tonnage: 4,664
Displacement: 7,360 tons
Machinery: Triple Expansion Engine, 3 Boilers
Horsepower/Speed: 3,800/15 knots
Fate: Scrapped, 1922

The third cargo ship built for Morgan Line service was EL RIO (The River) and she was the first ship built of steel at Newport News. Her contract was signed in January 1892, and her keel was laid just three months later. In evidence of improving facilities in the shipyard, her hull construction took only seven months and she was launched on October 26, 1892. EL RIO was christened by Miss Loulie Braxton, daughter of Col. Carter M. Braxton, who accompanied her.

Hull 5 was outfitted and completed trials and was delivered on February 9, 1893. EL RIO and her later sisters were fitted with but two masts, but they were still provided with auxiliary sails like Hulls 3 and 4.

The sleek new ship stayed in service between New York and New Orleans until her sale to the Navy in April 1898. She was converted by the shipyard to an auxiliary cruiser and, renamed DIXIE, was commissioned on April 19, 1898. She served in blockade and convoy duty in the Caribbean and participated in the capture of Ponce, Puerto Rico, receiving the surrenders of that town and La Playa.

She was briefly decommissioned in 1899, served as an Army transport, then was recommissioned in November 1899 for training duty. Between December 1899 and August 1900 she made a voyage to the Philippines via Suez; then she made two other voyages to the Mediterranean and to northern Europe.

Between 1902 and 1909 she was in and out of commission several times; then in February 1909 she was assigned as a destroyer tender to the Atlantic
(Continued on page 56)

EL CID
1893

EL CID (the Champion) was the fourth of the early Morgan Line steamers, and she had a longer career than any of her three sisters. Her contract was signed at about the same time as EL SUD was delivered and she was launched on May 31, 1893. Christened by Miss Lauretta Young, niece of Sommers N. Smith (the general superintendent of the shipyard), EL CID was completed and delivered in August 1893. The business climate was very bad in 1893, and the Morgan Line was probably glad to sell her to the Brazilian government in November.

During her brief merchant service, EL CID had, on her maiden trip, set a speed record of four days ten hours five minutes from New Orleans to New York and had prompted the press to say of her and her sisters, "the fleet is probably incomparable for the service on their speed and efficiency."

Purchased by the Brazilian government to help put down a revolution, EL CID was renamed NITCHEROY and was converted to a dynamite cruiser with a huge dynamite gun on her bow.

The U.S. Navy bought her back in July 1898 and commissioned her as the auxiliary cruiser BUFFALO. She made one trip to the Philippines, then traveled extensively as a naval training vessel in the Pacific. She served as a transport from 1906 until 1915, served with the Asiatic Fleet in China, then was converted to a destroyer tender and designated AD-8. She served in European waters during World War I, and then saw tender duty with the Pacific and Asiatic Fleets until 1922.

She was a barracks ship at San Diego until 1927 when she was sold. She passed to Philippine ownership and became a collier under the name SIRIUS in Far East service. After a many-faceted career in peace and war, the old veteran was finally scrapped in 1933.

EL SUD
1899

Four more steamers were ordered in 1898 by the Southern Pacific Co. for Morgan Line service to replace Hulls 3, 4, 5, and 6 which had been taken by the Navy for war service. The second group was identical in design to the first and had the same names. The keels for the first three of the second four ships were laid in late September 1898, and the second EL SUD and EL NORTE were launched on April 15, 1899. EL SUD was christened by Miss Jane H. Palen of Norfolk, sister of F.P. Palen who was draftsman-in-charge of the Engine Department at the shipyard.

The new EL SUD was ready for service in July 1899 and entered service on the Galveston-New York run. Her service was not interrupted by war, and her only known casualty was in 1915 when she stranded on the Galveston jetty in a hurricane.

In December 1925 she was sold to the Mallory Steamship Co. and was renamed PECOS. She served this owner with a number of other Newport News built ships, both passenger and cargo vessels, and passed with many of them to Clyde-Mallory Lines in 1932 and then to Agwilines in 1935. On May 10, 1935, she was sold to Italian shipbreakers for $23,000 and her long career came to an end.

EL NORTE
1899

EL NORTE
Hull No: 23
Owner: Southern Pacific Co.
Launched: April 15, 1899
Delivered: September 13, 1899
Dimensions: 405.75 x 48 x 33.75 ft
Gross Tonnage: 4,605
Displacement: 7,360 tons
Machinery: Triple Expansion Engine, 3 Boilers
Horsepower/Speed: 3,800/15 knots
Fate: Scrapped, 1934

The second EL NORTE was launched an hour after EL SUD on April 15, 1899. The honor of christening the new ship was bestowed on sponsor of the first EL NORTE, Miss Mary W. Orcutt of Elizabeth, NJ. After completing trials, the new EL NORTE was delivered on September 13, 1899, and entered coastal service with the Morgan Line.

Little is known of her career except that in 1907 she and sister EL SIGLO were chartered for the sugar trade. She remained in loyal service with her original owner on the New York, New Orleans, and Galveston route until 1934 when she was sold to Japanese shipbreakers and, renamed EL NORTE MARU, was taken to Japan and scrapped. Her condition in 1934 was evidently poor for her sale price was only $13,750, far below her original contract price of $600,000.

EL RIO
1899

EL RIO
Hull No: 24
Owner: Southern Pacific Co.
Launched: June 24, 1899
Delivered: October 19, 1899
Dimensions: 405.75 x 48 x 33.75 ft
Gross Tonnage: 4,604
Displacement: 7,360 tons
Machinery: Triple Expansion Engine, 3 Boilers
Horsepower/Speed: 3,800/15 knots
Fate: Collision, 1942

The second EL RIO had a long career and was the oldest Newport News ship to see World War II service. The keel for EL RIO and EL SUD were both laid on September 27, 1898, and EL RIO was ready for launch on June 24, 1899. She was christened by Miss Miriam Lodewick Post, sister of W.A. Post who was general superintendent of the shipyard.

Her trials completed, EL RIO joined the Morgan fleet in their coastal service in October 1899. Her career was unremarkable, although in October 1916 she picked up the crew of the sinking schooner T.W. DUNN on a voyage from New Orleans to Barcelona, Spain.

During the First World War she was acquired by the Navy, converted for service as a mine planter, and given the name HOUSATONIC (SP-1697). She was armed with a 5" gun, two 3" guns, and two machine guns and carried 100 men. She served in the Third Naval District from her commissioning on January 25, 1918, until she was returned to her owners on August 5, 1919.

In 1925 she passed to the Mallory Steamship Co. and was renamed BRAZOS. In 1932 her owner became the Clyde-Mallory Steamship Co.; then, in 1935 she was owned by Agwilines Inc. She was under charter to the New York and Porto Rico Line when she was struck and sunk without loss of life by an unidentified vessel about 150 miles southeast of Cape Hatteras on January 13, 1942.

EL RIO *Continued from page 54*

Fleet. During World War I she saw tender service at Queenstown, Ireland, and when peace came, she returned to the U.S. East Coast and was classified AD-1. After over twenty years of faithful Navy service, the old ship was decommissioned and sold for scrap in 1922.

EL CID
1899

EL CID

Hull No: 27
Owner: Southern Pacific Co.
Launched: October 7, 1899
Delivered: December 16, 1899
Dimensions: 405.75 x 48 x 33.75 ft
Gross Tonnage: 4,608
Displacement: 7,360 tons
Machinery: Triple Expansion Engine,
    3 Boilers
Horsepower/Speed: 3,800/15 knots
Fate: Scrapped, 1934

The second EL CID completed the second group of four cargo steamers built to replace the four Morgan Liners which were taken over by the Navy for Spanish-American war service. EL CID was christened by Miss Jessie Brahams at 10:00 A.M. on Saturday, October 7, 1899. This eighth Morgan Line ship built at

the shipyard had the shortest building time of the fleet of 12, taking just six months from keel to launch and two from launch to delivery.

EL CID was the last ship delivered by the yard in the 1800s and left the yard on December 16, 1899. She entered the New York to New Orleans service, and in 1902 she broke her later sister EL ALBA's speed record on that run by three hours, averaging 14.9 knots.

In November 1917 she was acquired by the Navy and was fitted out as a minelayer and renamed CANONICUS (CM-1696). With a complement of 368 officers and men, she operated out of Inverness, Scotland, and planted the mines of the North Sea barrage until January 1919. She made three trips between the East Coast and France before being returned to her owner in August 1919.

She continued with the Morgan Line in an uneventful career until being sold with three of her sisters in May 1934. She was sold to Japanese ship-breakers for only $13,750 and was taken to Japan for scrapping late in 1934.

EL VALLE
1901

EL VALLE

Hull No: 34
Owner: Southern Pacific Co.
Launched: March 9, 1901
Delivered: June 5, 1901
Dimensions: 405.75 x 48 x 33.75 ft
Gross Tonnage: 4,605
Displacement: 7,360 tons
Machinery: Triple Expansion Engine,
    3 Boilers
Horsepower/Speed: 3,800/15 knots
Fate: Scrapped, 1951

Hardly had the last of the second group of Morgan liners been launched when the Southern Pacific Co. ordered four more ships of this highly successful design by Horace See. EL VALLE (The Valley) was destined to be one of the most long-lived of the Morgan ships and to enjoy service with several owners. Hull 34

was christened on March 9, 1901, by Miss Maude Eleanor Converse, daughter of Capt. Converse of the battleship ILLINOIS, then being completed at the shipyard.

After outfitting and now-routine trials of her Newport News-built engine and boilers, EL VALLE joined the Morgan fleet in New York-New Orleans service in June 1901. Her service with her original owner was long and distinguished, and she kept her original name until 1941. In that year, she was sold to the Pan-Atlantic Steamship Co.—sold this time to the United Fruit Co.—and she stayed with them for two years.

In April 1947 she was again sold, transferred to Panamanian flag, and renamed ATZMAUT. In the service of the F & B Shipping Co. of Miami, she was engaged in transporting immigrants to Palestine to build the new nation of Israel. In early 1951 her usefulness was exhausted, and she was scrapped in Israel.

EL DIA
1901

EL DIA
Hull No: 35
Owner: Southern Pacific Co.
Launched: May 18, 1901
Delivered: September 15, 1901
Dimensions: 405.75 x 48 x 33.75 ft
Gross Tonnage: 4,616
Displacement: 7,360 tons
Machinery: Triple Expansion Engine, 3 Boilers
Horsepower/Speed: 3,800/15 knots
Fate: Scrapped, 1953

EL DIA (The Day) had the longest career of any of the 12 identical Morgan liners, and her career paralleled that of her sister EL VALLE and of several of her earlier sisters. EL DIA was christened by Mrs. Robert Stocker, wife of LCdr. Stocker who was stationed at Newport News. Hull 35 was launched on May 18, 1901,

and was ready for service the following September.

EL DIA stayed on the New York-New Orleans-Galveston run until 1917 when she was converted to a minelayer. Renamed ROANOKE, she entered naval service with three of her sister ships. Commissioned on January 25, 1918, she arrived in Scotland on May 18 and commenced planting the mines of the North Sea barrage. Early in 1919 she returned home, then made four trips to France as a transport, returning 5,500 troops home.

She was returned to her owner in September 1919 and, under her old name, served them until 1941, when she was sold with EL VALLE to the Pan-Atlantic Steamship Co. and was renamed PAN YORK. Her masts were cut down in 1941, and she was rebuilt in 1945 after being sold to the United Fruit Co.

In 1947 she was sold with her sister to the F & B Steamship Co. and was renamed KOMMIYUT. After several years of Palestine immigration transport, she was taken out of service and scrapped in 1953.

EL SIGLO
1901

EL SIGLO
Hull No: 36
Owner: Southern Pacific Co.
Launched: August 3, 1901
Delivered: November 30, 1901
Dimensions: 405.75 x 48 x 33.75 ft
Gross Tonnage: 4,613
Displacement: 7,360 tons
Machinery: Triple Expansion Engine, 3 Boilers
Horsepower/Speed: 3,800/15 knots
Fate: Scrapped, 1934

EL SIGLO (The Century) was the 11th cargo ship built at Newport News, and she was destined for service in both peace and war. Hull 36 was christened

by Miss Susan S. Usher, who was the daughter of LCdr. N.R. Usher of the new battleship ILLINOIS, on August 3, 1901. Completing successful trials during which she obtained a higher horsepower than any of her 11 sisters, she was delivered to the Morgan Line on November 30, 1901.

She saw 16 years of prosaic coastal service before being acquired for naval service in November 1917. She was converted to a minelayer and, renamed CANA-DAIGUA (CM-1694), she joined three other Morgan liners in laying the North Sea barrage. After 13 runs out of Inverness, she was converted to a transport and made four voyages to return troops from France.

She was returned to her owner in September 1919, and shortly thereafter was repaired and converted to oil fuel. After 15 more years with Morgan, she was sold for scrap with three of her sisters and was taken to Japan for demolition in late 1934.

EL ALBA
1902

EL ALBA

Hull No: 37
Owner: Southern Pacific Co.
Launched: November 2, 1901
Delivered: January 28, 1902
Dimensions: 405.75 x 48 x 33.75 ft
Gross Tonnage: 4,614
Displacement: 7,360 tons
Machinery: Triple Expansion Engine,
    3 Boilers
Horsepower/Speed: 3,800/15 knots
Fate: Scrapped, 1934

EL ALBA (The Dawn) was the last of the famous EL SUD-class freighters built at the shipyard. She became famous herself shortly after her delivery when she made a record passage from Galveston to New York in four days, 20 hours, and 38 minutes. EL ALBA was christened on November 2, 1901, by Miss Stella Brooks Miles, whose father was private secretary to Mr. Henry E. Huntington.

EL ALBA was completed and delivered on January 28, 1902, and joined her 11 running mates on the now-crowded route between New York and the Gulf ports. News clippings describe her career and reveal a series of casualties, none of which were fatal. In 1916 she suffered a bunker and cargo fire between New York and Galveston; then in May 1920, she had a fire in her cargo of rubber and cotton at New York. In January 1925 she was involved in a collision in New York Harbor and was damaged; then, exactly three years later she ran aground in the Houston channel and suffered $40,000 worth of damage. She was lucky, but her luck and her use fulness to the Morgan Line ran out in May 1934, when she too was sold to Japanese shipbreakers and taken to Japan for scrapping.

EL ORIENTE
1910

EL ORIENTE

Hull No: 132
Owner: Southern Pacific Co.
Launched: August 6, 1910
Delivered: October 24, 1910
Dimensions: 430 x 53 x 36 ft
Gross Tonnage: 6,008
Displacement: 10,030 tons
Machinery: Triple Expansion Engine,
    3 Boilers
Horsepower/Speed: 5,500/15.25 knots
Fate: Scrapped, 1947

EL ORIENTE (The East) had a career which remarkably paralleled that of her predecessor, EL MUNDO. EL ORIENTE's keel was laid on January 18, 1910, and she was launched on August 6, 1910. Hull 132 was christened by Miss Margaret H. Patton of East Orange, NJ, who was the daughter of Southern Pacific's New York agent. EL ORIENTE was com-pleted in October 1910 and entered uneventful New York-Texas service with her sister ships.

In July 1918 she was commissioned as a naval transport and saw duty ferrying cargo, animals, and later troops back and forth to France before being returned to her owners in September 1919. On December 14, 1928, she ran aground near Liberty Island in New York Harbor, and, after her cargo was lightered off, she was refloated and repaired.

In the 1930s she added Boston and other New England ports to her itinerary, and in May 1936 she went aground on the north side of the Cape Cod Canal but was successfully pulled off.

She went out of documentation in September 1941 but was operated by the U.S. Government during the war. She remained under American flag but was reported in decrepit condition with peeling paint, covered side ports, and no wearing pieces on her hull. In January 1946 with her wartime service over, she was placed in the James River fleet, where she stayed until being scrapped at Baltimore in 1947.

JEAN
1909

JEAN

Hull No: 117
Owner: A.H. Bull & Co.
Launched: June 19, 1909
Delivered: August 2, 1909
Dimensions: 328.08 x 46 x 24.25 ft
Gross Tonnage: 3,126
Displacement: 6,580 tons
Machinery: Triple Expansion Engine,
   2 Boilers
Horsepower/Speed: 1,200/10 knots
Fate: Scrapped, 1954

Seven years and 80 hulls passed between EL ALBA and the small cargo ship JEAN delivered in 1909. JEAN was the first of seven cargo vessels built for A.H. Bull & Co. between 1909 and 1934, and she had a very long career under a number of owners and flags. She was also the first freighter intended for foreign trade built in the United States in ten years. The keel for JEAN was laid on February 15, 1909, and she was

launched on June 19 of that year. Her sponsor was Miss Evelyn Ray Bull, daughter of Mr. A.H. Bull.

Although called a cargo ship, JEAN served as a collier for much of her career. After delivery to Bull in August 1909, she carried a cargo of coal from Baltimore to Tampa on her maiden voyage.

She was chartered by the Army in 1917; then in August 1918, she was commissioned for Navy service. JEAN was assigned to the Fifth Naval District and made trips to France and to South America.

She was returned to A.H. Bull & Co. in April 1919 and continued in prosaic service until 1926. In that year she was sold to Greek owners and was renamed MARGARITA CALAFATI. In 1928 her name was changed to GLADSTONE; then, in 1929 she was sold to M. Sanberg & Co., transferred to Latvian flag, and renamed SPORTS. She kept this unusual name and remained under Latvian registry until 1948, when her owner became the British Ministry of Transport; W.A. Souter & Co. managers.

In 1953 her ownership again changed, to Cia. Marittima Sports of Panama, and late in 1954 her luck ran out and she was sold for scrap and broken up.

RUTH
1910

RUTH
Hull No: 135
Owner: A.H. Bull & Co.
Launched: June 11, 1910
Delivered: August 8, 1910
Dimensions: 328.08 x 46 x 24.25 ft
Gross Tonnage: 3,102
Displacement: 6,610 tons
Machinery: Triple Expansion Engine, 2 Boilers
Horsepower/Speed: 1,200/10 knots
Fate: Scrapped, 1933

RUTH was the second ship built by the yard for A.H. Bull & Co., and she was built to carry phosphate rock from Florida to northern ports. Identical to JEAN, delivered to Bull the year before, RUTH was launched on June 11, 1910. The new ship was christened by her namesake, little Miss Ruth Priscilla Killeen, niece of the treasurer of the owning company. The new ship and her sister ship had the amidships superstructure and machinery and raised poop and forecastle which were to characterize general cargo ships for decades to follow.

RUTH entered her intended trade in August 1910 and plodded along for A.H. Bull & Co. until she was sold to the Meddo Steamship Co. of New York in May 1930. Renamed MEDDO, she served briefly with her new owner but was laid up in 1932 at New York. In 1933 she was removed from documentation and was scrapped.

HILTON
1911

HILTON
Hull No: 146
Owner: A.H. Bull & Co.
Launched: June 10, 1911
Delivered: July 8, 1911
Dimensions: 328.08 x 46 x 24.25 ft
Gross Tonnage: 3,102
Displacement: 6,610 tons
Machinery: Triple Expansion Engine, 2 Boilers
Horsepower/Speed: 1,200/10 knots
Fate: Scrapped, 1951

HILTON was the third of seven cargo ships built at Newport News for A.H. Bull & Co. between 1909 and 1934. Construction from keel to launch took only four months, and HILTON was launched from Shipway 4 by Miss Dorothy Bull on June 10, 1911. The new freighter was delivered to her owners less than a month later and entered service in southern, coastwise, and Puerto Rican trade.

Before World War I she was chartered to the Army; then in November 1918 she was commissioned as a naval transport at Cardiff, Wales. Based at Cardiff, she carried two cargoes to France before sailing home to be returned to Bull at Hampton Roads in April 1919.

She continued prosaic cargo service until being sold to the Eastern Transportation Co. in September 1935, converted to a barge of 2,801 GRT, and renamed HERCULES. She remained in service as a barge until being sold to the Norfolk Ship Salvage Co. which broke her up for scrap in 1951.

EVELYN
1912

EVELYN

Hull No: 156
Owner: A.H. Bull & Co.
Launched: May 9, 1912
Delivered: June 11, 1912
Dimensions: 328.17 x 46 x 25.5 ft
Gross Tonnage: 3,141
Displacement: 6,610 tons
Machinery: Triple Expansion Engine,
   2 Boilers
Horsepower/Speed: 1,200/10 knots
Fate: Scrapped, 1946

EVELYN was the fourth ship built for A.H. Bull & Co. by the shipyard, and she was to enjoy a more varied than average career. EVELYN was christened by her namesake, little Miss Evelyn Kiggins, granddaughter of A.H. Bull, on May 9, 1912. Completed just over a month later, EVELYN and her crew of 30 entered the southern, coastwise, and Puerto Rican trade with her sisters. She evidently did not see military service in World War I and never suffered a casualty except for a minor collision in the Chesapeake Bay in 1937. She and her sisters returned to the shipyard often during their careers for repairs and overhauls as their trade often brought them nearby.

EVELYN was acquired by the Navy in September 1942 and was converted for service as a "Q" ship to be used as bait for enemy submarines. She was armed with 4" guns and was renamed ASTERION (AK-63) for this duty. Unsuccessful in this service after six cruises, she was awarded one battle star and then was converted to a weather observation ship.

She was transferred to the Coast Guard at Boston in January 1944 and performed observation duties until she was decommissioned in July of that year. In 1946 the old veteran was sold and broken up for scrap.

CAROLYN
1912

CAROLYN

Hull No: 158
Owner: A.H. Bull & Co.
Launched: July 3, 1912
Delivered: July 20, 1912
Dimensions: 328.17 x 46 x 25.5 ft
Gross Tonnage: 3,141
Displacement: 6,610 tons
Machinery: Triple Expansion Engine,
    2 Boilers
Horsepower/Speed, 1,200/10 knots
Fate: War Loss, 1942

CAROLYN had a career similar to that of her sister ship EVELYN but came to a tragic end in war service. CAROLYN was christened and launched from Shipway 7 by Miss Carolyn Bull, also a granddaughter of A.H. Bull, on July 3, 1912. CAROLYN was delivered only 17 days later and entered service with her sisters.

Her career was uneventful, and she plodded along in cargo service until being acquired by the Navy early in 1942. Like EVELYN, she was converted for "Q" ship service, and was renamed ATIK. The "Q" ships were mystery ships which appeared to be cargo ships but baited submarines for the purpose of destroying them with their superior firepower. Just four days out of Portsmouth, NH, on a shakedown cruise, ATIK was torpedoed by the German submarine U-123. Damaged, she turned broadside and attempted to destroy the surfaced submarine, but it moved out of range. A few hours later the sub approached in darkness and torpedoed ATIK in her engine room, sending her to the bottom about 300 miles east of Norfolk. Neither wreckage nor survivors were found by sister ship ASTERION, and ATIK's crew of 141 apparently went down with her.

EL SOL
1910

EL SOL

Hull No: 130
Owner: Southern Pacific Co.
Launched: May 11, 1910
Delivered: August 20, 1910
Dimensions: 430 x 53 x 36 ft
Gross Tonnage: 6,008
Displacement: 10,030 tons
Machinery: Triple Expansion Engine,
   3 Boilers
Horsepower/Speed: 5,500/15 knots
Fate: Collision, 1927

EL SOL (The Sun) was the first of four identical cargo ships built for a good customer, the Southern Pacific Co., in 1910. These ships were somewhat larger than the 12 EL SUD-class ships that preceded them, and although they were sleek, they lacked the sailing ship looks of their earlier sisters. In marked contrast to the earlier ships, all four of the 1910 vessels went from the first keel to the last delivery in less than 13 months. The keel for EL SOL was laid on November 9, 1909. Launched on May 11, 1910, she was christened by

Miss Helen Torney, daughter of her owners' assistant manager.

The new ship was delivered on August 20, 1910, and entered service on the New York-New Orleans-Galveston route, under the management of Atlantic Steamship Lines, with her many older sisters. Early in World War I, she was chartered for Army service; then, in August 1918 she was commissioned as a naval vessel and made four trips to France with Army supplies. In April 1919 she became a troop transport and made two more voyages to France to return American troops home.

In September 1919 she was returned to her owners and took up her former service. EL SOL was lucky in her wartime service and escaped attack and damage by the enemy. She was not so fortunate in peacetime, however, and her end came practically at her owner's doorstep. She was rammed off the Statue of Liberty in New York harbor in fog on the morning of March 11, 1927, by the Black Diamond freighter SAC CITY and sank in just a few minutes with a gaping hole in her side. She was declared a total loss, but fortunately only one of her 47 crew members went down with her.

EL MUNDO
1910

EL MUNDO

Hull No: 131
Owner: Southern Pacific Co.
Launched: June 25, 1910
Delivered: September 25, 1910
Dimensions: 430 x 53 x 36 ft
Gross Tonnage: 6,008
Displacement: 10,030 tons
Machinery: Triple Expansion Engine,
    3 Boilers
Horsepower/Speed: 5,500/15.25 knots
Fate: Scrapped, 1947

EL MUNDO (The World) was the second of the 10,000 ton cargo ships delivered to Southern Pacific in 1910. She was destined to enjoy a long career, albeit with a rather decrepit old age. The contract for all four of the ships was signed on July 10, 1909, and EL MUNDO was launched less than a year later on June 25, 1910. Hull 131 was christened by Mrs. Samuel Ira Cooper, wife of the secretary to the owner's manager.

EL MUNDO entered the New York to Texas coastal trade the following September. Her career was uneventful for ten years; then an explosion occurred while she was at dock in New York on November 20, 1920, and, having caught fire, she was towed out and beached. She was salvaged and repaired and re-entered routine service. In October 1928 a fire broke out and damaged some of her cotton cargo while she was on a voyage from Houston and Galveston to New York.

In September 1941 she went out of documentation but was taken over by the Maritime Commission and transferred to Panamanian flag. Several reports indicated that her condition rapidly deteriorated, but she apparently served out the wartime years without mishap. The rusty old EL MUNDO was laid up in the James River in September 1945, where she stayed until being scrapped at Baltimore in 1947.

EL OCCIDENTE
1910

EL OCCIDENTE

Hull No: 133
Owner: Southern Pacific Co.
Launched: September 24, 1910
Delivered: December 2, 1910
Dimensions: 430 x 53 x 36 ft
Gross Tonnage: 6,008
Displacement: 10,030 tons
Machinery: Triple Expansion Engine,
    3 Boilers
Horsepower/Speed: 5,500/15.25 knots
Fate: War Loss, 1942

EL OCCIDENTE (The West) was the last of the second group of cargo ships built for Morgan interests, and she was one of but two ships built for these owners to become a war loss. EL OCCIDENTE was christened by Mrs. C.W. Jungen, wife of the owner's manager, on September 24, 1910.

She entered New York-Texas service in December 1910, where she remained until being commissioned as a naval transport in August 1918. She served principally as an animal transport and on one voyage to France, carried 800 horse and mule "passengers" and 1,467 tons of cargo. In 1919 she was converted to carry human passengers, and she made one more voyage before being returned to Southern Pacific in June 1919.

In December 1920, EL OCCIDENTE caught fire from an explosion aboard the barge BOLIKOW at Galveston but was repaired. In March 1926 she suffered a cargo fire at Key West but was apparently not heavily damaged; then, in October 1928 she collided with the Italian freighter PIETRO CAMPANELLA and her superstructure was damaged.

Like her predecessors, she went into government service in 1941, but unlike them, she was sent to the bottom of the North Atlantic on April 13, 1942, by enemy action.

COROZAL
1911

COROZAL

Hull No: 142
Owner: N.Y. & Porto Rico Co.
Launched: December 31, 1910
Delivered: February 19, 1911
Dimensions: 347.5 x 46.75 x 25 ft
Gross Tonnage: 3,063
Displacement: 7,030 tons
Machinery: Triple Expansion Engine,
   3 Boilers
Horsepower/Speed: 1,500/10 knots
Fate: Scrapped, 1958

COROZAL was the first of five identical cargo ships built for the New York & Porto Rico Steamship Co. between 1911 and 1915. Later the shipyard built the passenger liner COAMO as Hull 280 for this same owner. COROZAL and her sisters were of medium size, slightly larger than the Bull ships, and were intended for New York to Caribbean service. Named for a town in Puerto Rico, COROZAL was christened by Miss Bentley Robinson on December 31, 1910. The handsome new ship was completed just six weeks later and was delivered on February 19, 1911.

COROZAL's early career was uneventful. She was requisitioned for naval service in March 1918 and made three voyages to Nantes, France, with coal and then a fourth to Rochefort and Rotterdam. She was returned to her owner in April 1919. In April 1928 she was involved in a collision and grounding but apparently was not heavily damaged.

In April 1935 she passed to the ownership of Agwilines, and her uneventful career carried her safely through World War II. In February 1946 she was sold to the Chung Hsing Company of Shanghai and was renamed YUNG HSING. In 1950 she passed to Panamanian ownership and was renamed FAIRSIDE; then in 1951 she reverted to Chinese ownership and was renamed LIN CHEN.

Her active service continued until 1955 when she was removed from classification and was apparently laid up. Offical records do not reveal her ultimate fate but imply that she was scrapped around 1958.

MONTOSO
1911

MONTOSO

Hull No: 143
Owner: N.Y. & Porto Rico Co.
Launched: January 21, 1911
Delivered: March 5, 1911
Dimensions: 347.5 x 46.75 x 25 ft
Gross Tonnage: 3,063
Displacement: 7,030 tons
Machinery: Triple Expansion Engine,
    3 Boilers
Horsepower/Speed: 1,500/10 knots
Fate: Scrapped, 1953

MONTOSO was the second cargo ship built for the New York & Porto Rico Steamship Co., and her career closely paralleled that of her sister ship COROZAL. MONTOSO was christened on January 21, 1911, by Miss Mabel V. Basham and was ready for service when delivered the following March 5.

The new ship's service carried her from New York to Caribbean and Gulf Coast ports, and she apparently never suffered a casualty during her busy career. She was chartered by the Army for transport service early in World War I but was commissioned for naval service in December 1918 to carry ammunition and supplies. She made a voyage to Nantes, France, and on her return in January 1919, she located and towed the disabled steamer WEST HAVEN to Bermuda. She was returned to her owner the following March 13 and took up her old trade.

She passed to Agwilines ownership in 1935 and survived World War II, only to be sold to the Chung Hsing Steamship Co., renamed CHEE HSING, and transferred to Chinese flag in February 1946. In 1950 she was sold to the Grande Shipping Co. and, renamed STARSIDE, sailed under Panamanian flag. After over 40 years of hard service, the old ship was finally scrapped in 1953.

ISABELA
1911

ISABELA

Hull No: 145
Owner: N.Y. & Porto Rico Co.
Launched: June 24, 1911
Delivered: August 25, 1911
Dimensions: 347.5 x 46.75 x 25 ft
Gross Tonnage: 3,063
Displacement: 7,030 tons
Machinery: Triple Expansion Engine,
    3 Boilers
Horsepower/Speed: 1,500/10 knots
Fate: War Loss, 1942

The third cargo ship built for the New York & Porto Rico Steamship Co. was ISABELA, delivered in August 1911. ISABELA was christened by Miss Elizabeth Livesey on June 24, 1911. When delivered two months later, the new ship had the same sturdy good looks as her sister with a long unbroken sheer line and tall kingposts and stack. Employed by her owners, mostly in the New York to Puerto Rico trade, ISABELA evidently never suffered collision or casualty.

When war came, she was commissioned as a naval transport in April 1918 and made four voyages to France before being returned on February 14, 1919. She took up her former service with her original owner until February 1935, when she and her sisters passed to the ownership of Agwilines, Inc.

ISABELA had enjoyed a 30 year incident-free career but her luck did not hold. On May 18, 1942, she was sunk by enemy action about 20 miles off Navassa Island in the Caribbean, and three of her 37 crew were lost.

LORENZO
1913

LORENZO

Hull No: 163
Owner: N.Y. & Porto Rico Co.
Launched: January 25, 1913
Delivered: February 19, 1913
Dimensions: 347.5 x 46.75 x 25 ft
Gross Tonnage: 3,063
Displacement: 7,030 tons
Machinery: Triple Expansion Engine,
    3 Boilers
Horsepower/Speed: 1,500/10 knots
Fate: War Loss, 1918

LORENZO was the fourth of five identical cargo ships built for the New York & Porto Rico Steamship Co. between 1911 and 1915. The 3,063 ton freighter was launched by Miss Ruth Smith, daughter of Newport News' clerk of courts, on January 25, 1913. Outfitting was completed in brisk fashion, and LORENZO was delivered to her owners only 25 days after her launch.

The handsome new ship and her crew of 40 were not destined for a long career. After only 18 months of coastal, Caribbean, and Gulf service, LORENZO was seized by the British warship BERWICK at St. Lucia on September 12, 1914. Having been under charter to H.A.P.A.G. carrying 2,000 tons of coal and 150 tons of provisions for German cruisers, she was condemned by British Prize Court at Kingston, Jamaica, in September 1914. She was then taken over by the British government and was renamed HUNSGROVE. She served under British flag until she was torpedoed and sunk near Trevose Head, off the Southwest Coast of England, on June 8, 1918.

MARIANA
1915

MARIANA

Hull No: 188
Owner: N.Y. & Porto Rico Co.
Launched: May 22, 1915
Delivered: July 3, 1915
Dimensions: 347.5 x 46.75 x 25 ft
Gross Tonnage: 3,063
Displacement: 7,030 tons
Machinery: Triple Expansion Engine, 3 Boilers
Horsepower/Speed: 1,500/10 knots
Fate: War Loss, 1942

MARIANA was the last of five COROZAL-class freighters built for the New York & Porto Rico Steamship Co. between 1911 and 1915. A coal-burner like her sisters, MARIANA originally had a crew of 34. She was christened by Miss Almeria P. Bailey, daughter of the chief engineer of the shipyard, on May 22, 1915 and was launched from Shipway 3.

MARIANA entered service in July 1915 and sailed with the New York & Porto Rico Co. until July 1918, when she was chartered by the Navy and commissioned as a transport. She sailed from Baltimore with a cargo of over 3,000 tons of supplies and with a crew of 78. She was armed with two 4″ guns and made two voyages to Europe and served on local European supply routes.

She was decommissioned and returned to her owner at New York in April 1919. In 1936 her ownership passed to Agwilines, and she continued her usual service apparently untouched by casualty or incident. Her luck was not to last, however, since she was lost to enemy action somewhere in the North Atlantic on March 6, 1942. Details of her demise are sketchy, and it is assumed that her crew of 36 went down with her.

PETER H. CROWELL
1912

PETER H. CROWELL

Hull No: 161
Owner: Crowell & Thurlow Co.
Launched: December 12, 1912
Delivered: December 21, 1912
Dimensions: 382.17 x 46 x 24.25 ft
Gross Tonnage: 3,101
Displacement: 6,610 tons
Machinery: Triple Expansion Engine,
   2 Boilers
Horsepower/Speed: 1,200/10 knots
Fate: Scrapped, 1939

Between 1912 and 1917 the shipyard built four freighters and three colliers for the Crowell & Thurlow Steamship Co. of Boston. The first two freighters were identical to the ships built for A.H. Bull & Co. during the same period, and the first of these, PETER H. CROWELL, bore Hull No. 161. PETER H. CROWELL

was christened by Miss Florence A. Thurlow and was launched from Shipway 7 on December 12, 1912. Most of the outfitting work for this ship was completed on the ways, and delivery was made only nine days after launch. The shipyard was extremely busy at this time, and a launching or delivery occurred almost every month.

Although considered a cargo ship, PETER H. CROWELL spent most of her career in the coastal coal trade. She saw World War I service with the Navy from December 1917 to March 1919 and made several trips to France in convoy from New York. She was overhauled at New York and made one trip to San Diego early in 1919.

In 1924 she was sold to the Mystic Steamship Co. of Boston; then, in 1936 she passed to the Koppers Coal & Transportation Co. She underwent a major overhaul at Boston in 1933 but was never known to have suffered a serious casualty in her long career. After almost 30 years of faithful service under her original name, PETER H. CROWELL was scrapped in 1939.

LEWIS K. THURLOW
1913

LEWIS K. THURLOW

Hull No: 169
Owner: Crowell & Thurlow Co.
Launched: October 4, 1913
Delivered: November 14, 1913
Dimensions: 328.17 x 46 x 25.5 ft
Gross Tonnage: 3,178
Displacement: 6,610 tons
Machinery: Triple Expansion Engine, 2 Boilers
Horsepower/Speed: 1,200/10 knots
Fate: Scrapped, 1951

LEWIS K. THURLOW was the second general cargo ship built for the Crowell & Thurlow Co. of Boston, and she was similar in dimensions to PETER H. CROWELL, delivered in 1912, and to several of the ships built for A.H. Bull & Co. The new freighter was christened by Miss Grace B. Crowell on October 4, 1913, and was outfitted and completed sea trials just over a month later.

LEWIS K. THURLOW and her crew of 32 stayed in service with Crowell & Thurlow until November 1918 when, on a trip to Wales, she was acquired by the Navy and commissioned under the name L.K. THURLOW. She made one trip to France with a cargo of trucks and coal and then made a second trip; then, she returned to the United States with a cargo of 1,300 tons of airplane parts and reverted to her owner at Philadelphia in March 1919.

She had a remarkably uneventful career and served Crowell & Thurlow until January 1924, when she was sold to the Mystic Steamship Co. Although she was considered to be a freighter, she doubtless spent some of her career transporting coal for these owners. In 1937 she was sold to the Eastern Transportation Co. and was cut down to a barge of 2,914 GRT and renamed AJAX. Homeported in Wilmington, DL, she served with Eastern for almost 15 years before she was cut up for scrap in 1951.

MEDINA
1914

MEDINA

Hull No: 176
Owner: Mallory Steamship Co.
Launched: August 22, 1914
Delivered: September 29, 1914
Dimensions: 420.67 x 54.25 x 33.75 ft
Gross Tonnage: 5,426
Displacement: 9,245 tons
Machinery: Triple Expansion Engine, 4 Boilers
Horsepower/Speed: 4,100/14 knots
Fate: In Service

MEDINA was sister ship to the ill-fated NECHES, and she bacame one of the most long-lived products of Newport News shipbuilders. MEDINA was built for the Mallory Line and was christened by Miss Frances Stuart Semmes of Newport News on August 22, 1914.

The first of MEDINA's several careers was in New York to Galveston service with Mallory. She also sailed to Mexican ports, and in 1932 her owner became known as Clyde-Mallory Lines after a merger. Under Agwilines ownership after 1935, MEDINA spent some time under charter to the Cuba Mail Line in service between Caribbean ports and New York.

In 1947 she was sold and passed to Panamanian flag. She was converted from freight to passenger service in an Italian shipyard and, renamed ROMA, gained a long superstructure and a new modern look. In 1952 she was sold to Costa Lines of Genoa and was renamed FRANCA C. Carrying 900 passengers in two classes, she sailed between Genoa and South American ports. Her steam engine was replaced by a Fiat diesel and she was fitted with a squat modern stack. Late in the 1950s she became a one-class cruise ship in Mediterranean service. She retained her popularity and youthful appearance despite her years and was in Caribbean service during the 1970s.

Laid up in 1978, she astonished the maritime industry by finding a buyer who overhauled her and put her back into active service. Renamed DOULOS (Servant) and under Maltese registry, the 64 year-old veteran began a new career as an evangelical ship in the hands of Operation Mobilization in worldwide service.

NECHES
1914

NECHES

Hull No: 175
Owner: Mallory Steamship Co.
Launched: June 27, 1914
Delivered: August 20, 1914
Dimensions: 420.67 x 54.25 x 33.75 ft
Gross Tonnage: 5,426
Displacement: 9,245 tons
Machinery: Triple Expansion Engine, 4 Boilers
Horsepower/Speed: 4,100/14 knots
Fate: Collision, 1918

NECHES and MEDINA were two large freighters built for the Mallory Steamship Co. and delivered in 1914. Passenger liner HENRY R. MALLORY was of similar dimensions and was delivered to Mallory two years later. The two freighters had sharply contrast-

ing careers: NECHES was lost after only four years of service, but MEDINA was still in service over 70 years after her delivery.

NECHES was christened by Miss Alice Burwell Reed of Richmond on June 27, 1914. Less than two months later the new ship was delivered to the Mallory Line and entered service in coastal and international trade.

In January 1917 she and MEDINA were chartered for trade between New York and the River Plate. May 1918 found her in English waters, and she suffered her first and last mishap in collision with a British patrol vessel. In transport service for the U.S. Government, she was struck in dense fog while in convoy returning to America, and a hole was opened in her side. Despite heroic efforts by her crew and her naval armed guard to save her, she went down within a few hours—apparently without loss of life.

EDGAR F. LUCKENBACH
1916

EDGAR F. LUCKENBACH

Hull No: 190
Owner: Luckenbach Steamship Co.
Launched: March 29, 1916
Delivered: May 10, 1916
Dimensions: 442 x 57 x 42 ft
Gross Tonnage: 8,061
Displacement: 14,990 tons
Machinery: Triple Expansion Engine, 3 Boilers
Horsepower/Speed: 3,500/12 knots
Fate: Collision, 1939

Cargo ship EDGAR F. LUCKENBACH was unusual in that she was one of only two Newport News ships (with tug JOHN TWOHY, JR.) to have a male sponsor. This fine ship was built for coast-to-coast service via the Panama Canal, and no larger cargo vessel in terms of displacement was built at the shipyard until 1952. EDGAR F. LUCKENBACH was christened by Lewis Luckenbach, fifteen-year-old son of the ship's namesake, on March 29, 1916.

The handsome new flush-decked ship was completed and left the yard on May 10, 1916, with her owner's large white "L" on her tall stack. After little more than a year in her intended service, she was chartered by the Army for transport duty; then, in 1918 she was commissioned as a naval transport. She made two voyages to France in convoy, then in early 1919 was transferred to the Cruiser and Transport Force, and made five voyages to bring home wounded troops.

Untouched by the dangers of war, she was returned to Luckenbach in October 1919. She took up her former service and steamed uneventfully for almost 20 more years. In 1933 her gross tonnage was reduced to 6,002.

EDGAR F. LUCKENBACH's fairly long and uneventful career ended at New Orleans on July 21, 1939, when, attempting to avoid collision with the ferry NEW ORLEANS, she struck the Bienville St. Dock. With a 20 foot gash in her bow, she and her 8,000 ton cargo sank but no lives were lost.

WILLIAM A. McKENNEY
1916

WILLIAM A. McKENNEY

Hull No: 198
Owner: Crowell & Thurlow Co.
Launched: October 28, 1916
Delivered: November 29, 1916
Dimensions: 410.25 x 55 x 34.5 ft
Gross Tonnage: 6,256
Displacement: 12,800 tons
Machinery: Triple Expansion Engine, 3 Boilers
Horsepower/Speed: 2,100/10 knots
Fate: War Loss, 1942

WILLIAM A. McKENNEY and her sister FELIX TAUSSIG were two fine large cargo ships and were the last and largest of seven vessels built for the Crowell and Thurlow Steamship Co. of Boston between 1912 and 1917. WILLIAM A. McKENNEY was named for a director of the owning company and was christened by Miss Jeane Cartright Grabow of Boston on October 28, 1916. Just a month later the new ship was delivered and took up coastal service.

In late 1917 she was inspected for duty as a depot collier, and she was transferred to naval service in June 1918. Armed with one 5″ gun and one 3″ gun, WILLIAM A. McKENNEY made two trips to France with cargoes of rails, trucks, and supplies. She made one more postwar voyage to France with Army supplies before being returned to Crowell and Thurlow in January 1920.

The ship spent three more years with her original owner before she was sold to the Mystic Steamship Co. in 1924. In 1936 she passed to ownership of the Koppers Coal Co. of Pittsburg and, although built as a freighter, spent much of her time in coal service. In December 1941 Eastern Gas and Fuel Associates became her fourth owner.

Her career had thus far been without incident, but this was not to last. WILLIAM A. McKENNEY was attacked by the German submarine U-175 off the mouth of the Orinoco River in Venezuelan waters on October 4, 1942. Shelled and torpedoed by the submarine, the 26-year-old ship was quickly sent to the bottom of the South Atlantic.

FELIX TAUSSIG
1917

FELIX TAUSSIG

Hull No: 199
Owner: Crowell & Thurlow Co.
Launched: January 13, 1917
Delivered: February 14, 1917
Dimensions: 410.25 x 55 x 34.5 ft
Gross Tonnage: 6,253
Displacement: 12,800 tons
Machinery: Triple Expansion Engine, 3 Boilers
Horsepower/Speed: 2,100/10 knots
Fate: Scrapped, 1954

The keel for FELIX TAUSSIG was laid on August 7, 1916, and she was launched from Shipway 3 and christened by Miss Helen P. Taussig on January 13, 1917. The new ship was delivered just a month later and entered service with Crowell and Thurlow, only to be commissioned as a naval transport in August 1918.

Her wartime service began on a somewhat sour note, as she mistook the U.S. submarine chaser SC-209 for an enemy submarine and sank her with gun fire south of Long Island on August 27, 1918. During the rest of her war service, FELIX TAUSSIG made three voyages to France from Philadelphia before being returned to her owners on April 26, 1919.

She resumed her former service but was sold with her sisters, first to the Mystic Steamship Co. in 1924, then to Koppers Coal Co. in 1936, and to the Eastern Gas and Fuel Associates in 1942. In 1927 she set a lumber loading record at Frazer Mills, B.C., while chartered to the Isthmian Line.

FELIX TAUSSIG survived World War II without damage, then was sold to Compania Lama of Panama City for $280,000, renamed GEORGIE, and transferred to Panamanian flag in August 1946.

In April 1947 she ran aground in the English Channel on a voyage from Newport News to Denmark with a cargo of coal and her bottom was extensively damaged. Once freed, she delivered her cargo and then returned to Newport News for repair at the shipyard. Her captain praised her durable construction and noted that her original engine, then 30 years old, was still in good condition. She was repaired and went back into service in September 1947.

During 1948 she was sold to Katana S.d.N. Marittima of Catania, renamed ATA, and passed to Italian registry. After six years of service with this owner, the old veteran was broken up for scrap in Japan in 1954.

MUNAIRES
1918

MUNAIRES

Hull No: 207
Owner: Munson Steamship Co.
Launched: November 17, 1917
Delivered: January 12, 1918
Dimensions: 385 x 53 x 30 ft
Gross Tonnage: 5,095
Displacement: 10,410 tons
Machinery: Triple Expansion Engine, 2 Boilers
Horsepower/Speed: 2,400/11 knots
Fate: War Loss, 1942

MUNAIRES was the last ship delivered to the Munson Steamship Co. by the shipyard, and she was destined for the same prosaic service in peace and war as her sisters. MUNAIRES was christened without ceremony by Mrs. Frank C. Osborn, wife of Munson's assistant freight manager, on November 17, 1917, and was launched from Shipway 3 into the James at 10:00 A.M.

The new ship was completed in January 1918 but, like MUNINDIES before her, she was immediately acquired by the Navy for war service. She was armed with a 3″ and a 6″ gun and had a naval complement of 86, far in excess of her peacetime crew of 39 men. In war service with NOTS, she made five trips to France in convoy, each time carrying Army supplies. In January 1919 she sailed from New York to Argentina, stopping in Hampton Roads to load coal.

She was decommissioned and was returned to Munson in April 1919 at New York. Like MUNINDIES, her tonnage was reduced in 1920, and she served her original owner faithfully and apparently without incident for almost 20 years. In March 1937 she too was sold to Greek owners (for only $60,000) and, renamed PLEIADES, took up service with Proios Brothers of Piraeus. She apparently served this owner until 1941 and then passed to Japanese ownership.

Renamed No. 6 TAMON-MARU, she served the Hachiuma Steamship Co. for just over a year before she was torpedoed and sunk by the American submarine NAUTILUS (SS-168) off Hachinohe Port, northeast end of Honshu, on September 28, 1942.

MUNDELTA
1917

MUNDELTA

Hull No: 200
Owner: Munson Steamship Co.
Launched: March 15, 1917
Delivered: April 18, 1917
Dimensions: 385 x 53 x 30 ft
Gross Tonnage: 5,288
Displacement: 10,675 tons
Machinery: Triple Expansion Engine, 2 Boilers
Horsepower/Speed: 2,400/10.5 knots
Fate: War Loss, 1944

MUNDELTA was the first of a trio of cargo steamers built for the Munson Steamship Co. of New York, who also ordered the collier MUNALBRO in 1915. MUNDELTA carried the shipyard's Hull No. 200, and she and her sisters were typical three-islander cargo ships but were distinctive due to their elegant yacht-like sterns and a veritable forest of gooseneck ventilators along their entire length. Hull 200 was launched from Shipway 5 and was christened on March 15, 1917, by Mrs. W.D. Munson of New York, mother of Frank C. Munson who was owner of the steamship company.

MUNDELTA was completed and delivered to Munson only a month later, and after one year of general cargo service, she was acquired by the Navy for war transport service. After two voyages to France with Army supplies and mixed cargo, she was returned to Munson at New York in February 1919. MUNDELTA's original crew of 38 was apparently increased to 76 in 1920, and her tonnage was decreased at that time. From 1918 to 1925 her owner was known as the Mundelta Steamship Line, and she served routinely until her sale to British interests for $57,000 in December 1937.

Renamed MUNLOCK, she was owned by G.E. Marden and was homeported in Shanghai under British registry. It was reported that she was seized by Japanese forces on December 8, 1941, but details of her service and whereabouts after that date are not clear. After the war she was reported to have been lost in September 1944, having probably sunk somewhere in the Western Pacific.

MUNINDIES
1917

MUNINDIES

Hull No: 206
Owner: Munson Steamship Co.
Launched: October 17, 1917
Delivered: December 7, 1917
Dimensions: 385 x 53 x 30 ft
Gross Tonnage: 5,095
Displacement: 10,410 tons
Machinery: Triple Expansion Engine, 2 Boilers
Horsepower/Speed: 2,400/11 knots
Fate: War Loss, 1939

The second of the three cargo ships ordered by the Munson Steamship Co. in December 1915 was MUNINDIES—the keel for which was laid on Shipway 4 on May 21, 1917. The three Munson ships had two other sisters, AGWIDALE and AGWISTAR built for the Atlantic Gulf and West Indies Co., which were identical to them. All five were typical three-islander tramp steamers and several saw service in World War I.

MUNINDIES was launched on October 17, 1917, and was christened without ceremony by Mrs. Charles M. Dimm, wife of Munson's treasurer. The absence of ceremony was typical at this time due to the large amount of naval construction then underway in the shipyard.

MUNINDIES was completed and delivered to Munson on December 7, 1917, but was acquired by the Navy just ten days later and was commissioned as a naval transport. The ship was assigned to NOTS (Naval Overseas Transportation Service) and sailed to France from Philadelphia with 5,200 tons of Army cargo on January 4, 1918. With a complement of 62 and armed with a 4″ and a 3″ gun, MUNINDIES made three more trips to France and one to Argentina before her return to Munson in July 1919.

After her war service, the ship steamed dutifully for Munson without incident for almost twenty years. In 1922 her net tonnage was reduced by about 800 tons, and her peacetime complement went from 40 to 32 men. In April 1937 Munson sold her to a Greek owner, A. Roussas & Co. of Syra, who renamed her ELENA R. After brief service under Greek flag, the former MUNINDIES was sunk by a mine in November 1939, an early victim of World War II.

EL CAPITAN
1917

EL CAPITAN

Hull No: 204
Owner: Southern Pacific Co.
Launched: August 18, 1917
Delivered: September 20, 1917
Dimensions: 380 x 51 x 33.5 ft
Gross Tonnage: 5,216
Displacement: 9,420 tons
Machinery: Triple Expansion Engine, 2 Boilers
Horsepower/Speed: 2,350/11 knots
Fate: War Loss, 1942

EL CAPITAN (The Captain) was the last of 18 freighters built for Southern Pacific Co. interests between 1892 and 1917. The keel for this ship was laid on Shipway 5 on March 17, 1917, and she was ready for launching just five months later. EL CAPITAN was christened by Miss Katherine Anderson Jessup, niece of shipyard President H.L. Ferguson, on August 18, 1917.

Only a month later EL CAPITAN had been outfitted, completed trials, and was delivered to the U.S. Shipping Board for war service. In March 1918 she was transferred to the Navy and was commissioned as a naval transport (AK) and armed with a single 6″ gun on her stern. With a crew of 52, she made four voyages to France and England with supplies and equipment in 1918.

EL CAPITAN was decommissioned and returned to Southern Pacific at New York on February 1, 1919, and thereafter took up service on the New York-Texas run. In merchant service she sailed for the next 23 years without incident, except for being disabled at New York with an inoperative rudder in 1926.

In September 1941 her documents were surrendered at New York and she was transferred to Panamanian flag service with her sister EL ALMIRANTE. Her luck during World War II was no better than that of her sister. In convoy PQ-17 enroute to Murmansk, she took shelter in Matochkin Strait only to be bombed by Nazi planes during the night of July 9-10, 1942. EL CAPITAN and one other ship in the convoy were heavily damaged and were abandoned before sinking in the Strait.

EL ALMIRANTE
1917

EL ALMIRANTE

Hull No: 203
Owner: Southern Pacific Co.
Launched: June 23, 1917
Delivered: August 2, 1917
Dimensions: 380 x 51 x 33.5 ft
Gross Tonnage: 5,216
Displacement: 9,420 tons
Machinery: Triple Expansion Engine, 2 Boilers
Horsepower/Speed: 2,350/11 knots
Fate: Foundered, 1943

Sister ships EL ALMIRANTE and EL CAPITAN, delivered to the Southern Pacific Co. in 1917, were the last of a fleet of 18 ships built for one of the shipyard's best commercial customers. EL ALMIRANTE (The Admiral) and her sister were somewhat smaller than the four EL SOL-class ships which had been delivered in 1910 but were similar in design and appearance. The two ships were each built and delivered in about seven months at a time when the shipyard was in the midst of a boom brought on by the war in Europe.

EL ALMIRANTE was christened by Mrs. F.P. Palen, wife of the shipyard's vice president, on June 23, 1917, and was launched from Shipway 3 at 11:00 A.M. Following completion and successful sea trials, the new ship entered service on the New York-Texas run, starting her maiden voyage on August 16, 1917.

EL ALMIRANTE was to have a fairly long but very uneventful career. She apparently was not taken for war service and sailed on her usual route through the war and into the 1920s and 1930s. At various times during her career, she served the ports of Baltimore and Norfolk on her way from New York to New Orleans and Galveston. In late 1941 Southern Pacific put her under Panamanian flag, and she left her familar coastal route. Operated by the Maritime Commission, she was damaged in a collision and foundered in a storm on April 20, 1943, at 41° 8'N, 64° 27'W in the North Atlantic, while on a voyage in convoy from New York to the River Mersey.

AGWIDALE
1918

AGWIDALE

Hull No: 212
Owner: Atlantic, Gulf & West Indies Co.
Launched: September 5, 1918
Delivered: November 16, 1918
Dimensions: 385 x 53 x 30 ft
Gross Tonnage: 5,080
Displacement: 10,410 tons
Machinery: Triple Expansion Engine, 2 Boilers
Horsepower/Speed: 2,400/11 knots
Fate: Scrapped, 1960

AGWIDALE was the first of two cargo ships built at Newport News for the Atlantic, Gulf & West Indies Steamship Lines, which was to evolve later into the famous Agwilines, Inc. and become the owner of many Newport News-built ships. This owner also ordered two tankers at the shipyard which were delivered in 1923. The AGWIDALE and her sister AGWISTAR were sisters of the three Munson ships delivered in 1917 and 1918 and, although they were ordered in March 1917, their keels were not laid until well into 1918.

The construction of AGWIDALE and her sister was delayed by naval construction at the yard, and she was launched on September 5, 1918, by Mrs. Clifford D. Mallory, wife of the former vice president of the Clyde Steamship Co. AGWIDALE was painted in the "dazzle" camouflage colors of World War I and was delivered for naval service. Although commissioned on November 16, 1918, (five days after the Armistice), she made one trip to France with munitions and supplies in NOTS service before being returned to her owner in April 1919.

She was actually returned to the Mallory Steamship Co. and served them uneventfully until 1932. In that year her owner became known as Clyde-Mallory Lines and in 1935 became part of Agwilines, Inc. AGWIDALE survived World War II service under her original name and then was sold to Chinese interests in July 1946 for $95,000.

Renamed WEI MING, she served the Chung Hsing Mining Co. and then passed to the E-Hsiang Co. of Shanghai (and later of Hong Kong) in 1948. In 1960 the old ship was finally broken up for scrap.

AGWISTAR
1919

AGWISTAR

Hull No: 213
Owner: Atlantic, Gulf & West Indies Co.
Launched: December 21, 1918
Delivered: February 17, 1919
Dimensions: 385 x 53 x 30 ft
Gross Tonnage: 5,229
Displacement: 10,410 tons
Machinery: Triple Expansion Engine, 2 Boilers
Horsepower/Speed: 2,400/11 knots
Fate: Scrapped, 1953

AGWISTAR was the second freighter ordered by the Atlantic, Gulf and West Indies Steamship Lines in March 1917. She was launched from Shipway 5 on December 21, 1918, and was christened by Miss Robin Young. The new ship was delivered to the Mallory Steamship Co. on February 17, 1919, but she was not given the spectacular paint job that was provided for AGWIDALE.

In December 1920, AGWISTAR was conveyed to the New York and Cuba Mail Steamship Co., which was to be her owner and operator for most of her career. Although built as a freighter, she served as a tanker occasionally and in 1935 was chartered to the Richfield Oil Co., homeported in Los Angeles.

AGWISTAR apparently enjoyed almost 20 years of service without incident or casualty under her original name before being sold to Chinese owners for $115,000 in July 1946. Renamed CHONG HSING, she served the Chung Hsing Steamship Co. of Hong Kong with her sister until late in 1949, when she was sold to a Panamanian operator. With the new name FORTUNE STAR, she worked for the Far Eastern & Panama Transport Co. until being sold for scrap and broken up at Hong Kong in 1953.

MANUELA
1934

MANUELA

Hull No: 358
Owner: A.H. Bull & Co.
Launched: March 16, 1934
Delivered: May 30, 1934
Dimensions: 411 x 55 x 30.5 ft
Gross Tonnage: 4,773
Displacement: 10,611 tons
Machinery: Geared Turbines, 2 Boilers
Horsepower/Speed: 3,150/13 knots
Fate: War Loss, 1942

MANUELA was the last ship built at Newport News for the Bull Line and she was destined to have a brief career. The keel for Hull 358 was laid on November 6, 1933, and she was ready for launch on March 16, 1934. MANUELA was christened on that date by Mrs. John Bass, wife of the president of the Fajardo Sugar Co., and completed sea trials on May 28. She was delivered a few days later and left the shipyard for New York. The new ship had accommodations for 12 passengers and carried cargo in five holds with a total bale capacity of 396,000 cubic feet.

MANUELA stayed on the New York to Puerto Rico route all of her service life. In convoy on a voyage from Puerto Rico to New York on June 24, 1942, she was struck by a torpedo on her starboard side amidships off the North Carolina coast. Three men were killed by the explosion, but the rest of her crew of 37 were saved. MANUELA and her cargo of sugar sank one hour after the attack at 34°30'N, 75°40'W in the Atlantic.

ANGELINA
1934

ANGELINA

Hull No: 357
Owner: A.H. Bull & Co.
Launched: February 16, 1934
Delivered: April 25, 1934
Dimensions: 411 x 55 x 30.5 ft
Gross Tonnage: 4,773
Displacement: 10,611 tons
Machinery: Geared Turbines, 2 Boilers
Horsepower/Speed: 3,150/13 knots
Fate: War Loss, 1942

ANGELINA was the sixth of seven ships built at Newport News for A.H. Bull & Co., and she and her sister MANUELA were to have brief careers and come to tragic ends. ANGELINA was the first general cargo ship built in the United States since 1921 and the first built at the shipyard since 1919. Designed by Gibbs and Cox and shipyard designers, these ships had an unusual machinery arrangement with their turbines installed forward of their boilers. In fact, they were the first turbine-driven cargo ships built at Newport News, and their turbines were built at the shipyard.

ANGELINA was christened by Miss Carolyn Bull, daughter of the president of A.H. Bull & Co., on February 6, 1934. ANGELINA was completed and underwent trials on April 19 before being delivered on April 25, 1934. The handsome new ship left for New York and entered coastwise trade from that port to Puerto Rico, carrying loads mostly consisting of sugar and general cargo.

After eight uneventful years in this service ANGELINA came to a tragic end. Under requisition to the U.S. government, returning from England, she was torpedoed in mid-Atlantic on October 17, 1942. Hit at night and during a gale, ANGELINA went down quickly with 43 of her crew at 49°39'N, 30°20'W.

NIGHTINGALE
1939

NIGHTINGALE

Hull No: 373
Owner: W.R. Grace & Co.
Launched: April 28, 1939
Delivered: October 30, 1939
Dimensions: 459.25 x 63 x 40.5 ft
Gross Tonnage: 7,169
Displacement: 13,859 tons
Machinery: Geared Turbines, 2 Boilers
Horsepower/Speed: 6,000/15.5 knots
Fate: Scrapped, 1973

NIGHTINGALE was the first of five C-2 type cargo ships built at Newport News, and she was named for the famous clipper ship built in 1851. The C-2 ships were built to Maritime Administration design and were the fastest cargo ships under the American flag at the time, having a speed of 15.5 knots. The first four C-2 ships, Hulls 373-376, were actually built for the Maritime Administration to be operated by Grace Line in its South American trade.

NIGHTINGALE was christened by Mrs. S. Otis Bland, wife of Representative Bland of Virginia, and was launched from Shipway 6 on April 28, 1939. During her outfitting, huge American flags were painted on NIGHTINGALE's sides to identify her as a neutral, and she left the yard for Baltimore on October 30, 1939. She immediately entered Grace Line service between that port and the West Coast of South America via the Panama Canal.

Her name was changed to EMPIRE EGRET in 1941, and she was called upon to make voyages to Europe, the Middle East, and Asia as war approached. She was operated by the Ministry of War Transport under British flag until 1942 when Grace Line took her back and renamed her SANTA ISABEL. In late 1943 she was converted at New York for transport of 1,706 troops and during the following two years made numerous voyages to the West Pacific from California ports. In February 1946 she made a voyage from San Diego to Liverpool and Le Havre, then returned to New York in March.

Her name was changed to GUIDING STAR in March 1946 but in April she was placed in the James River Reserve Fleet. In June 1973 she was withdrawn from the fleet and sold for scrap.

STAG HOUND
1939

STAG HOUND

Hull No: 374
Owner: W.R. Grace & Co.
Launched: June 21, 1939
Delivered: December 4, 1939
Dimensions: 459.25 x 63 x 40.5 ft
Gross Tonnage: 7,169
Displacement: 13,859 tons
Machinery: Geared Turbines, 2 Boilers
Horsepower/Speed: 6,000/15.5 knots
Fate: Scrapped, 1974

STAG HOUND was the second C-2 freighter built by the shipyard for the Maritime Administration for operation by Grace Line. The sponsor for STAG HOUND was little Miss Martha Macy Hill of Norfolk, great-great-great granddaughter of the master of the clipper ship STAG HOUND. Miss Hill christened the new ship on June 21, 1939, and it was launched from Shipway 2 into the James River at 12:12 P.M.

After nearly six months of outfitting, STAG HOUND was delivered to Grace Line and went into their New York to South American service. This service was short-lived since the still-new freighter was purchased by the Navy in December 1940 and was placed in commission as a store ship.

In naval service she was renamed ALDEBARAN (AF-10) and was provided with four 5″ guns and a complement of 283 men. After two Pacific voyages in the first quarter of 1941, ALDEBARAN was converted to a fleet provision ship at Oakland, CA, and re-entered service in October. She made five round trips between San Francisco and Pearl Harbor by June 1942, then completed nine trips to the South Pacific and seven out of Pearl Harbor to the Marshalls, Eniwetok, and Ulithi. After April 1945 ALDEBARAN served the Fifth and Third Fleets in action against Okinawa and Japan. She was present at the Japanese surrender in September 1945 and, winning two battle stars, completed her wartime career having traveled over 250,000 miles without incident or need for major repairs. ALDEBARAN sailed in the Pacific until mid-1946, at which time she joined the Atlantic Fleet.

Based at Bayonne and Norfolk, she served naval ships and bases in the Caribbean and Mediterranean until she was laid up in the James River Reserve Fleet in June 1969. In November 1974 she was withdrawn from reserve and sold for scrap.

SANTA TERESA
1940

SANTA TERESA

Hull No: 376
Owner: W.R. Grace & Co.
Launched: December 15, 1939
Delivered: March 27, 1940
Dimensions: 459.25 x 63 x 40.5 ft
Gross Tonnage: 8,096
Displacement: 13,859 tons
Machinery: Geared Turbines, 2 Boilers
Horsepower/Speed: 6,000/15.5 knots
Fate: Scrapped, 1969

SANTA TERESA was the last C-2 freighter built for the Grace Line, and she was the last ship built at the shipyard for this owner until SANTA ROSA in 1958. When SANTA TERESA was launched on December 15, 1939, the first two ships in the series had been delivered and were already on the South American run. Hull 376 was launched at noon on that date by Miss Jean Roig, daughter of another vice president of the Grace Line. During the ceremony, a telegram from the president of the steamship company praised "the splendid workmanship which your great company has put into these vessels." A poem by Fairfax Downey commemorating the launching was read shortly afterwards.

The handsome new ship with her seven pairs of cargo booms completed trials on March 22 and left the shipyard on March 27, 1940. SANTA TERESA also remained in merchant service during World War II and escaped damage. She stayed in routine service with the Grace Line until 1963 when she was sold.

Her new owner was the Transasia Transport Co. of Wilmington, DL, who renamed her ELDORADO. The following year she passed to the ownership of Commodore Lines, also of Wilmington, and was renamed EXPRESS BALTIMORE. After a few more years of useful service, she was sold for scrap to a Taiwan breaker in February 1968.

SANTA ANA
1940

SANTA ANA

Hull No: 375
Owner: W.R. Grace & Co.
Launched: October 18, 1939
Delivered: February 15, 1940
Dimensions: 459.25 x 63 x 40.5 ft
Gross Tonnage: 8,096
Displacement: 13,859 tons
Machinery: Geared Turbines, 2 Boilers
Horsepower/Speed: 6,000/15.5 knots
Fate: Scrapped, 1968

The third C-2 built for Grace Line service in its South American trade was SANTA ANA, launched on October 18, 1939. The sponsor for Hull 357 was Miss

Adelaide B. Garni, 18 year old daughter of the vice president of the Grace Line. The new ship left for trials on January 30, 1940, and these went perfectly, except that dense fog extended them by a day.

Like her sisters, SANTA ANA was a cargo-only ship and had accommodations for 66 crew but none for passengers. SANTA ANA entered Grace Line service in mid-February and survived World War II in merchant service without damage. She stayed with her original owner under her original name until early 1965 when she was sold to the Vega Steamship Co. of New York and was renamed VEGA STAR. From 1967 to 1968 she was owned by Pleiades Steamship Co. and operated under Liberian registry. In mid-1968 she was sold by this last owner and was subsequently scrapped.

HAWAIIAN PACKER
1941

HAWAIIAN PACKER

Hull No: 388
Owner: Matson Navigation Co.
Launched: April 2, 1941
Delivered: June 16, 1941
Dimensions: 490.5 x 69.5 x 42.5 ft
Gross Tonnage: 10,394
Displacement: 18,260 tons
Machinery: Geared Turbines, 2 Boilers
Horsepower/Speed: 8,500/16.5 knots
Fate: Scrapped, 1984

HAWAIIAN PACKER was the second C-3 cargo ship built for Matson and she, like her sister HAWAIIAN PLANTER, was destined for a naval career. Hull 388 was launched by Mrs. Alexander G. Budge of Hawaii on April 2, 1941, and entered the James River from Shipway 6 at 12:15 P.M.

HAWAIIAN PACKER was acquired by the Navy just prior to completion during the following June and after dock trials was commissioned as the cargo ship DELTA (AK-29). Between her commissioning and May 1942 the new DELTA carried cargoes from ports on the East Coast to Halifax, Reykjavik, Argentina,

and Caribbean destinations. Between July 1942 and March 1943 she was converted for service as a repair ship and was redesignated AR-9. She spent the remainder of the war at Oran, Bizerte, and Pozzuoli repairing first amphibious craft then destroyers. DELTA returned to Norfolk for overhaul in April 1945 and in June went to Pearl Harbor for repair duty. In August 1945 she found herself at Yokosuka Naval Base in Japan for repair work, including the job of readying the Japanese battleship NAGATO for the atomic tests at Bikini. She saw service at Shanghai between March and June 1946, then was decommissioned and placed in reserve at Philadelphia in March 1947. She went back into service in November 1950 and, based at San Diego, went on deployment to the Far East.

During the Korean War she participated in the transport of refugee Vietnamese to South Vietnam following the partition of Indochina. In 1955 she was flagship to the Blockade and Escort Force in Korean waters; then, in November 1955 she sailed to Tacoma and was placed in reserve there. A veteran of multiple naval careers, DELTA was reactivated in October 1959 for duty at Long Beach. In 1979 she was moved to Bremerton, Washington, for use as a naval shoreside staff command ship, where she remained until she was scrapped in Taiwan in 1984.

HAWAIIAN PLANTER
1941

HAWAIIAN PLANTER

Hull No: 387
Owner: Matson Navigation Co.
Launched: February 14, 1941
Delivered: May 15, 1941
Dimensions: 490.5 x 69.5 x 42.5 ft
Gross Tonnage: 7,790
Displacement: 18,260 tons
Machinery: Geared Turbines, 2 Boilers
Horsepower/Speed: 8,500/16.5 knots
Fate: Scrapped, 1980

HAWAIIAN PLANTER was the first of two C-3 cargo ships built for the Matson Line, which had previously ordered four passenger ships from the shipyard in 1908 and 1913. As these were C-3 hulls, their principal dimensions and machinery were similar to the seven PRESIDENT JACKSON class passenger ships then building at the yard.

HAWAIIAN PLANTER was launched from Shipway 7 by Mrs. T. Alexander Walker, wife of the president of the Hawaiian Sugar Planters' Association, on February 14, 1941. The new ship completed all trials on May 13 in less than 12 hours and was delivered to Matson just two days later.

HAWAIIAN PLANTER was intended for merchant service from the East Coast to Hawaii, but the war intervened and she spent almost all of her career in Navy gray. She was purchased by the Navy in February 1943, was commissioned as BRIAREUS (AR-12) on November 15, 1943, and took up duty as a repair ship. Armed with a 5″ gun and a 3″ gun and with a complement of 903 men, she completed repairs on 142 ships in the South Pacific before the end of September 1944. She repaired damaged ships in the Solomons until July 1945 and moved to Leyte and then Okinawa.

She transferred to Norfolk in December 1945, then went out of commission in reserve in October 1946. She was recommissioned in September 1951, repaired ships of the Atlantic Fleet, and then was again decommissioned and placed in reserve in September 1955. In January 1977 BRIAREUS was transferred to Maritime Administration reserve; then in late 1980 she was sold for scrap.

IRENEE DU PONT
1941

IRENEE DU PONT

Hull No: 389
Owner: International Freighting Corp.
Launched: May 29, 1941
Delivered: August 1, 1941
Dimensions: 459.25 x 63 x 40.5 ft
Gross Tonnage: 6,126
Displacement: 13,859 tons
Machinery: Geared Turbines, 2 Boilers
Horsepower/Speed: 6,000/15.5 knots
Fate: War Loss, 1943

IRENEE DU PONT, the last of five C-2 cargo ships built at Newport News, was not built for the Maritime Commission but was ordered by the International Freighting Corp., a subsidiary of the Du Pont Co. She was one of the unluckiest ships ever built at the shipyard and had one of the shortest careers.

IRENEE DU PONT was ordered in April 1940, and her keel was laid on November 11 of the same year. The new ship was christened by Mrs. Ferdinand La Motte, Jr. of Wilmington, DL, on May 29, 1941, and was launched from Shipway 5. By July 30, IRENEE DU PONT was ready for trials and, these successfully completed, she was delivered to her highly pleased owner on August 1.

She was delivered with large American flags painted on her sides, and she appeared proud as she left the shipyard to serve her owner along the eastern coasts of North and South America. She and her crew of 42 enjoyed an uneventful ten months of service until June 11, 1942, when a fire broke out while she underwent major repair. IRENEE DU PONT was repaired and made a few more voyages, but she met her fate in the North Atlantic on March 17, 1943. Less than two years old, she was torpedoed and sunk by enemy action at 50°43'N, 35°02'W.

PARSIMINA
1947

PARSIMINA

Hull No: 458
Owner: United Fruit Co.
Launched: July 16, 1946
Delivered: January 16, 1947
Dimensions: 455.42 x 61 x 35.5 ft
Gross Tonnage: 7,067
Displacement: 12,590 tons
Machinery: Geared Turbines, 3 Boilers,
  Twin Screw
Horsepower/Speed: 12,000/18.5 knots
Fate: Scrapped, 1977

PARSIMINA was the first of three fruit cargo ships ordered by the United Fruit Co. in July 1945. These ships were slightly larger than the four TALAMANCA-class ships built for the Great White Fleet in the early 1930s and were the first merchant ships delivered at Newport News after the intensive naval newbuilding program during World War II.

The keel for PARSIMINA was laid on December 17, 1945, and she was christened by Mrs. Arthur A. Pollan of Boston, wife of the owner's vice president, on July 16, 1946. Named for a town in Limon Province, Costa Rica, PARSIMINA completed sea trials and left the yard on January 17, 1947. She sailed from Newport News to Puerto Cortes, Honduras, and loaded 70,000 stems of bananas and 5,000 plantains (banana plants) for New Orleans. PARSIMINA and her sisters were of the United Fruit Co.-designed FRA BERLANGA class and had 320,000 cubic feet of refrigerated cargo space and accommodations for 12 passengers. The handsome PARSIMINA served her owner dutifully through the 1950s and 1960s, bringing countless millions of bananas to northern markets.

After almost 25 years with United Fruit, she was sold to Caraibsche Sheepv.Maats, N.V. of Rotterdam and was transferred to Dutch flag in 1971. She served her Dutch owner under the name TOLTEC until she was sold for scrap in 1977.

HEREDIA
1947

HEREDIA

Hull No: 459
Owner: United Fruit Co.
Launched: September 12, 1946
Delivered: March 19, 1947
Dimensions: 455.42 x 61 x 35.5 ft
Gross Tonnage: 7,067
Displacement: 12,590 tons
Machinery: Geared Turbines, 3 Boilers,
    Twin Screw
Horsepower/Speed: 12,000/18.5 knots
Fate: Scrapped, 1977

The second cargo ship delivered to the United Fruit Co. in 1947 was HEREDIA, named for the capital of one of the principal provinces of Costa Rica. HEREDIA and her sisters were the fastest ships of their type in the world and were able to make better than 22 knots when necessary. The fruit cargo was protected by a cargo refrigerating system of the United Fruit Co.'s own design, and the ships featured an efficient conveyor system for loading and unloading up to 15 million bananas on each trip.

HEREDIA's keel was laid on January 28, 1946, and she was christened by Mrs. Hartley Rowe of Newton Centre, MA, wife of the owner's vice president and chief engineer, on September 12 of that year. After completing outfitting and cargo hold insulation, the new ship went on trials on March 18 and was delivered on March 19, 1947.

The graceful HEREDIA and her crew of 62 left the shipyard for Puerto Cortes, Honduras, where they loaded 75,000 stems of bananas and 6,700 stems of plantains. Less than one week after delivery, this cargo had been delivered to Mobile and HEREDIA began her second voyage. Hull 459 served her owners until, in 1971, she too was sold to the same Dutch owner as PARSIMINA. She served under Dutch flag as TANAMO until she was scrapped in 1977.

METAPAN
1947

METAPAN

Hull No: 460
Owner: United Fruit Co.
Launched: November 26, 1946
Delivered: May 7, 1947
Dimensions: 455.42 x 61 x 35.5 ft
Gross Tonnage: 7,067
Displacement: 12,590 tons
Machinery: Geared Turbines, 3 Boilers,
    Twin Screw
Horsepower/Speed: 12,000/18.5 knots
Fate: Scrapped, 1977

METAPAN was the last of three refrigerated cargo ships built at Newport News just after World War II. Named for a city in El Salvador, METAPAN was christened by Mrs. Matthew C. O'Hearn of Chevy Chase, MD, wife of the owner's Washington representative, on November 26, 1946.

METAPAN was completed and delivered on May 7, 1947, and she too sailed directly to Puerto Cortes from the shipyard. In addition to facilities to make their cargo comfortable, METAPAN and her sisters had modern attractive staterooms for 12 passengers. Notwithstanding the employees' unofficial motto, "Every Banana a Guest, Every Passenger A Pest," the ships of the Great White Fleet were renowned for their comfort and hospitality on the South and Central American routes.

METAPAN served her owners faithfully for almost 25 years until she was sold to the same Dutch owner as her sisters in 1971. She sailed under the name TINTO for six more years, then was scrapped in 1977 with the others.

OLD DOMINION MARINER
1952

OLD DOMINION MARINER

Hull No: 490
Owner: U.S. Maritime Administration
Launched: April 25, 1952
Delivered: October 8, 1952
Dimensions: 560.83 x 76 x 44.5 ft
Gross Tonnage: 9,216
Displacement: 21,050 tons
Machinery: Geared Turbines, 2 Boilers
Horsepower/Speed: 17,500/20 knots
Fate: Scrapped, 1986

OLD DOMINION MARINER was the first of 35 Mariner-class fast cargo ships ordered by the Maritime Administration in the first large government shipbuilding program since World War II. Five of these C4-S-1A ships were built at Newport News and all bore the nicknames of states. These freighters were the fastest and among the largest ships of their type, and they were provided with national defense features to facilitate their conversion in the event of war.

OLD DOMINION MARINER was launched from Shipway 7 on April 25, 1952, by Mrs. Thomas W.S. Davis, wife of the Assistant Secretary of Commerce for Domestic Affairs. The new Mariner completed trials 150 miles off the Virginia coast on October 2-3, 1952, and was the first of her class to be delivered. She was placed in the service of the National Shipping Authority, who named American President Lines as her general agent for carrying military cargoes for MSTS. She served with APL for less than two years before she was laid up in Suisun Bay, CA, for repairs.

She was placed back into operation under bareboat charter in January 1955, then was purchased by APL later that year and renamed PRESIDENT HAYES. In September 1974 she was sold to American Export Lines and renamed EXPORT DIPLOMAT; then in 1978 she was briefly chartered to Farrell Lines. She was renamed OLD DOMINION MARINER, then was laid up in the James River in late 1978. She remained idle until May 1986, when she was withdrawn from the reserve fleet and towed to Taiwan for scrapping.

TAR HEEL MARINER
1952

TAR HEEL MARINER

Hull No: 491
Owner: U.S. Maritime Administration
Launched: June 27, 1952
Delivered: November 28, 1952
Dimensions: 560.83 x 76 x 44.5 ft
Gross Tonnage: 9,128
Displacement: 21,050 tons
Machinery: Geared Turbines, 2 Boilers
Horsepower/Speed: 17,500/20 knots
Fate: Scrapped, 1980

TAR HEEL MARINER was the second Mariner-class general cargo ship built by the shipyard for the Maritime Administration and delivered in 1952. Like the other Mariners, Hull 491 had seven cargo holds and provisions for carrying refrigerated as well as liquid and dry cargoes. The keel for TAR HEEL MARINER was laid on August 27, 1951, and she was launched from Shipway 6 on a sultry June 27, 1952. The new ship was sponsored by Mrs. Herbert C. Bonner, wife of the congressman from North Carolina, and a large number of dignitaries from that state and from Washington, D.C., attended.

On completion in November 1952, TAR HEEL MARINER was assigned to the Pacific Far East Line and took up service with them carrying cargoes for MSTS. Like her sister, TAR HEEL MARINER served less than two years before being laid up in Suisun Bay in May 1954. In December 1956 she was purchased by Pacific Far East and was placed back in service. She was renamed WASHINGTON BEAR in 1960, then JOHN B. WATERMAN in 1972. She was sold to the Waterman Steamship Co. in May 1975, who sold her back to the Maritime Administration in 1977 but continued to operate her under charter. In July 1980 she was sold for scrapping in Taiwan.

VOLUNTEER MARINER
1953

VOLUNTEER MARINER

Hull No: 492
Owner: U.S. Maritime Administration
Launched: December 19, 1952
Delivered: August 14, 1953
Dimensions: 560.83 x 76 x 44.5 ft
Gross Tonnage: 9,128
Displacement: 21,050 tons
Machinery: Geared Turbines, 2 Boilers
Horsepower/Speed: 17,500/20 knots
Fate: Scrapped, 1980

VOLUNTEER MARINER was the third Mariner built at Newport News and she was perhaps the most colorful. Intended for service with the Matson Navigation Co., she sported their two-tone green and brown hull and blue and yellow stack. Like the others of her class, VOLUNTEER MARINER was designed to beat the foreign competition with her speed and size and to operate in time of war without need of convoy or escort.

The shipyard's third Mariner was christened by Mrs. Merlin O'Neill, wife of Admiral O'Neill who was Commandant of the Coast Guard, on December 19, 1952, and was launched from Shipway 6. Following completion and delivery on August 14, 1953, VOLUNTEER MARINER went into MSTS service with Matson but was laid up at Beaumont, TX, less than six months later on February 18, 1954. She was sold to American President Lines in July 1955 and entered their service as PRESIDENT JACKSON.

After almost 20 uneventful years with APL, she was sold to Waterman Steamship Corp. in July 1974 and was renamed JOSEPH HEWES. In November 1974 she was sold back to the Maritime Administration under their Trade In/Build Program, but she continued in service with Waterman under charter. In July 1980 she too was sold and was scrapped in Taiwan.

PALMETTO MARINER
1953

PALMETTO MARINER

Hull No: 493
Owner: U.S. Maritime Administration
Launched: June 30, 1953
Delivered: December 11, 1953
Dimensions: 560.83 x 76 x 44.5 ft
Gross Tonnage: 9,218
Displacement: 21,050 tons
Machinery: Geared Turbines, 2 Boilers
Horsepower/Speed: 17,500/20 knots
Fate: Scrapped, 1974

The fourth Newport News-built Mariner was PALMETTO MARINER whose keel was laid in Shipway 6 on October 20, 1952. Hull 493 was christened by Mrs. Sinclair Weeks, wife of the Secretary of Commerce, on June 30, 1953. With the other Mariners, PALMETTO MARINER was one of the largest and fastest cargo ships in the world. At the time of her launching, others of her type had exceeded the speed of 22 knots and had demonstrated great economy of operation.

PALMETTO MARINER, named for the state of South Carolina, was completed and delivered to Pope and Talbot Lines for MSTS service in December 1953. Just over seven months later she was laid up at Olympia, WA, where she remained until her sale to American President Lines in March 1955. Renamed PRESIDENT ADAMS, she stayed in continuous service with APL until she was sold to a Taiwan shipbreaker for scrap in May 1974.

CRACKER STATE MARINER
1954

CRACKER STATE MARINER

Hull No: 494
Owner: U.S. Maritime Administration
Launched: April 6, 1954
Delivered: May 29, 1954
Dimensions: 560.83 x 76 x 44.5 ft
Gross Tonnage: 9,219
Displacement: 21,050 tons
Machinery: Geared Turbines, 2 Boilers
Horsepower/Speed: 17,500/20 knots
Fate: Laid Up, 1978

CRACKER STATE MARINER was the last of five Mariners built at Newport News and one of but two of these to survive scrapping in the 1970s. The keel for Hull 494 was laid on July 13, 1953, and she was ready for launching on April 6, 1954. CRACKER STATE MARINER was christened by Mrs. Richard H. Poff, wife of the congressman from Virginia, and a large contingent from Washington, D.C., was in attendance. After the ship slid into the James River, a strong breeze caught her and moved her several hundred feet, but she was caught by tugs without incident.

In late May, CRACKER STATE MARINER was delivered to the South Atlantic Steamship Line but her service with them was brief, and she was laid up at Beaumont, TX, the following November. She was sold to American President Lines in April 1956 and was renamed PRESIDENT COOLIDGE and served them routinely for the next 18 years. In September 1974 she was sold to American Export Lines and was renamed EXPORT DEFENDER. She was sold back to the government in March 1974 but continued service with American Export Lines, then Farrell Lines under charter.

She was renamed CRACKER STATE MARINER in 1978 and was laid up in the James River Reserve Fleet in December of that year. She was repaired as part of the Ready Reserve Fleet program and continued in layup into the mid-1980s.

CALIFORNIA
1962

CALIFORNIA

Hull No: 551
Owner: States Steamship Co.
Launched: July 28, 1961
Delivered: January 18, 1962
Dimensions: 565 x 76 x 44.5 ft
Gross Tonnage: 12,693
Displacement: 22,629 tons
Machinery: Geared Turbines, 2 Boilers
Horsepower/Speed: 17,500/19.8 knots
Fate: Laid Up, 1979

In February 1960 the shipyard was awarded a contract for the construction of four modified Mariner-type freighters for the States Steamship Co., the first of which was CALIFORNIA. Two others of the same design were built on the West Coast, and all were intended for operation in the Pacific between the U.S. West Coast and the Far East.

The keel for the first freighter built at Newport

News in seven years was laid in January 1961, and she was launched from Shipway 8 on July 28, 1961. CALIFORNIA was christened by Miss Daphne Kerr, granddaughter of States Lines founder Charles E. Dant, and her twin sister Diana served as Maid of Honor.

The new ship completed trials and was delivered on January 18, 1962, with a gleaming coat of white paint on her topsides and superstructure. She and her sister ships were provided with many advanced features, including facilities and gear to handle container cargo, eight deep tanks for liquid cargo and a 60-ton heavy lift cargo gear.

CALIFORNIA enjoyed successful, if uneventful, service with States Lines until 1974 when her name was changed to SANTA RITA. In August 1979 her owner defaulted on her mortgage, and she was transferred to the Maritime Administration and renamed CALIFORNIA. After 1979 she remained in layup at Suisun Bay, CA, except for shipyard withdrawal for deactivation during the second half of 1980.

OREGON
1962

```
                  OREGON

Hull No: 552
Owner: States Steamship Co.
Launched: September 16, 1961
Delivered: April 19, 1962
Dimensions: 565 x 76 x 44.5 ft
Gross Tonnage: 12,691
Displacement: 22,629 tons
Machinery: Geared Turbines, 2 Boilers
Horsepower/Speed: 17,500/19.8 knots
Fate: Laid Up, 1985
```

The second modified Mariner-type ship built for the States Steamship Co. was Hull 552, named OREGON. It was said that each of the four ships was named for the state from which it would sail. The keel for Hull 552 was laid on March 1, 1961, and she was launched from Shipway 9 on September 16, 1961. The sponsor for OREGON was Miss Diana Kerr and her twin sister Daphne served as Maid of Honor, in a reversal of their roles at the launching of CALIFORNIA the previous July.

For the next seven months shipyard craftsmen outfitted OREGON with accommodations for 60 crew and provided spacious and attractive cabins and public rooms for 12 passengers. Unusual for a cargo vessel, public rooms included a main lounge, dining salon, and observation lounge; all were decorated with planters and many murals and paintings of Oregon scenes.

OREGON completed successful sea trials on April 12-13, 1962, and was delivered to States Lines on April 19. She stayed in routine Pacific service with her original owner until 1977 when she was sold to Moore-McCormack Lines and was renamed MORMACTIDE. She remained with Moore-McCormack until it was absorbed by United States Lines in 1983, then continued in service with them until she was laid up in the James River Reserve Fleet in 1985.

HAWAII
1962

```
                  HAWAII

Hull No: 554
Owner: States Steamship Co.
Launched: February 9, 1962
Delivered: August 16, 1962
Dimensions: 565 x 75 x 44.5 ft
Gross Tonnage: 12,691
Displacement: 22,629 tons
Machinery: Geared Turbines, 2 Boilers
Horsepower/Speed: 17,500/19.8 knots
Fate: Laid Up, 1985
```

HAWAII was the last of the four Mariners built for States Steamship Co. Her launching came on a cold and wet February day which contrasted with her name and her intended operating route.

HAWAII was christened by Mrs. J.R. Dant, wife of the president of States Lines, and was successfully launched on February 9, 1962. At a post-launching luncheon, leis were distributed and the mood was festive despite the weather. The sleek new HAWAII was completed and sailed for successful sea trials on August 10. She was delivered to her owner on August 16 and left the yard for the West Coast the following day.

HAWAII served her owner uneventfully for the next 14 years; then, in 1976 she was also sold to Moore-McCormack Lines and was renamed MORMACSEA. In new colors she served Moore-McCormack faithfully and without incident until 1983 when she passed to United States Lines. She served this owner until 1985 when she was laid up in the James River Reserve Fleet.

WASHINGTON
1962

WASHINGTON

Hull No: 553
Owner: States Steamship Co.
Launched: December 15, 1961
Delivered: June 26, 1962
Dimensions: 565 x 76 x 44.5 ft
Gross Tonnage: 12,691
Displacement: 22,629 tons
Machinery: Geared Turbines, 2 Boilers
Horsepower/Speed: 17,500/19.8 knots
Fate: Laid Up, 1985

WASHINGTON was the third Maritime Administration C4-S-lu Mariner-type freighter built for States Lines. Her keel was laid on May 29, 1961, and she was ready for launch the following December 15. Hull 553 was sponsored by Mrs. William H. Martin of Santa Monica, niece of J.R. Dant, president of States Lines. A pin in the launching mechanism jammed and delayed the actual launch for five minutes, despite the sponsor's gallant attempt to push the ship into the river by herself.

WASHINGTON was completed during the next six months and was provided with the same rakish superstructure and six sets of twin kingposts joined by crosstrees as were her sisters. She was also fitted with 11 pairs of normal booms and one heavy lift boom forward of her house. Like the others, her stack was decorated with a red seahorse, trademark of States Lines, and her hull was painted white with blue trim.

WASHINGTON entered the Pacific service of her owner and served them uneventfully until 1977. In that year she passed to the ownership of Moore-McCormack Lines and was renamed MORMACWAVE. In 1983 she passed to United States Lines and remained in their service until she entered the James River Reserve Fleet in September 1985.

PIONEER MOON
1962

PIONEER MOON

Hull No: 556
Owner: United States Lines
Launched: April 27, 1962
Delivered: August 21, 1962
Dimensions: 560.5 x 75 x 42.5 ft
Gross Tonnage: 11,244
Displacement: 21,053 tons
Machinery: Geared Turbines, 2 Boilers
Horsepower/Speed: 16,500/20 knots
Fate: Laid Up, 1981

On September 7, 1960, the shipyard signed a contract for the construction of five freighters for United States Lines, having beat out ten other bidders with a contract price of $10,413,000 each. These ships, later known as the "Challenger" class, were the first of United States Lines' 46-ship long range replacement program. Designed by Gibbs and Cox, these were considered by many to be the handsomest freighters built at Newport News since the Morgan Line ships.

The keel was laid for Hull 556 on September 18, 1961, and she was ready for launch seven months later. United States Lines' original plan was to name the first ship AMERICAN CHALLENGER and to place her in Atlantic service, but the loss in a storm of their ship PIONEER MUSE led to the name PIONEER MOON for Hull 556. PIONEER MOON was launched by Mrs. Clarence D. Martin, wife of the Under Secretary of Commerce for Transportation, on a sunny April 27, 1962. Attending the launching was Gen. John M. Franklin, Chairman of United States Lines, who had also been present at the launchings of AMERICA in 1939 and UNITED STATES in 1951. In a move that confounded shipyard workers (especially painters) the ship's name was changed back to AMERICAN CHALLENGER during her outfitting period and she was placed in Atlantic service after her delivery on August 21, 1962.

On her first transatlantic voyage, completed on September 21, she claimed a round-trip speed record of 24.11 knots, the highest ever for a cargo ship. After completion of Hull 557 as AMERICAN CHALLENGER in October, Hull 556 again took the name PIONEER MOON and transferred to Pacific service. In mid-1963 she set a new speed record from Yokohama to New York, making her a record holder in both oceans. In September 1971 she was long-term chartered to the Military Sealift Command until 1981. She was laid up at San Francisco in November 1981, then in 1983 was transferred to the reserve fleet at Suisun Bay, CA.

AMERICAN CHALLENGER
1962

AMERICAN CHALLENGER
Hull No: 557
Owner: United States Lines
Launched: June 15, 1962
Delivered: October 23, 1962
Dimensions: 560.5 x 75 x 42.5 ft
Gross Tonnage: 11,186
Displacement: 21,053 tons
Machinery: Geared Turbines, 2 Boilers
Horsepower/Speed: 16,500/20 knots
Fate: Laid Up, 1982

The second fast freighter built for United States Lines was Hull 557, named AMERICAN CHALLENGER. The keel for this ship was laid on December 18, 1961, and in seven months the sleek hull was ready for launch. Mrs. Fred Korth, wife of the Secretary of the Navy, launched AMERICAN CHALLENGER at 12:30 P.M. on June 15, 1962.

As this ship was to permanently carry the name of the class, an unusually large number of guests from New York and Washington, D.C., attended the ceremony. The "Challenger" class ships had a total dry cargo capacity of 686,986 cubic feet—26,000 cubic feet of which were refrigerated. Additionally, a deep tank capacity of 1,035 tons was provided for either liquid or dry cargo. Six cargo holds were served by 10-ton and 15-ton booms and one 70-ton heavy lift boom, the largest fitted to a cargo ship at that time.

AMERICAN CHALLENGER completed sea trials on October 16-17 and was delivered on October 23, 1962, freeing Hull 556 to enter Pacific service as PIONEER MOON. The new ship's relatively high speed was expected to cut two days off the normal ten day transatlantic voyage, and this proved to be the case in service. AMERICAN CHALLENGER sailed in routine Atlantic service until being chartered to the Military Sealift Command in September 1971. She delivered stores to the Navy around the world until she was laid up in 1982; then she joined the James River Reserve Fleet in July 1983.

AMERICAN CHARGER
1962

AMERICAN CHARGER
Hull No: 558
Owner: United States Lines
Launched: August 29, 1962
Delivered: December 18, 1962
Dimensions: 560.5 x 75 x 42.5 ft
Gross Tonnage: 11,186
Displacement: 21,053 tons
Machinery: Geared Turbines, 2 Boilers
Horsepower/Speed: 16,500/20 knots
Fate: Laid Up, 1981

The third Challenger-class freighter for United States Lines was AMERICAN CHARGER. The keel for Hull 558 was laid on February 12, 1962, and she was ready for launching on August 29 of that year. Mrs. Thomas D. Morris, wife of the Assistant Secretary of Defense for Installations and Logistics, christened the new ship.

During outfitting AMERICAN CHARGER was fitted, as were the others, with triple hatch covers over two of her holds, which enabled loading cargo directly into her wings rather than via the centerline. Hull 558 exceeded her required speed on trials on December 11-12 and was delivered to United States Lines on December 18, 1962.

From the time of her delivery to 1971, AMERICAN CHARGER served in the North Atlantic trade for which she was designed and carried hundreds of cargoes of all descriptions without incident. On August 19, 1971, she was long-term chartered to the Military Sealift Command and afterwards delivered military cargoes to American bases in many areas of the world. In 1981 she was withdrawn from service and was laid up; then she joined the reserve fleet at Suisun Bay, CA, in 1983.

AMERICAN CHAMPION
1963

AMERICAN CHAMPION

Hull No: 559
Owner: United States Lines
Launched: December 14, 1962
Delivered: March 8, 1963
Dimensions: 560.5 x 75 x 42.5 ft
Gross Tonnage: 11,186
Displacement: 21,053 tons
Machinery: Geared Turbines, 2 Boilers
Horsepower/Speed: 16,500/20 knots
Fate: Laid Up, 1983

AMERICAN CHAMPION was the fourth fast freighter launched for United States Lines in 1962. This was a busy time for the shipyard as nine cargo ships were launched between July 1961 and February 1963. The keel for Hull 559 was laid on June 18, 1962, and she was launched the following December 14.

Sponsor for AMERICAN CHAMPION was Mrs. Herbert C. Bonner, wife of Rep. Bonner of North Carolina, and over 120 Carolinian invited guests attended.

Hull 559 completed sea trials and left the shipyard on March 8, 1963. As handsome as the others of her class, her rakish stack and sleek superstructure gave an illusion of speed even when she stood at anchor. Her sampan stack was her inheritance from other famous Gibbs and Cox, Newport News products: AMERICA, UNITED STATES, SANTA ROSA, and SANTA PAULA.

After delivery AMERICAN CHAMPION served United States Lines on the Atlantic for almost 20 years. In June 1980 she was chartered as part of the Near-Term Rapid Deployment Force with 12 other ships and deployed to the Indian Ocean for that service as a T-AK with a crew of 56 men, but in July 1983 she ended active service and was laid up in the James River Reserve Fleet.

AMERICAN CHIEFTAIN
1963

AMERICAN CHIEFTAIN

Hull No: 560
Owner: United States Lines
Launched: February 8, 1963
Delivered: April 24, 1963
Dimensions: 560.5 x 75 x 42.5 ft
Gross Tonnage: 11,186
Displacement: 21,053 tons
Machinery: Geared Tubrines, 2 Boilers
Horsepower/Speed: 16,500/20 knots
Fate: Laid Up, 1983

AMERICAN CHIEFTAIN was the fifth and last cargo liner built at Newport News for United States Lines and her delivery left the shipyard without a merchant ship on the ways for the first time in 16 years. Hull 560 was built on Shipway 8, and she was launched with a flourish on February 8, 1963.

AMERICAN CHIEFTAIN was christened by Mrs. Thomas N. Downing, wife of the congressman from Virginia's First District, and a large number of guests from Newport News and Hampton as well as from Washington, D.C., attended.

Successful trials were held on April 22-23 and the new ship was delivered to her owner on April 24. Equipped, like her four sisters, with a special 70-ton Newport News Heavy Lift boom between holds 3 and 4 and with 20 other 10-ton and 15-ton booms, she entered service on the North Atlantic early in May.

The Challenger-class ships were the first general cargo ships built under federal subsidy which were not provided with passenger accommodations, signalling the end of a long tradition. AMERICAN CHIEFTAIN, like her predecessors, served on the Atlantic route until being chartered for Military Sealift Command service for ten years in August 1971. In July 1983 she was laid up in the James River Reserve Fleet.

ALASKAN MAIL
1968

ALASKAN MAIL

Hull No: 587
Owner: American Mail Line
Launched: April 16, 1968
Delivered: October 29, 1968
Dimensions: 605 x 82 x 46 ft
Gross Tonnage: 15,949
Displacement: 31,995 tons
Machinery: Geared Turbines, 2 Boilers
Horsepower/Speed: 24,000/21 knots
Fate: In Service

ALASKAN MAIL was the first of four C5-S-75a breakbulk cargo vessels built under a contract signed with the American Mail Line on June 9, 1966. Costing a total of $81 million, these were the largest general cargo ships in the world when built. Designed by the J.J. Henry Co., the ships featured dry cargo bale of over a million cubic feet in seven holds. Additionally, 21,090 cubic feet of refrigerated volume and space for 332 containers were provided.

The keel for ALASKAN MAIL was laid on August 21, 1967. Hull 587 was launched by Mrs. E.L. Bartlett, wife of the senator from Alaska, on April 16, 1968, and the new ship finished outfitting and completed trials on the following October 8.

After delivery on October 29, 1968, ALASKAN MAIL steamed west and took up service on American Mail Lines routes from the Pacific Northwest to the Far East. Serving on Federal Maritime Board Trade Route No. 29 to Japan, Korea, China, Hong Kong, Indonesia, Malaya, India and Pakistan, ALASKAN MAIL established an excellent safety record in view of the diversity of cargoes carried and ports served.

In 1973 her owner was merged with its parent company, American President Lines, and her name was later changed to PRESIDENT ADAMS. She continued in routine service into the 1980s, and in 1983 she was chartered to the Military Sealift Command as part of the Near-Term Prepositioned Force, stationed in the Indian Ocean.

INDIAN MAIL
1968

INDIAN MAIL

Hull No: 588
Owner: American Mail Line
Launched: July 27, 1968
Delivered: December 31, 1968
Dimensions: 605 x 82 x 46 ft
Gross Tonnage: 15,949
Displacement: 31,995 tons
Machinery: Geared Turbines, 2 Boilers
Horsepower/Speed: 24,000/21 knots
Fate: In Service

The second C-5 cargo ship built at Newport News for American Mail Line was INDIAN MAIL whose 76-ton keel was laid on Shipway 6 on November 13, 1967. By the time of her launching, INDIAN MAIL was in an advanced state of completion with her superstructure, kingposts, and stack in place. Hull 588 was christened by Mrs. Warren G. Magnuson, wife of the

senator from the state of Washington on July 27, 1968. The ceremony was attended by a number of dignitaries, including the Indian Ambassador, U.S. Secretary of Transportation, and American Mail Line's president.

Outfitting work proceeded after launch, and following successful trials on December 20, INDIAN MAIL was delivered on December 31, 1968. Like the others of her class, INDIAN MAIL was provided with 21 sets of 15 and 20-ton booms and a single 70-ton boom of Newport News design which served two holds. All the C-5 ships were provided with a unique "air glide" system for moving containers in the holds. This system was intended to maximize container capacity on the ships, but due to design and operational problems in service it was later inactivated.

In 1978 her name was changed to PRESIDENT JACKSON, and she was operated by American President Lines, Ltd. Afterwards she sailed routinely in Far East service and made several round-the-world voyages with specialized cargoes.

HONG KONG MAIL
1969

HONG KONG MAIL

Hull No: 590
Owner: American Mail Line
Launched: February 8, 1969
Delivered: July 25, 1969
Dimensions: 605 x 82 x 46 ft
Gross Tonnage: 15,949
Displacement: 31,995 tons
Machinery: Geared Turbines, 2 Boilers
Horsepower/Speed: 24,000/21 knots
Fate: In Service

Fourth of five C-5 cargo ships for American Mail Line was HONG KONG MAIL, whose keel was laid on July 30, 1968, just three days after the launch of INDIAN MAIL from the same shipway. HONG KONG MAIL was christened by Mrs. Thomas M.

Pelly, wife of Congressman Pelly of the state of Washington, on February 8, 1969. Ceremonies were marked by a festive air including colorful posters depicting Hong Kong, lanterns, and a Far East style launching ball which streamed forth confetti and streamers from the ship's bow.

HONG KONG MAIL was outfitted and ready for sea trials on May 27. The new ship, like her sisters, was provided with luxurious accommodations for 12 passengers and her public rooms were spacious and attractive. HONG KONG MAIL was completed and delivered on July 25, 1969, and left for Far East service.

Originally home-ported at Portland, OR, her home port was changed to Oakland, CA, and her name was changed to PRESIDENT WILSON in 1978. Later based in Seattle, WA, she continued in routine service with American President Lines.

KOREAN MAIL
1969

KOREAN MAIL

Hull No: 589
Owner: American Mail Line
Launched: November 9, 1968
Delivered: April 25, 1969
Dimensions: 605 x 82 x 46 ft
Gross Tonnage: 15,949
Displacement: 31,995 tons
Machinery: Geared Turbines, 2 Boilers
Horsepower/Speed: 24,000/21 knots
Fate: In Service

At the midpoint of the five-ship building program for American Mail Line, the keel for KOREAN MAIL was laid on April 22, 1968—just a week after the launching of ALASKAN MAIL. Just over six months later, Hull 589 was christened by Mrs. John Harllee, wife of the Federal Maritime Commission chairman, on November 9. The launching was attended by the Korean ambassador and his wife, and during the ship's slide into the James a large ball hanging on the bow burst open and released a shower of streamers in Far East fashion. Mr. Worth B. Fowler, president of American Mail Line, was present and praised the shipyard for the recently delivered ALASKAN MAIL with which he said his company was "overjoyed" in every respect.

After a four month outfitting period, KOREAN MAIL had her trials on March 6, 1969, and was delivered on April 25. She too entered trade on F.M.B. Route 29 as one of the world's largest breakbulk cargo carriers capable of carrying general cargo, containers, bulk grain, rail cars, aircraft, and outsize industrial machinery.

Over the years a number of interesting cargoes were carried by KOREAN MAIL and her class including 90 ft passenger hydrofoils for Hong Kong and thirty-six 85 ft commuter rail cars destined for Cleveland, carried from Japan to Tacoma.

In 1978 her name was changed to PRESIDENT TAYLOR, and she remained in routine service with American President Lines. Carrying a cargo of grain, she was intercepted and searched by the Iranian Navy in the Gulf of Oman in January 1986 but was released after a fruitless two-hour search for armaments.

AMERICAN MAIL
1969

AMERICAN MAIL

Hull No: 593
Owner: American Mail Line
Launched: May 3, 1969
Delivered: October 22, 1969
Dimensions: 605 x 82 x 46 ft
Gross Tonnage: 15,949
Displacement: 31,995 tons
Machinery: Geared Turbines, 2 Boilers
Horsepower/Speed: 24,000/21 knots
Fate: In Service

Last of the American Mail superliners was AMERICAN MAIL. The contract for this ship had been signed on November 30, 1966, five months after that for the first four ships. The keel for Hull 593 was laid on November 20, 1968, and she was launched on May 3, 1969. The sponsor for AMERICAN MAIL was Mrs. Henry Jackson, wife of Senator Jackson from the state of Washington, and she sent the new ship down Shipway 7 into the James River at 11:30 A.M. on launch day.

The sleek new ship completed trials on August 7, 1969, but was not delivered until the following October 22. She too entered Far East service and passed to American President Lines when her owner merged with its parent company on October 1, 1973. In 1978 her name was changed to PRESIDENT CLEVELAND, and she continued in routine service in the Pacific with occasional round-the-world voyages.

TANKERS
W.S. PORTER
1906

W.S. PORTER

Hull No: 44
Owner: Associated Oil Co.
Launched: August 25, 1906
Delivered: November 1, 1906
Dimensions: 399.17 x 49.75 x 30.25 ft
Gross Tonnage: 4,902
Displacement: 10,400 tons
Machinery: Triple Expansion Engine,
   3 Boilers
Horsepower/Speed: 2,500/11 knots
Fate: War Loss, 1944

W.S. PORTER was the first of 86 tankers built at Newport News between 1906 and 1979. This ship was originally ordered by the Saginaw Oil Co. in 1902, but work was stopped after construction was well underway. A contract to complete the ship was signed in November 1905 with the Associated Oil Co., and W.S.

PORTER gained the unusual distinction of being the only Newport News ship whose keel was laid twice.

Hull 44 was christened on August 25, 1906, by little Miss Jacquelyn Bickford, daughter of the shipyard's general counsel. W.S. PORTER gained another distinction moments after her christening when she stuck on the ways about fifty feet short of floating off. Six days later the tanker was floated off undamaged by means of shoring and with the help of tugs. The rest of her construction was fortunately routine, and she was delivered on November 1, 1906.

On her delivery voyage from New York to San Francisco, she towed a large tug and arrived on January 18, 1907, after 61 days at sea. W.S. PORTER served the Associated Oil Co. on the West Coast without incident for almost 20 years before being sold to Petroleum S.A.N. of Genoa and transferred to Italian registry in April 1925. She sailed for this owner in the Mediterranean under the name FRISCO for almost 20 more years until becoming a war loss in August 1944.

SUN
1907

SUN

Hull No: 64
Owner: Sun Co.
Launched: January 19, 1907
Delivered: April 8, 1907
Dimensions: 405.42 x 49.75 x 30.25 ft
Gross Tonnage: 4,836
Displacement: 10,600 tons
Machinery: Triple Expansion Engine,
　　3 Boilers
Horsepower/Speed: 2,000/10 knots
Fate: War Loss, 1943

On April 23, 1906, a contract was signed with the Sun Co. for construction of the shipyard's second tanker, later named SUN. This ship had the same beam and depth as W.S. PORTER but was six feet longer. Her keel was laid in June, and she was ready for launch on January 19, 1907. SUN was christened by Miss Ethel Pew, daughter of the oil company's president, and entered the James at 12:55 P.M. on that date. After completing sea trials on April 3, 1907, SUN was delivered to the Sun Co. on April 8.

Although she was originally intended for the Pacific Coast oil trade, SUN spent most of her career plodding uneventfully between Gulf and Mexican ports and Philadelphia. Her owner became known as the Sun Oil Co. in 1924 and in 1916 had founded their own shipyard on the Delaware River which later built many of her running mates.

When SUN was sold to Italian owners in January 1927, she was considered old and small. Her new owner was Cia. Italiana Trasporto Oli/Minerali of Genoa. Renamed GIORGIO, she served this owner on many long voyages between the Mediterranean and the Persian Gulf, European Continent, United States, and West Indies during the 1930s but became a war loss in 1943.

TEXAS
1908

TEXAS

Hull No: 82
Owner: Texas Co.
Launched: April 21, 1908
Delivered: July 18, 1908
Dimensions: 413.25 x 52 x 30 ft
Gross Tonnage: 5,106
Displacement: 11,150 tons
Machinery: Triple Expansion Engine,
   3 Boilers
Horsepower/Speed: 2,800/11 knots
Fate: Stranded, 1927

On June 10, 1907, the shipyard obtained a contract for the construction of a tanker for the Texas Co., which was to be the first of seven built for that company between 1908 and 1956. The new ship was later named TEXAS and was slightly larger than the first two tankers built at the shipyard. She was typical of her type and period with seven main cargo tanks divided by a centerline longitudinal bulkhead, two decks, and an expansion trunk on centerline between decks. Like several of the other early tankships built at Newport News, she was provided with auxiliary sails on her foremast and mizzen mast.

The keel for TEXAS was laid in September 1907, and she was christened on April 21, 1908, by Miss Helen Hardy, daughter of the congressman from Texas. The new ship was delivered the following July and entered trade between Gulf ports and the U.S. East Coast.

She served the Texas Co. for almost 20 years and was renamed GEORGIA in 1916, TEXACO in 1918, then GEORGIA again in 1919. Her home port was Port Arthur, TX. In 1927 she was sold to the N.V. Dutch Tanker Co. of Amsterdam and was transferred to Dutch registry. She enjoyed brief service between the Middle East and Northern Europe before being wrecked on Haisbro Sands, East Coast of England, on November 20, 1927, while bound from Abadan, Iran, to Grangemouth, Scotland, with a load of crude oil.

J.A. CHANSLOR
1910

J.A. CHANSLOR

Hull No: 129
Owner: Associated Oil Co.
Launched: February 12, 1910
Delivered: March 24, 1910
Dimensions: 400.5 x 52 x 30 ft
Gross Tonnage: 4,938
Displacement: 10,100 tons
Machinery: Triple Expansion Engine,
    4 Boilers
Horsepower/Speed: 2,000/10 knots
Fate: Stranded, 1919

The fourth tanker built at Newport News was J.A. CHANSLOR, ordered by the Associated Oil Co. in May 1909. This ship was given Hull No. 129 and had the same beam and depth as TEXAS which preceded it, but was slightly shorter. J.A. CHANSLOR had six pairs of main cargo tanks, was fitted with summer tanks amidships, and had a total capacity of 44,690 barrels of oil cargo.

Her keel was laid in August 1909, and she was christened and launched on February 12, 1910, by Mrs. Albert Lloyd Hopkins, wife of the assistant general manager of the shipyard. Mrs. J.A. Chanslor, wife of the president of the oil company, was to have been the ship's sponsor but was unable to attend because of illness. Completed on March 24, 1910, J.A. CHANSLOR entered regular trade on the West Coast between California and Washington ports with a crew of 41.

Her career proceeded uneventfully for almost ten years until the stormy night of December 19, 1919. On that night, she and 38 members of her crew were lost when, bound in ballast from Portland to San Francisco, she ran aground and was wrecked off Cape Blanco. She struck a reef and broke in two a few minutes later. Thirty men went down with her stern section in the choppy sea and eight more were lost from her lifeboats, leaving only three survivors.

WM. F. HERRIN
1911

WM. F. HERRIN

Hull No: 141
Owner: Associated Oil Co.
Launched: February 4, 1911
Delivered: March 20, 1911
Dimensions: 400.5 x 52 x 30 ft
Gross Tonnage: 4,938
Displacement: 10,100 tons
Machinery: Triple Expansion Engine,
    4 Boilers
Horsepower/Speed: 2,000/10 knots
Fate: Scrapped, 1950

Shortly after delivery of J.A. CHANSLOR, the Associated Oil Co. ordered an identical second ship which was later named WM. F. HERRIN. The keel was laid for this vessel on June 30, 1910, and she was christened by Miss Emily Bailey and launched from Shipway 4 on February 4, 1911. WM. F. HERRIN was fitted with eight cargo booms and was practically identical to her sister ship, but she was provided with eight pairs of cargo tanks in her tweendeck wings instead of the usual dry cargo spaces. After trials and delivery in late March, the new tanker sailed for the West Coast and took up trade there between Oregon and California ports.

Her career was uneventful and, after the loss of J.A. CHANSLOR in 1919, she continued until sold to an Italian owner in March 1928. She was renamed COLORADO and served with Petroleum Soc. Anon. di Navigazione of Genoa. In 1941 she took the name TYPHOON, and shortly thereafter, she passed to Panamanian registry; then, in 1942 she was acquired by the U.S. War Shipping Administration for war service.

In October 1943 the Navy chartered her and renamed her VILLALOBOS (IX-145), then placed her in Pacific service. She continued to be known by the name TYPHOON under charter and supported the invasion of the Gilberts, Marshalls, Guam, and Saipan. She was commissioned and took her Navy name late in 1944, then remained in Pacific service until war's end, which found her at Subic Bay in the Philippines, winner of three battle stars for her naval service. Inspection found the old ship in poor condition, and she was decommissioned in February 1946.

She stayed laid up at Subic until she was transferred back to her former Italian owners for further merchant service. This was not to be, however, because her former owners found her in a decrepit half-sunk condition at Subic where she lay, her future undecided, until she was broken up in 1950.

ILLINOIS
1913

ILLINOIS

Hull No: 162
Owner: Texas Co.
Launched: April 10, 1913
Delivered: May 17, 1913
Dimensions: 413 x 52 x 30.75 ft
Gross Tonnage: 5,225
Displacement: 11,130 tons
Machinery: Triple Expansion Engine,
    3 Boilers
Horsepower/Speed: 2,800/11 knots
Fate: War Loss, 1917

One of the shortest-lived of all Newport News tankers was ILLINOIS which was delivered to the Texas Co. in 1913. This ship was practically identical to TEXAS, which had been delivered to the same owner in 1908, but she was three inches longer and nine inches deeper. The keel for ILLINOIS was laid on September 9, 1912, and she was christened by Miss Elizabeth M. Drake of New York on April 10, 1913, and was launched from Shipway 3.

After delivery the following May 17, the new tanker took up trade with her sister between Gulf ports and Philadelphia and New York. Her career was uneventful but it was to be a short one. March 1917 found her in European waters with the then-neutral American flag painted on her sides along with the bold letters "ILLINOIS-USA." This provided little protection as she was attacked in daylight by a German submarine in the English Channel on March 8, 1917. Dramatic photos of her demise show that she settled by the stern, rolled over to port, then sank with her bow in the air. Fortunately, there was no fire, and all of her crew survived without casualties.

TOPILA
1913

TOPILA

Hull No: 167
Owner: East Coast Oil Co.
Launched: June 12, 1913
Delivered: July 22, 1913
Dimensions: 395 x 59 x 28 ft
Gross Tonnage: 5,125
Displacement: 9,760 tons
Machinery: Triple Expansion Engine,
    2 Boilers
Horsepower/Speed: 2,350/11 knots
Fate: Scrapped, 1950

TOPILA was one of two nearly identical tankers delivered to Southern Pacific Co. interests in 1913 and 1917. The shipyard obtained a contract for her construction from the East Coast Oil Co. on July 1, 1912, and laid her keel on the following November 2. She was the smallest tanker yet built at the shipyard, but she had the distinction of being the first one built for operation with oil fuel. TOPILA was launched from Shipway 5 on June 12, 1913, having been sponsored by Miss Margaret E. Reynolds of Newport News. The new tanker was outfitted and after trials was delivered on July 22.

She entered the coastal oil trade between Gulf ports and the East Coast and served her owner uneventfully until the late summer of 1917 when she was acquired by the Navy at Philadelphia for war service. Fitted with two 5″ guns, she carried many oil cargoes for the Navy and was one of the first ships assigned to the Naval Overseas Transportation Service (NOTS) at its formation in January 1918. She made three trips to Europe, then served between Port Arthur and the East Coast before being returned to Southern Pacific in June 1918. In 1929 she was apparently chartered to the Atlantic Richfield Co. with her later Newport News-built sister TORRES and took up service on the West Coast.

In October 1935 both ships were sold to Atlantic Richfield but retained their original names. The sturdy TOPILA served on the West Coast throughout the 1930s and luckily escaped damage on her usual routes through the end of World War II. In June 1947 she was sold to Compania Uruguaya de Comercio y Maritima S.A. and, renamed JORGE S., was transferred to Panamanian registry. This owner, an Onassis group company, operated her until she was scrapped in 1950, ending a remarkably long service career for a riveted tanker.

JOHN D. ARCHBOLD
1914

JOHN D. ARCHBOLD

Hull No: 170
Owner: Standard Oil Co.
Launched: January 28, 1914
Delivered: March 17, 1914
Dimensions: 474.5 x 60 x 36.17 ft
Gross Tonnage: 8,374
Displacement: 16,670 tons
Machinery: Quadruple Expansion Engine,
 3 Boilers
Horsepower/Speed: 2,800/10.5 knots
Fate: War Loss, 1917

JOHN D. ARCHBOLD was an important ship for Newport News not only because she was the largest tanker built there to her time, but especially since she was the first built for the shipyard's best commercial customer, the Standard Oil Co. Between 1914 and 1965, fully 41 tankers were delivered to this owner, and more than half of them were still in service into the 1980s.

JOHN D. ARCHBOLD and two sister ships built at the shipyard were large for their day and were built as coal burners. They had nine pairs of main cargo tanks and summer tanks and were provided with a pump room amidships.

The keel for JOHN D. ARCHBOLD was laid in June 1913, and the ship was launched by Mrs. Michael Murray VanBeunen, daughter of John D. Archbold, on January 28, 1914. After delivery on March 17, 1914, the tanker took up routine service between Gulf ports and Standard Oil's refinery at Bayonne, NJ.

Her career on this route was routine, but it was not to be a long one. On June 16, 1917, she was torpedoed by a German submarine at 47°41′N, 60°1′W, off the coast of Brittany and became one of the first American ships lost after the United States entered the war on April 6, 1917.

JOHN D. ROCKEFELLER
1914

JOHN D. ROCKEFELLER

Hull No: 177
Owner: Standard Oil Co.
Launched: August 8, 1914
Delivered: September 11, 1914
Dimensions: 474.5 x 60 x 36.17 ft
Gross Tonnage: 8,374
Displacement: 16,670 tons
Machinery: Quadruple Expansion Engine,
    3 Boilers
Horsepower/Speed: 2,800/10.5 knots
Fate: Scrapped, 1954

The early Standard Oil Co. tankers were named after company executives and JOHN D. ROCKEFELLER, named for the company's founder, was no exception. This ship was identical to JOHN D. ARCHBOLD which preceded it and ANTWERPEN which followed, and it was destined to have a long career under several owners and flags.

The contract for JOHN D. ROCKEFELLER was signed on October 2, 1913, and her keel was laid on the following December 1. Mrs. A.C. Bedford, wife of the vice president and director of the owning company, christened the tanker on August 8, 1914. After completion and delivery to the Standard Oil Co. fleet a month later, JOHN D. ROCKEFELLER entered service between Gulf Coast and East Coast ports.

She stayed with her original owner until October 1924 when she was sold to the Malabar Steamship Co. and was renamed MALABAR. She stayed with this owner until the mid-1930s, then passed to the ownership of the Seminole Steamship Co. in 1937 and to the Grosvenor-Dale Co. in 1941. She operated through the war undamaged and in March 1946 was sold to the China Tanker Co. of Shanghai (later of Kaohsiung) and placed under Chinese flag. Renamed YUNG TSIN, she stayed with this owner, trading mostly between Europe and the Far East, until she was finally scrapped in Formosa in 1954.

ANTWERPEN
1916

ANTWERPEN

Hull No: 191
Owner: Standard Oil of NJ
Launched: July 22, 1916
Delivered: August 24, 1916
Dimensions: 474.5 x 60 x 36.17 ft
Gross Tonnage: 7,955
Displacement: 16,650 tons
Machinery: Quadruple Expansion Engine,
    3 Boilers
Horsepower/Speed: 2,600/10.5 knots
Fate: War Loss, 1916

ANTWERPEN was the last of the trio of JOHN D. ROCKEFELLER-class tankers delivered to the Standard Oil Co. between 1914 and 1916, and she was to have one of the shortest careers of any Newport News ship.

Ordered for the American Petroleum Co. of Rotterdam, a Standard Oil affiliate, ANTWERPEN was transferred to Dutch flag before her delivery in 1916. Like many of the early tankers built at the shipyard, ANTWERPEN was constructed using the newly developed Isherwood System of longitudinal framing, and she additionally was provided with 28 separate cargo tanks and the ability to burn either coal or oil fuel.

The keel for ANTWERPEN was laid on November 1, 1915, and she was launched on July 22, 1916. Her sponsor was Mrs. F.D. Asche, who returned to Newport News two years later to launch a slightly larger tanker named after her husband. ANTWERPEN completed outfitting and trials and was delivered on August 24, 1916. She left the shipyard on that date and, on her maiden voyage, was sunk by enemy action, meeting her fate on September 12, 1916.

CHARLES PRATT
1916

CHARLES PRATT

Hull No: 186
Owner: Standard Oil of NJ
Launched: February 12, 1916
Delivered: March 18, 1916
Dimensions: 516.5 x 68 x 38 ft
Gross Tonnage: 10,050
Displacement: 21,250 tons
Machinery: Triple Expansion Engines,
    3 Boilers, Twin Screw
Horsepower/Speed: 3,000/10.5 knots
Fate: War Loss, 1940

CHARLES PRATT was the first of eight similar tankers delivered to the Standard Oil Co. and two other owners between 1916 and 1923. Her contract was signed on January 11, 1911, and her keel was laid on the following April 26. The hull construction of CHARLES PRATT was unusual in that she was built with three longitudinal bulkheads and had two decks. Above her lower deck, coal bunkers were located outboard and her expansion trunks were inboard. Below this deck were summer tanks outboard and main cargo tanks inboard. She was one of the largest tankers of her day, and shipyard naval architect William Gatewood made

a special trip to London to obtain approval of her design.

CHARLES PRATT was christened by Miss Mary Caroline Pratt, granddaughter of Mr. Pratt, on February 12, 1916. The new twin tanker was delivered and entered Standard's Gulf Coast-East Coast service on March 18 of that year. With Bayonne, NJ, as her hailing port, she served her original owner routinely for the next 25 years.

In 1923 her shelter deck was opened up and her gross tonnage decreased to 8,982 tons. From 1927 to 1935 her owner was known as the Standard Shipping Co., then became Standard Oil Co. of New Jersey. In July 1939 she was sold to the Panama Transport Co., a Standard affiliate, and passed to Panamanian registry.

After repairs at the shipyard in November 1940, she left for what was to be one of her last voyages. She arrived at Aruba and loaded cargo for Sierra Leone in Africa. On December 22 she was struck by a torpedo and was set on fire a day out from her destination. All but two of her crew were able to escape in her lifeboats before a second torpedo hit and, strangely, put out the fire. Almost a week passed before her crew was picked up by British steamers, none the worse for their ordeal. CHARLES PRATT, however, went to the bottom, her neutral flag having provided her with little protection against the enemy's torpedoes.

H.H. ROGERS
1916

H.H. ROGERS

Hull No: 187
Owner: Standard Oil of NJ
Launched: April 27, 1916
Delivered: May 25, 1916
Dimensions: 516.5 x 68 x 38 ft
Gross Tonnage: 10,050
Displacement: 21,250 tons
Machinery: Triple Expansion Engines,
    3 Boilers, Twin Screw
Horsepower/Speed: 3,000/10.5 knots
Fate: War Loss, 1943

H.H. ROGERS was the second tanker delivered to Standard Oil in 1916, and her career closely paralleled that of her sistership CHARLES PRATT. The contracts for both ships were signed on the same day, but H.H. ROGERS' keel was laid about three weeks after that of her sister. Mrs. William E. Benjamin, daughter of Mr. Rogers, was selected as sponsor and christened the ship on April 27, 1916.

After completion and delivery on May 25, H.H. ROGERS sailed with Standard Oil Co. fleet routinely for almost 27 years. Her tonnage was also reduced in 1923 and after 1927 she called Wilmington, DL, her home port.

When war came to Europe, she was transferred to neutral Panamanian registry but was heavily involved in wartime supply. From 1939 to 1943 she made 32 voyages and carried over 3.2 million barrels of cargo. Her trips were mostly on her usual routes, but she also made several trips to Europe, often carrying war supplies.

February 1943 found her in convoy with 40 other ships en route from Belfast to the United States. In heavy weather and 600 miles west of Irish coast, she was struck on her port side by a torpedo on February 21. Her fireroom and engine room flooded and she sank quickly, but miraculously none of her crew was lost.

F. Q. BARSTOW
1917

F.Q. BARSTOW

Hull No: 197
Owner: Standard Oil of NJ
Launched: March 17, 1917
Delivered: April 12, 1917
Dimensions: 516.5 x 68 x 38 ft
Gross Tonnage: 10,289
Displacement: 21,250 tons
Machinery: Triple Expansion Engines,
    3 Boilers, Twin Screw
Horsepower/Speed: 3,000/10.5 knots
Fate: Scrapped, 1946

The fourth CHARLES PRATT-class tanker built for Standard Oil of NJ was F.Q. BARSTOW, whose contract was signed on July 28, 1915, the same day as that for WM. G. WARDEN. Her keel was laid in Shipway 7 on May 16, 1916, and she was launched on March 17, 1917. The sponsor for F.Q. BARSTOW was Mrs. W.A. Barstow, who christened the ship at about 3:30 P.M. on that date.

The new tanker was delivered on the following April 12, and she started the same routine service along the Gulf and East coasts as her sisters. Like them, she had her shelter deck opened up in 1923, reducing her gross tonnage from 10,289 to 9,003. Her career very closely paralleled that of her immediate predecessor, and she served Standard Oil of NJ through the 1920s and 1930s without incident.

As war came, she made 63 voyages and carried 6.5 million barrels of cargo safely between 1939 and 1944. In May 1942 she rescued 29 survivors of the torpedoed Dutch ship HECTOR between New York and Caripito. She made 16 voyages in 1943; then, in April 1944 she too was sold to the government for wartime service. She survived the war undamaged only to be scrapped in 1946.

WM. G. WARDEN
1917

WM. G. WARDEN

Hull No: 196
Owner: Standard Oil of NJ
Launched: December 18, 1916
Delivered: February 2, 1917
Dimensions: 516.5 x 68 x 38 ft
Gross Tonnage: 10,289
Displacement: 21,250 tons
Machinery: Triple Expansion Engines,
    3 Boilers, Twin Screw
Horsepower/Speed: 3,000/10.5 knots
Fate: Scrapped, 1947

WM. G. WARDEN was unusual in that her career began and ended at Newport News. WM. G. WARDEN was the third of six tankers of the CHARLES PRATT class. Her contract was signed on July 28, 1915, and her keel was laid on March 15 of the following year.

When her launch date arrived on December 18, 1916, WM. G. WARDEN had a difficult time getting into the water. She was christened by Miss Sarah McLean of Philadelphia on the appointed date but, due to the wind and tide, was not launched that day. A northwester blew on the following day, and the launch was again postponed to December 18. By that time, the grease on the ways had become so cold and hard that she refused to move when the launching triggers were released and had to be started with jacks. Fortunately, the rest of her construction was routine, and she was delivered to Standard Oil Co. of NJ on February 2, 1917.

She served her owner faithfully for the next 37 years, calling at ports from Houston and Port Arthur to New York, Boston, and Providence. She was lucky and escaped war damage, making 64 voyages and carrying 6.8 million barrels of cargo between 1939 and 1943.

She was chartered to the War Shipping Administration in April 1942, then was sold to the government in March 1944. During the last two years of the war, she made many trips from Gulf Coast oil ports to Cristobal, Canal Zone, with oil and deck cargo.

She was laid up in the James River after the war, then was sold to the shipyard for scrapping—arriving on December 17, 1946, just a day short of the thirtieth anniversary of her difficult launching. After over 500 tons of weight were removed, she was placed in dry dock and cut in half; then Shipways 8 and 9 were flooded, and half of the old ship was placed in each. By the end of February, 1947, the job was complete and WM. G. WARDEN was reduced to scrap.

O.B. JENNINGS
1917

O.B. JENNINGS

Hull No: 201
Owner: Standard Oil of NJ
Launched: August 25, 1917
Delivered: October 31, 1917
Dimensions: 516.5 x 68 x 38 ft
Gross Tonnage: 10,289
Displacement: 21,250 tons
Machinery: Triple Expansion Engines,
    3 Boilers, Twin Screw
Horsepower/Speed: 3,000/10.5 knots
Fate: War Loss, 1918

O.B. JENNINGS was the fifth CHARLES PRATT-class tanker built at Newport News, and she was the last one built for the Standard Oil Co. of NJ. Her keel was laid on Shipway 2 on January 11, 1917, and seven months later she was complete for launch. O.B. JENNINGS was christened by Miss Jeanette Jennings, daughter of Walter Jennings who was a director of the owner, on August 25, 1917, and was successfully launched into the James.

The new tanker completed outfitting and trials and was delivered on October 31, 1917, for what was to be a tragically short career. Her first papers were issued to the U.S. Shipping Board's Emergency Fleet Corporation, but just a week later her ownership reverted to Standard Oil of NJ. She entered coastal service and served her owner uneventfully until she was torpedoed by the German submarine U-140 off the Virginia Capes on August 4, 1918, and was sent to the bottom. Struck down less than a year after her launching, she was gone, but fortunately only one of the 50 men aboard was lost with her.

TORRES
1917

TORRES

Hull No: 202
Owner: Southern Pacific Co.
Launched: May 12, 1917
Delivered: June 28, 1917
Dimensions: 395 x 59 x 28 ft
Gross Tonnage: 4,943
Displacement: 9,760 tons
Machinery: Triple Expansion Engine,
    2 Boilers
Horsepower/Speed: 2,350/11 knots
Fate: Scrapped, 1950

TORRES was ordered by the Southern Pacific Co. late in 1915 and, except for an apparent lack of World War I naval service, her career paralleled that of her sister ship TOPILA remarkably closely. The keel for TORRES was laid on Shipway 4 on November 20, 1916, and she was christened by Miss Gertrude E.

Loomis, daughter of the shipyard's electrical engineer, on May 12, 1917.

The new tanker entered the East Coast oil trade after delivery the following June 28 and survived World War I without damage. TORRES continued with Southern Pacific for over 12 years until she was apparently chartered to the Atlantic Richfield Co. of Los Angeles with TOPILA and another vessel in 1929. She took up West Coast service and stayed with Atlantic Richfield until 1940. In that year she was sold to Bermuth, Lembecke Co. of New York, and her home port was moved from Portland, OR, to Wilmington, DL.

She traded along the East Coast and survived another World War undamaged, then was sold to Compania des Opercaiones Maritimes of Panama and was transferred to Panamanian flag in October 1946. She sailed for this owner between the U.S., West Indies, and Mediterranean Sea for four years before being broken up for scrap at Trieste late in 1950.

J.C. DONNELL
1918

J.C. DONNELL

Hull No: 205
Owner: Atlantic Refining Co.
Launched: November 24, 1917
Delivered: January 21, 1918
Dimensions: 516.5 x 68 x 38 ft
Gross Tonnage: 10,241
Displacement: 21,200 tons
Machinery: Quadruple Expansion Engines,
    3 Boilers, Twin Screw
Horsepower/Speed: 3,000/10.5 knots
Fate: Scrapped, 1947

J.C. DONNELL, similiar in dimensions to CHARLES PRATT, was ordered by the Atlantic Refining Co. on November 26, 1915, but, probably due to the press of wartime work at the shipyard, her keel was not laid until March 22, 1917. The tanker was launched on November 24, 1917, and was delivered on the following January 21. The sponsor for J.C. DONNELL was Mrs. Otto D. Donnell of Findlay, OH, who christened the ship before its launch from Shipway 7.

Delivered ten months before the Armistice, the new tanker fortunately escaped wartime damage and went on to serve her original owner for almost 30 years. With a cruising radius of 8,000 miles, she spent most of her career in East Coast trade but was on the West Coast during the early 1940s.

She was acquired by the Navy through the War Shipping Administration in January 1943 and was commissioned as PASIG (AO-89). Intended for use as an oil storage facility near New Caledonia in the Pacific, she was not needed and was returned to Atlantic Refining Co. late in 1943. After this brief naval career, she continued to serve her original owner as J.C. DONNELL until she was scrapped in 1947.

H.M. FLAGLER
1918

H.M. FLAGLER

Hull No: 208
Owner: Standard Oil of NJ
Launched: April 27, 1918
Delivered: July 17, 1918
Dimensions: 477.75 x 60 x 37.17 ft
Gross Tonnage: 8,207
Displacement: 16,850 tons
Machinery: Quadruple Expansion Engine,
   3 Boilers
Horsepower/Speed: 2,600/10.5 knots
Fate: Scrapped, 1949

First of yet another class of tankers built at Newport News for the Standard Oil Co. of NJ, H.M. FLAGER was somewhat smaller than the CHARLES PRATT class which preceded her. The new ships were almost 40 feet shorter and eight feet narrower than the previous ones.

The contracts for H.M. FLAGLER and her first sister ship F.D. ASCHE were signed on April 20, 1916, but the keel for the first one was not laid until September 4 of the following year. Delayed by destroy-er construction at the shipyard, the construction of H.M. FLAGLER proceeded apace once started, and she was ready for launch by April 1918. The long tanker, first of ten of her class, was sponsored by Miss Mary Harkness Flagler, daughter of H.H. Flagler, and was smoothly launched from Shipway 5 at 11:10 A.M. on April 27, 1918. H.M. FLAGLER entered Standard's coastal service after delivery on July 17 and served for many years calling at New York, Wilmington, Boston, Baltimore, Baton Rouge, Galveston, and Houston.

With the coming of war, H.M. FLAGLER was transferred to Standard Oil's Panamanian affiliate Panama Transport Co. and continued to sail under her original name. She was operated by the Imperial Oil Co. and was time chartered to the U.S. government in late 1941, making trips to such distant ports as Palestine, Cartagena, Hailfax, and Le Havre during the war. She was extremely busy and carried 49 cargoes totalling 3.8 million barrels of oil between 1939 and 1945. During the war she was manned by Canadian, American, Danish, and British crews and she survived the war without a scratch. Returning to more conventional trade after the war, she served under Panamanian flag for four more years before being scrapped in 1949.

F.D. ASCHE
1918

F.D. ASCHE

Hull No: 209
Owner: Standard Oil of NJ
Launched: October 24, 1918
Delivered: December 10, 1918
Dimensions: 477.75 x 60 x 37.17 ft
Gross Tonnage: 8,293
Displacement: 16,850 tons
Machinery: Quadruple Expansion Engine,
    3 Boilers
Horsepower/Speed: 2,600/10.5 knots
Fate: Scrapped, 1959

F.D. ASCHE was the second tanker delivered to the Standard Oil Co. in 1918, and she was sister ship to H.M. FLAGLER and to the eight naval oilers which followed in 1919 and 1920. Her keel was laid on December 10, 1917, and she was launched by the following October. F.D. ASCHE was sponsored by Mrs. F.D. Asche and slipped off Shipway 7 at noon on October 24, 1918. The tanker was completed and was delivered to Standard Oil exactly a year after her keel had been laid, and she took up routine coastal service.

Her first three years were uneventful, but in October 1921 she was caught in a hurricane off the Florida coast while in ballast and was driven aground on October 27. She suffered massive bottom damage, but after a heroic salvage effort, she was refloated and was towed to New York and then to Newport News on the cushion of air in her tanks. She entered Dry Dock 3 on January 19, 1922, and provided four months of much needed work in view of the imminent cancellation of naval work at the shipyard.

She stayed in dock until May 12, then was redelivered to her owner, only to be sold to Danish interests and renamed SCANDIA the following September. She stayed with this affiliate of her original owner until 1940, at which time she passed into the service of the British Ministry of War Transport.

After war service without casualty, she returned to her former owner. SCANDIA served with Det Danske Petroleum until 1951 when she was sold to Cia. Maritima Iguano and, renamed AMADA, was placed under Panamanian flag. She served this owner in European, Mediterranean, and Mideast trade until being sold for scrap in 1959.

TIPPECANOE
1920

TIPPECANOE

Hull No: 254
Owner: U.S. Shipping Board
Launched: June 5, 1920
Delivered: August 4, 1920
Dimensions: 477.75 x 60 x 37.17 ft
Gross Tonnage: 8,266
Displacement: 16,850 tons
Machinery: Geared Turbines, 3 Boilers
Horsepower/Speed: 2,600/10.5 knots
Fate: Scrapped, 1946

TIPPECANOE was the seventh Shipping Board tanker built at the shipyard and, like several of her sisters, she was destined to spend much of her life laid up in "Red Lead Row." The keel for TIPPECANOE was laid down on October 1, 1919, and she was launched from Shipway 5 on June 5, 1920. The sponsor for this ship was Miss Harriet V. Gatewood, daughter of the works manager of the shipyard.

TIPPECANOE differed from earlier tankers of the PATOKA class in that she was fitted with geared steam turbine propulsion, the first Newport News tanker so engined.

The new ship was completed and was delivered to the Shipping Board on August 4, 1920, but was not commissioned as a naval oiler until March 1940. She had been acquired by the Navy at Mare Island in March 1922 but remained inactive there for 18 years.

After her commissioning on March 6, 1940, TIPPECANOE was designated AO-21. She was armed with two 5" guns and two 3" guns. She operated between the West Coast and Hawaii until March 1942 when she steamed for the South Pacific. She served the carriers LEXINGTON, YORKTOWN, ENTERPRISE, and HORNET and their escorts for a few months, then returned to Pearl Harbor. After August 1942, TIPPECANOE was assigned to duty in the Aleutians, where she stayed until the end of the war.

In August 1945 she started several months of service with the occupation forces in Japan; then, in late November she sailed for San Francisco and deactivation. She was decommissioned at Mare Island in March 1946, and her relatively short career came to a close when she was sold for scrap the following November.

PATOKA
1919

PATOKA

Hull No: 248
Owner: U.S. Shipping Board
Launched: July 26, 1919
Delivered: September 3, 1919
Dimensions: 477.75 x 60 x 37.17 ft
Gross Tonnage: 8,267
Displacement: 16,850 tons
Machinery: Quadruple Expansion Engine,
   3 Boilers
Horsepower/Speed: 2,600/10.5 knots
Fate: Scrapped, 1948

PATOKA was the first of eight tankers delivered to the U.S. Shipping Board in 1919 and 1920 for service as naval oilers. The contract for all eight ships was signed on October 10, 1918, and the keel for PATOKA was laid on the following December 16. Despite the heavy volume of other work then in progress at the shipyard, Hull 248 was christened and launched on July 26, 1919 by Miss Margaret V. Cornbrook, daughter of the shipyard's superintendent of hull construction, and entered the James River from Shipway 7 at 9:32 A.M.

After completion, trials and delivery on September

3, PATOKA was acquired by the Navy, commissioned on October 13, and designated AO-9. She was armed with two 5″ and four 40mm guns for naval service. PATOKA went quickly into naval service, making trips to Scotland, Italy, and Turkey during her first year. She served on both the East and West Coasts until 1924 when she was selected to be a tender for the airship SHENANDOAH. She was fitted out for this duty at the Norfolk Navy Yard, and a huge mooring mast for the airship was erected on her stern. She served as tender to several Navy airships until she was decommissioned and placed in reserve in August 1933.

She was recommissioned at Puget Sound in November 1939, classified as a seaplane tender, and designated AV-6. PATOKA was moved to Norfolk during the summer and again became a fleet oiler, AO-9. She delivered fuel and cargo to bases and ships of the fleet and made two round trips to Brazil before America entered the war. She was overhauled at Norfolk in April and May 1944 then, reclassified AG-125, sailed via Guam for Okinawa for duty as a minecraft tender.

After the war ended she served with occupation forces in Japan until returning to the U.S. in March 1946. PATOKA was decommissioned on July 1, 1946, and was laid up, then was sold for scrap in March 1948.

RAMAPO
1919

RAMAPO

Hull No: 249
Owner: U.S. Shipping Board
Launched: September 11, 1919
Delivered: October 22, 1919
Dimensions: 477.75 x 60 x 37.17 ft
Gross Tonnage: 8,246
Displacement: 16,850 tons
Machinery: Quadruple Expansion Engine,
   3 Boilers
Horsepower/Speed: 2,600/10.5 knots
Fate: Scrapped, 1953

The second of the Shipping Board tankers was RAMAPO which, like her seven sisters, was destined to serve her country well in World War II and to survive undamaged. The keel for Hull 249 was laid in Shipway 5 on January 15, 1919. Construction proceeded apace, and RAMAPO was christened by Miss Isabel W. Scott of Richmond and was launched on September 11, 1919.

The new tanker was completed on October 22 and was commissioned as AO-12 on November 15. Armed with 5″ guns at her bow and stern, RAMAPO began her career in the Caribbean, then traveled up and down the East Coast and to Europe before 1922. In that year she was transferred to the Pacific and served the Pacific Fleet for the next six years. In 1928 she was assigned to the Asiatic Fleet, and she thereafter averaged four Far East trips each year for the next nine years, serving as a survey ship and taking data for the U.S. Hydrographic Office. She briefly served in the Aleutians in 1937 but thereafter returned to Far East service.

Early in 1941 RAMAPO was assigned to Hawaiian shuttle service, and on the morning of December 7, 1941, she found herself at Pearl Harbor. She was undamaged in the attack there and escaped damage during the war while serving the Navy by supplying Aleutian stations and ships until September 1945. She was decommissioned at San Francisco in January 1946 and was transferred to the Maritime Commission the following July.

Winner of one battle star in World War II, the veteran RAMAPO was sold to the MarTrade Corporation of New York in 1949 and entered merchant service. She served in worldwide trade with this owner under American flag before passing to Liberian registry in 1951. Owned first by P.C. Nicurezo and later by the Three Stars Co., she plied between Europe, the Mediterranean and the Far East before being sold for scrap late in 1953.

RAPIDAN
1919

RAPIDAN

Hull No: 250
Owner: U.S. Shipping Board
Launched: October 25, 1919
Delivered: November 26, 1919
Dimensions: 477.75 x 60 x 37.17 ft
Gross Tonnage: 8,333
Displacement: 16,850 tons
Machinery: Quadruple Expansion Engine,
   3 Boilers
Horsepower/Speed: 2,600/10.5 knots
Fate: Scrapped, 1947

The third PATOKA-class tanker built for the U.S. Shipping Board's Emergency Fleet Corp. for naval service was RAPIDAN (AO-18), which was destined to spend much of her life idle in the James River. The keel for Hull 250 was laid in Shipway 2 on February 2, 1919, and in eight months she was ready to be launched. The honor of christening RAPIDAN was given to Miss May Davis Hopkins of Newport News, daughter of the late president of the shipyard, A.L. Hopkins, who was lost on the LUSITANIA; she sent the ship down the ways on October 25, 1919.

The proud new ship was delivered to the Shipping Board a month later but was not commissioned until January 1922. She remained in commission less than six months, then was laid up in the James River Fleet. She was not called to duty again until January 1940, at which time she was placed in Gulf Coast-East Coast service. She served the Atlantic Fleet until 1942, was overhauled, then made a trip to Casablanca. RAPIDAN was damaged by an underwater explosion in May 1943, was repaired, then was transferred to the Pacific in March 1944.

She finished out the war in the Aleutians, then returned to the East Coast for deactivation in September 1946. In September 1947 the old RAPIDAN, veteran of war in two theatres, was sold and scrapped.

SALINAS
1920

SALINAS

Hull No: 251
Owner: U.S. Shipping Board
Launched: May 5, 1920
Delivered: May 13, 1920
Dimensions: 477.75 x 60 x 37.17 ft
Gross Tonnage: 8,246
Displacement: 16,850 tons
Machinery: Quadruple Expansion Engine,
    3 Boilers
Horsepower/Speed: 2,600/10.5 knots
Fate: Scrapped, 1960

SALINAS was the fourth of the Shipping Board tankers built at the shipyard. The keel for SALINAS was laid on April 10, 1919, and, due to the fact that Shipway 9 and its overhead gantries were still under construction, she was virtually ready for trials when launched. The sponsor for Hull 251 was little Miss Isabel Ferguson, daughter of shipyard president and general manager Homer L. Ferguson, and she sent the new ship down the ways at 3:00 P.M. on May 5, 1920. She had originally been given the name HUDSONIAN, but when commissioned as a naval oiler (AO-19) in November 1921, she carried the name SALINAS.

She was in commission for only six months when she was decommissioned in June 1922 at Norfolk, and she stayed in reserve for four years. She was recommissioned in June 1926 and served the Navy by carrying fuels from Caribbean and Texas oil ports to both coasts, the Canal Zone, and the Caribbean.

She was extremely busy during World War II and had at least one serious brush with disaster. In convoy on a voyage from Iceland to Newfoundland, she was hit by two enemy torpedoes on October 30, 1941. The submarine surfaced and fired three more torpedoes which missed, then was chased away by SALINAS' guns and by her escorts. Said to be the only tanker to ever survive hits by two torpedoes, SALINAS continued in the Atlantic until April 1944, was transferred to the Pacific, and served out the war in Alaskan waters.

She was decommissioned at San Francsico in January 1946, then served the Hillcone Steamship Co. of that city as a merchant tanker until 1955. In that year she was sold to the Houston Shipping Co. and transferred to Liberian registry. She served this owner in the U.S. West Indies until she was sold and broken up for scrap in 1960.

SAPELO
1920

SAPELO

Hull No: 252
Owner: U.S. Shipping Board
Launched: December 24, 1919
Delivered: January 30, 1920
Dimensions: 477.75 x 60 x 37.17 ft
Gross Tonnage: 8,246
Displacement: 16,850 tons
Machinery: Quadruple Expansion Engine,
    3 Boilers
Horsepower/Speed: 2,600/10.5 knots
Fate: Scrapped, 1946

The keel for SAPELO, the fifth Shipping Board tanker, was laid on Shipway 4 on May 3, 1919, and she was ready for launch on December 24 of that year. The sponsor for SAPELO was Miss Mary Anne Mallison, daughter of the naval inspector of ordnance at the shipyard.

The new tanker was delivered to the Shipping Board on January 30, 1920, and was commissioned as AO-11 on February 19. After two transatlantic trips in 1920 to supply British and American forces and to return war dead, SAPELO settled into routine duty along the Gulf and East Coasts with an occasional European trip. After April 1924 she served most of the time in the Pacific, but returned to the East Coast on occasion. In July 1932 SAPELO was formally transferred to the Pacific but in 1933 she sailed to Philadelphia and was decommissioned and laid up.

She was recommissioned as war clouds gathered in August 1940 and during the first years of conflict, served along the East Coast and made trips to Canada and Iceland. She survived several dangerous convoys to and from Europe in which many other ships were lost, and she finished up the war back at her old stations along the Gulf and East Coasts and in the Caribbean. SAPELO was decommissioned in October 1945 and was sold for scrap in May 1946.

SEPULGA
1920

SEPULGA

Hull No: 253
Owner: U.S. Shipping Board
Launched: April 21, 1920
Delivered: May 27, 1920
Dimensions: 477.75 x 60 x 37.17 ft
Gross Tonnage: 8,266
Displacement: 16,850 tons
Machinery: Quadruple Expansion Engine,
   3 Boilers
Horsepower/Speed: 2,600/10.5 knots
Fate: Scrapped, 1946

SEPULGA, sixth of the Shipping Board tankers slated for naval service, had her keel laid on Shipway 7 on August 20, 1919, and eight months later was ready for launching. Hull 253 was christened by Miss Louise Graham, daughter of the naval inspector of machinery at the Shipyard, on April 21, 1920. By the end of the following month SEPULGA had completed trials and was delivered to the Shipping Board. While her original name was FLEETCO, the new tanker was commissioned as SEPULGA (AO-20) and joined the Navy in December 1921.

Her first tour was not a long one, for after only four months of service she was laid up at Mare Island, where she remained for the next 18 years. She was recommissioned on February 5, 1940, and, operating for the Naval Transportation Service, delivered fuel, supplies, and passengers from the West Coast to Pacific bases.

Except for brief duty in the Aleutians in 1942, SEPULGA spent much of the war in the central Pacific and after October 1944 served as headquarters and station ship at Ulithi. With only six years of useful service behind her, the old oiler was decommissioned in March 1946 and was sold for scrap the following December.

TRINITY
1920

TRINITY

Hull No: 255
Owner: U.S. Shipping Board
Launched: July 3, 1920
Delivered: September 4, 1920
Dimensions: 477.75 x 60 x 37.17 ft
Gross Tonnage: 8,266
Displacement: 16,850 tons
Machinery: Geared Turbines, 3 Boilers
Horsepower/Speed: 2,600/10.5 knots
Fate: Scrapped, 1954

TRINITY was the eighth and last Shipping Board tanker built at Newport News and, like TIPPECANOE she had steam turbine propulsion. Like her close sister, most of her career was spent idle, but she was much more active in World War II.

Her keel was laid on November 10, 1919, and she was launched from Shipway 2 on the following July 3. The sponsor for TRINITY was Miss Anne Sophie Christiansen, daughter of the superintendent of machinery at the shipyard. TRINITY was completed and was delivered directly to the Navy and was commissioned on September 4, 1920.

She made her maiden voyage to the Mediterranean, remaining there until April 1921. Based at Norfolk and designated AO-13, she operated on the East Coast until December 1923 when she was decommissioned and laid up at the Philadelphia Navy Yard. She remained idle there until recommissioned on June 21, 1938, then served on the East Coast for six months.

Early in 1939 she was transferred to the Pacific, and after brief service in the Alaskan area, she was assigned to the Asiatic Fleet. Based in the Philippines, she narrowly missed being caught in the attack at Cavite in December 1941. She also narrowly missed being destroyed by three torpedoes fired at her in the Dutch East Indies in January 1942.

After her war service, she returned to Mare Island in February 1946 and was decommissioned on May 28. She fortunately escaped scrapping and was sold to the Hillcone Steamship Co. of San Francisco in August 1948. Retaining the name TRINITY, she served this owner on the West Coast until 1951.

In February of that year, she was sold to the Colonial Steamship Co. and was renamed SEABEAVER. She stayed with Colonial until July 1952, then was sold to Pelivalle Compania Naviera, S.A. and, renamed AYSNETI, transferred to Panamanian registry. With this her last owner, she returned to a career of long voyages throughout the Western Hemisphere before finally being broken up for scrap in 1954.

AGWISTONE
1922

AGWISTONE

Hull No: 259
Owner: Atlantic, Gulf & West Indies Co.
Launched: February 8, 1921
Delivered: July 26, 1922
Dimensions: 516.5 x 68 x 38 ft
Gross Tonnage: 10,398
Displacement: 21,250 tons
Machinery: Triple Expansion Engines,
    3 Boilers, Twin Screw
Horsepower/Speed: 3,000/10.5 knots
Fate: Scrapped, 1949

On December 24, 1919, the shipyard obtained a contract for the construction of two merchant tankers which were virtually identical to CHARLES PRATT. These ships were built for the Atlantic, Gulf & West Indies Co., and they were named after executives of the AGWI Line and affiliates. The keel for the first ship, later named AGWISTONE, was laid on May 19, 1920, and she was launched from Shipway 7 on February 8, 1921, by Miss Barbara Stone of New York.

AGWISTONE completed trials in March but, probably owing to the post war shipping slump which had idled 17 percent of the world's ships, she and her sister ship were not delivered until July 1922 and remained idle at the shipyard until early in 1923. She went into coastal trade for the AGWI Line until being sold to the Beacon Oil Co., an affiliate of the Standard Oil Co. of NJ, in December 1929.

Renamed BEACON, she served this owner and later the Colonial Beacon Oil Co. and the Standard Shipping Co. before becoming part of the Standard Oil Co. of NJ fleet in 1936. With but a few overseas trips, BEACON stayed in domestic service until the beginning of World War II, then carried many cargoes to the armed forces in three oceans.

In February 1943 she and her crew pioneered the underway fueling at sea of naval vessels which later became an important technique used by navies around the world. In that same month she was witness to the torpedoing of her Newport News-built sister H.H. ROGERS while enroute from Londonderry to New York.

During the rest of the war, she was active in the Atlantic, Mediterranean, Indian Ocean, and Persian Gulf, and she carried over 8 million barrels of cargo on 79 voyages from 1939 to 1945. At war's end she was serving the Pacific between Balboa and Pearl Harbor. She went back into domestic service after the war, where she remained until scrapped in 1949.

AGWISMITH
1922

AGWISMITH

Hull No: 260
Owner: Atlantic, Gulf & West Indies Co.
Launched: March 26, 1921
Delivered: July 26, 1922
Dimensions: 516.5 x 68 x 38 ft
Gross Tonnage: 10,398
Displacement: 21,250 tons
Machinery: Triple Expansion Engines,
 3 Boilers, Twin Screw
Horsepower/Speed: 3,000/10.5 knots
Fate: Scrapped, 1954

Like her preceding sister, AGWISMITH's career got off to a slow start, but then she enjoyed a long and varied service life under several owners. The keel for Hull 260 was laid in Shipway 5 on June 17, 1920. AGWISMITH was christened by Miss Katherine Williams Smith, daughter of the president of the Ward Line, on March 26, 1921.

The new ship completed trials shortly thereafter but, like her sister ship, had her delivery delayed and did not leave the shipyard until February 1923. She also did not remain long with the AGWI Line and was sold to the California Petroleum Co. and was renamed HELEN VINMONT in 1926. This owner was an affiliate of the Texas Co. and put her into service on routes on both coasts and to South America.

In 1930 her name was changed to CALIFORNIA, and her ownership was changed to that of the Texas Co. In the early 1930s she traded in the Pacific and to the Far East, and she survived the war undamaged in the service of the Texas Co.

In 1951 she was sold to Cia. Maritima Isthmania and was transferred to Liberian registry. She served this owner under the name ARION until she was broken up for scrap in 1954.

WM. ROCKEFELLER
1921

WM. ROCKEFELLER

Hull No: 262
Owner: Standard Oil of NJ
Launched: October 5, 1921
Delivered: November 9, 1921
Dimensions: 572.5 x 75 x 43.25 ft
Gross Tonnage: 14,055
Displacement: 29,000 tons
Machinery: Triple Expansion Engines,
 3 Boilers, Twin Screw
Horsepower/Speed: 3,800/10.75 knots
Fate: War Loss, 1942

WM. ROCKEFELLER, named for the younger brother of John D. Rockefeller, had the same good fortune in peacetime service as her sister ship JOHN D. ARCHBOLD but was not so fortunate in wartime. The huge tanker's keel was laid on the same day as that of her sister, December 15, 1920. Her construction proceeded at a slightly slower pace than that of Hull 261, and she was launched on October 5, 1921. Sponsor for WM. ROCKEFELLER was Miss Isabel Rockefeller. Both of these ships had teak pilot houses and were the showpieces of Standard Oil's fleet.

After delivery just over a month after launch, the new tanker entered coastal trade between Gulf and East Coast ports during the 1920s and 1930s and into the first years of World War II.

From 1939 until June 1942, she carried over seven million barrels of cargo on a total of 49 voyages, but on her 50th wartime trip her luck ran out. She had delivered a cargo of fuel oil to Cape Town, South Africa in March 1942, then had returned to Guiria, Venezuela on June 2. She sailed for Aruba with a cargo of crude oil, then took on her last cargo of fuel oil. She sailed for New York on June 19. When 16 miles northeast of Diamond Shoal on June 28, she was torpedoed by the German submarine U-701, and a huge explosion and intense fire resulted. Despite considerable effort to fight the fire, the crew was forced to abandon ship, and WM. ROCKEFELLER later sank without loss of life. The loss of this fine ship was avenged just nine days later when U-701 was herself sunk in these same waters by depth charge from an Army patrol plane.

JOHN D. ARCHBOLD
1921

JOHN D. ARCHBOLD

Hull No: 261
Owner: Standard Oil of NJ
Launched: August 20, 1921
Delivered: September 24, 1921
Dimensions: 572.5 x 75 x 43.25 ft
Gross Tonnage: 14,055
Displacement: 29,000 tons
Machinery: Triple Expansion Engines,
    3 Boilers, Twin Screw
Horsepower/Speed: 3,800/10.75 knots
Fate: Scrapped, 1962

By far the largest tankers built at Newport News until 1949, JOHN D. ARCHBOLD and sister WM. ROCKEFELLER, at 22,600 DWT and approaching 600 feet long, were among the largest in the world when delivered in 1921. The two ships were ordered by the Standard Oil Co. of NJ on February 2, 1920, and the keel for JOHN D. ARCHBOLD was laid on December 15 of that year. The second Standard Oil tanker to bear this name (Hull 170 was the first), JOHN D. ARCHBOLD was christened by Mrs. Harold W. Chapin on August 20, 1921.

Notwithstanding the shipping crisis then underway, the new ship went directly into service after her delivery in September of that year. She remained in prosaic coastwise service until April 1942 when she was time chartered to the War Shipping Administration. She made her first ocean crossing in November 1942 when she carried a cargo of fuel oil to Glasgow. She stayed in North Atlantic service for a year, then transferred to the Pacific, only to return to the Atlantic a year later.

During the war years, she carried a total of 70 cargoes totalling almost 10 million barrels of fuel, most of which was delivered to bases in the Pacific. She returned to regular coastal service with Standard Oil after the war and remained until she was transferred to their Panamanian affiliate, Panama Transport Co., in 1949.

Around 1950 she was transferred to another affiliate, the Anglo American Oil Co., and was operated under British flag as ESSO LIVERPOOL until early 1953. At that time she ended 32 years of Standard Oil service and was sold to Steamship Enterprises of Panama and again transferred to Panamanian flag. Renamed LIVERPOOL, she steamed another nine years with this owner until, tired veteran, she was scrapped in Italy in 1962.

J.H. SENIOR
1924

J.H. SENIOR

Hull No: 273
Owner: Standard Oil of NJ
Launched: January 5, 1924
Delivered: February 23, 1924
Dimensions: 220.17 x 38 x 16.5 ft
Gross Tonnage: 1,155
Displacement: 2,287 tons
Machinery: Diesel-Electric
Horsepower/Speed: 455/8.5 knots
Fate: Scrapped, 1973

The longest-lived of any Newport News-built tanker, J.H. SENIOR was ordered by the Standard Oil Co. of NJ on June 15, 1923. Hull 273 was actually a self-propelled barge, and she was also the smallest powered tank vessel built at the shipyard.

The keel for J.H. SENIOR was laid on October 27, 1923, and she was ready to launch less than three months later. She was launched by Miss Adele Senior, and Mr. and Mrs. J.H. Senior were in attendance at the ceremony on January 5, 1924. After fitting out with diesel-electric machinery, the new vessel was delivered to her owners on February 23 and began what was to be a long if uneventful life.

She apparently served on the East Coast and inland waterways for her whole career. In 1930 her name was given to a large tanker (which was lost in a tragic collision and fire in 1943), and she was given the unglamorous name PETROLIA NO. 10. In 1938 she was renamed ESSO DELIVERY NO. 10 and was joined by a slightly larger Newport News-built sister named ESSO DELIVERY NO. 11. She made it through World War II undamaged in domestic service and was repowered in 1944, her horsepower increasing from 445 to 750. She served Esso's Inland Waterways Dept. and was renamed ESSO JAMES in 1961, then transferred to Humble Oil Co. briefly in 1960.

In 1961 she ended her long association with Standard Oil of NJ interests and was sold and renamed JAMES. A year later she was sold to Maritime Carriers of New York and was renamed SENIOR. She served this owner until the late 1960s, when she was chartered for use as a fender during construction at the Delaware Memorial Bridge. Her useful career at an end, she was finally sold for scrap in 1973.

ESSO DELIVERY NO. 11
1938

ESSO DELIVERY NO. 11

Hull No: 367
Owner: Standard Oil of NJ
Launched: December 8, 1937
Delivered: February 8, 1938
Dimensions 259.75 x 43.5 x 18.3 ft
Gross Tonnage: 1,707
Displacement: 3,570 tons
Machinery: Diesel-Electric
Horsepower/Speed: 1,000/10.5 knots
Fate: Scrapped, 1953

After the delivery of J.H. SENIOR in 1924, no new orders for tank vessels were obtained until motor oil barge ESSO DELIVERY NO. 11 was ordered by the Standard Oil Co. of NJ in April 1937. This ship was somewhat larger than her predecessor and, at 1,000 HP, had over twice the power. The keel for ESSO DELIVERY NO. 11 was laid in Shipway 8 on September 15, 1937, and she was launched by Mrs. H.S. Atchison on December 8 of that year and was delivered on the following February 8. Of all-welded construction, the new vessel had six main cargo tanks divided by a centerline longitudinal bulkhead and was certified for service in the Chesapeake Bay and for short coastal voyages.

ESSO DELIVERY NO. 11 was acquired by the Navy in April 1943 and was commissioned as AROOSTOOK (AOG-14). Armed with a single 3″ gun, she was sent to the Mediterranean and ferried gasoline between North African, Italian, Greek, and French ports. She sustained enemy air attack at Bari, Italy, in December 1943 but was not badly damaged.

She was decommissioned in January 1945 and was transferred to the French under Lend-Lease. Renamed LAC PAVIN, she served the French Navy as an oiler until she was broken up in 1953.

ESSO RICHMOND
1940

ESSO RICHMOND

Hull No: 370
Owner: Standard Oil of NJ
Launched: September 29, 1939
Delivered: April 20, 1940
Dimensions: 553 x 75 x 39 ft
Gross Tonnage: 11,316
Displacement: 23,359 tons
Machinery: Geared Turbines, 4 Boilers,
   Twin Screw
Horsepower/Speed: 13,500/18 knots
Fate: Scrapped, 1970

On January 3, 1938, the shipyard signed a contract with the Standard Oil Co. of NJ for the construction of three large, fast, twin screw tankers, which were identical to nine others ordered simultaneoulsy from other shipyards. These turbine-driven ships of 16,300 DWT were designed with national defense features and all three of the Newport News-built ships soon saw military service.

The keel for the first ship was laid in Shipway 9 on January 16, 1939, and she was named ESSO RICHMOND and was christened by Mrs. Joseph P. Kennedy on the following September 29. Attending Mrs. Kennedy at the ceremony were her father and mother and her daughter Eunice, who served as maid of honor.

After trials on April 18-19, ESSO RICHMOND was delivered to her owners and left the shipyard on April 20. She operated with the Esso fleet only until October, then was sold to the Maritime Commission, acquired by the Navy, and was renamed KASKASKIA and designated AO-27. She was armed with two 5″ guns and two 3″ guns and was provided with a naval complement of 272 men. KASKASKIA carried fuels between West Coast ports and Hawaii, Alaska, and Pacific Islands during the war. She steamed proudly into Tokyo Bay on September 10, 1945, to join the Occupation Force.

She remained in the Far East for a year before returning to California in September 1946. She continued in Naval service in the Pacific and during the Korean War operated out of Sasebo, Japan. KASKASKIA made three deployments to Korea, winning seven battle stars to add to the nine which she had won in World War II service.

She was placed out of commission in April 1955, re-entered service with MSTS in January 1957, was decommissioned in December 1957, then was recommissioned in December 1961 due to the Berlin Crisis. She served along the East Coast and with the Sixth Fleet in the Mediterranean into the 1960s and participated in several space recoveries during the period. The old KASKASKIA was finally stricken from the Navy List on December 19, 1969 and was sold for scrap in 1970.

ESSO RALEIGH
1940

ESSO RALEIGH

Hull No: 371
Owner: Standard Oil of NJ
Launched: January 26, 1940
Delivered: June 21, 1940
Dimensions: 553 x 75 x 39 ft
Gross Tonnage: 11,316
Displacement: 23,359 tons
Machinery: Geared Turbines, 4 Boilers,
    Twin Screw
Horsepower/Speed: 13,500/18 knots
Fate: Scrapped, 1975

Second of the Esso national defense tankers built prior to World War II was ESSO RALEIGH, the keel for which was laid on Shipway 6 on May 8, 1939. ESSO RALEIGH was launched on January 26, 1940, by Mrs. William L. Inslee, wife of the traffic division manager, Marine Department, of the owner.

Delivered to the Esso fleet on June 21, 1940, ESSO RALEIGH served her owner for less than a year and carried only 26 cargoes before being commissioned as the naval fleet oiler GUADALUPE (AO-32) in June 1941. She made six voyages on the East Coast then, taking six PT boats as deck cargo, was sent to the Pacific in August. She returned to the East Coast and was armed, then sailed to the Pacific in January 1942. She helped develop techniques for fueling at sea, then participated virtually in every major operation of the Pacific War.

GUADALUPE was involved in collision with another tanker in January 1945 in Luzon Strait and received a damaged bow, putting her out of action for a month. She stayed in the Pacific after the war and made a trip to Norfolk and back via the Persian Gulf and Suez in 1948. She was active during the Korean War and later supported American forces during the Vietnam Conflict. After 34 years of faithful service, GUADALUPE was stricken from the Navy list on May 15, 1975, and was subsequently sold for scrap.

ESSO COLUMBIA
1941

ESSO COLUMBIA

Hull No: 372
Owner: Standard Oil of NJ
Launched: September 18, 1940
Delivered: April 28, 1941
Dimensions: 553 x 75 x 39 ft
Gross Tonnage: 12,176
Displacement: 23,359 tons
Machinery: Geared Turbines, 4 Boilers,
    Twin Screw
Horsepower/Speed: 13,500/18 knots
Fate: Scrapped, 1970

The third large tanker ordered by the Standard Oil Co. of NJ in 1938 was named ESSO COLUMBIA but never saw service with the Esso fleet, being delivered directly to the Navy when completed in 1941. The keel for Hull 372 was laid on February 5, 1940, and she was launched the following September 18 by Mrs. Eugene Holman, wife of a director of Standard Oil Co. of NJ.

Like the other two ships ordered with her, ESSO COLUMBIA was built under a Maritime Administration contract and was destined for naval service. Instead of being delivered for merchant service, she was commissioned as AO-26 on April 28, 1941. Named SALAMONIE, she served along the East Coast until November 1942 when she made a trip to Casablanca and several to England in convoy. In July 1944 she sailed for the Pacific and service with the Seventh Fleet. She supported the fleet in the Leyte invasion and in the Philippines.

After the Japanese surrender, she supported occupation forces at Shanghai, then returned to the U.S. for an overhaul. She returned and spent two and a half years carrying fuel between the Persian Gulf and naval bases in the Far East before being transferred to the Atlantic Fleet in May 1949.

During the next two decades SALAMONIE served with the Second Fleet in the Caribbean and with the Sixth Fleet in the Mediterranean. She was placed in reserve in August 1968 and was decommissioned the following December. She was placed in the James River Reserve Fleet and stayed there until September 1970 when she was sold and was towed to Rotterdam to be scrapped.

ESSO SUEZ
1949

ESSO SUEZ

Hull No: 475
Owner: Esso Shipping Co.
Launched: January 14, 1949
Delivered: April 1, 1949
Dimensions: 628 x 82.5 x 42.5 ft
Gross Tonnage: 17,062
Displacement: 34,145 tons
Machinery: Geared Turbines, 2 Boilers
Horsepower/Speed: 12,500/16 knots
Fate: Scrapped, 1984

On January 29, 1948, the shipyard signed a contract for two tankers with the Standard Oil Co. of NJ, ending a severe shortage of newbuilding work at the yard following World War II. Over the next six years the yard was to deliver a total of 19 ships of this class for three owners, and these were to become among the most highly regarded of Newport News products.

The first Newport News-built ship of this type was ESSO SUEZ, the keel for which was laid on July 7, 1948. Built on Shipway 9, ESSO SUEZ was in an advanced state of outfitting when christened by Mrs. F.H. Bedford, wife of a director of the owner on January 14, 1949. ESSO SUEZ was the second of the 26,000 DWT class, as ESSO ZURICH had been launched at

Sun on December 4.

ESSO SUEZ was completed quickly and made better than 17 knots on her trial trip in late March. She was delivered on April 1, 1949, and by that time the yard had obtained contracts for nine more of her type. After delivery the new ship was placed in the domestic service of the Esso Shipping Co. under American flag, but she made trips to Europe and the Far East during her first year.

On April 20, 1951, she was involved in a collision with ESSO GREENSBORO near Morgan City, LA, in dense fog. Both ships caught fire and two men were killed on ESSO SUEZ but 37 died on ESSO GREENSBORO. Repairs to ESSO SUEZ took four months; then she was returned to service.

During her lifetime, she stayed mostly in the U.S. and West Indies trade, and in 1962 her name was changed to ESSO JACKSONVILLE to better suit her domestic career. She was operated by Humble Oil and Refining Co. until 1964 when she was sold to Pioneer Tankers, Inc. and was renamed OCEAN PIONEER.

In 1968 she was again sold, this time to Hudson Waterways Corporation of New York, and she was renamed TRANSPANAMA. She stayed with Hudson Waterways until 1976 when she was sold to Sabine Towing & Transportation Co. Renamed SAN MARCOS, she stayed with Sabine into the 1980s and continued to provide dependable service, but in 1984 she was finally retired and scrapped in Taiwan.

ESSO MONTEVIDEO
1949

ESSO MONTEVIDEO
Hull No: 476
Owner: Esso Shipping Co.
Launched: February 25, 1949
Delivered: May 26, 1949
Dimensions: 628 x 82.5 x 42.5 ft
Gross Tonnage: 17,062
Displacement: 34,145 tons
Machinery: Geared Turbines, 2 Boilers
Horsepower/Speed: 12,500/16 knots
Fate: Scrapped, 1976

The second ship in the yard's postwar tanker building program was ESSO MONTEVIDEO which was ordered with ESSO SUEZ in January 1948. The keel for ESSO MONTEVIDEO was laid in the outboard end of Building Dock 11 on August 26, 1948, and by February of the following year all 23 of her subassemblies had been erected, tested, and partially outfitted. Hull 476 was floated and moved to the inboard end of the dock on February 25, 1949, for

christening by Mrs. F.W. Pierce, wife of a director of the Standard Oil Co. of NJ.

The new ship completed outfitting and successful trials and was delivered to the oil company on the following May 26. Unlike her sister, ESSO MONTEVIDEO was placed under Panamanian flag with Esso's Panama Transport Co. She made several voyages to Europe in the first few years of her career, and in September 1952 she grounded in the harbor at Charleston, SC, but was freed without major damage.

She stayed with Panama Transport Co. until 1964, then transferred to the Esso Transport & Tanker Co. where she stayed for the next 10 years. Her voyages carried her far and wide and she served Esso in Europe, the Mediterranean, the West Indies, Canada, Argentina, on the Pacific Coast, and in the Far East.

She sailed under Panamanian flag until 1973 when she was converted for use as a non-self-propelled tank-cleaning barge for use in Swedish waters. Based off Gothenburg, she served in this capacity until she suffered a hull fracture in 1976. Leaking oil, she was condemned and was subsequently scrapped.

ESSO CRISTOBAL
1949

ESSO CRISTOBAL
Hull No: 477
Owner: Esso Shipping Co.
Launched: April 29, 1949
Delivered: July 15, 1949
Dimensions: 628 x 82.5 x 42.5 ft
Gross Tonnage: 17,062
Displacement: 34,145 tons
Machinery: Geared Turbines, 2 Boilers
Horsepower/Speed: 12,500/16 knots
Fate: Scrapped, 1972

Happily for the shipyard, new tanker orders came almost monthly in 1948, and on February 20 a contract was signed with Esso for two more 26,000 DWT tankers. The third in the series was ESSO CRISTOBAL, the keel for which was laid on Shipway 8 on November 15, 1948. Due to efficiencies gained by building several identical ships simultaneously and to the use of rigid assembly and outfitting schedules, ESSO CRISTOBAL was on the stocks less than six months. She was christened by Mrs. John R. Suman, wife of another Standard Oil Co. of NJ director, on a

sunny April 29, 1949, and slipped gracefully into the James River.

By now, construction of these ships was becoming routine and the shipyard was full of tanker subassemblies. In one area of the yard the ships' smokestacks were finished and painted and several of them together with their huge Esso ovals presented a striking appearance. By the time of ESSO CRISTOBAL's delivery on July 15, 1949, the Esso newbuilding program had grown to ten ships and a contract had been signed with a Greek owner for an 11th.

ESSO CRISTOBAL entered service with the Panama Transport Co. fleet under Panamanian flag and remained with them for over 12 years, making voyages in both the Atlantic and the Pacific Oceans, and ranging as far away as the Far East. She suffered several mishaps—a grounding in October 1950 and a collision in 1952—but she was not seriously damaged.

In the early 1960s most of her voyages were in Argentine waters, and in 1962 she transferred to Standard Oil Co. of NJ's Argentinian affiliate Petromar, S.A. and was renamed PETROMAR ROSARIO. She stayed with Petromar in routine service for almost ten years, then in 1971 was sold to the Royal Trading & *(Continued on page 135)*

ESSO STOCKHOLM
1949

ESSO STOCKHOLM

Hull No: 478
Owner: Esso Shipping Co.
Launched: July 1, 1949
Delivered: August 26, 1949
Dimensions: 628 x 82.5 x 42.5 ft
Gross Tonnage: 17,062
Displacement: 34,145 tons
Machinery: Geared Turbines, 2 Boilers
Horsepower/Speed: 12,500/16 knots
Fate: Scrapped, 1978

Fourth of the Esso "supertankers" built at Newport News was ESSO STOCKHOLM, the keel for which was laid on Shipway 9 on January 19, 1949. Hull 478 was structurally complete and ready for launching on the following July 1, and her sponsor was Mrs. Emile E. Soubry, wife of an Esso director. Although the launching ceremony was delayed for awhile, the ship was dramatically christened by Mrs. Soubry, whose skirts flew high into the air.

After launching, ESSO STOCKHOLM was moved to the south end of the shipyard and by August 26 she had been outfitted, tested, and tried; then she was delivered to the Panama Transport Co. fleet. The new ship was destined for a long and varied career and spent over two decades in service with the Esso fleet, carrying countless cargoes of both crude oil and products. In her early years, she apparently made voyages to the Far East, but most of her career was spent in the Western Hemisphere.

In 1960 her name was changed to ESSO COLON; then, in 1970 she was sold to the Alliance Navigation Co. of Panama and was renamed ALLIANCE SUCCESS. After two years with Alliance, she was sold to Gallantry Navigation Co., also of Panama, and was renamed HONG KONG GALLANTRY. In 1974 she was again sold, this time to Northeast Petroleum Industries, and she remained under Panamanian registry. She sailed under the name TASMAN VOYAGER for four years with this owner before being broken up in 1978.

ESSO GENOVA
1949

ESSO GENOVA

Hull No: 480
Owner: Esso Shipping Co.
Launched: September 8, 1949
Delivered: November 11, 1949
Dimensions: 628 x 82.5 x 42.5 ft
Gross Tonnage: 17,062
Displacement: 34,145 tons
Machinery: Geared Turbines, 2 Boilers
Horsepower/Speed: 12,500/16 knots
Fate: Scrapped, 1976

Just a week before the keel was laid for ESSO SUEZ, the shipyard received an order for six additional 26,000 ton tankers from the Standard Oil Co. of NJ, bringing the total to ten ordered for the Esso fleet. These ships were in great demand as they had 70 percent more capacity than the standard T-2 type and had only about a foot more draft; and also offered a 20 percent reduction in transportation costs over the T-2s.

The first ship of this group of six ordered on June 29, 1948, was ESSO GENOVA, the keel for which was laid on Shipway 8 on May 3, 1949, only four days after ESSO CRISTOBAL had been launched from it. ESSO GENOVA was the first of the 26,000 DWT tankers whose steam turbines were manufactured by the shipyard; the machinery for the previous ships had been ordered from General Electric. All of these ships subsequent to ESSO GENOVA also had Newport News machinery, the dependability and efficiency of which enhanced the reputation of the shipyard over the years.

ESSO GENOVA was launched on September 8, 1949, by Mrs. B.B. Howard, wife of a director and former Marine Department head of the owners. Unlike several of her sisters, which were launched late, ESSO GENOVA was launched two minutes ahead of schedule, but those on the sponsor's stand were given ample warning.

Hull 480 was completed and delivered to her owners on November 11, 1949, a scant six months after her keel had been laid. Like many of the other ships, she was assigned to the Panama Transport Co. and flew the Panamanian flag. She served the Esso fleet faithfully and, after voyages to the Far East early in her career, she traded mostly between the U.S., Canada, and the West Indies with an occasional South American trip. Her name was changed to ESSO BOGOTA in 1963, and she sailed for Standard Oil Co. of NJ affiliates until she was scrapped in 1976.

ESSO LIMA
1949

ESSO LIMA

Hull No: 481
Owner: Esso Shipping Co.
Launched: October 12, 1949
Delivered: December 21, 1949
Dimensions: 628 x 82.5 x 42.5 ft
Gross Tonnage: 17,062
Displacement: 34,145 tons
Machinery: Geared Turbines, 2 Boilers
Horsepower/Speed: 12,500/16 knots
Fate: Scrapped, 1984

The sixth of the Esso "supertankers" built at Newport News was ESSO LIMA which was given Hull No. 481. Her keel was laid in Building Dock 11 on May 16, 1949. This dock was used for the construction of ESSO MONTEVIDEO which had been launched on February 25, then was the site of the ill-fated construction of the aircraft carrier UNITED STATES (CVA-58) whose contract was cancelled on April 23.

Built in place of the carrier, the hull of ESSO LIMA was completed quickly, and the new tanker was launched on October 12 by Mrs. M.G. Gamble, wife of the marine director of the Standard Oil Co. of NJ.

Like ESSO GENOVA, ESSO LIMA had a very short construction time and was ready for trials on December 13, 1949. The trials of ESSO LIMA were well documented in the press because special tests were held to establish the efficiency of the Newport News-built turbines. During the last hour of her four-hour endurance trial, ESSO LIMA's fuel consumption measured .498 pounds per shaft horsepower per hour indicating a very high efficiency for the yard-built machinery.

ESSO LIMA completed trials then was delivered to the Esso Shipping Co. and placed in domestic service under the American flag on December 21. Her trade routes were between the East and Gulf Coasts and the West Indies, and she served first the Esso Shipping Co. and later the Humble Oil & Refining Co.

She was involved in collision with a barge at Baltimore in July 1952 but was not damaged, and her career was generally routine. In 1972 she left Esso service and was sold to the Sabine Towing & Transportation Co. Renamed SABINE, she remained in service into the 1980s on her familiar domestic routes, but in 1984 was finally withdrawn from service and scrapped in Taiwan.

ESSO BERMUDA
1950

ESSO BERMUDA

Hull No: 482
Owner: Esso Shipping Co.
Launched: November 22, 1949
Delivered: January 27, 1950
Dimensions: 628 x 82.5 x 42.5 ft
Gross Tonnage: 17,062
Displacement: 34,145 tons
Machinery: Geared Turbines, 2 Boilers
Horsepower/Speed: 12,500/16 knots
Fate: Scrapped, 1976

ESSO BERMUDA was the seventh 26,000 DWT tanker for Esso, and she had one of the shortest building times of the 19 of her class which were built at the shipyard. Her keel was set down on Shipway 9 on July 6, 1949, and she was launched less than five months later on November 22. Mrs. A.T. Proudfit, wife of the president of the Creole Petroleum Co., was the sponsor for ESSO BERMUDA. The weather for all of the Esso launchings had been good, but this launch day the temperature was 35F and a 20-knot north wind was blowing. There was some apprehension over launching this ship in such a wind, but the task was completed without incident.

Hull 482 was moved south to her outfitting pier by the tugs with some difficulty, and the rest of her construction and trials were routine. ESSO BERMUDA was delivered to the Esso Shipping Co. and placed in domestic trade under American registry on January 27, 1950.

All of her service life was spent with the Esso fleet, and she stayed mostly in coastal trade except for some Pacific and Far East trips in the 1960s. In 1960 she passed to Humble and was renamed ESSO DALLAS, which was more appropriate for her domestic assignment, but in 1972 she went to Esso Transport Co. and flew the Panamanian flag. After over 25 years of dependable service to the Esso fleet, the former ESSO BERMUDA was scrapped in 1976.

ESSO HAVANA
1950

ESSO HAVANA

Hull No: 483
Owner: Esso Shipping Co.
Launched: December 16, 1949
Delivered: March 3, 1950
Dimensions: 628 x 82.5 x 42.5 ft
Gross Tonnage: 17,062
Displacement: 34,145 tons
Machinery: Geared Turbines, 2 Boilers
Horsepower/Speed: 12,500/16 knots
Fate: In Service

The eighth 26,000 DWT tanker constructed for the Esso Shipping Co. was ESSO HAVANA, which had been ordered with five others on June 29, 1948. The keel for Hull 483 was laid in Building Dock 10 on August 9, 1949, just four days after it had been vacated by ATLANTIC EMPEROR. By December 16, ESSO HAVANA was ready to be floated out the dock herself.

She was christened on that date by Mrs. Hines H.

Baker of Houston, wife of the president of Humble Oil & Refining Co. Mrs. Baker was provided with a bottle which seemed equally as hard as the hull of the tanker, for she was obliged to hurl it at the bow three times before it broke, and the ship was well under way when it did. Mr. Baker was present at this launching as was Eugene Holman, president of the Standard Oil Co. of NJ. ESSO HAVANA completed by-now routine outfitting and trials and was delivered on March 3, 1950.

Her first ten years of service with the Esso Shipping Co. saw her trading mostly along the East and Gulf coasts and in the West Indies. She transferred to Humble in 1960, and her name was changed to ESSO MIAMI in 1961 after the Cuban Missile Crisis.

During the 1960s she saw some Pacific and Far East service, but she mainly sailed on her old routes. In 1973 she briefly carried her owners' new corporate name as EXXON MIAMI but later in that year was sold to Sabine Towing and Transporation Co. and was renamed PECOS. With her home port as Baltimore, she continued to serve Sabine into the mid-1980s.

ESSO NEW YORK
1950

ESSO NEW YORK

Hull No: 484
Owner: Esso Shipping Co.
Launched: February 9, 1950
Delivered: April 14, 1950
Dimensions: 628 x 82.5 x 42.5 ft
Gross Tonnage: 17,062
Displacement: 34,145 tons
Machinery: Geared Turbines, 2 Boilers
Horsepower/Speed: 12,500/16 knots
Fate: Drillship, 1975

ESSO NEW YORK was the ninth of ten 26,000 DWT tankers built at Newport News for Esso and delivered in 1949 and 1950. The keel for this ship was laid on Shipway 8 on September 14, 1949, just six days after the launch of ESSO GENOVA from it. ESSO NEW YORK was launched on February 9, 1950, by Mrs. John W. Brice, wife of a director of the Standard Oil Co. of NJ. The new ship slid gracefully into the James River under drizzly skies at 11:45 A.M., and the launching was witnessed by a number of out-of-town guests.

ESSO NEW YORK was essentially completed on April 11, 1950, and underwent sea trials on that date.

As with the preceding nine ships of this type, performance of her turbines and auxiliary machinery on trials was outstanding. In particular, performance of the ship's Newport News steam turbines was attributed to improvements in design resulting from the shipyard's steam turbine research program begun in 1937.

After trials ESSO NEW YORK was delivered to the Esso Shipping Co. on April 14, 1950, and entered domestic service. Serving mostly between the East and Gulf Coasts, she was transferred to the Humble Oil & Refining Co. in 1960 and served them until 1974. She saw some Pacific and West Coast service late in her Esso career but in 1974 was sold to Fluor Drilling Services for conversion to an oil drillship. This conversion was done in 1975 by Taiwan Shipbuilding Corp. and involved removal of her stern and addition of diesel-electric propulsion machinery, a heliport, drilling equipment, and quarters for 115 crew on her former cargo section.

Renamed WODECO VIII and later WESTERN OFFSHORE NO. VIII, the now-13,858 GRT ship remained in service in Chinese waters into the mid-1980s, capable of drilling up to 25,000 ft. deep in waters up to 600 ft. in depth. In 1985 she was sold to a Danish owner and renamed DAN DUCHESS, remaining active past her 35th birthday.

ESSO SANTOS
1950

ESSO SANTOS

Hull No: 485
Owner: Esso Shipping Co.
Launched: March 21, 1950
Delivered: May 19, 1950
Dimensions: 628 x 82.5 x 42.5 ft
Gross Tonnage: 17,062
Displacement: 35,145 tons
Machinery: Geared Turbines, 2 Boilers
Horsepower/Speed: 12,500/16 knots
Fate: Scrapped, 1972

Last of the ten-ship fleet of Esso tankers delivered at Newport News in 1949 and 1950, the keel for ESSO SANTOS was laid in Building Dock 11 on October 17, 1949. Hull 475 could not be pulled up into the forward end of the dock for christening as had the other ships built there, since that end was occupied by the construction of caissons for the York River Bridge. The ceremony was instead held on barges moored at the bow of the ship, and ESSO SANTOS was christened by Mrs. William J. Haley, wife of an Esso official, on March 21, 1950. Mrs. Haley was the first left-hander to sponsor a Newport News ship in many years and, as the many photographers present had taken the usual places to her right, there was a frantic rush to positions on her left as she grasped the bottle in her left hand.

After successful launch, outfitting, and trials, the new ESSO SANTOS was delivered to the Panama Transport Co. on May 19. She steamed for Esso under the Panamanian flag in worldwide service for the next 22 years. In November 1956 she collided with another ship in New York harbor but was not seriously damaged. In 1961 her owner became the Esso Transport and Shipping Co., and later it became the Esso Transport Co.

Her itinerary was quite varied late in her career, and in 1965 she made voyages in U.S., West Indies, European, Baltic, Canadian, Argentine, South African, and Far East waters. With deliveries of new "handy-size" diesel tankers to Esso in the early 1970s, ESSO SANTOS became surplus, and she was sold for scrap and broken up in Taiwan in 1972.

ESSO NEWARK
1952

ESSO NEWARK

Hull No: 499
Owner: Esso Shipping Co.
Launched: April 18, 1952
Delivered: August 19, 1952
Dimensions: 628 x 82.5 x 42.5 ft
Gross Tonnage: 17,062
Displacement: 34,640
Machinery: Geared Turbines, 2 Boilers
Horsepower/Speed: 12,500/16 knots
Fate: Scrapped, 1984

Just one year after trials and delivery of ESSO SANTOS, the last of ten 26,000 DWT tankers delivered to Esso between 1949 and 1950, the Esso Shipping Co. placed orders for six more identical ships on May 8, 1951.

The first of these additional six was ESSO NEWARK, whose keel was laid in Shipway 10 on November 29, 1951. This dock had been the scene five months earlier of the launch of the liner UNITED STATES on June 23. Construction of tankers of this class was, by then, routine and ESSO NEWARK was ready for christening on April 18, 1952. Sponsor for Hull 499 was Mrs. David A. Shepherd, wife of a director of the Standard Oil Co. of NJ, who christened the ship after three swings of the champagne bottle.

Following uneventful trials on August 14, ESSO NEWARK was delivered to the Esso Shipping Co. on August 19, 1952. Following a parallel career with several of her Newport News-built sisters, she served Esso on the East and Gulf Coasts and transferred to the Humble Oil and Refining Co. in 1960.

In 1973 her owner became the Exxon Shipping Co. and her name was changed to EXXON NEWARK. In October 1982 she underwent her seventh ABS special survey and became the first ship in her owner's fleet to do so. She remained in service into 1984 as the oldest ship in the Exxon fleet, then was sold to Taiwanese breakers and scrapped in 1984.

ESSO CHESTER
1952

ESSO CHESTER
Hull No: 500
Owner: Esso Shipping Co.
Launched: August 8, 1952
Delivered: October 10, 1952
Dimensions: 628 x 82.5 x 42.5 ft
Gross Tonnage: 17,062
Displacement: 34,640 tons
Machinery: Geared Turbines, 2 Boilers
Horsepower/Speed: 12,500/16 knots
Fate: Scrapped, 1984

Newport News Shipbuilding's 500th hull was ESSO CHESTER, which was the 12th ship in Esso's 1948-1954 newbuilding program at the shipyard. The keel for Hull 500 was laid on Shipway 9 on December 31, 1951. Due to intense activity in the shipyard, including delivery of superliner UNITED STATES and cargo ships of the Mariner class, ESSO CHESTER was not launched until August 8, 1952. Sponsor for ESSO CHESTER was Mrs. Stanley C. Hope, wife of the president of the Esso Standard Oil Co. As was the case for several others of the Esso launchings at the shipyard, the sponsor's plane arrived late, requiring a 15 minute postponement of the ceremony.

Notwithstanding ESSO CHESTER's relatively long building period on the ways, the ship completed outfitting and trials in a more timely manner and was delivered to the Esso fleet on October 10, 1952. She was placed in domestic service with the Esso Shipping Co. between the East Coast and Gulf Coast with frequent calls in the West Indies and remained there for all of her Esso career. She was operated by Humble in the 1960s, and in 1973 her name was changed to EXXON CHESTER.

In June 1979 she collided with and sank the freighter REGAL SWORD in fog off Cape Cod. She sustained serious damage and required extensive repairs, but no lives were lost in the incident.

In 1980 she was converted to carry asphalt as well as products, and she was fitted with a bow thruster. She remained in service through 1983 as the second oldest tanker in Exxon's domestic fleet, then was sold with EXXON HUNTINGTON to Spanish breakers in 1984.

ESSO BANGOR
1953

ESSO BANGOR
Hull No: 501
Owner: Esso Shipping Co.
Launched: November 25, 1952
Delivered: January 16, 1953
Dimensions: 628 x 82.5 x 42.5 ft
Gross Tonnage: 17,062
Displacement: 34,640 tons
Machinery: Geared Turbines, 2 Boilers
Horsepower/Speed: 12,500/16 knots
Fate: Scrapped, 1984

ESSO BANGOR was another of the Newport News-built 26,000 DWT tankers to remain in service with her original owners into the 1980s. The keel for Hull 501 was laid on Shipway 8 on June 16, 1952, just four days prior to delivery of UNITED STATES. Construction of ESSO BANGOR proceeded more rapidly than her predecessor, and she was launched on November 25, 1952. Mrs. Eger V. Murphree, wife of the president of the Standard Oil Development Co., was sponsor for ESSO BANGOR and she performed her task flawlessly. The shipyard's Board of Directors, which had held a meeting at the yard that morning, was present at the ceremony.

Following completion of outfitting work, trials of ESSO BANGOR were held on January 14, 1953, and the new ship was delivered just two days later. ESSO BANGOR served in the U.S. Esso fleet throughout her career along the Gulf and East Coasts and in the West Indies. With her fleet mates she took the Exxon name in 1973 and became EXXON BANGOR.

Her career was a routine one. She never suffered major damage and was not converted, but provided over 30 years of dependable service to her owner. She was sold in early 1984, was briefly named BANGOR, then was towed to Japan and scrapped.

ESSO GLOUCESTER
1953

ESSO GLOUCESTER

Hull No: 502
Owner: Esso Shipping Co.
Launched: March 17, 1953
Delivered: May 1, 1953
Dimensions: 628 x 82.5 x 42.5 ft
Gross Tonnage: 17,064
Displacement: 34,640 tons
Machinery: Geared Turbines, 2 Boilers
Horsepower/Speed: 12,500/16 knots
Fate: Scrapped, 1977

ESSO GLOUCESTER enjoyed a somewhat more varied career than most of her Newport News sisters but met an earlier fate. ESSO GLOUCESTER's keel was laid on Shipway 9 on October 15, 1952, and she was launched by Mrs. James C. Anderson, wife of the comptroller of the Standard Oil Co. of NJ, on March 17, 1953. A smaller party of Esso guests than usual was in attendance, and Hull 502 was launched at noon without ceremony. A colorful watercolor painting of ESSO GLOUCESTER and tugs escorting her to the outfitting berth was done by local artist T.C. Skinner, and flags in the painting were at half mast due to the death of shipyard chairman Homer L. Ferguson on March 14.

ESSO GLOUCESTER underwent routine trials on April 29 and was delivered on May 1, 1953. The new ship served the Esso Shipping Co., then Humble, on domestic routes until the early 1970s.

In 1970 her name was changed to ENCO GLOUCESTER; then, in 1971 she was transferred to Esso's Liberian-flag affiliate Esso Tankers Inc. and was again named ESSO GLOUCESTER. She remained in international service with Esso Tankers until 1977 when she was removed from service and sold for scrap.

ESSO HUNTINGTON
1953

ESSO HUNTINGTON

Hull No: 503
Owner: Esso Shipping Co.
Launched: August 18, 1953
Delivered: October 9, 1953
Dimensions: 628 x 82.5 x 42.5 ft
Gross Tonnage: 17,064
Displacement: 34,640 tons
Machinery: Geared Turbines, 2 Boilers
Horsepower/Speed: 12,500/16 knots
Fate: Scrapped, 1984

ESSO HUNTINGTON was the fifth 26,000 DWT tanker contracted for in May 1951. Hull 503 and her namesake West Virginia city owed their name to the shipyard and C & O founder Collis P. Huntington. The keel for ESSO HUNTINGTON was laid on Shipway 8 on March 2, 1953, and she was launched on the following August 18. Sponsor for ESSO HUNTINGTON was Mrs. Leo D. Welch, wife of the treasurer and a director of the Standard Oil Co. of NJ, and as usual, tug HUNTINGTON caught the ship after its slide.

Trials and delivery for the ship occurred on October 6 and October 9 respectively, and Esso's newest tanker entered domestic service with the Esso Shipping Co. She worked with Esso Shipping, Humble, and later Exxon Shipping Co. on the East and Gulf Coasts and in the West Indies into the 1980s.

In 1973 her name became EXXON HUNTINGTON, and in 1980 she underwent conversion for service as a chemical carrier as well as a tanker. Her cargo tanks were increased in number from 30 to 46 during this conversion, and her gross tonnage increased to 17,548. As with all of her sister ships, changing load line regulations over the years had increased her original 26,800 DWT to almost 29,000 DWT.

EXXON HUNTINGTON remained in service with her original owner into 1984. Late in that year she was sold with EXXON CHESTER and was scrapped in Spain.

ESSO FLORENCE
1954

ESSO FLORENCE

Hull No: 504
Owner: Esso Shipping Co.
Launched: November 20, 1953
Delivered: January 15, 1954
Dimensions: 628 x 82.5 x 42.5 ft
Gross Tonnage: 17,064
Displacement: 34,640 tons
Machinery: Geared Turbines, 2 Boilers
Horsepower/Speed: 12,500/16 knots
Fate: Laid Up, 1982

ESSO FLORENCE was the last of sixteen 26,000 DWT Esso tankers delivered at Newport News between 1949 and 1954, and she had one of the best keel-to-delivery times for a ship of her size in the shipyard's history. The keel for this ship was laid on Shipway 9 on June 27, 1953, and she was sponsored by Mrs. Peter T. Lamont, wife of a Standard Oil Co. of NJ official, on November 20. ESSO FLORENCE was in an advanced stage of outfitting at launch, and after completing trials she was delivered on Janaury 15, 1954.

The new ship served the Esso Shipping Co. fleet on the familiar Gulf and East Coast and West Indies routes for most of her career. She saw some Pacific Coast service with Humble in the late 1960s, and her name was changed to EXXON FLORENCE in 1973.

During the severe winter of 1977, she moved much-needed fuels from Exxon's Bayway, NJ, refinery to terminals on Long Island and up to Bucksport, ME, a job usually accomplished by tugs and barges. In May 1982 EXXON FLORENCE made her last voyage with Exxon, from Baytown, TX, to Los Angeles, then was turned over to the Maritime Administration and laid up at their fleet in Suisun Bay, CA. She was replaced by a new specialty ship, and her operators sentimentally noted her loss saying, "she was a good ship, and she performed her duties admirably." Renamed FLORENCE, she remained at Suisun Bay into the mid-1980s.

ESSO CRISTOBAL Continued from page 128

Transport Co. and took the name YORK under Panamanian flag. After a few more voyages with this owner, the former ESSO CRISTOBAL was broken up for scrap in Taiwan in 1972.

CALIFORNIA
1954

CALIFORNIA

Hull No: 498
Owner: Texas Co.
Launched: December 18, 1953
Delivered: February 5, 1954
Dimensions: 565 x 75 x 40.5 ft
Gross Tonnage: 12,790
Displacement: 24,840 tons
Machinery: Geared Turbines, 2 Boilers
Horsepower/Speed: 13,650/18 knots
Fate: In Service

Last of the four fast tankers ordered by Texaco in 1951 was CALIFORNIA, whose keel was laid on Shipway 7 on July 27, 1953. Hull 498 was christened by Mrs. Josephine Welch Wood, wife of a vice-president of the Texas Co., on December 18, 1953, and was smoothly launched under sunny skies.

On sea trials conducted on February 2, CALIFORNIA's machinery gave the same smooth performance and good steam rate which had been experienced with the first three ships. The compact high speed-high performance Newport News turbines for these ships were similar to those fitted to the Esso ships and provided 13,650 normal and 15,000 maximum SHP with steam at 570 psig and 840F.

CALIFORNIA was delivered to the Texas Co. on February 5, 1954, and took up domestic service on the East, Gulf, and later Pacific Coasts. In 1960 she too had the Texaco name added to hers and became TEXACO CALIFORNIA. She was also enlarged and modernized in 1973 and her carrying capacity was increased to 42,742 DWT. She stayed with Texaco and sailed with three of her Newport News sisters as the largest of their fleet into the mid-1980s.

ATLANTIC EMPEROR
1949

ATLANTIC EMPEROR

Hull No: 479
Owner: Atlantic Maritime Co.
Launched: August 5, 1949
Delivered: October 1, 1949
Dimensions: 628 x 82.5 x 42.5 ft
Gross Tonnage: 17,094
Displacement: 34,145 tons
Machinery: Geared Turbines, 2 Boilers
Horsepower/Speed: 12,500/16 knots
Fate: Scrapped, 1972

Three tankers of the ESSO SUEZ class were built for non-Esso owners and the first of these was ATLANTIC EMPEROR, built for Atlantic Maritime Company, a Livanos Group firm. The keel for this ship was laid in Building Dock 10 on February 21, 1949, and she was floated out on the following August 5. Sponsor for ATLANTIC EMPEROR was the diminutive Mrs.

Aristo Onassis, who successfully christened the tanker on the second swing.

This ship had a different color scheme from her Esso sisters and was fitted with a streamlined stack which, like her bow, was decorated with the letter "L" surrounded by the Greek geometrical design known as the "Ring of Life." On the day of her delivery a Greek Orthodox service was held on her deck, and she left the shipyard on October 1, 1949, under charter to Gulf Oil.

ATLANTIC EMPEROR operated with Livanos interests in both hemispheres under Liberian registry for her entire career. She had the misfortune to run aground at New York in October 1950, then again in the Suez Canal in 1953, but was repaired successfully. In December 1954 she suffered heavy weather damage and had her decks set down, but she was repaired at Palermo the following April.

Unlike most of her sisters, ATLANTIC EMPEROR remained with her original owner and kept her original name throughout her life. After 23 years of hard service, she was scrapped in Taiwan in 1972.

NORTH DAKOTA
1953

NORTH DAKOTA

Hull No: 495
Owner: Texas Co.
Launched: December 18, 1952
Delivered: March 6, 1953
Dimensions: 565 x 75 x 40.5 ft
Gross Tonnage: 12,790
Displacement: 24,840 tons
Machinery: Geared Turbines, 2 Boilers
Horsepower/Speed: 13,650/18 knots
Fate: Scrapped, 1984

On June 19, 1951, the shipyard was awarded a contract for the construction of four tankers for the Texas Co., the first ships built for that company since the ill-fated ILLINOIS delivered in 1913. These and a fifth ship ordered later were of Newport News design and, at 18,000 DWT, were smaller than the Esso tankers recently delivered but were high powered for their size and had a speed of 18.5 knots.

NORTH DAKOTA was the first of the Texaco ships and her keel was laid on Shipway 5 on June 30, 1952. The new ship was ready for launching on December 18 and was christened by Mrs. Elizabeth Walsh Long, wife of the executive vice-president of the Texas Co. A large contingent of Texas Co. guests attended the launching, and the ceremony was made colorful by the bright orange construction paint on NORTH DAKOTA's hull and a large Texaco symbol on her stem.

The new ship was outfitted and completed trials on March 2-3, 1953, and was delivered to Texaco on March 6. During her career with her original owner, NORTH DAKOTA was in domestic service on all three coasts. In 1954 she ran aground at New York and underwent hull repairs, which included replacement of her bilge keels. In 1960 she and her fleetmates adopted the name "Texaco", and she became TEXACO NORTH DAKOTA.

In October 1973 an onboard explosion in the Gulf of Mexico killed three of her crew and injured two others. In 1980 she collided with a platform under construction in the Gulf of Mexico and suffered heavy structural damage. In 1981 she was sold to Sabine Towing and Transportation Co., and her name was changed to BLANCO. Repairs to her were found to be uneconomical, and she was sold for scrap in 1984.

NEW YORK
1953

NEW YORK

Hull No: 496
Owner: Texas Co.
Launched: June 2, 1953
Delivered: July 31, 1953
Dimensions: 565 x 75 x 40.5 ft
Gross Tonnage: 12,740
Displacement: 24,840 tons
Machinery: Geared Turbines, 2 Boilers
Horsepower/Speed: 13,650/18 knots
Fate: In Service

Second of the Texaco tankers ordered in 1951 was NEW YORK whose keel was laid on Shipway 5 on December 22, 1952, just four days after the launch of NORTH DAKOTA. This ship and her four sisters were considered relatively small and were referred to as "floating service stations," designed to carry mixed cargoes of refined products in a total of 27 tanks.

NEW YORK was launched on a sunny June 2, 1953, by Mrs. Madeline G. Baker of New York City,

wife of another executive vice president of the Texas Co. The ceremony was a colorful one, and a large number of guests and spectators attended.

NEW YORK was completed and underwent trials on July 28. Sea trials for NORTH DAKOTA had been rough, but they were ideal for those of NEW YORK, and she obtained a maximum speed of over 20 knots, making her the fastest tanker built at Newport News.

The second Texaco ship was delivered on July 31, 1953, and went into domestic service. She served on all three coasts and in 1960, she also added to her name and became TEXACO NEW YORK.

In 1972 her forward cargo section was removed and scrapped, and her stern was mated to a new bow built at Maryland Shipbuilding and Dry Dock Co. The enlarged TEXACO NEW YORK had all of her accommodations aft and gained a new taller stack. Her post-conversion appearance was quite modern, and she gained 157 feet in length, 15 in beam and eight in depth. Her gross tonnage increased to 23,461 and her carrying capacity to 42,667 DWT, making her the largest ship in Texaco's domestic fleet. She continued in service with her original owner into the mid-1980s.

CONNECTICUT
1953

CONNECTICUT

Hull No: 497
Owner: Texas Co.
Launched: September 11, 1953
Delivered: November 6, 1953
Dimensions: 565 x 75 x 40.5 ft
Gross Tonnage: 12,790
Displacement: 24,840 tons
Machinery: Geared Turbines, 2 Boilers
Horsepower/Speed: 13,650/18 knots
Fate: In Service

The third high-speed 565-foot tanker delivered to the Texas Co. in 1953 was CONNECTICUT, which was given Hull No. 497. The keel for this ship was laid on Shipway 5 on March 25, 1953, just a week after the launch of ESSO GLOUCESTER from it. CONNECTI-CUT was structurally complete and in bright orange primer when launched on September 11, 1953. Mrs. Olive Kay Dorwin, wife of the vice president and

general counsel for the Texas Co., was sponsor for CONNECTICUT. After launching, the new vessel was first taken to Pier 2 for installation of her reduction gear, then was moved to Pier 10 for outfitting.

Hull 497 completed trials, then was delivered to the Texaco fleet on November 6, 1953. Like the other ships of her class, CONNECTICUT had accommodations for a crew of 47 and for two passengers. She could carry 12 grades of cargo and was able to discharge all her tanks in less than 14 hours with onboard pumps. She had a modern streamlined appearance with raked and curved superstructures and had a curved stem and cruiser stern. After delivery, CONNECTICUT took up domestic service between the Gulf and East Coasts and later also saw service on the West Coast.

In 1959 she became known as TEXACO CON-NECTICUT; then, in 1971 she was "jumboized" with a longer, wider, and deeper forebody, and her capacity, like that of three of her sisters, was increased to 42,721 DWT. With a greatly altered and modernized appearance, she continued to serve Texaco into the mid-1980s.

FLORIDA
1956

FLORIDA

Hull No: 515
Owner: Texas Co.
Launched: April 26, 1956
Delivered: July 14, 1956
Dimensions: 565 x 75 x 40.5 ft
Gross Tonnage: 12,803
Displacement: 24,839 tons
Machinery: Geared Turbines, 2 Boilers
Horsepower/Speed: 13,650/18 knots
Fate: In Service

On March 29, 1955, the shipyard received an order from the Texas Co. to build a fifth high-speed tanker of the NORTH DAKOTA class. This was the first tanker contract in almost three years and marked the beginning of a boom in construction of this type of ship which lasted five years and produced 15 ships.

The keel for the fifth Texaco ship was laid on Shipway 7 on November 22, 1955 and before launching, it was given the name FLORIDA. Hull 515 was christened by Mrs. Rhoda Allen Worden, wife of a Texas Co. vice president, on April 26, 1956. The sleek ship slid into the James River at 11:30 A.M. on that date, decorated with a large Texaco star on her bow. FLORIDA was outfitted and tested in less than three months and was delivered to Texaco on July 14, 1956.

During her early career the ship was active on both the East, Gulf, and Pacific Coasts. In 1960 her name was changed to TEXACO FLORIDA, then in 1971 her forebody was replaced by one 538 feet in length, increasing her length to 723 feet and her capacity to 41,400 DWT. She was provided with a bulbous bow, and her cargo tanks consisted of six center tanks and 12 wing tanks, all 90 feet long. After the conversion, TEXACO FLORIDA went back onto her old familiar trade routes and served Texaco reliably into the mid-1980s.

FLYING A NEW YORK
1954

FLYING A NEW YORK

Hull No: 508
Owner: Tide Water Associated Oil
Launched: February 3, 1954
Delivered: March 26, 1954
Dimensions: 628 x 82.5 x 42.5 ft
Gross Tonnage: 17,055
Displacement: 35,035 tons
Machinery: Geared Turbines, 2 Boilers
Horsepower/Speed: 12,500/16 knots
Fate: In Service

On June 9, 1952, the shipyard signed a contract for the construction of two tankers for the Tide Water Associated Oil Co., Eastern Division. These ships were essentially identical to the ESSO SUEZ class but had a slightly greater draft and displaced slightly over 35,000 long tons.

The first of the Tide Water ships was named FLYING A NEW YORK, and her keel was laid on Shipway 8 on August 31, 1953. Hull 508 was christened by Mrs. David R. Grace, wife of the president of the

Broad Tankers Corp., on February 3, 1954. Launchings were frequent occurrences at Newport News at this time, and this one was held on a Wednesday and attracted only a small crowd. The somewhat drab appearance of the ship at launch was brightened by the huge "Flying A" symbol on her stack.

The new tanker was outfitted and underwent successful trials on March 23, then was delivered on March 26. FLYING A NEW YORK was assigned to Tide Water's service between the Gulf of Mexico and the Atlantic Coast, with her home port at Wilmington, DL. In 1956 she was assigned to the Broad Tankers Corp., a Tide Water affiliate.

In 1967 her ownership was changed to the Tidewater Oil Co.; then, the following year her owner became known as the Getty Oil Co. and she was renamed NEW YORK GETTY. She saw some Pacific Coast service early in her career but mostly stayed in service between the Gulf and East Coasts and in the West Indies. She served Getty until 1982, at which time she was sold to Crest Tankers, Inc. and was renamed BEAUJOLAIS. She continued to serve this owner into the mid-1980s.

FLYING A DELAWARE
1954

FLYING A DELAWARE

Hull No: 509
Owner: Tide Water Associated Oil
Launched: May 19, 1954
Delivered: July 2, 1954
Dimensions: 628 x 82.5 x 42.5 ft
Gross Tonnage: 17,055
Displacement: 35,035 tons
Machinery: Geared Turbines, 2 Boilers
Horsepower/Speed: 12,500/16 knots
Fate: Scrapped, 1984

FLYING A DELAWARE was the second ship ordered by Tide Water Associated Oil Co. in 1952, and she was the last of 19 of the highly successful 26,000 DWT "supertankers" built at Newport News. The keel for FLYING A DELAWARE was laid on Shipway 7 on December 21, 1954. Unlike that of her sister ship, the launching for FLYING A DELAWARE was a gala occasion with many out-of-town guests in attendance. Hull 509 was christened by Mrs. D.T. Staples, wife of the president of the Tide Water Associated Oil Co., on May 19, 1954. In addition to the stack insignia, the ship had a huge "Flying A" symbol painted on her bow.

After trials on June 29 in the Atlantic Ocean, FLYING A DELAWARE was delivered to Tide Water on July 2, 1954, and went into coastal service with the Eastern Tank Ship Co. Her service was routine until November 1966 when, loaded with a cargo from Brownsville, TX, she ran aground five miles south of Cape Henlopen, DL. Fortunately, she was refloated without major damage or loss of cargo.

In 1968 her ownership changed to that of the Getty Oil Co. and she was renamed DELAWARE GETTY. She stayed under this name until 1982 when she was sold to Crest Tankers, Inc. with her sister and was renamed POMMARD. Under this name she continued on her old routes and provided dependable service for two more years before being scrapped in 1984.

CRADLE OF LIBERTY
1954

CRADLE OF LIBERTY

Hull No: 512
Owner: Grand Bassa Tankers
Launched: July 23, 1954
Delivered: October 15, 1954
Dimensions: 707 x 93 x 48.5 ft
Gross Tonnage: 22,610
Displacement: 49,636 tons
Machinery: Geared Turbines, 2 Boilers
Horsepower/Speed: 20,000/17.5 knots
Fate: In Service

The third Grand Bassa ship built at Newport News in 1954 had the longest service life of her class and, like her predecessor, was lengthened, widened, and deepened when she was 20 years old. The keel for this ship, named CRADLE OF LIBERTY in honor of the city of Boston, was laid on Shipway 8 on February 8, 1954. Launch day for this ship was July 23, 1954, and the wife of Cities Service Oil Co. president Henry E. Brandli was appointed as sponsor. One of the largest tankers in the world when launched, CRADLE OF LIBERTY was capable of transporting over 14 million gallons of fuel and was fitted with a dehumidifying system to reduce corrosion in her tanks.

After delivery on October 15, 1954, the ship made voyages on the East Coast-Gulf Coast route and also saw service in the Far East. Serving Cities Service under Liberian flag, she traded all over the world. In 1974, like her preceding sister, she gained a new forebody which increased her capacity from 38,900 DWT to 69,312 DWT and added 120 feet to her length.

She continued with Grand Bassa under Panamanian flag until 1981. In January of that year, she ran aground in the East River in New York and was heavily damaged. She was sold to Cove Liberty Corp. of New York and was reconstructed and renamed COVE LIBERTY. After being redelivered in January 1982 and transferred to the American flag, she continued in service with Cove into the mid-1980s.

W. ALTON JONES
1954

W. ALTON JONES

Hull No: 510
Owner: Grand Bassa Tankers
Launched: April 20, 1954
Delivered: June 15, 1954
Dimensions: 707 x 93 x 48.5 ft
Gross Tonnage: 22,596
Displacement: 49,636 tons
Machinery: Geared Turbines, 2 Boilers
Horsepower/Speed: 20,000/17.5 knots
Fate: Drillship, 1976

In November 1952 the shipyard obtained a contract for four 38,900 DWT high speed tankers from Grand Bassa Tankers, a Cities Service Co. affiliate. These ships were later said to be the fastest single-screw tankers yet built, and they were the second largest tankers ever built in the U.S. to that time and among the largest in the world. Their design was the product of collaboration between the owner's naval architects and shipyard designers, and their maximum horsepower of 22,000 was far above the shipyard's previous maximum of 15,000 for tankers.

The first of these ships was W. ALTON JONES, the keel of which was laid down in Shipway 10 on

November 2, 1953. Due to the size of this ship, her christening was a huge affair. W. ALTON JONES was christened by the wife of the ship's namesake and chairman of the Cities Service Co., who was present at the ceremony. The huge ship was in an advanced state of completion when launched on April 20, 1954, and she was delivered to Grand Bassa on June 15 after having averaged 18.85 knots on trials. W. ALTON JONES received a gala welcome in New York City on June 20, then settled into a routine service between the Persian Gulf and the U.S.

After all this fanfare, the tanker had a rather routine service life with Grand Bassa Tankers under Liberian flag. In 1959 her name was given to a new ship and she became known as CITIES SERVICE VALLEY FORGE. She served her original owner for almost 20 years until 1973 when she was sold to Fluor Drilling Services of New Orleans.

She was taken to Japan, where she was converted at Kobe to an oil drilling ship. Her stern was scrapped, but her forebody was joined to a new stern fitted with six diesels driving six generators, which powered four 3,800 SHP propulsion motors on twin shafts. With a greatly altered appearance and the new name WESTERN OFFSHORE NO. IX, she continued to serve Fluor in Venezuelan then East African waters into the mid-1980s.

STATUE OF LIBERTY
1954

STATUE OF LIBERTY

Hull No: 511
Owner: Grand Bassa Tankers
Launched: June 2, 1954
Delivered: August 16, 1954
Dimensions: 707 x 93 x 48.5 ft
Gross Tonnage: 22,610
Displacement: 49,636 tons
Machinery: Geared Turbines, 2 Boilers
Horsepower/Speed: 20,000/17.5 knots
Fate: Scrapped, 1983

The second 38,900 DWT tanker built for Grand Bassa Tankers was STATUE OF LIBERTY, named in honor of Cities Service founder Henry L. Doherty, who aided in raising funds to provide floodlights for the Statue of Liberty. When the keel was laid for Hull 511 on Shipway 9 on December 14, 1953, it was for the largest commercial ship ever built on that facility. Sponsor for STATUE OF LIBERTY was Mrs. Burl S.

Watson, wife of the president of the Cities Service Co., and she christened the new ship on June 2, 1954. A large number of guests attended the ceremony, including W. Alton Jones, chairman of the owning company.

After a short outfitting period and trials, STATUE OF LIBERTY was delivered on August 16, 1954. She was considered a very large ship for her time "capable of carrying enough gasoline to fly a Stratocruiser 301 times around the world."

STATUE OF LIBERTY, like her sisters, flew the Liberian flag for most of her career but was registered in Panama after 1980. Her voyages were truly worldwide and in 1967 she traded to Britain, the Continent, the Mediterranean, Africa, the West Indies, the Far East and Australia.

In 1975 she was lengthened, widened, and deepened in Japan by addition of a new forebody, and her tonnage was inceased to 33,449 GRT and 69,176 DWT. She continued to serve Grand Bassa Tankers faithfully after this conversion until she was broken up for scrap in 1983.

LIBERTY BELL
1954

LIBERTY BELL

Hull No: 513
Owner: Grand Bassa Tankers
Launched: October 19, 1954
Delivered: December 15, 1954
Dimensions: 707 x 93 x 48.5 ft
Gross Tonnage: 22,610
Displacement: 49,636 tons
Machinery: Geared Turbines, 2 Boilers
Horsepower/Speed: 20,000/17.5 knots
Fate: Scrapped, 1977

The keel for the last of four tankers built for Grand Bassa was laid on Shipway 9 on April 19, 1954. This ship was later named LIBERTY BELL in honor of the city of Philadelphia. The 707-foot ship was christened by Mrs. Christopher Story, wife of the vice

president of the Cities Service Oil Co., on October 19, 1954. A large crowd of visitors and guests were in attendance for the launching, which was to be the last at Newport News for almost two years.

The new LIBERTY BELL completed trials and was delivered to Grand Bassa on December 15, 1954. Like the other ships of her class, LIBERTY BELL had accommodations for 54 crew and four passengers. She was powered with DeLaval turbines of 20,000 SHP and made a trial speed of 18.8 knots.

The new ship entered service early in 1955 under charter to Cities Service and during her first year made voyages between the East Coast and Gulf Coast ports and to the Far East. In subsequent years her service was truly worldwide and carried her to Europe, Africa, South America, and the West Coast. She was apparently never involved in a major accident and served her original owner faithfully until she was scrapped in 1977.

ESSO GETTYSBURG
1957

ESSO GETTYSBURG

Hull No: 519
Owner: Esso Shipping Co.
Launched: October 11, 1956
Delivered: March 1, 1957
Dimensions: 715 x 93 x 48.58 ft
Gross Tonnage: 24,543
Displacement: 50,145 tons
Machinery: Geared Turbines, 2 Boilers
Horsepower/Speed: 26,500/18.3 knots
Fate: In Service

On August 1, 1955, the shipyard was low bidder on two tankers for the Esso Shipping Co., which were to be the largest Esso tankers ever built to that time and the largest tankers flying the American flag. The first of these was ESSO GETTYSBURG, the keel for which was laid on Shipway 8 on April 16, 1956. Designed by their owner, ESSO GETTYSBURG and her sisters were the most powerful single-screw ships yet built at the shipyard, and their Newport News-built turbines later gave them a trial speed of over 19 knots. They were built under the Maritime Administration's "trade-in-and-build" program and were pro-

vided with national defense features.

Sponsor for ESSO GETTYSBURG was Mrs. W.R. Stott, wife of a director of the Standard Oil Co. of NJ, and she sent the ship down the ways at 11:30 A.M. on October 11, 1956.

Reflecting improvements in accommodations on merchant ships made in the 1950s, the quarters on ESSO GETTYSBURG were all arranged for single occupancy and were very comfortably appointed. She was delivered on March 1, 1957, and, commanded by Esso's senior master Captain Jens G. Olsen, delivered her first cargo of crude oil to the Esso Bayway (NJ) refinery on March 12.

ESSO GETTYSBURG settled into routine crude service between the Gulf and East Coasts, competing with land-based pipelines; her 30 cargo tanks gave her a capacity of about 37,800 DWT.

Her only serious mishap was on January 24, 1971, when she ran aground at the mouth of New Haven harbor. Heavy bottom damage caused her to spill 385,000 gallons of fuel oil into the harbor, but after repairs at Baltimore she returned to service.

In 1973 her name became EXXON GETTYS-BURG, and in the late 1970s and early 1980s she remained in the specialty/products trade with Exxon in coastwise service.

ESSO WASHINGTON
1957

ESSO WASHINGTON

Hull No: 520
Owner: Esso Shipping Co.
Launched: February 15, 1957
Delivered: May 17, 1957
Dimensions: 715 x 93 x 48.58 ft
Gross Tonnage: 24,543
Displacement: 50,145 tons
Machinery: Geared Turbines, 2 Boilers
Horsepower/Speed: 26,500/18.3 knots
Fate: In Service

Second of the 37,800 DWT tankers delivered to Esso in 1957 was ESSO WASHINGTON which was given Hull No. 520. The keel for this ship was laid on Shipway 9 on July 9, 1956, and she was ready for launch by February 15 of the following year. Sponsor for ESSO WASHINGTON was Mrs. George Koegler, widow of the former deputy general counsel of the Standard Oil Co. of NJ. Unlike the previous ship, ESSO WASHINGTON was launched with her stack in place, and she presented an imposing sight as she slid into the James River with bunting at her bow and an ensign at her stern.

After outfitting and trials, the new ship was delivered and joined the Esso fleet on May 17, 1957. She was active in crude and products service on both the Atlantic and Pacific Coasts early in her career, then later served mostly between Gulf of Mexico and East Coast ports. In 1973 her name was changed to EXXON WASHINGTON and she continued in product service through the 1970s.

In 1981 she and her two following sisters were converted at Newport News for crude service from the Hondo Field off southern California to Baytown, TX, via the Panama Canal. The conversion consisted of the addition of crude oil washing and inert gas systems and brought her up to regulatory requirements to again carry crude oil. She continued in Exxon's Hondo trade into the mid-1980s.

ESSO JAMESTOWN
1957

ESSO JAMESTOWN

Hull No: 527
Owner: Esso Shipping Co.
Launched: October 1, 1957
Delivered: December 20, 1957
Dimensions: 715 x 93 x 48.58 ft
Gross Tonnage: 23,486
Displacement: 50,145 tons
Machinery: Geared Turbines, 2 Boilers
Horsepower/Speed: 26,500/18.3 knots
Fate: In Service

On May 25, 1956, the shipyard received an order for an additional two 37,800 DWT tankers for the Esso Shipping Co. The keel for the first of these, ESSO JAMESTOWN, was laid on Shipway 8 on March 18, 1957. The four ships of this class all were named for places of historical significance, and that of Hull 527 was significant in that her launch and delivery occurred during the year of the Jamestown Festival. The sponsor of ESSO JAMESTOWN was Mrs. Harold W. Fisher, wife of the joint managing director of Iraq Petroleum Co., and the Fishers flew to Newport News from their home in England for the ceremony. After the successful launch on a rainy October 1, 1957, the launching party and guests were treated to a luncheon at the Williamsburg Inn, then toured Jamestown Festival Park.

After delivery on December 20, 1957, ESSO JAMESTOWN settled into the crude trade between Gulf ports to Esso's East Coast refineries with occasional trips to the West Coast. In 1973 her name was changed to EXXON JAMESTOWN and in 1981, her operation no longer being competitive with the pipelines, she was also converted at Newport News for the carriage of Hondo crude. She suffered no major mishaps during her career and remained in the West Coast-Gulf Coast via Panama trade into the mid-1980s.

ESSO LEXINGTON
1958

ESSO LEXINGTON

Hull No: 528
Owner: Esso Shipping Co.
Launched: January 28, 1958
Delivered: April 25, 1958
Dimensions: 715 x 93 x 48.58 ft
Gross Tonnage: 23,486
Displacement: 50,145 tons
Machinery: Geared Turbines, 2 Boilers
Horsepower/Speed: 26,500/18.3 knots
Fate: In Service

Fourth and last of the 37,800 DWT ships built for Esso was ESSO LEXINGTON, which had been ordered with ESSO JAMESTOWN on May 25, 1956. The keel for Hull 528 was laid on Shipway 9 on July 29, 1957, and by January 28, 1958, the new ship was ready for launch. Mrs. Myron A. Wright, wife of the producing coordinator for the Standard Oil Co. of NJ, was

sponsor for ESSO LEXINGTON, and she made good her promise "to splash champagne all over," dousing many on the platform. This ship slid down the ways 44 years to the day after the shipyard's first Esso ship, JOHN D. ARCHBOLD, was launched in 1914 and was the 37th ship built at Newport News for the Esso fleet.

After a relatively short outfitting period, ESSO LEXINGTON underwent sea trials in unusually bad weather on April 22-23, then was delivered to Esso on April 25, 1958. She joined the Esso fleet on the next day and was said to be (with her three sisters) the most powerful single-screw vessel afloat at the time.

After delivery she spent virtually all her career in first crude and later products trade between the Gulf and East Coasts and West Indies. In 1973 her name became EXXON LEXINGTON, and in 1981 she too was converted at Newport News for the Hondo crude trade. Otherwise virtually unaltered, and with her Newport News-built machinery providing trouble-free dependability, she remained in the Hondo trade into the mid-1980s.

G.S. LIVANOS
1958

G.S. LIVANOS

Hull No: 530
Owner: Ocean Tanker Line Ltd.
Launched: June 5, 1958
Delivered: August 27, 1958
Dimensions: 712 x 93 x 48.5 ft
Gross Tonnage: 23,626
Displacement: 52,302 tons
Machinery: Geared Turbines, 2 Boilers
Horsepower/Speed: 20,000/17 knots
Fate: Scrapped, 1984

Newport News Hull 530 was G.S. LIVANOS, second of two 41,000 DWT tankers for Ocean Tanker Line, Ltd. The keel for this ship was laid on Shipway 6 on September 30, 1957, and she was the largest ship built there to that time. Sponsor for G.S. LIVANOS was Mrs. Clinton C. Johnson, wife of the vice president

of the Chemical Corn Exchange Bank of New York. Mr. Stavros S. Livanos and his son George S. Livanos, the ship's namesake, were present at the launching on June 5, 1958.

After completion and sea trials on August 8, the new ship was delivered to her owner on August 27, 1958. G.S. LIVANOS entered worldwide service, and voyages during her first few years took her to the United Kingdom, Mediterranean, U.S. Pacific Coast, and the Far East. In later years she added Europe, the Baltic, Africa, the U.S. East Coast, and the West Indies to her itinerary.

In 1973 she ended her career with Ocean Tanker and passed to the Tank Oil Corp. of Monrovia. Remaining under Liberian registry, she was renamed SOUTH-WEST CAPE in 1973. Changing regulations had increased her gross tonnage to 25,988 and her deadweight to 44,216, and she continued in routine service with Tank Oil until she was sold to Taiwanese breakers in 1984.

ARIETTA S. LIVANOS
1958

ARIETTA S. LIVANOS

Hull No: 529
Owner: Ocean Tanker Line Ltd.
Launched: March 21, 1958
Delivered: June 30, 1958
Dimensions: 712 x 93 x 48.5 ft
Gross Tonnage: 23,626
Displacement: 52,302 tons
Machinery: Geared Turbines, 2 Boilers
Horsepower/Speed: 20,000/17 knots
Fate: Scrapped, 1979

The shipyard signed a contract for two ships for Ocean Tanker Line, Ltd. on July 30, 1956. These ships were similar in dimensions to the W. ALTON JONES class previously delivered, but they were fuller at the ends, increasing their capacity to 41,000 DWT. The keel for the first of these ships, ARIETTA S. LIVANOS, was laid in Shipway 10 on July 29, 1957.

The new tanker, largest yet built at the yard, was christened by her namesake, Mrs. Arietta S. Livanos, on March 21, 1958. Mrs. Livanos was the wife of Stavros G. Livanos, owner of the steamship line, and she was the first sponsor in memory to give her own name to a ship.

ARIETTA S. LIVANOS completed sea trials on June 6, then was delivered to her owner on June 30, 1958. After a brief layup at the shipyard, the new tanker entered service on August 2, flying the Liberian flag and making the long voyages for which she had been designed.

Her early career was routine, but on October 22, 1966, she collided with the German ship ANNELISE off the French coast during a voyage from Mena al Ahmadi to Rotterdam with a load of crude oil. ARIETTA S. LIVANOS was hit in way of her engine room and at first was reported sinking, but she was towed first to Brest then to Rotterdam.

She was sold "as is" to Royal Transport and Trading Co. and was repaired and renamed ATLANTIC. She returned to service briefly but was laid up in 1972. In 1973 she received a new forebody in Greece, and her capacity was increased to 52,400 DWT. A new owner, Progressive Navigation Co., renamed her PENNSYLVANIA during the same year.

During the next few years, she passed through the ownership of Seagull Maritime Enterprises and GATX Bulk Carrier Number Six, who operated her under Liberian flag until she was scrapped in 1979.

SANSINENA
1958

SANSINENA

Hull No: 531
Owner: Barracuda Tanker Corp.
Launched: August 7, 1958
Delivered: October 24, 1958
Dimensions: 810 x 104 x 60 ft
Gross Tonnage: 37,203
Displacement: 77,029 tons
Machinery: Geared Turbines, 2 Boilers
Horsepower/Speed: 22,750/17.2 knots
Fate: Exploded, 1976

A good year for tankers at the shipyard was 1956, and on August 20 a contract was signed with Barracuda Tanker Corp. for the construction of three 60,000 DWT ships, the largest ever built in the U.S. to that time. Designed by the shipyard and fitted with Newport News-built turbines of 22,750 SHP, these ships were ordered for charter to the Union Oil Co. for crude service between the Persian Gulf and West Coast ports. All three were named after Union Oil producing fields in California, and the first was named SANSINENA.

The keel for this vessel was laid on Shipway 8 on

October 7, 1957, and she was launched on August 7, 1958. Sponsor for SANSINENA was Mrs. Reese H. Taylor, wife of the chairman of Union Oil. The SANSINENA's 24 ft diameter propeller, the world's largest, was in place at the time of launching. Outfitting was complete by the following October, and following successful trials on October 19-20, SANSINENA was delivered on October 24, 1958.

The new ship left the shipyard on the following day for her maiden voyage to the Persian Gulf via the Suez Canal, then loaded crude oil, and proceeded to a Union Oil refinery on the West Coast. She settled into routine service on this route and stayed there for the next 18 years with occasional assignments to other routes. She was not "jumboized" with her two sisters in Japan in 1965, but changing regulations increased her dead weight to over 70,000 tons over the years.

Her unspectacular career came to a spectacular end at Los Angles on December 17, 1976. Just after unloading a full cargo of Indonesian light crude at her Union Oil berth, an explosion caused by a spark in one of her center tanks caused her to break in two and sink. The violence of the explosion blew off both of her deckhouses and caused nine deaths and over 50 injuries. Totally demolished, she was later cut down and scrapped.

TORREY CANYON
1958

TORREY CANYON

Hull No: 532
Owner: Barracuda Tanker Co.
Launched: October 28, 1958
Delivered: January 9, 1959
Dimensions: 810 x 104 x 60 ft
Gross Tonnage: 37,203
Displacement: 77,029 tons
Machinery: Geared Turbines, 2 Boilers
Horsepower/Speed: 22,750/17.2 knots
Fate: Stranded, 1967

TORREY CANYON was the second tanker ordered by Barracuda in 1956 and, like her predecessor, she met a violent end—because of which her name became perhaps the most infamous in tanker history. The keel for TORREY CANYON was laid on Shipway 9 on February 5, 1958, and she was christened with California champagne on October 28 of that year by Mrs. Arthur C. Stewart, wife of the vice president, director, and executive committee chairman of the Union Oil Co.

TORREY CANYON was delivered to Barracuda on January 9, 1959, and, like her predecessor, made her maiden voyage from Newport News to the Persian Gulf, thence to California with cargo.

The career of this ill-fated ship was quite routine until her demise in 1967. In 1965 the then-67,000 DWT TORREY CANYON and her later sister LAKE PALOURDE were jumboized in Japan to 118,000 DWT ships in a conversion of unprecedented scale.

TORREY CANYON's career continued without incident until March 18, 1967. On that date she was steaming under charter to the British Petroleum Co. from Merra-al-Ahmad to Milford Haven with 118,000 tons of Kuwait crude when she ran aground near Seven Stones in the Scilly Isles off Britain's southwest coast in clear weather. A huge oil slick, which eventually covered 350 square miles and caused heavy pollution to the British coast, began to spill out immediately. Although there was no loss of life to the ship's crew, the heavy pollution made the wreck of the TORREY CANYON one of the most notorious marine disasters in history and led to improved standards of construction and operation of tankers over the following years.

LAKE PALOURDE
1959

LAKE PALOURDE

Hull No: 533
Owner: Barracuda Tanker Co.
Launched: March 16, 1959
Delivered: May 25, 1959
Dimensions: 810 x 104 x 60 ft
Gross Tonnage: 37,203
Displacement: 77,029 tons
Machinery: Geared Turbines, 2 Boilers
Horsepower/Speed: 22,750/17.2 knots
Fate: Scrapped, 1984

Third of the Barracuda supertankers ordered in 1956 was LAKE PALOURDE, which was the only ship of her class to enjoy a long career without a disastrous end. The keel for Hull 533 was laid on Shipway 8 on August 12, 1958, just five days after the launch of SANSINENA from that facility. LAKE PALOURDE was christened by Mrs. Horace C. Flanigan, wife of a Union Oil Co. director and mother of Peter M. Flanigan, president of Barracuda Tankers, on March 16, 1959. Outfitting was completed rapidly, and the

third Barracuda tanker underwent trials on May 5-6 and was delivered on May 25, 1959.

After delivery she too made her maiden voyage to the Persian Gulf, then delivered a load of crude to Union Oil in California. After six years of routine service, LAKE PALOURDE was also converted in Japan in 1965, and her capacity was increased to 118,000 DWT. Her new forebody enabled her to carry 51,000 tons of additional cargo at only about one knot less speed, and the entire conversion took only slightly more than four months. After her conversion LAKE PALOURDE returned to worldwide service for Barracuda under Liberian registry.

After the TORREY CANYON disaster, LAKE PALOURDE was seized in a French port and was held until her insurers paid $7.5 million to the British and French in settlement for damage caused by her sister ship.

LAKE PALOURDE was provided with an inert gas system in 1978 to prevent accidents like that which befell SANSINENA, and she continued in service with Barracuda until 1982. She was laid up at Portland, OR, in that year; then, in 1984 she was towed to Taiwan for scrapping.

THETIS
1959

THETIS

Hull No: 535
Owner: Rye Marine Corp.
Launched: April 24, 1959
Delivered: September 15, 1959
Dimensions: 712 x 93 x 48.5 ft
Gross Tonnage: 23,612
Displacement: 52,302 tons
Machinery: Geared Turbines, 2 Boilers
Horsepower/Speed: 20,000/17 knots
Fate: In Service

On December 5, 1956, the shipyard obtained a contract with Rye Marine Corp. for the construction of a 41,000 DWT tanker similar to the ARIETTA S. LIVANOS previously ordered by Ocean Tanker Line. The new ship, subsequently named THETIS after a sea nymph of Greek mythology, was also owned by Greek interests but was built for American flag service.

The keel for THETIS was laid on Shipway 6 on September 29, 1958, and the new tanker was christened on April 24, 1959. Sponsor for THETIS was Mrs.

Anthony D. Manthos of Rye, NY, wife of a principal of Rye Marine Corp., owners, and K and M Management Corp., operators.

THETIS was the first new ship ever built for Manthos interests, and she joined a sizeable fleet of purchased vessels after her delivery on September 15, 1959. Her colorful bow and stack insignia, derived from a combination of the house flags of the Kulukundis and Manthos interests, gave THETIS a distinctive look.

The tanker had been inactive at the shipyard for almost three months before her delivery, but she went to work in the fall of 1959 and sailed routinely with Rye Marine for almost 15 years, serving both U.S. coasts.

In 1975 she was sold to the American Trading and Transportation Co. and was renamed WASHINGTON TRADER. After extensive steel renewals at the shipyard following her sale, the ship operated in the Alaska crude trade, then later was employed carrying Trans-Panama crude from Chiriqui Grande to the Gulf and East Coast refineries under charter to Exxon. In 1983 she was overhauled at Baltimore and was fitted with an inert gas system to enable her to operate safely into the mid-1980s.

ACHILLES
1960

ACHILLES

Hull No: 536
Owner: Newport Tankers Corp.
Launched: April 13, 1960
Delivered: June 7, 1960
Dimensions: 712 x 93 x 48.5 ft
Gross Tonnage: 23,612
Displacement: 52,302 tons
Machinery: Geared Turbines, 2 Boilers
Horsepower/Speed: 20,000/17 knots
Fate: Scrapped, 1984

Just a month after completion of THETIS, the shipyard signed another contract with K and M interests for the construction of a sister ship, later named ACHILLES. Owner for this 41,000 DWT vessel was Newport Tankers Corp., and like her sister, ACHILLES was intended for American flag service.

The keel for Hull 536 was laid on Shipway 6 on September 14, 1959, and she was launched on April 13, 1960. Sponsor for ACHILLES was Mrs. Manuel E.

Hadjilias of London, and many of the K and M principals who had been present at the launch of the THETIS were in attendance.

The names of the two ships were closely linked in Greek mythology: Thetis being the sea nymph who held her infant son Achilles by the heel as she dipped him into the River Styx, protecting him from harm. ACHILLES was protected from harm by the traditional launching ceremony and was out fitted and completed sea trials on June 1. A charter was obtained and the tanker left the shipyard on July 5, 1960, in her handsome gray and red livery with the distinctive K and M markings.

After delivery, ACHILLES settled into a remarkably routine career, sailing for her original owners under her orignal name well past her 20th birthday. Voyages took her from the Middle East and Far East to both U.S. coasts early in her career, and later her service was mostly on domestic routes. She continued to sail with distinction and completed her 24th year with her original owner and name before being sold to Bangladesh breakers in 1984.

ESSO BOSTON
1960

ESSO BOSTON

Hull No: 541
Owner: Esso Standard Division
Launched: September 28, 1960
Delivered: November 22, 1960
Dimensions: 740 x 102 x 50 ft
Gross Tonnage: 29,675
Displacement: 62,105 tons
Machinery: Geared Turbines, 2 Boilers
Horsepower/Speed: 19,000/17.5 knots
Fate: In Service

ESSO BOSTON was the second 48,800 DWT supertanker ordered by Esso in December 1956. The keel for Hull 541 was laid on Shipway 9 on January 11, 1960, and the 740-foot black and maroon ship was ready for launch on the following September 28. A large party of guests from New York, Boston, and Houston were on hand as Mrs. George M. Parker christened the huge ship at noon. Mrs. Parker, wife of the president of Esso Export Corp., was aided and

advised by the sponsors of four other Newport News-built Esso ships who were present at the launching of ESSO BOSTON.

After outfitting at a southside berth, ESSO BOSTON completed successful sea trials in variable weather on November 9-10 and was delivered to Humble on November 22, 1960. Hull 541, like her sister, was built with safety and efficiency as primary considerations. Their hull design was optimized to provide speed, economy, and good seakeeping, and they were provided with unusual cutaway sterns to minimize propeller-induced vibration.

ESSO BOSTON's maiden voyage took her to Baton Rouge where, after an open house, she loaded oil for her first trip up the East Coast. After a gala open house at Boston, she settled into prosaic service on the coastal route. In 1973 her name was changed to EXXON BOSTON and her operator became the Exxon Shipping Co. With her sister she withdrew from the coastal trade in the late 1970s and, after conversion, was placed in the Hondo crude trade, where she remained into the mid-1980s.

NATIONAL DEFENDER
1959

NATIONAL DEFENDER

Hull No: 537
Owner: National Transport Corp.
Launched: August 19, 1959
Delivered: October 23, 1959
Dimensions: 810 x 104 x 60 ft
Gross Tonnage: 36,905
Displacement: 82,678 tons
Machinery: Geared Turbines, 2 Boilers
Horsepower/Speed: 22,750/17.1 knots
Fate: In Service

The 1950s were years of superlatives for Newport News-built tankers with ship after ship snatching the "largest" title from its predecessors. NATIONAL DEFENDER, ordered by the National Transport Corp. on December 21, 1956, was the last of these and was the largest tanker in terms of displacement launched at Newport News until the ULCCs of the late 1970s. The large number of tanker orders held by the shipyard caused the keel laying for the NATIONAL DEFENDER to be delayed until November 17, 1958, by which time a contract for a sister ship, Hull 538, had been cancelled.

The launching of NATIONAL DEFENDER was quite colorful, and due to the ship's size, it was an important media event. The "new queen of the American merchant fleet" was christened by Mrs. John Theodoreacopulos, wife of the chairman of National Transport Corp., on August 19, 1959.

After highly successful trials of the ship's Newport News-built machinery on October 19-20, NATIONAL DEFENDER was delivered on October 23, 1959. Delay in obtaining a charter for the new ship postponed her departure from the shipyard until March 16, 1960, but she made up for lost time a month later when she set a record by lifting 40,353 tons of corn from Baton Rouge to Uruguay, the largest single grain cargo carried to that time.

After an initial diversion to the grain trade, NATIONAL DEFENDER settled into routine service and served her original owner for 13 years. Voyages during this time took her to both U.S. coasts, the Plate, Far East, Mediterranean, and the Middle East. In 1973 she passed to the Vancor Steamship Co. of New York, and her name was changed to VANTAGE DEFENDER. Five years later she was sold to Cove Ventures of New York and was renamed COVE LEADER.

In the late 1970s she was fitted with segregated ballast, crude oil tank washing, and inert gas systems, bringing her up to modern safety and pollution standards. She continued in crude service between the Gulf and East Coasts into the mid-1980s.

ESSO BALTIMORE
1960

ESSO BALTIMORE

Hull No: 540
Owner: Esso Standard Division
Launched: April 28, 1960
Delivered: July 15, 1960
Dimensions: 740 x 102 x 50 ft
Gross Tonnage: 29,675
Displacement: 62,105 tons
Machinery: Geared Turbines, 2 Boilers
Horsepower/Speed: 19,000/17.5 knots
Fate: In Service

On December 14, 1956, the shipyard obtained a contract for five 48,800 DWT tankers from an old customer, the Standard Oil Co. of NJ, for service with the Esso Standard Division of Humble Oil & Refining Co. These ships were assigned Hull Nos. 540-544 but only the first two, named ESSO BALTIMORE and ESSO BOSTON, were built.

The keel for ESSO BALTIMORE was not laid on Shipway 8 until September 9, 1959, due to the press of other tanker work at the shipyard. Sponsor for ESSO BALTIMORE was Mrs. Morgan J. Davis, wife of the president of Humble Oil & Refining Co., and she sent the giant tanker down the ways on April 28, 1960, amid great fanfare.

During outfitting, it became apparent that this ship and her sister represented a departure from previous Esso tankers, for they featured modern streamlined stacks and superstructures; offered individual air conditioned quarters; and lacked the traditional forward dry cargo hold and booms formerly provided. ESSO BALTIMORE's 19,000 SHP Newport News-built turbines were put to the test during sea trials on July 11-12, 1960, and the ship was delivered on July 15.

She sailed later that day for Baltimore and an open house which drew 17,000 vistors. She then sailed for New York and joined the Esso fleet after another successful open house there. Designed to be the largest and most efficient oil tanker able to operate in the Gulf Coast-East Coast trade, her 35 cargo tanks gave her a total capacity of 417,842 U.S. barrels.

She stayed on her intended routes for almost 20 years until her operation in competition with land-based pipelines became unprofitable in the late 1970s. Her name was changed to EXXON BALTIMORE in 1973, and her later operator was the Exxon Shipping Co. After her withdrawal from her original route, she was converted for the carriage of Hondo crude from Santa Barbara to Baytown via the Panama Canal, where she served with four of her Newport News sisters into the mid-1980s. In 1985 she was reclassified as a products ship and, fitted with heating coils, began to carry heavy fuels and asphalt cargoes.

ATLANTIC PRESTIGE
1962

ATLANTIC PRESTIGE

Hull No: 564
Owner: Atlantic Refining Co.
Launched: August 17, 1962
Delivered: November 27, 1962
Dimensions: 667.33 x 82.5 x 46 ft
Gross Tonnage: 19,885
Displacement: 41,346 tons
Machinery: Geared Turbines, 2 Boilers
Horsepower/Speed: 13,750/16 knots
Fate: In Service

On May 19, 1961, the shipyard obtained a contract from the Atlantic Refining Co. for what might be called its last conventional tanker. This 32,600 DWT ship, later named ATLANTIC PRESTIGE, was the last tank ship built at Newport News which had a midship superstructure and conventional hull form which had characterized the shipyard's first 78 tankers.

The keel for ATLANTIC PRESTIGE was laid on December 20, 1961, and by the following August 17 the ship was ready for launch. The sponsor for Hull 564 was chosen by a unique lottery system among 373 Atlantic seagoing personnel. Winner was Mrs. Herman G. Fredeluces, wife of a crew member of ATLANTIC ENGINEER, and she performed her task ably at a small ceremony. To commemorate this launching, the oil company gave away special drinking glasses at their area service stations for three days surrounding the event.

The new ATLANTIC PRESTIGE underwent sea trials of her shipyard-built machinery on November 19-20, then was delivered to Atlantic on November 27, 1962. The new ship's maiden voyage was in ballast to Atlantic's refinery at Port Arthur, TX, where she picked up a load of product to carry up the East Coast. Her service was largely routine except for groundings in 1972 and 1975 and a collision which sank the tug LIPAN in 1974 without loss of life.

She stayed in routine service with Atlantic and later Arco, and in 1976 her name was changed to ARCO PRESTIGE. In 1981, after almost 20 years with her original owner, she was sold to the American Trading Transportation Co. and was renamed PENN-SYLVANIA TRADER. Homeported at Wilmington, DL, she continued in dependable service to her new owner.

ESSO HOUSTON
1964

ESSO HOUSTON

Hull No: 573
Owner: Humble Oil & Refining Co.
Launched: September 26, 1964
Delivered: December 11, 1964
Dimensions: 800 x 116 x 54.5 ft
Gross Tonnage: 35,291
Displacement: 81,783 tons
Machinery: Geared Turbines, 1 Boiler
Horsepower/Speed: 19,000/16.5 knots
Fate: In Service

ESSO HOUSTON and her sister marked a turning point in tanker construction at Newport News. The two 66,700 DWT ships were the first tankers built at the shipyard to have all-aft superstructures and to be provided with protruding bulbous bows to enhance their speed in ballast. Their design included features which contributed to efficient and economical operation including a single-boiler automated plant and turbine-driven deepwell cargo pumps in lieu of pump rooms. In addition, the two ships were of 116 ft beam and were the first Newport News-built tankers which were too wide to pass through the Panama Canal.

The keel for ESSO HOUSTON was laid on Shipway 8 on January 27, 1964. Construction of this ship and her sister was unique in that all 159 large subassemblies were treated with Humble coating systems before their transfer to the shipway. Launch of Esso's largest tanker to date took place on September 26, 1964. Sponsor for ESSO HOUSTON was Mrs. Carl F. Reistle, wife of Humble's chairman of the board, and she was honored by the attendance of a large crowd of Esso guests and Newport News shipbuilders and their families.

ESSO HOUSTON's outfitting was continued at Pier 1, and successful sea trials were completed on December 7-8, followed by delivery on December 11, 1964. The superlative new ship entered the Esso fleet immediately, serving between the Gulf and East Coasts in competition with the newly laid Colonial Pipeline.

Her name was changed to EXXON HOUSTON in 1973, and she stayed on her original route until the late 1970s when she was no longer competitive with the pipeline. She was provided with segregated ballast and inert gas systems to bring her up to date and was placed in North Slope crude service in 1978. Steaming between the Alaskan port of Valdez and Exxon's refineries on the West Coast, EXXON HOUSTON continued in reliable service to the fleet past her 20th birthday.

ESSO NEW ORLEANS
1965

ESSO NEW ORLEANS

Hull No: 576
Owner: Humble Oil & Refining Co.
Launched: January 23, 1965
Delivered: April 9, 1965
Dimensions: 800 x 116 x 54.5 ft
Gross Tonnage: 35,285
Displacement: 81,783 tons
Machinery: Geared Turbines, 1 Boiler
Horsepower/Speed: 19,000/16.5 knots
Fate: In Service

A second 66,700 DWT tanker, later named ESSO NEW ORLEANS, was ordered on January 10, 1964, and her keel was laid on Shipway 9 (next to ESSO HOUSTON in Shipway 8) on the following June 1. Launching for the ESSO NEW ORLEANS on January 23, 1965 was unique. Sponsor for the 800-foot ship was Mrs. J.K. Jamieson, wife of the executive vice president and director of the Standard Oil Co. of NJ, and a large crowd was in attendance. Shipyard president Donald Holden made a remark about "tigers in the ship's tanks" as he introduced the sponsor, and as Mrs. Jamieson christened the ship and it started its slide, all but a few were in for a surprise. As ESSO NEW ORLEANS glided down the ways, the head of a large Esso tiger appeared on her bow, a 35-foot tiger tail dropped out of her starboard hawse pipe, and a huge tiger's roar was heard, giving a spectacular finish to the launching.

After this fanfare the new tanker routinely completed outfitting, underwent trials on April 4-5, and was delivered to Humble on April 9, 1965. Like ESSO HOUSTON, she was provided with extensive safety and economy features and had 21 large tanks in lieu of the more usual 30 or so. Due to automation, her crew was greatly reduced in comparison with those of more conventional ships.

After delivery the ESSO NEW ORLEANS settled into routine service in competition with the pipeline between the Gulf and East Coasts. With her sisters, she took the Exxon name in 1973 and became EXXON NEW ORLEANS. She too was fitted with segregated ballast and inert gas systems, and on August 4, 1977, she became the first Exxon ship to load North Slope crude at Valdez for shipment to Exxon's refinery at Benicia, CA.

She was rocked by an explosion while undergoing repairs at Portland, OR, on August 12, 1982, and seven workers were injured, but she was not seriously damaged. She continued in the Alaska-West Coast crude trade into the mid-1980s.

EL PASO HOWARD BOYD
1979

EL PASO HOWARD BOYD

Hull No: 610
Owner: El Paso LNG Co.
Launched: March 4, 1978
Delivered: June 29, 1979
Dimensions: 948.5 x 135 x 85 ft
Gross Tonnage: 69,472
Displacement: 97,215 tons
Machinery: Geared Turbines, 2 Boilers
Horsepower/Speed: 40,000/19.75 knots
Fate: Laid Up, 1980

The third and last LNG carrier built at Newport News was EL PASO HOWARD BOYD, the keel for which was laid in Shipway 12 on April 18, 1977. This ship was christened by Mrs. Lucille Belhumeur Boyd, wife of El Paso's chairman and namesake of the ship, on March 4, 1978.

Outfitting on the huge ship, equivalent in size to a 160,000 DWT tanker, proceeded quickly. Due to the nature of their cargo which "boiled off" during the voyage, the LNG ships were fitted with boilers which could burn either oil or "boiled off" natural gas. The ships were extremely powerful, with 40,000 SHP steam turbines driving a single 25 ft diameter propeller, and had an operating speed of 18.5 knots.

EL PASO HOWARD BOYD was completed and delivered on June 29, 1979, and entered service in July. She lifted only ten cargoes of Algerian LNG before being withdrawn from service in April 1980. She too was laid up at Newport, RI, and also remained there after her transfer to GEN MAR and her renaming to GAMMA in July 1983.

EL PASO SOUTHERN
1978

EL PASO SOUTHERN

Hull No: 608
Owner: El Paso LNG Co.
Launched: January 22, 1977
Delivered: May 31, 1978
Dimensions: 948.5 x 135 x 85 ft
Gross Tonnage: 69,472
Displacement: 97,215 tons
Machinery: Geared Turbines, 2 Boilers
Horsepower/Speed: 40,000/19.75 knots
Fate: Laid Up, 1980

A "new chapter in shipbuilding history at Newport News" opened on September 30, 1972, when the shipyard signed a $297.7 million contract with El Paso for the construction of three liquid natural gas (LNG) carriers under Maritime Administraton subsidy. These ships were intended to carry LNG from Arzew, Algeria, to terminals at Cove Point, MD, and Savannah, GA, but they were not destined for trouble-free careers. For construction of these and other energy ships of the 1970s, the shipyard had previously begun work on a new 271-acre commercial shipyard north of the existing yard with a huge 1,600 ft dry dock. The superstructures for all three ships were built at Beaufort, NC, and barged to the shipyard.

The first keel block for the first ship, later named EL PASO SOUTHERN, was laid in the gigantic new Shipway 12 on November 8, 1975. EL PASO SOUTHERN was launched on a bitterly cold January 22, 1977. Sponsor for the ship was Mrs. Jan Diesel, wife of shipyard chairman and chief executive officer John P. Diesel. Mrs. Diesel launched the 125,000 cubic meter capacity LNG-ship by cutting a symbolic hawser and freeing the ship in the dock.

High winds and bitter cold prevented moving the ship until the next day, but outfitting proceeded later and EL PASO SOUTHERN completed trials and was delivered on May 31, 1978. The 949-ft ship underwent gas trials after delivery, then entered service in October 1978. After carrying only 19 cargoes of LNG, the ship was idled by a dispute between El Paso and Algeria over the price of Algerian LNG in April 1980. Talks with the Algerians reached a stalemate, and in October 1980 EL PASO SOUTHERN was laid up at Newport, RI, with her two Newport News-built sisters. In July 1983 the ship was sold to the GEN MAR Corp. and was renamed SOUTHERN but remained in lay-up.

EL PASO ARZEW
1978

EL PASO ARZEW

Hull No: 609
Owner: El Paso LNG Co.
Launched: August 6, 1977
Delivered: December 8, 1978
Dimensions: 948.5 x 135 x 85 ft
Gross Tonnage: 69,472
Displacement: 97,215 tons
Machinery: Geared Turbines, 2 Boilers
Horsepower/Speed: 40,000/19.75 knots
Fate: Laid Up, 1980

The shipyard's new Shipway 12 was designed to accommodate the construction of one and one-half large ships simultaneously, enabling the keel of the second LNG ship to be laid on September 8, 1976, more than three months prior to launching of the first ship. The second ship, named EL PASO ARZEW, was christened with champagne on August 6, 1977, by Mrs. Abdel Aziz Maoui, wife of the Algerian ambassador. In attendance were over 15,000 people who came for the launching and for a gala open house for the new Commercial Shipyard.

After launching, the ship was moved to a nearby outfitting berth for completion and installation of her cargo containment system. The containment system utilized for the Newport News-built LNG ships was a "waffle membrane" system built under license from the French firm Technigaz. The system consisted of a unique stainless steel membrane provided with corrugations to allow thermal contraction when in contact with the supercold (-260°F.) LNG. Installation of the membrane and its supporting balsa wood insulation system called for new skills and methods which were developed for the task.

EL PASO ARZEW completed outfitting and trials and was delivered on December 8, 1978. The new ship entered service in January but carried only 18 cargoes, about two-thirds to Cove Point and the rest to Savannah, before being idled in April 1980 by the dispute with Algeria. EL PASO ARZEW was also laid up at Newport, RI, the following October and remained in lay-up after her sale to GEN MAR. Her name was changed to ARZEW in July 1983.

U.S.T. PACIFIC
1979

U.S.T. PACIFIC

Hull No: 614
Owner: Connecticut National Bank
Launched: September 8, 1979
Delivered: December 7, 1979
Dimensions: 1187.5 x 228 x 95 ft
Gross Tonnage: 189,416
Displacement: 449,840 tons
Machinery: Geared Turbines, 2 Boilers
Horsepower/Speed: 45,000/15.9 knots
Fate: Laid Up, 1981

The second ULCC built at Newport News was U.S.T. PACIFIC, the contract for which was signed on June 29, 1974. The contract for a third ship for Zapata Ocean Carriers was signed on the same day but was later cancelled. The keel for U.S.T. PACIFIC was laid in Shipway 12 on January 8, 1979, and the giant was christened a short nine months later by Mrs. Charles de Bretterville, who was drenched with champagne at the traditional ceremony on September 8, 1979.

The obvious reason for the rapid construction of U.S.T. PACIFIC was the impending change in regulations for the design of oil tankers which required, among other things, the installation of a double bottom in the cargo section of a ship of her size delivered after December 31, 1979. Outfitting and trials were therefore completed quickly and U.S.T. PACIFIC was delivered on December 7, 1979, for operation by the Interocean Management Corporation.

Like her sister ship, Hull 614 had 27 huge cargo and clean ballast tanks, the largest of which were 143.33 ft long. She was also fitted with General Electric steam turbines of 45,000 SHP and a single six-bladed propeller measuring an astounding 31.5 ft in diameter which drove her at a respectable 15.9 knots despite her size.

U.S.T. PACIFIC entered service immediately after her delivery and made only two voyages with cargo, from the Persian Gulf to the Caribbean, before June 1980. She served as a storage vessel in the Gulf of Mexico until February 1981, when she too was slated for lay-up. She sailed in ballast to Singapore and Labuan, Malaysia via the Persian Gulf, then was laid up at Labuan in May 1981.

U.S.T. ATLANTIC
1979

U.S.T. ATLANTIC

Hull No: 613
Owner: Connecticut National Bank
Launched: October 14, 1978
Delivered: March 7, 1979
Dimensions: 1187.5 x 228 x 95 ft
Gross Tonnage: 189,417
Displacement: 449,840 tons
Machinery: Geared Turbines, 2 Boilers
Horsepower/Speed: 45,000/15.9 knots
Fate: Laid Up, 1981

On June 29, 1974, the shipyard received an order from VLCC I Corporation for the construction of the new commerical shipyard's first oil tanker, later named U.S.T. ATLANTIC. Two more sister ships were ordered two months later but one of these was later cancelled. These tankers, known as Ultra Large Crude Carriers or ULCCs, were the largest ships ever built in the Western Hemisphere and their dimensions were staggering. At 398,000 DWT, they were capable of carrying six times as much oil as the shipyard's previous ESSO HOUSTON class and drew 74 feet of water when fully loaded. Built from a shipyard-developed design, these ships matched the size and capabilities of the new facilities at Newport News.

The keel for U.S.T. ATLANTIC was laid in Shipway 12 on September 14, 1977, just over a month after the launching of EL PASO ARZEW. The final subassembly for the huge ship was erected a year to the day after the keel. As with the LNG carriers, the huge deckhouses for the ULCCs were built and outfitted in North Carolina, barged to Newport News, then placed aboard, using the yard's 900-ton gantry crane.

U.S.T. ATLANTIC was floated out of Shipway 12 on October 14, 1978, following a small private ribbon-cutting ceremony. The ship's sponsor was Mrs. W.R. Phillips, wife of the shipyard's vice president for waterfront operations, and she performed the traditional champagne christening when the ship was delivered on March 7, 1979.

The largest vessel ever to fly the American flag entered service immediately and made five voyages from the Persian Gulf to Europe and the Caribbean. She served as a storage vessel in the Gulf of Mexico and Caribbean during the last quarter of 1980, made one more voyage to the Persian Gulf in 1981, then reverted to service as a storage vessel in the Gulf of Mexico. In June 1981 she departed in ballast for the Far East and, arriving in August, was laid up at Labuan, Malaysia, near Brunei.

LUMBER CARRIERS & COLLIERS
FRANCIS H. LEGGETT
1903

FRANCIS H. LEGGETT

Hull No: 43
Owner: Hammond Lumber Co.
Launched: January 31, 1903
Delivered: April 21, 1903
Dimensions: 258.75 x 41 x 19 ft
Gross Tonnage: 1,606
Displacement: 3,610 tons
Machinery: Triple Expansion Engine,
    2 Boilers
Horsepower/Speed: 1,000/10 knots
Fate: Foundered, 1914

Hull 43, FRANCIS H. LEGGETT, was the first lumber carrier built at Newport News and she met an early, tragic end. Built for the Hammond Lumber Co. of San Francisco, the LEGGETT was the first vessel built at the yard to use oil fuel, and she was fitted with cabins for about 50 passengers. Francis H. Leggett (daughter of the ship's namesake) was to have launched the new ship but could not be present, so Mrs. Archer M. Huntington, who was vacationing in the area, did the honors on January 31, 1903.

FRANCIS H. LEGGETT sailed on her maiden voyage for the West Coast on April 30, 1903, with two locomotives and a large shipment of rails aboard but had to return to the shipyard for restowage of this cargo. The ship entered the service of the Hammond Lumber Co. carrying lumber from Washington and Oregon to California ports.

After over ten years of routine service with Hammond, then with the Leggett Steamship Co. and the Hicks-Hauptman Transportation Co., FRANCIS H. LEGGETT was lost in a gale on September 18, 1914, just 60 miles from the mouth of the Columbia River. The seas swept off the ship's cargo hatches and she filled with water and went down with 65 passengers and crew, leaving only two survivors.

GEORGE W. FENWICK
1908

GEORGE W. FENWICK

Hull No: 79
Owner: Hammond Lumber Co.
Launched: October 26, 1907
Delivered: January 28, 1908
Dimensions: 295.75 x 43 x 21 ft
Gross Tonnage: 2,009
Displacement: 4,950 tons
Machinery: Triple Expansion Engine,
  2 Boilers
Horsepower/Speed: 1,350/11.23 Knots
Fate: War Loss, 1942

First of a pair of similar lumber carriers built for two owners, Hull 79, like FRANCIS H. LEGGETT, was built for the Hammond Lumber Co. Miss Mary D. Gatewood, daughter of shipyard naval architect William Gatewood, christened GEORGE W. FENWICK on October 26, 1907. Designed at the shipyard, the FENWICK and her sister NANN SMITH were rather long and narrow, and their hulls resembled those of the sailing lumber schooners which they doubtless replaced.

The new lumber ship was delivered on January 28, 1908, and left the yard with a crew of 26 men, bound for the Pacific Coast. After eight years of service with Hammond and the Fenwick Steamship Co., GEORGE W. FENWICK was sold to a Norwegian owner and sailed under that flag until 1921 with the name TRORBJORG.

Returning to American ownership of the Sudden and Christianson Co., the ship was renamed CATHERINE G. SUDDEN until she was again sold in 1939, this time to a Greek owner. Renamed HELLENIC TRADER, the old lumber carrier enjoyed only a few more years of service before she was torpedoed and sunk in the Red Sea on June 6, 1942.

NANN SMITH
1907

NANN SMITH

Hull No: 80
Owner: C.A. Smith Timber Co.
Launched: October 5, 1907
Delivered: December 12, 1907
Dimensions: 295.75 x 43 x 21 ft
Gross Tonnage: 2,009
Displacement: 4,950 tons
Machinery: Triple Expansion Engine,
    2 Boilers
Horsepower/Speed: 1,350/11.75 knots
Fate: War Loss, 1917

Built for the C.A. Smith Timber Co. of Minneapolis, NANN SMITH was practically identical to GEORGE W. FENWICK and in fact was the first of the two to be launched. One of but a few Newport News-built ships to have a namesake sponsor, the new lumber carrier was launched by little Miss Nann Smith, daughter of the owner's president, on October 5, 1907. Like her sister ship, NANN SMITH was fitted with six 60 ft booms and had three masts and a sailing rig.

The new ship entered the Pacific Coast lumber trade after delivery late in 1907. In March 1909 she passed to the Inter-Ocean Transportation Co. of St. Paul; her home port was officially listed as St. Paul until 1914 when it became Marshfield, OR. In July 1916, NANN SMITH, like her sister ship, was sold to Norwegian owners after having made two trips to Chile to carry nitrate to the United States. Her career under the Norwegian flag was short-lived, for the following spring she was declared a war loss from enemy action.

ADELINE SMITH
1912

ADELINE SMITH

Hull No: 159
Owner: C.A. Smith Timber Co.
Launched: October 26, 1912
Delivered: November 27, 1912
Dimensions: 310.5 x 44.5 x 21.5 ft
Gross Tonnage: 2,168
Displacement: 5,375 tons
Machinery: Triple Expansion Engine,
    4 Boilers
Horsepower/Speed: 1,800/11 knots
Fate: Scrapped, 1949

Last of the Newport News-built lumber carriers and the largest, ADELINE SMITH was the only one of the four to survive both World Wars. Miss Adeline Smith, who had attended her sister Nann at the launching of NANN SMITH, christened her own ship early on the morning of October 26, 1912.

The new ship left the yard but a month later and sailed for the West Coast after stopping at Sparrows Point, MD, to pick up a consignment of machinery and rails for Marshfield, OR. ADELINE SMITH was in routine lumber service on the Pacific Coast for almost 35 years, first with Smith, then with the Inter-Ocean Transportation Co. In 1917 she was sold to the Dollar Steamship Line and renamed STANLEY DOLLAR. In 1923 she was sold again, to W.R. Chamberlin, and was renamed W.R. CHAMBERLIN, JR. after a major modernization and conversion to oil fuel.

In 1943 she went out of documentation at San Francisco and was requisitioned by the Navy, renamed TACKLE, and converted to a salvage vessel designated ARS-37. She served with the Eighth Fleet between Italy and North Africa until August 1944. She participated in the landings on Southern France in September 1944 and was heavily damaged by a mine but was successfully repaired. She remained in the Mediterranean until returning to Norfolk in May 1945, having received two battle stars for her wartime service.

Declared unfit for further service, TACKLE was decommissioned on September 13, 1945, and was struck from the Navy list on October 11. The old ship was laid up by the Maritime Commission until she was sold and scrapped in 1949.

EDWARD PIERCE
1914

EDWARD PIERCE

Hull No: 182
Owner: Crowell & Thurlow Co.
Launched: October 24, 1914
Delivered: November 6, 1914
Dimensions: 375 x 49 x 30 ft
Gross Tonnage: 4,387
Displacement: 9,220 tons
Machinery: Triple Expansion Engine,
    2 Boilers
Horsepower/Speed: 1,700/10 knots
Fate: Scrapped, 1949

The new collier was launched by Miss Mary Bradford Pierce, daughter of the company's president and the ship's namesake, before a large crowd at 12:30 A.M. on October 24, 1914. EDWARD PIERCE was fitted with two large kingposts and eight 5-ton booms for unloading coal, and her appearance was similar to that of a tanker with machinery aft and a midships deckhouse.

She entered service along the East Coast in late 1914 with her home port as Boston and with a crew of 35. After ten years of routine service with Crowell and Thurlow, EDWARD PIERCE was involved in a collision in Boston harbor in 1924 and sank. She was refloated and repaired and in that same year was sold to the Mystic Steamship Co. of Boston.

In 1936 she was sold to the Koppers Coal Co., then in 1941 to Eastern Gas and Fuel Associates. Continuing in routine coastal service with her original machinery, the old ship was finally dismantled in Boston in 1949 after more than 1,000 voyages.

First of four identical merchant colliers built at Newport News, EDWARD PIERCE and two of her sisters were built for the Crowell and Thurlow Co. of Boston, who also had four cargo ships built at the yard.

WALTER D. NOYES
1915

WALTER D. NOYES
Hull NO: 189
Owner: Crowell & Thurlow Co.
Launched: June 19, 1915
Delivered: July 29, 1915
Dimensions: 375 x 49 x 30 ft
Gross Tonnage: 4,388
Displacement: 9,220 tons
Machinery: Triple Expansion Engine, 2 Boilers
Horsepower/Speed: 1,700/10 knots
Fate: Scrapped, 1951

WALTER D. NOYES, the second of three identical colliers built for the Crowell and Thurlow Co., was launched on June 19, 1915, by Miss Elva S. Noyes, daughter of Walter D. Noyes for whom the ship was named. Delivered only a month later, WALTER D. NOYES began her coasting coal trade which was to make her, like her sisters, a frequent visitor to the coal piers at Newport News and Norfolk.

The new collier survived World War I undamaged, but was involved in a collision with a passenger ship, CITY OF SAVANNAH, near Boston on March 30, 1924. After repair of considerable damage, WALTER D. NOYES returned to regular service. She was sold to the Mystic Steamship Co. in this year, then to the Koppers Coal Co. in 1936. Retaining her original name, she was again sold, in 1936, to Eastern Gas and Fuel Associates of Boston.

After almost 35 years of service as a collier with a crew of 37, the old ship was sold to the Eastern Transportation Co. of Baltimore in 1949 and was cut down to a barge of 4,263 GRT with a crew of nine. Her days in this service were limited, however, and she was scrapped at Baltimore in 1951.

STEPHEN R. JONES
1915

STEPHEN R. JONES
Hull No: 192
Owner: Crowell & Thurlow Co.
Launched: October 23, 1915
Delivered: November 11, 1915
Dimensions: 375 x 49 x 30 ft
Gross Tonnage: 4,388
Displacement: 9,220 tons
Machinery: Triple Expansion Engine, 2 Boilers
Horsepower/Speed: 1,700/10 knots
Fate: Stranded, 1942

Third and last of the Crowell and Thurlow colliers, STEPHEN R. JONES had a collision-prone career, which was to be suddenly ended by a freak accident. Christened and launched from Shipway 7 by Miss Carol Cushman of Boston, STEPHEN R. JONES slid into the James on October 23, 1915.

Only three weeks later the new collier entered service on the coastal run between the Hampton Roads coal terminals and New England ports. Like her sisters, STEPHEN R. JONES was built as a coal burner and had two single ended boilers 15 ft in diameter.

She was acquired by the Navy at Philadephia in May 1918 and was commissioned as a Naval Overseas Transportation Service ship. She made four round trips to France with army supplies before being returned to her owner in March 1919. In 1924 the collier passed to the Mystic Steamship Co., then along with her sisters went to the Koppers Coal Company in 1936.

In the first of several such incidents, she ran aground in October 1929 off Conimicut Point, MA, but was successfully freed. On February 3, 1939, she collided with the Norwegian freighter VITO in New York harbor but suffered only minor damage. She was sold to Eastern Gas and Fuel Associates in 1941.

Another collision on June 28, 1942, proved fatal, as STEPHEN R. JONES collided with the granite left bank of the Cape Cod Canal near Bourne, MA, and settled on her side, closing the canal. Since the canal was a vital inland route for war traffic, it was decided to demolish the wreck by blowing it down with explosives, and the Navy completed this task on July 31, 1942.

MUNALBRO
1916

MUNALBRO

Hull No: 194
Owner: Munson Steamship Co.
Launched: May 6, 1916
Delivered: May 25, 1916
Dimensions: 375 x 49 x 30 ft
Gross Tonnage: 4,293
Displacement: 9,220 tons
Machinery: Triple Expansion Engine,
    2 Boilers
Horsepower/Speed: 1,700/10 knots
Fate: Scrapped, 1954

The collier MUNALBRO was identical to the three built for Crowell and Thurlow in 1914 and 1915 except that she was fitted with twelve 5-ton booms and a 30 ton boom. MUNALBRO was built for the Munson Steamship Line of New York, which shortly afterward ordered three cargo ships from the shipyard. MUNALBRO was launched by Mrs. H.A. Bromell, wife of the vice president of the owning company, on May 6,

1916, and began what was to be the longest career of the four colliers on May 25, 1916.

Her ownership passed several times between Munson and Munalbro Steamship Corp., which was created by Munson as her owning company. She was acquired from Munson by the Navy in September 1918 and made two convoy trips to France with army supplies.

Decommissioned in March 1919, MUNALBRO was returned to her owners to complete what was to be a 20-year career with them. Renamed JAMES L. RICHARDS in 1936, she joined her Newport News-built sisters with the Koppers Coal Co., then passed to Eastern Gas and Fuel Associates with them in 1941.

Surviving the war, she was transferred to the U.S. Maritime Commission in 1946. In 1948 she reappeared in the registers cut down to a barge of 4,281 GRT and a crew of ten, owned by L. Edward Hooper of Norfolk. In 1950 she was sold to Waterways Transportation Co. of Baltimore, then in 1951 to Coastwise Transportation Line of New York. She was finally scrapped at New York in 1954.

FERRIES
BINGHAMTON
1905

BINGHAMTON

Hull No: 49
Owner: Hoboken Ferry Co.
Launched: February 20, 1905
Delivered: March 25, 1905
Dimensions: 231 x 43.25 x 18 ft
Gross Tonnage: 1,462
Displacement: 1,050 tons
Machinery: Compound Engines,
    2 Boilers, Double-Ended
Horsepower/Speed: 1,400/12 knots
Fate: Restaurant, 1975

The third of five boats built for the Hoboken ferry was launched by Miss Charlotte Emery, daughter of the Hoboken chief engineer. BINGHAMTON's career was more eventful than her two predecessors, and she outlasted the entire fleet. On the night of August 7, 1905, she caught fire at the Hoboken terminal and was badly damaged but was saved and repaired. A sister ferry, HOPATCONG was lost in the same fire. In November 1912 BINGHAMTON's whistle stuck as she was leaving her slip, and she was struck by both a steamboat and a car float and was slightly damaged.

After 64 years of service, BINGHAMTON was sold in 1969 for use as a floating restaurant and bar. Ferry Binghamton, Inc. bought her in 1974 and opened her as Binghamton's in 1975 at Edgewater, NJ. Later placed on the National Register of Historic Places, she remained in this "service" as a nostalgic reminder of bygone days on the Hudson.

SCRANTON
1905

SCRANTON
Hull No: 47
Owner: Hoboken Ferry Co.
Launched: October 29, 1904
Delivered: January 31, 1905
Dimensions: 231 x 43.25 x 18 ft
Gross Tonnage: 1,462
Displacement: 1,050 tons
Machinery: Compound Engines,
2 Boilers, Double-Ended
Horsepower/Speed: 1,400/12 knots
Fate: Sank, 1968

SCRANTON was the first of five practically identical ferries built for the Hoboken Ferry Co. Built of steel, she was the first spoon-bow type ferry and was the model for all ferries subsequently built for her owner. It is unclear who was asked to launch SCRANTON, but Miss Mary E. Johnson may have christened her on October 29, 1904.

SCRANTON served on the Manhattan to Hoboken route in New York Harbor which was run by the Delaware, Lackawanna & Western Railroad. The new ferry settled into an uneventful 60-year career, at first running 24 hours every day. Later, as the bridge and tunnel system expanded in New York, SCRANTON and her sisters were cut back to five 12-hour days. By 1967 only two boats were running, and service was stopped soon thereafter.

SCRANTON was sold for use as an exhibit hall, but broke her moorings in a storm in 1968 and sank off Pier 16, Hoboken. Unsuccessful attempts were made to raise her, and she was subsequently scrapped in place.

ELMIRA
1905

ELMIRA
Hull No: 48
Owner: Hoboken Ferry Co.
Launched: January 5, 1905
Delivered: February 24, 1905
Dimensions: 231 x 43.25 x 18 ft
Gross Tonnage: 1,462
Displacement: 1,050 tons
Machinery: Compound Engines,
2 Boilers, Double-Ended
Horsepower/Speed: 1,400/12 knots
Fate: Scrapped, 1983

ELMIRA, identical to SCRANTON, was launched on January 5, 1905, possibly by Miss Mary E. Johnson. The new ferry began her long and monotonous service in early March 1905. The New York and Hoboken Ferry Co. had been bought by the Delaware, Lackawanna & Western Railroad Co. in 1903 and had its origins with John Stevens' steam launch of 1804.

ELMIRA enjoyed over 60 years of service on the Hoboken route and, like her sisters, retained her original machinery throughout her career. On November 22, 1967, ELMIRA left New York with a load of commuters on the last run of the Hoboken Ferry, amid fanfare and nostalgia. She was sold in 1968 to E.O. Wickberg of Perth Amboy, NJ, for use as a floating restaurant and bar, but the plan was disapproved by the city fathers, and the old ferry was permanently laid up in 1971 and was again put up for sale. In the summer of 1983, she was sold to Witte's Salvage and was broken up at their scrap yard at Rossville, Staten Island.

SCANDINAVIA
1905

SCANDINAVIA
Hull No: 50
Owner: Hoboken Ferry Co.
Launched: March 11, 1905
Delivered: April 24, 1905
Dimensions: 231 x 43.25 x 18 ft
Gross Tonnage: 1,462
Displacement: 1,050 tons
Machinery: Compound Engines,
2 Boilers, Double-Ended
Horsepower/Speed: 1,400/12 knots
Fate: Scrapped, 1967

Last of the first four boats which had been ordered by Hoboken Ferry Co. in March 1904, SCANDINAVIA entered service in May 1905. The name of her sponsor is not known and her early service was apparently uneventful. Like her sisters, she was designed by Gardner & Cox of New York and was provided with handsome cabins with 408 seats on main deck and 578 on the upper deck. In 1936 her name was changed to POCONO. A year before, the Hoboken Ferry Co. had raised its fare to a nickel to quiet numerous complaints from passengers weary of having to find four coins to pay the four cent fare. With the end of service in 1967, POCONO was laid up at Witte's and was eventually scrapped.

ITHACA
1906

ITHACA

Hull No: 62
Owner: Delaware, Lackawanna & W.R.R.
Launched: June 16, 1906
Delivered: September 9, 1906
Dimensions: 232 x 43.25 x 18 ft
Gross Tonnage: 1,462
Displacement: 1,015 tons
Machinery: Compound Engines,
    2 Boilers, Double-Ended
Horsepower/Speed: 1,400/12 knots
Fate: Burned, 1946

A fifth ferry was ordered in November 1905 for service on the Hoboken to Manhattan run. ITHACA was launched by Miss Ruth Werner of New York. During her trip from Newport News, ITHACA got in a race from the Narrows to Manhattan with the Staten Island ferry BROOKLYN; the winner is unknown. On St. Patrick's Day in 1914, ITHACA collided with a car float of the CRRNJ. A freight car on the float crashed through the cabin of the ferry and killed three men and injured four. ITHACA once carried a broom at her masthead as the fastest boat in the Hoboken Ferry fleet after she won a 134 mile race from Hoboken to Newburgh, NJ, on October 1, 1909.

While in drydock at West Brighton, Staten Island, on August 11, 1946, ITHACA was almost completely destroyed by fire. She was tied up for about a year and was subsequently scrapped.

TUGBOATS
DOROTHY
1891

DOROTHY

Hull No: 1
Owner: James Sheffield
Launched: December 17, 1890
Delivered: April 30, 1891
Dimensions: 90 x 19 x 10.75 ft
Gross Tonnage: 130
Displacement: 180 tons
Machinery: Quadruple Expansion Engine,
   1 Boiler
Horsepower/Speed: 250/10 knots
Fate: Restored, 1976

Named for the daughter of William C. Whitney, DOROTHY was sponsored by Miss Etta Koninsky. The shipyard's first vessel, the tug was built for James Sheffield for railroad towing service in New York's East River and Hell Gate with the New York & Northern Railway Co. Designed by Horace See, DOROTHY was considered innovative and powerful in 1891, and she was the first tug ever fitted with a quadruple expansion engine.

In 1893 her owner was absorbed by the New York Central, and in 1900 she was renamed NEW YORK CENTRAL NO. 3. In 1912 she was sold to Joseph M. Clark of Norfolk and was renamed J. ALVAH CLARK. She worked under this name towing barges up and down the Chesapeake Bay and the East Coast for over 50 years under various owners including the Clark, Wood, Norfolk Lighterage, and Curtis Bay Towing Cos.

She joined the Navy in October 1917 and performed tug and towing duties in Hampton Roads, served on net patrol, and transported guards to merchant vessels under the designation SP-1248 until she was sold back to Clark in July 1919. She was dieselized in 1936 and was fitted with a steel "coffin hull" in 1946. In 1962 she was sold to Jesse Simpkins and renamed JESSE JR.; then, in 1963 she was sold to R.K. Davis and renamed JANET S.

In 1964 her machinery was damaged in a minor accident and her towing career came to an end. She was laid up and sank, but in 1974 she was salvaged and sold back to her builder. In 1976 she was restored to her original appearance and was placed on display as a tribute to Newport News shipbuilders.

EL TORO
1891

EL TORO

Hull No: 2
Owner: Pacific Improvement Co.
Launched: January 12, 1891
Delivered: May 20, 1891
Dimensions: 90 x 19 x 10.75 ft
Gross Tonnage: 130
Displacement: 180
Machinery: Quadruple Expansion Engine,
   1 Boiler
Horsepower/Speed: 250/10 knots
Fate: Scrapped, 1982

Ordered for service as a tug and fireboat at the Morgan Line's Hudson River pier, Hull No. 2 was christened by Miss Margaret Seidler on January 12, 1891. EL TORO was identical to her sister DOROTHY except for her colors, stack, and gilded bull's head atop her pilothouse.

After seven years of New York service, EL TORO was purchased by the Navy, renamed ACCOMAC, and sent to Key West for harbor tug and dispatch boat service during the Spanish-American War. It is said that during the war she gallantly captured three Spanish schooners and put prize crews aboard. After brief harbor service at Havana, she served as a yard tug at Pensacola. She was assigned to service at the Boston Navy Yard in 1911, renamed NOTTOWAY in 1918, then was designated YT-18 in 1920.

In 1947 she was sold to Arthur W. Hall of Boston who renamed her EL TORO; then, in 1949 she was sold to the Norfolk Dredging Co. and returned to her home state. She was dieselized and renamed VIRGINIA in 1950.

In 1960 she sank at her pier during a hurricane and was sold to Harbor Towing Co. of Baltimore. She was then repowered and modernized and was placed back into towing service. In January 1976 she again sank at her pier. She was subsequently sold to Jesse Simpkins, renamed WA HOO, and laid up in Norfolk. Her engine and towing bitts were removed, and she lay derelict at Simpkins yard until she was scrapped in November 1982.

JOHN H. ESTILL
1894

JOHN H. ESTILL

Hull No: 12
Owner: Savannah Pilots Assn.
Launched: September 18, 1894
Delivered: November 25, 1894
Dimensions: 130 x 23 x 13.5 ft
Gross Tonnage: 243
Displacement: 335 tons
Machinery: Compound Engine, 1 Boiler
Horsepower/Speed: 710/14 knots
Fate: Scrapped, 1952

Named for the owner of the *Savannah News*, Hull 12 was sponsored by Miss Helen Thompson on September 18, 1894. JOHN E. ESTILL was one of the earliest steel steam pilot boats, called "finest in the country" when many pilot boats were still under sail. True to this tradition, she was built with a sailing rig, in addition to her engine, but the sailing rig was removed by 1912. She was the longest tug or pilot boat ever built at Newport News and was the only one built at a profit among the early boats.

She served in Savannah Harbor until 1915 when she was sold to Henry J. Schutte and placed in towing service at Galveston under the name LEOPOLD ADLER. In 1924 she was sold to the Wilmington Towing Co. (NC) and was renamed MARY COLLINS; then, in 1925 her name again became LEOPOLD ADLER. From 1930 to 1951 she was owned by R.R. Stone of Wilmington and was engaged in towing service. After 58 years of service with her original engine, the old boat was sold to W.S. Sanders of Norfolk in 1952 and was dismantled for scrap.

ALBERT F. DEWEY
1895

ALBERT F. DEWEY

Hull No: 13
Owner: Albert F. Dewey
Launched: January 31, 1895
Delivered: April 15, 1895
Dimensions: 95 x 19 x 9.5 ft
Gross Tonnage: 134
Displacement: 239 tons
Machinery: Triple Expansion Engine,
   1 Boiler
Horsepower/Speed: 257/abt.10 knots
Fate: Unknown

Launched by Miss Louise Parker of Newport News, Hull 13 was named for her owner who ordered her for towing service with the Charlotte Harbor Lighterage and Stevedore Co. of Punta Gorda, FL. She was fairly typical of her type, except that she sported a gilded stag on her pilothouse top instead of the more traditional eagle.

She served in Florida waters until 1905, then was sold to the U.S. Army Engineers and renamed C. DONOVAN. She worked in the New Orleans and Galveston engineer district until 1936 when she was sold to Jahncke Service Corp. of New Orleans and renamed ALBERT F. DEWEY. In June 1941 she was sold to the Minder Construction Corp. for use in a national defense project in the West Indies.

On her trip from New Orleans to St. Lucia for this service, she experienced a hectic voyage which her crew attributed to the "unlucky 13." The 45 year old tug was evidently in unseaworthy condition, and after several days of severe weather her crew abandoned her at Antilla, Cuba. They claimed "there were 13 of us in the crew, we sailed 13 days after signing on, the captain's birthday came on the 13th of July, the boat's hull has the number 13 on it, and the letter M on the funnel is the 13th letter in the alphabet." Records indicate that she eventually reached her destination and was sold back to the Engineers on July 9, 1941, but details of her final disposition are incomplete.

SOMMERS N. SMITH
1896

SOMMERS N. SMITH

Hull No: 17
Owner: Pilots' Benevolent Assn.
Launched: May 30, 1896
Delivered: September 14, 1896
Dimensions: 118 x 21 x 15 ft
Gross Tonnage: 211
Displacement: 311 tons
Machinery: Compound Engine, 1 Boiler
Horsepower/Speed: 400/12 knots
Fate: Scrapped, 1937

Suffering the most inauspicious beginning of any Newport News-built ship, Hull 17 slipped in her launching cradle immediately after launch, took on water through open portholes, and sank. She was later raised undamaged and was completed. SOMMERS N. SMITH was named for the general superintendent of the shipyard, and these events must have been a great source of embarrassment to him. She was built as a pilot boat and was sponsored by Mrs. Henry B. Plant, wife of the president of her owners. Notwithstanding her ungainly launch, SOMMERS N. SMITH had a graceful hull, reminiscent of a sailing pilot boat, and in fact she was rigged for sailing.

She served as a pilot boat at Pensacola until 1899 when she was sold to William J. Minford of Philadelphia and put into towing service. In 1912 she was sold to Charles E. Davis of that port; then, in 1915 she was sold to the Eastern Transportation Co. of Wilmington (DL) and renamed EASTERN. She served with Eastern in general towing service along the East and Gulf coasts until she was scrapped in 1937.

EL AMIGO
1899

EL AMIGO

Hull No: 30
Owner: Southern Pacific Co.
Launched: June 24, 1899
Delivered: September 9, 1899
Dimensions: 100 x 22 x 12 ft
Gross Tonnage: 150
Displacement: 234 tons
Machinery: Compound Engine, 1 Boiler
Horsepower/Speed: 522/10.4 knots
Fate: Scrapped, 1950

EL AMIGO was ordered for Morgan Line Service to replace EL TORO, which had been sold to the Navy. She was slightly larger than her predecessor, but her engine was more than twice as powerful. Hull 30 was launched by Miss Emma Rowbottom, daughter of the superintendent of machinery at the yard, on June 24, 1899. EL AMIGO served her owner at their Hudson River pier in New York for over 30 years, then in 1931 was sold to M & J Tracy and renamed ANN MARIE TRACY. Under this name she worked at general harbor towing service with Tracy for 17 years.

Early in the morning of October 2, 1948, she collided with the Liberty tanker ELIZA JANE NICHOLSON off Pier 64 in the Hudson River and sank with nine of her crew. A Coast Guard inquiry later placed the blame for the collision on lack of good judgment by the pilots of both vessels, and the pilot of the tanker was charged with negligence. ANN MARIE TRACY was raised on October 4, 1948, and was laid up. She was finally scrapped in 1950.

BATH
1908

BATH

Hull No: 84
Owner: Delaware, Lackawanna & W.R.R.
Launched: January 18, 1908
Delivered: April 9, 1908
Dimensions: 101 x 25 x 13 ft
Gross Tonnage: 204
Displacement: 381 tons
Machinery: Compound Engine, 1 Boiler
Horsepower/Speed: 600/abt.10 knots
Fate: In Service

Launched from an adjacent shipway shortly before her sister CORNING, Hull 84 was probably christened by Miss Coley, who accompanied the owner's representative. Like her sister tug, BATH worked in railroad service in New York Harbor with her original owner until 1957. A handsome portrait of her was done by the painter Jacobsen in 1918.

In 1958 she was sold to Portsmouth Navigation Co. of Portsmouth, NH, and shortly thereafter, her old steam engine was replaced with an 1,800 horsepower diesel. Her harbor tug service at Portsmouth consisted of docking and undocking ships at that port and at the naval shipyard there. Her owner was affiliated with the Moran Towing and Transportation Co., and she continued in service at Portsmouth into the 1980s under her original name.

CORNING
1908

CORNING
Hull No: 83
Owner: Delaware, Lackawanna & W.R.R.
Launched: January 18, 1908
Delivered: March 18, 1908
Dimensions: 101 x 25 x 13 ft
Gross Tonnage: 204
Displacement: 381 tons
Machinery: Compound Engine, 1 Boiler
Horsepower/Speed: 600/abt. 10 knots
Fate: Laid Up, 1985

CORNING and her sister BATH were the hardiest of the Newport News built tugs, and both remained in service into the 1980s. CORNING was launched by either the owner's representative Captain Emery or by Miss Coley, who accompanied him to Newport News. It is generally believed that she launched one of the tugs, as both were launched on the same day. CORNING was launched without incident about 20 minutes after BATH at 10:20 A.M. on January 18, 1908.

The tug was delivered two months after launch and went into railroad tug service in New York harbor. She remained in this service until 1958 when she was sold to the Peninsula Towing Co. of Florida. She was dieselized and in 1960 passed to Capital Towing of Port Everglades and Baton Rouge. After service as a docking tug and in towing work on the Mississippi, she was sold to Westlake Marine Corp. of Lake Charles, LA, in 1977. She was again sold, to Bisso Towboat Co. of New Orleans, in 1979 and remained in service under the name BISSO. Relegated mainly to standby service, she was laid up and stripped in 1985 in preparation for her planned scrapping in 1986.

P.R.R. NO. 26
1925

P.R.R. NO. 26
Hull No: 295
Owner: Pennsylvania Railroad Co.
Launched: October 31, 1925
Delivered: November 19, 1925
Dimensions: 105.18 x 24 x 13.5 ft
Gross Tonnage: 186
Displacement: Abt. 360 tons
Machinery: Diesel-Electric
Horsepower/Speed: 750/abt. 10 knots
Fate: Sunk, 1982

Sister of Hull 294, P.R.R. NO. 26 was launched at 8:35 A.M. on the same day and was delivered on November 19, 1925. She had no sponsor and, like her sister, was delivered without machinery. Both of the tugs were similar in design to other tugs in the Pennsylvania fleet, and both featured the tall pilot-houses with many windows characteristic of railroad tugs.

Along with her sister, P.R.R. NO. 26 served the Pennsylvania until its demise in the late 1960s. Her ungraceful name was changed to ELMIRA in 1930 and her career was uneventful. She was laid up in a scrapyard in Jersey City until at least 1972, then was sold to Henry W. McDowell of Savannah. McDowell also bought DETROIT, which was of similar design and was built in 1924 in Mariner's Harbor, New York. Neither boat ever returned to active service, and ELMIRA was reportedly towed offshore and sunk as a reef in 1982.

P.R.R. NO. 20
1926

P.R.R. NO. 20
Hull No: 314
Owner: Pennsylvania Railroad Co.
Launched: May 20, 1926
Delivered: May 30, 1926
Dimensions: 80 x 19 x 12.5 ft
Gross Tonnage: 95
Displacement: Abt. 200 tons
Machinery: Diesel-Electric, Double-Ended
Horsepower/Speed: 250/abt. 10 knots
Fate: Scrapped, 1976

Identical to her sister, P.R.R. NO. 20 was launched from the same shipway 20 minutes later at 4:02 P.M. on May 20, 1926, without benefit of a formal cermony or sponsor. It was said around the harbor that these boats "didn't know whether they were comin' or goin'" because of their double-ended design. In 1930 her name became COLOMBUS, and she served with the Pennsylvania in New York until going out of documentation in February 1970. She was laid up, then was reportedly scrapped at Witte's Salvage at Rossville, in 1976.

JOHN TWOHY, JR.
1909

JOHN TWOHY, JR.

Hull No: 118
Owner: Twohy Tow Boat Co.
Launched: April 10, 1909
Delivered: May 15, 1909
Dimensions: 103.5 x 23.5 x 11.33 ft
Gross Tonnage: 133
Displacement: 270 tons
Machinery: Compound Engine, 1 Boiler
Horsepower/Speed: 250/abt.10 knots
Fate: Scrapped, 1970

Her owner, also known as the Lambert's Point Tow Boat Co., ordered JOHN TWOHY, JR. for service in the Hampton Roads area. She was named for and christened by the small son of the owner's president who was one of but two male sponsors of Newport News ships (the other was for Hull 190). JOHN TWOHY, JR. had another distinction in that she was the only wooden vessel ever built at the yard. The tug was built under an informal agreement with Captain Twohy: part of this was that she would be fitted with a new boiler and an engine removed from another tug. The new tug served in harbor and general towing service until she was sold to McAllister Brothers in 1911 and renamed J.P. McALLISTER.

After working for McAllister in the New York area for many years, a fire started aboard her during the night of May 18, 1934, and she burned without loss of life. The three barges which she had been towing were saved and her hulk was towed to Gravesend Bay and beached. Just four months later another Newport News ship, the MORRO CASTLE (Hull 337), was lost in the most famous of shipboard fires but a few miles to the south.

J.P. McALLISTER was salvaged and rebuilt and went back to work in 1944 with a new 600 IHP steam engine. She served McAllister faithfully until she was laid up in the mid-1960s and scrapped in 1970.

P.R.R. NO. 18
1925

P.R.R. NO. 18

Hull No: 294
Owner: Pennsylvania Railroad Co.
Launched: October 31, 1925
Delivered: November 11, 1925
Dimensions: 105.18 x 24 x 13.5 ft.
Gross Tonnage: 186
Displacement: Abt. 360 tons
Machinery: Diesel-Electric
Horsepower/Speed: 750/abt.10 knots
Fate: Scrapped, 1970

With her sister P.R.R. NO. 26, P.R.R. No. 18 was ordered for service with one of the largest tug fleets in New York Harbor. They were ordered and built as hulls only, and their engines were installed by their owner after delivery. They were similar in design to P.R.R. NO. 16, which had been placed in service in 1924 and was claimed to be the first diesel-electric tug ever built. The new tugs were launched together without sponsors and P.R.R. NO. 18 slid down the ways at 8:02 A.M. on October 31, 1925.

After being towed to her owner's yard at Hoboken, NJ, the tug was fitted with machinery and placed into service. Built during the transition of tugs from steam to diesel power, these new tugs nonetheless, retained the tall stacks more characteristic of steamers as this gave them a more powerful appearance.

P.R.R. NO. 18 served her owners faithfully and uneventfully for over 40 years with her original engine. Her name became FORT WAYNE in 1930. In the late 1960s with the breakup of the Pennsylvania Railroad (then Penn Central), FORT WAYNE was laid up and went out of documentation. She reportedly sank at Jersey City, then was raised and scrapped there in 1970.

P.R.R. NO. 15
1926

P.R.R. NO. 15

Hull No: 313
Owner: Pennsylvania Railroad Co.
Launched: May 20, 1926
Delivered: May 30, 1926
Dimensions: 80 x 19 x 12.5 ft
Gross Tonnage: 95
Displacement: Abt. 200 tons
Machinery: Diesel-Electric, Double-Ended
Horsepower/Speed: 250/abt. 10 knots
Fate: Scrapped, 1972

P.R.R. NO. 15 and her sister P.R.R. NO. 20 were launched without sponsors and were delivered together without machinery a week later. They were most unusual as they were double-enders with propellers and rudders on either end, and they were not fitted with stacks. Their former owners recall that their design was intended to allow them to reverse easily, and their small size made them ideal for service as drill tugs, able to move in and out among congested piers. P.R.R. NO. 15 was given the name TOLEDO in 1930 and served the Pennsylvania until being removed from documentation in February 1972. She was laid up and then scrapped at Jersey City after almost 50 years of service to her original owner.

W.J. HARAHAN
1928

W.J. HARAHAN

Hull No: 327
Owner: Chesapeake & Ohio Railway
Launched: March 31, 1928
Delivered: April 26, 1928
Dimensions: 109.5 x 28 x 14.5 ft
Gross Tonnage: 266
Displacement: 485 tons
Machinery: Compound Engine, 1 Boiler
Horsepower/Speed: 800/10 knots
Fate: In Service

W.J. HARAHAN, first of five identical steam tugs built for the C & O, was floated from Shipway 8 at 1:30 P.M. on March 31, 1928, without a sponsor. The tug was the first steel boat in the C & O fleet and, due to the abundance of coal at her piers, she was a coal-fired steamer. She had a very large boiler (16 ft dia. x 12 ft)

and was the model for future C & O tugs.

She served at Newport News until 1941 when she was comandeered for war service under Lend-Lease and went to Britain. She served the British Ministry of War Transport handling vessels in the English Channel during the war. In 1945 she was returned to the U.S. Government and placed in service at the Maritime Administration's Hudson River Reserve Fleet.

In 1949 the tug was sold to McAllister Brothers and was renamed MARGARET M. McALLISTER. She served in New York for two years and in 1951 was placed in service with McAllister in Norfolk. She also served in Philadelphia, and in 1957 she entered McAllister's shipyard, and her steam machinery was replaced with a Cleveland 1,750 BHP diesel. Hull modifications at this time included replacement of her stack and mast and removal of the after ten feet of her deckhouse. After conversion she continued in yeoman service in New York Harbor into the mid-1980s.

GEORGE W. STEVENS
1937

GEORGE W. STEVENS

Hull No: 365
Owner: Chesapeake & Ohio Railway
Launched: September 8, 1937
Delivered: October 14, 1937
Dimensions: 109.5 x 28 x 14.5 ft
Gross Tonnage: 262
Displacement: 504 tons
Machinery: Compound Engine, 1 Boiler
Horsepower/Speed: 800/10 knots
Fate: In Service

GEORGE W. STEVENS was ordered by the C & O in 1937 to replace a slightly smaller wooden tug of the same name. Both tugs were named after a former president of the railroad as was C & O practice. The new tug was identical in design to W.J. HARAHAN built nine years earlier, and she had a coal-fired steam plant like all C & O tugs built before the 1950s. These tugs were fitted with fire fighting nozzles and featured one atop the deckhouse aft, useful for fighting fires under the railroad's piers. The GEORGE W. STEVENS worked for the C & O at Newport News for over 30 years, docking and undocking coal and cargo ships and towing car floats and barges across Hampton Roads. Over the years the C & O tugs were occasionally called into service to help the shipyard tugs with a big job.

In the late 1960s the C & O steam fleet began to be replaced with more modern diesel tugs. In July 1968 GEORGE W. STEVENS was sold to Albert W. Pelligrini and was placed under Panamanian flag. She was apparently converted to diesel power and reportedly remained in service into the 1980s.

F.M. WHITAKER
1937

F.M. WHITAKER

Hull No: 366
Owner: Chesapeake & Ohio Railway
Launched: September 8, 1937
Delivered: October 29, 1937
Dimensions: 109.5 x 28 x 14.5 ft
Gross Tonnage: 267
Displacement: 511 tons
Machinery: Compound Engine, 1 Boiler
Horsepower/Speed: 800/10 knots
Fate: In Service

Launched without ceremony on the same day as her sister, F.M. WHITAKER also replaced an older wooden tug. She also followed the design of W.J. HARAHAN, and her superstructures were painted the bright orange of the C & O passenger coaches; the orange was used on the railroad's tugs until the early 1950s. Large portholes below the pilothouse gave light to the galley and messroom forward in the main deckhouse, and the tall stack gave F.M. WHITAKER and her sisters a powerful appearance. Typical of railroad tugs, the tall pilothouse had generously sized windows all around.

F.M. WHITAKER also served the C & O for over 30 years at Newport News. In the early 1950s, in addition to a new color scheme, most of the tugs were converted to liquid fuel and their stacks were somewhat shortened. In 1966 F.M. WHITAKER was sold to the Florida Towing Co. of Jacksonville and took up harbor service there. Her new owners found her steam machinery useful because its steam was available to other vessels.

After years of this service, F.M. WHITAKER went out of documentation and was laid up at Jacksonville. In 1981 she was redocumented at New Orleans under the ownership of E.N. Bisso and Son and was renamed GLADYS B. Dieselized, she remained in service into the mid-1980s.

HUNTINGTON
1933

HUNTINGTON

Hull No: 356
Owner: Newport News Shipbuilding
Launched: October 11, 1933
Delivered: November 18, 1933
Dimensions: 109 x 29 x 14.5 ft
Gross Tonnage: 271
Displacement: 489 tons
Machinery: Compound Engine, 1 Boiler
Horsepower/Speed: 800/10 knots
Fate: In Service

As much a part of the shipyard scene as Dry Dock No. 1, HUNTINGTON served her builders faithfully for over 50 years. Although official records indicate that the tug was launched without a sponsor, it is generally believed that Anne Ferguson, granddaughter of shipyard president Homer L. Ferguson, did the honors.

HUNTINGTON was similar in design to W.J. HARAHAN, except that she was built one foot broader in the beam. In 1950 her steam engine was replaced with an 800 BHP diesel, and in the 1970s her traditional brown and black colors with bright brasswork were painted blue and white. In later years she was considered underpowered and there was some talk of selling her.

She was mostly relegated to standby service for her newer and more powerful sister JOHN P. DIESEL. She brushed against some of the world's most famous hulls in her lifetime and was the tug sent to bring DOROTHY home in 1974. She continued as a waterfront tradition in the 1980s and hoped for many more years of service with her builder.

R.J. BOWMAN
1948

R.J. BOWMAN

Hull No: 467
Owner: Chesapeake & Ohio Railway
Launched: February 26, 1948
Delivered: July 2, 1948
Dimensions: 109.5 x 28 x 14.5 ft
Gross Tonnage: 260
Displacement: 504 tons
Machinery: Compound Engine, 1 Boiler
Horsepower/Speed: 800/10 knots
Fate: Sank, 1981

Last tug delivered by the shipyard, R.J. BOWMAN was delivered a week after her sister A.T. LOWMASTER. Named after a former vice president of the C & O, she was built at a time of C & O expansion during a boom in the coal exporting business. R.J.

BOWMAN and her sister were an anachronism, in that they were built as coal-fired steamers 20 years after diesel engines became standard for tugs. The C & O always operated steam tugs until its merger with the B & O in the mid-1960s. R.J. BOWMAN was the last C & O tug to be converted to oil fuel and she was the last of the four Newport News-built tugs still in C & O service to be sold.

Also, the last steam tug in operation in Hampton Roads, she spent her final years in standby service there, then was sold to Ross Towboat Co. of Boston. She was moved to Boston and was laid up there, going out of documentation in 1973. In the spring of 1980 the Ross fleet was sold to Boston Fuel Transportation Inc., but R.J. BOWMAN was not part of the deal and was retained by former Ross owner Mary DeVeau. Laid up and deteoriating at a ramshackle East Boston pier, the old tug was sunk by vandals on August 1, 1981.

A.T. LOWMASTER
1948

A.T. LOWMASTER

Hull No: 468
Owner: Chesapeake & Ohio Railway
Launched: February 26, 1948
Delivered: June 25, 1948
Dimensions: 109.5 x 28 x 14.5 ft
Gross Tonnage: 260
Displacement: 504 tons
Machinery: Compound Engine, 1 Boiler
Horsepower/Speed: 800/10 knots
Fate: In Service

Ordered by the C & O during a very lean time for the shipyard, A.T. LOWMASTER and R.J. BOWMAN were probably the last steam tugs ever built in the U.S. A.T. LOWMASTER was named for a former president of the railroad, and she and her sister were built and floated off Shipway 8 together without ceremony on February 26, 1948. The new tugs were the last of six of a class which began with W.J. HARAHAN, and they were also fitted with 20″ x 44″/30″ engines and with large boilers measuring 16 ft in diameter and 12 ft long. They were built for coal fuel but were converted to oil around 1950. It is widely remembered that there were problems with the engines on trials, possibly since they were the first ones built at the shipyard since 1938.

A.T. LOWMASTER stayed in the service of the C & O at Newport News until 1968 when she was replaced with a diesel tug and was sold to Edward W. Sanchez of New Bedford, MA. Her steam engine was replaced with a 2,000 BHP diesel, and she served with the Red Star Towing Co. at New Haven, CT. In 1976 she was sold again, this time to Great Lakes Barge, Ltd. of Sault St. Marie, Canada. She remained in service in Canadian waters into the mid-1980s under the name WILFRED M. COHEN.

YACHTS
DOLPHIN
1922

DOLPHIN

Hull No: 263
Owner: Mortimer L. Schiff
Launched: April 8, 1922
Delivered: June 2, 1922
Dimensions: 180.82 x 24 x 14.17 ft
Gross Tonnage: 496
Displacement: 493 tons
Machinery: Diesels, Twin Screw
Horsepower/Speed: 1,100/14.75 knots
Fate: Stranded, 1960

A contract for the yacht DOLPHIN was obtained in October 1921 in a market devoid of larger merchant shipbuilding contracts. DOLPHIN was ordered by banker Mortimer L. Schiff, who was a member of the New York Yacht Club and a founder of the Boy Scouts of America. The new yacht was launched on April 8, 1922, by Miss Alice L. Cox, Mr. Schiff's niece.

Having completed outfitting, the sleek new yacht with her crew of 21 left Newport News just two months after launch, bound for her owner's home at Oyster Bay, L.I., New York. Her speed was a respectable 14.75 knots, and she spent six seasons with Mr.

Schiff on Long Island Sound until 1929 when she was replaced with a larger DOLPHIN II.

She was sold to John W. Hubbard of Pittsburgh and renamed RAMONA. After ten years under Mr. Hubbard's ownership, she was sold to a Canadian owner in June 1940 and was armed for war service. During World War II she served the Canadian Navy as the armed yacht LYNX.

She was found to be too old for war service and was sold to W.D. Branson in 1942 for use as a fruit carrier between Mexico and Toronto. She was caught up in a "banana war" trade dispute and sank at her pier in a Caribbean port under mysterious circumstances but was raised and repaired.

Later sold to Cia. Central de Navegation of Honduras, she was renamed ELENA and served them until 1951 when she passed to Samana Lines and was renamed SAMANA QUEEN. Just a year later she was sold to Rican Star Lines of Costa Rica and was renamed RICAN STAR. She kept this name in 1959 when she was sold to Pacific Shipping Co. and was converted to a shrimp carrier under Australian flag. Her long odyssey came to an end on May 24, 1960, when she wrecked off the central Queensland coast and was abandoned as a total loss.

OHIO
1922

OHIO

Hull No: 265
Owner: Edward W. Scripps
Launched: September 16, 1922
Delivered: November 16, 1922
Dimensions: 172 x 26 x 15.58 ft
Gross Tonnage: 514
Displacement: 641 tons
Machinery: Diesels, Twin Screw
Horsepower/Speed: 700/12.5 knots
Fate: Stranded, 1953

Motor yacht OHIO was ordered by journalist Edward W. Scripps of Cincinnati and was christened by Miss Isabel Ferguson, daughter of shipyard president Homer L. Ferguson. OHIO was designed by the famous New York firm of Cox and Stevens and was built under their supervision. Mr. Scripps traveled widely aboard OHIO and died aboard her in Monrovia

Bay off Liberia on March 12, 1926.

She was renamed MIRAMICHI in 1927 and remained in the Scripps family for another year; then, in 1928 she was sold to Henry Walbridge of New York. Her new owner renamed her WALUCIA III and kept her until 1933 when she was sold to a British owner. She passed to other owners in the 1930s and also carried the names KALLISTO and ENTROPHY.

In 1940 the U.S. Navy bought the yacht EN-TROPHY from Robert V.G. Furman of Schnectady, NY, and classified her as a submarine chaser, PC-459. She was fitted out for Navy service and sent to Caribbean waters. In February 1941 she was reclassified patrol yacht PY-18 and named TURQUOISE. She spent the war in the Caribbean area, never seeing serious action, and was transferred under Lend-Lease to the Equadorian Navy in 1944. She served Equador as NUEVE DE OCTOBRE through 1949, then was formally purchased by that government and renamed ESMERALDAS. In 1953 she ran aground in the Guayas River and was declared a total loss.

NENEMOOSHA
1925

NENEMOOSHA

Hull No: 281
Owner: Alfred I. DuPont
Launched: November 22, 1924
Delivered: February 15, 1925
Dimensions: 130.08 x 22.10 x 11.5 ft
Gross Tonnage: 232
Displacement: 178 tons
Machinery: Diesels, Twin Screw
Horsepower/Speed: 360/12 knots
Fate: Unknown

The smallest of the Newport News-built yachts, NENEMOOSHA was ordered by industrialist and inventor Alfred I. DuPont of the Delaware DuPonts, who was a member of the New York Yacht Club. The yacht was christened by Mrs. DuPont, and on February 15, 1925, left the yard with her crew of seven, bound for her home port of Wilmington, DL.

She served Mr. DuPont along the East Coast and at his estate near Jacksonville, FL. When he died in 1935, she remained in the DuPont family, was re-engined to 800 HP, and served out of Wilmington until 1942. In that year NENEMOOSHA was requisitioned by the War Shipping Administration and served the Maritime Training Service under the name WILLIAM WEBB. She remained a merchant marine training vessel through the war, then was sold to Cala Corp. of Miami. Again under her original name, the yacht was converted for cargo service and sailed under the Philippine flag into the mid 1950s. Registers of shipping do not indicate further service or her ultimate fate.

PAWNEE
1926

PAWNEE

Hull No: 293
Owner: Harry P. Bingham
Launched: November 10, 1925
Delivered: January 15, 1926
Dimensions: 160 x 26.5 x 15.5 ft
Gross Tonnage: 456
Displacement: 655 tons
Machinery: Diesels, Twin Screw
Horsepower/Speed: 900/13.75 knots
Fate: In Service

Motor yacht PAWNEE was built for banker Harry Payne Bingham of New York for an oceanographic research trip to the Gulf of California. She was launched on November 10, 1925, by his daughter Barbara and was delivered just over two months later. Mr. Bingham was an avid sportsman and cruised extensively with his new yacht and its crew of 22.

In 1929 PAWNEE was sold to Mr. Henry D. Lloyd of Boston and Newport and was renamed HARDI BAIOU, replacing a smaller yacht with the same name. She served her new owner in New England waters until 1936 when she was sold to the Virginia Pilot Association and renamed VIRGINIA. She was converted for service as a pilot cutter but retained her outward appearance. She served on permanent station at Cape Henry and was re-engined in 1955.

Active with the VPA until the late 1960s, VIRGINIA was donated to Maryland Sea Service of Baltimore for use in merchant marine training. Continuing through the mid-1970s, she was sold to Jesse Simpkins of Norfolk and remained laid up at his Elizabeth River pier until 1980, when she was "sold South." Leaving Norfolk in January 1981, she was damaged and was abandoned under suspicious circumstances. She was later sold to Edbern Shipping Co. and, homeported at Nassau, Bahamas, continued as an "island hopper" under the name ANDRO.

SAVARONA
1926

SAVARONA

Hull No: 303
Owner: Richard M. Cadwalader
Launched: March 20, 1926
Delivered: October 1, 1926
Dimensions: 185.28 x 27 x 15.67 ft
Gross Tonnage: 559
Displacement: 805 tons
Machinery: Diesels, Twin Screw
Horsepower/Speed: 1,600/16 knots
Fate: Sunk, 1968

Launched with eight other vessels on the biggest launch day in the shipyard's history, SAVARONA was built for Richard M. Cadwalader of Philadelphia to a design of Cox and Stephens. The new yacht was christened by Miss Helen Tyson on March 20, 1926. SAVARONA was designed for relatively high speed and had a great cruising radius of 9,000 miles. She served only a short while with her original owner and was sold first to James Elverson and then to Eugene F. McDonald, founder and president of Zenith Radio Corp. She experienced several changes in name; first to SEQUOIA, then to ALLEGRO, and finally to the biblical MIZPAH, which name she was to retain for almost 40 years.

She cruised around Florida, on the Great Lakes, and on the high seas until she was acquired by the Navy in 1942. She became PY-29 and served first as a convoy escort, then as a training ship, and finally as flagship for Destroyer Force, Atlantic Fleet.

In September 1946 MIZPAH left the Navy, was converted for cargo service, and entered an unlikely new career as a bananna boat trading between Honduras and Tampa. Painted white, she was first owned by Merren Shipping Co. then Hamilton Bros., and she sailed under the Honduran flag.

In October 1967, out of service, she was sold to Eugene Kinney who was a nephew of her former owner E.F. McDonald. Unable to rennovate her as a yacht, Kinney donated her hull for use as a sunken reef, and she was sunk off Palm Beach in April 1968.

ARCADIA
1926

ARCADIA

Hull No: 304
Owner: Galen L. Stone
Launched: April 3, 1926
Delivered: September 1, 1926
Dimensions: 188 x 27.5 x 15.67 ft
Gross Tonnage: 578
Displacement: 733 tons
Machinery: Diesels, Twin Screw
Horsepower/Speed: 1,600/16 knots
Fate: Scrapped, 1969

Motor yacht ARCADIA was ordered by banker Galen L. Stone of Boston in September 1925 at the height of the shipyard's yacht building program. ARCADIA, like several of the other yachts then under construction at the yard, was designed by Cox and Stevens. She was launched by Mrs. Carrie L. Stone, wife of her owner, and was delivered less than five

months later. ARCADIA's service with Mr. Stone was quite brief as he died about four months after she was completed. The still-new yacht passed to Margaret S. Hardwick of Boston and stayed in her service until 1940, cruising between New England and Florida. Documents show that she was on the West Coast at least once, in 1930.

In June 1940 she was sold and went into service as the armed yacht ELK with the Royal Canadian Navy. She served in antisubmarine, convoy, and training duty in both Caribbean and Canadian waters during World War II.

In 1946 she reappeared in the registers as GRAND MANAN III in cargo and passenger service with Saint John Marine Transports Ltd. of Saint John, New Brunswick, Canada. She was still under Canadian flag and had been converted for this service and had new engines. For over 22 years she served as a ferry between Blacks' Harbour, St. John, and Grand Manan. In 1969 the old yacht was dismantled and sold for scrap.

JOSEPHINE
1926

JOSEPHINE

Hull No: 305
Owner: E.S. Burke, Jr.
Launched: March 20, 1926
Delivered: June 19, 1926
Dimensions: 140.25 x 24 x 13.06 ft
Gross Tonnage: 337
Displacement: 400 tons
Machinery: Diesels, Twin Screw
Horsepower/Speed: 450/12.5 knots
Fate: Scrapped, 1952

JOSEPHINE was the first of three yachts launched in the "most unique multiple launching in the noteworthy history of American shipbuilding." Her owner, sportsman and banker Edmund S. Burke, Jr. of Cleveland and New York, ordered this compact but seaworthy yacht to the design of Cox and Stevens. In spite of her size, JOSEPHINE featured all of the luxury of larger yachts, including a library finished in walnut and a living room paneled in teak. Five staterooms were provided for the owner and his guests.

Mrs. Burke (for whom the yacht was named) was to have been the sponsor but records indicate that the Burkes' daughter Patty did the honors shortly after noon on March 20, 1926. The gleaming white yacht was delivered three months after launching and left the yard with a crew of 13.

JOSEPHINE served only two seasons with the Burkes, then was sold to Uzal H. McCarter of New York in September 1927. In June 1932 she was again sold, to Henry B. Plant, and was renamed MASCOTTE. She was home ported in New London but cruised as far south as Miami. In June 1939 MASCOTTE was again sold, this time to L.H. Prichard and C.R. Anthony, then, in April 1940 she was sold for $87,500 to the Canadian government.

She served during World War II with the Royal Canadian Navy as the armed yacht REINDEER. She had a very busy wartime career and engaged in patrol, convoy, and training duty until war's end. In June 1946 she was sold to W.N. MacDonald of Sydney, N.S., and joined his passenger and cargo fleet. Apparently little used, she was reportedly abandoned and scrapped around 1952.

ARAS
1926

ARAS

Hull No: 308
Owner: Hugh J. Chisholm
Launched: March 20, 1926
Delivered: June 11, 1926
Dimensions: 162 x 26 x 14.5 ft
Gross Tonnage: 444
Displacement: 540 tons
Machinery: Diesels, Twin Screw
Horsepower/Speed: 950/13.5 knots
Fate: Sank, 1930

One of the most interesting of the Newport News-built yachts, ARAS was the third and last yacht launched on March 20, 1926. She was christened by the wife of her owner, wood pulp magnate Hugh J. Chisholm of New York and Portland, ME. She was designed for cruising with a family including small children and had a cheerful children's room on her main deck. Five staterooms and five baths were provided and a double bottom was fitted, which was unusual protection for a yacht.

ARAS served the Chisholms until March 1930 when she was sold and replaced by a much larger vessel of the same name, which later became the presidential yacht WILLIAMSBURG. ARAS' new owner, Charles S. Howard, took her west and her new home port was San Francisco. She was renamed VALIANT and after only a few months with Howard, she exploded and caught fire off Catalina Island on December 13, 1930. She subsequently sank without loss of life, ending the shortest career of any of her Newport News sisters.

ROBADOR
1926

ROBADOR

Hull No: 316
Owner: Robert Law, Jr.
Launched: May 29, 1926
Delivered: August 17, 1926
Dimensions: 161.33 x 26 x 14.75 ft
Gross Tonnage: 433
Displacement: 573 tons
Machinery: Diesels, Twin Screw
Horsepower/Speed: 900/14 knots
Fate: Scrapped, 1956

Last of the diesel yachts built at Newport News, ROBADOR was built for enthusiastic yachtsman and financeer Robert Law, Jr. Mr. Law was not present when the new yacht was launched by Miss Eleanor Mary Wilkie of New York on May 29, 1926. ROBADOR was also the last of the five Cox and Stevens designs

built at the yard, and excellent photos of her plush interior have survived.

She served Mr. Law for the rest of the 1926 season and for the next two seasons, based at the Indian Harbor Yacht Club on Long Island Sound. In August 1928 she was sold to William J. Matheson, renamed SEAFORTH, and moved to a new home port at Miami. In July 1931 she was again sold, to Herman W. Falk of Milwaukee, and she stayed with her new owner without change of name for 10 years.

March 1941 saw her surrendered to the Navy, renamed CYMOPHANE, and designated PYC-26. Her wartime service saw her in convoy escort duty along the East Coast and later involved her in experimental work for submarine training. In June 1948 she left Navy service and thereafter took up service with Circle Line Sightseeing Yachts of New York City. She took back her civilian name of SEAFORTH and served with the Circle Line until she was dismantled for scrap in the summer of 1956.

VIKING
1929

VIKING

Hull No: 328
Owner: George F. Baker, Jr.
Launched: December 15, 1928
Delivered: April 27, 1929
Dimensions: 272.08 x 36.56 x 18.5 ft
Gross Tonnage: 1,300
Displacement: 1,625 tons
Machinery: Turbo-Electric, Twin Screw
Horsepower/Speed: 2,600/15.5 knots
Fate: Collision, 1944

Without question one of the most beautiful ships ever built at Newport News, steam yacht VIKING was designed by Theordore D. Wells and built for millionaire banker George F. Baker, Jr., both of New York. Mr. Baker's daughter Florence launched the huge yacht and it was delivered just over four months later. Mr. Baker was a former commodore of the New York Yacht Club who had sailed on several yachts defending the America's Cup, but he did not make Baker's Chocolate, as was believed by many shipyard workers.

VIKING was one of the finest private vessels in the world and was the first to employ turbo-electric machinery, which had been built by General Electric. The new yacht was both graceful and rakish, and her bow was decorated with a Viking figurehead of teak carved by master shipyard wood carver William Geggie.

Her owner's assets survived the Depression, and Mr. Baker and his crew of 45 spent the 1930s fishing on long cruises to the Mediterranean, down the West Coast of South America, and to several Pacific Islands. On a round-the-world cruise, Mr. Baker died aboard his beloved yacht in Honolulu harbor in 1937. She passed to Norman B. Woolworth in the same year and was renamed NOPARO.

In December 1940 she was sold to the Navy and converted for duty as patrol gunboat ST. AUGUSTINE, PG-54. She was assigned to patrol and convoy escort duty, and her war service was routine until the night of January 6, 1944. She had been leading a convoy of merchant ships from New York to Guantanamo, Cuba, when, southeast of Cape May, NJ, she was rammed amidships by the tanker CAMAS MEADOWS. She sank from the collision within five minutes, and only 30 of her 145 crewmen survived the cold stormy sea.

BAY & RIVER STEAMERS
NEWPORT NEWS
1895

NEWPORT NEWS

Hull No: 14
Owner: Norfolk and Washington Steamboat Co.
Launched: April 9, 1895
Delivered: June 15, 1895
Dimensions: 247 x 37 x 16.5 ft
Gross Tonnage: 1,535
Displacement: 1,320 tons
Machinery: Triple Expansion Engine,
    2 Boilers
Horsepower/Speed: 2,460/22 knots
Fate: Burned, 1924

Bay steamer NEWPORT NEWS was the first ship to carry the young shipbuilding city's name and was the first of her type built at the yard. She was designed as a 22 knot propeller steamer for overnight service on the Potomac River and the Chesapeake Bay, and she had accommodations for about 300 passengers.

NEWPORT NEWS was christened by Miss N. Gertrude Woodbury, niece of the vice president of the Norfolk and Washington Steamboat Co., in the presence of several thousand spectators on April 9, 1895. The new steamer was delivered with a gleaming white hull and superstructure, a gilded pilothouse eagle, and gilded carved decorations on her bow and stern. She was a comfortable vessel, and her public rooms and cabins were stylishly decorated.

Entering service on the overnight run between Norfolk, Old Point Comfort, Alexandria, and Washington, NEWPORT NEWS served her owner for over 25 years, occasionally returning to the shipyard for repairs and with launching excursion parties. She was joined in service by the yard-built SOUTHLAND in 1908.

In 1910 she sustained heavy damage in a collision in Hampton Roads with the British steamship LORD ROBERTS; then in 1918 she was involved in a pier fire at Washington. In the latter episode her superstructure was heavily damaged, but she was rebuilt and placed back in service as MIDLAND in 1919. Her days were numbered, however, and she again caught fire on January 26, 1924, and was destroyed. Her hulk was laid up at Alexandria for a few years until she was finally scrapped.

MARGARET
1896

MARGARET

Hull No: 20
Owner: Plant Investment Co.
Launched: May 30, 1896
Delivered: October 14, 1896
Dimensions: 182 x 25 x 8.25 ft
Gross Tonnage: 674
Displacement: 390 tons
Machinery: Compound Engine, 1 Boiler,
    Side Wheels
Horsepower/Speed: 550/11.5 knots
Fate: Sank, 1924

Launched shortly after the tug SOMMERS N. SMITH from the same shipway, MARGARET was lucky that the tug drifted downstream before sinking. Side wheel steamer MARGARET was launched on May 30, 1896, by Mrs. H.B. Plant, her namesake and wife of the president of the Plant Investment Co. In an unusual episode, the new steamer was later pulled back up onto the shipway and her length was increased by 40 feet before she was delivered. Her owner had also ordered the yard's first passenger ship (and least profitable contract), LA GRANDE DUCHESSE. Steamer MARGARET had 12-ft diameter side wheels with eight feathering buckets each and made a respectable 11.5 knots.

She was homeported in New Haven and served her original owner until 1902 when she was sold to the Atlantic Coast Line of Tampa. In 1904 she passed to the People's Steamboat Co. of Norwich, CT. She passed to Mexican ownership in 1906 and was renamed TLACATOLPAN; then, in 1908 she was sold to the Pontchartrain Transporation Co. of New Orleans. In 1913 she was sold to the Lamsville and Jeffersonville Ferry Co. of Louisville, KY, where she served until 1916 under the name CARMANIA. She was sold to the Baltimore and Philadelphia Steamboat Co. in 1916, and her home port was Philadelphia until she was again sold in 1919 to the White-Gans Corp. of New York. This veteran of many owners and 28 years of service sank at her dock at Fall River, MA, on March 12, 1924, without loss of life.

JAMESTOWN
1906

JAMESTOWN

Hull No: 61
Owner: Norfolk & Washington Steamboat Co.
Launched: March 17, 1906
Delivered: June 20, 1906
Dimensions: 262 x 63 x 14.5 ft
Gross Tonnage: 1,337
Displacement: 1,122 tons
Machinery: Compound Engine, 4 Boilers
    Side Wheels
Horsepower/Speed: 2,000/18 knots
Fate: Converted, 1930

The side wheel bay steamer JAMESTOWN was ordered for the inauguration of day service from Washington to Hampton Roads in connection with the Jamestown Tercentennial of 1907. She was built with many fire-safety innovations following the burning of the GENERAL SLOCUM in 1904 in which over 1,000 lives were lost. JAMESTOWN was launched on March 17, 1906, by little Miss Judith Norment, daughter of a vice president of the steamboat company.

Well before completion, JAMESTOWN underwent a special trial to prove her contract speed of 18 knots. She joined NEWPORT NEWS in service in June 1906 and served through the Jamestown celebration, then was sold to the Argentine Navigation Co. (Nicolas Mihanovich) and renamed COLONIA in November 1909. Her new owner put her into "tauronautica" service, carrying up to 1,500 excursionists from Buenos Aires to his large resort "Real de San Carlos," which featured an 8,000-seat bullring.

Highly successful at this, she served Mihanovich under the Argentine flag until she was sold to Benito Canale of Buenos Aires in 1925. In 1927 she was sold to S.J. Borzone, also of Buenos Aires, and was active until 1930. Records indicate that she was cut down to a lighter in that year but do not reveal her ultimate fate.

SOUTHLAND
1909

SOUTHLAND

Hull No: 107
Owner: Norfolk & Washington Steamboat Co.
Launched: October 3, 1908
Delivered: February 15, 1909
Dimensions: 305 x 51 x 17.75 ft
Gross Tonnage: 2,081
Displacement: 1,830 tons
Machinery: Quadruple Expansion Engine,
    4 Boilers
Horsepower/Speed: 3,000/17.4 knots
Fate: Scrapped, 1955

Ordered by the Norfolk & Washington Steamboat Co. in 1908, SOUTHLAND was the largest of the seven bay and river craft built by the yard. The long and graceful steamer was launched on October 3, 1908, by Miss Ida Norment Smith, daughter of the secretary-treasurer of the owner. SOUTHLAND was a fine addition to the fleet and she entered service in 1909.

She served on the run between Washington and Norfolk as one of the "Honeymoon Fleet" until she was requisitioned for war service in 1942. She became part of a fleet of eight inland steamers outfitted in Baltimore for the Atlantic crossing and for war service with the British Ministry of War Transport. The converted ships sailed from St. John's, Newfoundland, on September 21, 1942. Three of the steamers were torpedoed and sunk but SOUTHLAND survived. She was used by the Royal Navy in British waters until 1944, then was converted to carry 554 passengers at Glasgow and was transferred to the U.S. Navy.

She served the Twelfth Fleet in Europe until 1945 and, since there was doubt that she could safely cross the Atlantic, she was sold in England in August 1945. Her new owner was the Fu Chung International Corp. of Hong Kong, and she sailed to the Far East via the Suez in 1947. She was renamed HUNG YUNG and later served with the Pao Ching Co., also of Hong Kong, in river service before reportedly being scrapped in 1955.

CAROLINA
1911

CAROLINA

Hull No: 150
Owner: Albemarle Steam Navigation Co.
Launched: October 25, 1911
Delivered: November 4, 1911
Dimensions: 130 x 25 x 9 ft
Gross Tonnage: 334
Displacement: 354 tons
Machinery: Compound Engine, 1 Boiler
Horsepower/Speed: 225/9.1 knots
Fate: Scrapped, 1974

CAROLINA was one of two small river steamers ordered for service with the Albemarle Steam Navigation Co. of Franklin, VA. CAROLINA was intended for service between Edenton and Murfreesboro, NC, and she had cabins for 18 passengers. She was launched by little Miss Mary Dillard and entered service in late 1911.

The short, stubby little vessel carried passengers and freight throughout the year, and in season she handled peanuts, cotton, and fertilizer. CAROLINA stayed in this service until 1917 when she and VIRGINIA joined the Army as passenger and freight steamers for the Quartermaster Corps. In 1922 both boats were sold to the Buxton Line of Norfolk and resumed merchant service.

In 1937 she was sold to R.O. Colonna of Norfolk and was cut down to a barge. She served in this capacity until 1951 when she was sold to the Atlantic Fishing Co. of Norfolk and was repowered and put into service as a menhaden fishing boat with the name W.W. COLONNA. Under this name she served several owners for fifteen years, including Atlantic and Haynie of Reedville, VA and Pascagoula, MS. In 1974 she was sold to a Panamanian owner, then was later reported scrapped.

VIRGINIA
1911

VIRGINIA

Hull No: 151
Owner: Albemarle Steam Navigation Co.
Launched: October 25, 1911
Delivered: November 18, 1911
Dimensions: 115 x 25 x 9 ft
Gross Tonnage: 292
Displacement: 313 tons
Machinery: Compound Engine, 1 Boiler
Horsepower/Speed: 200/8.4 knots
Fate: Foundered, 1942

VIRGINIA was ordered with CAROLINA for the Albemarle Steam Navigation Co., but she was 15 feet shorter, making her the smallest of the Newport News-built bay and river steamers. She was intended for service on the Blackwater River between Franklin, VA, and Tunis, NC, and her shorter length enabled her to safely navigate sharp bends on the narrow river. VIRGINIA had cabins for 16 passengers and was similar in design to CAROLINA. She was christened by Miss Mary Dillard, daughter of Capt. James B. Dillard, USA, who was on duty at the yard. Miss Dillard had also christened CAROLINA earlier the same day.

The new steamer followed her sister into the Army, then to service with the Buxton Line. In 1934 she was renamed SEMINOLE and was sold to R.W. and E.M. Gatewood. In their service she was almost destroyed by fire at Pungo Ferry, North Landing River, NC, on June 16, 1939, without loss of life. In 1941 she was rebuilt as a barge and re-entered service as SEMINOLE, 173 GRT, under the ownership of J.O. Webster of Miami. Her new career was not to last long, as she foundered about 50 miles east of Miami on October 4, 1942.

YORKTOWN
1928

YORKTOWN

Hull No: 325
Owner: Chesapeake Steamship Co.
Launched: February 25, 1928
Delivered: May 17, 1928
Dimensions: 277.25 x 53 x 18 ft
Gross Tonnage: 1,547
Displacement: 2,240 tons
Machinery: Triple Expansion Engine,
    4 Boilers
Horsepower/Speed: 2,700/15.5 knots
Fate: War Loss, 1942

Last of the Newport News-built bay steamers, YORKTOWN was christened by Miss Ruth Miller Green on a snowy Saturday, February 25, 1928. The aptly-named YORKTOWN was built for York River service between West Point and Baltimore. She was closely modeled on the line's earlier CITY OF RICH-MOND and was a replacement for the lost CITY OF ANNAPOLIS. A train connection at West Point made it a comfortable trip from Baltimore to Richmond. The new YORKTOWN was a comfortable vessel with accommodations for 330 passengers and 53 crew.

She served on the West Point-Baltimore route for nine years and brought many visitors to the Yorktown Sesquicentennial in 1931. In 1937 YORKTOWN was moved to the Bay route between Baltimore and Old Point Comfort and Norfolk following the loss by fire of the line's CITY OF BALTIMORE. In the merger of 1941, she passed to the Old Bay Line.

The war years found her requisitioned by the War Shipping Administration and, like SOUTHLAND, outfitted for service with the British Ministry of War. Her superstructure was boarded up, and she was armed and painted gray for the Atlantic crossing. Under the command of a British crew, she set out from St. John's, Newfoundland, with seven other steamers on September 21, 1942. On the fifth day out she was torpedoed by German submarine U-619 off the Irish coast, and she sank in just 90 seconds. Nineteen of her crew took to rafts and were saved 46 hours after she sank.

DREDGES & A CABLE SHIP
CAYO PIEDRA
1907

CAYO PIEDRA

Hull No: 75
Owner: American Locomotive Co.
Launched: March 21, 1907
Delivered: April 3, 1907
Dimensions: 125 x 41.25 x 12 ft
Gross Tonnage: —
Displacement: 569 tons
Machinery: None
Horsepower/Speed: -/-
Fate: Unknown

CAYO PIEDRA was the first dredge built at Newport News and little is known of her history. She was a "dipper" type dredge featuring a power shovel which excavated bottom material for transfer into barges. She was ordered by the American Locomotive Co. of Richmond for service with the Director General of Public Works of the Republic of Cuba. The shipyard built her hull only, and her dredging machinery was built and installed by American Locomotive Co. The construction of CAYO PIEDRA was superintended by R.W. Hunt & Co., Engineers, of Chicago, and she was built to specifications drawn up by the Atlantic Equipment Co. She was launched without ceremony on March 21, 1907, and was delivered less than two weeks later. Registers of shipping do not reveal details of her service history or ultimate fate.

CLATSOP
1908

CLATSOP

Hull No: 87
Owner: U.S. War Department
Launched: May 16, 1908
Delivered: September 2, 1908
Dimensions: 183 x 38 x 23 ft
Gross Tonnage: 1,100
Displacement: 1,365 tons
Machinery: Compound Engine, 2 Boilers
Horsepower/Speed: 800/abt. 10 knots
Fate: Scrapped, 1961

The second of her type, the largest, and the only self-propelled dredge built at Newport News, CLAT-SOP was christened by Miss Virginia Warwick on May 16, 1908. CLATSOP was a suction hopper dredge fitted with side dragarms manipulated by large booms fitted aft. She carried eight officers and 37 men and entered service with the U.S. War Department (Army Corps of Engineers) in late 1908. She served in the Portland District on the Columbia and Williamette rivers for many years before moving to the Philadelphia District around 1937. In 1936 she helped four other hopper dredges move over 8 million cubic yards of the material to build the Golden Gate Exposition site at San Francisco.

CLATSOP evidently served in the Philadelphia area until after World War II, then was sold to a Chicago owner and renamed SANDPILOT. She worked on Lake Michigan and around the mouth of the Chicago River for the Construction Aggregates Corp. until she was sold for scrap in 1961.

NORFOLK
1925

NORFOLK

Hull No: 282
Owner: Atlantic Gulf & Pacific Co.
Launched: February 23, 1925
Delivered: June 1, 1925
Dimensions: 162 x 38 x 14 ft
Gross Tonnage: —
Displacement: Abt. 600 tons
Machinery: None
Horsepower/Speed: -/-
Fate: Unknown

Like CAYO PIEDRA, little is known about dredge NORFOLK, delivered in 1925. NORFOLK was built without propelling machinery or boilers, but she was fitted with a 26-inch dredge pump powered by a six-cylinder 1,150 BHP diesel engine. The dredge was launched from Shipway 4 on February 23, 1925, without a sponsor or ceremony. NORFOLK was a cutterhead hydraulic dredge and featured a steel hull and house, A-frame, ladder, and spuds. In normal service she discharged dredged material through a floating pipeline to a disposal area. When originally ordered, NORFOLK's dimensions were 152 x 38 x 12.5 ft, but her design was enlarged and provided with greater freeboard prior to construction.

NORFOLK was placed in service on the East Coast and gained a reputation for being good for digging hard materials, but she was considered somewhat under-powered. Shortly before V-J Day in 1945, she was commandeered by the Navy and taken to the Philippines under the command of an AG&P crew. She worked at Manicani, Cavite, and Manila until her crew returned to the U.S. in June 1946, and details of her further service are unknown.

RAYMOND
1926

RAYMOND

Hull No: 292
Owner: U.S. War Department
Launched: March 20, 1926
Delivered: September 5, 1926
Dimensions: 177.5 x 40 x 14.67 ft
Gross Tonnage: —
Displacement: 1,950 tons
Machinery: None
Horsepower/Speed: -/-
Fate: Scrapped, 1980

Like CLATSOP before her, RAYMOND was ordered by the U.S. War Department, Army Corps of Engineers. She was designed as a 20-inch cutterhead hydraulic dredge, and she was fitted with a large ten cylinder diesel engine for her dredge pump. Her overall length with cutter extended was 234 ft, and she featured two 34-inch diameter spuds over 70 ft long to hold her in place while dredging. RAYMOND was named for General Charles W. Raymond and was launched by his granddaughter, Miss Caroline Raymond, on March 20, 1926, a day when a number of vessels were launched at Newport News. The new dredge was delivered six months after launch and took up station in the Houston Ship Channel in company with tug C. DONOVAN, built as Hull 13.

RAYMOND was moved to the Pacific in 1944 and saw military service. After World War II she went to Okinawa for use in a number of harbor and channel projects for about five years. In 1955 the dredge was sold to the government of Korea and was renamed ASAN-MAN-HO by President Syngman Rhee in commemoration of a great Korean naval victory in the Middle Ages. The old dredge was overhauled by the Koreans and was put to work cleaning sand from Pusan Harbor. ASAN-MAN-HO worked on a number of projects along the Korean coast.

In 1967 she was transferred to the Korea Dredging Corp., and in subsequent years she worked on land reclamation and maintenance and channel dredging at Inchon and Pohang. Worn out after almost 55 years of hard work, the former RAYMOND was scrapped by her owner in 1980.

JOSEPH HENRY
1909

JOSEPH HENRY

Hull No: 114
Owner: U.S. War Department
Launched: December 30, 1908
Delivered: March 31, 1909
Dimensions: 167.58 x 32 x 16.33 ft
Gross Tonnage: 601
Displacement: 800 tons
Machinery: Compound Engines, 2 Boilers,
    Twin Screw
Horsepower/Speed: 1,000/11.3 knots
Fate: Laid Up, 1983

Little JOSEPH HENRY was the only cable layer ever built at Newport News, and her unusual design resulted in an unprofitable contract for the shipyard. JOSEPH HENRY was built for the Submarine Cable Service of the U.S. Army Signal Corps., intended to lay cable for fire control systems in New York Harbor and along the East Coast. She was launched by little Lillian May Boag, daughter of U.S. inspector Boag, who superintended construction for the government, and left the yard in 1909.

JOSEPH HENRY saw extensive service with the Army until the end of World War II when she was sold to the Greek government and renamed THALIS O. MILISSIOS. She became Greece's first cable ship and took over maintenance of a large network of inter-island submarine cables. In Greek service, she laid over 140 new cables and performed more than 630 repairs to existing cables. Hard at work in Greece with her original machinery, the little cable layer was one of the oldest Newport News ships still in active service

and retained her original appearance. Homeported in Piraeus, THALIS O. MILISSIOS worked for the Hellenic Telecommunications Organization until she was laid up in 1983.

Hull No: 299
Owner: R.B. Knox
Launched: September 4, 1925
Delivered: September 4, 1925
Dimensions: 80 x 30 x 7 ft
Displacement: Abt. 150 tons
Machinery: None
Fate: Unknown

The last and smallest of the dredges built at Newport News, Hull 299 had the dubious distinction of being delivered without a name. Hull 299 was a hydraulic dredge, and she was also unique in that her hull was made up of six pontoons, which were bolted together. She was designed by S.L.G. Knox, consulting engineer and brother of her owner, who represented the Duluth Superior Dredging Co. The dredge pontoons, trusses, gantries, spud supports and house framing were fabricated and assembled, then disassembled and "launched" into seven freight cars.

This "launching" had no sponsor, and the dredge was "delivered" as soon as it was loaded from Shipway 9 onto the rail cars. Hull 299 was moved to Tampa for consignment to the Florida and Southern Dredging Co., but official records do not indicate her service history or ultimate fate.

CAROLINA
1914

CAROLINA

Hull No: 172
Owner: New York & Porto Rico Co.
Launched: —
Delivered: March 1, 1914
Dimensions: 404 x 47.67 x 36.5 ft
Gross Tonnage: 5,017
Displacement: 5,780 tons
Machinery: Triple Expansion Engine,
   4 Boilers
Horsepower/Speed: 6,820/17.27 knots
Fate: War Loss, 1918

The shipyard's first conversion job large enough to merit a hull number was that of the remodeling of CAROLINA, built in the yard in 1896 as LA GRANDE DUCHESSE, Hull 15. It was remembered that this was the yard's first passenger ship and one on which it had considerable difficulty and lost a great deal of money. Hull 15 had become CITY OF SAVANNAH in 1901, then CAROLINA in 1906 when purchased by the New York and Porto Rico Steamship Co. It was this company who contracted with the shipyard in May 1913 to remodel CAROLINA into a single screw ship, install a new engine and boilers, and perform extensive alterations. Her original quadruple expansion engines were replaced with a triple, and her four single-end boilers were replaced with two single- and two double-enders. Her twin 14.25 ft propellers were replaced with a single 17-ft diameter screw in an unusual conversion. Her accommodations were extensively remodeled, and her draft increased from 17.83 ft to 22.5 ft.

She left the yard on March 1, 1914, leaving the shipyard management pleased that they had finally turned a profit on her. Her new career as a single screw ship was short-lived, as she was torpedoed and sunk on June 2, 1918.

STANDARD
1886

STANDARD

Hull No: 195
Owner: Standard Oil Co. of NJ
Launched: —
Delivered: February 18, 1916
Dimensions: 545 x 68.68 x 31.75 ft
Gross Tonnage: 9,724
Displacement: Abt. 23,500 tons
Machinery: Quadruple Expansion Engine,
    3 Boilers
Horsepower/Speed: 3,300/10 knots
Fate: Scrapped, 1954

On July 13, 1915, the shipyard signed a contract with the Standard Oil Co. of NJ for extensive repairs and alterations to the bulk oil steamer STANDARD. This vessel was the former JUPITER, built at Kiel, Germany, in 1914. During the course of this work, the ship's depth was reduced from 34.63 ft to 31.75 ft and her gross tonnage from 10,073 to 9,724. While in Dry Dock 3 on August 24, 1915, the ship slipped off her keel blocks, but fortunately, the damage was not major and no lives were lost.

Delivered on February 18, 1916, with three new single-ended boilers built at the shipyard, STANDARD and her crew of 44 resumed service with the Standard Oil fleet. She remained in routine service with her owner until sold to Panamanian registry in 1939 for $270,000. She sailed for the Panama Transport Co. during the 1940s, then with the American European Tanker Co. during the 1950s before being sold for scrap in 1954.

LEVIATHAN
1923

LEVIATHAN

Hull No: 264
Owner: United States Lines
Launched: —
Delivered: May 16, 1923
Dimensions: 950.58 x 100 x 73.11 ft
Gross Tonnage: 59,956
Displacement: 66,800 tons
Machinery: Geared Turbines, 46 Boilers,
   Quadruple Screw
Horsepower/Speed: 100,000/22 knots
Fate: Scrapped, 1938

LEVIATHAN, formerly the German liner VATER-LAND, was known locally as "the ship that saved the shipyard." With an apparently fatal lull in naval shipbuilding due to the Naval Holiday, this $8 million reconditioning contract signed by the yard on February 15, 1922, kept half of its work force of 4,000 occupied for over a year and helped avoid massive layoffs.

The ship was enormous, and the work to be done was called "the largest single job of reconditioning in the history of the United States, and probably the world." During the reconditioning, the ex-German ship was completely redecorated by American artists, and she was provided with a large tiled pool. She was converted from coal to oil fuel, and more than 500 miles of new wiring were installed. As the Germans refused to provide the original plans for the ship for a reasonable price, they were completely redrawn by naval architect William Francis Gibbs and his staff from measurements taken on board. The LEVIA-THAN's conversion resulted in more than a $1.2 million loss for the shipyard, but it stayed in business during this difficult time.

At the completion of this demanding and difficult job, over 40,000 people visited the ship and she was delivered on May 16, 1923. She took up service on the New York-Channel Ports-Bremen run until being withdrawn from service in 1934. Never a financial success, she was scrapped in Scotland in 1938.

REPUBLIC
1924

REPUBLIC

Hull No: 272
Owner: United States Lines
Launched: —
Delivered: April 11, 1924
Dimensions: 615.25 x 68 x 52 ft
Gross Tonnage: 17,911
Displacement: 29,250 tons
Machinery: Quadruple Expansion Engines,
    6 Boilers, Twin Screw
Horsepower/Speed: 7,500/13.5 knots
Fate: Scrapped, 1952

The U.S. Lines passenger ship REPUBLIC arrived for a similar reconditioning only a day after the sailing of LEVIATHAN, bringing with her another much-needed year's work for 2,000 yard craftsmen. Originally built in Ireland in 1907 as SCOTIAN, she was acquired by the Hamburg American Line and renamed PRESIDENT GRANT. She was seized in 1914 at New York and saw extensive service as a troopship until 1921.

Her conversion for service with U.S. Lines was similar to that of LEVIATHAN. She was converted to oil fuel and fitted out for cabin class service. Two of her masts were removed, and she was fitted with two new single-ended boilers and four double-enders.

On completion she entered the North Atlantic service with LEVIATHAN. She reverted to Army service in 1931 and made several trips to the Far East, then was placed in New York-Honolulu service. She served the Navy in World War II in the Pacific.

In February 1945 she was returned to the Army for conversion to a hospital ship but instead reverted to troopship service for another year. She was laid up in March 1946 and, veteran of an extremely varied career, was scrapped at Baltimore in 1952.

AMERICA
1928

AMERICA

Hull No: 322
Owner: United States Lines
Launched: —
Delivered: March 3, 1928
Dimensions: 687 x 74.25 x 52.48 ft
Gross Tonnage: 21,145
Displacement: 34,575 tons
Machinery: Quadruple Expansion Engines,
    8 Boilers, Twin Screw
Horsepower/Speed: 17,500/17.5 knots
Fate: Scrapped, 1957

Not to be confused with the more famous yard-built AMERICA of 1940 (Hull 369), this vessel was the ex-German AMERIKA built in Ireland in 1905 for the Hamburg-America Line. She was seized at Boston in 1917 and took up service with the Navy as a transport, making nine round trips to Europe in her first year. She struck and sank the British freighter INSTRUCTOR in July 1918 but incurred only superficial damage. She sank at her pier in Hoboken, NJ, on October 15, 1918, but was raised and refitted to make eight more European round trips. She was operated by U.S. Lines from 1921 in North Atlantic service.

While at the shipyard undergoing repairs on March 10, 1926, she was extensively damaged by fire. She was rebuilt as Hull 322, being completely reconditioned and redecorated but not converted for oil fuel.

After reconditioning she re-entered service on March 3, 1928. She was transferred to the U.S. Shipping Board in 1931 and was laid up. In 1940 she was transferred to the War Department, and, after an extensive overhaul, entered troop service under the name EDMUND B. ALEXANDER. After more extensive service as a troopship, she was laid up in 1948, then was sold for scrap in 1957 after 52 years of life.

PRESIDENT JOHNSON
1929

PRESIDENT JOHNSON

Hull No: 330
Owner: Dollar Steamship Line
Launched: —
Delivered: January 19, 1929
Dimensions: 615.67 x 65 x 43.25 ft
Gross Tonnage: 14,500
Displacement: 26,900 tons
Machinery: Quadruple Expansion Engines,
    8 Boilers, Twin Screw
Horsepower/Speed: 10,000/15 knots
Fate: Scrapped, 1952

Built as MANCHURIA in 1904 by New York Ship-building Co. at Camden, NJ, this vessel served the Pacific Mail Steamship Co. and the Atlantic Transport Co., until acquired by the Navy and converted for troop service in April 1918. After making 13 round trips to Europe, MANCHURIA was returned to her owner in September 1919. She served on the North Atlantic with American Line until 1923 when she entered New York to San Francisco service with Panama Pacific Line.

She was sold to the American Foreign Steamship Co. (Dollar Line) in 1928 and, renamed PRESIDENT JOHNSON, arrived at the shipyard on November 3. The $400,000 contract for her reconditioning called for the renewal and redecorating of all public rooms and provision for new accommodations for 760 steerage passengers. First class staterooms were extensively refitted, and a new deckhouse with Veranda Bar was added. A new pool was added, and the boiler and engine casing bulkheads were moved two feet inboard, a difficult task. The work was completed in 62 working days to the great satisfaction of the owner. She entered round-the-world service with the Dollar Line until transferred to American President Lines in July 1941.

In November of that year, she was acquired by the Army and served as a troop carrier in the Pacific during World War II. In 1947 she was sold to the Tagus Navigational Co. of Panama and was renamed SANTA CRUZ. She served for a few years as an immigrant transport between Italy and South America before being scrapped in 1952.

PRESIDENT FILLMORE
1930

PRESIDENT FILLMORE

Hull No: 341
Owner: Dollar Line
Launched: —
Delivered: January 11, 1930
Dimensions: 615.67 x 65 x 51.25 ft
Gross Tonnage: 15,575
Displacement: 26,900 tons
Machinery: Quadruple Expansion Engines,
    8 Boilers, Twin Screw
Horsepower/Speed: 10,000/15 knots
Fate: Scrapped, 1947

Fourth and last Dollar Line ship reconditioned at Newport News in the late 1920s, PRESIDENT FILL-MORE started life as MONGOLIA, sister ship to MANCHURIA, built in 1904 and previously reconditioned at the yard as PRESIDENT JOHNSON. These two ships were among the largest and fastest in the American fleet when built. MONGOLIA served with the Pacific Mail Co. until 1915, then passed to the Atlantic Transport Co. After World War I transport service, she served on the North Atlantic with American Line, then after 1925 in the Pacific for Panama Pacific Line.

In 1929 she became a Dollar liner and was renamed PRESIDENT FILLMORE. The contract for her reconditioning was signed on March 29, 1929, and she entered the yard in September. The work done on her was extensive and was similar to that performed on the others.

She left the yard on January 11, 1930, and re-entered round-the-world service out of San Francisco. She was laid up in 1931 and transferred to American President Lines in 1938. In February 1940 she was sold to Wallem & Co. of Panama for $300,000 and transferred to Panamanian flag.

PRESIDENT FILLMORE sank at her berth at Baltimore in March 1940 but was raised and towed to Newport News for repairs. She was renamed PANA-MANIAN and survived the war undamaged; she was laid up at Hong Kong in 1946, then scrapped at Shanghai in 1947.

WARD
1929

WARD

Hull No: 332
Owner: U.S. Shipping Board
Launched: —
Delivered: August 1, 1929
Dimensions: 412.25 x 55 x 34.83 ft
Gross Tonnage: 6,203
Displacement: 13,141 tons
Machinery: Geared Diesel
Horsepower/Speed: 3,950/12.5 knots
Fate: Scrapped, 1949

Sister ship of CITY OF ELWOOD and built at New Orleans in 1921, WARD's contract for dieselization was signed at the same time as that of her sister. The contract for WARD called for the same work as for CITY OF ELWOOD and official trials were held on August 1, 1929. WARD was handed back to her owners the same day and re-entered routine merchant service. She was operated by the Shipping Board and by the Maritime Commission through the 1930s. Early in 1940 she was sold to the American Export Lines who renamed her EXTON. She was pressed back into government service during the war and again took the name WARD. She was finally sold for scrap in 1949.

CITY OF ELWOOD
1929

CITY OF ELWOOD

Hull No: 331
Owner: U.S. Shipping Board
Launched: —
Delivered: June 12, 1929
Dimensions: 412.25 x 55 x 34.83 ft
Gross Tonnage: 6,203
Displacement: 13,141 tons
Machinery: Geared Diesel
Horsepower/Speed: 3,950/12.5 knots
Fate: Scrapped, 1946

This large cargo ship was built at New Orleans in 1920 by Doullut and Williams Shipbuilding for the U.S. Shipping Board. Little is known of her career. The shipyard signed a contract with the Shipping Board on October 20, 1928, which called for the replacement of the ship's steam engine with a diesel and for a general reconditioning. The ship's engine was replaced with a Busch-Sulzer six-cylinder 30″ x 52″ engine, and her accommodations were rennovated and four cabins were added, making her practically a new ship at completion.

After sea trials which indicated a three knot gain in speed over her former powerplant, she left the yard on June 12, 1929, and re-entered service. After many years of routine service with the Shipping Board and later with the Maritime Commission, she was dismantled and scrapped in 1946.

PRESIDENT HARRISON
1929

PRESIDENT HARRISON

Hull No: 333
Owner: Dollar Lines
Launched: —
Delivered: April 29, 1929
Dimensions: 522.67 x 62 x 42 ft
Gross Tonnage: 10,533
Displacement: 20,900 tons
Machinery: Quadruple Expansion Engines,
    6 Boilers, Twin Screw
Horsepower/Speed: 7,000/15 knots
Fate: War Loss, 1944

Dollar liner PRESIDENT HARRISON was built by New York Shipbuilding Corp. of Camden, NJ, in 1921 as WOLVERINE STATE. Originally owned by the U.S. Shipping Board, she passed to the Dollar Line in late 1923. Contracts for reconditioning of this ship and PRESIDENT JOHNSON and PRESIDENT GARFIELD were all signed in November 1928, while that for PRESIDENT FILLMORE was made the following March. PRESIDENT HARRISON originally had been laid down as a troopship; but, as the war was won before she was delivered, she was completed as a passenger/cargo ship.

She entered the yard on February 3, 1929, after completion of her 16th round-the-world voyage for essentially the same type of reconditioning as PRESIDENT JOHNSON. All of her first class staterooms were removed and replaced, and all public rooms were renewed and redecorated. Safety equipment was upgraded, and PRESIDENT HARRISON left the yard essentially a new ship.

She was returned to her owners for Pacific Ocean trade out of San Francisco and continued in routine service until 1941. On December 8, 1941, her crew scuttled her off Shanghai after hearing of the attack on Pearl Harbor and declaration of war. She was captured by the Japanese and was repaired and placed in troop transport service as KACHIDOKI MARU. In convoy enroute to Japan from Singapore, she was torpedoed and sunk by the U.S. submarine PAMPANITO (SS-383) on September 12, 1944.

PRESIDENT GARFIELD
1929

PRESIDENT GARFIELD

Hull No: 334
Owner: Dollar Line
Launched: —
Delivered: July 13, 1929
Dimensions: 522.67 x 62 x 42 ft
Gross Tonnage: 10,558
Displacement: 20,900 tons
Machinery: Quadruple Expansion Engines,
    6 Boilers, Twin Screw
Horsepower/Speed: 7,000/15 knots
Fate: Scrapped, 1948

The third Dollar liner to be reconditioned at the shipyard, PRESIDENT GARFIELD was originally built in 1921 as BLUE HEN STATE, and she was a sister ship of PRESIDENT HARRISON. Originally designed as a troopship for the U.S. Shipping Board, she too was completed as a merchant vessel. She entered service with Dollar Line out of San Francisco in 1924 and continued in round-the-world service until entering the yard for reconditioning on May 4, 1929.

Her renovation was very similar to that of the other Dollar Line ships, and she was re-delivered on July 13, 1929. The passenger and cargo vessel went back to her former service and was transferred to American President Lines in 1938 and renamed PRESIDENT MADISON when a new PRESIDENT GARFIELD was delivered by Newport News in 1941.

On April 11, 1942, she left merchant service and was sold to the War Shipping Administration for Navy service. She was renamed KENMORE (AP-62) and transported troops and equipment in the Pacific until being converted to a hospital ship and renamed REFUGE (AH-11) in 1944. She made four voyages returning casualties from Europe to the United States, was overhauled, then entered hospital service in the Pacific theater in November 1944.

At the conclusion of the war, she returned patients and troops to San Francisco and Seattle until being decommissioned at Seattle. She received one battle star for her World War II service. Renamed PRESIDENT MADISON and laid up at Olympia, WA, in 1946, the old ship was sold for scrap and broken up at Vancouver, WA, in February 1948.

SALTA
1949

SALTA

Hull No: 472
Owner: Rio De La Plata, S.A.
Launched: —
Delivered: April 4, 1949
Dimensions: 492 x 69.5 x 42.5 ft
Gross Tonnage: 12,053
Displacement: 13,790 tons
Machinery: Geared Turbines, 2 Boilers
Horsepower/Speed: 8,500/17.25 knots
Fate: Scrapped, 1966

Last of the escort carriers converted for merchant service and the second to be converted to an immigrant ship, Hull 472 was built as JAMAICA (CVE-43) by Seattle-Tacoma Shipbuilding Corp. in 1943. She saw service with the Royal Navy as SHAH (D.21), in

hunter-killer antisubmarine service in the Atlantic, and later in the Indian Ocean. She returned to Norfolk in December 1945, was laid up, then was sold to the shipyard on June 20, 1947.

The yard signed a contract with Rio De La Plata in April 1948 for conversion of two vessels and SALTA was delivered on April 4, 1949. The transformation of SALTA was similar to that of CORRIENTES, and work on these and the other three escort carrier conversions filled in huge gaps in the yard's workload after World War II.

After delivery, SALTA joined CORRIENTES and six other ships in immigrant passenger service from Spain and Italy to the interior of Argentina. In routine service in 1964, she saved the lives of 478 survivors of the fire-swept cruise liner LAKONIA. Worn and weary veteran of varied service, the SALTA was broken up for scrap in 1966.

JACONA
1930

JACONA

Hull No: 343
Owner: New England Public Service Co.
Launched: —
Delivered: November 7, 1930
Dimensions: 396 x 53 x 29.33 ft
Gross Tonnage: 5,128
Displacement: Abt. 6,400 tons
Machinery: 10,000 KW Turbogenerators,
    4 Boilers
Horsepower/Speed: -/- knots
Fate: In Service

This cargo ship, pulled from the James River Reserve Fleet in 1930, was the center of a pioneering installation said to be the world's first floating power plant. JACONA was built for the U.S. Shipping Board by Todd-Tacoma in 1919 and had been in general cargo service until laid up. The New England Public Service

Co. of Augusta, ME, conceived the idea of a floating power plant from the Navy's successful use of LEXINGTON (CV-2) at Tacoma, WA, in 1929.

JACONA entered the yard in mid-1930, and her engine and boilers were removed. Four new-oil-burning generators were installed, and accommodations were modified to house a crew of 19 men. At completion, full power generation into the local power company's system was not possible due to the limited size of the yard's feeders, so the generators were tested one at a time.

JACONA left the shipyard under tow on November 7, 1930, and took up station in Maine. Later, she was moved to New Hampshire, and in 1945 she was transferred to Army service. She served at Pearl Harbor, Okinawa, Nagasaki, and Korea for ten years until she was transferred to the Navy in 1955 and was designated YFP-1. Based at Okinawa, she was eventually replaced by a land-based plant. Still in excellent condition, the old JACONA was transferred to the government of the Philippines in 1971.

URUGUAY
1938

URUGUAY

Hull No: 377
Owner: U.S. Maritime Commission
Launched: —
Delivered: September 2, 1938
Dimensions: 601.09 x 80 x 52 ft
Gross Tonnage: 20,184
Displacement: 30,260 tons
Machinery: Turbo-Electric, 12 Boilers,
    Twin Screw
Horsepower/Speed: 13,500/18 knots
Fate: Scrapped, 1964

URUGUAY was built by the yard in 1928 as CALIFORNIA, Hull 315. She and her sisters, VIR-GINIA and PENNSYLVANIA (later BRAZIL and ARGENTINA), were Moore-McCormack Lines' "Good Neighbor Fleet," which enjoyed great popularity on the South American run. Arriving at the yard for reconditioning on June 20, 1938, CALIFORNIA's face-lift began the same day. Just 74 days later, the big ship left Newport News with a new swimming pool on the promenade deck aft, 52 first class staterooms converted into 26 more comfortable suites, and an enclosed well deck forward. Two new propellers of Newport News design were installed, air conditioning equipment was fitted for her tourist dining room, and hull and machinery were extensively overhauled. The most notable change in her outward appearance was the removal of her dummy after stack and enclosure of the forward stack with a more streamlined outer casing.

The ship left the yard as URUGUAY on September 2, 1938, and resumed service. URUGUAY joined the Army in 1942 and made a number of voyages to Europe and the Far East. She was returned to merchant service after the war and rejoined the "Good Neighbor Fleet." The fleet was laid up in the James River Reserve Fleet in the late 1950s, and all three ships were scrapped in 1964.

AMERICA
1946

AMERICA

Hull No: 461
Owner: U.S. Maritime Commission
Launched: —
Delivered: October 31, 1946
Dimensions: 723 x 93.25 x 45.46 ft
Gross Tonnage: 26,315
Displacement: 35,440 tons
Machinery: Geared Turbines, 6 Boilers,
    Twin Screw
Horsepower/Speed: 34,000/23 knots
Fate: Laid Up, 1981

One of the most famous and beloved of all Newport News ships, AMERICA was originally built as Hull 369 and delivered in July 1940. She entered the North Atlantic trade with United States Lines, but her new career was cut short only a year later when she was requisitioned for war service with the Navy, designated P-23, and renamed WEST POINT. Painted gray, she raced all over the world for 56 months, and during her wartime career carried over 350,000 troops and steamed almost a half million miles.

On February 28, 1946, she re-entered the shipyard for a much-needed overhaul and for conversion back to merchant service. Given Hull No. 461 for this extensive work, her interior and exterior were restored to their former elegance in seven months. Exterior work included removal of wartime equipment such as gun foundations, rafts, porthole patch plates, and wind breaks. Over 10,000 sq ft of her wooden decks were renewed and all of her exterior equipment was overhauled. Interior work was extensive, as virtually all of her staterooms had been removed; and her public rooms had been modified to accommodate 8,000 passengers, a vast number for her size. Over 1,000 men worked aboard through the summer and fall, and she was completed and delivered on October 31, 1946, and began her maiden postwar Atlantic crossing on November 10.

She was sold to the Chandris Line in 1964 and transferred to Greek flag with the name AUSTRALIS. She was engaged in cruise service in the Pacific and Far East until 1977. An attempt to put her back in service with an American firm with her original name in 1978 was unsuccessful, and she was sold back to Chandris and renamed ITALIS shortly thereafter. She was overhauled and her dummy forward stack was removed. Renamed NOGA, she remained laid up in Greek waters, was sold, and was renamed ALFERDOSS in 1984.

ARTILLERO
1947

ARTILLERO

Hull No: 462
Owner: Dodero Navigation
Launched: —
Delivered: December 16, 1947
Dimensions: 491.83 x 69.5 x 42.5 ft
Gross Tonnage: 7,858
Displacement: 18,223 tons
Machinery: Geared Turbines, 2 Boilers
Horsepower/Speed: 8,500/16.5 knots
Fate: Stranded, 1967

Originally built as the escort aircraft carrier VERMILLION (CVE-52) in 1943, this ship was transferred to Great Britain and saw war service as SMITER (D.55). After wartime service, she was returned to the U.S. Navy and put up for sale. She was the first of five escort carriers purchased by the shipyard after the war for conversion to merchant service, and this was essentially the same for all five of the ships.

All structure above the shelter deck was removed including island, flight deck, and sponsons. Removal of 1,600 tons of concrete ballast by dynamiting and a great number of interior bulkheads by more conventional means were formidable tasks. In about ten months the war-weary carriers were transformed into sleek modern C-3 cargo ships for the Dodero Navigation Co. of Argentina.

ARTILLERO was, at the time of her arrival at Buenos Aires in January 1948, the largest cargo vessel in Argentina's fleet and she received a gala welcome. She immediately went into service between Buenos Aires and New York, expediting the export of badly needed foods to the rest of the world. She sailed with Dodero until 1958, then passed to Flota Argentina de Navegacion Ultramar. In 1963 she was sold again, to Empressa Lineas Maritimas Argentinas.

After 16 years in Argentine service, she was sold to Philippine President Lines in 1966 and renamed PRESIDENT GARCIA. On July 18, 1967, she ran aground in Saint's Bay on the south coast of Gurnsey and was damaged beyond repair. Sold to a German scrap yard, she was broken up at Hamburg in 1968.

CORACERO
1948

CORACERO

Hull No: 463
Owner: Dodero Navigation
Launched: —
Delivered: January 12, 1948
Dimensions: 491.83 x 69.5 x 42.5 ft
Gross Tonnage: 7,858
Displacement: 18,233 tons
Machinery: Geared Turbines, 2 Boilers
Horsepower/Speed: 8,500/16.5 knots
Fate: Scrapped, 1973

Sister ship to Hull 462, CORACERO was originally built by Seattle-Tacoma Shipbuilding Co. in 1943 as ST. SIMON (CVE-51). She was transferred to Great Britain under Lend-Lease in December 1943 and saw war service with the Royal Navy as ARBITER (D.31). She performed Channel escort duty and later served as an aircraft ferry in the Pacific. She returned to the U.S. Navy at Norfolk in March 1946, was laid up in the James River Reserve Fleet, then was sold to the shipyard with SMITER on December 9, 1946.

She entered Building Dock 10 early in 1947 and had her flight deck and fixed ballast removed, along with her island and sponsons. After several months of pierside work, she returned to Dock 10 to receive a new deckhouse. When her conversion was completed, CORACERO, like her sisters, featured modern navigational equipment and cabins and attractive public rooms for 12 passengers.

After a successful trial trip off the Virginia Capes, CORACERO was delivered to Dodero Navigation Company on January 9, 1948. She served with Dodero until 1958, then passed through the same series of owners as ARTILLERO and became PRESIDENT MACAPAGAL of Philippine President Lines in 1966. She was renamed LUCKY TWO in 1972 and was broken up for scrap in 1973.

LANCERO
1948

LANCERO

Hull No: 464
Owner: Dodero Navigation
Launched: —
Delivered: February 9, 1948
Dimensions: 491.83 x 69.5 x 42.5 ft
Gross Tonnage: 7,858
Displacement: 18,223 tons
Machinery: Geared Turbines, 2 Boilers
Horsepower/Speed: 8,500/16.5 knots
Fate: Scrapped, 1973

LANCERO, built at Seattle-Tacoma Shipbuilding Corp. in 1943 as DELGADA (CVE-40), was the last of the three escort carriers converted to cargo ships at the shipyard in 1948. She saw service with the Royal Navy as SPEAKER (D.40) and returned to the U.S. Navy at Norfolk in July 1946. Laid up in the James River Fleet, she too was sold to the shipyard on April 16, 1947.

She was stripped of her wartime equipment and structures and was converted in a manner similar to her sisters ARTILLERO and CORACERO. Her handsomely decorated dining salon, lounge, and smoking room—like those of her sisters—were provided with attractive oil paintings by local artist T.C. Skinner and featured modern decorative colors.

LANCERO left Newport News on February 9, 1948, as a handsome addition to the Dodero Fleet. She passed through the same succession of owners as her sisters and became PRESIDENT OSMENA of the Philippine President Line in 1966. After being renamed LUCKY THREE in 1972, she was scrapped in 1973.

CORRIENTES
1949

CORRIENTES

Hull No: 465
Owner: Rio De La Plata, S.A.
Launched: —
Delivered: January 19, 1949
Dimensions: 492 x 69.5 x 42.5 ft
Gross Tonnage: 12,053
Displacement: 13,790 tons
Machinery: Geared Turbines, 2 Boilers
Horsepower/Speed: 8,500/17.25 knots
Fate: Scrapped, 1964

Built at Seattle-Tacoma Shipbuilding Corp. in 1943 as TRACKER (BAVG-6), this escort carrier saw World War II service with the Royal Navy in the North Atlantic, Arctic, and during the Normandy Invasion. She was returned to the U.S. Navy in November 1945 and was laid up in the James River. She was purchased by the shipyard in May 1946, and unlike the previous three escort carriers converted at the yard, she and a fifth sister were transformed into immigrant passenger ships with a capacity of 1,350 persons.

After the now-routine removals were completed, the ship underwent extensive conversion for passenger service. Only No. 1 hold was retained for cargo, and the other holds on the ship were converted for crew and passenger cabins, a hospital, and baggage and other spaces. A long deckhouse was added, topped by a modern elliptical stack. New equipment for fresh water, refrigeration, and ventilation was provided and the ship's accommodations, while not luxurious, were comfortable.

When completed in January 1949, the sleek "new" ship entered service with Rio De La Plata, S.A., a subsidiary of Dodero, carrying immigrants from Italy and Spain to Argentina. She stayed in passenger service between these countries until she was sold for scrap and broken up in 1964.

GENERAL SIMON B. BUCKNER
1948

GENERAL SIMON B. BUCKNER

Hull No: 466
Owner: U.S. Army
Launched: —
Delivered: February 12, 1948
Dimensions: 608.82 x 75.5 x 52.5 ft
Gross Tonnage: 16,020
Displacement: 19,766 tons
Machinery: Turbo-Electric, 4 Boilers,
   Twin Screw
Horsepower/Speed: 18,000/20.8 knots
Fate: Laid Up, 1970

Built at Bethlehem-Alameda as the Navy troopship ADMIRAL E.W. EBERLE (AP-123) and launched by Mrs. Earl Warren in 1944, this was the first of five Army troopships converted from wartime to peacetime service at the shipyard. These were known as P-2 transports, and they were converted from troopships with a capacity of 4,463 troops to a peacetime capacity of 2,035 troops, passengers, staff, and crew.

The ADMIRAL E.W. EBERLE was manned by the Coast Guard as part of the Naval Transportation Service in World War II. During the war she made one transpacific voyage and two Atlantic round trips. Late in the war, she made three trips from Seattle to Japan and Korea. She was transferred to the Army in May 1946. She was partially converted at Todd Shipyards in Los Angeles in 1946 and made four more Pacific trips before arriving at Newport News on May 15, 1947.

Work done at the yard was extensive, including conversion of 100-person staterooms into family cabins and the provision of public rooms. During conversion, the Army name GENERAL SIMON B. BUCKNER was given to the ship, and she departed on February 13, 1948, for service between New York and German ports. In 1950 the ship was transferred back to the Navy and was assigned to the Military Sea Transportation Service (MSTS).

After many more years of service, she was transferred to the Maritime Administration in 1969 and was subsequently laid up in the James River Reserve Fleet where she remained into the 1980s.

GENERAL EDWIN D. PATRICK
1948

GENERAL EDWIN D. PATRICK

Hull No: 469
Owner: U.S. Army
Launched: —
Delivered: April 29, 1948
Dimensions: 608.82 x 75.5 x 52.5 ft
Gross Tonnage: 16,020
Displacement: 19,766 tons
Machinery: Turbo-Electric, 4 Boilers,
    Twin Screw
Horsepower/Speed: 18,000/20.8 knots
Fate: Laid Up, 1968

Army troopship GENERAL EDWIN D. PATRICK began life as ADMIRAL C.F. HUGHES (AP-124) at Bethlehem-Alameda Shipyard in 1944. She was commissioned into Navy service with a Coast Guard crew on January 31, 1945, and immediately made three voyages with troops from California to Pearl Harbor and Guam. She made a trip to France to carry troops to the Far East, then made three more trips from the West Coast to the Philippines and one to Yokohama.

She was transferred to the Army in May 1946 and entered the shipyard on June 2. As was the case with all of the P-2 transports converted at the yard, many thousands of items of ship's equipment had to be removed and stored during the work. Every available warehouse was filled, and half of the lay-off section of the Mold Loft and the former Boiler Shop were used for storage. She was provided with the same public rooms as the other ships, including a children's play room which featured colorful decorations of fish, teddy bears, and chickens, along with its tiny furniture. A fenced play area was provided on Bridge Deck.

After conversion, GENERAL EDWIN D. PATRICK was returned to the Army on April 29, 1948. She was reacquired by the Navy in March 1950 and, operated by MSTS, earned three battle stars for her Korean War service. She continued in service until being transferred to the Maritime Administration on September 20, 1968, and laid up in the Suisun Bay, CA, where she remained into the mid-1980s.

GENERAL DANIEL I. SULTAN
1948

GENERAL DANIEL I. SULTAN

Hull No: 470
Owner: U.S. Army
Launched: —
Delivered: June 24, 1948
Dimensions: 608.82 x 75.5 x 52.5 ft
Gross Tonnage: 16,039
Displacement: 19,766 tons
Machinery: Turbo-Electric, 4 Boilers,
    Twin Screw
Horsepower/Speed: 18,000/20.8 knots
Fate: Laid Up, 1968

The third of five Army P-2 transports converted by the yard after World War II was built as ADMIRAL W.S. BENSON (AP-120) by Bethlehem-Alameda Shipyard in 1944. During the war the ship saw service with the Naval Transportation Service and made two trips to India, one to France, and four across the Pacific. She was decommissioned on June 3, 1945, and was transferred to the Army.

Like the other P-2 transports, her conversion to peacetime service was done in two phases. First, only that work required to convert the ship for quick return to Army service was done at a West Coast shipyard; then, when the ship was no longer urgently needed for repatriation of troops, the more extensive and permanent work was completed. The second phase was, by far, the major part of the work, and each job was worth about $5 million. Like other conversions, these came at a time when work was sorely needed by the shipyard.

Renamed GENERAL DANIEL I. SULTAN, the ship left the yard on June 1948 looking more like a sleek ocean liner than a military transport. The conversion had included, in addition to extensive interior rennovation, a considerable amount of exterior structural work. GENERAL DANIEL I. SULTAN was handed back to the Army on June 24, 1948.

She went back into Navy service with the MSTS in 1950 and received two battle stars for service in the Korean War. She continued in service and carried troops to Vietnam before being transferred to the Maritime Administration on November 7, 1968. She was later laid up at Suisun Bay, CA, where she remained into the 1980s.

GENERAL HUGH J. GAFFEY
1948

GENERAL HUGH J. GAFFEY

Hull No: 471
Owner: U.S. Army
Launched: —
Delivered: August 19, 1948
Dimensions: 608.82 x 75.5 x 52.5 ft
Gross Tonnage: 16,039
Displacement: 19,766 tons
Machinery: Turbo-Electric, 4 Boilers,
    Twin Screw
Horsepower/Speed: 18,000/20.8 knots
Fate: Barracks Ship, 1978

The fourth P-2 transport to be converted at the yard after World War II began life as ADMIRAL W.L. CAPPS (AP-121) at Bethlehem-Alameda Shipyard in 1944. She made three transatlantic and three transpacific voyages in 1944 and 1945, then made two trips to San Francisco returning troops from Okinawa and Japan.

She was transferred to Army service in May 1946 and entered the shipyard for conversion shortly thereafter. She received the same outfitting for peacetime transport of soldiers, wives, and families as the other P-2 ships at the shipyard. A new smoking room, lounge, auditorium, children's play room, and enclosed promenade were installed. Her accommodations, while not luxurious, were handsome and comfortable.

She was returned to Army service as GENERAL HUGH J. GAFFEY on August 19, 1948. Like her sisters, she returned to Navy service in March 1950 for use as a civil service transport operated by MSTS. She was transferred to the custody of the Maritime Administration on November 27, 1968, and was laid up at Suisun Bay, CA. In 1978 she was withdrawn and converted to a barracks ship for use at the Naval Shipyard, Bremerton, WA. After seven years there, she was moved to Yokosuka, Japan, for similar service in 1985.

GENERAL WILLIAM O. DARBY
1948

GENERAL WILLIAM O. DARBY

Hull No: 473
Owner: U.S. Army
Launched: —
Delivered: October 14, 1948
Dimensions: 608.82 x 75.5 x 52.5 ft
Gross Tonnage: 16,039
Displacement: 19,766 tons
Machinery: Turbo-Electric, 4 Boilers,
    Twin Screw
Horsepower/Speed: 18,000/20.8 knots
Fate: Barracks Ship, 1981

The fifth and last of the Army P-2 transports converted at the yard was built at Bethlehem-Alameda Shipyard in 1945 as ADMIRAL W.S. SIMMS (AP-127). Commissioned on September 27, 1945, she made four trips from the West Coast to the Philippines, Korea, and Okinawa before being decommissioned on June 21, 1946. She was the last of eight P-2 "Admiral" class troopships built at Alameda, and the first phase of her conversion to peacetime service was completed at Bethlehem's San Pedro yard in May 1946. The planning for the postwar Army transport fleet had been under way even during their return of troops from overseas.

Prepared for continued service, she left the yard on October 14, 1948, as the renamed GENERAL WILLIAM O. DARBY with her gleaming white enlarged superstructure and tall buff-colored stacks with red, white and blue bands. She was reacquired by the Navy in March 1950 for Korean War service with the MSTS. She was stricken from the Navy list in 1969, transferred to the Maritime Administration, and laid up in the James River.

In 1981 she was taken out of the reserve fleet and converted for service as a Navy barracks ship for use at the Naval Shipyard, Portsmouth, VA; then, she was moved to Newport News Shipbuilding to serve as housing for ship's force during overhaul of NIMITZ from June 1983 to July 1984. Returned to Portsmouth, she again came to Newport News for the overhaul of DWIGHT D. EISENHOWER in October 1985.

CARPENTER
1949

CARPENTER

Hull No: 474
Navy No: DDK-825
Launched: —
Delivered: December 15, 1949
Dimensions: 390.5 x 40.82 x 24.0 ft
Displacement: 3,040 tons
Armament: 4 3″ Guns, 4 21″ TT
Machinery: Geared Turbines, 4 Boilers,
   Twin Screw
Horsepower/Speed: 12,500/35 knots
Fate: In Commission

CARPENTER was a GEARING-class destroyer whose construction was begun at the Consolidated Shipbuilding Co. at Orange, TX, in 1945. Her contract was cancelled early in 1946 but then started again until the ship was transferred to the Navy in October 1946.

When delivered by tug to Newport News on November 6, 1947, CARPENTER was about 70 percent complete and was in good condition due to the installation of a dehumidifying system. She was completed by the yard as the first ship of a new class of hunter-killer (antisubmarine) destroyers which bore her name. She was fitted with the latest weapons and secret sonar devices and was commissioned at the Norfolk Naval Shipyard on December 15, 1949, with Cdr. J.B. Grady in command. The shipyard delivered CARPENTER with mixed pride and regret, since at her completion there were no Navy contracts in hand for the first time in 22 years.

CARPENTER joined the Pacific Fleet after shakedown and was based at Pearl Harbor. She saw service with TF 77 and participated in several shore bombardments and patrol cruises in the Taiwan Strait. She received five battle stars for her Korean War service.

From the end of the war to 1960, CARPENTER operated between Pearl Harbor and the Far East in training and exercises. After almost 20 more years in similar service, she was sold to the Turkish Navy on February 20, 1981, and was renamed ANITTEPE (D-347).

ANKARA
1949

ANKARA

Hull No: 487
Owner: Turkish Government
Launched: —
Delivered: April 12, 1949
Dimensions: 409.33 x 62.0 x 30.5 ft
Gross Tonnage: 6,179
Displacement: 8,650 tons
Machinery: Geared Turbines, 3 Boilers,
    Twin Screw
Horsepower/Speed: 8,500/18 knots
Fate: Scrapped, 1981

One of the most famous of Newport News ships, ANKARA was built as IROQUOIS (Hull 306) in 1927. She served her original owner, the Clyde Line, between New York and Florida ports until 1940.

In that year she was acquired by the Navy and converted to the hospital ship SOLACE (AH-5). She was probably the busiest hospital ship of World War II, as she treated more than 25,000 patients and steamed more than 170,000 miles in the Pacific. She was laid up in the James River Reserve Fleet after the war and was sold to Turkish Maritime Lines in April 1948.

Her conversion to ANKARA for service between Istanbul, Alexandria, and Marseilles was the last of 25 major and minor postwar conversions done at the yard. She arrived at the yard quite different in appearance than when she left in 1927. Her after stack had been removed and she had become a naval ship. On the inside, her original ornate wooden interior had been stripped out in 1940. The conversion work in 1948 was considerable and cost more than her original construction. Modern accommodations were provided for 175 first class, 152 second class, and 72 steerage class passengers; and the most contemporary furnishings, colors, and decorative methods were used.

She entered Turkish service in April 1949 and continued until laid up in Istanbul in 1977. She was finally sold for scrap and broken up in 1981.

LAKE CHAMPLAIN
1952

LAKE CHAMPLAIN

Hull No: 489
Navy No: CV-39
Launched: —
Delivered: September 19, 1952
Dimensions: 871.82 x 101 x 54.52 ft
Displacement: 38,436 tons
Armament: 12 5″ Guns
Machinery: Geared Turbines, 8 Boilers,
    Quadruple Screw
Horsepower/Speed: 150,000/33 knots
Fate: Scrapped, 1972

Originally delivered by the Norfolk Navy Yard in June 1945, LAKE CHAMPLAIN was the first of three aircraft carriers modernized at Newport News in the early 1950s. After less than two years in "Magic Carpet" service returning servicemen home from Europe and having set a speed record for crossing the Atlantic, LAKE CHAMPLAIN was laid up at Norfolk in February 1947.

A contract for her reactivation and modernization for Korean War service was signed by the shipyard on August 18, 1950. The work was worth $38 million and kept about 2,000 yard workers busy until late 1952. The ship's flight deck and its supporting structure were strengthened. Heavier catapults, elevators, and other facilities were provided to service the then-relatively new jet aircraft which had come into service since 1947.

A like-new LAKE CHAMPLAIN left the yard on September 19, 1952. She was made the flagship of Carrier Task Force 77 and saw Korean service until July 1953. She was converted to an anti-submarine carrier in 1957 and successfully recovered Alan Sheppard's Mercury capsule "Freedom 7" in 1960. LAKE CHAMPLAIN participated in the Cuban blockade in 1962. She participated in training and exercise duty until serving as the prime recovery ship for Gemini 5.

She was deactivated and decommissioned in May 1966 at Philadelphia and was stricken from the Navy list on December 1, 1969. In 1972 she was sold and was subsequently scrapped at Kearny, NJ.

RANDOLPH
1953

RANDOLPH

Hull No: 505
Navy No: CV-15
Launched: —
Delivered: July 1, 1953
Dimensions: 871.82 x 101 x 54.52 ft
Displacement: 38,436 tons
Armament: 12 5″ Guns
Machinery: Geared Turbines, 8 Boilers,
    Quadruple Screw
Horsepower/Speed: 150,000/32 knots
Fate: Scrapped, 1975

Completed in late 1944 as Newport News Hull 398, RANDOLPH saw considerable action during her nine-month service in World War II and earned three battle stars for it. She was hit by a kamikaze aircraft in March 1945 and served with Halsey's famous Third Fleet. Many of her strikes were against the Japanese mainland and Japanese shipping. She arrived at Norfolk in October 1945 and made two trips in "Magic Carpet" service returning American military person-nel from Europe. She later became a training ship, then was placed in reserve at Philadelphia in February 1946.

A contract was awarded to the shipyard to modernize RANDOLPH on June 5, 1951. The carrier was towed to Newport News and entered Shipway 10 shortly after the launch of the liner UNITED STATES from it. RANDOLPH had originally been built in Shipway 10, and she spent a large part of her modernization there. Her work was similar to that for LAKE CHAMPLAIN and INTREPID, also done at the yard, and she was returned to the Navy on July 1, 1953. She served with the Sixth Fleet, then in 1955 was again modernized and provided with an angled flight deck at the Norfolk Navy Yard.

She spent several more years in the Mediter-ranean, then became the recovery ship for Astronauts Virgil Grissom in 1961 and John Glenn in 1962. She served in the Cuban blockade, then returned for more service in the Mediterranean and Caribbean.

In February 1969 she was decommissioned and laid up at Philadelphia, and in June 1973 she was stricken from the Navy list. In April 1975 she was sold and was subsequently scrapped.

INTREPID
1954

INTREPID

Hull No: 507
Navy No: CV-11
Launched: —
Delivered: June 18, 1954
Dimensions: 871.82 x 103 x 54.52 ft
Displacement: 41,434 tons
Armament: 12 5″ Guns
Machinery: Geared Turbines, 8 Boilers,
    Quadruple Screw
Horsepower/Speed: 150,000/33 knots
Fate: Museum Ship, 1982

The third and last ESSEX-class aircraft carrier to be modernized at the yard during the Korean War was the famous INTREPID, completed at Newport News in 1943 as Hull 394. INTREPID saw extensive action in the Pacific war, and her planes destroyed 650 enemy aircraft and sank or damaged 289 enemy ships. She was put in reserve at San Francisco in 1946 but was taken out late in 1950 and arrived at Newport News in the spring of 1951.

After her conversion at the shipyard, she returned to service until being again modernized in 1956-1958 at the New York Naval Shipyard and fitted with an angled flight deck. She was redesignated as an anti-submarine carrier (CVS) in 1962 and in that year recovered Astronaut Scott Carpenter. Later she re-covered Astronauts Gus Grissom and John Young's Gemini capsule.

INTREPID was again modernized in 1965, then deployed for three tours of duty in Vietnam. She served in Atlantic and Mediterranean waters in anti-submarine duty. She was retired in 1974 but served as the host ship for the Bicentennial Exposition in Philadelphia in 1976. In March 1982 she was towed from Philadelphia to Bayonne, NJ, and was reactivated for duty as a museum ship. She began this service at New York on July 4, 1982.

JOHN SERGEANT
1956

JOHN SERGEANT

Hull No: 518
Owner: U.S. Maritime Administration
Launched: —
Delivered: September 26, 1956
Dimensions: 467.25 x 56.90 x 37.33 ft
Gross Tonnage: 7,780
Displacement: 13,570 tons
Machinery: Geared Gas Turbine, 2 Boilers
Horsepower/Speed: 6,000/18 knots
Fate: Scrapped, 1974

In August 1955 the shipyard received a contract from the Maritime Administration to convert the Liberty ship JOHN SERGEANT from steam to gas turbine propulsion. This, the first shipboard installation of its kind, involved removing the original engine and boiler and replacing them with a 6,000 horsepower open cycle gas turbine unit. In addition to the machinery modifications, the ship was provided with a new bow section which extended her length by 25 ft, had her hull and decks strengthened, and had her superstructure enlarged. The gas turbine machinery was built by General Electric, and the ship was provided with a reversible pitch propeller made by the S. Morgan Smith Co. Rudder, shafting, and gears were all improved to accommodate the increase in power from 2,160 to 6,000 shaft horsepower.

On trials in September 1956, JOHN SERGEANT's speed was observed at 18 knots, up from her original 11 knots. She entered general cargo service with U.S. Lines late in 1956 and remained with them until laid up in the James River Reserve Fleet in 1959. She was finally sold for scrap by the Maritime Administration in 1974.

MATSONIA
1957

MATSONIA

Hull No: 523
Owner: Matson Navigation Co.
Launched: —
Delivered: May 10, 1957
Dimensions: 638.67 x 79 x 44.5 ft
Gross Tonnage: 18,656
Displacement: 26,141 tons
Machinery: Geared Turbines, 12 Boilers,
    Twin Screw
Horsepower/Speed: 22,000/20 knots
Fate: In Service

Originally built as MONTEREY by Bethlehem-Quincy in 1932, MATSONIA saw troop-carrier service during World War II. After the war, about $5 million was spent on her reconversion to merchant service but the work was halted in 1947. She had been stripped of wartime equipment and was laid up at San Francisco,

so she was not much more than an empty shell when she arrived at Newport News for completion of the work on April 20, 1956. Much of her machinery had been removed and overhauled after the war but had not been reinstalled. Part of the work at Newport News included the installation of a modern clipper bow. Her empty cabins, public rooms, and passageways were transformed such that at delivery she was one of the most modern and comfortable ships afloat.

At the completion of this, the largest such project in U.S. merchant marine history, the gleaming white MATSONIA was christened by Mrs. Neal S. Blaisdell, wife of the mayor of Honolulu, at the yard on May 17, 1957. The like-new ship entered the California-Hawaii service with accommodations for 770 passengers.

In 1963 she was renamed LURLINE, and she remained with Matson until she was sold to Ajax Navigation Co., transferred to Greek flag, and renamed BRITANIS in 1970. She continued with that company cruise service in the Caribbean into the 1980s.

AIRCRAFT CARRIERS
RANGER
1934

RANGER

Hull No: 353
Navy No: CV-4
Launched: February 25, 1933
Commissioned: June 4, 1934
Dimensions: 769 x 80 x 51 ft
Displacement: 15,758 tons
Armament: 8 5" Guns
Machinery: Geared Turbines, 6 Boilers,
   Twin Screw
Horsepower/Speed: 53,500/29.25 knots
Fate: Scrapped, 1947

On November 1, 1930, the shipyard received a $15.2 million contract for the first Navy ship designed and built from the keel up as an aircraft carrier. This ship, named RANGER, was the culmination of Navy design studies dating back to 1922 and was preceded by LANGLEY, a converted collier, as well as LEXINGTON and SARATOGA, converted battle cruisers.

Originally designed as a flush deck ship with folding stacks, RANGER was provided with an island while under construction, which gave her a weight problem all of her life. She displaced 15,758 tons and

introduced the open hangar deck and the gallery deck to aircraft carrier design.

The keel for the innovative RANGER was laid on Shipway 8 on September 26, 1931, and she was launched by Mrs. Herbert Hoover on February 25, 1933. The new ship, with her complement of 1,788 men and her 736 ft flight deck, was commissioned as CV-4 at the Norfolk Navy Yard on June 4, 1934, with Capt. Arthur L. Bristol commanding.

After commissioning, RANGER served in the Atlantic until March 1935, then transferred to Pacific service. She sailed along the west coast of North and South America and to Hawaii for four years, then returned to the Atlantic in 1939. She saw Neutrality Patrol and wartime duty in the Atlantic until 1942, was overhauled at the Norfolk Navy Yard early in 1942, then ferried 140 Army P-40s to Accra, on the Gold Coast of Africa, in two trips. She was the only large American carrier in the Atlantic Fleet and led a task force including four escort carriers, which provided air power in support of the invasion of German-held French Morocco in November 1942. RANGER launched 496 combat sorties during this operation and later became known as "The Mighty 'R'."

(Continued on page 239)

YORKTOWN
1937

YORKTOWN

Hull No: 359
Navy No: CV-5
Launched: April 4, 1936
Commissioned: September 30, 1937
Dimensions: 824.75 x 82.25 x 52.5 ft
Displacement: 23,547 tons
Armament: 8 5″ Guns
Machinery: Geared Turbines, 9 Boilers,
    Quadruple Screw
Horsepower/Speed: 120,000/32.5 knots
Fate: War Loss, 1942

On August 3, 1933, Newport News was low bidder for two aircraft carriers which became the famous YORKTOWN (CV-5) and ENTERPRISE (CV-6). These ships, at 20,000 tons, were considerably larger than RANGER and were the first carriers designed with the benefit of operational experience. They were provided with steam turbine machinery of 120,000 horsepower and quadruple screws and were capable of a speed of 32.5 knots. While complete plans and specifications had been furnished by the Navy for RANGER, only preliminary information was available for the new ships. Newport News designers and engineers therefore completed both contract and detail design, setting a precedent for virtually every class of U.S. carrier to follow. The result was a three-elevator ship with catapults on two decks, an island, open bow, and capacity for 85 airplanes.

The keel for YORKTOWN was laid on Shipway 8 on May 21, 1934, and the shipyard's largest hull to that date was ready for launch less than two years later. First Lady Mrs. Eleanor Roosevelt served as sponsor for the new carrier on April 4, 1936. After completion of successful trials, YORKTOWN was commissioned at Norfolk on September 30, 1937, with Capt. Ernest D. McWhorter in command.

Entire volumes have been written about the service career of the gallant YORKTOWN. She was attached to the Atlantic Fleet in routine training operations until April 1939, was transferred to the Pacific for two years, then returned to the Atlantic in April 1941. She conducted four patrols there before the attack on Pearl Harbor, then departed Norfolk for her destiny in the Pacific on December 16, 1941. Early in the war she escorted a number of troop convoys; then, she executed the first U.S. carrier attack of the war in the Marshalls and Gilberts in February 1942.

(Continued on page 239)

ENTERPRISE
1938

ENTERPRISE

Hull No: 360
Navy No: CV-6
Launched: October 3, 1936
Commissioned: May 12, 1938
Dimensions: 824.75 x 82.25 x 52.5 ft
Displacement: 23,547 tons
Armament: 8 5" Guns
Machinery: Geared Turbines, 9 Boilers,
    Quadruple Screw
Horsepower/Speed: 120,000/ 32.5 knots
Fate: Scrapped, 1958

The second YORKTOWN-class ship built at Newport News was ENTERPRISE (CV-6), which was to become one of the most famous fighting ships in U.S. history. The keel for ENTERPRISE was laid on Shipway 9 on July 16, 1934, and she was launched on October 3, 1936. Mrs. Claude A. Swanson, wife of the Secretary of the Navy, was sponsor and Mrs. Woodrow Wilson attended the ceremony. Like her sister ship, ENTERPRISE was armed with eight 5" guns and twenty-two .50 cal machine guns and had a complement of 306 officers and 2,613 enlisted men. Successful acceptance trials were held on April 12-14, 1938, and the new ENTERPRISE was placed in commission at Norfolk on May 12, with Capt. N.H. White commanding.

After spending her first year in the Atlantic, the carrier began duty in the Pacific in April 1939, and she conducted training operations which were to later prove invaluable. When the Japanese attacked Pearl Harbor, ENTERPRISE was enroute to Hawaii from Wake Island and her aircraft sortied against the attackers.

During the war, she became known as the "Galloping Ghost of the Oahu Coast," and she was in the thick of virtually every major naval battle in the Pacific. She steamed over a quarter of a million miles during the war and her battle record was impresssive. She was damaged fifteen times in combat but dished out many times more damage on the enemy, claiming 911 Japanese planes, 71 ships sunk, and 192 ships damaged. The Japanese reported her sunk on six occasions but she fought on.

ENTERPRISE pioneered 24-hour carrier operations which helped turn the tide in the Pacific and made carriers the leaders in naval warfare. She was awarded the Presidential Unit Citation for her service as well as the Navy Unit Commendation and an impressive 20 battle stars.

She entered "Magic Carpet" service after the war and brought more than 10,000 veterans home from Europe. Battle weary, the "Big E" was decommissioned on February 17, 1947, and remained in reserve until she was sold for scrap in 1958.

HORNET
1941

HORNET

Hull No: 385
Navy No: CV-8
Launched: December 14, 1940
Commissioned: October 20, 1941
Dimensions: 824.75 x 82.25 x 52.5 ft
Displacement: 23,927 tons
Armament: 8 5″ Guns
Machinery: Geared Turbines, 9 Boilers,
    Quadruple Screw
Horsepower/Speed: 120,000/32.5 knots
Fate: War Loss, 1942

The Navy's seventh aircraft carrier was built at another shipyard, but, beginning with HORNET (CV-8) in 1941, the next eight were built at Newport News. The shipyard obtained a contract for HORNET on April 10, 1939, and her keel was laid down on Shipway 8 on the following September 25.

Although similar to YORKTOWN and ENTERPRISE, HORNET was considered by the Navy to be in a class by herself. Her flight deck was slightly wider than her predecessors, and her complement was 160 officers and 1,729 enlisted men. HORNET was fitted with two catapults on her flight deck and was the only Newport News carrier with shipyard-built machinery.

After just under 15 months on the ways, HORNET

was launched on December 14, 1940. Mrs. Frank Knox, wife of the Secretary of the Navy, served as sponsor for the new carrier. HORNET completed trials on September 25, 1941, and was commissioned three months ahead of schedule at Norfolk on October 20, 1941. Capt. Marc A. Mitscher, a veteran of the Navy's first transatlantic flight in 1918, was HORNET's first skipper.

The training period of the new carrier was interrupted by the attack on Pearl Harbor in December. In February 1942 an experiment was conducted in which two B-25 bombers were launched from HORNET's deck in preparation for an important future mission. She left the Atlantic for the Pacific war on March 4, 1942, and loaded 16 B-25 bombers at San Francisco later that month. On April 18 these planes were launched for the daring raid on Tokyo led by LCol. "Jimmy" Dolittle; however, over a year passed and HORNET was lost in combat before her role in this secret mission was made public.

HORNET was destined for a gallant wartime career but not for a long one. She arrived on site one day after the Battle of the Coral Sea but was in the thick of the fighting at Midway. All 15 planes of her famed Torpedo Squadron Eight were lost to enemy fighters on June 4, 1942, but her others helped sink four Japanese carriers and other ships and made Midway the decisive battle of the Pacific war.

(Continued on page 239)

ESSEX
1942

ESSEX

Hull No: 392
Navy No: CV-9
Launched: July 31, 1942
Commissioned: December 31, 1942
Dimensions: 855.82 x 93 x 54.5 ft
Displacement: 33,292 tons
Armament: 12 5″ Guns
Machinery: Geared Turbines, 8 Boilers,
    Quadruple Screw
Horsepower/Speed: 150,000/33 knots
Fate: Scrapped, 1975

First of a class of 24 ships, ESSEX became known as the "Fightingest Ship in the Navy" and participated in fully 68 combat operations in the Pacific. CV-9 was ordered together with YORKTOWN, INTREPID, and cruisers BIRMINGHAM and MOBILE on July 3, 1940, and at 27,100 tons, she was considerably larger than her predecessors. She and her class were to become the backbone of the Navy's Pacific carrier operations during World War II.

The keel for ESSEX was laid on Shipway 8 on April 28, 1941, and she was launched on July 31, 1942. Mrs. Artemus L. Gates, wife of the Assistant Secretary of the Navy for Air, was sponsor for the shipyard's fifth carrier. During the ship's fifteen months on the ways, the attack on Pearl Harbor took place, and LANGLEY and YORKTOWN were lost. During her outfitting period, LEXINGTON, WASP, and HORNET were lost; and after commissioning on December 31, 1942, under the command of Capt. D.B. Duncan, she underwent shakedown, then steamed to the Pacific the following May.

ESSEX participated in virtually every action during the remainder of the Pacific war and won a Presidential Unit Citation and thirteen battle stars for her service.

After assaults at Marcus Island, Wake, Rabaul, Kwajalein Atoll, Truk, and Saipan, she underwent overhaul from February to May 1944 at San Francisco. During the Okinawa campaign in 1944, she operated combat planes for an unprecedented 79 consecutive days. Her air groups destroyed over 1,500 enemy aircraft and over 100 enemy ships and damaged many more. Her gunners shot down 33 enemy aircraft but were unable to stop a kamikaze which hit her flight deck on November 25, 1944. This attack caused heavy damage, killing 15 men and wounding 44, but ESSEX's crew repaired her deck and miraculously had her back in action within an hour. Fortunately this was her only major hit of the war.

(Continued on page 239)

YORKTOWN
1943

YORKTOWN

Hull No: 393
Navy No: CV-10
Launched: January 21, 1943
Commissioned: April 15, 1943
Dimensions: 855.82 x 93 x 54.5 ft
Displacement: 33,292 tons
Armament: 12 5″ Guns
Machinery: Geared Turbines, 8 Boilers,
    Quadruple Screw
Horsepower/Speed: 150,000/33 knots
Fate: Museum Ship, 1975

Hardly had the first YORKTOWN (CV-5) settled to the bottom of the Pacific in June 1942 when sentiment arose in the shipyard to give her name to another Newport News-built aircraft carrier. A letter from shipyard employees sought to rename ESSEX, but this was not possible, so the name of the second ESSEX-class carrier was changed from BON HOMME RICHARD to YORKTOWN (CV-10) in September 1942.

The keel for the second YORKTOWN was laid on December 1, 1941, just days before the attack on Pearl Harbor, and that of INTREPID (CV-11) was laid on the same day. The new YORKTOWN gained several nicknames during her career, the first of which was "The Eager Ship." During her launching ceremony on January 21, 1943, she began to move minutes ahead of schedule, but her experienced sponsor First Lady Mrs. Eleanor Roosevelt quickly broke the bottle on her bow before she got away. A total of only 17 months passed between the laying of YORKTOWN's keel and her commissioning under Capt. J.J. Clark on April 15, 1943, a record never equalled in carrier construction.

After shakedown in the Atlantic, the new YORK-TOWN left for the Pacific via Panama on July 6, 1943. Her first action was at Marcus Island on August 31 and, like ESSEX, she was involved in almost every engagement in the Pacific from that time until Tokyo Bay. As the war progressed, YORKTOWN had many narrow escapes from damage and became known as the "Lucky Y." Engaged in strikes against Japan in March 1945, she was struck by a bomb which hit her signal bridge, killing five men and wounding 26, but she remained operational and continued fighting.

During the rest of the war, she was known as the "Fighting Lady," and she later starred in a Hollywood film of that name. During World War II, YORKTOWN earned 11 battle stars and the Presidential Unit Citation for her gallantry.

(Continued on page 239)

RANGER *Continued from page 233*

She returned to Norfolk in late November and was overhauled; then, after delivering 75 planes to Casablanca and patrolling in New England waters, she joined the British Home Fleet in August 1943. She steamed into Norwegian waters with her task force in October and launched attacks against German shipping which did considerable damage.

For the first half of 1944, she engaged in training and aircraft ferry operations in the Atlantic; then, in May of that year, she underwent modernization at Norfolk. In July, RANGER sailed for the Pacific where she engaged in night fighting training operations on the West Coast until war's end.

She returned to the East Coast in October 1945 and was decommissioned on October 18, 1946. Winner of two battle stars for her World War II action, the weary RANGER was sold and scrapped at Philadelphia in 1947.

YORKTOWN *Continued from page 234*

YORKTOWN's combat career lasted only four months but her achievements were remarkable. She pioneered carrier task force operations in the Pacific and participated in the campaigns of Coral Sea and Midway, which halted Japanese expansion. During the Coral Sea campaign in May 1942, YORKTOWN joined the first carrier duel in history, and her planes and those from LEXINGTON sank the Japanese carrier SHOHO. As carrier warfare was in its infancy, several Japanese pilots mistook YORKTOWN for one of their own and attempted to land on her deck, only to be welcomed by fire from her guns. After hasty damage repairs at Pearl Harbor, YORKTOWN joined the Battle of Midway with sisters ENTERPRISE and HORNET in June 1942.

During the fierce battle, she was hit by three bombs and two torpedoes, flooded to third deck, and lost power. Salvage crews fought bravely to save the mortally wounded YORKTOWN, but she was struck by two more torpedoes on June 6. The gallant YORK-TOWN capsized and sank in 3,000 fathoms at 7:00 A.M. on June 7, 1942, with her battle flags still flying.

HORNET *Continued from page 236*

Action in the Solomons in August left HORNET as the only U.S. carrier operating in the South Pacific. She joined repaired ENTERPRISE in October, and they met the Japanese fleet head-on in the Battle of Santa Cruz on the 26th. Planes from HORNET heavily damaged one enemy carrier and a cruiser, but she herself was subjected to a dive bombing and torpedo attack which so heavily damaged her that she had to be abandoned. HORNET had been hit by six large bombs, nine torpedoes, and two enemy planes which crashed aboard her; however, it took hits from over 400 American 5″ shells and from four more enemy torpedoes before she finally sank on October 27, 1942.

ESSEX *Continued from page 237*

War's end found her at Tokyo Bay, and after the surrender she steamed to Bremerton, WA, for deactivation. She was placed in reserve in January 1947, then was reactivated in January 1951, having been fitted with a new flight deck and a streamlined island. She won four more battle stars and the Navy Unit Commendation for Korean War action, then saw training action.

In 1955 she was extensively overhauled at Puget Sound and was provided with an angled flight deck. She was transferred to the Atlantic in 1956 and supported the U.S. mission in Beirut in 1958. In 1960 she was converted to an ASW carrier and became CVS-9, homeported at Quonset Point. She underwent FRAM conversion in 1962 and served for seven more years before being withdrawn from service in June 1969. Placed in reserve, she was finally stricken and scrapped in 1975.

YORKTOWN *Continued from page 238*

She was engaged in passenger service immediately after the war, then was placed in the Pacific Reserve Fleet in January 1947. After almost five years at rest, she was recommissioned in December 1952, but she reentered the fleet too late to see action in the Korean War. In 1955 YORKTOWN received a new flight deck to facilitate jet aircraft operations; then, in 1957 she was reclassified as an ASW carrier and was redesignated as CVS-10. In April 1965 she saw her first deployment to Vietnam, which became her main operating area for the next three years, enabling her to receive five more battle stars.

In 1968 YORKTOWN enjoyed two unusual missions: first as a platform for the filming of *Tora! Tora! Tora!*; then as a recovery ship for Apollo 8.

Early in 1969 she was transferred and took up service in the Atlantic, returning there after a 26-year absence. Homeported at Norfolk, YORKTOWN served the Atlantic Fleet in ASW exercises until she was decommissioned and laid up in the Atlantic Reserve Fleet in 1970. Her name was stricken in 1973, but she was saved from scrapping. The proud YORKTOWN was donated for use as a memorial and was dedicated at Charleston, SC, on the 200th anniversary of the Navy on October 13, 1975.

INTREPID
1943

INTREPID

Hull No: 394
Navy No: CV-11
Launched: April 26, 1943
Commissioned: August 16, 1943
Dimensions: 855.82 x 93 x 54.5 ft
Displacement: 33,292 tons
Armament: 12 5" Guns
Machinery: Geared Turbines, 8 Boilers,
    Quadruple Screw
Horsepower/Speed: 150,000/33 knots
Fate: Museum Ship, 1982

The keel for the third ESSEX-class aircraft carrier, later named INTREPID (CV-11), was laid down in Shipway 10 on December 1, 1941. Like her Newport News-built sisters, this ship was to become a legend of the Pacific war. INTREPID was the first large ship to be launched by flotation at Newport News and this occurred on April 26, 1943. Sponsor for CV-11 was Mrs. John H. Hoover, wife of VAdm. Hoover, and the ceremony was small and brief under wartime conditions. INTREPID was completed and commissioned on August 16, 1943, with Capt. Thomas L. Sprague commanding. She trained in the Caribbean, then sailed for Pearl Harbor via San Francisco in December.

INTREPID was to have a gallant wartime career but was damaged so many times that she became known as the "Unlucky I" or "Dry I" (a reference to her frequent drydockings to repair battle damage).

In February 1944 she was struck by an enemy torpedo and her rudder was damaged, but her crew ingeniously jury-rigged a sail which enabled her to return to Pearl Harbor. In October 1944 she helped sink the Japanese battleship MUSASHI, but on October 30 she was hit by a kamikaze and lost ten of her crew. On November 24 INTREPID was hit by two more suicide planes and was heavily damaged, losing 65 of her crew. In spite of the damage, she never lost power and all fires were extinguished within two hours. After repairs at San Francisco, she participated in attacks on Okinawa and Tokyo, and in April 1945 she helped sink the Japanese battleship YAMATO. INTREPID was again hit by a kamikaze off Okinawa on April 16 and eight men were killed, but fires were out in an hour and carrier operations resumed within three hours.

After the war ended she briefly served with the occupation force; then, she retired to the Pacific Reserve Fleet with five battle stars and the Navy Unit Commendation on her record. INTREPID was withdrawn from reserve and was modernized at Newport News as Hull 507, being provided with the Navy's first steam catapults. She operated in the Atlantic and Mediterranean in 1955 and 1956, then was refitted and given an angled flight deck at the New York Navy Yard.

(Continued on page 251)

HORNET
1943

Official U.S. Navy Photograph

HORNET

Hull No: 395
Navy No: CV-12
Launched: August 30, 1943
Commissioned: November 29, 1943
Dimensions: 855.82 x 93 x 54.5 ft
Displacement: 33,292 tons
Armament: 12 5″ Guns
Machinery: Geared Turbines, 8 Boilers,
    Quadruple Screw
Horsepower/Speed: 150,000/33 knots
Fate: Laid Up, 1970

The fourth ESSEX-class aircraft carrier built at Newport News was HORNET (CV-12), named in memory of the first carrier HORNET (CV-8) lost at Santa Cruz in 1942. When her keel was laid on Shipway 8 on August 3, 1943, HORNET was the fourth carrier under construction at the shipyard. The new HORNET was launched by Mrs. Frank M. Knox, who had sponsored the first carrier HORNET, on August 30, 1943. HORNET was quickly completed and was commissioned on November 29, 1943, under the command of Capt. Miles M. Browning.

After shakedown in the Atlantic the new carrier sailed for the Pacific in February 1944. She participated in the invasions of New Guinea and conducted raids against enemy bases in the Carolines during March, April, and May. Her planes scored many victories in the "Marianas Turkey Shoot" of June 1944, which left only 35 operational aircraft of the 430 with which the Japanese had entered the Battle of the Philippine Sea.

HORNET continued operations against enemy bases and shipping in the Philippines for several months. Early in 1945 she launched raids against Tokyo; then she supported the landings on Iwo Jima in late February. In April her planes supported the assault on Okinawa and also participated in attacks which sank the superbattleship YAMATO and her escorts.

In June 1945 HORNET was caught in a typhoon which damaged her flight deck and ended her combat career during which she had received the Presidential Unit Citation and seven battle stars. She was overhauled at San Francisco and, following four months of "Magic Carpet" troop service, she was decommissioned in January 1947 and was placed in reserve. HORNET was inactive until March 1951 when she sailed to the New York Navy Yard for conversion to an attack carrier (CVA).

She was recommissioned in September 1953 and, after an eight-month world cruise and brief duty in the Indian Ocean and in the Mediterranean, served in the Pacific until 1955. In December of that year, HORNET entered Puget Sound Naval Shipyard and was fitted with a modern closed bow and an angled flight deck.

She became an ASW carrier in 1958 and remained in the Pacific for the rest of her career. In 1966 she recovered an unmanned Apollo spacecraft near Wake, and during the next few years she made several deployments to Vietnam. In 1970 the old HORNET was withdrawn from service and was decommissioned and placed in the Pacific Reserve Fleet at Bremerton, WA.

FRANKLIN
1944

FRANKLIN

Hull No: 396
Navy No: CV-13
Launched: October 14, 1943
Commissioned: January 31, 1944
Dimensions: 855.82 x 93 x 54.5 ft
Displacement: 33,292 tons
Armament: 12 5" Guns
Machinery: Geared Turbines, 8 Boilers,
    Quadruple Screw
Horsepower/Speed: 150,000/33 knots
Fate: Scrapped, 1966

The keel for the fifth ESSEX-class aircraft carrier, later named FRANKLIN (CV-13) was laid in Shipway 11 on December 7, 1942, bringing the number of carriers being built at the yard to an unprecedented five. Later known as "Big Ben," the FRANKLIN became famous for withstanding terrible damage and surviving to steam home under her own power. FRANKLIN was floated out of Shipway 11 on October 14, 1943, and was sponsored by LCdr. Mildred H. McAfee, director of the WAVES.

The new carrier was commissioned on January 31, 1944, and after shakedown, joined TG 58.2 in the Pacific. In July 1944 she launched strikes against the three Jimas, then Guam and Rota in preparation for their invasion. In the Philippines in October, she was struck by an enemy plane and was also hit with a bomb which killed three of her crew and wounded 22. Her planes destroyed a number of ships and planes in Manila Bay.

During the action around Leyte in late October, she was hit by two suicide planes, one of which crashed through to her gallery deck, killing 56 men and wounding 60. FRANKLIN underwent temporary repairs at Ulithi, then was overhauled at Puget Sound.

By March 1945 she was back in action, launching attacks on the Japanese mainland. Only 50 miles from Japan, she was hit by two 500-pound bombs on March 19, which left her ablaze and dead in the water with 724 killed and 265 injured. The ship lost radio communication and took a 13 degree list, but 710 heroic crewman stayed with her and saved her. Miraculously, they patched her up and steamed her to Pearl Harbor, over 6,000 miles away, and the Navy and the American people lavished praise on her gallant crew and on her builder. She was cleaned up at Pearl Harbor, then sailed for New York Naval Shipyard and overhaul.

She was opened to the public as a heroine after the war but was decommissioned in February 1947 and was placed in reserve at Bayonne, NJ. Proud winner of four battle stars for her war service, the gallant FRANKLIN remained in reserve until she was stricken in 1964 and scrapped in 1966.

TICONDEROGA
1944

TICONDEROGA

Hull No: 397
Navy No: CV-14
Launched: February 7, 1944
Commissioned: May 8, 1944
Dimensions: 888 x 93 x 54.5 ft
Displacement: 33,292 tons
Armament: 12 5″ Guns
Machinery: Geared Turbines, 8 Boilers,
    Quadruple Screw
Horsepower/Speed: 150,000/33 knots
Fate: Scrapped, 1974

TICONDEROGA or "Big Ti" (CV-14) was the shipyard's tenth aircraft carrier, and she was completed almost exactly ten years after RANGER, its first. CV-14 was basically an ESSEX-class carrier but had a widened extreme-clipper bow and a flight deck extension which increased her length to 888 feet.

TICONDEROGA was originally laid down as HANCOCK on Shipway 9 on February 1, 1943, but her name was exchanged with that of CV-19 on the following May 1. Carrier construction went on around the clock during the war, and TICONDEROGA was ready for launch just 53 weeks after her keel was laid. Sponsor for the big ship was Miss Stephanie Pell, whose grandfather had restored Fort Ticonderoga and

was present at the ceremony on February 7, 1944. A romance was also launched that day, as Miss Pell met a "dashing" French naval officer who became her husband within a year. TICONDEROGA was completed quickly and was commissioned on May 8 with Capt. Dixie Kiefer commanding.

After shakedown in the West Indies, the new carrier departed Norfolk on July 30. She loaded supplies and aircraft at San Diego, then proceeded to Hawaii. After a month at Pearl Harbor, she raced westward to join in the assault on the Philippines. She and sister carriers ESSEX, YORKTOWN, and HORNET successfully screened MacArthur's assault on Mindoro in December; then, joined by ENTERPRISE in January 1945, the five Newport News-built fighters struck against the Japanese at Luzon. The action moved to the South China Sea where "Big Ti's" planes attacked an enemy convoy and sank a claimed ten ships.

On January 21 her luck went sour, and she was hit by two suicide planes which killed or wounded 345 of her crew. Ship's force fought valiantly and saved TICONDEROGA from sinking while Capt. Kiefer, seriously wounded, refused medical attention for 12 hours until the situation was under control. TICONDEROGA retired to Puget Sound for repairs, then rejoined the war in May. She spent the last days of the war in Japanese home waters and won a total of five battle stars for her service.

(Continued on page 251)

RANDOLPH
1944

RANDOLPH

Hull No: 398
Navy No: CV-15
Launched: June 28, 1944
Commissioned: October 9, 1944
Dimensions: 888 x 93 x 54.5 ft
Displacement: 33,292 tons
Armament: 12 5" Guns
Machinery: Geared Turbines, 8 Boilers,
    Quadruple Screw
Horsepower/Speed:150,000/33 knots
Fate: Scrapped, 1975

Carrier RANDOLPH (CV-15), named for the famous frigate of 1776, was ordered with carriers HORNET, FRANKLIN, and TICONDEROGA and light cruisers BILOXI and HOUSTON on September 9, 1940. Due to intense activity in the shipyard, the laying of her keel in Shipway 10 was not scheduled until May 10, 1943. RANDOLPH was floated from the shipway on June 28, 1944, after christening by Mrs. Guy M. Gillette, wife of the senator from Iowa. As was the usual practice during the war years, formal sea trials were waived, and the new carrier was placed in commission on October 9, 1944, with Capt. Felix Baker commanding.

RANDOLPH reached San Francisco on December 31 and left for Ulithi, arriving on February 10, 1945. She launched attacks on the Jimas and on Tokyo, but while at anchor at Ulithi on March 11, she was hit in her side by a kamikaze and 25 men were killed and 106 were wounded. Repaired, she joined the assault on Okinawa and then concentrated attacks on the Japanese mainland through the end of the war.

"Candoo Randoo" left the Pacific and saw "Magic Carpet" service from the Mediterranean returning American servicemen to the U.S. In 1946 and 1947 she served as a training ship for midshipmen; then, in February 1948 she was decommissioned and was placed in reserve at Philadelphia.

In October 1952 she was reclassified CVA-15 and was again placed in commission. She deployed with the 6th Fleet in the Mediterranean in 1954, then was overhauled and fitted with an angled flight deck at Norfolk late in 1955. In 1956 she was the first carrier to fire a Regulus guided missile. RANDOLPH was present at the Suez crisis in 1956 and covered the evacuation of American personnel from Alexandria.

For the next decade, the carrier served routinely in the Mediterranean and the Atlantic, homeported at Norfolk. She was the recovery ship for astronauts Grissom and Glenn and their Mercury spacecraft in 1961 and 1962, and operated in the Caribbean during the Cuban Missile Crisis.

In August 1968 it was decided to deactivate 50 ships to reduce expenditures and RANDOLPH was on the list. She was again placed in reserve at Philadelphia where she lay from February 1969 until she was sold for scrap in April 1975.

BOXER
1945

BOXER

Hull No: 410
Navy No: CV-21
Launched: December 14, 1944
Commissioned: April 16, 1945
Dimensions: 888 x 93 x 54.5 ft
Displacement: 33,292 tons
Armament: 12 5″ Guns
Machinery: Geared Turbines, 8 Boilers,
    Quadruple Screw
Horsepower/Speed: 150,000/33 knots
Fate: Scrapped, 1971

BOXER (CV-21) was the 12th aircraft carrier built at Newport News and, although she was built during World War II, she was the first one completed too late to see combat in that conflict. BOXER was ordered with light cruisers AMSTERDAM, PORTSMOUTH, and VICKSBURG just a week after the attack on Pearl Harbor, but her keel was not laid until September 13, 1943. Miss Ruth D. Overton, daughter of the senator from Louisiana, launched Hull 410 from Shipway 8 on December 14, 1944, and a large crowd attended the ceremony. A huge banner on her bow at launch proclaimed "Here we go to Tokyo... Help to Sink the Rising Sun." BOXER was completed in April 1945, trials were waived, and she was commissioned at Norfolk on April 16, with Capt. D.F. Smith commanding.

She joined the Pacific Fleet in August at San Diego, then was based at Guam for a year, being at anchor in Tokyo Bay for the Japanese surrender. She returned to the West Coast in September 1946 and served there until she returned to the Far East in January 1950.

In July 1950 BOXER made a record crossing of the Pacific in less than nine days, carrying 150 airplanes and 1,000 troops for the Korean Conflict. Her return trip to the U.S. was completed in only seven days, ten hours, and 36 minutes. She was repaired, then returned to the Far East to support the landing in Inchon in September. Known as the "Busy Bee," she was overhauled at San Diego, then returned for three more tours to Korea where she served until the end of the fighting, winning eight battle stars for her efforts.

For BOXER, 1952 was an eventful year: in August, a hangar deck fire killed nine men; then, a few weeks later, she became the first ship to use guided missiles in combat.

She alternated duty stations between the West Coast and the Far East and was reclassified as an ASW carrier (CVS-21) in 1955, then as an amphibious assault ship (LPH) in 1958. In that year she moved to Norfolk, her new homeport, and the rest of her career was spent in the Atlantic and the Caribbean. BOXER underwent a FRAM modernization in 1962 but was stricken in 1969 and was subsequently scrapped in 1971.

MIDWAY
1945

MIDWAY

Hull No: 439
Navy No: CVB-41
Launched: March 20, 1945
Commissioned: September 10, 1945
Dimensions: 968 x 113 x 57.5 ft
Displacement: 56,957 tons
Armament: 18 5″ Guns
Machinery: Geared Turbines, 12 Boilers,
    Quadruple Screw
Horsepower/Speed: 212,000/33 knots
Fate: In Commission

MIDWAY (CVB-41) and sister CORAL SEA (CVB-43), delivered in 1945 and 1947 respectively, represented a turning point in aircraft carrier design and construction. The shipyard had been given a contract in 1941 to design a larger, more protected, and more advanced carrier class and MIDWAY was the result. A total of six of the class were ordered (four from Newport News), but three were canceled as the war drew to a close.

The keel for MIDWAY was laid in Shipway 11 on October 27, 1943; and during her construction, subassemblies weighing as much as 100 tons were erected, huge units by 1940s standards.

MIDWAY was the largest warship in the world at the time of her delivery and also was the most completely welded large ship yet built. She and her sister, unlike previous carriers built at the shipyard, had armored flight decks and were provided with multiple longitudinal bulkheads for torpedo protection. They were the first U.S. warships designed with a beam (113 ft) too large to enable them to transit the Panama Canal.

MIDWAY was floated in Shipway 11 on March 20, 1945. The new ship was christened by Mrs. Bradford Williams Ripley II, widow of a Navy flier killed in the Pacific in 1943. Present at the ceremony was Lt. George H. Gay, lone survivor of Torpedo Squadron Eight which was lost at Midway. Due to unfavorable wind, the huge new carrier was not moved out of her berth on launching day; however, once moved, outfitting proceeded and she was commissioned on September 10, 1945, with Capt. Joseph F. Bolger in command.

(Continued on page 251)

CORAL SEA
1947

CORAL SEA

Hull No: 440
Navy No: CVB-43
Launched: April 2, 1946
Commissioned: October 1, 1947
Dimensions: 968 x 113 x 57.5 ft
Displacement: 56,957 tons
Armament: 18 5″ Guns
Machinery: Geared Turbines, 12 Boilers,
    Quadruple Screw
Horsepower/Speed: 212,000/33 knots
Fate: In Commission

CORAL SEA (CVB-43) was the second MIDWAY-class aircraft carrier built at Newport News and was the last of the shipard's "wartime" carrier building program. CORAL SEA was laid down in Shipway 10 on July 10, 1944, and was christened by Mrs. Thomas C. Kinkaid, wife of Adm. Kinkaid, who commanded in the Battle of Coral Sea in 1942. The launching took place on April 2, 1946, and it was a complex operation due to the relative sizes of the ship and the building dock. Shipway 10 was smaller than the dock used to build MIDWAY, and CORAL SEA overhung the ship-way in both length and breadth. With water ballast,

CORAL SEA weighed 42,462 tons at launch, the heaviest ever launched in the country.

During outfitting, the ship's enormous 212,000 SHP steam turbine powerplant and 12 boilers were installed and, although the war emergency was over, her formal sea trials were waived. CORAL SEA joined the Navy in ceremonies on October 1, 1947, ending eight years of continuous carrier building at Newport News in which "two miles of carriers" requiring 75 million man-hours of labor were constructed.

The 60,000 ton CORAL SEA, commanded by Capt. A.P. Storrs III, began her career with the Atlantic Fleet in the Caribbean area, then was deployed with the Sixth Fleet in the Mediterranean.

She saw occasional duty in the Caribbean and with NATO forces in the Atlantic during the 1950s and was visited by Tito of Yugoslavia, Franco of Spain, and the King and Queen of Greece in the Mediterranean. She evacuated Americans during the Suez Crisis in 1956, then returned to Norfolk in February 1957.

Rounding Cape Horn and visiting South American ports en route, CORAL SEA arrived at Bremerton, WA, in April 1957 for major conversion. During a three year stay at Puget Sound Naval Shipyard, she was fitted with three steam catapults, a closed bow, and an improved elevator system.

(Continued on page 251)

LEYTE
1946

LEYTE

Hull No: 446
Navy No: CV-32
Launched: August 23, 1945
Commissioned: April 11, 1946
Dimensions: 888 x 93 x 54.5 ft
Displacement: 33,292 tons
Armament: 12 5″ Guns
Machinery: Geared Turbines, 8 Boilers,
    Quadruple Screw
Horsepower/Speed: 150,000/33 knots
Fate: Scrapped, 1971

LEYTE (CV-32) was Newport News' ninth and last ESSEX-class aircraft carrier, and, like BOXER, she was completed too late to serve in World War II. She and the larger MIDWAY and CORAL SEA which followed were named for the famous battles during the war in which Newport News-built carriers so distinguished themselves. A sister ship to LEYTE, to be named IWO JIMA (CV-46), was laid down in January 1945 but was cancelled in August when 28.5 percent completed.

LEYTE herself was laid down on Shipway 9 on February 21, 1944, as CROWN POINT but her name was changed to LEYTE in May 1945. She was launched from Shipway 9 on August 23, 1945, and was the last Newport News built aircraft carrier to be launched from an inclined shipway. Sponsor for LEYTE was Mrs. Alice Dillon Mead, wife of the

senator from New York.

The new carrier was completed in the spring and was commissioned at Portsmouth on April 11, 1946, with Capt. Henry F. MacComsey commanding. Present at the cermony was Adm. Marc A. Mitscher, then commander of the Eighth Fleet, who had commanded HORNET (CV-8) at the Battle of Midway.

The new LEYTE made a cruise to South America with battleship WISCONSIN during her first year. She served in routine training missions in the Atlantic and the Mediterranean and left Norfolk in September 1950 to join TF 77 in Korean waters. After a stop in Japan in October, she deployed for 92 days and launched almost 4,000 sorties against the North Koreans, receiving two battle stars.

After this, she returned for overhaul at Norfolk, then alternated between her homeport there and the Mediterranean until February 1953. At that time, she was slated for reserve status, but instead it was decided to convert her for ASW service. An explosion occurred aboard LEYTE while under conversion at Boston in October and a fire resulted in which 37 men died.

After this tragedy, the conversion was completed and she moved to Quonset Point, RI, for ASW service as CVS-32. After five years of this service, she decommissioned in May 1959 and was laid up at Bayonne, NJ. She remained inactive there until she was stricken in 1969. In September 1970 she was sold for scrap, and later her boilers were removed and installed as steam auxiliaries at the shipyard where she was built.

FORRESTAL
1955

FORRESTAL

Hull No: 506
Navy No: CVA-59
Launched: December 11, 1954
Commissioned: October 1, 1955
Dimensions: 1039 x 129.33 x 60.82 ft
Displacement: 75,900 tons
Armament: 8 5″ Guns
Machinery: Geared Turbines, 8 Boilers,
    Quadruple Screws
Horsepower/Speed: 260,000/33 knots
Fate: In Commission

Following the excitement of the christening of superliner UNITED STATES three weeks before, Newport News shipbuilders received exciting news on July 12, 1951: the award of a contract for the design and construction of a new large aircraft carrier. On July 30 President Truman authorized that the ship would be named FORRESTAL (CVA-59) after the first Secretary of Defense, James V. Forrestal.

The keel for the world's largest ship was laid in Shipway 11 on July 14, 1952. FORRESTAL and three other ships of her class had a standard displacement of 56,000 tons (compared with 45,000 for MIDWAY) and their extreme width across their angled flight decks was almost 250 ft. They were provided with four deck-edge elevators and four steam catapults as well

as enclosed bows, armored flight decks, and advanced underwater protection systems. FORRESTAL was the first aircraft carrier designed and built for jet aircraft.

The new supercarrier was christened at ceremonies on December 11, 1954, and her sponsor was Mrs. James V. Forrestal, widow of the late Secretary.

FORRESTAL was removed from Shipway 11 to her southside outfitting berth on December 12. Within a year the new ship was ready for trials, and these were held in two phases on August 29-31 and September 21-23, 1955. At the conclusion, a giant broom was raised on FORRESTAL's mast to indicate a "clean sweep" of her trials. CVA-59 was commissioned at the Norfolk Naval Shipyard on October 1, commanded by Capt. R.L. Johnson.

Her first year was spent in the Caribbean and in the Atlantic training Navy fliers in use of her advanced features. She deployed to the Mediterranean early in 1957 and joined the Sixth Fleet. She stood off the entrance to the Mediterranean during the Suez and Lebanon crises of 1956 and 1958, but was not called on to actively participate.

FORRESTAL was originally fitted with eight 5″ MK42 guns (two on each quarter), but the forward mounts and their sponsons were later removed to improve her seaworthiness and speed in rough weather, and the aft mounts were replaced with Sea Sparrow missile launchers in 1967.

(Continued on page 251)

RANGER
1957

RANGER

Hull No: 514
Navy No: CVA-61
Launched: September 29, 1956
Commissioned: August 10, 1957
Dimensions: 1045.88 x 129.33 x 60.82 ft
Displacement: 75,900 tons
Armament: 8 5″ Guns
Machinery: Geared Turbines, 8 Boilers,
    Quadruple Screw
Horsepower/Speed: 280,000/35 knots
Fate: In Commission

RANGER (CVA-61) was the third ship of the FORRESTAL class; SARATOGA (CVA-60) and INDEPENDENCE (CVA-62) were built at the New York Naval Shipyard. These three ships had more powerful propulsion plants than FORRESTAL, but they featured the same massive armored flight decks of 1.75-inch plating which, unlike those of earlier carriers, were strength decks integral with their hulls.

RANGER was ordered on February 3, 1954, and was laid down in Shipway 10 on the following August 2. In an operation repeated for several other carriers at Newport News, her midship section was floated out of Shipway 10 and was moved to the larger Shipway 11 after the launch of the preceeding ship from it. In this way at least six months of construction time was

saved. Hull construction essentially complete, RANGER was launched on September 29, 1956. Mrs. Arthur Radford, wife of the chairman of the Joint Chiefs of Staff, christened RANGER on an overcast day before a far smaller crowd than had attended ceremonies for FORRESTAL two years earlier.

RANGER, the eighth Navy ship to bear her name, completed successful trials in July 1957 and was placed in commission under Capt. C.T. Booth II on August 10. A number of officers who had served on the first carrier RANGER were present both during trials and at the commissioning.

The new RANGER underwent shakedown with the Atlantic Fleet at Guantanamo, completed final acceptance trials in June 1958, then sailed for her homeport of Alameda, CA and joined the Pacific Fleet. After pilot training exercises along the West Coast and near Hawaii, she deployed to the Far East with the Seventh Fleet as flagship of Carrier Division 2 in February 1959. She made several deployments to the Far East before the Tonkin Gulf incident of August 1964 and was sent there from Hawaii immediately afterward to become flagship, Fast Carrier Task Force 77.

RANGER launched attacks against Vietnamese enemy targets until April 1965 when an engine room fire caused her to be withdrawn to San Francisco for repair and overhaul. In 1966 she and her Carrier Air Wing 14 were awarded the Navy Unit Commendation for service in the Vietnam area.

(Continued on page 259)

INTREPID *Continued from page 240*

Reclassified as an ASW carrier (CVS) in 1961, INTREPID was recovery ship for the Mercury VII and Gemini III spacecraft in the early 1960s, and she served the Pacific Fleet on three deployments to Vietnam from 1966 to 1968. She then rejoined the Atlantic Fleet with homeport at Quonset Point, RI, and was in ASW service in the Atlantic until she was decommissioned in 1974.

INTREPID was selected by Congress to be the Navy and Marine Corps Bicentennial Exposition Ship at Philadelphia in 1975-1976 and was visited by thousands during that celebration. This duty prepared her for her next assignment, for she was saved from scrapping and was converted to an sea, air, and space museum. Famous veteran of war and peace, INTREPID was opened at New York on July 4, 1982, and began yet another career.

TICONDEROGA *Continued from page 243*

Like many of her sisters, TICONDEROGA saw some troop repatriation duty; then, she was decommissioned in January 1947. She was reactivated at New York in September 1954 and, homeported at Norfolk, operated in the Atlantic until 1956. In that year she was modernized at Norfolk Naval Shipyard and received an angled flight deck and a closed bow, then was moved to the Pacific. Fate found her present at the Gulf of Tonkin incident in August 1964, and she served for five years in Vietnamese waters and was awarded 12 battle stars for her efforts.

She was converted to an ASW carrier in 1970 and deployed twice more to the Far East, recovering astronauts and spacecraft from the Apollo 16 and Apollo 17 moon missions. In late 1974 TICONDEROGA's age was showing, and the old veteran was decommissioned and sold for scrapping.

MIDWAY *Continued from page 246*

The war over, MIDWAY's career was routine. Homeported at Norfolk, she served as a training ship in the Atlantic, and in 1947 she test-fired a captured German V-2 rocket from her flight deck. Beginning in 1947 she began yearly missions to the Mediterranean, and in 1952 she engaged in maneuvers with NATO vessels in the North Sea. She made a world cruise in 1955, operated in the Pacific, then underwent overhaul at Puget Sound, and was provided with a modern closed bow and an angled flight deck.

Serving in the Pacific with the Seventh Fleet from 1958, her planes were credited with the downing of the first three MIGs destroyed by American forces in Southeast Asia. She entered the naval shipyard at San Francisco in February 1966 for major modernization, then re-entered the fleet in 1970.

MIDWAY probably underwent more modernization than any aircraft carrier in history, having had her elevator arangements, catapults, electronics, and armament completely updated to handle the most modern aircraft in the fleet. In October 1973, MIDWAY was homeported at Yokosuka, Japan, the only U.S. carrier to be based in a foreign port. She remained active in the Pacific and Indian Oceans into the mid-1980s, and celebrated her 40th birthday in September 1985.

CORAL SEA *Continued from page 247*

She was recommissioned in January 1960 and rejoined the Navy with the Seventh Fleet in the Far East. She served off the West Coast and in the Western Pacific through the 1960s and 1970s and saw action during the Vietnam War. In 1977 she became a training carrier for reserve air groups and did not have a permanent wing aboard. After two years of this service, she took aircraft aboard from ENTERPRISE, then in overhaul, and again became fully operational.

With completion of CARL VINSON (CVN-70) in 1983, CORAL SEA was transferred to the East Coast and entered the Norfolk Naval Shipyard for a major overhaul and modernization to operate F-18 jets. This completed in January 1985, she rejoined the fleet only to be involved in a collision with a merchant ship off Cuba the following April 12. Her damaged bow repaired, she deployed to the Mediterranean in October, paying her first visit there in 30 years. Early in 1986 she was active off the coast of Libya during tense times between that country and the U.S.

FORRESTAL *Continued from page 249*

In June 1967 she deployed to Vietnamese waters, and on July 29 she suffered the worst naval disaster since World War II. Engaged in flight operations, she was ravaged by fire and explosions which began with the rupture of a fuel tank on her flight deck and ultimately resulted in 145 deaths. Her aircraft all but destroyed, she put in to Subic, Philippines, then was repaired at the Norfolk Naval Shipyard.

After overhaul she served along the East Coast and in the Mediterranean, and in 1976 she hosted the Bicentennial Naval Review at New York. She entered Philadelphia Naval Shipyard early in 1983 for a 30 month Ship Life Extension Program (SLEP) overhaul. FORRESTAL completed this extensive overhaul in May 1985, and with 15 years added to her expected service life, rejoined the Atlantic Fleet. Proudly carrying her motto "First in Defense," she celebrated her 30th birthday in September 1985.

ENTERPRISE
1961

ENTERPRISE

Hull No: 546
Navy No: CVAN-65
Launched: September 24, 1960
Commissioned: November 25, 1961
Dimensions: 1101.5 x 129.25 x 60.82 ft
Displacement: 85,350 tons
Armament: None
Machinery: Geared Turbines, 8 Reactors,
   Quadruple Screw
Horsepower/Speed: 280,000/35 knots
Fate: In Commission

In the mid-1950s, anticipating the construction of nuclear-powered ships, Newport News created its Atomic Power Division (APD) and helped design and build the Large Ship Reactor for the Navy in Idaho. This effort was rewarded on November 15, 1957, with the award of a contract for the construction of the giant ENTERPRISE (CVAN-65). This revolutionary ship was a great milestone for Newport News ship-builders, thereafter the sole builders of carriers for the Navy. Everything about the largest warship in the world was impressive, from her 1,100-ft length and

85,000 ton displacement to her eight-reactor power-plant and 200,000-mile range. In order to keep construction costs down, she was not provided with armament, but space for future installation of the Terrier missile system was provided. The contract award followed development of contract plans for the Navy by shipyard designers and engineers.

The keel for Hull 546 was laid in Shipway 11, newly enlarged for the building of this great ship, on February 4, 1958. Despite her size and complexity and the introduction of nuclear power, ENTERPRISE was completed in about the same time as the average for the conventional FORRESTAL- and KITTY HAWK-class carriers. The huge ship was christened on September 24, 1960, by Mrs. William B. Franke, wife of the Secretary of the Navy. It was a beautiful early fall day and, in the presence of over 15,000 spectators, the new carrier was saluted by a water salvo from the missile tubes of FBM submarine ROBERT E. LEE in Shipway 10.

ENTERPRISE was moved to her outfitting berth on September 25 and began 14 months of outfitting and trials, culminating in her commissioning on November 25, 1961, under the command of Capt. V.P. de Poix.

(Continued on page 259)

AMERICA
1965

AMERICA

Hull No: 561
Navy No: CVA-66
Launched: February 1, 1964
Commissioned: January 23, 1965
Dimensions: 1047.5 x 129.33 x 60.82 ft
Displacement: 77,600 tons
Armament: Terrier Missiles
Machinery: Geared Turbines, 8 Boilers,
    Quadruple Screw
Horsepower/Speed: 280,000/30+ knots
Fate: In Commission

On November 25, 1961, Newport News was awarded the contract for the conventionally-powered aircraft carrier CVA-66, later named AMERICA by President John F. Kennedy. This ship, given Hull No. 561, was an improved FORRESTAL or KITTY HAWK-class ship capable of supporting 95 aircraft and fitted with two twin Terrier surface-to-air missile launchers. Like others of her class, she was powered with four geared Westinghouse turbines developing 280,000 SHP driving quadruple screws. AMERICA also had an improved elevator arrangement with two units forward of her island, one aft, and one on her port aft quarter. AMERICA was fitted with a bow sonar dome, novel for a U.S. carrier, and she was the last carrier fitted with the hinged masts required for passing under the Brooklyn Bridge to access the New York Navy Yard.

Hull 561 was laid down in Shipway 10 on January 9, 1961. The Navy's newest carrier was christened by Mrs. David L. McDonald, wife of the Chief of Naval Operations, on February 1, 1964. Several thousand witnessed the event which climaxed when a 21 by 38-ft eight-color map of the United States swung down from AMERICA's bow. Later in the year, the carrier AMERICA was photographed alongside the famous liner AMERICA, in the shipyard for annual overhaul.

The carrier AMERICA completed her preliminary acceptance trials on December 1-3, 1964, with more than 2,000 shipyard, Navy, and vendor personnel aboard, and was placed in commission at the Norfolk Naval Shipyard on January 23, 1965. AMERICA's first commanding officer was Capt. L.K. Heyworth.

After her commissioning, AMERICA served ably with the Atlantic fleet, providing the deterrent symbolized in her motto, "Don't Tread On Me." She made three deployments to Vietnam in 1968, 1970, and 1972
(Continued on page 259)

JOHN F. KENNEDY
1968

JOHN F. KENNEDY

Hull No: 577
Navy No: CVA-67
Launched: May 27, 1967
Commissioned: September 7, 1968
Dimensions: 1040 x 128.5 x 60.82 ft
Displacement: 78,300 tons
Armament: None
Machinery: Geared Turbines, 8 Boilers,
    Quadruple Screw
Horsepower/Speed: 280,000/30+ knots
Fate: In Commission

A few months after the dramatic events of November 1963, the shipyard won a contract for the construction of a conventionally-powered aircraft carrier which was later named JOHN F. KENNEDY (CVA-67). This ship, assigned Hull No. 577, was basically a KITTY HAWK-class ship, but appropriations were delayed by debate over whether to provide her with nuclear propulsion, so she essentially became a one-class ship. Her design featured canted stacks, a fixed mast, and the first use of the C13 Mod 1 catapult which enabled her to launch large aircraft at anchor even in no-wind

conditions. JOHN F. KENNEDY was built without a major defense weapons system as an economy measure, but three Sea Sparrow BPDMS missile launchers were installed a year after her commissioning.

The keel for Newport News' 20th carrier was laid on inclined Shipway 8 on October 22, 1964. This facility was used since Shipway 11 was then occupied by ENTERPRISE, which was in the yard for refueling and overhaul. On May 15, 1965, the drydock work had been completed on ENTERPRISE and the midsection of JOHN F. KENNEDY was floated into Shipway 11. By the summer of 1966, construction had progressed to the flight deck of the new ship and work had begun on her island structure. The ship's eight boilers were built in the shipyard's shops and each weighed 112 tons.

The christening of JOHN F. KENNEDY on May 27, 1967, was one of the most memorable events in the shipyard's history. Caroline Kennedy christened the new carrier in the presence of a crowd of more than 32,000 which included the late President's family and President Johnson. The event was a bittersweet affair and the President concluded his principal address by saying, "Let this ship we christen in his name be a testament that his countrymen have not forgotten."

(Continued on page 260)

NIMITZ
1975

NIMITZ

Hull No:594
Navy No: CVAN-68
Launched: May 13, 1972
Commissioned: May 3, 1975
Dimensions: 1092 x 134 x 64 ft
Displacement: 90,702 tons
Armament: Sea Sparrow Missiles
Machinery: Geared Turbines, 2 Reactors,
    Quadruple Screw
Horsepower/Speed: 260,000/30+ knots
Fate: In Commission

Firmly established as the Navy's sole builder of aircraft carriers, the shipyard was awarded a contract on March 31, 1967, for the construction of the nuclear-powered carrier CVAN-68, later named NIMITZ. This ship like its famous namesake, gained the reputation of always being in the "thick of it." Engineering and design work began immediately on the new carrier which was to become the first of a class of the largest and most advanced warships ever produced. The main improvements over previous designs consisted of a two-reactor propulsion plant with a 13-year refueling cycle, increased hangar room due to elevator placement, improved protection and armor, and a more compact island. Complement on the NIMITZ-class ships grew to 6,286, almost 1,400 more than on ENTERPRISE.

The keel for NIMITZ was set down in Shipway 11 on June 22, 1968, and it was authenticated by Sen. Henry M. Jackson with the assistance of RAdm. Chester W. Nimitz, Jr. and VAdm. Hyman G. Rickover. NIMITZ was christened on May 13, 1972, sponsored by Mrs. Catherine Nimitz Lay, daughter of FAdm. Nimitz. Construction proceeded, but delivery was seriously delayed by late arrival of major components of the ship's nuclear powerplant. As a result, the new carrier did not undergo sea trials until March 1975 and was not placed in commission until May 3, 1975.

After her commissioning under the command of Capt. Bryan W. Compton, NIMITZ began training cruises to the Mediterranean. In September 1979, she left Norfolk for what was to be another routine deployment to the Mediterranean. Shortly afterwards, however, the Iranian Hostage Crisis and the Soviet invasion of Afganistan occurred, and NIMITZ was dispatched to the Indian Ocean and Arabian Sea with Newport News-built cruisers CALIFORNIA (CGN-36) and TEXAS (CGN-39).

After operating for a record 125 days at sea NIMITZ and her consorts were relieved by another Newport News-built trio consisting of DWIGHT D. EISENHOWER (CVN-69), SOUTH CAROLINA (CGN-37), and VIRGINIA (CGN-38); and sailed for home. They were greeted with a tumultous welcome in Hampton Roads, led by President Carter, on May 26, 1980, after a nine-month deployment and 144 days at sea.

(Continued on page 260)

DWIGHT D. EISENHOWER
1977

DWIGHT D. EISENHOWER
Hull No: 599
Navy No: CVN-69
Launched: October 11, 1975
Commissioned: October 18, 1977
Dimensions: 1092 x 134 x 64 ft
Displacement: 91,209 tons
Armament: Sea Sparrow Missiles
Machinery: Geared Turbines, 2 Reactors,
    Quadruple Screw
Horsepower/Speed: 260,000/30+ knots
Fate: In Commission

Newport News shipbuilders were awarded a contract for CVN-69, their second NIMITZ-class nuclear aircraft carrier, in 1969. Shortly after contract award, the new ship was named DWIGHT D. EISENHOWER, after the 34th President.

The keel-laying for the nation's third nuclear carrier was attended by members of the families of Presidents Eisenhower and Nixon. Construction on the ship proceeded in Shipway 10 since CVN-69 was a virtual twin of NIMITZ, which was building in the adjacent dock. After the launch of NIMITZ in May 1972, the midbody of DWIGHT D. EISENHOWER was moved to the larger Shipway 11 in the by-now routine fashion.

The launching of CVN-69, like that of NIMITZ, was delayed by the delivery of nuclear powerplant components, and she was not launched until October 11, 1975. It was a great day for the shipyard, the Navy, and the country as the keel was laid for the CARL VINSON (CVN-70) during double ceremonies. After the principal address by Vice President Nelson Rockefeller, DWIGHT D. EISENHOWER was christened by Mrs. Eisenhower amid great celebration before a large crowd.

The ship was outfitted and underwent tests and trials over the next two years and was placed in commission on October 18, 1977, under the command of Capt. William E. Ramsey.

DWIGHT D. EISENHOWER underwent shakedown in the Atlantic during the last months of 1977, trained during 1978, then made her first deployment to the Mediterranean in January 1979. On May 7, 1980, she relieved NIMITZ in the Arabian Sea in the wake of the Iranian Hostage Crisis. She thereafter made annual deployments to the troubled Mediterranean until she returned to Newport News for overhaul in October 1985.

Said to have traveled almost a million miles since her commissioning, she entered Shipway 11 on October 26 for a 15-month stay in the yard.

CARL VINSON
1982

CARL VINSON

Hull No: 611
Navy No: CVN-70
Launched: March 15, 1980
Commissioned: March 13, 1982
Dimensions: 1092 x 134 x 64 ft
Displacement: 91,209 tons
Armament: Sea Sparrow Missiles
Machinery: Geared Turbines, 2 Reactors,
    Quadruple Screw
Horsepower/Speed: 260,000/30+ knots
Fate: In Commission

Next in the shipyard's long line of carriers was CARL VINSON (CVN-70), which was authorized in FY 1974. The third NIMITZ-class ship was named after Rep. Carl Vinson of Georgia who championed a strong Navy in Congress from 1914 to 1964. CARL VINSON became the first American naval ship to be named after a living person since the Revolutionary War and was the first to have its namesake present at launching.

The keel for CVN-70 was authenticated by Rep. Carl Vinson himself on October 11, 1975, prior to ceremonies on the same day for launching of the DWIGHT D. EISENHOWER. Carrier CARL VINSON was launched from Shipway 11 on March 15, 1980, in the presence of the 96-year-old Rep. Vinson. Sponsor for CARL VINSON was Mrs. Molly Snead, Vinson's longtime friend and nurse, and she performed her duties ably. During the ceremony, Sen. John W. Warner presented a Joint Resolution of Congress honoring Rep. Vinson.

During the next two years outfitting proceeded, the Navy crew slowly moved aboard, and tests and trials were completed. CARL VINSON was completed and was commissioned on March 13, 1982 with Capt. Richard L. Martin commanding.

She underwent shakedown off the East Coast, became fully operational, and then sailed for duty with the Pacific Fleet in the spring of 1983. Homeported at Alameda, CARL VINSON made her first deployment to the Far East late in 1984. She returned home in May 1985 and participated in Navy Day ceremonies in San Francisco Bay in October with her Newport News fleetmates ENTERPRISE and ARKANSAS.

THEODORE ROOSEVELT
1986

THEODORE ROOSEVELT

Hull No: 624
Navy No: CVN-71
Launched: October 27, 1984
Commissioned: Fall 1986
Dimensions: 1092 x 134 x 64 ft
Displacement: 91,209 tons
Armament: Sea Sparrow Missiles, CIWS
Machinery: Geared Turbines, 2 Reactors,
    Quadruple Screw
Horsepower/Speed: 280,000/30+ knots
Fate: Under Construction

The contract for the fourth NIMITZ-class aircraft carrier was awarded to Newport News on September 30, 1980. This ship had originally been cancelled in the late 1970s in favor of two medium carriers (CVV) but was reinstated and was followed by two more NIMITZ-class ships in the early 1980s. The keel for the shipyard's fifth nuclear carrier, named THEODORE ROOSEVELT (CVN-71), was laid down in Shipway 12 on October 30, 1981. This marked the first naval construction in the North Yard, originally built for commercial shipbuilding, and use of the "superlift" capacity of the 900-ton gantry crane which was expected to enable a 17-month reduction in construction time for the carrier. Use of the shipyard's Computer Aided Design and Manufacturing (CADAM) system was also a key to the rapid construction and planned early delivery of THEODORE ROOSEVELT.

As expected, construction on the new ship progressed much more quickly than on previous ships of her class, and she was readied for launching in the fall of 1984.

With over 15,000 in attendance, Mrs. Barbara Lehman, wife of the Secretary of the Navy, christened THEODORE ROOSEVELT on President Roosevelt's birthday, October 27, 1984. In a gala ceremony, Secretary of Defense Caspar Weinberger delivered the principal address and Navy F-14 jets roared overhead and thrilled the crowd.

THEODORE ROOSEVELT was then moved to her outfitting berth in the North Yard, and work was continued toward her fall 1986 delivery.

RANGER *Continued from page 250*

RANGER returned to the West Coast late in 1966, underwent overhaul at Puget Sound, then engaged in intensive training with the new Corsair II jet and UH-2C Seasprite rescue helicopter. She relieved CONSTELLATION in November 1967 and engaged in operations against North Vietnam from Yankee Station for five months. RANGER made a total of seven deployments to the Western Pacific before 1974 and earned a total of 13 battle stars for her Vietnam service. Like others of her class, she had her guns replaced by Sea Sparrow missile launchers in the 1970s.

RANGER was plagued by bad luck during a deployment to the Arabian Sea in 1983. She collided with the oiler WICHITA enroute, damaging an elevator; then while on station on November 1, her machinery spaces caught fire and killed six of her crewmen.

RANGER returned to San Diego via Subic early in 1984 after 121 days at sea, believed to be a record for non-nuclear carriers. She entered Puget Sound Naval Shipyard on April 15 for ROH which was completed in mid-1985, her SLEP overhaul having been deferred until 1992.

ENTERPRISE *Continued from page 252*

After commissioning, ENTERPRISE began an exhaustive series of trials and tests in the Atlantic. Flight operations were first held from her deck in January 1962, and in February she served as a tracking station for John Glenn's historic "Friendship 7" orbital mission. She participated in the naval blockade during the Cuban Missile Crisis in 1962 and was dispatched to the Far East in the wake of the PUEBLO incident.

Based at Alameda, CA, she sailed around the world, unreplenished, with nuclear escorts LONG BEACH (CGN-9) and BAINBRIDGE (CGN-25) in "Operation Sea Orbit" in 1963. ENTERPRISE served with distinction in the Vietnam War, but a weapons explosion reminiscent of the FORRESTAL disaster struck her in 1969 and killed 27 of her crew and destroyed 15 of her aircraft.

She returned to Newport News in 1964 and 1969 for care at the hands of her proud builders. In 1975 she aided in the evacuation of Saigon, then continued service in the Pacific. From 1979 to 1982 ENTERPRISE underwent a major refit and overhaul at Puget Sound Naval Shipyard, during which her island was radically reconfigured and her unusual "billboard" antennae and antenna dome were removed.

With altered appearance, the "Big E" rejoined the fleet in March 1982 and continued to serve and to receive acclamation into her third decade in commission. She deployed to the Indian Ocean from Alameda on May 30, 1984, and relieved AMERICA, then returned on December 20 and began preparations for scheduled repairs beginning in January. These completed, she engaged in local operations there and made her 12th deployment in 1985. In November of that year, she ran aground 100 miles west of San Diego and had a 60-ft gash torn in her side. Quickly repaired, she prepared for her next West Pac deployment.

AMERICA *Continued from page 253*

and alternately saw service off the East Coast and in the Mediterranean with the Second and Sixth fleets. The final attacks on Vietnam by shipboard planes were made from her decks in 1973; then, she was overhauled in 1975 for modifications required to carry the new F-14 "Tomcat" and S-3A "Viking" aircraft. During her 1981 deployment to the Indian Ocean, AMERICA became the first carrier to transit the Suez Canal in both directions. In 1984 she made a long deployment to the Mediterranean Sea and Indian Ocean, returning to Norfolk in November.

She underwent routine repairs at the Norfolk Naval Shipyard beginning in January 1985, then led one of three NATO battle groups in the giant Operation Sea Safari in the Atlantic later in the year.

AMERICA was visited by First Lady Nancy Reagan off the Maryland coast in July, then joined the giant Operation Ocean Safari across the Atlantic to Northern Europe in August and September. Near year's end she was in port in Norfolk for a well-earned rest with her Newport News sisters JOHN F. KENNEDY, NIMITZ, and DWIGHT D. EISENHOWER. Early in 1986, she deployed to the Mediterranean and joined CORAL SEA for strikes on Libya in response to terrorist acts sponsored by that country.

JOHN F. KENNEDY *Continued from page 254*

NIMITZ *Continued from page 255*

JOHN F. KENNEDY was completed during the next 15 months and underwent highly successful trials off the Virginia Capes in July and August 1968. She was commissioned at the shipyard on September 7 and was placed under the command of Capt. Earl P. Yates. President Kennedy's family returned for the ceremony and thousands attended the ship's open house.

The new "Big John" spent her first year in shakedown and training off the East Coast, then made a cruise to the Mediterranean in April 1969. She was welcomed everywhere by admirers of her namesake and later became a familiar sight in the Mediterranean. Her Med deployment in September 1970 was of an emergency nature and took her to cover the Middle East crisis in that year. Her third Mediterranean cruise, begun in December 1971, was extended to ten months to allow other carriers to participate in Vietnam action.

In November 1976 she was involved in a serious collision with BELKNAP (CG-26) off Sicily, which destroyed that ship's superstructure and caused eight deaths and 25 injuries. JOHN F. KENNEDY was not seriously damaged herself and, after repairs, continued service in the Mediterranean and along the East Coast.

In September 1983 she left Norfolk for a 219-day deployment off Lebanon during which one of her aircraft was shot down over Syria. She remained in the Med until late April 1984, then entered overhaul at Norfolk Naval Shipyard on October 5 of that year, staying there until late 1985. At year's end she was moored at the Norfolk Naval Station preparing for her next overseas deployment.

True to her reputation, NIMITZ was back in the thick of it in August 1981 when two of her planes downed two attacking Libyan jets. The only major accident in NIMITZ's first decade occurred in May 1981 when one of her aircraft crash-landed on her flight deck, causing an explosion and fire that killed 14 of her crewmen and injured 45. In tribute to her staunch construction and able crew, she was repaired at Norfolk and sailed just two days later.

During the summer of 1983 NIMITZ returned to Newport News for overhaul and entered Shipway 11 where she was born 11 years before. Redelivered to the Navy in July 1984, she returned to the Atlantic Fleet to serve until her transfer to the Pacific when THEODORE ROOSEVELT commissioned late in 1986. She was reported in the Mediterranean during the TWA hostage crisis in June 1985 and returned to Norfolk in October of that year.

BATTLESHIPS
KEARSARGE
1900

KEARSARGE

Hull No: 18
Navy No: BB-5
Launched: March 24, 1898
Commissioned: February 20, 1900
Dimensions: 375.33 x 72.17 x 34.42 ft
Displacement: 11,550 tons
Armament: 4 13″, 4 8″, 14 5″ Guns
Machinery: Triple Expansion Engines,
     5 Boilers, Twin Screw
Horsepower/Speed: 10,000/16 knots
Fate: Scrapped, 1955

In the fall of 1895, Newport News was low bidder on two battleships for the Navy, which were later named KEARSARGE (BB-5) and KENTUCKY (BB-6). The resulting contract was of great importance to the young shipyard and marked its entry into the construction of large naval vessels. These ships were said to be the first battleships wholly designed in the U.S. and built of American materials.

The keels of both ships were laid down on June 30, 1896, and they were launched in a gala double ceremony on March 24, 1898. KEARSARGE was christened by Mrs. Herbert Winslow, daughter-in-law of Capt. Winslow who had commanded the famous KEARSARGE during the Civil War. During outfitting, KEARSARGE was fitted with her innovative double turrets which consisted of 8-inch turrets mounted over 13-inch ones with two guns in each one.

KEARSARGE was completed and was commis-sioned on February 20, 1900; she was the only U.S. battleship ever built which was not named for a state. Typical of her time, she was painted white and had handsome hull decorations in gold.

With Capt. William M. Folger in command, KEARSARGE became the flagship of the North Atlantic Fleet. She retained this position until March 1904; and during her first few years, she made a number of goodwill voyages to Europe and was visited by royalty in Germany, Portugal, and Greece. Off Cuba in April 1906, an explosion of one of her 13″ charges killed ten of her crew. In December 1907 she began an around-the-world cruise with the Great White Fleet, which lasted until February 1909. KEARSARGE was modernized from 1909 to 1915, then took part in operations during the Mexican Revolution in 1915.

As World War I approached, the now-old ship served as an engineering training ship; then, in May 1920 she was decommissioned for conversion to a crane ship. Her superstructure was removed and a 250-ton revolving crane was mounted onto her hull. Two blisters were fitted to her hull to add stability and her beam increased from 72 to 92 ft. Redesignated AB-1, her most famous exploit was the raising of the submarine SQUALUS in 1939.

In 1941 her name was given to an aircraft carrier and she became known as CRANE SHIP NO. 1. She spent three years on the West Coast after World War II, then finished her career in the Boston Naval Shipyard. Almost 60 years old and still with her original powerplant, she was stricken and was sold for scrap in 1955.

KENTUCKY
1900

KENTUCKY

Hull No: 19
Navy No: BB-6
Launched: March 24, 1898
Commissioned: May 15, 1900
Dimensions: 375.33 x 72.17 x 34.42 ft
Displacement: 11,538 tons
Armament: 4 13", 4 8", 14 5" Guns
Machinery: Triple Expansion Engines,
    5 Boilers, Twin Screw
Horsepower/Speed: 10,000/16 knots
Fate: Scrapped, 1924

The second battleship built at Newport News was KENTUCKY (BB-6). This ship was identical to KEARSARGE and was launched on the same day as she was. Sponsor for KENTUCKY was Miss Christine Bradley, daughter of the governor of the ship's namesake state. At the insistence of the Women's Christian Temperance Union, Miss Bradley baptized KENTUCKY with pure Kentucky spring water instead of the traditional alcoholic champagne. This was highly controversial and, as the huge ship began to slide, it was unofficially showered with a fusillade of Kentucky whiskey in small bottles thrown by a veritable army of "colonels."

Even after this glorious start, KENTUCKY was to have a short and somewhat unlucky career. The new battleship was commissioned on May 15, 1900, Capt. Colby M. Chester in command. KENTUCKY sailed for the Far East via Suez in October and served in that area as flagship of the Southern Squadron until March 1904. At that time she sailed home, again via Suez, for overhaul at the New York Navy Yard.

She spent the next few years in the Atlantic and in the Caribbean, and she landed troops at Havana in October 1906 for action in the Cuban Insurrection. She continued exercises along the Atlantic coast until 1907, visited the Jamestown Exposition, then joined KEARSARGE and the Great White Fleet for their famous world cruise. The ships returned in February 1909 and, after overhaul at Philadelphia, KENTUCKY was decommissioned until June 1912.

She remained inactive or out of commission until June 1915, at which time she began a series of militia training cruises. In September 1915 she sailed to the Gulf of Mexico to stand by during the Mexican Revolution.

KENTUCKY spent World War I in training duty along the East Coast and never saw battle. Her contribution was to train thousands of Navy men for war and she did her job well. She was repaired at Boston in late 1918, then continued her training duties, which included an occasional cruise with midshipmen.

She entered the Philadelphia Navy Yard in August 1919 and was decommissioned for the last time on May 29, 1920. In 1924 KENTUCKY was sold and scrapped in accordance with the Washington Treaty of 1922 which limited naval armaments.

ILLINOIS
1901

ILLINOIS

Hull No: 21
Navy No: BB-7
Launched: October 4, 1898
Commissioned: September 16, 1901
Dimensions: 375.33 x 72.17 x 34.42 ft
Displacement: 11,625 tons
Armament: 4 13", 14 6" Guns; 4 18" TT
Machinery: Triple Expansion Engines,
    8 Boilers, Twin Screw
Horsepower/Speed: 10,000/16 knots
Fate: Scrapped, 1956

Battleship ILLINOIS, first of three ships of her class, was awarded to Newport News on September 26, 1896. She and her two sisters built at other yards had the same dimensions as KEARSARGE and KENTUCKY but were less heavily armed. Protective armor on the ILLINOIS class, at 16.6", was a half inch thinner than that of the previous ships.

The keel for ILLINOIS was laid down on February 10, 1897, and she was launched on October 4, 1898. Miss Nancy Leiter of Chicago was sponsor for ILLINOIS.

The Navy's newest battleship completed trials on June 12, 1901, and was commissioned on the following September 16. With Captain G.A. Converse in command, the ship became flagship of the European Squadron at Naples. ILLINOIS ran aground in Norwegian waters in July 1902 and underwent repairs at Chatham, England.

After repairs she resumed duty in the Mediterranean, then was transferred to the North Atlantic in January 1903. She joined several of her Newport News-built sisters for the great round-the-world cruise in 1907, and she and two other U.S. battleships aided victims of the Sicilian earthquake in January 1909.

ILLINOIS returned to Hampton Roads with the Great White Fleet in February but was decommissioned at Boston during the following August. She was recommissioned in 1912 and participated in fleet exercises, making two summer cruises to the Mediterranean with midshipmen in 1913 and 1914.

ILLINOIS was again decommissioned in 1919, at the Philadelphia Navy Yard, then was used as a militia training ship until 1924. She was not scrapped as were many of her fleetmates but was converted for use as a floating armory at the New York Navy Yard and was assigned to the New York Naval Reserve. ILLINOIS remained in this noncombatant status at New York for over thirty years. Her name was given to a new battleship in 1941 and she was reclassified IX-15 and was renamed PRAIRIE STATE. She remained on active duty as a training and then a barracks ship until the end of 1955. After over 50 years of service, she was scrapped at Baltimore in 1956.

MISSOURI
1903

MISSOURI

Hull No: 25
Navy No: BB-11
Launched: December 28, 1901
Commissioned: December 1, 1903
Dimensions: 393.75 x 72.17 x 34.5 ft
Displacement: 12,240 tons
Armament: 4 12″, 16 6″, 6 3″ Guns; 2 18″ TT
Machinery: Quadruple Expansion Engines,
    12 Boilers, Twin Screw
Horsepower/Speed: 15,500/18 knots
Fate: Scrapped, 1922

The first battleship MISSOURI, one of three MAINE-class battleships ordered from three different shipyards in 1898, was awarded to Newport News on December 30, 1898. These ships were larger than their predecessors but their largest guns were reduced to 12″ bore. They were considerably more powerful and were faster than the earlier battleships and could carry over 1,800 tons of coal in their bunkers. The keel for MISSOURI was laid on February 7, 1900, and she was launched on December 28, 1901. Mrs. Marion Galludet, daughter of the senator from Missouri, was sponsor

for the ship. Capt. William S. Cowles commanded the new MISSOURI after her commissioning on December 1, 1903.

The new ship was to have a brief and somewhat unlucky career. She was assigned to the North Atlantic Fleet, and during gunnery practice in April 1904, a mishap in her after turret set off a powder fire which suffocated 36 of her crew. After repairs at Newport News, MISSOURI saw duty in the Mediterranean then operated along the eastern seaboard until 1907. She too took part in the great cruise of 1907-1909, then was placed in reserve with her sister ILLINOIS at Boston in May 1910. She recommissioned the following year and resumed duty with the Atlantic Fleet. She again decommissioned, at Philadelphia, in September 1912. MISSOURI was in and out of commission several more times before the beginning of World War I and made a training cruise to the West Coast via Panama with midshipmen in 1915. She operated as a training vessel in the Chesapeake Bay, based at Yorktown, during the war. After the Armistice she made four voyages to France to return troops from "over there." MISSOURI was decommissioned for the last time at the Philadelphia Navy Yard in September 1919, then was sold for scrap in 1922.

VIRGINIA
1906

VIRGINIA

Hull No: 40
Navy No: BB-13
Launched: April 5, 1904
Commissioned: May 7, 1906
Dimensions: 441.25 x 76 x 41.33 ft
Displacement: 14,970 tons
Armament: 4 12″, 8 8″, 12 6″ Guns; 4 21″ TT
Machinery: Triple Expansion Engines,
    24 Boilers, Twin Screw
Horsepower/Speed: 18,000/18 knots
Fate: Sunk, 1923

First of her class of five ships was battleship VIRGINIA, which was authorized by Congress in 1899. With the addition of 8″ guns, these ships were more heavily armed than their immediate predecessors, and they were considerably larger and more powerful. Like the preceding MAINE class, the VIRGINIA class had armor with a maximum thickness of 12 inches. The contract for VIRGINIA was signed on February 15, 1901, and her keel was laid on May 21, 1902. The launching on April 5, 1904, was declared a legal holiday by the General Assembly, and the ceremony was attended by tens of thousands. Sponsor for VIRGINIA was little Miss Mathilde Gay Montague, daughter of the governor. This lady returned to Newport News 70 years later in 1974 to attend the christening of another VIRGINIA, the nuclear powered cruiser commissioned in 1976.

Battleship VIRGINIA was completed and commissioned on May 7, 1906, with Capt. Seaton Schroeder commanding. After shakedown off the New England coast, the new ship anchored off President Theodore Roosevelt's home on Long Island in September for a review. Except for a period in dock at New York, VIRGINIA spent the next months in Cuban waters, then was overhauled at Norfolk. She took part in the great naval review of 1907 in Hampton Roads and late in that year made ready for her round-the-world cruise with the Great White Fleet.

After her return and review in February 1909, VIRGINIA entered the Norfolk Navy Yard for extensive repairs, which lasted for four months. The next year was spent in routine operation off the East Coast, broken by her first voyage to Europe in late 1909. During the next few years VIRGINIA served along the East Coast and in the Cuban area, making several deployments to Mexico during unrest there. She was in drydock at Boston when the U.S. entered World War I in 1917, and she sent boarding parties to seize German

(Continued on page 275)

LOUISIANA
1906

LOUISIANA

Hull No: 45
Navy No: BB-19
Launched: August 27, 1904
Commissioned: June 2, 1906
Dimensions: 456.33 x 76.5 x 43.08 ft
Displacement: 16,000 tons
Armament: 4 12", 8 8", 12 7", 20 3" Guns;
    4 21" TT
Machinery: Triple Expansion Engines,
    12 Boilers, Twin Screw
Horsepower/Speed: 16,500/18 knots
Fate: Scrapped, 1923

The sixth battleship built at Newport News was LOUISIANA, which was one of two CONNECTICUT-class ships authorized in July 1902. Later, four more of this class were built and Newport News was also awarded MINNESOTA (BB-22). The contract for LOUISIANA was signed on October 15, 1902, and her keel was laid down on February 7 of the following year. The new battleship was christened and launched on August 27, 1904. Sponsor for LOUISIANA was Miss Juanita LaLande of New Orleans, who had been honored by the governor of Louisiana to perform that duty. The ship was completed and underwent trials late in 1905, then was commissioned on June 2, 1906, with Capt. A.R. Couden in command.

After shakedown, LOUISIANA was dispatched to Havana to stand by during the insurrection there in September 1906. The ship carried a peace commission which included then-Secretary of War W.H. Taft, and this commission set up a provisional government for Cuba. In November of the same year, LOUISIANA carried President Theodore Roosevelt to inspect construction progress on the Panama Canal and stopped at Puerto Rico on the return trip to enable him to pay a visit there. A year later, she too joined the Great White Fleet in its historic circumnavigation, returning in February 1909. She was overhauled after this voyage, then joined the Atlantic Fleet and sailed to Europe. She visited a number of northern European ports during the summer of 1911 and was herself visited by royalty from Denmark, Sweden, Germany, and Russia. From 1913 to 1915 LOUISIANA served in home waters and was dispatched to Mexico three times during unrest there. She was placed in reserve at Norfolk in late 1915 and was inactive for the next few years, except for summer training cruises. She served as an engineering and gunnery training ship during the first year of World War I and later saw convoy escort duty. LOUISIANA saw service as a troopship in 1919 and made four trips to France to bring Americans back from "over there." The veteran ship entered the Philadelphia Navy Yard and was decommissioned on October 20, 1920. LOUISIANA remained at Philadelphia until November 1923 when she was sold and scrapped.

MINNESOTA
1907

MINNESOTA

Hull No: 46
Navy No: BB-22
Launched: April 8, 1905
Commissioned: March 9, 1907
Dimensions: 456.33 x 76.5 x 43.08 ft
Displacement: 16,000 tons
Armament: 4 12", 8 8", 12 7", 20 3" Guns;
    4 21" TT
Machinery: Triple Expansion Engines,
    12 Boilers, Twin Screw
Horsepower/Speed: 16,800/18 knots
Fate: Scrapped, 1924

MINNESOTA was the fifth of six CONNECTI-CUT-class battleships ordered by the Navy, and she was the second of her class, after LOUISIANA, to be built at Newport News. MINNESOTA was authorized by Congress in March 1903, and her contract was signed on June 20 of that year. The keel for the shipyard's seventh battleship was laid on October 29, 1903, and she was launched on April 8, 1905. Sponsor for MINNESOTA was Miss Rose Marie Schaller, daughter of the senator from Minnesota. The new battleship was outfitted and tested by late 1906 and

was commissioned on March 9, 1907, commanded by Capt. J. Hubbard.

Having barely completed shakedown, MINNE-SOTA participated in the great naval review in Hampton Roads in 1907, then left with many of her sisters for their cruise around the world. After her return in 1909, she served along the East Coast and, like some of her sisters, was called upon to stand by first in Cuban, then in Mexican waters, during periods of unrest in those places. In November 1916, MINNE-SOTA became flagship, Reserve Force, Atlantic Fleet; then, five months later she rejoined the active fleet as an engineering and gunnery training ship in the Atlantic.

On September 29, 1918, she struck a German mine off the Delaware/Maryland coast and was seriously damaged without loss of life. She limped into the Philadelphia Navy Yard for repairs which lasted five months, then was assigned to troop transport duty. Between March and July 1919, MINNESOTA made three trips to France, returning over 3,000 troops to the U.S. Thereafter she served once more as a training ship, but her days were numbered. She was decommissioned on December 1, 1921, and a victim of the Washington Treaty, was sold for scrap at Philadelphia in 1924.

DELAWARE
1910

DELAWARE

Hull No: 86
Navy No: BB-28
Launched: February 6, 1909
Commissioned: April 4, 1910
Dimensions: 510 x 84.75 x 44.5 ft
Displacement: 20,009 tons
Armament: 10 12″, 14 5″ Guns; 2 21″ TT
Machinery: Triple Expansion Engines,
    14 Boilers, Twin Screw
Horsepower/Speed: 25,000/21 knots
Fate: Scrapped, 1924

First of a class of two battleships authorized in 1906, DELAWARE was the eighth of her type built at Newport News. These were the first American battleships to exceed 500 ft in length, and they were fast and powerful for their day. The contract for DELAWARE was signed on August 6, 1907, and her keel was laid on the following November 11. She was launched in ceremonies on February 6, 1909, and was sponsored by Miss Anna P. Cahall of Bridgeport, DL, niece of the governor of that state. The new battleship completed construction and trials and was commissioned on April 4, 1910. Commanded by Capt. C.A. Grove, the new DELAWARE visited the city of Wilmington in her namesake state, then sailed with the Atlantic Fleet to England and France. She returned for exercises in Cuban waters in late 1911, then sailed from Norfolk to Brazil and Chile. In June 1911 she was at Portsmouth, England, for the naval review following the coronation of George V.

Following this first year of widespread travel, DELAWARE spent the next five years mostly involved in fleet exercises and training in home waters off the East Coast. She visited France in 1913, then was dispatched to Mexico during unrest there in 1914 and 1915. DELAWARE was one of the few Newport News-built battleships to see World War I service at the scene of the fighting in Europe. She joined the British Grand Fleet in December 1917 in Scottish waters and sailed in convoy escort to Norway. In February 1918 she was twice attacked by a German submarine but escaped damage. After three convoy escort trips, DELAWARE helped to screen ships engaged in laying the great North Sea mine barrage in mid-1918.

DELAWARE spent what were to be her last few years in routine maneuvers and exercises off the East Coast and in the Caribbean. Her last voyage was a cruise to Europe with midshipmen in the summer of 1923, during which she visited Denmark, Scotland, and Spain. In September 1923 she was stripped of her armament at the Boston Navy Yard; then, she was decommissioned on November 10, 1923. In accord with the Washington Treaty, DELAWARE was sold and scrapped during the following year.

TEXAS
1914

TEXAS

Hull No: 147
Navy No: BB-35
Launched: May 18, 1912
Commissioned: March 12, 1914
Dimensions: 573 x 94.75 x 48.67 ft
Displacement: 27,000 tons
Armament: 10 14", 21 5" Guns; 4 21" TT
Machinery: Triple Expansion Engines,
    14 Boilers, Twin Screw
Horsepower/Speed: 30,000/21 knots
Fate: Memorial, 1948

Probably the most famous of all the battleships built at Newport News was TEXAS, which survived as a memorial over 70 years after her commissioning in 1914. TEXAS was the second of two NEW YORK-class ships authorized by Congress in June 1910.

In just a few years, U.S. battleships had increased greatly in size and power, and these ships were the first in the fleet with 14" guns. TEXAS and her sister were fitted with reciprocating engines and were coal burners; their traditional machinery was capable of an impressive 30,000 SHP.

The contract for TEXAS was signed on December

17, 1910, and her keel was laid down on the following April 17. The great ship was on the stocks for just over a year before her launch on May 18, 1912. Miss Claudia Lyon, daughter of the Republican national committee-man from Texas, served as sponsor for TEXAS on that date.

With the first U.S. 14" guns afloat, TEXAS was commissioned on March 12, 1914, and began 32 years of active duty with the Navy. She sailed from Hampton Roads under the command of Capt. Albert W. Grant on March 12 and spent three weeks at New York to complete her armament. She left hastily for deployment to Mexico during unrest there in June and July of 1915, then settled into more or less routine operation with the Fleet.

She was scheduled for deployment to Britain after the beginning of World War I, but she ran aground on Block Island in September 1917, and her departure was delayed for repairs until the following January. She joined the British Grand Fleet and saw convoy duty, then later escorted ships laying the North Sea mine barrage. She joined the Fleet to meet the German Fleet for its surrender in November 1918, then served as an escort for President Wilson's arrival in France.

(Continued on page 275)

PENNSYLVANIA
1916

PENNSYLVANIA

Hull No: 171
Navy No: BB-38
Launched: March 16, 1915
Commissioned: June 12, 1916
Dimensions: 608 x 96.67 x 45.08 ft
Displacement: 31,400 tons
Armament: 12 14", 14 5", 4 3" Guns; 2 21" TT
Machinery: Geared Turbines, 12 Boilers,
    Quadruple Screw
Horsepower/Speed: 32,000/21 knots
Fate: Sunk, 1948

Battleship PENNSYLVANIA represented a milestone in large warship construction at Newport News. She was described as the "most powerful warship in the world" when her contract was let to the shipyard on February 28, 1913, and she deserved this title in several ways. Her steam turbines were the largest fitted to a Newport News ship to that date, and she was the first U.S. vessel to mount all triple turrets and twelve 14" guns. She was one of the Navy's first oil-burners, and this, ironically, kept her out of the action in World War I. The keel for PENNSYLVANIA was laid on October 27, 1913, and she was ready for launch on March 16, 1915. Her massive 18" armor was too heavy

for the launching ways, and wooden planking was subsituted on her sides for the launch. Sponsor for PENNSYLVANIA was Miss Elizabeth Kolb of Philadelphia, who had been selected by the governor of Pennsylvania for the duty. A large crowd, including many Pennsylvania guests, attended the launching, and for the first time, motion pictures were taken of a launch at the shipyard.

PENNSYLVANIA was completed rapidly and was commissioned on June 12, 1916, with Capt. H.B. Wilson commanding. The new battleship, sister to the unfortunate ARIZONA built at the New York Navy Yard, became flagship of the Atlantic Fleet in October 1916. When the U.S. entered the war with Germany the following April, PENNSYLVANIA was unable to join the Grand Fleet, since she was an oil-burner and no tankers were available to accompany her to Europe. She busied herself with training and maneuvers in home waters for over a year until she accompanied President Wilson to France in December 1918. In 1922 she was assigned to the Pacific Fleet and spent most of the 1920s along the West Coast and in the Hawaiian area. PENNSYLVANIA underwent a major overhaul and modernization at the Philadelphia Navy Yard from 1929 to 1931, had her cage masts removed and tripod masts installed, then rejoined the Pacific Fleet where she saw routine service for ten years.

(Continued on page 275)

MISSISSIPPI
1917

MISSISSIPPI

Hull No: 185
Navy No: BB-41
Launched: January 25, 1917
Commissioned: December 18, 1917
Dimensions: 624 x 97 x 46.25 ft
Displacement: 32,000 tons
Armament: 12 14", 14 5", 4 3" Guns; 2 21" TT
Machinery: Geared Turbines, 9 Boilers,
   Quadruple Screw
Horsepower/Speed: 32,000/21 knots
Fate: Scrapped, 1956

MISSISSIPPI, authorized in 1914, was the 11th battleship built at Newport News. She and two other ships of the NEW MEXICO class which were built were similar in size and armament to the preceding PENNSLYVANIA class and, like all such naval vessels to follow, burned oil fuel. The contract for MISSISSIPPI was signed on November 23, 1914, and her keel was set down on April 5, 1915. Sponsor for the new battleship was Miss Camille McBeath, who had been chosen by the governor of the ship's namesake state for the honor. Miss McBeath sent MISSISSIPPI down the ways on January 25, 1917, and many digni-

taries from both Washington and Mississippi were in attendance.

The battleship was completed within a year and was commissioned on December 18, 1917. MISSISSIPPI's first few years, under the command of Capt. J.L. Jayne, were uneventful, and she spent much of her time in routine operations on the West Coast based at San Pedro. On June 12, 1924, tragedy struck her and 48 of her men who were killed after an explosion in one of her main turrets. Except for a trip to Australia in 1925, MISSISSIPPI remained on the West Coast with an occasional cruise to the Caribbean for the next 15 years.

She was modernized in 1936 and had her cage masts removed and new superstructure installed. She was transferred to the Atlantic in mid-1941 and made two deployments there before the attack on Pearl Harbor.

She left the Atlantic on December 9, 1941, and steamed for the Pacific, arriving at San Francisco in late January. MISSISSIPPPI saw extensive action in the Pacific during World War II and is said to have fired over a million shells at the Japanese. She participated in a number of campaigns including those in the Aleutians, Gilberts, Marshalls, and Philippines. In the Gilberts on November 20, 1943, she suffered another
(Continued on page 276)

MARYLAND
1921

MARYLAND

Hull No: 210
Navy No: BB-46
Launched: March 20, 1920
Commissioned: July 21, 1921
Dimensions: 624 x 96 x 46.25 ft.
Displacement: 32,619 tons
Armament: 8 16", 12 5", 4 3" Guns; 2 21" TT
Machinery: Turbo-Electric, 8 Boilers,
    Quadruple Screw
Horsepower/Speed: 31,000/21 knots
Fate: Scrapped, 1959

Four COLORADO-class battleships were authorized by Congress in August 1916, and two of these, MARYLAND and WEST VIRGINIA, were built at Newport News. These were the first ships to mount 16" main batteries and to have turbo-electric propulsion and electrically operated auxiliaries. Contracts for both the Newport News-built ships were awarded on December 5, 1916, and they were assigned hull numbers 210 and 211 by the shipyard. The keel for MARYLAND was laid on Shipway 6 on April 24, 1917, and she was launched on March 20, 1920. Christened on that date by Mrs. E. Brooks Lee, wife of the comptroller of the state of Maryland, the ship slipped smoothly into the James River.

The new battleship was commissioned under the command of Capt. C.F. Preston on July 21, 1921, and began what was to become a long and active career. First of the COLORADO class commissioned, MARYLAND spent her first few years regularly engaged in ceremonial duties in home and South American waters. She was assigned to the Pacific Fleet in 1923, made a trip to Australia in 1925, and carried President Hoover on part of his Latin American tour in 1928.

MARYLAND operated in the Pacific in routine maneuvers and training through the end of the 1930s and was moored at Pearl Harbor inboard of OKLAHOMA on December 7, 1941. Like PENNSLYVANIA, MARYLAND was protected against torpedo attack, but she did suffer two bomb hits. She was able to sail for repair at the Puget Sound Navy Yard and was modernized and readied for battle with the Japanese.

She left the yard in February 1942 and underwent a long period of training and escort duty in the South Pacific. She supported the invasions of the Gilberts, the Marshalls, and the Philippines with shore bombardment and was hit by an air-launched torpedo at Saipan in June 1944, which caused major damage. MARYLAND was repaired at Pearl Harbor, then supported landings in the Philippines and fought in the famous Battle of Surigao Strait in October 1944. She was hit by a kamikaze in November, which killed 31 of her crew, and again underwent repairs in Hawaii. She supported operations at Okinawa beginning in March 1945 and on April 7 was again struck by a suicide plane but kept on fighting.

At war's end, MARYLAND was placed in troop service and made five trips, repatriating more than 9,000 servicemen. She was placed in the Pacific Reserve Fleet at Bremerton and was decommissioned in April 1947. Winner of seven battle stars for her World War II service, "Fighting Mary" was withdrawn and scrapped in 1959.

WEST VIRGINIA
1923

WEST VIRGINIA

Hull No: 211
Navy No: BB-48
Launched: November 19, 1921
Commissioned: December 1, 1923
Dimensions: 624 x 96 x 46.25 ft
Displacement: 32,619 tons
Armament: 8 16″, 12 5″, 8 3″ Guns; 2 21″ TT
Machinery: Turbo-Electric, 8 Boilers,
    Quadruple Screw
Horsepower/Speed: 30,000/21 knots
Fate: Scrapped, 1959

WEST VIRGINIA, last of the "Old Battleships" built at Newport News, was the last capital ship completed under the Naval Holiday set by the Washington Treaty of 1922. She had been authorized by Congress in August 1916, but construction of badly-needed destroyers at the shipyard delayed her keel laying until April 12, 1920. Sister to MARYLAND, WEST VIRGINIA was lucky to be built at all since construction on six other similar ships, including IOWA at Newport News, was cancelled. Miss Alice Wright Mann of West Virginia was chosen by the Secretary of the Navy to sponsor WEST VIRGINIA, and she christened the ship on Shipway 6 on November 19, 1921.

The new battleship was completed and underwent successful trials in 1923, then was commissioned on December 1, 1923, with Capt. Thomas J. Senn in command. WEST VIRGINIA's first year was marred by a steering gear failure and grounding in Hampton Roads but she was not damaged. Her first two decades were spent mostly in training and fleet exercises, and except for a Pacific deployment in 1925, she stayed in the Atlantic with an occasional trip to Hawaii. Berthed at Pearl Harbor on the morning of December 7, 1941, WEST VIRGINIA was hit by seven torpedoes and two huge bombs which sank her and killed 105 of her men. Skillful action by her crew prevented her from capsizing, but her commanding officer, Capt. Mervyn S. Bennion, lost his life after a courageous defense of his ship.

After the attack, the monumental salvage job began and WEST VIRGINIA was refloated in May 1942. Salvage was made unpleasant by the fact that the bodies of 70 of the ship's crew were trapped in the wreckage, including those of three men in a storeroom who had checked off days on a calendar until they died on December 23.

The almost-destroyed WEST VIRGINIA rose from the ashes and, greatly modernized, emerged from the Puget Sound Navy Yard in July 1944 virtually a new ship. She left the West Coast, and after a stop at Hawaii, joined the fleet for action in the Philippines in *(Continued on page 276)*

INDIANA
1942

INDIANA

Hull No: 378
Navy No: BB-58
Launched: November 21, 1941
Commissioned: April 30, 1942
Dimensions: 680.5 x 108 x 52 ft
Displacement: 42,545 tons
Armament: 9 16", 20 5" Guns
Machinery: Geared Turbines, 8 Boilers,
    Quadruple Screw
Horsepower/Speed: 130,000/27 knots
Fate: Scrapped, 1962

INDIANA, last battleship built at Newport News, was called the "longest, widest, and luckiest" by her builders. Over 22 years had passed between award of WEST VIRGINIA in 1916 and the contract for INDIANA in 1938, and due to the Naval Holiday, no American battleship had been commissioned since 1923. Due to the volume of aircraft carrier, cruiser, and destroyer construction at the shipyard, the keel for INDIANA was not laid until November 20, 1939. Construction progressed rapidly thereafter, and by November 21, 1941, she was ready for launching. INDIANA was christened by Mrs. Margaret Schricker Robbins, daughter of the governor of Indiana, and over 500 Hoosiers arrived on two special trains to witness the

ceremony. Construction on the new battleship was accelerated after the attack on Pearl Harbor and INDIANA was commissioned on April 30, 1942, with Capt. A.S. "Tip" Merrill in command.

After shakedown in the Atlantic, she joined carriers ENTERPRISE and SARATOGA in the central Pacific. INDIANA supported strikes against the Solomons and Gilberts in 1942 and 1943 and moved with the fleet against the Marshalls in early 1944. She escaped serious battle damage but was involved in a collision with WASHINGTON (BB-56) in February 1944 and was forced to retire to Hawaii for repairs. She rejoined the fleet in late April and provided bombardment during advances on Truk and the Marianas. In June, INDIANA distinguished herself in the "Great Marianas Turkey Shoot" against Japanese naval aircraft; then, in August she moved on the Palaus and the Philippines. After action at Leyte in September, she left for repair on the West Coast, then returned in January 1945 for more fighting at Iwo Jima. INDIANA continued on to Okinawa, then to Japan itself, winning a total of nine battle stars during the war.

Virtually undamaged, she was put in the reserve fleet at Bremerton, then was decommissioned in September 1947. After almost 15 years of inactivity, the veteran INDIANA was finally withdrawn from the reserve fleet and was scrapped at San Francisco in 1962.

VIRGINIA *Continued from page 265*

ships in that port. After leaving Boston, VIRGINIA served as a gunnery training ship, then saw convoy escort duty in the Atlantic. She made five voyages to France after the war in "Magic Carpet" service to repatriate American troops. She brought 6,037 men home, then was decommissioned at Boston in August 1920.

VIRGINIA was placed on the sale list for scrapping, but fate had another mission for her. She and her sister ship NEW JERSEY were transferred to the War Department in August 1923 for use as targets off Cape Hatteras. Billy Mitchell's bombers attacked the two ships there on September 5, 1923, in order to demonstrate the power of aerial bombardment of naval vessels. A single 1,100-pound bomb hit the defenseless anchored VIRGINIA and virtually demolished her. She sank about 30 minutes later and was shortly followed to the bottom by her sister ship.

TEXAS *Continued from page 269*

TEXAS returned to the U.S. late in 1918 and, after repair, rejoined the Atlantic Fleet. In 1919 she became the first U.S. battleship to launch an airplane from her decks; then, she was reassigned to the Pacific Fleet until 1924.

TEXAS was extensively overhauled and modernized at the Norfolk Navy Yard in 1925. Her distinctive cage masts were replaced with a single huge tripod mast, and her fire control system was updated. After brief service in the Atlantic, she was assigned to the Pacific where she spent most of the next ten years. TEXAS became flagship for the U.S. Fleet in 1931 and served in the Pacific out of San Diego until she was transferred back to the Atlantic in 1937.

In 1939 she began service with the Neutrality Patrol and convoyed ships to Britain to help the war effort. TEXAS served ably in this assignment into 1942, at which time she was deployed for the invasion of North Africa. After supporting Operation Torch with shore bombardment, she resumed her convoy escort duties in the Atlantic and Mediterranean until the end of 1943. She was present and provided support at Normandy in June 1944, then bombarded Cherbourg late in that month. At Cherbourg she was hit several times by German shells but she completed her duty. She was repaired at Plymouth, then participated in the invasion of southern France in July 1944.

In September she returned to the U.S. and was repaired at New York, but her fighting days were far from over. TEXAS deployed to the Pacific early in 1945 and joined the island-hopping battle to Japan. She provided shore bombardment, first at Iwo Jima, then at Okinawa and in the Philippines.

After the war ended, TEXAS brought four shiploads of troops home to California; then, in January 1946 she sailed for Norfolk via Panama for deactivation. She was moored at Baltimore until the end of 1947; then, she was towed to Texas and was decommissioned and transferred to that state for service as a memorial at the San Jacinto Battleground.

PENNSYLVANIA *Continued from page 270*

When the Japanese attacked on December 7, 1941, PENNSYLVANIA was in dry dock at the Pearl Harbor Navy Yard. This was fortunate for her since torpedoes were unable to reach her in the dock, and her only major hit was a bomb to one of her 5″ mounts. After the attack, 29 of her men were dead and 38 were wounded, but she was able to sail to San Francisco for repairs only 13 days later.

Following repairs, she engaged in patrol and operations along the West Coast, then in April 1942 was sent to participate in fighting in the Aleutians. Almost 30 years old, PENNSYLVANIA saw her first action in bombardment in this campaign. After three missions to Alaska, she moved to the Hawaiian area to lead the long march to Japan. She participated in the assaults on the Gilberts, Marshalls, and Marianas, then in late 1944 provided shore bombardment at Leyte in the Philippines. She saw action at the Battle of Surigao Strait that decimated the Japanese fleet, then continued bombardment of Philippine targets. She was overhauled at San Francisco during the second quarter of 1945, then returned to the Western Pacific.

Her good luck ran out while she lay at anchor at Okinawa on August 12, as she was attacked by a Japanese torpedo plane and, hit aft, was heavily damaged. Twenty men were killed and ten were wounded, and PENNSYLVANIA did not reach Puget Sound for repairs until late October. Sufficient repairs were made to allow her to sail to Bikini to serve as a target ship for nuclear bomb testing there in July 1946; then, she was decommissioned on August 29. Winner of eight battle stars in World War II, the old PENNSYLVANIA was finally sunk near Kwajalein in the Marshalls on February 19, 1948.

turret explosion which killed 43 of her crew. MISSIS-SIPPI fought in the Battle of Surigao Strait, then was hit and damaged by a kamikaze in the Philippines in January 1945. She was repaired at Pearl Harbor, then steamed to Okinawa to provide shore bombardment in support of invading troops. She was hit by another suicide plane in June but kept on shelling the enemy.

MISSISSIPPI was present in Tokyo Bay for the surrender, then sailed for Norfolk on September 6, 1945. There she was converted to a weapons testing ship and was redesignated AG-128. She successfully launched the new Terrier missile in 1953 and carried so much secret equipment that the Navy restricted photographs of her.

Shipyard officials, some of whom had helped build her, attended a 37th birthday party held for her in 1954. Almost 40 years old, MISSISSIPPI was decommissioned in September 1956, and the veteran winner of eight battle stars in World War II was sold for scrap in November of the same year.

October. She provided shore bombardment at Leyte Gulf, fought in the Battle of Surigao Strait, and served at Mindoro before the end of 1944. She followed the war to its conclusion at Luzon, Iwo Jima, and Okinawa, then was present at the surrender in Tokyo Bay in September 1945. She had avenged her sinking by helping to sink the Japanese battleship YAMASHIRO in Surigao Strait and had won five battle stars, notwithstanding her late entry into the war.

WEST VIRGINIA made several voyages in "Magic Carpet" troop service before she was decommissioned on January 9, 1947, and was placed in the Pacific Reserve Fleet. The famous and beloved "Weevie" remained in reserve for the next 12 years, then was sold and scrapped at New York in 1959.

CRUISERS
WEST VIRGINIA
1905

WEST VIRGINIA

Hull No: 38
Navy No: ACR-5
Launched: April 18, 1903
Commissioned: February 23, 1905
Dimensions: 503.75 x 69.33 x 41.17 ft
Displacement: 13,660 tons
Armament: 4 8", 14 6" Guns; 2 18" TT
Machinery: Triple Expansion Engines,
    16 Boilers, Twin Screw
Horsepower/Speed: 23,000/22 knots
Fate: Scrapped, 1930

The first cruiser built at Newport News was the armored cruiser WEST VIRGINIA which was one of six PENNSYLVANIA-class ships authorized in 1899 and 1900. These ships had armor on their sides and decks and were, in fact, larger than many battleships of their day. The contract for WEST VIRGINIA and MARYLAND of this class was awarded to the shipyard in January 1901, and the keel for the first ship was laid on the following September 16. WEST VIRGINIA was launched with ceremony on April 18, 1903, and was christened by Miss Katherine White, daughter of the governor of West Virginia.

The new cruiser was commissioned on February 23, 1905, with Capt. C.H. Arnold in command. She was attached to the Atlantic Fleet for just over a year, then spent two years with the Asiatic Squadron. After overhaul in 1908, she spent six years with the Pacific Fleet, then was placed in reserve.

In 1916 she was dispatched to Mexico during trouble there. At this time she was renamed HUNTINGTON in honor of the West Virginia city and, incidentally, for the shipyard's founder, so that her former name could be used for the Newport News-built battleship WEST VIRGINIA. In 1917 HUNTINGTON was fitted with catapults for four seaplanes and then performed a series of experiments with seaplanes and balloons at Pensacola. Late in 1917 she was assigned to troop convoy service and made ten trips to Europe in 1917 and 1918. In November 1918 HUNTINGTON was converted for service as a troop transport, and she subsequently made six voyages as a troopship and brought over 12,000 men home from Europe. She was assigned to Cruiser Force in July 1919, then was decommissioned at Portsmouth, NH, in September 1920. After ten years in reserve, the old HUNTINGTON was scrapped in 1930 in accordance with the London Treaty for the reduction of naval armament.

MARYLAND
1905

MARYLAND
Hull No: 39
Navy No: ACR-8
Launched: September 12, 1903
Commissioned: April 18, 1905
Dimensions: 503.75 x 69.33 x 41.17 ft
Displacement: 13,749 tons
Armament: 4 8″, 14 6″, 18 3″ Guns; 2 18″ TT
Machinery: Triple Expansion Engines,
16 Boilers, Twin Screw
Horsepower/Speed: 23,000/22 knots
Fate: Scrapped, 1930

MARYLAND was the second cruiser built at Newport News, and she was the sister ship of WEST VIRGINIA which was constructed a few months ahead of her. These cruisers had a maximum thickness of armor of nine inches and literally bristled with a total of 60 guns. They were painted a bright white and were richly ornamented in the fashion of that time. The keel for MARYLAND was laid down on October 7, 1901, and the new ship was readied for launching on September 12, 1903. Sponsor for MARYLAND was Miss Jennie Scott Waters, daughter of a member of the staff of the governor of Maryland. MARYLAND completed trials in January 1905 and was commissioned on the following April 18 under the command of Capt. R.R. Ingersoll.

The new cruiser spent her first year-and-a-half in training and maneuvers in the Atlantic, then was assigned to the Asiatic Fleet in September 1906. She remained in the Pacific until the beginning of World War I and was active in missions to troubled Mexico and Nicaragua during these years. Renamed FREDERICK in 1917, also so that her old name could be used for a Newport News-built battleship, she joined her sisters in the Atlantic for escort duty during the war. She escorted troops returning from France on six voyages, then was placed in reduced commission at Philadelphia in mid-1919. In 1920 she carried the American Olympic Team to Belgium while on a training cruise; then in late 1920 she returned to the Pacific Fleet. FREDERICK remained in the Pacific on active duty until February 1922 when she was taken out of commission and was placed in reserve at Mare Island. In late 1929 she was stricken and was sold for scrapping early in the following year.

MONTANA
1908

MONTANA
Hull No: 58
Navy No: ACR-13
Launched: December 15, 1906
Commissioned: July 21, 1908
Dimensions: 504.5 x 72.5 x 42.17 ft
Displacement: 14,500 tons
Armament: 4 10″, 16 6″, 22 3″ Guns; 4 21″ TT
Machinery: Triple Expansion Engines,
16 Boilers, Twin Screw
Horsepower/Speed: 23,000/22 knots
Fate: Scrapped, 1935

MONTANA was the last armored cruiser ever built for the Navy, and she was the last cruiser completed at Newport News for 22 years. The keel for MONTANA was laid on April 29, 1905, and she was on the stocks for almost 20 months. MONTANA was launched on a cold December 15, 1906, and was christened by Miss Minnie Conrad of Great Falls, MT. The powerful new cruiser with four stacks was completed and passed her speed trials in April 1908, then was commissioned on July 21, with Capt. Alfred Reynolds commanding.

MONTANA's career was remarkably like that of her Newport News-built sister NORTH CAROLINA and she met the same fate. Her first few months were spent cruising off the East Coast; then, in April 1909 she sailed to the Middle East for protective duty after the Turkish Revolution. Later in 1909 and in 1910 MONTANA again cruised off the East Coast and also engaged in ceremonial duties. She was overhauled in 1911, then again deployed to the Middle East. During the next few years MONTANA operated in routine service along the East Coast and in the Caribbean. At the outbreak of World War I she served in escort duty along the Atlantic seaboard up to Nova Scotia; then, in 1919 she made six trips to France and returned 8,800 servicemen from "over there."

She arrived at the Puget Sound Navy Yard in August 1919 and was renamed MISSOULA in June 1920. Still at Puget Sound, the old cruiser was decommissioned on February 2, 1921. MISSOULA spent the next nine years in reserve, then was struck from the Navy list in July 1930. Like her sister before her, she was sold in accordance with the London Treaty of 1930 and was scrapped in 1935.

CHARLESTON
1905

CHARLESTON

Hull No: 41
Navy No: C-22
Launched: January 23, 1904
Commissioned: October 17, 1905
Dimensions: 424.25 x 65.08 x 40 ft
Displacement: 9,700 tons
Armament: 14 6", 18 3" Guns
Machinery: Triple Expansion Engines,
    16 Boilers, Twin Screw
Horsepower/Speed: 21,000/22 knots
Fate: Scrapped, 1930

The third cruiser built at Newport News was CHARLESTON, ordered in March 1901. Of ST. LOUIS class, this ship was a protected cruiser and was smaller than the two armored cruisers previously built at the shipyard and had no torpedo tubes. The keel for CHARLESTON was laid down on January 30, 1902, and her construction on the stocks took just under two years. The new cruiser was launched on January 23, 1904, and was sponsored by Miss Helen W. Rhett, daughter of the mayor of the city of Charleston, SC. After 18 more months of construction and outfit-

ting, CHARLESTON stood trials, then was commissioned on October 17, 1905. Under the command of Capt. H. Winslow the new ship underwent shakedown, then carried diplomats to Central America during her first year.

In late 1906 she began service with the Pacific Fleet, then in mid-1908 she transferred to the Asiatic Fleet. CHARLESTON remained in the Far East until late 1910, showing the flag at ports in China, Japan, Manchuria, and Russia; then, she returned to the West Coast and was decommissioned at Bremerton, WA. She was placed in commission in reserve in 1912 and served as a receiving ship at Bremerton, then as a submarine tender in 1916.

CHARLESTON was placed back in full commission when the U.S. entered World War I, and after patrol duty in the Caribbean, she escorted the first American troops to France in June 1917. In late 1918 she made two convoy trips to Nova Scotia, then made five trips to France in troop transport service. In July 1919 CHARLESTON returned to the West Coast, and after serving as administrative flagship for Commander, Destroyer Squadrons, Pacific Fleet for four years, she was decommissioned in December 1923. After almost seven years in the Reserve Fleet, CHARLESTON was sold for scrap in 1930.

NORTH CAROLINA
1908

NORTH CAROLINA

Hull No: 57
Navy No: ACR-12
Launched: October 6, 1906
Commissioned: May 7, 1908
Dimensions: 504.5 x 72.5 x 42.17 ft
Displacement: 14,500 tons
Armament: 4 10″, 16 6″, 22 3″ Guns; 4 21″ TT
Machinery: Triple Expansion Engines,
    16 Boilers, Twin Screw
Horsepower/Speed: 23,000/22 knots
Fate: Scrapped, 1930

Armored cruiser NORTH CAROLINA was the fourth cruiser built at Newport News. She and sister ship MONTANA were the last armored cruisers ever built for the Navy, as their type was replaced by development of the larger battle cruisers. Authorized in 1904, the keel for NORTH CAROLINA was laid down on March 21, 1905, and she was ready for launching 18 months later on October 6, 1906. Sponsor for the cruiser was Miss Rebekah Williams Glenn, daughter of the governor of North Carolina. Newspapers hailed NORTH CAROLINA as the "largest vessel in the United States Navy" and over 10,000 persons attended the ceremony. The new NORTH

CAROLINA underwent her speed trials in adverse conditions in early 1908 and had difficulty attaining her contract speed, but later made the grade and was commissioned on May 7 under the command of Capt. William A. Marshall.

NORTH CAROLINA had a short and relatively peaceful career. After shakedown, she carried President-elect Taft on an inspection trip to the Panama Canal, then made a cruise to the Mediterranean with her sister MONTANA in mid-1909. The two cruisers provided relief for victims of unrest in Turkey and protected American citizens from harm during this deployment to the Middle East. During the following years, NORTH CAROLINA engaged in training and ceremonial operations, and she returned the bodies of MAINE crewmen home from Cuba for burial. She returned to the Middle East in 1915 to protect American interests at the beginning of war in Europe; then, while serving as station ship at Pensacola, she became the first ship in history to launch an aircraft by catapult while under way. She served as an escort along the East Coast during World War I and for the first half of 1919 was in troop service, returning veterans to the U.S.

Renamed CHARLOTTE in 1920, she was decommissioned at Puget Sound in February 1921. After nine years in reserve at Bremerton, her name was stricken, and she was sold for scrap in 1930.

HOUSTON 1930

HOUSTON

Hull No: 323
Navy No: CA-30
Launched: September 7, 1929
Commissioned: June 17, 1930
Dimensions: 600 x 64.42 x 36 ft
Displacement: 11,574 tons
Armament: 9 8″, 4 5″ Guns; 6 21″ TT
Machinery: Geared Turbines, 8 Boilers,
    Quadruple Screw
Horsepower/Speed: 107,000/32.6 knots
Fate: War Loss, 1942

The first "modern" cruiser built at Newport News was the famous HOUSTON, ordered almost 20 years after the delivery of MONTANA in 1908. The keel for HOUSTON was laid down on Shipway 8 on May 1, 1928. Sponsor for HOUSTON was Miss Elizabeth Holcombe, daughter of a former mayor of Houston, and she christened the powerful ship with water from the Houston Ship Channel on September 7, 1929. The launching was a happy occasion at Newport News, since no major naval ship had been launched there since the battleship WEST VIRGINIA in 1921.

HOUSTON was completed and was commissioned on June 17, 1930, with Capt. J.B. Gay in command. The new cruiser underwent shakedown in the Atlantic, then sailed for the Pacific in January 1931 to become flagship, Asiatic Station. She returned to the West Coast late in 1933 and, as a unit of the Scouting Force, engaged in routine operations for the next eight years.

In the Philippines on December 7, 1941, HOUSTON immediately sailed for Australian waters to join the allied ABDA (American-British-Dutch-Australian) Force. This force, under the command of Adm. Doorman of the Dutch Navy, engaged the enemy early in the war and fought gallantly but was doomed from the start. Outnumbered and without air cover, the Allied fleet of five cruisers and ten destroyers met the enemy on February 28, 1942. One by one the Allied ships succumbed to devastating torpedo attacks until only HOUSTON and HMAS PERTH were left of the cruisers. Near midnight the two cruisers met the Japanese force in an attempt to destroy the Java invasion fleet and were able to sink one transport and beach three others. During this action PERTH was sunk by enemy torpedoes and HOUSTON followed shortly thereafter. HOUSTON sank a minesweeper and hit three destroyers but was herself fatally hit by four torpedoes and sank heroically just after midnight. Her fate was not made known for over nine months, and the full details of the gallantry of her men was not told until the survivors were freed from prison camps after the war. For her heroism, HOUSTON was awarded the Presidential Unit Citation. She was the first Newport News ship so honored.

AUGUSTA
1931

The second NORTHAMPTON-class cruiser built at Newport News was AUGUSTA, awarded to the shipyard on the same day as HOUSTON on June 13, 1927. AUGUSTA's keel was set down on Shipway 6 on July 2, 1928, and construction there took just under 19 months. AUGUSTA was launched on February 1, 1930, and was christened by Miss Evelyn McDaniel of Augusta, GA. The completed AUGUSTA joined the fleet on January 30, 1931, with Capt. J.O. Richardson in command.

The new ship was destined to have a proud career and began with a year with the Atlantic Fleet in routine operation. She transferred to the Asiatic Fleet, relieving HOUSTON as flagship in November 1933, and for a while she was commanded by the later-famous Chester W. Nimitz. She returned to the Atlantic in 1940 and was made flagship of the Atlantic Fleet. AUGUSTA sailed to Newfoundland with President Roosevelt aboard in August 1941 for the Atlantic Conference; then, when war broke out, she was assigned to carrier escort out of Bermuda. She participated in the Allied landings on North Africa in November 1942, then returned to the U.S. for repair at New York. She made two convoy escort voyages in early 1943, one of which was to escort QUEEN MARY carrying Winston Churchill; then, she joined the British fleet at Scapa Flow to help escort Murmansk-bound convoys. She was overhauled in late 1943, then participated in the Normandy landings in June 1944. The next month AUGUSTA moved to the Mediterranean where she supported the Allied landings in southern France in August and September.

She was overhauled at Philadelphia in late 1944 and early 1945, then carried President Truman to Belgium for the Potsdam Conference in July 1945 and returned him to Newport News in August. AUGUSTA was converted for "Magic Carpet" troop service after the war, then was decommissioned at Philadelphia on July 16, 1946. First slated for disposal, she was placed in reserve in 1951, and the proud winner of three battle stars was finally withdrawn and sold for scrap in 1959.

BOISE
1938

BOISE

Hull No: 361
Navy No: CL-47
Launched: December 3, 1936
Commissioned: August 12, 1938
Dimensions: 608.33 x 59.58 x 42 ft
Displacement: 11,581 tons
Armament: 15 6″, 8 5″ Guns
Machinery: Geared Turbines, 8 Boilers,
     Quadruple Screw
Horsepower/Speed: 100,000/33.6 knots
Fate: Scrapped, 1981

The contract for BOISE was awarded on August 22, 1934, and her keel was laid on April 1, 1935. She remained on the ways for 20 months until her launch on December 3, 1936. Sponsor for BOISE was Miss Salome Clark, daughter of Representative Clark of Idaho, and water from the Snake River was used for the ceremony. After more construction and outfitting and trials, the cruiser was commissioned on August 12, 1938, with Capt. B.V. McCandles commanding.

Following her shakedown cruise which took her to Africa, BOISE joined Battle Force, Pacific and, based at San Pedro, operated in the Pacific until December 1941. She was in the Philippines when war broke out but had the misfortune to strike an uncharted reef in January 1942, which necessitated repairs that kept her out of the action for five months.

After repair at the Mare Island Navy Yard, BOISE escorted a convoy to New Zealand, then engaged in a feint raiding cruise in July and August to draw Japanese attention away from the landings at Guadalcanal. In September she saw action at Guadalcanal and was hit by shells off Cape Esperance, which necessitated another trip home for repairs, this time to Philadelphia.

In June 1943, her repairs completed, BOISE sailed for the Mediterranean where she supported the landings on Sicily, Taranto, and Salerno. After these actions she again returned to the Pacific and distinguished herself by winning a total of 11 battle stars. She was in action off New Guinea for most of 1944 and late in that year fought in the campaigns of Leyte, Surigao Strait, and Mindoro. After duty near Borneo during the first half of 1945 and a tour of the Philippines with Gen. MacArthur aboard, BOISE returned to the West Coast. She remained there until the end of the war, then was transferred to the East Coast in October and was decommissioned at New York on July 1, 1946.

At a time when many of her sister ships were being scrapped, BOISE was sold to Argentina in January 1951 and became NUEVE DE JULIO. For service with the Argentine Navy, she was modernized and her superstructure was cut down, hull bulges were added, and her mast derricks and catapults were removed. Named for the Argentine Independence Day, she was commissioned on March 11, 1952, and began service which lasted almost 30 years with the Argentine Navy. She served along with class sister PHOENIX, which had been renamed GENERAL BELGRANO in 1956. By the late 1970s, NUEVE DE JULIO became too old for further service and was scrapped in 1981, escaping the action that claimed her sister during the Falklands War in 1982.

ST. LOUIS
1939

ST. LOUIS

Hull No: 362
Navy No: CL-49
Launched: April 15, 1938
Commissioned: May 19, 1939
Dimensions: 608.33 x 59.58 x 42 ft
Displacement: 11,780 tons
Armament: 15 6", 8 5" Guns
Machinery: Geared Turbines, 8 Boilers,
    Quadruple Screw
Horsepower/Speed: 100,000/33 knots
Fate: Sank, 1980

One of the Navy's most courageous World War II cruisers was ST. LOUIS, which was authorized in 1929 and was awarded to Newport News on October 16, 1935. The keel for Hull 362 was laid down on Shipway 6 on December 10, 1936, and her hull was readied for launching on April 15, 1938. Miss Nancy Lee Morrill of St. Louis was selected as sponsor for the cruiser, and she sent it down the ways with a splash of champagne on that date. After commissioning under the command of Capt. Charles H. Morrison on May 19, 1939, ST. LOUIS underwent shakedown in the Atlantic, then spent her first year with the Neutrality Patrol.

In late 1940 she moved to the Pacific where fate promised her an active and distinguished career. She operated from Hawaiian waters for the next year and was in the Pearl Harbor Navy Yard under repair on December 7, 1941, when the Japanese attacked. She splashed three enemy planes during the attack, then made for sea to search for the Japanese fleet. In the aftermath, ST. LOUIS provided escort for transports between the West Coast and Hawaii; then, she departed with YORKTOWN for attacks on the Marshalls and Gilberts. For most of the second half of 1942 she was active in the Aleutians; then, she began operations in the Solomons.

Active in almost every major engagement of the Pacific war, ST. LOUIS was heavily damaged on several occasions. In July 1943 she was on patrol in the "Slot" in the Solomons and was hit by a torpedo which damaged her bow. After repair at Mare Island, she returned to the Solomons for more action. In January 1944 she was hit by a bomb which killed 23 of her crew and injured 20, but she was back in action in less than a month. She supported the landings at Saipan and Guam, then was sent to the West Coast for overhaul in August and September. ST. LOUIS moved to the Philippines late in 1944 and while on patrol in the Surigao Strait in November was attacked by a swarm of suicide planes. Two of these were successful and again put her out of the action. After another repair period, she again returned to fight and in mid-March joined in strikes against Okinawa. During this action, she fired a total of 26,250 5" and 6" shells weighing over two million pounds at the enemy. For the remainder of the war, ST. LOUIS engaged in operations against the Japanese on the Asian mainland; then, she joined in "Magic Carpet" troop service until she was decommissioned at Philadelphia on June 20, 1946.

After winning 11 battle stars during World War II, it seemed that her career was over, but she was destined for many more years of service. She was sold to the government of Brazil and, after modernization, was commissioned as TAMANDARE' on January 29, 1951. She served with distinction with the Brazilian Navy for the next 15 years, then was offered at auction to scrappers in 1975. She was finally sold but, under tow to Taiwan in August 1980, she sank in the South Atlantic and escaped the burner's torch.

BIRMINGHAM
1943

BIRMINGHAM

Hull No: 390
Navy No: CL-62
Launched: March 20, 1942
Commissioned: January 29, 1943
Dimensions: 610 x 65.67 x 42 ft
Displacement: 12,006 tons
Armament: 12 6", 12 5" Guns
Machinery: Geared Turbines, 4 Boilers,
    Quadruple Screw
Horsepower/Speed: 100,000/32.5 knots
Fate: Scrapped, 1959

First of eight CLEVELAND-class cruisers built at Newport News during World War II was BIRMINGHAM, which was awarded to the shipyard along with one other cruiser and three aircraft carriers on July 3, 1940. The contract award for these ships was personally announced by President Roosevelt on his visit to Newport News in July 1940. The keel for BIRMINGHAM was laid on Shipway 2 on February 17, 1941, and construction there took just over 13 months. Sponsored by Mrs. W. Cooper Green, wife of the mayor of Birmingham, AL, BIRMINGHAM was launched on March 20, 1942. Under the shipyard's intense war production effort, the new cruiser was outfitted and tested in a few more months and was commissioned on January 29, 1943, with Capt. J. Wilkes in command. BIRMINGHAM was immediately assigned to the Atlantic Fleet and, after a minimum of shakedown, sailed for the Mediterranean to support the invasion of Sicily in July. She was then assigned to the Pacific Fleet, arriving at Pearl Harbor in September.

Like other cruisers in the Pacific, she was destined to see some of the hottest action of the war and to participate in most of the major campaigns. During the rest of 1943, BIRMINGHAM provided support to raids on Tarawa, Wake, and in the Solomons. In the latter action she was damaged by two bombs and a torpedo and had to retire to Mare Island for repairs. She returned to the fighting in February 1944 and supported invasions of Saipan, Tinian, and Guam; later in the year, she was active during raids on the Philippines, Okinawa, Luzon, and Formosa. During the Battle for Leyte Gulf, BIRMINGHAM suffered heavy damage from a magazine explosion aboard light carrier PRINCETON while bravely aiding that crippled vessel and 48 of her crew perished. Damage was so heavy that the cruiser again sailed to Mare Island for major repair. BIRMINGHAM rejoined the fleet in January 1945 and saw more action in the invasions of Iwo Jima and Okinawa in March and May. Near the end of the Okinawa sortie, she was hit forward by a suicide plane and returned to Pearl Harbor for repair. She returned to the western Pacific in August 1945 and, after a trip to Australian waters, sailed for San Francisco where she was decommissioned on January 2, 1947.

Recipient of nine battle stars for her World War II gallantry as well as the Navy Unit Commendation for her assistance to PRINCETON, the old BIRMINGHAM remained in reserve until she was stricken and scrapped in 1959.

MOBILE
1943

MOBILE
Hull No: 391
Navy No: CL-63
Launched: May 15, 1942
Commissioned: March 24, 1943
Dimensions: 610 x 65.67 x 42 ft
Displacement: 12,006 tons
Armament: 12 6", 12 5" Guns
Machinery: Geared Turbines, 4 Boilers, Quadruple Screw
Horsepower/Speed: 100,000/32.5 knots
Fate: Scrapped, 1960

The second CLEVELAND-class light cruiser awarded to Newport News on July 3, 1940, was MOBILE, which was assigned Hull No. 391. The keel for MOBILE was laid on Shipway 7 on April 14, 1941, and her hull was on the ways for 13 months. On May 15, 1942, Mrs. Harry T. Hartwell of Mobile christened the cruiser and sent her down the ways to the James River. As was the usual practice during the war years, formal trials were waived, and MOBILE was commissioned on March 24, 1943, with Capt. Charles J. Wheeler in command. After a brief shakedown on the East Coast, MOBILE departed for the Pacific where her speed and guns were needed most.

She was destined to see an unusually active battle career and to win 11 battle stars without ever sustaining major damage. Within a month after her arrival at Pearl Harbor in late July, MOBILE had participated in raids on Marcus Island and during the following month was in action at Tarawa and Wake. She was in action in the Marshalls in December and joined in the assault on Kwajalein Atoll in January. With TF 58 she provided support to operations in the Carolines and then the Marianas at Saipan, Tinian, and Guam. By her first birthday in March, MOBILE had steamed over 70,000 miles and had engaged the enemy in fully 11 sorties. Later in 1944 she escorted carriers and saw action in the Battle of the Philippine Sea, but she never sustained battle damage. She subsequently participated in the Battle for Leyte Gulf, then saw out the end of the war in Philippine waters.

After the war MOBILE was assigned to "Magic Carpet" duty for several voyages, the last of which found her at San Diego early in 1946. She then steamed to Puget Sound and was decommissioned on May 9, 1947. Veteran of a short but very active four-year combat career, MOBILE lay at Bremerton in reserve until early 1960 when she was withdrawn and sold for scrap.

BILOXI
1943

BILOXI

Hull No: 399
Navy No: CL-80
Launched: February 23, 1943
Commissioned: August 31, 1943
Dimensions: 610 x 65.67 x 42 ft
Displacement: 12,006 tons
Armament: 12 6″, 12 5″ Guns
Machinery: Geared Turbines, 4 Boilers,
    Quadruple Screw
Horsepower/Speed: 100,000/32.5 knots
Fate: Scrapped, 1961

Called "Lucky Lady" and "Busy Bee," BILOXI was the shipyard's third CLEVELAND-class cruiser built during World War II. She was indeed lucky and never lost a man to enemy action, although she was involved in almost every major operation in the Pacific after her arrival there. BILOXI was awarded to Newport News along with four carriers and the second cruiser HOUSTON on September 9, 1940, and her keel was laid on Shipway 4 on July 9, 1941. She was the third cruiser launched at the yard in less than a year when she slipped into the James River on February 23, 1943. BILOXI's sponsor was Mrs. Louis Braun, wife of

a former mayor of the city of Biloxi. The new ship was completed, trials were waived, and she was commissioned on August 31, 1943, with Capt. D.M. McCurl in command.

BILOXI had one of the shortest but busiest careers of any Newport News-built warship. She arrived in the Pacific in late 1943 and served almost continuously until the end of the war in either shore bombardment or in carrier escort and support. Her missions carried her to Truk, Saipan, Hollandia, Iwo Jima, Guam, Yap, Cichi Jima, Okinawa, Formosa, Leyte, Luzon, Indochina, Hong Kong, and finally Tokyo at war's end. BILOXI was struck by a kamikaze plane off Okinawa on March 27, 1945, but its 1,100-pound bomb was a dud and her crew, after disarming it, mounted it on her quarterdeck as a souvenir. A month later she was on the West Coast for overhaul, but she quickly returned to finish the war. She engaged in troop service briefly and stayed with the occupation force in Japan until November 1945; then, she returned to the U.S. for deactivation.

BILOXI was placed in reserve and was decommissioned at Puget Sound Naval Shipyard on October 29, 1946. Winner of nine battle stars for her World War II heroism, the short-lived veteran was finally stricken in 1961 and was subsequently scrapped.

HOUSTON
1943

HOUSTON
Hull No: 400
Navy No: CL-81
Launched: June 19, 1943
Commissioned: December 20, 1943
Dimensions: 610 x 65.67 x 42 ft
Displacement: 12,006 tons
Armament: 12 6″, 12 5″ Guns
Machinery: Geared Turbines, 4 Boilers, Quadruple Screw
Horsepower/Speed: 100,000/32.5 knots
Fate: Scrapped, 1959

The shipyard's fourth CLEVELAND-class light cruiser, awarded on September 9, 1940, carried Newport News Hull No. 400 and was originally named VICKSBURG. Her keel was laid on Shipway 2 on August 4, 1941, and on October 12, 1942, she was renamed HOUSTON, in memory of her shipyard-built sister HOUSTON which was lost in battle on the previous March 1. In the wake of the loss of the first HOUSTON, a great patriotic campaign was mounted in her namesake city to raise money for a replacement for her, and this was accomplished by a bond drive by the citizens of Houston. The second HOUSTON was launched on June 19, 1943, and was sponsored by Mrs. Claud B. Hamill, wife of Houston's War Bond Committee chairman. The cruiser was commissioned on December 20, 1943, with Capt. W.W. Behrens in command.

After shakedown and training on the East Coast, HOUSTON left for the Pacific in April 1944. She arrived at Majuro Atoll in late May and joined Vice Admiral Mitscher's carrier task force. She immediately saw action in the Marianas, then went on to fight at the Bonins, Guam, Tinian, Saipan, Rota, and Iwo Jima. HOUSTON moved with her task force to the Philippines in September and joined the attack on Formosa in October. On October 13, 1944, she came under attack from Japanese aircraft and was hit in her engine room by a torpedo. She lost power and assumed a 16-degree list, but her crew fought gallantly and saved her. Under tow three days later, she was again torpedoed and 55 of her crew were lost; but again her damage control crews saved her, and she eventually returned to New York for repair.

Having won three battle stars in the Pacific, her war efforts were over as she did not leave the New York Navy Yard until October 1945. Her survival was noted by the chief of the Bureau of Ships, who praised her builders and her staunch qualities. During the next two years, the rebuilt HOUSTON engaged in training cruises which took her twice to Europe and the Mediterranean. She entered the Philadelphia Navy Yard in August 1947 and was decommissioned there on the following December 15. Placed in reserve, she remained inactive at Philadelphia until she was stricken in March 1959 and was sold for scrap.

AMSTERDAM
1945

AMSTERDAM

Hull No: 408
Navy No: CL-101
Launched: April 25, 1944
Commissioned: January 8, 1945
Dimensions: 610 x 65.67 x 42 ft
Displacement: 12,006 tons
Armament: 12 6", 12 5" Guns
Machinery: Geared Turbines, 4 Boilers,
    Quadruple Screw
Horsepower/Speed: 100,000/32.5 knots
Fate: Scrapped, 1971

Cruisers AMSTERDAM and PORTSMOUTH and carrier BOXER were awarded to the shipyard on December 15, 1941. The keel for AMSTERDAM was not laid on Shipway 4 until March 3, 1943, just ten days after the launch of BILOXI from that facility. Construction on the CLEVELAND-class light cruiser took about 13 months and AMSTERDAM was launched on April 25, 1944. Mrs. William E. Hasenfuss of Amsterdam, NY,

acted as sponsor for the new ship; she was the mother of a soldier killed at Pearl Harbor and was Amsterdam's first Gold Star Mother of World War II. AMSTERDAM was completed late in 1944, trials were waived, and she was commissioned on January 8, 1945, with Capt. A.P. Lawton in command.

The Navy's newest cruiser almost missed the war and had one of the shortest careers of any Newport News-built warship. AMSTERDAM underwent shakedown and engaged in training exercises until mid-1945, then joined the action in the Pacific in July. Attached to Cruiser Division 18, she participated in Third Fleet attacks against the Japanese homeland in July and August. She entered Tokyo Bay three days after the surrender, then returned to the eastern Pacific and steamed between the West Coast and Hawaii until the end of 1945. AMSTERDAM was deactivated at San Francisco beginning in January 1946, then was decommissioned and placed in reserve on June 30, 1947. Winner of one battle star in World War II, the short-lived AMSTERDAM remained in reserve until she was withdrawn and scapped in 1971.

PORTSMOUTH
1945

PORTSMOUTH

Hull No: 409
Navy No: CL-102
Launched: September 20, 1944
Commissioned: June 25, 1945
Dimensions: 610 x 65.67 x 42 ft
Displacement: 12,006 tons
Armament: 12 6", 12 5" Guns
Machinery: Geared Turbines, 4 Boilers,
    Quadruple Screw
Horsepower/Speed: 100,000/32.5 knots
Fate: Scrapped, 1971

Light cruiser PORTSMOUTH was distinctive since she was the first Newport News ship to have two sponsors, this distinction being shared only with submarines SAM RAYBURN in 1963, LEWIS AND CLARK in 1964, and L. MENDEL RIVERS in 1973. The keel for PORTSMOUTH was laid on Shipway 2 on September 20, 1944, and few had hopes that she would see action in World War II. The shipyard's last CLEVELAND-class light cruiser to be launched stayed on the ways for 15 months. Sponsors for PORTS-MOUTH were Mrs. Marian Marvin Dale, wife of the mayor of Portsmouth, NH, and Mrs. Sarah Sanders

Leigh, wife of the former mayor of Portsmouth, VA. The cruiser was launched on September 20, 1944, by the two ladies with two bottles of champagne, and the ceremony was the first launching since Pearl Harbor to which the public was invited. After completion, trials were waived as usual, PORTSMOUTH joined the fleet on June 25, 1945, with Capt. H.B. Brumbaugh commanding.

True to prediction, the new cruiser was commissioned too late to participate in the war, so she had a short peacetime career. She underwent shakedown in the Caribbean and was homeported at Norfolk during the rest of 1945, then undertook a goodwill trip to African ports in mid-1946 and called at Naples and Palermo in the Mediterranean. The Mediterranean climate apparently agreed with her, and she returned to Italy the following fall. She returned to the U.S. in April 1947, then again cruised to the Med in November. PORTSMOUTH was overhauled at Boston in mid-1948 and then engaged in training cruises and exercises in the Atlantic and Caribbean until early 1949. She entered the Philadelphia Navy Yard in March 1949 for deactivation overhaul and was decommissioned there on June 15 of that year. PORTSMOUTH remained in the Atlantic Reserve Fleet at Philadelphia until late 1970 when she was stricken and was sold for scrap.

VICKSBURG
1944

VICKSBURG

Hull No: 411
Navy No: CL-86
Launched: December 14, 1943
Commissioned: June 12, 1944
Dimensions: 610 x 65.67 x 42 ft
Displacement: 12,006 tons
Armament: 12 6", 12 5" Guns
Machinery: Geared Turbines, 4 Boilers,
    Quadruple Screw
Horsepower/Speed: 100,000/32.5 knots
Fate: Scrapped, 1964

Light cruiser VICKSBURG was the shipyard's penultimate CLEVELAND-class cruiser built during World War II. Given the designation CL-86, this ship had her keel laid as CHEYENNE on October 26, 1942, but a month later her name was changed to VICKSBURG. Sponsor for the light cruiser was Miss Muriel Hamilton, daughter of the mayor of Vicksburg, MI. VICKSBURG was launched from Shipway 6 on December 14, 1943, and was outfitted and completed for commissioning on June 12, 1944.

The new VICKSBURG underwent shakedown in the Chesapeake Bay and in Caribbean waters, then operated off New England until mid-December. After overhaul at the Norfolk Navy Yard, VICKSBURG sailed for the Pacific, arriving at Pearl Harbor on January 17, 1944. After exercises off Hawaii, the cruiser left for action in the assault on Iwo Jima. She engaged in bombardment and supported the landings on Iwo Jima into March, then supported strikes against Okinawa. While at Okinawa, she fired over 2,300 5" and 6" shells at the enemy in one six-hour period. After supporting a minesweeping operation in the China Sea in June, VICKSBURG steamed for the Philippines where she stayed until the end of the war. In late September she stopped at Okinawa and picked up 2,200 passengers and returned them, under crowded conditions, to Hawaii in early October. Having won two battle stars during the war, VICKSBURG then engaged in ceremonial duties along the West Coast.

She was modernized at San Francisco from January to May of 1946, then became flagship, Third Fleet. After another year of routine service VICKSBURG was decommissioned and placed in reserve at San Francisco on June 30, 1947. Veteran of a brief but busy three-year career with the Navy, the cruiser remained in reserve until she was sold and scrapped in 1964.

DULUTH
1944

DULUTH

Hull No: 412
Navy No: CL-87
Launched: January 13, 1944
Commissioned: September 18, 1944
Dimensions: 610 x 65.67 x 42 ft
Displacement: 12,006 tons
Armament: 12 6", 12 5" Guns
Machinery: Geared Turbines, 4 Boilers,
    Quadruple Screw
Horsepower/Speed: 100,000/32.5 knots
Fate: Scrapped, 1960

Light cruiser DULUTH was the last CLEVELAND-class ship awarded to the Newport News shipyard, but she was delivered in 1944, before AMSTERDAM and PORTSMOUTH. Like many of her sisters, DULUTH was destined to spend most of her years at anchor in reserve. Her keel was laid on Shipway 3 on November 9, 1942, and her launching occurred on January 13, 1944. Mrs. Edward H. Hatch, wife of the mayor of the city of Duluth, served as sponsor for the cruiser. The ship was quickly completed and was commissioned on September 18, 1944, Capt. D.R. Osborn, Jr. commanding.

The new DULUTH saw training duty at Newport, RI, for several months after her commissioning, then sailed for the Pacific in April 1945. She joined the Fifth Fleet in May; then, her bow was heavily damaged in a typhoon in June, forcing her to retire to Guam for repairs. Not discouraged, DULUTH joined with Task Force 38 in final strikes on Japan. She entered Tokyo Bay on September 16 where she celebrated her first birthday on the 18th. She returned to the U.S. and arrived at Seattle in mid-October, after which she was based at San Pedro, CA. DULUTH spent most of 1946 on a tour of duty to the Far East and for the first half of 1947 she was at Pearl Harbor. She saw more Far East assignments through May 1948, then was based at Long Beach, CA. After a summer cruise to British Columbia in 1948, she engaged in operations in Alaskan waters early in 1949.

On June 25, 1949, DULUTH was decommissioned and was placed in reserve at San Francisco. Winner of two battle stars for her brief service in World War II, DULUTH was sold for scrap in November 1960.

NEWPORT NEWS
1949

NEWPORT NEWS

Hull No: 456
Navy No: CA-148
Launched: March 6, 1947
Commissioned: January 29, 1949
Dimensions: 716.5 x 76.42 x 45.08 ft
Displacement: 19,930 tons
Armament: 9 8″, 12 5″, 12 3″ Guns
Machinery: Geared Turbines, 4 Boilers,
    Quadruple Screw
Horsepower/Speed: 120,000/33.5 knots
Fate: Stricken, 1978

The last, biggest, and proudest conventionally-powered cruiser built by Newport News shipbuilders was NEWPORT NEWS, begun and completed after the end of World War II. This heavy cruiser was the first combatant named after the shipbuilding city, and her launching was celebrated in the shipyard's 50th year of naval construction. The contract for NEWPORT NEWS was awarded in April 1944, and her design incorporated many lessons learned during the war. In particular, her radar and rapid-fire 8″ guns were the most advanced of the time. The keel for NEWPORT NEWS was laid in Shipway 11 on October 1, 1945, and 17 months later she was ready for launching. Mrs. Homer L. Ferguson, wife of the long-time shipyard president, was chosen as sponsor for the huge ship, and the city's mayor proclaimed the day as "Newport News Cruiser Day." Mrs. Ferguson christened NEWPORT NEWS on March 6, 1947, in the presence of an enthusiastic crowd of 20,000 spectators.

The occasion was also Homer L. Ferguson's birthday, and he paid tribute to yard employees in his remarks. After this fanfare, NEWPORT NEWS was moved south for outfitting, which was completed some 22 months later. The new ship, designated CA-148, was commissioned at the shipyard on January 29, 1949, with Capt. Roland N. Smoot in command.

Her busy career began with shakedown in the Caribbean, after which she became flagship for the Atlantic Fleet. She made the first of many Mediterranean cruises in January 1950 and then became flagship for the Sixth Fleet. During the 1950s, NEWPORT NEWS alternated summer and winter between the Atlantic and the Mediterranean, and in 1957 and 1958 she stood by during the Syrian and Lebanon Crises.

In 1961 and 1962 she underwent minor conversion to outfit her as flagship for the Second Fleet; then, in 1964 and 1965 she saw major conversion to become the First Fleet flagship in the Pacific. Her twin bow gun mounts were removed and replaced with an antenna mast and her accommodations were improved for this service. She served as a fire support ship on several tours of duty to Vietnam, and while there, in October 1972 an explosion in her No. 2 turret killed a number of her crew and rendered that turret inoperable for the rest of her career. Undaunted, NEWPORT NEWS and her men continued to serve the Navy and their country until she was decommissioned on June 27, 1975. Several attempts were made to bring her home as a memorial but these were not successful and, after being stricken in 1978, she remained inactive at Philadelphia.

CALIFORNIA
1974

CALIFORNIA

Hull No: 595
Navy No: DLGN-36
Launched: September 22, 1971
Commissioned: February 16, 1974
Dimensions: 596 x 61.04 x 41.41 ft
Displacement: 10,050 tons
Armament: 2 MK 13 Launchers, 1 ASROC,
    2 MK 45 5″ Guns, 4 MK 32 TT
Machinery: Geared Turbines, 2 Reactors,
    Twin Screw
Horsepower/Speed: 60,000/30+ knots
Fate: In Commission

After a 21-year interval following completion of NEWPORT NEWS in 1949, the keel for CALIFORNIA was laid on January 29, 1970. Originally planned as a five-ship class, the last three of these sleek nuclear vessels were deferred and became the later VIRGINIA class of four ships. Originally delivered as guided missile frigates (DLGN), CALIFORNIA and her sister SOUTH CAROLINA were reclassified as cruisers (CGN) in 1975. They represented an improved TRUX-TUN design, and their reactors enabled a cruising range of over 700,000 miles in carrier escort. The keel for CALIFORNIA was laid and authenticated by Mrs.

Glenard P. Lipscomb, then construction proceeded toward launching. The then-frigate was launched from Shipway 9 on September 22, 1971. Proud sponsor of CALIFORNIA was First Lady Mrs. Patricia Nixon, and she did her job with a bottle of California champagne.

CALIFORNIA was completed and underwent successful sea trials on December 18, 1973, then was commissioned on February 16, 1974, under the command of Capt. Floyd H. Miller, Jr. The powerful new ship underwent shakedown and was assigned to duty in the Atlantic. CALIFORNIA later joined NIMITZ as escort and was with her for her famous nine-month deployment to the Indian Ocean in 1979 and 1980. On Memorial Day 1980 she entered Hampton Roads with NIMITZ and TEXAS to an emotional welcome home after the longest American naval deployment since World War II. After a well-deserved rest, she and her 540 crewmen continued in operation with fast carrier task forces. In 1981 she became the first nuclear ship since ENTERPRISE and her escorts to sail around the world. CALIFORNIA underwent a 16-month overhaul at Newport News and, on completion in 1983, transferred to her new home port of San Diego. She took part in four exercises in the Pacific in 1984, then deployed with the CONSTELLATION battle group in 1985.

SOUTH CAROLINA
1975

SOUTH CAROLINA

Hull No: 596
Navy No: DLGN-37
Launched: July 1, 1972
Commissioned: January 25, 1975
Dimensions: 596 x 61.04 x 41.41 ft
Displacement: 10,050 tons
Armament: 2 MK 13 Launchers, 1 ASROC,
    2 MK 45 5" Guns, 4 MK 32 TT
Machinery: Geared Turbines, 2 Reactors,
    Twin Screw
Horsepower/Speed: 60,000/30+ knots
Fate: In Commission

The second and final ship in the CALIFORNIA class was SOUTH CAROLINA, the contract for which was awarded on July 19, 1968. Like her sister, SOUTH CAROLINA was fitted with the latest in surface search, fire control, and air search radars. The keel for the multipurpose SOUTH CAROLINA was laid on Shipway 8 on December 1, 1970, and was authenticated by Mr. and Mrs. L. Mendel Rivers. Construction on the shipway took exactly 19 months, and SOUTH CAROL-INA was launched on a sunny July 1, 1972. Mrs. J. Fred Buzhardt, wife of the general counsel for the Department of Defense, was sponsor for the ship and the principal address was delivered by Sen. Strom Thurmond of South Carolina. A crowd of about 4,000 spectators enjoyed the sliding launch.

SOUTH CAROLINA completed outfitting and trials and was commissioned on January 25, 1975, with Capt. William C. Neel commanding. After commissioning, the new warship cruised to Charleston to visit her namesake state. Later in 1975 she was assigned to the Atlantic Fleet nuclear task force, and with EISENHOWER and VIRGINIA, relieved NIMITZ, CALIFORNIA, and TEXAS in April 1980 after their long deployment. After 86,000 miles of steaming and 12 crossings of the Equator, she returned to Norfolk on December 22 of that year and underwent a yard period during which the Harpoon weapons system was installed. In 1982 SOUTH CAROLINA was the first U.S. Navy ship on station for operations off Lebanon; then, in March 1983 she began overhaul. This lasted until July 1984, at which time she resumed operations with the Atlantic Fleet. In 1985 she deployed to the Mediterranean with NIMITZ and ten other ships, returning to Norfolk in October.

TEXAS
1977

TEXAS

Hull No: 606
Navy No: CGN-39
Launched: August 9, 1975
Commissioned: September 10, 1977
Dimensions: 585 x 63 x 42 ft
Displacement: 10,500 tons
Armament: 2 MK 26 Launchers,
    2 MK 45 5" Guns, 6 MK 32 TT
Machinery: Geared Turbines, 2 Reactors,
    Twin Screw
Horsepower/Speed: 60,000/30+ knots
Fate: In Commission

TEXAS, authorized in 1971, was the second VIRGINIA-class cruiser built at Newport News. She was laid down on August 18, 1973, and her keel was authenticated by Mrs. William P. Clements, Jr., a Texas native and the wife of the Deputy Secretary of Defense. After almost two years on the ways, TEXAS was launched on August 9, 1975. Mrs. Dolph Brisco, wife of the governor of Texas, was sponsor of TEXAS; and during the christening, it was recalled that the last TEXAS launched at Newport News was the famous battleship of 1914, still preserved as a memorial in her namesake state. After completion and successful trials, the new TEXAS was commissioned on September 10, 1977, with Capt. Peter B. Fiedler commanding.

She engaged in shakedown and training off the Virginia Capes and in the Caribbean and then underwent her Post Shakedown Availability (PSA) at the shipyard from March to July 1978. She continued in lone exercises for the remainder of the year, then later joined NIMITZ and CALIFORNIA to form an all-nuclear Carrier Battle Group. TEXAS deployed to the Indian Ocean with this group in mid-1979, then led their proud parade into Hampton Roads on Memorial Day 1980 after their record nine-month patrol. Her operations were classified in 1981 and 1982, but in March 1983 she departed with CARL VINSON and ARKANSAS on a round-the-world cruise, which ended at their new homeport of San Diego. She deployed with the CARL VINSON battle group again in October 1984, then in 1985 entered Puget Sound Navy Yard for an overhaul which was scheduled to last until December 1986.

VIRGINIA
1976

VIRGINIA

Hull No: 601
Navy No: CGN-38
Launched: December 14, 1974
Commissioned: September 11, 1976
Dimensions: 585 x 63 x 42 ft
Displacement: 10,500 tons
Armament: 2 MK 26 Launchers,
　　2 MK 45 5″ Guns, 6 MK 32 TT
Machinery: Geared Turbines, 2 Reactors,
　　Twin Screw
Horsepower/Speed: 60,000/30+ knots
Fate: In Commission

Four improved CALIFORNIA-class cruisers were built by the shipyard between 1976 and 1980, and the first of these was VIRGINIA, awarded on December 21, 1971. These ships were ten feet shorter than CALIFORNIA and SOUTH CAROLINA due to the deletion of independent ASROC launchers from their armament. While the previous ships had helicopter landing facilities only, the VIRGINIA--class ships were provided with full helo capability and hangar. The keel for VIRGINIA was laid on August 19, 1972, and she was launched with much ceremony and local patriotism on December 14, 1974. Sponsor for VIRGINIA was Miss Virginia S. Warner, daughter of Secretary of the Navy (and later Senator) John Warner. Mrs. Gay Montague Moore, who had christened battleship VIRGINIA at the shipyard in 1904, attended the ceremony. After 21 more months of construction and outfitting, VIRGINIA completed trials and was commissioned on September 11, 1976, with Capt. George W. Davis, Jr. in command.

After shakedown and training, which lasted a year, the new cruiser joined the Atlantic Fleet, home-ported at Norfolk. In 1978 she participated in a NATO exercise which took her to several European ports. Early in 1979, she deployed to the Mediterranean; then, in mid-1980 she sailed to the Indian Ocean with carrier EISENHOWER and SOUTH CAROLINA to relieve NIMITZ, TEXAS, and CALIFORNIA. She returned home with them in December, then operated in the Caribbean and along the East Coast in 1981. VIRGINIA deployed to the Med in January 1982 and returned in July; then, she spent most of 1983 in operations off Lebanon. Deployed until December 1, she returned to Norfolk, then entered Norfolk Naval Shipyard in mid-1984 for a 16-month overhaul which completed in November 1985.

MISSISSIPPI
1978

MISSISSIPPI
Hull No: 607
Navy No: CGN-40
Launched: July 31, 1976
Commissioned: August 5, 1978
Dimensions: 585 x 63 x 42 ft
Displacement: 10,500 tons
Armament: 2 MK 26 Launchers, 2 MK 45 5″ Guns, 6 MK 32 TT
Machinery: Geared Turbines, 2 Reactors, Twin Screw
Horsepower/Speed: 60,000/30+ knots
Fate: In Commission

MISSISSIPPI was the third VIRGINIA-class nuclear-powered cruiser built at Newport News between 1972 and 1980. Like the others, she was fitted with a huge bow dome to accommodate her AN/SQS-53A sonar. CGN-40 was authorized in 1972, and her keel was laid down on February 22, 1975. As construction of her type was by now becoming routine, she spent only 17 months on the ways and was launched on July 31, 1976. Sponsor for MISSISSIPPI was Miss Janet Finch, daughter of Mississippi Governor Cliff Finch, and the principal speaker at the ceremony was Senator John Stennis, also of the ship's namesake state. The ceremony was held amid controversy resulting from a $894 million contract dispute involving several ships between the shipyard and the Navy, and in his address Senator Stennis urged a quick and equitable settlement. Controversy or not, MISSISSIPPI was successfully launched and was moved southside for outfitting and completion.

Commissioned on August 5, 1978, under the command of Capt. Peter M. Hekman, MISSISSIPPI underwent shakedown and training on the East Coast, and then, homeported at Norfolk, joined the Atlantic Fleet in 1978. She was very active during her first few years in commission. In 1984 she deployed to Northern Europe with DWIGHT D. EISENHOWER, participated in two exercises during the summer, was in the Mediterranean in October, then engaged in joint U.S.-Israeli exercises in December. In October 1985 she anchored off Yorktown and helped celebrate the 204th anniversary of the Battle of Yorktown. At year's end she prepared for overhaul, scheduled to begin at Norfolk Naval Shipyard early in 1986.

ARKANSAS
1980

ARKANSAS
Hull No: 612
Navy No: CGN-41
Launched: October 21, 1978
Commissioned: October 18, 1980
Dimensions: 585 x 63 x 42 ft
Displacement: 10,500 tons
Armament: 2 MK 26 Launchers, 2 MK 45 5″ Guns, 6 MK 32 TT
Machinery: Geared Turbines, 2 Reactors, Twin Screw
Horsepower/Speed: 60,000/30+ knots
Fate: In Commission

The sixth and last CGN built at Newport News in the 1970s was ARKANSAS. She was authorized in 1975 after having been authorized, then cancelled, in 1971; but five more ships designated CGN-42 through CGN-46 were put off indefinitely by the Navy. ARKANSAS, at first, was built under a court order after the shipyard tried unsuccessfully to stop work on her amid controversy over claims against the Navy for cost overruns on four ships. The keel for this controversial ship was laid on January 17, 1977, and she was ready for launch on October 21, 1978. Mrs. Betty Bumpers of Arkansas was chosen to christen the cruiser and her husband, Sen. Dale Bumpers, gave the principal address at the ceremony. After Mrs. Bumpers crashed the bottle and ARKANSAS began to slide, a huge banner saying "Beat Texas" was raised on board. A cheer of "Sooiiee...Pig...Sooiiee" rose from the 1,500 spectators, but the Texas Longhorns beat the Arkansas Razorbacks later that afternoon just the same.

After this excitement, ARKANSAS underwent outfitting, tests, and trials and was commissioned, under the command of Capt. Dennis S. Read, on October 18, 1980. After her shakedown and training period in the Atlantic, CGN-41 joined the Pacific Fleet in 1981. She too was busy during her first few years. In 1984 she deployed to the Pacific and Indian Oceans from May to December with ENTERPRISE. On November 3 she made the first transit of the Suez Canal by a nuclear ship, then returned to Alameda at year's end. She deployed again in 1985, then joined ENTERPRISE and CARL VINSON for Navy Day ceremonies in San Francisco Bay in October of that year.

SUBMARINES
SIMON LAKE X & Sisters
1905

SIMON LAKE X & Sisters

Hull No: 51-55
Owner: Lake Torpedo Boat Co.
Launched: October 27, 1904
Delivered: February 23, 1905
Dimensions: 73 x 11.25
Displacement: 154 tons
Armament: 3 18" TT
Machinery: Gasoline Engines, Twin Screw
Horsepower/Speed: 240/8.5 (4.5) knots
Fate: Stricken, 1913-1915

The first submarines built at Newport News were Hulls 51-55, completed in 1904 and 1905 for pioneer Simon Lake and his Lake Torpedo Boat Co. These were similar to his PROTECTOR which had been secretly sold to the Russian Navy in 1904. PROTECTOR was successful, so the Russians ordered the five which were built at the shipyard. The Lake submarines were very advanced for their time and, with their circular hulls and even keel design, were forerunners of the nuclear ships of fifty years later. Like PROTECTOR, they were provided with three torpedo tubes and a diving chamber and had retractable wheels for running along the bottom.

The contract to build Hulls 51-55 was awarded on

April 30, 1904, and construction began shortly afterward. They were not built on shipways but in the old Beam Shed, and all were built to be loaded aboard ship for delivery to Russia. Hull 53 was completed and, named SIMON LAKE X, was launched from a shipway in the conventional manner. Miss Mildred Lake, daughter of Simon Lake, christened the boat on October 27, 1904, and naval constructor (later shipyard president) Homer L. Ferguson of Washington, D.C., was an honored guest.

Successful trials in local waters were held for SIMON LAKE X, and this proved the acceptability of all five hulls . Hulls 51 and 52 were loaded aboard barge KENNEBEC on October 27, and Hulls 54 and 55 went aboard barge ADRIA on January 2, 1905. SIMON LAKE X was delivered on February 23 and was also shipped to Russia. Delivered too late to take part in the Russo-Japanese War for which they had been built, the five boats nonetheless were accepted and joined the Imperial Russian Navy in 1904 as BYCHOK, KEFAL, PLATUS, PLOTVA, and SIG. All were assembled at Libau (now Liepaja) Arsenal on the Baltic, and all but SIG were shipped to Vladivostok on specially-built rail cars during the summer of 1905. SIG served in the Baltic fleet, and the others were with the Siberian Fleet until they all became obsolete and were stricken between 1913 and 1915.

LAKE
1906

LAKE

Hull No: 56
Owner: Lake Torpedo Boat Co.
Launched: February 27, 1906
Delivered: June 25, 1906
Dimensions: 85.82 x 11.25 ft
Displacement: 180 tons
Armament: 3 18" TT
Machinery: Gasoline Engines, Twin Screw
Horsepower/Speed: 240/8.5 (4.5) knots
Fate: Stricken, 1913-1915

On February 6, 1905, Simon Lake ordered a sixth submarine from Newport News. This boat, later named LAKE, was about 13 feet longer than Hulls 51-55 previously built, but was similar to them in most other respects. The keel for LAKE was laid on March 1, 1905, and she was launched from a shipway on February 27, 1906, evidently without a sponsor. LAKE was completed and left the shipyard under her own power on June 25, 1906. Simon Lake had originally intended to submit LAKE for Navy trials in hopes of fulfilling his lifelong dream of building submarines for his own country. Since this boat was not completed in time for the trials, the Navy refused him and so LAKE was also sold to the Russians. It is believed that she too was transported across the continent to Vladivostok and was stricken with her sisters before 1915.

TUNA
1912

TUNA

Hull No: 120
Owner: Lake Torpedo Boat Co.
Launched: January 10, 1912
Delivered: May 15, 1912
Dimensions: 161 x 13 ft
Displacement: 516 tons
Armament: 4 18" TT
Machinery: Gasoline Engines, Twin Screw
Horsepower/Speed: 1,200/14 (10) knots
Fate: Sank, 1919

TUNA was the second Newport News-built submarine which Simon Lake succeeded in selling to the Navy in 1912. The keel for this boat was laid on October 20, 1909, and she was launched on January 10, 1912. Miss Marjorie F. Miller acted as sponsor for TUNA, which had been renamed G-2 two months before the launching. The new submarine was deli-

vered to Lake on May 15 and sailed northward to be outfitted at the New York Navy Yard. During her acceptance trials, she had the misfortune to run aground off Atlantic City but was freed without damage. Designated SS-27, she was placed in commission on February 6, 1915, with Lt. R.C. Needham commanding.

Homeported at Portsmouth, VA, G-2 engaged in exercises along the East Coast during her first year in commission. She underwent major overhaul at the New York Navy Yard until the end of June 1917, then was assigned to the submarine flotilla at New London. She operated in both instructional and experimental duty while at New London, helping to build the U.S. submarine force and to develop and test new weapons for use for and against her type. G-2 was decommissioned on April 2, 1919, and was detailed for target service in Niantic Bay, CT. Under inspection by a maintenance crew on July 30, she suddenly sank at her mooring, carrying three men down with her.

SEAL
1911

SEAL

Hull No: 119
Owner: Lake Torpedo Boat Co.
Launched: February 8, 1911
Delivered: July 29, 1911
Dimensions: 161 x 13 ft
Displacement: 516 tons
Armament: 6 18″ TT
Machinery: Gasoline Engines, Twin Screw
Horsepower/Speed: 1,200/14 (10) knots
Fate: Sunk, 1921

With submarine SEAL, ordered from the shipyard in December 1908, Simon Lake finally succeeded in selling a boat of his design to the U.S. Navy. This boat and her sister TUNA, ordered in January 1909, were much larger than Hulls 51-55 built previously for Lake, and both were accepted by the Navy. The keel for SEAL was laid on February 2, 1909, and she was launched on February 8, 1911. Miss Margaret V. Lake served as sponsor for the submarine designed by her father. Fitted with unusual deck-mounted torpedo tubes, in addition to the usual hull tubes, SEAL was delivered to Lake and left the shipyard on July 29, 1911. On acceptance trials SEAL reached a depth of 256 feet, almost doubling the existing record. She was renamed G-1 for naval service and was commissioned at New York on October 28, 1912, with Lt. K. Whiting in command.

G-1 gained an interesting distinction when she was designated SS-19-½, possibly the only Navy ship ever to carry a fraction in her official designation. She was assigned to the Atlantic Torpedo Fleet and engaged in patrols and exercises along the East Coast until October 1915. At that time she became a school ship at the then-new base at New London where, except for occasional experimental test duty, she remained until she was decommissioned in March 1920. G-1 was not scrapped but was assigned to target duty after her decommissioning. She was towed to Narragansett Bay and was sunk with ordnance by GREBE (AM-43) on June 21, 1921, thus ending her relatively short career.

SHARK
1961

SHARK

Hull No: 545
Navy No: SSN-591
Launched: March 16, 1960
Commissioned: February 9, 1961
Dimensions: 252 x 31.58 ft
Displacement: 3,500 tons
Armament: 6 21″ TT
Machinery: Geared Turbines, Reactor
Horsepower/Speed: 15,000/16+ (30+) knots
Fate: In Commission

Almost 45 years after the last Lake-type submarine left Newport News, the shipyard was awarded its first nuclear contract for a SKIPJACK-class submarine later named SHARK (SSN-591). The six SKIP-JACK submarines which were built in four shipyards were the Navy's first nuclear boats with ALBACORE-type high speed hulls and were termed "flying submarines" and "the world's fastest." They were also the first with sail-mounted diving planes. The contract

for SHARK was awarded on February 5, 1957, and her keel was laid on February 24 of the following year. She was launched from Shipway 5 on March 16, 1960, and was sponsored by Mrs. Marjorie R. Shane, widow of the commander of the former SHARK (SS-314) which was lost in World War II. SHARK won wide praise on her trials and was commissioned at the shipyard on February 9, 1961, with LCdr. John F. Fagan, Jr. commanding.

She completed shakedown, underwent her post-shakedown availability (PSA) at Newport News, then in August 1961 became the first nuclear submarine to deploy to the Mediterranean. Homeported at Norfolk, she served the Atlantic Fleet and engaged in ASW training and exercises with frequent Mediterranean and Northern European deployments. By 1967 she had won two Navy Unit Commendations. SHARK underwent her first refueling overhaul at Norfolk in 1967 and her second in Mississippi in 1974. In 1982 her home port was temporarily shifted to Vallejo, CA, for her third refueling overhaul. One of the oldest operational submarines in the nuclear Navy, SHARK remained fully active as she approached her 25th birthday.

ROBERT E. LEE
1960

ROBERT E. LEE

Hull No: 547
Navy No: SSBN-601
Launched: December 18, 1959
Commissioned: September 16, 1960
Dimensions: 381.67 x 33 ft
Displacement: 6,700 tons
Armament: 16 Polaris, 6 21" TT
Machinery: Geared Turbines, Reactor
Horsepower/Speed: 15,000/20 (30+) knots
Fate: Laid Up, 1983

The shipyard's first nuclear ship was Polaris submarine ROBERT E. LEE (SSBN-601). Although the contract for SHARK had been awarded almost 18 months earlier than that of ROBERT E. LEE, the Polaris program had priority and the latter ship was completed first. ROBERT E. LEE and her four sisters built at other shipyards were of modified SKIPJACK-class design with a 130-foot missile section containing 16 Polaris tubes added amidships. ROBERT E. LEE became the third Polaris submarine to join the fleet and was the first nuclear ship built in the South. Her keel was laid on Shipway 5 on August 25, 1958, less than a month after her contract was signed on July 30. Her construction was expedited and she was launched on December 18, 1959. The christening ceremony for ROBERT E. LEE was a festive one in the tradition of the Old South, and General Lee's granddaughter Mrs. Hanson E. Ely, Jr. served as sponsor.

ROBERT E. LEE fired a water salvo from her missile tubes during the launching of ENTERPRISE (CVAN-65) and completed highly successful sea trials before being commissioned at the shipyard on September 16, 1960. Like other Polaris ships she was operated with two crews in alternating 60-day patrols, and her first commanders were Cdr. Reuben F. Woodal (Blue Crew) and Cdr. Joseph Williams, Jr. (Gold Crew).

ROBERT E. LEE fired her first missile off Cape Canaveral in December 1960 and underwent her PSA at Newport News in February 1961. She was assigned to Submarine Squadron 14 operating out of Holy Loch, Scotland, in July and commenced the first of many deterrent patrols on August 9. During her career ROBERT E. LEE completed 55 such patrols on both sides of the globe. She underwent her first refueling overhaul at the Mare Island Naval Shipyard in 1965-1966 and was modified for the improved Polaris A-3 system. She continued with Squadron 14 and completed her 33rd patrol before her second refueling at the Puget Sound Naval Shipyard in 1971. She operated on the East Coast until late 1973, then was transferred to the Pacific, arriving at Guam in October. ROBERT E. LEE underwent her third refueling at Mare Island in 1977 but was not converted to the Poseidon missile system because of her age.

With the arrival of the first Trident missile submarines in 1981 and 1982, ROBERT E. LEE's days were numbered. She completed the Navy's last Polaris patrol on October 1, 1981, marking the end of a fleet total of 1,245 patrols and over 24,000 man-years at sea with the Polaris system. She was redesignated SSN-601 on March 1, 1982 then operated on the West Coast as an attack submarine with a consolidated crew for the next year. In February 1983, ROBERT E. LEE entered Puget Sound Naval Shipyard for inactivation. Her reactor was defueled, her missile section was removed, and she was decommissioned at Bremerton, WA, on November 30, 1983, in a ceremony held aboard MISSOURI (BB-63). ROBERT E. LEE was then laid up there awaiting disposal after defending her country for over 20 years.

SAM HOUSTON
1962

SAM HOUSTON

Hull No: 548
Navy No: SSBN-609
Launched: February 2, 1961
Commissioned: March 6, 1962
Dimensions: 410.42 x 33 ft
Displacement: 8,000 tons
Armament: 16 Polaris, 4 21" TT
Machinery: Geared Turbines, Reactor
Horsepower/Speed: 15,000/20 (30+) knots
Fate: In Commission

The second Polaris Fleet Ballistic Missile (FBM) submarine built at Newport News was SAM HOUSTON (SSBN-609), awarded on July 1, 1959. SAM HOUSTON was one of five ETHAN ALLEN-class ships built at Newport News and General Dynamics/ Electric Boat. These were based on the PERMIT attack submarine design but were the first ships specifically designed as FBM submarines. They were about 30 ft longer than the previous class and had a deeper diving capability.

The keel for SAM HOUSTON was laid on December 28, 1959, and she was launched on February 2, 1961. Mrs. John B. Connally, Jr., wife of the Secretary of the Navy, sponsored SAM HOUSTON and FAdm. Chester W. Nimitz, a Texas native, delivered the principal address at the ceremony. The Navy's seventh FBM submarine completed trials on January 23, 1962,

and was commissioned in Dry Dock 2 on March 6 with Capt. W.P. Willis, Jr. (Blue) and Cdr. Jack H. Hawkins (Gold) in command. After shakedown and missile firing trials, SAM HOUSTON was deployed to Holy Loch and began her first patrol.

Over the years she conducted a total of 54 strategic deterrent patrols in both the Atlantic and in the Pacific. In mid-1963 SAM HOUSTON became the first FBM submarine to enter the Mediterranean and to make a port call while on patrol. After four years overseas, she returned to Portsmouth Naval Shipyard for refueling overhaul in August 1966. She returned to Holy Loch in May 1968 and continued with Squadron 14 until she joined Squadron 16 in the Mediterranean in August 1970. After her second refueling overhaul, which began at Charleston Naval Shipyard in November 1972, SAM HOUSTON was transferred to the Pacific and began operations from Guam in 1976. In August 1979 she fired an MK 37 exercise torpedo, which was picked up by a Soviet ship. An international incident resulted but was resolved by the Department of State and the weapon was recovered.

SAM HOUSTON completed her last Polaris patrol in August 1980 and was reclassified SSN-609 in November. Based at Bremerton, WA, she engaged in classified operations in 1983, then in September of that year began conversion as an amphibious transport for a commando/anti-terrorist team in the Pacific area. This work completed in late 1985, SAM HOUSTON continued in her 23rd year of service to her country.

JOHN MARSHALL
1962

JOHN MARSHALL

Hull No: 549
Navy No: SSBN-611
Launched: July 15, 1961
Commissioned: May 21, 1962
Dimensions: 410.42 x 33 ft
Displacement: 8,000 tons
Armament: 16 Polaris, 4 21″ TT
Machinery: Geared Turbines, Reactor
Horsepower/Speed: 15,000/20 (30+) knots
Fate: In Commission

JOHN MARSHALL (SSBN-611) was the second ETHAN ALLEN-class FBM submarine built at Newport News. Ships of this class were originally fitted with the Polaris A-1 missile and were later improved to the Polaris A-3 with 2,500 nautical mile capability. The keel for JOHN MARSHALL was laid on April 4, 1960, and she was launched on July 15, 1961. Sponsor for the nation's ninth Polaris submarine was Mrs. Robert F. Kennedy, wife of the Attorney General of the United States, and Mr. Kennedy delivered the principal address. JOHN MARSHALL was completed within a year and was placed in commission ahead of schedule on May 21, 1962. The sponsor, the Attorney General, and Chief Justice Earl Warren attended the ceremony in which Cdr. Robert W. Stecher (Blue) and Cdr. Robert D. Donovan (Gold) were placed in command.

The new submarine completed shakedown along the East Coast then underwent her PSA at the shipyard until mid-December. She began her first deterrent patrol from Charleston, SC, on New Year's Eve, 1962 and completed it at Holy Loch on the following March 8. JOHN MARSHALL completed 17 such patrols before beginning her first refueling overhaul and Polaris A-2 conversion at Newport News in December 1966. She left the shipyard in April 1968 and, after trials of her new missile system off Cape Canaveral, resumed patrols out of Holy Loch. She completed 22 more of these before her second refueling in 1974. This overhaul was accomplished at Mare Island Naval Shipyard and also included conversion to the Polaris A-3. She completed this in May 1976 and was assigned to the Pacific Fleet, operating from Guam. JOHN MARSHALL continued her patrols until she completed her 54th in December 1980. She was converted to SSN-611 in 1981 and moved to the Atlantic to deploy to the Mediterranean in December. She returned to Charleston in mid-1982 and was based there until she sailed to Bremerton, WA, for her third refueling overhaul which commenced in September 1983. During this yard period she underwent conversion to carry commando troops of the Delta Force team in the Atlantic area. Her overhaul and conversion completed in late 1985, she began her new duties as an amphibious transport.

THOMAS JEFFERSON
1963

THOMAS JEFFERSON

Hull No: 555
Navy No: SSBN-618
Launched: February 24, 1962
Commissioned: January 4, 1963
Dimensions: 410.42 x 33 ft
Displacement: 8,000 tons
Armament: 16 Polaris, 4 21" TT
Machinery: Geared Turbines, Reactor
Horsepower/Speed: 15,000/20 (30+) knots
Fate: Laid Up, 1985

On July 22, 1960, Newport News was awarded the contract for its third and last ETHAN ALLEN-class FBM submarine, later named THOMAS JEFFERSON (SSBN-618). This ship was laid down on Shipway 5 on February 3, 1961, and proceeded rapidly to her launching on February 24, 1962. THOMAS JEFFERSON was sponsored by Mrs. Robert McNamara, wife of the Secretary of Defense. The new submarine was completed within a year and was commissioned 48 days ahead of schedule on January 4, 1963, with Capt. Leon H. Rathbun, Jr. (Blue) and Cdr. Charles Priest, Jr. (Gold) in command.

THOMAS JEFFERSON underwent shakedown and PSA, then was assigned to Submarine Squadron 14 in October. A controversy arose early in her career when a plastic model construction kit appeared which provided details of her machinery and weapons, but this passed as she began her first Polaris patrol. She underwent her first refueling overhaul at the shipyard in 1967 and 1968, then resumed her patrols. Her 36th and last patrol in the Atlantic ended at Norfolk in March 1974; then she was reassigned to the Pacific Fleet in June. THOMAS JEFFERSON was refueled and converted to the Polaris A-3 system at Mare Island Naval Shipyard from July 1974 to November 1975.

After shakedown and missile firing trials she sailed west to continue her strategic deterrent patrols. Her 52nd and last such mission ended at Pearl Harbor in November 1980, after which she was converted to SSN-618. THOMAS JEFFERSON transferred to her new home port at Charleston in mid-1981. She participated in exercises with South American navies until September, circumnavigating their continent in the process. She was deployed to the Mediterranean in 1983 and supported AMERICA (CVA-66) in June of that year, receiving the Navy Expeditionary Medal for this duty. After another year of duty, she entered Puget Sound Naval Shipyard in 1984, and her spent fuel and missile compartment were removed. She was decommissioned at Bremerton on February 1, 1985, and was laid up awaiting disposal, having ably defended her country for 23 years.

JAMES MONROE
1963

JAMES MONROE

Hull No: 562
Navy No: SSBN-622
Launched: August 4, 1962
Commissioned: December 7, 1963
Dimensions: 425 x 33 ft
Displacement: 8,250 tons
Armament: 16 Polaris, 4 21″ TT
Machinery: Geared Turbines, Reactor
Horsepower/Speed: 15,000/20 (30+) knots
Fate: In Commission

JAMES MONROE (SSBN-622) was the first LAFAY-ETTE-class submarine built at Newport News. Ships of this class were the largest of the Polaris FBM submarines and ultimately ten of this size were built at Newport News. The keel for JAMES MONROE was laid down on Shipway 5 on July 31, 1961, and launch day came on August 4 of the following year. Mrs. Roswell L. Gilpatric, wife of the Deputy Secretary of Defense, was sponsor for JAMES MONROE, and a number of President Monroe's descendants attended the ceremony. The new JAMES MONROE was placed in commission at the shipyard on December 7, 1963, with Cdr. William H. Sandeford (Blue) and Cdr. Warren R. Cobean, Jr. (Gold) in command. During the ceremony the ship's ensign was raised, then lowered to half-staff in memory of the late President Kennedy.

After shakedown in the Atlantic and PSA, JAMES MONROE was assigned to Submarine Squadron 16 and completed 18 patrols from Holy Loch and Rota by 1968. Originally fitted with the A-2 missile system, she was converted to A-3 during her first refueling overhaul at Charleston in 1968 and 1969. In 1970 JAMES MONROE was assigned to Squadron 15 in the Pacific where she completed 17 more deterrent patrols by 1974. She returned to Newport News for her second refueling and conversion to the Poseidon missile system from 1974 to 1977, then continued her patrols with Squadrons 6 and 14. JAMES MONROE was named outstanding FBM submarine in the Atlantic Fleet in 1981 and completed her 50th patrol in that year. Winner of a number of Fleet awards for excellence in performance, engineering, and damage control readiness, she sailed from Holy Loch on her 65th patrol early in 1986.

HENRY CLAY
1964

HENRY CLAY

Hull No: 563
Navy No: SSBN-625
Launched: November 30, 1962
Commissioned: February 20, 1964
Dimensions: 425 x 33 ft
Displacement: 8,250 tons
Armament: 16 Polaris, 4 21″ TT
Machinery: Geared Turbines, Reactor
Horsepower/Speed: 15,000/20 (30+) knots
Fate: In Commission

The sixth Polaris submarine built at Newport News was HENRY CLAY (SSBN-625); her contract had been awarded with that of JAMES MONROE on February 3, 1961. The keel for HENRY CLAY was laid on October 23, 1961, and the nation's 18th FBM submarine was launched on a crisp November 30, 1962. Mrs. Green B. Gibson, great-granddaughter of Henry Clay, served as sponsor for the ship and her sister, Miss Henrietta Clay, was her maid of honor. As

HENRY CLAY rode down the ways, a "Beat Army" sign was raised aboard and drew a cheer from the crowd.

The new submarine underwent trials off the Virginia Capes on December 15, 1963, then was commissioned in Dry Dock 1 on February 20, 1964, with Cdr. Thomas A. Bryce (Blue) and Cdr. John C. Lewis (Gold) in command. HENRY CLAY completed her PSA at the shipyard, then deployed to her first deterrent patrol in the Atlantic. She completed her 18th patrol in October 1968, and entered Charleston Naval Shipyard for refueling and Polaris A-3 conversion. She resumed her patrols in the Pacific with Squadron 15 in August 1970 and completed 18 more before August 1977. HENRY CLAY underwent her second refueling overhaul and her conversion to Poseidon at Portsmouth Naval Shipyard in 1976 and 1977. She was then reassigned to the Atlantic Fleet and by the end of 1983 had completed her 58th strategic deterrent patrol in the defense of her country. Operating out of Holy Loch, she continued her patrols into the mid-1980s.

JAMES MADISON
1964

JAMES MADISON

Hull No: 565
Navy No: SSBN-627
Launched: March 15, 1963
Commissioned: July 28, 1964
Dimensions: 425 x 33 ft
Displacement: 8,250 tons
Armament: 16 Polaris, 4 21″ TT
Machinery: Geared Turbines, Reactor
Horsepower/Speed: 15,000/20 (30+) Knots
Fate: In Commission

The shipyard's seventh Polaris submarine, later named JAMES MADISON (SSBN-627), was laid down on March 5, 1962. The Polaris program dominated naval construction at Newport News in the early 1960s, and a full dozen FBM submarines were delivered from 1960 to 1965. JAMES MADISON was launched on March 15, 1963, and was sponsored by Mrs. A.S. "Mike" Monroney, wife of Senator Monroney of Oklahoma. The submarine was commissioned in Dry Dock 1 on July 28, 1964, with Cdr. Joseph L. Skoog, Jr. (Blue) and Cdr. J.B. Kearney (Gold) in command. At the

ceremony, Mrs. Monroney presented a naval message written by President Madison and a silver bowl to the ship.

JAMES MADISON completed shakedown with each of her two crews and in January 1965 sailed on her first strategic deterrent patrol in the Atlantic. She had made her tenth patrol by the end of 1966 and in February 1969 arrived at Groton for her first refueling overhaul. During this overhaul, which lasted until June 1970, she became the first ship to be converted to the Poseidon missile system. She also was the first to launch the new missile, doing so in August 1970. JAMES MADISON began the Navy's first Poseidon patrol and, operating out of Holy Loch, completed her 49th patrol in June 1979. In August of that year she returned to her birthplace at Newport News for her second refueling and for conversion to the more modern Trident missile system. With the distinction of being the oldest FBM submarine to be retrofitted with Trident, she left the shipyard in February 1982. After post-overhaul shakedown in the Atlantic, JAMES MADISON resumed her patrols and completed her 53rd by the end of 1983. Operating from the Navy's new Trident base at King's Bay, GA, she continued in the defense of her country into the mid-1980s.

JOHN C. CALHOUN
1964

JOHN C. CALHOUN

Hull No: 566
Navy No: SSBN-630
Launched: June 22, 1963
Commissioned: September 15, 1964
Dimensions: 425 x 33 ft
Displacement: 8,250 tons
Armament: 16 Polaris, 4 21" TT
Machinery: Geared Turbines, Reactor
Horsepower/Speed: 15,000/20 (30+) knots
Fate: In Commission

The fourth LAFAYETTE-class FBM submarine built at Newport News was JOHN C. CALHOUN (SSBN-630). Her keel was laid on June 4, 1962, and she was on the ways for just over a year before her launching on June 22, 1963. Sponsor for JOHN C. CALHOUN was Miss Rosalie J. Calhoun, great-great granddaughter of John C. Calhoun. The new submarine completed trials on June 14, 1964, and was com-missioned on September 15 with Cdr. Dean L. Axene (Blue) and Cdr. Frank Thurtell (Gold) commanding.

JOHN C. CALHOUN completed shakedown and PSA, then began her first patrol in March 1965. Deployed in the Atlantic, she underwent her first refueling and conversion to Poseidon at Mare Island Naval Shipyard in June 1969. She launched her first Poseidon missile off Cape Canaveral in April 1971, then resumed her patrols in the Atlantic. Completion of her 22nd deterrent patrol in May 1972 marked the 1,000th successful such mission for the nation's 41-ship FBM submarine fleet. JOHN C. CALHOUN received her second refueling at Portsmouth Naval Shipyard in 1977 and 1978, then resumed her routine. In 1980 she was converted to Trident at Charleston Naval Shipyard and in 1981 her 43rd patrol was the Navy's 1,999th. As she approached her 20th birthday, JOHN C. CALHOUN paid a visit to Morocco and completed her 52nd strategic deterrent patrol in 1983. She entered overhaul at Charleston Naval Shipyard in October 1984, expecting to complete in August 1986.

VON STEUBEN
1964

VON STEUBEN

Hull No: 567
Navy No: SSBN-632
Launched: October 18, 1963
Commissioned: September 30, 1964
Dimensions: 425 x 33 ft
Displacement: 8,250 tons
Armament: 16 Polaris, 4 21" TT
Machinery: Geared Turbines, Reactor
Horsepower/Speed: 15,000/20 (30+) knots
Fate: In Commission

The contract for VON STEUBEN (SSBN-632) was awarded with those of JAMES MADISON, JOHN C. CALHOUN, and SAM RAYBURN on July 20, 1961. The keel for this ship, named in honor of the German baron who trained American troops during the Revolution, was laid on September 4, 1962. VON STEUBEN was launched on October 18, 1963, and was christened by Mrs. Fred Korth, wife of the Secretary of the Navy. The principal address at the ceremony was given by CNO Adm. David L. McDonald, who had served on the shipyard-built carriers ESSEX and CORAL SEA. VON STEUBEN was completed within a year of her launching and was commissioned in Dry Dock 1 on September 30, 1964, with Cdr. John P. Wise (Blue) and Cdr. Jeffrey C. Metzel, Jr. (Gold) in command.

After commissioning, VON STEUBEN underwent shakedown and missile firing trials with each of her crews, then returned to Newport News for her PSA. Assigned to Submarine Squadron 18 with homeport at Charleston, she began patrols with her Polaris A-3 missiles in March 1965. Early in 1969 she was reassigned to Squadron 16 for patrols out of Rota; then, in November 1970 she began an 18-month period in the Electric Boat shipyard at Groton for refueling and conversion to the Poseidon C-3 missile system. After shakedown, VON STEUBEN continued her patrols, operating out of Charleston and Holy Loch. In January 1980 she returned to Newport News for her second refueling and for conversion to the Trident C-4 missile system. One of 12 ships of her class to be so converted, she completed her yard stay in June 1982 and fired her new missiles for the first time in November. Home-ported at Charleston, she completed her 54th deterrent patrol late in 1983. She celebrated her 20th birthday in 1984 and continued her missions in her nation's defense.

SAM RAYBURN
1964

SAM RAYBURN

Hull No: 568
Navy No: SSBN-635
Launched: December 20, 1963
Commissioned: December 2, 1964
Dimensions: 425 x 33 ft
Displacement: 8,250 tons
Armament: 16 Polaris, 4 21" TT
Machinery: Geared Turbines, Reactor
Horsepower/Speed: 15,000/20 (30+) knots
Fate: In Commission

The tenth Polaris submarine built at Newport News was SAM RAYBURN (SSBN-635), named in memory of the long-time Speaker of the House of Representatives. The keel for this ship was laid down on December 3, 1962, with a brief ceremony attended by Vice President Johnson, and she was launched on December 20 of the following year. Mrs. S.E. Bartley and Mrs. W.A. Thomas, sisters of the colorful "Mr. Sam," served as co-sponsors for SAM RAYBURN, and theirs was only the second such dual duty (after the launching of light cruiser PORTSMOUTH in 1944) in shipyard history.

After passing her acceptance trials with fewer discrepancies than any ship of her class to date, SAM RAYBURN was placed in commission at the shipyard on December 2, 1964. The 50th nuclear submarine in the Navy was placed under the command of Capt. Oliver H. Perry, Jr. (Blue) and Cdr. William A. Williams III (Gold) and in the care of their 268 crewmen. SAM RAYBURN was assigned to Squadron 18 for her first patrol, then transferred to Squadron 16 at Rota for her second through seventh. She returned to Squadron 18 for patrols until December 1969, at which time she began her first refueling overhaul and was converted to the Poseidon missile system at Portsmouth Naval Shipyard. In the early 1970s she engaged in special operations and routine patrols along the East Coast and in the Atlantic; then, she returned to Portsmouth Naval Shipyard in May 1979 to commence her second refueling. She was not converted to Trident and completed her shipyard stay in October 1979. SAM RAYBURN continued her deterrent patrols with Squadron 14 out of New London and Holy Loch and returned from her 54th such mission in late 1983. After refit and routine repairs, she sailed for her 55th patrol early in 1984. Scheduled for overhaul and conversion to an SSN in FY 1986, she completed her 21st year of service to her country in 1985.

SIMON BOLIVAR
1965

SIMON BOLIVAR

Hull No: 569
Navy No: SSBN-641
Launched: August 22, 1964
Commissioned: October 29, 1965
Dimensions: 425 x 33 ft
Displacement: 8,250 tons
Armament: 16 Polaris, 4 21" TT
Machinery: Geared Turbines, Reactor
Horsepower/Speed: 15,000/20 (30+) knots
Fate: In Commission

The 11th FBM submarine built at Newport News in the 1960s was SIMON BOLIVAR (SSBN-641), named after the South American statesman and revolutionary. The contract for this ship was awarded on August 1, 1962, and the keel was laid on Shipway 5 on April 17, 1963. Mrs. Thomas C. Mann, wife of the Assistant Secretary of State for Inter-American Affairs, served as sponsor when SIMON BOLIVAR was launched on August 22, 1964. The nation's 31st Polaris submarine underwent successful trials in September 1965 and was commissioned on October 29 with Cdr. Charles H. Griffiths (Blue) and Cdr. Charles A. Orem (Gold) commanding.

After completing shakedown and missile firing trials, SIMON BOLIVAR returned to Newport News for PSA. In April she and her Blue Crew deployed for her first deterrent patrol in the Atlantic. Operating with Squadron 18 out of Charleston, she continued her patrols routinely until she returned to Newport News in February 1971 for refueling and Poseidon conversion. This work was completed in May 1972, and after shakedown, she returned to her usual duty. Having completed her 40th strategic deterrent patrol in January 1979, SIMON BOLIVAR entered Portsmouth Naval Shipyard for conversion to the Trident missile system. She launched her first Trident in April 1981, then resumed her patrols. During 1983 SIMON BOLIVAR visited Groton and engaged in midshipmen cruises in the summer and paid a visit to Morocco in November. On December 29, 1983, she deployed on her 50th deterrent patrol in her nation's defense. In February 1985 she entered Portmouth Naval Shipyard for an overhaul scheduled to complete in December 1986.

LEWIS AND CLARK
1965

LEWIS AND CLARK

Hull No: 570
Navy No: SSBN-644
Launched: November 21, 1964
Commissioned: December 22, 1965
Dimensions: 425 x 33 ft
Displacement: 8,250 tons
Armament: 16 Polaris, 4 21" TT
Machinery: Geared Turbines, Reactor
Horsepower/Speed: 15,000/20 (30+) knots
Fate: In Commission

The 12th Polaris FBM submarine built at Newport News was LEWIS AND CLARK (SSBN-644), named for the famous Virginia-born explorers. The keel for LEWIS AND CLARK was laid on July 23, 1963, and she was launched on November 21, 1964. Mrs. W. Goodrich Sale, great-great-grandniece of Meriwether Lewis, and Mrs. Martin F. Engman, Jr., great-great granddaughter of William Clark, served as co-sponsors for LEWIS AND CLARK and became the third such duo in shipyard history. The only Polaris submarine named after two men, LEWIS AND CLARK was commissioned on December 22, 1965, with Cdr. John F. Fagan, Jr. (Blue) and Cdr. Kenneth A. Porter (Gold) in command.

The new submarine began her patrols in the Atlantic in mid-1966 and, by the time of her first refueling overhaul at Portsmouth Naval Shipyard in mid-1971, she had completed 18 such missions. LEWIS AND CLARK was converted to the Poseidon missile system during this shipyard period and emerged in July 1972 with greatly enhanced deterrent power. Calling at both Charleston and Holy Loch during the next few years, she completed her 49th patrol in mid-1981. In July of that year she returned to her birthplace at Newport News to begin her second refueling overhaul. Not slated for retrofit with the Trident system, she left the shipyard and underwent trials in October and November 1983, then entered port at Charleston for the holidays. Commencing her 50th deterrent patrol early in 1984, LEWIS AND CLARK continued to serve her country faithfully in the manner of the pioneers after which she was named.

GEORGE C. MARSHALL
1966

GEORGE C. MARSHALL

Hull No: 574
Navy No: SSBN-654
Launched: May 21, 1965
Commissioned: April 29, 1966
Dimensions: 425 x 33 ft
Displacement: 8,250 tons
Armament: 16 Polaris, 4 21" TT
Machinery: Geared Turbines, Reactor
Horsepower/Speed: 15,000/20 (30+) knots
Fate: In Commission

On July 29, 1963, the shipyard was awarded a contract for the construction of its 13th and 14th FBM submarines, later named GEORGE C. MARSHALL (SSBN-654) and GEORGE WASHINGTON CARVER (SSBN-656). The keel for GEORGE C. MARSHALL was laid on March 2, 1964, and she was launched on May 21, 1965. Mrs. George C. Marshall sponsored the submarine named for her husband, and the principal address at the ceremony was given by former Secretary of State Dean Acheson. Cadets from Gen. Marshall's alma mater, VMI, added color to the event. The new GEORGE C. MARSHALL completed trials in March 1966 and was placed in commission on April 29 with Cdr. Warren R. Cobean (Blue) and Cdr. Willard E. Johnson (Gold) in command.

One of the last Polaris FBM submarines to be delivered to the Navy, she began patrols in the Atlantic with her A-3 missiles and by September 1971 had completed 20 such missions. Late in 1971 GEORGE C. MARSHALL entered Puget Sound Naval Shipyard for refueling and conversion to the 2,900-mile Poseidon missile system. She left the shipyard and began her 21st patrol in September 1973, completing it at Rota in October. Calling at Rota, Charleston, and Holy Loch between patrols, she finished her 50th deployment at Groton in mid-1981 and engaged in midshipman operations in the summer of that year. After completing her 51st patrol, GEORGE C. MARSHALL arrived at Newport News for her second refueling and for conversion to the 4,000-mile Trident missile system. This work was accomplished late in 1983, and after shakedown and missile firing trials, she deployed to the Atlantic for her 52nd strategic deterrent patrol. Continuing in the defense of her country, she celebrated her 20th birthday in April 1986.

GEORGE WASHINGTON CARVER
1966

GEORGE WASHINGTON CARVER

Hull No: 575
Navy No: SSBN-656
Launched: August 14, 1965
Commissioned: June 15, 1966
Dimensions: 425 x 33 ft
Displacement: 8,250 tons
Armament: 16 Polaris, 4 21″ TT
Machinery: Geared Turbines, Reactor
Horsepower/Speed: 15,000/20 (30+) knots
Fate: In Commission

The 14th and last Polaris submarine built at Newport News was GEORGE WASHINGTON CARVER (SSBN-656), the keel for which was laid on August 24, 1964. This ship was launched less than a year later on August 14, 1965, and singer Marian Anderson served as sponsor. After completing trials on May 8, 1966, GEORGE WASHINGTON CARVER was placed in commission on June 15 with Capt. R.D. Donavan (Blue) and LCdr. Carl J. Lidel (Gold) commanding.

She began her first patrol in the Atlantic in December and completed 20 such missions before her first refueling overhaul. She was refueled and converted to Poseidon at Electric Boat in 1972 and 1973 and launched her first Poseidon missile in May 1973. Calling at Rota and New London between missions, GEORGE WASHINGTON CARVER continued her patrols routinely for the next nine years. Her 34th patrol, completed in 1977, was the Navy's 1,500th FBM patrol, and she finished her 52nd mission in August 1982. In November of that year, GEORGE WASHINGTON CARVER returned to her birthplace at Newport News to begin her second refueling overhaul. She remained in the shipyard for all of 1983 and most of 1984, then resumed her vital role in her nation's defense as she approached the 20th anniversary of her commissioning in 1986.

RAY
1967

RAY

Hull No: 572
Navy No: SSN-653
Launched: June 21, 1966
Commissioned: April 12, 1967
Dimensions: 292 x 31.67 ft
Displacement: 4,060 tons
Armament: 4 21″ TT, SUBROC
Machinery: Geared Turbines, Reactor
Horsepower/Speed: 15,000/20 (30+) knots
Fate: In Commission

The keel for the shipyard's third nuclear attack submarine, later named RAY (SSN-653), was laid on January 4, 1965. One of nine STURGEON-class ships ultimately built at Newport News, RAY and her sisters were fitted with the "Subsafe" features developed after the loss of THRESHER in 1963. They were also provided with advanced bow-mounted sonar, which required that their torpedo tubes be installed amidships. RAY, with one of the shortest names in shipyard history, was launched on June 21, 1966, and was christened by Mrs. Thomas H. Kuchel, wife of Sen. Kuchel of California. The new RAY was commissioned at ceremonies in the shipyard on April 12, 1967, and was placed under the command of Cdr. A.L. Kelln. During the ceremony it was noted that RAY was delivered well ahead of schedule and only a month behind the class prototype STURGEON.

After commissioning, RAY joined the Atlantic Fleet and began operations, which took her to Scotland in 1969 and to the Mediterranean in 1973. She spent 1971 at Norfolk Naval Shipyard in overhaul, then engaged in two NATO exercises in the Atlantic in 1972. By the end of 1976, she had won her fourth Navy Unit Commendation. In 1975 and 1976 RAY was at Charleston Naval Shipyard for her first refueling overhaul, and in 1977 she deployed to the Mediterranean. During this deployment in September, she struck a submerged seamount between Sardinia and Africa. Three of her crew were injured, and she was towed to port in Italy, then sailed for Charleston and permanent repair. Her sonar dome and sphere were removed, and she underwent other repairs before returning to service in November 1978. In 1979 RAY engaged in classified operations, then visited Scotland and Germany. She underwent a routine overhaul at Charleston in 1980 and 1981, then engaged in classified operations vital to the defense of her country during the next several years. In November 1983, she entered Charleston Naval Shipyard for overhaul, which completed in August 1985.

QUEENFISH
1966

QUEENFISH

Hull No: 571
Navy No: SSN-651
Launched: February 25, 1966
Commissioned: December 6, 1966
Dimensions: 292 x 31.67 ft
Displacement: 4,060 tons
Armament: 4 21″ TT, ASROC
Machinery: Geared Turbines, Reactor
Horsepower/Speed: 15,000/20 (30+) Knots
Fate: In Commission

The second nuclear attack submarine built at Newport News was QUEENFISH (SSN-651), which was awarded on March 26, 1963. Because of the priority given to the Polaris program, the keel for this STURGEON-class ship was not laid until May 11, 1964, and she was not launched until February 25, 1966. Rep. Julia Butler Hansen of the state of Washington served as sponsor for QUEENFISH. SSN-651 embarrassed both her builders and the Navy when, with Adm. Rickover aboard, she refused to submerge on her first diving trial and had to return to the shipyard for reballasting. After completing trials in October, the new submarine was commissioned on December 6, 1966, with Cdr. Jackson B. Richard in command. At the ceremony it was noted that QUEENFISH, although the ninth ship of her class, was the first to be placed in commission.

Assigned to the Pacific Fleet with homeport at Pearl Harbor, QUEENFISH engaged in routine operations in the Pacific until she departed Pearl for an extended mission to the Arctic in July 1971. Having been built with specialized equipment for operations in ice, she followed the track of NAUTILUS made 12 years earlier and surfaced within 500 yards of the North Pole on August 5. By the end of 1972 QUEENFISH had won two Navy Unit Commendations for this and for other classified operations. She underwent her first refueling overhaul at Puget Sound Naval Shipyard in 1973 and 1974, then returned to operations out of Pearl Harbor. By the end of the 1970s, she had made six deployments to the western Pacific and had won a total of five Navy Unit Commendations for her missions. In 1981 she returned to Puget Sound for a non-refueling overhaul and underwent modifications to her sonar and fire control systems. QUEENFISH completed her shipyard period in January 1983 and left for her eighth WestPac deployment in December. She and her 107 crewmen returned from this mission the following June and began preparations for their next assignment in the Pacific. QUEENFISH continued in her country's service as her 20th birthday approached in 1986.

LAPON
1967

<table>
<tr><td colspan="2">LAPON</td></tr>
<tr><td>Hull No:</td><td>578</td></tr>
<tr><td>Navy No:</td><td>SSN-661</td></tr>
<tr><td>Launched:</td><td>December 16, 1966</td></tr>
<tr><td>Commissioned:</td><td>December 14, 1967</td></tr>
<tr><td>Dimensions:</td><td>292 x 31.67 ft</td></tr>
<tr><td>Displacement:</td><td>4,060 tons</td></tr>
<tr><td>Armament:</td><td>4 21″ TT, SUBROC</td></tr>
<tr><td>Machinery:</td><td>Geared Turbines, Reactor</td></tr>
<tr><td>Horsepower/Speed:</td><td>15,000/20 (30+) knots</td></tr>
<tr><td>Fate:</td><td>In Commission</td></tr>
</table>

On May 28, 1964, Newport News was awarded a contract for the construction of three STURGEON-class nuclear attack submarines. The first of these was LAPON (SSN-661), whose keel was laid on July 26, 1965. LAPON was launched on December 16, 1966, and was christened by Mrs. Charles D. Griffin. The attack submarine was placed in commission less than a year later on December 14, 1967, with Cdr. Chester M. Mack in command.

The 74th nuclear submarine to join the Navy, LAPON was assigned to the Atlantic Fleet with homeport at Norfolk. She spent her first year in training and exercises along the East Coast, then in 1970 made her initial deployment to the Mediterranean, first of her class to do so. After overhaul at Portsmouth Naval Shipyard in 1971, she again deployed to the Mediterranean in 1972. By the end of that mission, she had become one of only three active submarines to hold the Presidential, Navy, and Meritorious Unit Commendations. LAPON returned to Newport News for her first refueling overhaul from 1975 to 1977. She was damaged when she struck a pier at St. Croix in November 1977 and was repaired at Norfolk Naval Shipyard, then deployed to the Mediterranean in mid-1978. She engaged in operations in the North Atlantic in 1979, then made her fourth Mediterranean deployment in 1980. LAPON continued in alternative local and overseas operations until her third major overhaul, which commenced in 1983. This completed, she continued operations in the Atlantic in defense of her country. In 1985 she deployed to the Indian Ocean, circumnavigating the globe before her return to Norfolk late in the year.

HAMMERHEAD
1968

<table>
<tr><td colspan="2">HAMMERHEAD</td></tr>
<tr><td>Hull No:</td><td>579</td></tr>
<tr><td>Navy No:</td><td>SSN-663</td></tr>
<tr><td>Launched:</td><td>April 14, 1967</td></tr>
<tr><td>Commissioned:</td><td>June 28, 1968</td></tr>
<tr><td>Dimensions:</td><td>292 x 31.67 ft</td></tr>
<tr><td>Displacement:</td><td>4,060 tons</td></tr>
<tr><td>Armament:</td><td>4 21″ TT, SUBROC</td></tr>
<tr><td>Machinery:</td><td>Geared Turbines, Reactor</td></tr>
<tr><td>Horsepower/Speed:</td><td>15,000/20 (30+) knots</td></tr>
<tr><td>Fate:</td><td>In Commission</td></tr>
</table>

The second nuclear attack submarine awarded to Newport News on May 28, 1964, was HAMMERHEAD (SSN-663). The keel for this ship was laid down on November 29, 1965, and she was launched on April 14, 1967. HAMMERHEAD was sponsored by Mrs. O. Clark Fisher, wife of Rep. Fisher of Texas. After outfitting and trials the submarine was commissioned on June 28, 1968, with Cdr. E. Frederick Murphy, Jr. commanding.

HAMMERHEAD was assigned to the Atlantic Fleet, and homeported at Norfolk, alternated operations and exercises along the East Coast and in the Caribbean with deployments to the Mediterranean during her first few years. In October 1970 she sailed on an extended mission to the Arctic. She surfaced at the North Pole on November 30, surfaced a record number of times, and spent more time under the ice than any of her predecessors. In 1971 HAMMERHEAD engaged in classified operations overseas, and the next year she underwent an extensive overhaul at Portsmouth Naval Shipyard. She sailed along the East Coast and in the Caribbean in 1973, then deployed overseas in 1974 and 1975. In October 1976 HAMMERHEAD returned to Newport News for her first refueling overhaul. This was completed in 1978; then, for part of that year and in 1979 she was engaged in classified operations. She deployed for NATO exercises in European waters in 1980, then made her first trip to the western Pacific in 1981. In 1982 she deployed to the North Atlantic from May to July, then returned to local operations out of Norfolk. In November 1983 HAMMERHEAD was again deployed to the Mediterranean and continued operations in defense of her country. In 1985 she entered Mare Island Naval Shipyard for overhaul, which was scheduled to complete in September 1986.

SEA DEVIL
1969

SEA DEVIL

Hull No: 580
Navy No: SSN-664
Launched: October 5, 1967
Commissioned: January 30, 1969
Dimensions: 292 x 31.67 ft
Displacement: 4,060 tons
Armament: 4 21" TT, SUBROC
Machinery: Geared Turbines, Reactor
Horsepower/Speed: 15,000/20 (30+) knots
Fate: In Commission

SEA DEVIL (SSN-664) was the last of three STURGEON-class nuclear attack submarines awarded to the shipyard in May 1964, and she was also its 20th nuclear submarine. The keel for SEA DEVIL was laid on Shipway 6 on April 6, 1966, and she was launched on October 5, 1967. Mrs. Ignatius Galantin, wife of the Chief of Naval Material, served as sponsor for SEA DEVIL. The new submarine was placed in commission in ceremonies at the shipyard on January 30, 1969, and it was noted that although Newport News was one of five shipyards participating in the SSN-637 program,

it had delivered half of the ten ships commissioned to that date.

SEA DEVIL was placed under the command of LCdr. Richard A. Currier and was assigned to Submarine Squadron 6 with homeport at Norfolk. The 80th nuclear submarine in the Navy, SEA DEVIL engaged in local operations and shakedown in local waters during her first months in commission. She soon joined her sister ships in regular deployments to the North Atlantic and to the Mediterranean. SEA DEVIL underwent overhaul from late 1977 to early 1978 and later in 1978 operated in both Mediterranean and European waters. After her summer deployment to the Mediterranean in 1981, SEA DEVIL was transferred to Squadron 4 and her homeport was moved to Charleston. She entered Charleston Naval Shipyard in October 1981 for her first refueling and left the yard three months ahead of schedule in April 1983. SEA DEVIL completed her shakedown on a trip to New London, then sailed to the Caribbean in time to witness the first nighttime launch of the Space Shuttle in August. Newly refueled and refitted, she looked forward to more years of uninterrupted service to the Navy.

SPADEFISH
1969

SPADEFISH

Hull No: 581
Navy No: SSN-668
Launched: May 15, 1968
Commissioned: August 14, 1969
Dimensions: 292 x 31.67 ft
Displacement: 4,060 tons
Armament: 4 21" TT, SUBROC
Machinery: Geared Turbines, Reactor
Horsepower/Speed: 15,000/20 (30+) knots
Fate: In Commission

SPADEFISH (SSN-668) was the sixth STURGEON-class nuclear attack submarine built at Newport News during the 1960s. Contracts for SPADEFISH and her later sister FINBACK (SSN-670) were awarded to the shipyard on March 9, 1965, and the first keel was laid on December 21, 1966. SPADEFISH was launched on May 15, 1968, and Mrs. Charles T. Booth II, wife of the commander of the Atlantic Fleet Naval Air Force,

served as sponsor. The new SPADEFISH joined the Atlantic Fleet on August 14, 1969, under the command of Cdr. G.M. Henson.

SPADEFISH underwent her PSA at the shipyard in 1970 and began a series of yearly deployments to the North Atlantic, which lasted until her first overhaul at Norfolk Naval Shipyard in 1973 and 1974. She left the shipyard in July 1974 and operated on the East Coast until mid-1975. SPADEFISH engaged in classified and special operations at home and abroad for the next two years, then returned to Newport News in January 1978 for her first refueling overhaul. SPADEFISH left the shipyard ready for another ten years of service and commenced classified operations which lasted until the end of 1982. From February to May 1983, she made a solo deployment overseas and visited Scotland and France. She spent the remainder of the year in local operations out of Norfolk and on exercises in the Caribbean. At year's end SPADEFISH readied herself for another overseas deployment during 1984 and for celebration of her 15th birthday in that year.

FINBACK
1970

FINBACK

Hull No: 582
Navy No: SSN-670
Launched: December 7, 1968
Commissioned: February 4, 1970
Dimensions: 292 x 31.67 ft
Displacement: 4,060 tons
Armament: 4 21" TT, SUBROC
Machinery: Geared Turbines, Reactor
Horsepower/Speed: 15,000/20 (30+) knots
Fate: In Commission

The last submarine built at Newport News in the productive 1960s was FINBACK (SSN-670), which was also the sixth of the shipyard's nine STURGEON-class ships. The keel for FINBACK was laid on June 26, 1967, and she was launched on December 7, 1968. She was said to be the the first Navy warship launched on December 7 since the end of World War II. Mrs. Charles Baird, wife of the Under Secretary of the Navy, was selected to serve as sponsor for FINBACK. During her construction, FINBACK was fitted to carry the 50-foot Deep Submergence Rescue Vessel which gave her the capability to rescue the crews of stricken submarines. The usual extensive trials were completed in October 1979 and FINBACK was placed in commission on February 4, 1970, with Cdr. Robert C. Austin in command.

She completed shakedown and PSA during 1970, then began regular deployments with the Atlantic Fleet to Europe and the Mediterranean. FINBACK was overhauled at Norfolk Naval Shipyard from July 1974 to May 1975, then sailed southward. This trip was memorable, since on July 10 she was seen departing Port Canaveral with a topless dancer on her port diving plane. In a highly controversial action, her commanding officer was relieved of command, but her crew put the incident behind them and carried on. During the first half of 1976 FINBACK deployed to the Mediterranean, and she was in the Caribbean for the rest of the year. She made a long deployment to Europe in 1977 and in July 1978 returned to Newport News for her first refueling. This took until the end of 1978, then FINBACK rejoined the Atlantic Fleet. She deployed to the Mediterranean during each of the next three years and in 1983 stayed in local waters and in the Caribbean. She and her crew celebrated her 15th birthday in February 1985 and later that year were in port at Norfolk preparing for their next sojourn overseas.

RICHARD B. RUSSELL
1975

RICHARD B. RUSSELL

Hull No: 598
Navy No: SSN-687
Launched: January 12, 1974
Commissioned: August 16, 1975
Dimensions: 300.5 x 31.67 ft
Displacement: 4,060 tons
Armament: 4 21" TT, SUBROC
Machinery: Geared Turbines, Reactor
Horsepower/Speed: 15,000/20 (30+) knots
Fate: In Commission

RICHARD B. RUSSELL (SSN-687), named for the late senator from Georgia, was the last of nine STURGEON-class nuclear attack submarines built at Newport News. Her keel was laid on October 19, 1971, and she was launched in ceremonies on January 12, 1974. Sponsor for RICHARD B. RUSSELL was Mrs. Herman E. Talmadge, wife of Sen. Talmadge of Georgia. The new submarine completed official trials on June 15, 1975, and was commissioned on August 16 under the command of Cdr. John C. Brons.

Assigned to the Atlantic Fleet with homeport at New London, RICHARD B. RUSSELL completed shakedown and underwent her PSA at the shipyard from March to May 1976. After local and Caribbean operations, she deployed to the Mediterranean for the first time in October 1976. She engaged in NATO operations in Northern European waters during the fall of the next year, and also deployed to that area during 1978. After a shipyard period at Charleston in 1979, she again deployed to the Mediterranean for the first half of 1980, then operated along the East Coast until year's end. RICHARD B. RUSSELL engaged in confidential operations in 1981; then, she entered Mare Island Naval Shipyard in January 1982 for her first major non-refueling overhaul. After completion of her shipyard work in October 1983, her homeport was moved to Vallejo, CA. RICHARD B. RUSSELL was then assigned to serve as a test platform for submarine rescue and research and development projects, and as 1983 drew to a close, she and her crew prepared for their first deployment to the Pacific. In August 1985 she and her men celebrated completion of her tenth year of service to her country.

L. MENDEL RIVERS
1975

L. MENDEL RIVERS

Hull No: 597
Navy No: SSN-686
Launched: June 2, 1973
Commissioned: February 1, 1975
Dimensions: 300.5 x 31.67 ft
Displacement: 4,060 tons
Armament: 4 21″ TT, SUBROC
Machinery: Geared Turbines, Reactor
Horsepower/Speed: 15,000/20 (30+) knots
Fate: In Commission

The last two STURGEON-class nuclear attack submarines built at Newport News were L. MENDEL RIVERS (SSN-686) and RICHARD B. RUSSELL (SSN-687), awarded on July 25, 1969. They were also the last of their class and were only the second and third U.S. Navy attack submarines named for persons rather than for sea creatures. They, with eight others of the 37-ship STURGEON class, were slightly longer than the first 27. The keel for L. MENDEL RIVERS was laid down on June 26, 1971, and after construction under the motto, "Get the RIVERS in the river," launching took place on June 2, 1973. Mrs. Margaret

Rivers Eastman and Mrs. Lois Rivers Ravenel, daughters of the late Congressman Rivers, co-sponsored the submarine named for their father and became the fourth dual sponsors in shipyard history.

After outfitting and trials, the new L. MENDEL RIVERS was placed in commission on February 1, 1975, under the command of Cdr. Roderic L. Wolfe and joined the Atlantic Fleet. L. MENDEL RIVERS completed shakedown and PSA during 1975, then began classified operations which lasted until the end of 1977 and included two deployments to the Mediterranean. She engaged in local operations out of Norfolk during part of 1978 and was deployed to Northern Europe for the first time in August of that year. She returned in November and operated along the East Coast until her next deployment to the Mediterranean a year later. L. MENDEL RIVERS returned from this mission in April 1980, then stayed in local waters and in the Caribbean for the rest of the year. She underwent her first major overhaul at Charleston Naval Shipyard from March 1981 to September 1982, then engaged in local and Caribbean operations for the rest of that year. As the new year began, L. MENDEL RIVERS and her crew prepared for another long overseas deployment in their nation's defense and anticipated celebration of her tenth birthday in 1985.

LOS ANGELES
1976

LOS ANGELES

Hull No: 600
Navy No: SSN-688
Launched: April 6, 1974
Commissioned: November 13, 1976
Dimensions: 360 x 33 ft
Displacement: 6,900 tons
Armament: 4 21″ TT, SUBROC/Harpoon
Machinery: Geared Turbines, Reactor
Horsepower/Speed: 35,000/20 (32+) knots
Fate: In Commission

The award of a contract for the construction of five nuclear attack submarines on January 8, 1971, marked an important milestone in the history of Newport News Shipbuilding. These ships were the first of the Newport News-designed LOS ANGELES (SSN-688) class "fast" submarines, the first class for which the shipyard was "lead yard." They were considerably larger and more powerful than their predecessors and were designed to carry the new MK 48 torpedo and the Tomahawk cruise missile.

Assigned Hull No. 600, the keel for LOS ANGELES was laid down on January 8, 1972. The submarine was launched on April 6, 1974, and was christened by Mrs. Anne Armstrong, counselor to the President. The sponsor was unable to launch LOS ANGELES with 12 strong swings of the champagne bottle but was successful with the first blow of a spare bottle. LOS ANGELES was completed in mid-1976 and was placed in commission on November 13 of that year under the command of Cdr. John E. Christensen.

The new submarine underwent shakedown in the Atlantic, had her PSA at the shipyard during the first quarter of 1978, then left for duty with the Pacific Fleet. Homeported at Pearl Harbor, LOS ANGELES visited her namesake city on her way west, then engaged in exercises in mid-Pacific until the end of the year. In mid-1979 she was deployed to the Indian Ocean and returned to Pearl Harbor in August. LOS ANGELES made her second deployment under the "Ready SSN" program and in January 1980 made a high speed transit to the Indian Ocean. She visited Australia during this deployment, then returned to Hawaii for a shipyard availability. At the end of her sixth year in commission, LOS ANGELES was enroute to her fourth deployment to the western Pacific and the Indian Ocean, and 16 of her sister ships had already joined the fleet.

BATON ROUGE
1977

BATON ROUGE

Hull No: 602
Navy No: SSN-689
Launched: April 26, 1975
Commissioned: June 25, 1977
Dimensions: 360 x 33 ft
Displacement: 6,900 tons
Armament: 4 21" TT, SUBROC, Harpoon
Machinery: Geared Turbines, Reactor
Horsepower/Speed: 35,000/20 (32+) knots
Fate: In Commission

The second LOS ANGELES-class submarine built at Newport News was BATON ROUGE (SSN-689). The keel for this ship was laid on November 18, 1972, and she was launched on April 26, 1975. Mrs. F. Edward Hebert, wife of Rep. Hebert of Louisiana, served as sponsor for BATON ROUGE. SSN-689 was placed in commission in the shipyard on June 25, 1977, with Cdr. Thomas C. Maloney in command.

Assigned to Submarine Squadron 6, BATON ROUGE operated in the Atlantic on shakedown until her PSA at Newport News, which began in February 1978. In October 1978 BATON ROUGE deployed to the Mediterranean for six months, returning to Norfolk the following March. In July 1979 she was assigned to the new 688-class Squadron 8, and in the fall of that year she engaged in exercises in European waters. BATON ROUGE deployed to the Indian Ocean in February 1980, then returned around-the-world to Norfolk the following August. After routine availibility there, she operated in the Atlantic from Halifax to the Bahamas for the first eight months of 1981, then again deployed to the Indian Ocean. BATON ROUGE was back in Norfolk for the holidays and in 1982 engaged in exercises in both the Caribbean and in European waters. She underwent her first major overhaul in 1984 and 1985, then returned to her missions for the defense of her country.

MEMPHIS
1977

MEMPHIS

Hull No: 603
Navy No: SSN-691
Launched: April 3, 1976
Commissioned: December 17, 1977
Dimensions: 360 x 33 ft
Displacement: 6,900 tons
Armament: 4 21" TT, SUBROC, Harpoon
Machinery: Geared Turbines, Reactor
Horsepower/Speed: 35,000/20 (32+) knots
Fate: In Commission

Third of the five SSN-688-class submarines awarded to Newport News on January 8, 1971, was MEMPHIS (SSN-691). The keel for MEMPHIS was laid on June 23, 1973, and the new attack submarine was launched on April 3, 1976. Sponsor for MEMPHIS was Mrs. Cathy Beard, wife of Tennessee Congressman Beard. MEMPHIS was commissioned at the shipyard on December 17, 1977, and was placed under the command of Cdr. Gerald D. Hicks.

Assigned to Squadron 6, MEMPHIS underwent shakedown in the Atlantic, then returned to Newport News for PSA from August to December 1978. After operations in the Atlantic and Caribbean early in 1979, MEMPHIS made her first deployment to the Mediterranean in June. Returning to Norfolk in November, she was assigned to the new Squadron 8. In 1980 MEMPHIS began the year in exercises in the Caribbean; then, in September she deployed to the Indian Ocean via the Mediterranean. Circumnavigating the globe, she returned to Norfolk on March 7, 1981, after having spent 140 days at sea and having steamed over 50,000 miles. After a shipyard period, MEMPHIS engaged in local and Caribbean operations until October, then again deployed overseas. She returned to the Mediterranean from March to August 1982 and engaged in two months of special operations overseas. In 1983 MEMPHIS underwent a routine availability at Norfolk Naval Shipyard until May, then engaged in operations in the Caribbean during the summer. At year's end, she and her men were in port preparing for another long overseas deployment. In 1985 she began overhaul at Norfolk Naval Shipyard, which was scheduled to complete in 1986.

CINCINNATI
1978

CINCINNATI

Hull No: 604
Navy No: SSN-693
Launched: February 19, 1977
Commissioned: May 26, 1978
Dimensions: 360 x 33 ft
Displacement: 6,900 tons
Armament: 4 21″ TT, SUBROC, Harpoon
Machinery: Geared Turbines, Reactor
Horsepower/Speed: 35,000/20 (32+) knots
Fate: In Commission

The shipyard's fourth SSN-688-class submarine was CINCINNATI (SSN-693), the keel for which was laid just after the launching of LOS ANGELES on April 6, 1974. CINCINNATI herself was launched on February 19, 1977, and was sponsored by Mrs. Nancy Keating, wife of the president of the Cincinnati Enquirer. The new Secretary of the Navy, W. Graham Claytor, delivered the principal address at the ceremony. Just over four years after her keel was laid, CINCINNATI was commissioned on May 26, 1978, with Cdr. Gilbert Wilkes, III in command.

Assigned to Squadron 6, the new submarine and her crew engaged in shakedown operations and exercises in the Atlantic and Caribbean until she returned to Newport News for her PSA in February 1979. This completed in May, she was assigned to the new Squadron 8 in August, then began her first deployment to the Mediterranean in November. CINCINNATI returned to Norfolk six months later, and after a period of upkeep, engaged in local and Caribbean operations and in midshipmen cruises for the rest of 1980. In January 1981 she deployed to the Indian Ocean, returning to Norfolk in August after circumnavigating the world and logging over 60,000 miles. CINCINNATI then underwent availability at Norfolk Naval Shipyard, which lasted until the end of the year. Operations in the Caribbean and special operations occupied her until August 1982, at which time she deployed to Scotland. She returned to Norfolk in October and operated in local waters until the following January. Beginning 1983 in the Caribbean, CINCINNATI made a rapid recall voyage to Europe and remained overseas until March. In June and July she was again at Norfolk Naval Shipyard; then, in October she deployed to the Mediterranean, remaining there into 1984. In October 1985 she entered Norfolk Naval Shipyard for overhaul and was expected to remain there until 1987.

BIRMINGHAM
1978

BIRMINGHAM

Hull No: 605
Navy No: SSN-695
Launched: October 29, 1977
Commissioned: December 16, 1978
Dimensions: 360 x 33 ft
Displacement: 6,900 tons
Armament: 4 21″ TT, SUBROC, Harpoon
Machinery: Geared Turbines, Reactor
Horsepower/Speed: 35,000/20 (32+) knots
Fate: In Commission

Last of the first group of five LOS ANGELES-class submarines ordered by the Navy on January 8, 1971, was BIRMINGHAM (SSN-695), which was laid down on April 26, 1975, immediately following the launch of BATON ROUGE. BIRMINGHAM was launched on October 29, 1977, and was christened by Mrs. Maryon P. Allen, wife of the late Sen. Allen of Alabama. The new submarine was commissioned at the shipyard on December 16, 1978, under the command of Cdr. Paul L. Callahan.

Homeported at Norfolk, BIRMINGHAM engaged in exercises and shakedown operations for most of 1979, then returned to Newport News for her PSA in September. In July 1980, she began her first deployment to the Mediterranean, which lasted until January 1981. Her sonar dome was damaged during this deployment, and on her return to Norfolk in February, she entered Norfolk Naval Shipyard for repairs. BIRMINGHAM left the shipyard in April and in May operated in waters around Florida. She joined a major fleet exercise in October 1981, during which she sank a target destroyer with her Harpoon missiles. Before year's end, she was awarded the Navy Unit Commendation for her 1980 deployment. In early 1982 BIRMINGHAM took part in a major exercise in the Caribbean, then entered Norfolk Naval Shipyard for a routine availability which lasted until July. After a few months of local operations out of Norfolk, she sailed for her second overseas deployment in November. This
(Continued on page 319)

SAN FRANCISCO
1981

SAN FRANCISCO

Hull No: 616
Navy No: SSN-711
Launched: October 27, 1979
Commissioned: April 24, 1981
Dimensions: 360 x 33 ft
Displacement: 6,900 tons
Armament: 4 21" TT, Harpoon
Machinery: Geared Turbines, Reactor
Horsepower/Speed: 35,000/20 (32+) knots
Fate: In Commission

SAN FRANCISCO (SSN-711) was the first of five more SSN-688-class submarines ordered from Newport News on August 1, 1975. The keel for SAN FRAN-CISCO was laid on May 26, 1977, and launching occurred on October 27, 1979. The submarine was sponsored by Mrs. Robert Y. Kaufman, wife of VAdm.

Kaufman, and was commissioned at Norfolk on April 24, 1981. The new Secretary of Defense Caspar Weinberger spoke at the ceremony in which Capt. James A. Marshall was placed in command of SAN FRANCISCO.

In testimony to her capabilities, the new SSN engaged in confidential operations throughout her first year in commission. Assigned to the Pacific Fleet, she engaged in special operations in January 1982, then operated locally in Hawaiian waters until May. On May 26 she left her homeport of Pearl Harbor for operations with the Seventh Fleet in the West Pacific and Indian Oceans. During this deployment LOS ANGELES made port calls in Japan, the Philippines, Guam, Diego Garcia, and Perth. She returned to Pearl Harbor in November 1982 and began a period of upkeep in preparation for her next mission. Remaining active in the Pacific, she made several more deployments before her fifth birthday in 1986.

ATLANTA
1982

ATLANTA

Hull No: 617
Navy No: SSN-712
Launched: August 16, 1980
Commissioned: March 6, 1982
Dimensions: 360 x 33 ft
Displacement: 6,900 tons
Armament: 4 21" TT, Harpoon
Machinery: Geared Turbines, Reactor
Horsepower/Speed: 35,000/20 (32+) knots
Fate: In Commission

The seventh LOS ANGELES-class submarine built at Newport News was ATLANTA (SSN-712), which was laid down on August 17, 1978. ATLANTA was launched just under two years later on August 16, 1980, and was sponsored by Mrs. Sam Nunn, wife of the senator from Georgia. Commissioned on March 6,

1982, ATLANTA and her 11 officers and 115 enlisted men were placed under the command of Cdr. Robin J. White.

The new attack submarine was assigned to the Atlantic Fleet with homeport at Norfolk, and completed her PSA at the shipyard from May to October 1982. The first SSN-688-class ship certified for all three of the MK 48 torpedo, Harpoon, and Tomahawk weapons systems, ATLANTA joined in a major fleet ASW exercise in January and February 1983. During later exercises in May she sank target ship BUSHNELL (ex-AS-15) with two MK 48 torpedos. ATLANTA departed Norfolk in June for her first overseas deployment, a five-month assignment to the eastern Atlantic and Mediterranean. She made port calls in Scotland, England, and Norway during this deployment and returned to Norfolk in November. The first Navy ship also fitted for land attack Tomahawk missiles, she made operational test launches of antiship cruise missiles off the Florida coast in September 1984.

HOUSTON
1982

HOUSTON

Hull No: 618
Navy No: SSN-713
Launched: March 21, 1981
Commissioned: September 25, 1982
Dimensions: 360 x 33 ft
Displacement: 6,900 tons
Armament: 4 21″ TT, Harpoon
Machinery: Geared Turbines, Reactor
Horsepower/Speed: 35,000/20 (32+) knots
Fate: In Commission

Nuclear attack submarine HOUSTON (SSN-713), Newport News' eighth LOS ANGELES-class ship, was laid down on January 29, 1979. Construction on the ways took just under 26 months, and HOUSTON was launched on March 21, 1981. Sponsor for the submarine was Mrs. Barbara Bush, wife of the new Vice President who delivered the principal address at the ceremony. The sophisticated HOUSTON was placed in commission at Norfolk on September 25, 1982, with Capt. G.H. Mensch in command. The new submarine experienced early trouble with her reduction gears which delayed her assignment to the Atlantic Fleet until December, but in the new year she engaged in operations and shakedown in the Caribbean until April. HOUSTON returned to Newport News for her PSA which lasted until October, then was certified to carry Tomahawk cruise missiles in her torpedo tubes. Permanently assigned to the Pacific Fleet, she left Norfolk in early November and steamed to her new homeport of San Diego via the Panama Canal. HOUSTON arrived in California on November 23, 1983, and then began preparations for her first overseas deployment, which was completed in 1984.

NORFOLK
1983

NORFOLK

Hull No: 619
Navy No: SSN-714
Launched: October 31, 1981
Commissioned: May 21, 1983
Dimensions: 360 x 33 ft
Displacement: 6,900 tons
Armament: 4 21″ TT, Harpoon
Machinery: Geared Turbines, Reactor
Horsepower/Speed: 35,000/20 (32+) knots
Fate: In Commission

Newport News' ninth SSN-688-class submarine was NORFOLK (SSN-714), named for the home of the world's largest naval installation. The keel for this ship was laid on August 1, 1979, and NORFOLK was launched on October 31, 1981. Mrs. Jane Dalton Weinberger, wife of the new Secretary of Defense, served as sponsor for NORFOLK. She and Secretary Weinberger attended commissioning ceremonies for NORFOLK at the Norfolk Naval Station on May 21, 1983, and the secretary, in his address, praised the new submarine's capabilities. Under the command of Capt. Kenneth R. Karr, NORFOLK and her crew joined the Atlantic Fleet and engaged in certification trials of weapons and propulsion systems as well as fleet ASW exercises during their first months in commission. In October 1983 NORFOLK returned to Newport News for her PSA, which took her into 1984.

BIRMINGHAM *Continued from page 317*

mission lasted until February 1983, at which time BIRMINGHAM and her men returned to their home port and readied themselves for their next assignment. She continued in her duties and prepared for overhaul, scheduled to begin at Portsmouth Naval Shipyard in July 1986.

BUFFALO
1983

BUFFALO
Hull No: 620
Navy No: SSN-715
Launched: May 8, 1982
Commissioned: November 5, 1983
Dimensions: 360 x 33 ft
Displacement: 6,900 tons
Armament: 4 21″ TT, Harpoon
Machinery: Geared Turbines, Reactor
Horsepower/Speed: 35,000/20 (32+) knots
Fate: In Commission

The tenth LOS ANGELES-class submarine built at Newport News was BUFFALO (SSN-715), which was laid down on January 25, 1980. BUFFALO was christened by Mrs. Joanne Kemp, wife of Rep. Kemp of New York, on May 8, 1982. During the ship's outfitting period, her crew won the esteem of local residents by working with Newport News youths, ten of whom were made honorary crew members based on their good grades and attitudes. BUFFALO was placed in commission at the Norfolk Naval Station on November 15, 1983 with Cdr. Michael Hewitt in command and joined the Atlantic Fleet with homeport at Norfolk.

SALT LAKE CITY
1984

SALT LAKE CITY
Hull No: 621
Navy No: SSN-716
Launched: October 16, 1982
Commissioned: May 12, 1984
Dimensions: 360 x 33 ft
Displacement: 6,900 tons
Armament: 4 21″ TT, Harpoon
Machinery: Geared Turbines, Reactor
Horsepower/Speed: 35,000/20 (32+) knots
Fate: In Commission

On September 15, 1977, Newport News shipbuilders were awarded contracts for three more LOS ANGELES-class attack submarines. The first of these was SALT LAKE CITY (SSN-716) which was laid down on August 26, 1980. Launched on October 16, 1982, SALT LAKE CITY was christened by Mrs. Kathleen Garn, wife of Sen. Garn of Utah. She and Senator Garn attended the commissioning of SALT LAKE CITY at the Norfolk Naval Station on May 12, 1984, at which time Capt. Richard I. Itkin was placed in command. SALT LAKE CITY was temporarily assigned to Squadron 6, Atlantic Fleet but completed her PSA at Newport News and moved to the West Coast for permanent duty with the Pacific Fleet in 1985.

OLYMPIA
1984

OLYMPIA
Hull No: 622
Navy No: SSN-717
Launched: April 30, 1983
Commissioned: November 17, 1984
Dimensions: 360 x 33 ft
Displacement: 6,900 tons
Armament: 4 21″ TT, Harpoon
Machinery: Geared Turbines, Reactor
Horsepower/Speed: 35,000/20 (32+) knots
Fate: In Commission

The second LOS ANGELES-class submarine awarded to Newport News on September 15, 1977 was

OLYMPIA (SSN-717). The keel for this, the shipyard's 35th submarine, was laid on March 31, 1981, and she was launched on April 30, 1983. OLYMPIA was christened by Mrs. Dorothy Williams, wife of Chief of Naval Material Adm. John G. Williams. Both Adm. and Mrs. Williams were natives of the state of Washington and the ceremony was a colorful and patriotic one. OLYMPIA was completed by an enthusiastic team of shipyard workers who called themselves the "O Team" and she was delivered to the Navy in November 1984. She was commissioned at the Norfolk Naval Station on November 17, 1984, and was placed under the command of Capt. William Hughes. OLYMPIA was assigned to the Atlantic Fleet for the duration of her shakedown and PSA period.

HONOLULU
1985

HONOLULU

Hull No: 623
Navy No: SSN-718
Launched: September 24, 1983
Commissioned: July 6, 1985
Dimensions: 360 x 33 ft
Displacement: 6,900 tons
Armament: 4 21" TT, Harpoon
Machinery: Geared Turbines, Reactor
Horsepower/Speed: 35,000/20 (32+) knots
Fate: In Commission

HONOLULU (SSN-718) was the third LOS AN-GELES-class submarine awarded to Newport News on September 15, 1977, and her keel was laid down on November 10, 1981, on the shipway recently vacated by sister ship NORFOLK. HONOLULU was launched on September 24, 1983, and was sponsored by Mrs. Joan B. Clark, wife of the assistant to the President for National Security Affairs. The ceremony, done with Hawaiian flair, was a festive event. After the launching, HONOLULU was moved to her outfitting pier for completion. She was commissioned under the command of Capt. Robert M. Mitchell at the Norfolk Naval Base in ceremonies on July 6, 1985, and was assigned to the Pacific Fleet after her shakedown on the East Coast.

CHICAGO
1986

CHICAGO

Hull No: 625
Navy No: SSN-721
Launched: October 13, 1984
Commissioned: 1986
Dimensions: 360 x 33 ft
Displacement: 6,900 tons
Armament: 4 21" TT, Harpoon, Tomahawk (VLS)
Machinery: Geared Turbines, Reactor
Horsepower/Speed: 35,000/20 (32+) knots
Fate: Under Construction

CHICAGO was the first SSN-688-class submarine fitted with the shipyard-designed Vertical Launch System (VLS) for Tomahawk cruise missiles. Previous ships had been certified to carry Tomahawk as part of their torpedo load, but CHICAGO and later ships carried a full load of torpedoes as well as the cruise missiles. The keel for CHICAGO was laid down on January 5, 1983, and she was readied in record time for launching on a windy October 13, 1984, the 209th birthday of the Navy. Sponsor for CHICAGO was Mrs. Vicky Ann Paisley, wife of the Assistant Secretary of the Navy for Research, Engineering, and Systems. Mrs. Paisley broke the christening bottle on the second swing and sent CHICAGO down the ways to her outfitting berth. The new CHICAGO was scheduled to be commissioned under the command of Cdr. Robert B. Avery in 1986.

Newport News' 14th LOS ANGELES-class submarine, named CHICAGO (SSN-721), was awarded with two others of her class on August 31, 1981.

KEY WEST
1986

OKLAHOMA CITY
1987

KEY WEST
Hull No: 626
Navy No: SSN-722
Launched: July 20, 1985
Commissioned: 1986
Dimensions: 360 x 33 ft
Displacement: 6,900 tons
Armament: 4 21″ TT, Harpoon, Tomahawk (VLS)
Machinery: Geared Turbines, Reactor
Horsepower/Speed: 35,000/20 (35+) knots
Fate: Under Construction

OKLAHOMA CITY
Hull No: 627
Navy No: SSN-723
Launched: November 2, 1985
Commissioned: 1987
Dimensions: 360 x 33 ft
Displacement: 6,900 tons
Armament: 4 21″ TT, Harpoon, Tomahawk (VLS)
Machinery: Geared Turbines, Reactor
Horsepower/Speed: 35,000/20 (35+) knots
Fate: Under Construction

The 15th 688-class attack submarine built at the shipyard was KEY WEST (SSN-722), which was laid down on July 6, 1983. She was the second LOS ANGELES-class submarine to be fitted with the VLS system for Tomahawk cruise missiles and was launched on a sultry July 20, 1985. Sponsor for KEY WEST was Mrs. Virginia Innes-Brown Conn, wife of the Assistant Secretary of the Navy for Financial Management. After 18 months of outfitting and trials, the new KEY WEST was scheduled for commissioning under the command of Cdr. Warren N. Lipscomb, Jr. late in 1986.

Third of the three LOS ANGELES-class attack submarines awarded to Newport News in August 1981 was OKLAHOMA CITY (SSN-723). The keel for the shipyard's 16th 688-class ship was laid on January 4, 1984 and she was readied for launch on November 2, 1985. OKLAHOMA CITY was sponsored by Mrs. Linda Nickles, wife of Sen. Don Nickles of Oklahoma, and was launched to "Oklahoma," played and sung by the shipyard's Centennial Band and Chorus. The new ship was scheduled to be commissioned in 1987 under Cdr. Joseph J. Kroll, Jr. and was to be the first Newport News-built submarine with her VLS system fully operational at delivery.

NEWPORT NEWS
1987

NEWPORT NEWS
Hull No: 628
Navy No: SSN-750
Launched: March 15, 1986
Commissioned: 1987
Dimensions: 360 x 33 ft
Displacement: 6,900 tons
Armament: 4 21″ TT, Harpoon, Tomahawk (VLS)
Machinery: Geared Turbines, Reactor
Horsepower/Speed: 35,000/20 (35+) knots
Fate: Under Construction

Nuclear attack submarine NEWPORT NEWS, the 17th LOS ANGELES-class ship built at the shipyard, was awarded on April 19, 1982. The third Navy ship to be named for the shipbuilding city, NEWPORT NEWS was laid down on March 3, 1984. In a ceremony which anticipated the shipyard's 100th anniversary celebration in 1986, the submarine's keel was authenticated by yard employee Nickey N. Atkins on March 3, 1984. NEWPORT NEWS was one of the last ships ever launched from a sliding shipway at the yard, before introduction of the new land level ship construction facility. She was christened with great ceremony by Mrs. Rosemary Trible on March 15, 1986. The new NEWPORT NEWS was scheduled to be commissioned under the command of Cdr. Mark B. Keef late in 1987.

DESTROYERS
ROE
1910

ROE

Hull No: 115
Navy No: DD-24
Launched: July 24, 1909
Commissioned: September 17, 1910
Dimensions: 294 x 26.33 x 16.08 ft
Displacement: 742 tons
Armament: 4 3"Guns, 6 18" TT
Machinery: Direct Drive Turbines,
    4 Boilers, Triple Screw
Horsepower/Speed: 12,000/29.5 knots
Fate: Scrapped, 1934

The first of a long line of 31 destroyers built at Newport News was ROE, one of three of her class delivered to the Navy in 1910 and 1911. These were the first steam turbine-powered ships built at the yard and their turbines were constructed in the shipyard's shops.

The contract for the first two ships was signed on October 12, 1908, and the keel for ROE was laid on January 18, 1909. Named for RAdm Francis A. Roe of Civil War fame, the new destroyer was on the stocks only six months before she was launched on July 24,

1909. Sponsor for ROE was Mrs. Anne Martin Hall, wife of the inspector of machinery for the Navy at the shipyard.

Notwithstanding the novelty of her direct-drive steam turbine machinery, ROE underwent successful trials on July 16, 1910, and achieved 31 knots on her speed runs, which were three knots more than required.

ROE was commissioned on September 17, 1910, with Lt. C.H. Woodward in command and began a series of exercises in the Atlantic and in the Caribbean, which lasted three years. The still-new destroyer was placed in reserve at Philadelphia in November 1913, then went in and out of reserve over the next three years.

ROE was put back in full commission in March 1917, and later that year she went to France for escort and patrol service. She stayed in Europe for a year, then returned to the U.S. and more reserve status until 1924. In that year she was assigned to the Coast Guard which operated her until 1930 in the famous "Rum War" against liquor smugglers.

ROE was returned to the Navy in October of that year, but she was again laid up. In May 1934 the old destroyer was sold and scrapped in accordance with the London Treaty of 1930.

TERRY
1910

TERRY (DD-25) was the second destroyer built at the shipyard. These early destroyers were known as "torpedo boat destroyers" and their high forecastle, open superstructure, and three tall stacks gave them a distinctive appearance.

TERRY was named for Cdr. Edward Terry of Civil War fame, and her keel was laid down on February 8, 1909. She was six months on the ways before her launching on August 21. TERRY was christened by Mrs. George H. Rock, wife of the naval constructor at the shipyard. The new destroyer was commissioned on October 18, 1910, with LCdr. Martin E. Trench commanding.

For her first few years, TERRY spent her summers in New England waters and her winters in the Caribbean. Based at Charleston, SC, she was in reserve but was occasionally active from 1913 to 1916. In June 1916, TERRY struck a reef while on maneuvers in Haitian waters and sank to her main deck. She was salvaged, repaired at Charleston, and in 1917 engaged in escort duty along the East Coast.

In early 1918, TERRY began operations from Irish ports in convoy escort duty. Her World War I career was uneventful, and she returned to the U.S. in late 1918, only to be decommissioned and laid up at Philadelphia in November 1919.

She was transferred to the Coast Guard in June 1924 and served in their "Rum War" against smugglers during the Prohibition years. The worn out TERRY was returned to the Navy in October 1930, and in May 1934 she was sold for scrap.

MONAGHAN
1911

On June 23, 1909 the shipyard received a contract for its third destroyer, later named MONAGHAN after Ens. John R. Monaghan, who was killed in action in Samoa in 1899. This ship was virtually identical to the ROE-class ships but was sometimes considered the first of her own class of five ships which were authorized in 1909.

The keel for MONAGHAN was laid on May 31, 1910, and her hull construction took almost nine months. She was sponsored by Miss Eleanor R. Monaghan, sister of Ens. Monaghan, and was launched on February 18, 1911. MONAGHAN was completed six months later and was commissioned on June 21, 1911, with LCdr. W.P. Cronan commanding.

The new destroyer and her sisters were among the Navy's first oil fueled ships and MONAGHAN was called "queen of all the oil burners of the Navy" after, according to her crew, she made over 34 knots on trials.

MONAGHAN joined the Atlantic Fleet and engaged in routine operations along the East Coast until she was assigned to troop convoy escort duty at the outbreak of World War I. She was active in European waters during the last year of the war, then returned home to be decommissioned in November 1919.

MONAGHAN lay idle at Philadelphia until she was drafted into the Coast Guard for service in the "Rum War" in 1924. She served in the Atlantic and along the Gulf coast during the 1920s, intercepting and searching some of the hundreds of small vessels which engaged in liquor smuggling during Prohibition. This "war" service was hard on both ships and men, and in 1931 MONAGHAN was declared unfit for further service and was returned to the Navy. Her name was assigned to a new destroyer in 1933, and the tired old MONAGHAN was sold and scrapped in 1934.

FANNING
1912

FANNING

Hull No: 144
Navy No: DD-37
Launched: January 11, 1912
Commissioned: June 21, 1912
Dimensions: 294 x 26.33 x 16.08 ft
Displacement: 742 tons
Armament: 5 3" Guns, 6 18" TT
Machinery: Direct Drive Turbines,
    4 Boilers, Triple Screw
Horsepower/Speed: 12,000/29.5 knots
Fate: Scrapped, 1934

The fourth of the early destroyers built at Newport News was FANNING, named after Lt. Nathaniel Fanning, who was commissioned by John Paul Jones for his heroism during the battle with SERAPIS in 1779. FANNING was similar to the three destroyers previously built at the shipyard but was considered of the PAULDING class of which 13 ships were built in several shipyards. FANNING was the forerunner of the large number of destroyers built at Newport News during World War I as she was provided with a fourth stack and was a "four-piper."

The keel for FANNING was laid down on April 29, 1911, and she was launched on January 11, 1912, by Mrs. Kenneth McAlpine, wife of the navy inspector of machinery at the shipyard. The new destroyer completed trials on May 29 and was commissioned on June 21, 1912, with Lt. W.N. Jeffers in command.

FANNING spent her first few years along the East Coast in training and exercises, then took up escort and submarine search duty as World War I intensified in 1916. In late 1916, she worked with oiler JASON to develop methods for underway refueling.

FANNING was called to war in June 1917 and sailed to Ireland to engage in antisubmarine warfare. Her depth charges damaged the German submarine U-58 in November 1917, and she captured its crew when it sank. She was not able to engage the enemy directly again, but busied herself in escort, patrol, and rescue duty for the duration of the war.

FANNING remained in European waters until March 1918, then returned to the U.S., only to be decommissioned at Philadelphia in November 1919. She also was transferred to the Coast Guard in 1924 and served with them until 1930 when she was returned to the Navy. "Old 37" was then laid up until she was sold for scrap in May 1934.

RADFORD
1918

RADFORD

Hull No: 218
Navy No: DD-120
Launched: April 5, 1918
Commissioned: September 30, 1918
Dimensions: 314.33 x 31 x 20.67 ft
Displacement: 1,207 tons
Armament: 4 4", 2 3" Guns; 12 21" TT
Machinery: Direct Drive Turbines,
    4 Boilers, Twin Screw
Horsepower/Speed: 25,000/33 knots
Fate: Sunk, 1936

The second of the WICKES-class flush-deck destroyers built at Newport News in 1918 and 1919 was RADFORD, which was named after RAdm. William Radford of Mexican War and Civil War fame. The keel for RADFORD was laid down on Shipway 2 on October 2, 1917, and she was launched on April 5, 1918. Sponsor for RADFORD was Miss Mary L. Radford,

and only a brief naming ceremony was held due to wartime conditions at the shipyard.

RADFORD underwent trials on September 26 and was commissioned at Portsmouth on September 30 with LCdr. Arthur S. Carpenter in command. Except for a convoy escort trip to Europe in mid-1919, RADFORD operated along the East Coast and in the Caribbean with Destroyer Force, Atlantic Fleet, during her first year.

She joined Destroyer Force, Pacific Fleet, in August 1919; and, homeported at San Diego, she participated in maneuvers and exercises along the West Coast until she was laid up in June 1922. RADFORD lay at anchor at San Diego until April 1932 when she was slated for conversion as a target towing ship. Unfortunately for her, this conversion was cancelled and she remained in reserve.

Veteran of only a short four years of active service, RADFORD was withdrawn from the reserve fleet in August 1936 and was taken to sea and sunk in accordance with the London Treaty of 1930.

LAMBERTON
1918

HULL 226, ABBOT

LAMBERTON

Hull No: 217
Navy No: DD-119
Launched: March 30, 1918
Commissioned: August 22, 1918
Dimensions: 314.33 x 31 x 20.67 ft
Displacement: 1,207 tons
Armament: 4 4", 2 3" Guns
Machinery: Direct Drive Turbines,
    4 Boilers, Twin Screw
Horsepower/Speed: 25,000/33 knots
Fate: Scrapped, 1947

LAMBERTON (DD-119) was the first of 25 destroyers built at Newport News between 1918 and 1920. The first 11 of these hulls were WICKES-class ships, while the remaining 19 were of the shipyard-led CLEMSON class. These destroyers were sorely needed by the Navy and the shipyard was directed to give their construction priority over all other naval work.

The contract for LAMBERTON and five sister ships was awarded on June 29, 1917, and the keel for the first hull was laid on Shipway 1 on the following October 1. LAMBERTON was named for RAdm. Benjamin P. Lamberton who was Adm. Dewey's chief of staff aboard OLYMPIA at the Battle of Manila Bay. Miss Isabel S. Lamberton, granddaughter of RAdm. Lamberton, was chosen as sponsor, and she christened the destroyer on March 30, 1918.

LAMBERTON completed trials on August 17 and was commissioned five days later, with LCdr. Frank L. Slingluff in command. The new four-piper with her classic flush deck and small enclosed superstructure spent less than a year with the Atlantic Fleet before being transferred to the Pacific. LAMBERTON cruised the West Coast in training and exercises for three years, then was placed in reserve at San Diego in June 1922.

She was placed back in commission in late 1930 and resumed her operations on the West Coast, then was modified as a target towing ship and was reclassified AG-21 in April 1932.

Late in the 1930s LAMBERTON was placed in minesweeping duty and was redesignated DMS-2. She patrolled Hawaiian waters for almost a year after the outbreak of war, then engaged in escort and patrol duty in the Alaskan theatre until mid-1943.

After serving out the war back in target towing service out of San Diego, LAMBERTON was decommissioned in December 1946. Winner of one battle star in World War II, the old destroyer was sold for scrap in May 1947.

MONTGOMERY
1918

MONTGOMERY

Hull No: 219
Navy No: DD-121
Launched: March 23, 1918
Commissioned: July 26, 1918
Dimensions: 314.33 x 31 x 20.67 ft
Displacement: 1,207 tons
Armament: 4 4″, 2 3″ Guns; 12 21″ TT
Machinery: Direct Drive Turbines,
    4 Boilers, Twin Screw
Horsepower/Speed: 25,000/33 knots
Fate: Scrapped, 1946

The third WICKES-class destroyer built at Newport News during World War I was MONTGOMERY (DD-121). This ship was named for RAdm. John B. Montgomery, and it was sponsored by his great-granddaughter, Mrs. Andrew W. Jones, on March 23, 1918. MONTGOMERY was quickly completed and was commissioned on July 26 with LCdr. W.R. Purnell commanding.

The new destroyer was completed too late to see combat but, after shakedown and training, engaged in antisubmarine patrols along the East Coast until mid-1919. In July 1919 she was transferred to the Pacific and operated along the West Coast until she was decommissioned and placed in reserve at San Diego with several of her Newport News-built sisters in 1922.

MONTGOMERY lay at anchor at San Diego until she was converted to a minelayer in 1930 and was recommissioned as DM-17. She served out of Pearl Harbor as a light minelayer for the next six years but was again decommissioned and laid up at San Diego in December 1937.

(Continued on page 333)

BREESE
1918

BREESE

Hull No: 220
Navy No: DD-122
Launched: May 11, 1918
Commissioned: October 23, 1918
Dimensions: 314.33 x 31 x 20.67 ft
Displacement: 1,207 tons
Armament: 4 4″, 2 3″ Guns; 12 21″ TT
Machinery: Direct Drive Turbines,
    4 Boilers, Twin Screw
Horsepower/Speed: 25,000/33 knots
Fate: Scrapped, 1946

BREESE (DD-122) was the fourth of the six WICKES-class torpedo boat destroyers ordered from the shipyard on June 29, 1917. She was named after Capt. Kidder R. Breese, and her keel was laid on Shipway 4 on November 10, 1917. The keel for GAMBLE was laid on the same shipway on the next day, and both were launched on May 11, 1918. Mrs. J. Gilbert McIlvaine, daughter of Capt. Breese, was chosen as sponsor for BREESE.

The destroyer was rapidly completed and underwent trials on October 19, then was commissioned on October 23, with Lt. J.M.B. Smith commanding. Like her sisters, BREESE spent her first year in the Atlantic, then moved to a long career in the Pacific. Like the others, she went out of commission in the 1920s, then was converted as a light minelayer in 1931. She also served out of Pearl Harbor and was laid up in 1937, only to be reactivated in 1939. She was credited with the "splash" of an enemy plane at Pearl Harbor on December 7, 1941, and assisted in the sinking of several midget submarines.

BREESE was very active during the war in the Pacific. Following a collision in August 1942, BREESE had one of her four stacks removed while she was being repaired. After leaving the U.S., she spent 42 months in minelaying activities in the Pacific, and her crew claimed to have laid more mines than any other ship. She was active with her sisters MONTGOMERY, GAMBLE, and RAMSAY in many of the major actions of the Pacific war and won an impressive ten battle stars for her efforts.

After finishing up the war in sweeping activities in the East China Sea, BREESE returned to the West Coast in November 1945. She steamed to New York in December and was decommissioned in January 1946. The busy BREESE was sold the following May and was subsequently scrapped.

GAMBLE
1918

GAMBLE

Hull No: 221
Navy No: DD-123
Launched: May 11, 1918
Commissioned: November 29, 1918
Dimensions: 314.33 x 31 x 20.67 ft
Displacement: 1,207 tons
Armament: 4 4", 2 3" Guns; 12 21" TT
Machinery: Direct Drive Turbines,
    4 Boilers, Twin Screw
Horsepower/Speed: 25,000/33 knots
Fate: War Loss, 1945

Another of the Newport News-built destroyers to become minelayers in the 1930s was GAMBLE (DD-123), which was named for two brothers who were heroes of the War of 1812. The keel for GAMBLE was laid on Shipway 4 alongside that of BREESE on November 11, 1918, and both were launched on May 11, 1918. Miss Evelyn H. Jackson, who was related to Secretary of the Navy Josephus Daniels, was sponsor for GAMBLE.

After sea trials on November 22-24, the destroyer was commissioned on November 29 at Norfolk, with Cdr. H.J. Abbett in command. GAMBLE underwent shakedown and training in the Atlantic for ten months, then joined her sisters at San Diego in August 1919.

She was put in reserve in December of that year, was reactivated in October 1920, then was decommissioned at San Diego in June 1922. Like her sisters, she remained in reserve through the 1920s, then was converted as a minesweeper (DM-15) in 1930. She also was decommissioned between 1937 and 1939, then was in the fighting at Pearl Harbor on December 7, 1941.

GAMBLE was extremely busy during the war and won seven battle stars. In August 1942, she took the enemy submarine I-123 under attack east of Guadalcanal and sank her in a swirl of oil and debris. In May 1943 she, BREESE, and PREBLE laid over 250 mines in the path of the "Tokyo Express" in less than 20 minutes, which later sank three Japanese destroyers. GAMBLE went on to perform minelaying, escort, bombardment, and antisubmarine duties across the Pacific, and in early 1945, found herself supporting the assault on Iwo Jima.

On February 18, her good luck ran out when she was hit by two 250-pound bombs dropped from a Japanese "Betty" and was set afire along her entire length. Miraculously, only six of her crew were killed, eight were injured, and GAMBLE was still floating on the next day. Her smoking hulk was towed to Saipan, and there was some hope that she might be repaired; but this was not to be, and she was sunk off Guam on July 16, 1945.

RAMSAY
1919

RAMSAY

Hull No: 222
Navy No: DD-124
Launched: June 8, 1918
Commissioned: February 15, 1919
Dimensions: 314.33 x 31 x 20.67 ft
Displacement: 1,207 tons
Armament: 4 4", 2 3" Guns; 12 21" TT
Machinery: Direct Drive Turbines,
    4 Boilers, Twin Screw
Horsepower/Speed: 25,000/33 knots
Fate: Scrapped, 1946

Sixth and last of the torpedo boat destroyers ordered by the Navy in June 1917 was RAMSAY (DD-124), which was named for RAdm. Francis M. Ramsay.

The keel for RAMSAY was laid on Shipway 3 on January 20, 1918, and that of HOPEWELL was set alongside a month later. The two ships were both launched on June 8, and RAMSAY was sponsored by RAdm. Ramsay's granddaughter, Miss Mary Virginia Ramsay of Norfolk. The ship completed outfitting and trials in February 1919 and was commissioned on the 15th of that month, with Cdr. H.H. Norton commanding.

The new RAMSAY spent her first six months in the Atlantic, and her duties included service as a weather ship in the Azores for the NC transatlantic flights in May 1919. She transferred to San Diego in August and served with Destroyer Force, Pacific, until she was decommissioned in June 1922.

She stayed in reserve until 1930 when she was converted as a light minelayer and was redesignated DM-16. With MONTGOMERY, BREESE, and GAM-
(Continued on page 333)

HOPEWELL
1919

HOPEWELL

Hull No: 223
Navy No: DD-181
Launched: June 8, 1918
Commissioned: March 22, 1919
Dimensions: 314.33 x 31 x 20.67 ft
Displacement: 1,207 tons
Armament: 4 4", 2 3" Guns; 12 21" TT
Machinery: Geared Turbines, 4 Boilers,
    Twin Screw
Horsepower/Speed: 26,000/35 knots
Fate: War Loss, 1941

Just three days before the first keel was laid for the first of the shipyard's World War I destroyers, LAMBERTON, the Navy awarded five more similar ships of the WICKES class to Newport News. The first of the second group was HOPEWELL—named, not for the Virginia city, but for Midshipman Pollard Hopewell, who was lost with the frigate CHESAPEAKE in 1813.

The keel for HOPEWELL was laid down on Shipway 3 on January 19, 1918, alongside RAMSAY, then under construction, and the two destroyers were both launched on the following June 8. Mrs. Grote M. Hutcheson of Newport News was appointed by the shipyard to sponsor HOPEWELL. After commissioning at Portsmouth on March 22, 1919, HOPEWELL served in the Atlantic under the command of LCdr. R.E. Rogers and in May 1919 was an observation ship for the NC transatlantic flights.

She spent her first few years in the Atlantic in training and maneuvers, then was decommissioned and laid up at Philadelphia in July 1922. She lay at anchor there for almost 18 years until she was recommissioned in June 1940. HOPEWELL served with the Neutrality Patrol in the Atlantic for only three months before she was transferred to the Royal Navy in the "destroyers-for-bases" transfer of 50 old destroyers to Britain.

In October 1940 she was commissioned HMS BATH, and in March 1941 she was transferred to the Royal Norwegian Navy. A month later she helped destroy a fish oil factory in occupied Norway, which was being used to manufacture explosives for the German war effort.

Engaged in convoy duty, she was torpedoed amidships while enroute to West Africa on August 19, 1941. Her back was broken by the attack, and she sank in only three minutes, carrying 86 of her crew of 128 down with her.

THOMAS
1919

THOMAS

Hull No: 224
Navy No: DD-182
Launched: July 4, 1918
Commissioned: April 25, 1919
Dimensions: 314.33 x 31 x 20.67 ft
Displacement: 1,207 tons
Armament: 4 4", 1 3" Guns; 12 21" TT
Machinery: Geared Turbines, 4 Boilers,
    Twin Screw
Horsepower/Speed: 26,000/35 knots
Fate: Scrapped, 1949

Destroyer THOMAS rounded out the first dozen of her type built at Newport News. She was named after Lt. Clarence C. Thomas, the first U.S. naval officer to lose his life in the World War, and her keel was laid on Shipway 2 on March 23, 1918.

THOMAS was launched on "Liberty Launching Day", July 4, 1918, along with sister ships HARADEN and ABBOT, and it was a gala event which contrasted with other wartime launchings at the shipyard. THOMAS was the first to go down the ways, and she was christened by Mrs. Evelyn M. Thomas, young widow of Lt. Thomas.

After her commissioning on April 25, 1919, THOMAS operated along the East Coast under the command of LCdr. Harry A. McLure, then was decommissioned and placed in reserve at Philadelphia in June 1922. Like her previous sister, THOMAS lay in "Red Lead Row" for 18 years before she was recommissioned in June 1940.

Also like her sister, she was transferred to Britain three months later, and she was renamed HMS ST. ALBANS for service with the Royal Navy. She and three of her Newport News-built sisters were placed in

(Continued on page 333)

HARADEN
1919

HARADEN

Hull No: 225
Navy No: DD-183
Launched: July 4, 1918
Commissioned: June 7, 1919
Dimensions: 314.33 x 31 x 20.67 ft
Displacement: 1,207 tons
Armament: 4 4" Guns; 4 21" TT
Machinery: Geared Turbines, 4 Boilers,
    Twin Screw
Horsepower/Speed: 26,000/35 knots
Fate: Scrapped, 1945

Ninth in the destroyer-building program at Newport News during World War I was HARADEN (DD-183), named for Capt. Johnathan Haraden, naval hero of the Revolutionary War. The keel for HARADEN was laid down on Shipway 1 on March 30, 1918, and she was launched on "Liberty Launching Day," July 4, with THOMAS and ABBOTT. Other shipyards around the country also launched ships on this gala day. HARADEN was sponsored by Miss Mabel B. Stephens, a descendant of Capt. Haraden, and keels for three

more destroyers were laid on the shipways within a few days after the multiple launching.

HARADEN was completed and was commissioned at the Norfolk Navy Yard on June 7, 1919, with LCdr. R.H. Booth in command. The new destroyer was immediately sent to Europe and served in the Adriatic Sea for her first four months, after which she operated along the East Coast until she was decommissioned in July 1922. She rusted at Philadelphia with many of her sisters for 17 years before being recommissioned in December 1939.

After a series of training and patrol cruises, HARADEN was transferred to Britain in September 1940 and was assigned to the Canadian Navy and renamed HMCS COLUMBIA. She stayed busy during the war years, serving in convoy escort in the Atlantic between England and the U.S.

After almost four years of escort and antisubmarine duty without mishap, COLUMBIA went aground off the coast of Newfoundland in February 1944 and was heavily damaged. She was only partially repaired and served out the war as a fuel and ammunition hulk in Nova Scotia. She was ultimately returned to the U.S. after the war and was sold for scrap in August 1945.

ABBOT
1919

ABBOT

Hull No: 226
Navy No: DD-184
Launched: July 4, 1918
Commissioned: July 19, 1919
Dimensions: 314.33 x 31 x 20.67 ft
Displacement: 1,207 tons
Armament: 4 4", 2 3" Guns; 12 21" TT
Machinery: Geared Turbines, 4 Boilers,
    Twin Screw
Horsepower/Speed: 26,000/35 knots
Fate: Scrapped, 1945

ABBOT, named for Commodore Joel Abbot, who served in the War of 1812 and commanded frigate MACEDONIAN to Japan in 1852, was the tenth destroyer built at Newport News during World War I. Her keel was laid down on Shipway 2 on April 5, 1918, and she was ready for launch less than three months later.

ABBOT was christened by Miss Louise Abbot Cooke of Pittsburgh, great-granddaughter of Commodore Abbot. The sponsor later organized a group of ladies who knitted 116 pairs of stockings for ABBOT's crewmen. ABBOT was outfitted and completed and underwent trials on July 15, 1919, then was commissioned four days later with LCdr. W.N. Richardson, Jr. commanding.

The new ABBOT followed a career typical of her type at the time and served with the Atlantic Fleet for less than three years before being laid up at Philadelphia in 1922. She was not recommissioned until June 1940 and three months later was transferred to the Royal Navy and was renamed HMS CHARLESTOWN. She laid mines with the 17th British Destroyer Division off the coast of Scotland and saw convoy escort duty in the North Atlantic until late 1944.

In December of that year, she collided with the merchant steamship FLORIZEL off the southeast coast of England and was damaged. She was laid up at Grangemouth, Scotland, after this incident and was subsequently scrapped in 1945.

BAGLEY
1919

BAGLEY

Hull No: 227
Navy No: DD-185
Launched: October 19, 1918
Commissioned: August 27, 1919
Dimensions: 314.33 x 31 x 20.67 ft
Displacement: 1,207 tons
Armament: 4 4", 2 3" Guns; 12 21" TT
Machinery: Geared Turbines, 4 Boilers,
    Twin Screw
Horsepower/Speed: 26,000/35 knots
Fate: Scrapped, 1945

The last ship in the Navy's huge 111-destroyer WICKES class was BAGLEY, whose keel was laid on Shipway 4 at Newport News on May 11, 1918. BAGLEY was named in honor of Ens. Worth Bagley, who was the first American naval officer to lose his life in action during the Spanish-American War. Ens. Bagley's mother served as sponsor for the new destroyer and christened it on October 19, 1918. BAGLEY was completed by the summer of 1919 and was commissioned on August 27 with Cdr. R.L. Walker commanding.

In the mold cast by others of her type, she served with the Atlantic Fleet along the East Coast and in the Caribbean before being laid up at Philadelphia in July 1920. BAGLEY remained in reserve for many years, and her name was given to a new destroyer in 1935. She was renamed DORAN in December 1939 and was reactivated and served with the Atlantic Squadron until she was transferred to the Royal Navy at Halifax in September 1940.

The old destroyer was renamed HMS ST. MARY'S and was placed in mine laying and convoy escort service in the North Atlantic and in British home waters. In August 1941, she collided with the transport ROYAL ULSTERMAN and withdrew for repairs which lasted four months. She continued with the Royal Navy until February 1944, then was laid up on the Tyne in northern England for the duration of the war.

In one account of her wartime service, she was caught in a gale bet ween England and Iceland for 36 hours and plowed ahead, only to lose 50 miles of headway during the storm.

Worn out from her wartime experiences, ST. MARY'S was returned to the U.S. after the end of the Atlantic war and was subsequently scrapped.

CLEMSON
1919

CLEMSON

Hull No: 228
Navy No: DD-186
Launched: September 5, 1918
Commissioned: December 29, 1919
Dimensions: 314.33 x 31 x 20.67 ft
Displacement: 1,277 tons
Armament: 4 4", 3 3" Guns; 12 21" TT
Machinery: Geared Turbines, 4 Boilers,
    Twin Screw
Horsepower/Speed: 27,000/35 knots
Fate: Scrapped, 1946

On February 15, 1918, a contract was awarded to Newport News for the construction of 20 destroyers of the CLEMSON class, 156 of which were ultimately built there and at other shipyards. After the Armistice in November 1919, six of the Newport News ships were cancelled at the suggestion of the shipyard as an economy measure. The ships of the CLEMSON class had more powerful machinery than their predecessors and were capable of a speed of 35 knots. CLEMSON herself was named for Midshipman Henry A. Clemson, who lost his life when SOMERS sank at Vera Cruz in 1846.

The keel for the lead ship of the large class of new destroyers was laid on Shipway 4 alongside that of BAGLEY on May 11, 1918. CLEMSON was christened by Miss Mary C. Daniels, niece of the Secretary of the Navy, and was launched on September 5, 1918. The freighter AGWIDALE was launched at the shipyard on the same day, and the informal ceremonies were typical of those in wartime Newport News.

CLEMSON was completed and underwent trials on November 11, 1919, then was commissioned on December 29 under the command of LCdr. G.C. Dichman. She was active along the East Coast and around Cuba until she was decommissioned at Philadelphia in June 1922. In November 1939 CLEMSON was reclassified as AVP-17 and was converted for service as an aircraft tender.

She was reclassified again as AVD-4 in August
(Continued on page 333)

DAHLGREN
1920

> ### DAHLGREN
> Hull No: 229
> Navy No: DD-187
> Launched: November 20, 1918
> Commissioned: January 6, 1920
> Dimensions: 314.33 x 31 x 20.67 ft
> Displacement: 1,277 tons
> Armament: 4 4", 3 3" Guns; 12 21" TT
> Machinery: Geared Turbines, 4 Boilers,
>   Twin Screw
> Horsepower/Speed: 27,000/35 knots
> Fate: Scrapped, 1946

Second of the CLEMSON-class destroyers built at Newport News was DAHLGREN, named after the famous RAdm. John A. Dahlgren, who greatly advanced the science of naval ordnance. DAHLGREN's keel and that of GOLDSBOROUGH were laid on Shipway 3 on June 8, 1918, and both ships were launched on November 20 of that year. Mrs. Josiah Pierce, daughter of RAdm. Dahlgren, was chosen as sponsor for DAHLGREN, and the ship was launched in a simple wartime ceremony.

DAHLGREN completed trials on December 30, 1919, and was commissioned on January 6, 1920, with Cdr. L. Sahm commanding. She served with the Atlantic Fleet along the East Coast and in the Gulf of Mexico for over two years before she was laid up at Philadelphia in June 1922.

Ten years later she was recommissioned and sent to the West Coast where, except for a brief period in 1934, she was based until July 1937. Two of her boilers were replaced by units operating at 1,300 PSI and 910°F, and she became an experimental engineering ship for the next two years.

She later tested variable-pitch propellers and saw occasional escort duty before being assigned to the Gulf Sea Frontier at Key West to serve with SEMMES in the development of antisubmarine warfare. She often also made patrols and in July 1942 she rescued 57 survivors of the torpedoed PENNSYLVANIA SUN.

In March 1945, DAHLGREN was reclassified as a miscellaneous auxiliary and was redesignated as AG-91. She served out the war at the Mine Warfare Test Station at Solomon's Island, MD, then was ordered to the Navy Yard at Philadelphia for decommissioning in November 1945. The hard-working DAHLGREN remained at Philadelphia until she was sold for scrapping in June 1946.

GOLDSBOROUGH
1920

> ### GOLDSBOROUGH
> Hull No: 230
> Navy No: DD-188
> Launched: November 20, 1918
> Commissioned: January 26, 1920
> Dimensions: 314.33 x 31 x 20.67 ft
> Displacement: 1,277 tons
> Armament: 4 4", 1 3" Guns; 12 21" TT
> Machinery: Geared Turbines, 4 Boilers,
>   Twin Screw
> Horsepower/Speed: 27,000/35 knots
> Fate: Scrapped, 1946

The shipyard's third CLEMSON-class destroyer built during World War I was GOLDSBOROUGH (DD-188), which was named in memory of RAdm. Louis M. Goldsborough, commander of the North Atlantic Blockading Squadron during the Civil War.

The keel for GOLDSBOROUGH was laid on Shipway 3 with that of DAHLGREN on June 8, 1918, and the two destroyers were both launched on November 20. Miss Lucetta P. Goldsborough, niece of RAdm. Goldsborough, served as sponsor for GOLDSBOROUGH, and the destroyer was completed and was commissioned on January 26, 1920, with Cdr. F.M. Robinson commanding.

GOLDSBOROUGH served the Atlantic Fleet along the East Coast and in the Caribbean until she was decommissioned and laid up at Philadelphia in July 1922. She lay in waiting until she was redesignated AVP-18 in November 1939, then was converted as a seaplane tender destroyer designated AVD-5 in August 1940. GOLDSBOROUGH served again with the Atlantic Fleet, steaming as far as Iceland and Greenland in her duties until being transferred to the Pacific in late 1941.

After serving in the Galapagos Islands, she transferred to the Caribbean area and did duty tending aircraft and escorting convoys until November 1943.

(Continued on page 333)

MONTGOMERY *Continued from page 327*

Following a truly checkerboard career, MONT-GOMERY reactivated in late 1939 and, after a year on the West Coast, returned to Pearl Harbor. She was there on December 7, 1941, and after the attack she engaged in antisubmarine sweeps and convoy escort duty.

MONTGOMERY was active during the Solomons campaign and in late 1942 made a two-month sortie to Alaska to lay mines in the Aleutians. She was in collision with another minelayer at Guadalcanal in August 1943, and her bow was damaged, then repaired on the West Coast.

During the remainder of the war, MONTGOMERY was active across the Pacific and won four battle stars for her exploits. In October 1944 she was herself struck by a floating mine while at anchor in the Carolines, and her machinery spaces were flooded, and four of her crew were killed. She limped to the West Coast in February 1945, but the decision was made to retire her. In March 1946 the veteran MONTGOMERY was sold and scrapped after almost three decades with the Navy.

RAMSAY *Continued from page 328*

BLE, she made up Mine Division Two and was homeported at Pearl Harbor.

RAMSAY was decommissioned with the other ships from 1937 to 1939, then with them returned to Hawaiian waters. She sortied from Pearl Harbor just two hours after the Japanese attack and possibly sank a midget submarine.

She spent the early months of the war in escort and antisubmarine duty in Hawaiian waters, then sailed westward in February 1942. RAMSAY engaged in minelaying activities in the central Pacific and occasionally saw escort service until September 1942 when she transferred to the Aleutians. She underwent repairs on the West Coast at the end of 1942, then returned to Alaskan waters until September 1943. She stayed with the fleet across the Pacific and won three battle stars during the war.

She was reclassified AG-98 in June 1945 and was decommissioned at San Diego in October. The old RAMSAY was ultimately sold for scrap in November 1946.

THOMAS *Continued from page 329*

escort service; then, in April 1941 she too was transferred to Norway.

Soon after joining the Royal Norwegian Navy, ST. ALBANS collided with and sank minesweeper HMS ALBERIC and had to retire for extensive repairs. In June she recovered survivors from the torpedoed EMPIRE DEW, and two months later she helped sink German submarine U-401. ST. ALBANS was damaged in a gale in October, but she proved seaworthy and survived.

She remained in escort and antisubmarine duty for the next two years before being laid up in British waters in January 1944. Her career was not over, however, for she was transferred to the Soviet Navy in July and, renamed DOSTOINYI ("Worthy"), served Russia until she was handed back to Britain in February 1949. Veteran of service with four navies, the old destroyer was scrapped soon afterward.

CLEMSON *Continued from page 331*

1940 and for the next three years served with the Atlantic Fleet in the Caribbean and in Brazilian waters. In mid-1943 CLEMSON was converted back to a destroyer and again became DD-186. She served in a group with BOGUE (CVE-9) for six months and assisted in sinking eight German submarines, then was in escort duty to North Africa.

In March 1944 she was again converted, this time to a high speed transport, and was reclassified APD-31. Continuing her varied career, she served in the Pacific as mother ship for UDT Team 6, which cleared many beaches before the invasions of Allied troops.

At war's end, she was in the midst of still another conversion, back to DD-186, when work was stopped and she was decommissioned. Winner of nine battle stars for her action and sharing the Presidential Unit Citation for her duty with BOGUE, the weary CLEMSON was sold for scrap in November 1946.

GOLDSBOROUGH *Continued from page 332*

At that time she reverted to a destroyer and regained her old number for service with the task force built around CORE (CVE-13).

After several Atlantic patrols, GOLDSBOROUGH was converted as a high speed transport and was redesignated APD-32 in March 1944. She transferred to the war in the Pacific and operated in transport, escort, and bombardment service until the end of hostilities, winning five battle stars for her efforts.

Except for being hit in her forward stack by an enemy shell at Leyte Gulf in October 1944, GOLDS-BOROUGH escaped damage in the war and survived to return to the West Coast in July 1945. She was redesignated DD-188 at San Diego but was decommissioned in October. In November 1946, GOLDSBOROUGH was sold, and she was subsequently scrapped at New York.

SEMMES
1920

SEMMES
Hull No: 231
Navy No: DD-189
Launched: December 21, 1918
Commissioned: February 21, 1920
Dimensions: 314.33 x 31 x 20.67 ft
Displacement: 1,277 tons
Armament: 5 4″, 1 3″ Guns; 12 21″ TT
Machinery: Geared Turbines, 4 Boilers, Twin Screw
Horsepower/Speed: 27,000/35 knots
Fate: Scrapped, 1947

The fifteenth ship in the shipyard's World War I destroyer-building program was SEMMES, named after RAdm. Raphael Semmes, CSN, who commanded the James River Squadron in the Civil War. The keel for SEMMES was laid down on Shipway 2 along with that of her sister SATTERLEE on July 10, 1918, and both were launched on December 21, 1918. SEMMES was sponsored by Mrs. John H. Watkins, granddaughter of RAdm. Semmes.

After trials on February 10, 1920, SEMMES was commissioned on February 21 with Cdr. H.H. Norton in command. She operated out of Norfolk with the Atlantic Fleet until she was laid up in April 1922 at Philadelphia, where she remained idle for ten years.

In April 1932 she was commissioned as a Coast Guard destroyer, and she served in that capacity for two years before being converted as an experimental ship. As AG-24, SEMMES tested submarine sound equipment.

During World War II she was active with DAHLGREN with the Gulf Sea Frontier at Key West and performed antisubmarine training missions and patrols along the East Coast. In May 1942 she collided with and sank the British ship SENATEUR DUHAMEL and was withdrawn for major repairs.

After the end of the war in Europe, SEMMES continued her experiments with underwater sound equipment and served the Fleet Sonar School and the Submarine School. In June 1946 she was decommissioned and was once again laid up at Philadelphia. SEMMES was sold the following November and was broken up for scrap at Philadelphia in 1947.

SATTERLEE
1919

SATTERLEE
Hull No: 232
Navy No: DD-190
Launched: December 21, 1918
Commissioned: December 23, 1919
Dimensions: 314.33 x 31 x 20.67 ft
Displacement: 1,277 tons
Armament: 4 4″, 1 3″ Guns; 12 21″ TT
Machinery: Geared Turbines, 4 Boilers, Twin Screw
Horsepower/Speed: 27,000/35 knots
Fate: War Loss, 1942

SATTERLEE, named for Capt. Charles Satterlee, who was lost with the cutter TAMPA (built at Newport News as MIAMI) when she was torpedoed in 1918, was the shipyard's 20th destroyer. The keel for SATTERLEE was laid down on Shipway 2 on July 10, 1918, the same day as those for SEMMES and MASON were laid. SATTERLEE and SEMMES were both launched on December 21, 1918, and Miss Rebecca E. Satterlee sponsored the ship named for her father.

Following completion and trials on December 15-17, 1919, SATTERLEE was placed in commission on December 23 with Cdr. Reed M. Fawell commanding. The new destroyer was active in the Atlantic and Caribbean for over two years until she was laid up at Philadelphia in July 1922. During this time she participated in training and maneuvers and was at the America's Cup races off New York in July 1920. She remained inactive for over 17 years, then was recommissioned and placed in Neutrality Patrol duty in the Caribbean.

In October 1940 SATTERLEE was transferred to Britain and became HMS BELMONT. She was placed in convoy escort duty with the Royal Navy and, except for involvement in a collision in March 1941, her service was uneventful. Her routine was tragically broken on January 31, 1942, when, escorting a troop convoy across the North Atlantic, she was torpedoed and sunk with all hands.

MASON
1920

MASON

Hull No: 233
Navy No: DD-191
Launched: March 5, 1919
Commissioned: February 28, 1920
Dimensions: 314.33 x 31 x 20.67 ft
Displacement: 1,277 tons
Armament: 4 4", 3 3" Guns; 12 21" TT
Machinery: Geared Turbines, 4 Boilers,
    Twin Screw
Horsepower/Speed: 27,000/35 knots
Fate: War Loss, 1941

The keel for MASON, named for John Young Mason who was Secretary of the Navy under Presidents Tyler and Polk, was laid on Shipway 1 on July 10, 1918. MASON was launched by herself on March 5, 1919, and was sponsored by Miss Mary Mason Williams, great-granddaughter of Secretary Mason.

After trials on February 24, MASON was commissioned on February 28, 1920, with Lt. Carl F. Holden commanding. The new destroyer spent an uneventful two years along the eastern seaboard until she was decommissioned and laid up at Philadelphia in July 1922.

MASON was placed back in commission after a wait of 17 years, and resumed her career in December 1939. In October 1940 she was transferred to Britain at Halifax, Nova Scotia, and became HMS BROADWATER. For the rest of 1940 and the first half of 1941, she was in escort service around Africa to the Middle East; then, in June 1941 she was transferred to the Newfoundland Escort Force.

On October 17 she attacked a German submarine which was harassing her North Atlantic convoy, but the next day she herself came under submarine attack. She was torpedoed by U-101 and sank with 42 of her crew on October 18, 1941.

GRAHAM
1920

GRAHAM

Hull No: 234
Navy No: DD-192
Launched: March 22, 1919
Commissioned: March 13, 1920
Dimensions: 314.33 x 31 x 20.67 ft
Displacement: 1,277 tons
Armament: 4 4", 3 3" Guns; 12 21" TT
Machinery: Geared Turbines, 4 Boilers,
    Twin Screw
Horsepower/Speed: 27,000/35 knots
Fate: Scrapped, 1922

GRAHAM (DD-192) had the shortest career of any Newport News-built destroyer. Named after Secretary of the Navy William A. Graham, who organized Perry's Japan expedition of 1853, GRAHAM was the 22nd destroyer built at the shipyard. Her keel was laid on Shipway 4 on September 10, 1919, and she was launched on March 22, 1919, with minimum ceremony. Mrs. Annie Graham Smallwood, granddaughter of Secretary Graham, was appointed by the Navy Department to sponsor GRAHAM. After completion of her trials on March 9, 1920, the destroyer was commissioned on March 13, 1920, with LCdr. Paulus P. Powell commanding.

The proud new GRAHAM was destined for a short career. One of her first assignments was as a moving picture ship for the America's Cup races in July 1920. Then she was assigned to the Atlantic Torpedo Fleet. In this assignment, she conducted exercises and maneuvers along the East Coast and in Caribbean waters. She joined in exercises in 1921 which took her through the Panama Canal to Peru, then in the summer of 1921 took part in bombing tests of captured German warships off the Virginia capes.

In November 1921 her complement was reduced in anticipation of her decommissioning, but she was damaged in collision with the steamer PANAMA off the coast of New Jersey in December and put in to New York for repairs. At a time when many of her contemporaries were being laid up in accordance with the Washington Treaty for the reduction of naval armament, it was decided not to repair GRAHAM. Thus denied a further career and a chance for wartime service, the still-new GRAHAM was sold for scrap in September 1922.

ABEL P. UPSHUR
1920

ABEL P. UPSHUR

Hull No: 235
Navy No: DD-193
Launched: February 14, 1920
Commissioned: November 23, 1920
Dimensions: 314.33 x 31 x 20.67 ft
Displacement: 1,277 tons
Armament: 4 4″, 1 3″ Guns; 12 21″ TT
Machinery: Geared Turbines, 4 Boilers,
    Twin Screw
Horsepower/Speed: 27,000/35 knots
Fate: Scrapped, 1945

ABEL P. UPSHUR, named for the Secretary of the Navy and Secretary of State who was killed in the gun explosion on PRINCETON in 1844, was laid down on Shipway 10 on August 19, 1918. Sister ship HUNT was laid down on the same shipway on that date, and the two destroyers were both launched on February 14, 1920. Mrs. Elizabeth Upshur Benson of Richmond, great-grandniece of Secretary Upshur, served as sponsor for ABEL P. UPSHUR. Trials were held on May 18,

and after a period of inactivity, the new destroyer was commissioned on November 23, 1920, with Lt. V.H. Godfrey in command.

ABEL P. UPSHUR served with the Atlantic Fleet for less than two years before being laid up in August 1922. She trained naval reservists from Washington, D.C., from March 1928 to October 1930. Then she was assigned to the Coast Guard until May 1934.

ABEL P. UPSHUR was laid up for five more years until she was reactivated in December 1939 and joined the Neutrality Patrol.

In September 1940 she and many of her sisters were transferred to Britain in exchange for Atlantic bases and she became HMS CLARE. She served the Royal Navy in convoy escort duty in the Atlantic and Mediterranean for the next four years. In February 1941 CLARE was involved in collision with a merchant vessel and was put out of action until the following October. She participated in the North African and Sicilian landings in 1942 and 1943.

In May 1944 she became an aircraft target ship, and she remained in this service until war's end. Laid up in Scotland in August 1945, CLARE was subsequently moved to England and scrapped.

HUNT
1920

HUNT

Hull No: 236
Navy No: DD-194
Launched: February 14, 1920
Commissioned: September 30, 1920
Dimensions: 314.33 x 31 x 20.67 ft
Displacement: 1,277 tons
Armament: 4 4″, 1 3″ Guns; 12 21″ TT
Machinery: Geared Turbines, 4 Boilers,
    Twin Screw
Horsepower/Speed: 27,000/35 knots
Fate: Scrapped, 1945

With completion of HUNT in 1920, Newport News shipbuilders had two dozen destroyers to their credit. This ship was named in honor of William Henry Hunt who was Secretary of the Navy and ambassador to Russia in the 1880s. The keel for HUNT was laid on Shipway 10 on August 19, 1918, and she was launched with ABEL P. UPSHUR on February 14, 1920. Miss Virginia Livingston Hunt, granddaughter of Secretary Hunt, christened the new destroyer.

HUNT completed trials on June 3 and left the

shipyard five days later, but was not commissioned until September 30, 1920. Under the command of Lt. Roswell H. Blair, HUNT served with the Atlantic Fleet until being decommissioned and laid up at Philadelphia in August 1922. She was reactivated in September 1930 and was operated by the Coast Guard until she was again laid up in May 1934. Like many of her sisters, she was placed back in Navy commission in early 1940 and joined the Neutrality Patrol.

In October 1940 she was transferred to Britain at Halifax and was renamed HMS BROADWAY. Assigned to escort and antisubmarine duty, she helped capture submarine U-101 in May 1940 and sink U-89 in May 1943. During the war her bow carried two "eyes" which her commanding officer had painted on in imitation of oriental junks in search of sea devils. This apparently worked against submarines as well as sea devils and contributed to BROADWAY's success.

In September 1943 the old destroyer became an aircraft target ship, in which service she remained until the end of the war. Just after the German surrender she was dispached to Norway to escort a convoy of her former enemy submarines back to Germany. She was laid up later in 1945 and was subsequently sold for scrap.

WELBORN C. WOOD
1921

WELBORN C. WOOD

Hull No: 237
Navy No: DD-195
Launched: March 6, 1920
Commissioned: January 14, 1921
Dimensions: 314.33 x 31 x 20.67 ft
Displacement: 1,277 tons
Armament: 4 4″, 3 3″ Guns; 12 21″ TT
Machinery: Geared Turbines, 4 Boilers,
   Twin Screw
Horsepower/Speed: 27,000/35 knots
Fate: Scrapped, 1947

WELBORN C. WOOD was the shipyard's 25th destroyer, and the tenth to serve in the Royal Navy in World War II. This ship, designated DD-195, was named in memory of Midshipman Wood, who was killed in action in the Philippines in 1899.

The keel for WELBORN C. WOOD was laid down on Shipway 11 with that of GEORGE E. BADGER on September 24, 1918, and the two destroyers were launched together on March 6, 1920. Miss Virginia Mary Tate of Jasper, GA, was chosen as sponsor of WELBORN C. WOOD. Following trials on June 22, the new ship was inactive until she was commissioned on January 14, 1921, with LtJG. Leon W. Mills commanding.

Typical of many of her sisters, WELBORN C. WOOD served with the Atlantic Fleet until she was laid up with them at Philadelphia in August 1922. She was reactivated in October 1930 and was commissioned as CG-19 for Prohibition enforcement service with the Coast Guard. After the repeal of Prohibition in 1933, WELBORN C. WOOD returned to layup in May 1934.

In September 1939 she was again placed in commission and served in the Neutrality Patrol until she was transferred to Britain in September 1940. Renamed HMS CHESTERFIELD, she got off to an inglorious start by twice colliding with sistership HMS CHURCHILL (ex-HERNDON), but then served routinely in the North Atlantic in convoy escort for much of the war. In another unfortunate incident, she was damaged by her own depth charges while attacking a German submarine and had to retire for repairs for much of 1943.

Late in the war, she joined several of her sisters in duty as an aircraft target ship. Then she was laid up in Scotland in January 1945. The old CHESTERFIELD, veteran of many careers, was finally scrapped in 1947.

GEORGE E. BADGER
1920

GEORGE E. BADGER

Hull No: 238
Navy No: DD-196
Launched: March 6, 1920
Commissioned: July 28, 1920
Dimensions: 314.33 x 31 x 20.67 ft
Displacement: 1,277 tons
Armament: 4 4″, 3 3″ Guns; 12 21″ TT
Machinery: Geared Turbines, 4 Boilers,
   Twin Screw
Horsepower/Speed: 27,000/35 knots
Fate: Scrapped, 1946

GEORGE E. BADGER, designated DD-196, was named after Secretary of the Navy and later Sen. Badger of North Carolina. The keel for this ship was laid with that of WELBORN C. WOOD on September 24, 1918, and the two destroyers were launched from Shipway 11 on March 6, 1920. Sponsored by Miss Mary Badger Wilson, granddaughter of Secretary Badger, the ship glided into the James at 10:30 A.M. on that date.

GEORGE E. BADGER completed trials and left the shipyard on July 21, 1920. She was commissioned on July 28 under the command of LCdr. Albert G. Berry, Jr. and began service with the Atlantic Fleet which lasted less than a year.

She was laid up at Philadelphia in June 1921, recommissioned for Coast Guard service in October 1930, and returned to layup in May 1934.

Redesignated AVP-16 in October 1939, GEORGE E. BADGER recommissioned in January 1940 as a small seaplane tender, then was redesignated AVD-3 in August 1940 for service as a seaplane tender destroyer. She tended seaplanes in Icelandic and Newfoundland waters until early 1942, then served in escort duty in the Atlantic through June 1943.

She joined with BOGUE (CVE-9) and her sister destroyer CLEMSON in a hunter-killer task group in
(Continued on page 339)

BRANCH
1920

BRANCH

Hull No: 239
Navy No: DD-197
Launched: April 19, 1919
Commissioned: July 26, 1920
Dimensions: 314.33 x 31 x 20.67 ft
Displacement: 1,277 tons
Armament: 4 4″, 1 3″ Guns; 12 21″ TT
Machinery: Geared Turbines, 4 Boilers,
    Twin Screw
Horsepower/Speed: 27,000/35 knots
Fate: War Loss, 1943

BRANCH (DD-197) was named after John Branch, who was first a U.S. senator, then was Secretary of the Navy from 1829 to 1831. The keel for this destroyer was laid down on Shipway 4 on October 28, 1918, and she was launched on April 19, 1919. BRANCH was sponsored by Miss Laurie O'Brien Branch, grandniece of Secretary Branch.

During trials on March 30, 1920, BRANCH attained the speed of 36.24 knots, making her the fastest of the World War I destroyers built at Newport News. She was commissioned on July 26, 1920, and joined the Atlantic Fleet with Cdr. F.H. Roberts in command.

Just a year later, she was operating in reduced commission with a partial crew; then, she was laid up at Philadelphia in August 1922. BRANCH lay at anchor for over 17 years until her recommissioning in December 1939 and assignment to the Neutrality Patrol.

She was transferred to Britain at Halifax in October 1940 and was renamed HMS BEVERLEY for service with the Royal Navy. BEVERLEY was assigned to convoy escort duty in the Atlantic and on the northern route to Russia. She was involved in battle with several enemy submarines in February 1943 but was not damaged.

Her luck ran out in April of the same year. Escorting a convoy of 49 ships across the Atlantic in a heavy fog, she collided with one of them and lost use of her degaussing and antisubmarine warfare systems. On April 11, BEVERLEY was torpedoed by a U-boat in the North Atlantic east of Newfoundland. Hit by two enemy torpedoes, she sank almost instantly, taking 139 of her crew with her.

HERNDON
1920

HERNDON

Hull No: 240
Navy No: DD-198
Launched: May 31, 1919
Commissioned: September 14, 1920
Dimensions: 314.33 x 31 x 20.67 ft
Displacement: 1,277 tons
Armament: 4 4″, 3 3″ Guns; 12 21″ TT
Machinery: Geared Turbines, 4 Boilers,
    Twin Screw
Horsepower/Speed: 27,000/35 knots
Fate: War Loss, 1945

HERNDON, penultimate destroyer built at Newport News during World War I, was laid down on Shipway 3 along with DALLAS on November 25, 1918. She was named in memory of Navy explorer and hero Cdr. William L. Herndon.

HERNDON and DALLAS were both launched on May 31, 1919, and Miss Lucy Taylor Herndon christened the destroyer named for her uncle. Both ships were completed in April 1920, and HERNDON was commissioned at Norfolk on the following September 14 after a period of inactivity.

She was placed under the command of LCdr. L.H. Thebaud and served in reserve training duty until she was laid up at Philadelphia in June 1922. HERNDON was in service with the Coast Guard from 1930 until 1934 in their "Rum War" against smugglers, then was laid up for five more years.

In December 1939 she was recommissioned and joined the Neutrality Patrol in the Caribbean. In September 1940, less than a week before her 20th birthday, HERNDON was transferred to the Royal Navy and was renamed HMS CHURCHILL. She served in convoy escort and antisubmarine duty and was visited by Winston Churchill in August 1941.

CHURCHILL enjoyed an active career under several flags during the war and participated in the invasion of North Africa. In November 1942 she was transferred to the Royal Canadian Navy, and in May 1944 she went into the service of the Russian Navy. Renamed DELATELNYI ("Active"), she was escorting a convoy into the White Sea when she was torpedoed and sunk by a U-boat on January 16, 1945.

DALLAS
1920

<table>
<tr><td colspan="2">DALLAS</td></tr>
<tr><td>Hull No:</td><td>241</td></tr>
<tr><td>Navy No:</td><td>DD-199</td></tr>
<tr><td>Launched:</td><td>May 31, 1919</td></tr>
<tr><td>Commissioned:</td><td>October 29, 1920</td></tr>
<tr><td>Dimensions:</td><td>314.33 x 31 x 20.67 ft</td></tr>
<tr><td>Displacement:</td><td>1,277 tons</td></tr>
<tr><td>Armament:</td><td>4 4" Guns; 4 21" TT</td></tr>
<tr><td>Machinery:</td><td>Geared Turbines, 4 Boilers, Twin Screw</td></tr>
<tr><td>Horsepower/Speed:</td><td>27,000/35 knots</td></tr>
<tr><td>Fate:</td><td>Scrapped, 1945</td></tr>
</table>

The 25th and last flush-deck "four piper" destroyer built at Newport News during World War I was DALLAS (DD-199). This ship was named for Capt. Alexander J. Dallas, who died in 1844 in the sloop VANDALIA; and she was laid down with HERNDON on Shipway 3 on November 25, 1918. Both destroyers were launched on May 31, 1919, and Miss Wathen Dallas Strong, great-granddaughter of Capt. Dallas, was sponsor for DALLAS. As it had been decided not to build six more of these destroyers, shipyard hull numbers 242 through 247 were never used for construction and DALLAS was the last in the series.

After trials on April 27, 1920, DALLAS was placed in commission on October 29 with Lt. E.H. Roach in command. The new destroyer operated out of Charleston, SC, until she was laid up at Philadelphia with her sisters in June 1922.

Unlike the others, she was recommissioned in April 1925 and operated in the Atlantic and Caribbean until 1931. In January 1932 DALLAS transferred to the West Coast for two years. She returned to the East Coast for much of 1934, then served for four more years out of San Diego, sailing as far from home as Hawaii and Alaska for exercises. She returned to Philadelphia in November 1938 and was laid up for only six months before she was put in escort and patrol service with the Atlantic Fleet.

DALLAS had an outstanding wartime career. She spent the early months of the war in escort and anti-submarine duty. Then in October 1942 she fought her way up a river in French Morocco to deliver an Army Raider battalion. For this brave venture, she was awarded the Presidential Unit Citation. She continued her regular duties for a few months, then participated in the invasions of Sicily and the Italian mainland in 1943. DALLAS ended the war on the East Coast in escort service.

Her name was changed to ALEXANDER DALLAS in March 1945 to avoid confusion with that of a cruiser then under construction. Winner of four battle stars and the Presidential Unit Citation for her World War II service, the old destroyer was decommissioned at Philadelphia in July 1945 and was later sold for scrap.

GEORGE E. BADGER *Continued from page 337*

the Atlantic and sank U-613 in the Azores in July. She continued with BOGUE and several other destroyers and helped sink another submarine, U-172, in December 1943.

After several convoy escort trips to North Africa, GEORGE E. BADGER was converted at Norfolk for service as a high-speed transport and was redesignated APD-33 in May 1944. She then sailed to the Pacific to begin another career and arrived at Guadalcanal in August. She screened other ships during bombardments and gathered intelligence at Leyte in October 1944, then went on to serve at Iwo Jima and Okinawa, winning a total of eight battle stars and sharing the Presidential Unit Citation for her extensive wartime service.

She returned to the U.S. in July 1945, was again designated DD-196, then was decommissioned at San Francisco in October. After a few months well-deserved rest, the old GEORGE E. BADGER was sold and scrapped in mid-1946.

MUSTIN
1939

MUSTIN

Hull No: 363
Navy No: DD-413
Launched: December 8, 1938
Commissioned: September 15, 1939
Dimensions: 348.33 x 36 x 19.67 ft
Displacement: 1,960 tons
Armament: 4 5" Guns; 8 21" TT
Machinery: Geared Turbines, 3 Boilers,
    Twin Screw
Horsepower/Speed: 50,000/35 knots
Fate: Sunk, 1948

Over 16 years after the last of the World War I destroyers left Newport News, a contract was awarded for the construction of MUSTIN and RUSSELL, two ships which were destined to distinguish themselves in World War II. This contract was dated October 12, 1936, and the keels for these SIMS-class destroyers were laid down on Shipway 9 on December 20, 1937. MUSTIN was named for Capt. Henry C. Mustin, who was one of the Navy's first aviators. Mrs. Lloyd M. Mustin, daughter-in-law of Capt. Mustin, christened MUSTIN when the two ships were launched on December 8, 1938.

MUSTIN was commissioned on September 15, 1939, with LCdr. James S. Freeman commanding, and was soon assigned to Neutrality Patrol duty in the Atlantic. After war broke out in the Pacific she was placed in convoy escort duty between Hawaii and the West Coast until April 1942.

She missed the battle of Midway but engaged in patrols around Hawaii until August. In that month she sailed into battle with HORNET (CV-8).

In October, when HORNET was fatally damaged during the Battle of Santa Cruz, MUSTIN recovered 337 of her crewmen, then helped sink her with torpedoes. During the battle, MUSTIN had downed five enemy planes. She was in the thick of the fighting during the campaigns in the Gilberts and the Marshalls, then went on to New Guinea, and then Leyte where she downed three more Japanese planes. She was active until late May and won a total of 13 battle stars for her gallantry.

The end of the war found her on the West Coast under repair, but she returned for occupation duty in Japan for the last three months of 1945.

During the summer of 1946 MUSTIN was used as a target in the atomic tests at Bikini, then she was decommissioned there on August 29. She remained in the Marshalls until she was sunk by naval gunfire near Kwajalein on April 18, 1948.

RUSSELL
1939

RUSSELL
Hull No: 364
Navy No: DD-414
Launched: December 8, 1938
Commissioned: November 3, 1939
Dimensions: 348.33 x 36 x 19.67 ft
Displacement: 1,960 tons
Armament: 5 5″ Guns; 8 21″ TT
Machinery: Geared Turbines, 3 Boilers, Twin Screw
Horsepower/Speed: 50,000/35 knots
Fate: Scrapped, 1947

RUSSELL was the last destroyer built at Newport News. Her keel was laid on Shipway 9 alongside that of MUSTIN on December 20, 1937, and the two were launched on December 8, 1938. RUSSELL was named after RAdm. John Henry Russell, who had a distinguished naval career from 1841 to 1886. RUSSELL was sponsored by Mrs. Charles H. Marshall, granddaughter of RAdm. Russell.

After successful sea trials on October 17, 1939, the new destroyer was commissioned on November 3 with LCdr. J.C. Pollock commanding. Like MUSTIN, RUSSELL was considerably larger and more powerful than the destroyers previously built at the shipyard and was armed with 5″ guns.

RUSSELL was also assigned to the Neutrality Patrol, then was sent to the Pacific after the attack on Pearl Harbor. She became Newport News' busiest destroyer, winning 16 battle stars in World War II. RUSSELL was in the fighting at the Battle of the Coral Sea and saved 170 men from LEXINGTON (CV-2), then recovered 492 from YORKTOWN (CV-5) at the Battle of Midway. She seemed destined for rescue service and came to the aid of HORNET (CV-8) at the Battle of the Santa Cruz Islands in October 1942.

After overhaul on the West Coast and patrol duty in the Aleutians in mid-1943, RUSSELL was back in action in the assaults on the Gilberts and the Marshalls, then went on to the Philippines and Okinawa. In December 1945 she joined other destroyers to sink enemy destroyer HINOKI in the Philippines.

RUSSELL was under repair at Seattle when the war in the Pacific came to an end, and on November 15, 1945, she was decommissioned there. Still young but weary from her wartime exploits, RUSSELL was sold for scrap in September 1947.

GUNBOATS & A MONITOR
NASHVILLE
1897

NASHVILLE

Hull No: 7
Navy No: PG-7
Launched: October 19, 1895
Commissioned: August 19, 1897
Dimensions: 233.67 x 38 x 25.08 ft
Armament: 8 4″ Guns
Displacement: 1,364 tons
Machinery: Quadruple Expansion Engines,
     6 Boilers, Twin Screw
Horsepower/Speed: 2,488/16.3 knots
Fate: Scrapped, 1957

One of the most famous of all Newport News ships, NASHVILLE, was said to have fired the first shot of the Spanish-American War. Hull 7 was the first naval ship constructed by the shipyard, although she was delivered after the gunboats WILMINGTON and HELENA which were ordered later.

With great ceremony, NASHVILLE was launched by Miss Maria Guild on October 19, 1895. WILMINGTON followed her down the same shipway later on the same day. NASHVILLE was commissioned on August 19, 1897, with Cdr. Washburn Maynard commanding.

In the spring of 1898, the new gunboat was stationed at Key West anticipating the outbreak of war with Spain. On April 22, with a large American naval force, she set out to blockade Cuba. That same day she fired three shots across the bow of the Spanish steamer BUENA VENTURA, which stopped and hauled down her colors and was captured. For the rest of the war, NASHVILLE stayed in blockade duty and captured three more ships.

She served in the Philippines and China in 1900 and 1901, then moved to the Mediterranean for a year. She served in the Caribbean and spent four years out of commission between 1901 and 1909. From 1909 to 1911 she was in militia training duty on the Great Lakes at Chicago. She was extensively overhauled in 1911 and then served in the Gulf and Caribbean until 1917.

During the early years of World War I, she was assigned to European submarine patrol and convoy escort duty. She was decommissioned on October 29, 1918, and was later sold to the Richmond Cedar Works and cut down to a barge. She was renamed RICHMOND CEDAR WORKS NO. 4 and served her new owner until 1954 when she was taken out of service. In 1957 she was sold for scrap.

WILMINGTON
1897

WILMINGTON

Hull No: 8
Navy No: PG-8
Launched: October 19, 1895
Commissioned: May 13, 1897
Dimensions: 251.82 x 40.11 x 17.67 ft
Armament: 8 4″ Guns
Displacement: 1,342 tons
Machinery: Triple Expansion Engines,
　　6 Boilers, Twin Screw
Horsepower/Speed: 1,600/15.08 knots
Fate: Sunk, 1947

On her way to an epic career, WILMINGTON was christened by Miss Anne B. Gray shortly after the launch of NASHVILLE on October 19, 1895. Slightly larger than NASHVILLE, WILMINGTON had a single tall funnel. Commissioned on May 13, 1897, under Cdr. Chapman C. Todd, she joined the North Atlantic Squadron, then was sent south for Cuban blockade duty. During the war with Spain she captured several vessels, cut a submarine cable, and participated in a spectacular attack with HELENA and two other ships on the harbor and shipping at Manzanillo, Cuba.

After the war, WILMINGTON embarked on a goodwill tour of South American ports and made a 4,600 mile round trip on the Amazon. On October 16, 1900, she departed Brazil for the Far East via Suez.

She spent many years on patrol and "flag-showing" duties in waters around China and the Philippines until 1922 when she returned to the U.S. for service as a training ship on the Great Lakes, operating out of Toledo. She remained on the Lakes in spring and summer training cruise duty through the 1920s and 1930s.

She was renamed DOVER in 1941, and in 1942 a 5″ gun was fitted forward. She served in Canadian and New England waters until early 1943 when she was sent south for duty as an armed guard training ship. She remained in that service until the end of the war, then was decommissioned on December 20, 1945.

At the time of her decommissioning, this well-traveled veteran was the oldest ship in full commission in the Navy. On December 30, 1946, she was sold to a San Francisco scrapper. She was partially scrapped there; then, in early 1947 her hulk was used to lift a sunken vessel and both were sunk in deep water, ending service which spanned three wars and five decades.

HELENA
1897

HELENA

Hull No: 9
Navy No: PG-9
Launched: January 30, 1896
Commissioned: July 8, 1897
Dimensions: 251.82 x 40.11 x 17.67 ft
Armament: 4 4", 1 3" Guns
Displacement: 1,342 tons
Machinery: Triple Expansion Engines,
    6 Boilers, Twin Screw
Horsepower/Speed: 1,600/15.5 knots
Fate: Scrapped, 1934

Sister of WILMINGTON and last of the series of three gunboats for the Navy, HELENA—under the command of Cdr. W.T. Swinburne—was launched by Miss Agnes Bell Steele on January 30, 1896, and was commissioned on July 8, 1897.

After brief service in the North Atlantic, she took up blockade duty around Cuba. During the Spanish-American War, she exchanged fire with the enemy batteries at Fort Tunas; and, with WILMINGTON, she attacked Manzanillo and destroyed shipping there.

In November 1898 she sailed for Manila via Suez to aid in suppressing the Philippine Insurrection, arriving in February 1899. She participated in troop movements and bombardment in Philippine waters until the end of the trouble there.

She served in Chinese waters from October 1900 until December 1902. She was placed out of commission for a short time but spent most of the next thirty years serving in the Yangtze River and South China patrol. On May 27, 1932, the old gunboat was decommissioned and struck from the Navy list and on July 7, 1934, she was sold for scrap.

ARKANSAS
1902

ARKANSAS

Hull No: 26
Navy No: BM-7
Launched: November 10, 1900
Commissioned: October 28, 1902
Dimensions: 255.08 x 50 x 15 ft
Armament: 2 12″, 4″ Guns
Displacement: 3,180 tons
Machinery: Triple Expansion Engines,
    4 Boilers, Twin Screw
Horsepower/Speed: 1,717/12 knots
Fate: Scrapped, 1922

ARKANSAS was the only monitor ever built at Newport News. She was ordered shortly after the sinking of MAINE, and three similar monitors were built simultaneously in other yards. ARKANSAS was the lead vessel in this series, all of which were intended for coastal defense. She was christened by Miss B.N. Jones on November 10, 1900, and was placed in commission on October 28, 1902, with Cdr. C.E. Vreeland commanding.

Known as "New Navy" monitors, the ARKANSAS class had a single turret, aft of which was a superstructure, mast, and a tall funnel. They were armed with two 12″ guns and assorted 4″ and 6-pounders and the development and installation of an electric turning gear for ARKANSAS' turret was an historic development.

The new monitor served as an instruction and cruise ship for the U.S. Naval Academy with occasional duty with the Coast Service along the East and Gulf Coasts.

In March 1909 she was renamed OZARK and reassigned to the D.C. Naval Militia until March 1913. Late in that year she was converted to a submarine tender and served with the Atlantic Fleet and in the Chesapeake Bay into 1916. In 1917 she cruised off the Mexican coast aiding in the protection of shipping, and in 1918 continued in the Caribbean area.

She returned to Norfolk in 1919 and was decommissioned at Philadelphia in August of that year. She was sold for scrap in January 1922.

AMPHIBIOUS SHIPS
EASTWAY
1943

EASTWAY

Hull No: 401
Navy No: LSD-9
Launched: May 21, 1943
Commissioned: September 14, 1943
Dimensions: 457.75 x 72 x 37 ft
Displacement: 7,498 tons
Armament: 1 5″ Gun
Machinery: Geared Turbines, 2 Boilers,
    Twin Screw
Horsepower/Speed: 7,000/17 knots
Fate: Scrapped, 1972

During World War II the shipyard built 11 dock landing ships (LSDs) for the Navy. These ships were designed to provide docking facilities for landing craft and were also employed to carry the craft into combat. They were provided with huge wells and stern gates for their mission and were invaluable during the war. The first Newport News-built LSDs were delivered to the British government as soon as they were completed.

The keel for the first of these was laid down on November 23, 1942. Originally to be named HMS BATTLEAXE, this ship was christened as EASTWAY (LSD-9) at her launch on May 21, 1943. Sponsor for EASTWAY was Mrs. W.W. Field, daughter of Gen. J.R. Kilpatrick. The LSD was completed and was transferred to the Royal Navy under lend-lease on September 14, 1943.

Later commissioned as HMS EASTWAY (F-130), she served with distinction in the Normandy invasion during the following June and in the landings in Southern France two months later. After this, EASTWAY served in British waters transporting equipment and troops across the English Channel.

Her wartime missions completed, EASTWAY was returned to the U.S. Navy in 1947 and was laid up. Declared surplus with many other ships after the war, she was sold to the Greek government in May 1947 and was converted for merchant service. As HYPERION she served in civilian status until 1955 when she once again became a naval vessel.

Renamed NAFKRATOUSSA (L-153), she was in naval service with Greece until she was replaced by ex-FORT MANDAN (LSD-21) in 1971. A year later the old veteran LSD was sold and scrapped.

HIGHWAY
1943

HIGHWAY

Hull No: 402
Navy No: LSD-10
Launched: July 19, 1943
Commissioned: October 19, 1943
Dimensions: 457.75 x 72 x 37 ft
Displacement: 7,498 tons
Armament: 1 5″ Gun
Machinery: Geared Turbines, 2 Boilers,
   Twin Screw
Horsepower/Speed: 7,000/17 knots
Fate: Scrapped, 1960

The second LSD built at Newport News during World War II was HIGHWAY (LSD-10). The keel for this ship was laid with that of EASTWAY on November 23, 1942. HIGHWAY was launched on July 19, 1943, and was christened by Mrs. R.M. Challoner, Jr.

Originally named CLAYMORE, HIGHWAY was transferred to the Royal Navy at her completion on October 19, 1943, and was commissioned as HMS HIGHWAY (F-140). After commissioning, HIGHWAY and her British crew steamed to the Far East and served with the East Indies Fleet until March 1944. They then joined the Mediterranean Fleet and participated in the landings on southern France in August. HIGHWAY and her men later returned to the Far East and served there until the end of the war.

In April 1946 HIGHWAY was returned to the U.S. Navy at Norfolk, then was laid up. She was sold to Atlas Metals Corp. in 1948; then, in 1953 she went to the Suwannee Steamship Co. and was converted and placed into merchant service as a car ferry.

Renamed ANTONIO MACEO, she sailed under the Honduran flag between American and Cuban ports, carrying loaded railroad cars and general cargo.

In 1957 she passed to TMT Trailer Ferry, Inc. and became the American-flag TMT FLORIDA QUEEN. The old LSD continued in merchant service with TMT until 1960 when she was sold to be broken up for scrap.

NORTHWAY
1944

NORTHWAY

Hull No: 403
Navy No: LSD-11
Launched: November 18, 1943
Commissioned: February 15, 1944
Dimensions: 457.75 x 72 x 37 ft
Displacement: 7,498 tons
Armament: 1 5″ Gun
Machinery: Geared Turbines, 2 Boilers,
   Twin Screw
Horsepower/Speed: 7,000/17 knots
Fate: Scrapped, 1975

The third LSD built at Newport News during World War II was NORTHWAY (LSD-11), which was laid down on May 24, 1943. This ship, originally named HMS CUTLASS, was launched on November 18, 1943, and was sponsored by Mrs. Tracy C. Miner, Jr., daughter of RAdm. O.L. Cox, supervisor of shipbuilding at the shipyard.

NORTHWAY was completed early in 1944 and left Newport News for service with the Royal Navy on February 15, 1944. Her delivery was timely, as NORTHWAY arrived overseas in time to train and ready herself and her crew for the D-Day invasion in June. After the landings on Normandy, she busied herself by ferrying men and material across the English Channel until the end of the war.

NORTHWAY and her British crew arrived back in Newport News on December 14, 1946, and she was returned to the custody of the U.S. government. She was decommissioned and was placed in reserve, but in 1953 was sold to the Suwannee Steamship Co. with her sister HIGHWAY and was converted to the car ferry JOSE MARTI. She made only one trip for this owner, then was laid up at Jacksonville, FL, for two more years.

In mid-1955 she was sold to the West India Fruit & Steamship Co. and was extensively converted at the shipyard to become the automobile, car, and passenger ferry CITY OF HAVANA. She was fitted out to carry 500 passengers and 100 automobiles and, under the Liberian flag, began service between Florida ports and Havana in January 1956.

She continued in service until 1962 when she was sold to the West German Navy for use as a depot ship. Designated WS-1, she served in this capacity until she was sold to Greek mercantile interests in 1966, then was reconverted for further as a car ferry.

She was sold to the Atlantic Steam Navigation Co. of London and took up coasting service between Britain, Brest, and the River Elbe. Renamed CELTIC FERRY, she remained in the service until she was scrapped in 1975.

OCEANWAY
1944

OCEANWAY

Hull No: 404
Navy No: LSD-12
Launched: December 29, 1943
Commissioned: March 29, 1944
Dimensions: 457.75 x 72 x 37 ft
Displacement: 7,498 tons
Armament: 1 5" Gun
Machinery: Geared Turbines, 2 Boilers,
    Twin Screw
Horsepower/Speed: 7,000/17 knots
Fate: Sunk, 1969

The fourth and last LSD built at Newport News and transferred to Great Britain under Lend-Lease was OCEANWAY (LSD-12). The keel for this ship was laid on July 23, 1943, and launching took place on December 29, 1943. OCEANWAY, originally named HMS DAGGER, was christened by Mrs. Herman T. Gordy, secretary to RAdm. O.L. Cox.

The new HMS OCEANWAY (F-143) left the shipyard on March 29, 1944, and steamed to join the Normandy invasion fleet. During the landings in June, she was with other British ships under the command of RAdm. John W. Hall, Jr. and landed men and supplies on Omaha Beach.

Like her sisters, OCEANWAY served in British home waters and ferried troops and supplies to France until the end of the war. She was returned to the U.S. Navy in February 1947 and was placed in reserve.

Later that year, she was sold to the government of Greece and was converted for merchant service. As OKEANOS, she served Greek interests until 1952 when she was sold back to the Navy.

Converted back to an amphibious ship, she was transferred to the French Navy in May 1952 and became FOUDRE (A-646). She was later reclassified L-9020, but in 1966 she was replaced by a new French-built LSD. Decommissioned in December 1968, the old LSD was sunk as a target off Toulon by U.S. and French warships during the following year.

CASA GRANDE
1944

CASA GRANDE

Hull No: 405
Navy No: LSD-13
Launched: April 11, 1944
Commissioned: June 5, 1944
Dimensions: 457.75 x 72 x 37 ft
Displacement: 7,498 tons
Armament: 1 5" Gun
Machinery: Geared Turbines, 2 Boilers,
    Twin Screw
Horsepower/Speed: 7,000/17 knots
Fate: Laid Up, 1970

CASA GRANDE (LSD-13) was the first of the 12 LSDs built at Newport News to be commissioned in the U.S. Navy instead of going to Britain. Originally intended to be named HMS SPEAR, then HMS PORTWAY, she took her name from the Casa Grande Indian dwelling in Arizona.

CASA GRANDE was laid down on November 23, 1943, and was launched on April 11, 1944. Mrs. Gerard Delapalme, daughter of Adm. LeBreton, served as sponsor for the LSD.

CASA GRANDE was placed in commission on the day before D-Day under the command of LCdr. F.E. Strumm, USNR. She left for the Pacific on July 19 and arrived in time to participate in the assault on Leyte in October. In January 1945 CASA GRANDE was in Lingayen Gulf supporting another invasion and in April was in the action at Okinawa.

After the war, she supported occupation forces in the Pacific, having won three battle stars for her wartime service. CASA GRANDE was decommissioned at Norfolk in October 1946 but was recommissioned there in November 1950. During the 1950s, she engaged in missions to Newfoundland and Greenland and trained in the Caribbean; then, in the 1960s she served the Sixth Fleet in the Mediterranean.

Homeported at Norfolk, CASA GRANDE remained active until she was decommissioned in 1968 and was placed in the James River Reserve Fleet in 1970. She was withdrawn by the Navy in March 1983 for stripping but was placed back in the reserve fleet in April 1984.

RUSHMORE
1944

RUSHMORE

Hull No: 406
Navy No: LSD-14
Launched: May 10, 1944
Commissioned: July 3, 1944
Dimensions: 457.75 x 72 x 37 ft
Displacement: 7,498 tons
Armament: 1 5″ Gun
Machinery: Geared Turbines, 2 Boilers,
   Twin Screw
Horsepower/Speed: 7,000/17 knots
Fate: Laid Up, 1971

RUSHMORE (LSD-14) was the sixth of her type built at Newport News during World War II. Originally named HMS SWORD, then HMS SWASHWAY, she got her permanent name from the Mount Rushmore Memorial in South Dakota.

RUSHMORE was laid down on December 31, 1943, and was christened on May 10, 1944, by Miss Eleanor Blewett of Newport News, daughter of shipyard official (and later president) W.E. Blewett, Jr.

The new LSD was commissioned on July 3, 1944, and was placed under the command of LCdr. E.A. Jansen, USNR. RUSHMORE departed for the Pacific on August 5 and arrived in time to participate in the amphibious landings at Leyte Gulf during October. She later saw action at Palawan and Mindanao in February and March 1945 and in Borneo in May. She won three battle stars for her efforts, and after the surrender she stayed with the occupation force in Japanese waters.

In August 1946 she was put in reserve at Pascagoula, MS, where she remained until recommissioned in September 1950. She served with the Atlantic fleet and made cruises to the Mediterranean, Arctic, and Caribbean areas.

Based at Little Creek, VA, RUSHMORE continued her career through the 1960s with deployments to the Mediterranean with the Sixth Fleet. After her return from the Mediterranean in April 1970, she was ordered inactivated and she was decommissioned on the following September 30. In February 1971 the veteran RUSHMORE was placed in the James River Reserve Fleet where she remained into the 1980s.

SHADWELL
1944

SHADWELL

Hull No: 407
Navy No: LSD-15
Launched: May 24, 1944
Commissioned: July 24, 1944
Dimensions: 457.75 x 72 x 37 ft
Displacement: 7,498 tons
Armament: 1 5″ Gun
Machinery: Geared Turbines, 2 Boilers,
   Twin Screw
Horsepower/Speed: 7,000/17 knots
Fate: Fire Test Ship, 1985

First named HMS TOMAHAWK, then HMS WATERWAY, LSD-15 was eventually named SHADWELL after the birthplace of Thomas Jefferson in Albermarle County, VA. SHADWELL was the last of the seven LSDs ordered on September 10, 1941, and she was the last of those intended for transfer to Britain but retained.

She was laid down on January 17, 1944, and was launched on May 24, 1944, after christening by Miss Mary Greenman of Arlington, VA. SHADWELL was quickly completed and was commissioned exactly two months later with LCdr. William K. Brooks commanding.

Late in August, SHADWELL sailed for the Pacific and prepared for action in the Luzon invasion planned for January 1945. On January 24, SHADWELL ran into bad luck and was hit by an air-dropped torpedo while steaming in the Philippines. A huge 60-foot hole was blasted in her bottom; she was in desperate condition, but her crew worked through the night and saved her. Amazingly, there were only three casualties and no fatalities, and SHADWELL was able to sail to Puget Sound Navy Yard for repairs.

She returned to the Far East in August and served the occupation forces until her return to the U.S. for inactivation in mid-1946.

SHADWELL was laid up at Orange, TX, until September 1950; then she was recommissioned and joined the Atlantic Fleet. Like others of her class, she served in the western Atlantic and Caribbean during
(Continued on page 358)

CABILDO
1945

CABILDO

Hull No: 448
Navy No: LSD-16
Launched: December 28, 1944
Commissioned: March 15, 1945
Dimensions: 457.75 x 72 x 37 ft
Displacement: 7,498 tons
Armament: 1 5" Gun
Machinery: Geared Turbines, 2 Boilers,
    Twin Screw
Horsepower/Speed: 7,000/17 knots
Fate: Sunk, 1985

CABILDO (LSD-16) was the shipyard's eighth LSD and she was named after the historic old town hall of New Orleans. She was assigned Hull No. 448 since forty numbers had been assigned to cruisers, carriers, LSTs, and destroyer escorts since SHADWELL (Hull 407). CABILDO was ordered with five other LSDs (two were later cancelled) and was laid down on July 24, 1944. She was launched on December 28 of the same year and was sponsored by Miss Anne B. Pendleton, daughter of a shipyard superintendent.

CABILDO was commissioned on March 15, 1945, and was placed under the command of Cdr. E.B. Holdorff. The LSD arrived at Pearl Harbor on June 8, then sailed westward to begin service at Guam and Okinawa. Typical of her type, she provided docking and repair facilities for smaller craft and carried troops and equipment where required. Completed too late to see combat, CABILDO carried on these duties, then served as a receiving and repair ship in Japanese waters until she returned to the U.S. in mid-1946 for decommissioning.

She was recommissioned at San Diego in October 1950 and served in the Korean War, winning two battle stars for her efforts. CABILDO made a number of Far East deployments during the 1950s and 1960s from her homeport of San Diego. In 1955 she was provided with a helicopter platform which enabled her to help develop the vertical envelopment concept of amphibious warfare.

CABILDO continued in commission until she was laid up in the Suisun Bay Reserve Fleet in 1970. She remained there until she was stricken from the Navy List in October 1976, then was designated as a missile target ship in 1982. The old LSD proved to be a durable target, but was finally sunk in the Pacific in September 1985.

CATAMOUNT
1945

CATAMOUNT

Hull No: 449
Navy No: LSD-17
Launched: January 27, 1945
Commissioned: April 9, 1945
Dimensions: 457.75 x 72 x 37 ft
Displacement: 7,498 tons
Armament: 1 5" Gun
Machinery: Geared Turbines, 2 Boilers,
    Twin Screw
Horsepower/Speed: 7,000/17 knots
Fate: Scrapped, 1983

CATAMOUNT, the shipyard's ninth LSD, was named after the famous tavern at Bennington, VT, where claims to the territory of Vermont were resolved in 1765 by the states of New York and New Hampshire. The keel for this LSD was laid down on August 7, 1944, and she was launched on January 27, 1945. Mrs. Dave E. Satterfield, Jr. of Richmond served as sponsor for CATAMOUNT.

LSD-17 was placed in commission on April 9, 1945, with Cdr. C.A. Swafford commanding. CATAMOUNT soon sailed for the Pacific and served out the war in the Far East ferrying landing craft and equipment to Guam, the Philippines, and Japan. She returned to Hampton Roads in February 1946 and was attached to the Atlantic Fleet until the beginning of the Korean War.

In August 1950 CATAMOUNT sailed from Norfolk and steamed for Kobe, Japan, via San Diego. She landed Marines at Wonsan, then served as mother ship to a fleet of minesweepers at Chinnampo in November.

CATAMOUNT returned to San Diego in June 1951 for repairs and then made two more deployments to Korea, winning a total of seven battle stars in the war.

(Continued on page 358)

COLONIAL
1945

COLONIAL

Hull No: 450
Navy No: LSD-18
Launched: February 28, 1945
Commissioned: May 15, 1945
Dimensions: 457.75 x 72 x 37 ft
Displacement: 7,498 tons
Armament: 1 5" Gun
Machinery: Geared Turbines, 2 Boilers,
    Twin Screw
Horsepower/Speed: 7,000/17 knots
Fate: Laid Up, 1970

The tenth LSD built at Newport News during World War II was COLONIAL (LSD-18), which was named after Colonial National Historical Park. COLONIAL was laid down on Shipway 6 on August 21, 1944, and was launched on February 28, 1945. Mrs. Learned L. Dean, wife of Cdr. Dean of the SOS Office at the shipyard, sponsored COLONIAL.

The new LSD was commissioned under the command of LCdr. J.A. Patterson, USNR, on May 15, 1945. COLONIAL arrived at Pearl Harbor in September and so did not see action in World War II. She stayed in the Pacific for only four months, ferrying landing craft to the western ocean, until she returned to Norfolk in January 1946.

She served the Atlantic Fleet until August 1950, at which time she sailed to the Korean War. COLONIAL landed troops, tanks, and equipment at Inchon, Wonsan, and Iwon before the end of the year. For the rest of this deployment and for much of another, she served as mother ship for minesweepers clearing Korean harbors. She received seven battle stars for her Korean War exploits, then continued in the Pacific during the 1950s and 1960s.

COLONIAL underwent a FRAM II modernization in the early 1960s, which extended her service life and enabled her to serve in the Vietnamese War. She was inactivated and decommissioned in June 1970 and was placed in reserve in the fleet at Suisun Bay, CA. Although stricken from the Navy List in October 1976, COLONIAL remained in the Reserve Fleet into the 1980s.

COMSTOCK
1945

COMSTOCK

Hull No: 451
Navy No: LSD-19
Launched: April 28, 1945
Commissioned: July 2, 1945
Dimensions: 457.75 x 72 x 37 ft
Displacement: 7,498 tons
Armament: 1 5" Gun
Machinery: Geared Turbines, 2 Boilers,
    Twin Screw
Horsepower/Speed: 7,000/17 knots
Fate: Scrapped, 1985

The 11th and last of the LSDs built by the shipyard was COMSTOCK (LSD-19), named after the Comstock Lode in Nevada. Two more ships of this type were cancelled as the war drew to a close, and the massive wartime shipbuilding program wound down.

The keel for COMSTOCK was laid down on Shipway 7 on January 3, 1945. She was launched on April 28, 1945, and was christened by Mrs. Henry O. Redue, Jr., daughter of RAdm. Cox, supervisor of shipbuilding at Newport News.

The new COMSTOCK was commissioned on July 2, 1945, with LCdr. J.C. Rochester in command. COMSTOCK left for the Pacific on September 6 and arrived at Okinawa on October 20. She stayed with the occupation force for only a few months, then steamed to Puget Sound Naval Shipyard for conversion to a boat pool ship.

COMSTOCK made several deployments to the Far East before the beginning of the Korean War, so in 1950 she was ready for combat duty there. She was active in the invasions of Inchon and Wonsan, then supported minesweeping operations in Korean waters. She made a total of four deployments to the Korean theater during the war and won ten battle stars for her efforts.

In 1954 COMSTOCK served in Operation "Passage to Freedom," which evacuated Vietnamese civilians from Haiphong. She made many more deployments to the Far East and saw extensive Vietnam service before she was decommissioned and laid up in January 1970. Stricken in 1976, she remained laid up and was finally scrapped in 1985.

LST-383
1942

HULL 414, LST-384

LST-383

Hull No: 413
Navy No: LST-383
Launched: September 28, 1942
Commissioned: October 27, 1942
Dimensions: 327.75 x 50 x 25.17 ft
Displacement: 3,776 tons
Armament: 2 Twin 40mm, 4 Single 40mm Guns
Machinery: Geared Diesels, Twin Screw
Horsepower/Speed: 1800/10.5 knots
Fate: Scrapped, 1951

LST-383 was the first of 18 tank landing ships built at Newport News during World War II. Such a high priority was placed on the construction of these ships that the keel of HORNET (CV-12) was floated out of the newly constructed Shipway 11 so that six LSTs could be built there ahead of her. The shipyard's performance in the building of the vitally-needed LSTs was just short of a miracle.

The contract for their construction was awarded on May 21, 1942, and the keel for LST-383 was laid less than a month later on June 16. This was the first of 1,051 LST keels which would eventually be laid by many shipyards around the country. Within four days, seven more LST keels had been laid at Newport News, five of them in the shipway with LST-383.

All six of these were launched by flotation on September 28, 1942, after christenings by daughters of shipyard officials. Miss Pamela Cole served as sponsor for the shipyard's first LST.

LST-383 was commissioned on October 27 and was the first of her type delivered to the Navy. After tests in the Hampton Roads area, LST-383 sailed for the war in Europe. She participated in the Sicilian Invasion in June 1943 and was the first to land at Salerno in September. From January to March 1944, LST-383 was in action against Anzio and Nettuno, then she sailed to England to prepare for the Normandy invasion in June.

Winner of four battle stars, she was transferred to the Royal Navy in November 1944 and served out the war under British flag. She was sold to the Netherlands East Indies Customs in June 1946 and served them as ALBATROS (LST-1) until she was reportedly sold for scrap in 1951.

LST-384
1942

Newport News' second LST was also laid down on June 16, 1942, and was launched with five others on September 28, 1942, after christening by Miss Alice Palen.

LST-384 was commissioned on November 2, 1942, and served in Europe during the war. She participated in the landings on Sicily in July 1943, on Salerno in September 1943, and on Anzio-Nettuno in January and February 1944. LST-384 also landed troops and equipment on Normandy in June 1944 and won her fourth battle star there.

Near the end of the war in Europe, she was moved to the Far East for service with the occupation force. Then in late 1945 she returned to the U.S. Decommissioned in April 1946 and veteran of but three years of active duty, LST-384 was sold for scrap in 1948.

LST-385
1942

LST-385 was laid down on June 19, 1942, and was launched with five others on the following September 28. The shipyard's third LST was christened by Miss Janet L. Peebles and was placed in commission on November 6.

LST-385 served in the European theater during World War II and was awarded five battle stars for participation in landings on Sicily, Salerno, Anzio-Nettuno, and Normandy as well as for convoy service in November 1943.

She was transferred to Britain in November 1944, then was returned to the Navy in March 1946. In December 1947, LST-385 was sold to Philippine interests but her ultimate fate is unknown.

LST-386
1942

The keel for LST-386 was laid in Shipway 11 on June 19, 1942, and she was floated out with five sisters on September 28 after christening by Miss Mary R. Scott. LST-386 was commissioned on November 10, 1942, and sailed for the war in Europe soon thereafter.

The new LST joined many of her sisters in the Mediterranean and was in action during operations on Tunisia, Sicily, Salerno, and Anzio-Nettuno in 1942 and 1943. LST-386 had a makeshift "flight deck" installed in 1943, which enabled her to carry and launch four L-4 "Cub" observation planes during the Sicilian operation. She carried troops and equipment to the beaches of Normandy in June 1944, then was transferred to Britain in December.

She later was returned to Navy custody, then was sold to Frozen Foods Co. of Scotland in June 1947. She was in merchant service with this firm until she was sold for scrap in 1950.

LST-387
1942

LST-387 was laid down in Shipway 11 on June 20, 1942, and she was launched with five others on September 28. This LST was christened by Miss Roberta A. Fitzhugh. Since the six ships were floated simultaneously from the huge Shipway 11, it was necessary for the sponsors to go aboard them to break their champagne bottles on the bows while standing on deck.

LST-387 was commissioned on November 17, 1942, and soon left Newport News for duty in Europe. She had not been there long until she was attacked on June 22, 1943, by a German submarine while steaming from Arzew to the Sicilian Invasion. Hit by one torpedo, her stern was heavily damaged and 23 of her crew were killed and 21 were wounded. After being taken in tow and repaired, she became a receiving ship at Bizerte. She was provided with a repair crew and maintained landing craft at Bizerte and later at Palermo.

LST-387 returned to Norfolk in June 1945 and was decommissioned in May 1946. In December 1947 she was sold and was subsequently scrapped at Philadelphia.

LST-388
1942

LST-388 was the last of the first fleet of six LSTs built together in Shipway 11 in 1942. Her keel was laid on June 20, and she was christened by Miss Barbara A. Besse on September 28.

Commissioned on November 20, LST-388 sailed for the Mediterranean to join several of her sisters. She participated in operations on Tunisia, Sicily, and Salerno in 1943 and joined the invasion of Normandy on D-Day in 1944.

LST-388 returned to the U.S. after the war ended in Europe, then was sent to the Pacific to participate in atomic tests in July 1946 as a non-target ship.

In January 1947 she was decommissioned, and in April 1948 she was transferred to the Maritime Administration and was sold and was later presumably scrapped.

LST-389
1942

The next four LSTs built at Newport News were constructed on inclined shipways, while the first six occupied Shipway 11. They were not launched with the conventional triggers but were instead released by cutting sole pieces.

LST-389 was laid down on June 20, 1942, and was christened by Miss Clara E. Ashe on October 15. The LST was placed in commission on November 24 under the command of Lt. George G. Carpenter, USNR.

LST-389 followed her other sisters to the Mediterranean and participated in the Sicilian and Salerno landings in July and September of 1943. She also supported the invasion of Normandy in June 1944, then returned to the U.S. a year later.

As the war with Japan ended, her orders to the Pacific were cancelled, and she was decommissioned in March 1946. LST-389 was laid up on the St. John's River in Florida. She was named BOONE COUNTY in 1955 but was struck from the Navy list in June 1959.

In May 1960 she was transferred to the Greek Navy and was renamed LESBOS (L-172). She remained active in naval service into the 1980s.

LST-390
1942

LST-390 was laid down beside LST-389 on June 20, 1942, and was launched with her on October 15. Miss Robin Holzbach served as sponsor for LST-390. Quickly fitted out, the new ship became the first Newport News-built LST to serve in the Pacific war. She was commissioned on November 28 under the command of Lt. W.J.C. Baker, USNR, and left for the Pacific soon thereafter.

LST-390 earned three battle stars for operations at Cape Torokina in November and December 1943, at Saipan in June 1944, and at Iwo Jima in February 1945. She also was awarded the Navy Unit Commendation with 15 other ships for her actions in the Solomons campaign from March 1943 to May 1944.

After the war she remained with the occupation force until March 1946, serving as a hospital ship designated LSTH-390. She returned to the U.S. and was decommissioned in March 1946, then was stricken in September 1947. The veteran LST-390 was sold in April 1948 and was subsequently scrapped at Seattle.

LST-391
1942

LST-391 and LST-392 were also built together on an inclined shipway, while the first six of their type were occupying Shipway 11. Both were laid down on July 14, 1942, and were launched by cutting sole pieces on October 28. LST-391 was sponsored by Miss Katherine W. Blewett, who christened her in the conventional manner.

The LST was quickly completed and was placed in commission on December 3. LST-391 served in the European war and participated in operations on Sicily, Salerno, and Normandy, earning three battle stars for her efforts.

After the war she returned to the U.S. and was laid up. In 1955 she was named BOWMAN COUNTY when all Navy LSTs were given names. Then in 1960 she was transferred to the Greek Navy with her sister LST-389. Renamed RODOS (L-157), she continued to serve the Royal Hellenic Navy into the 1980s.

LST-392
1942

LST-392 was built alongside LST-391 and was also laid down on July 14, 1942, and christened on October 28. Miss June L. Irvine acted as sponsor for the shipyard's tenth LST.

LST-392 was commissioned on December 7, 1942, and was placed under the command of Lt. Louis R. Lemaire, Jr., USNR. She fought in the war in Europe and earned four battle stars for service in operations on Tunisia, Sicily, and Salerno in 1943 and on Normandy in 1944. LST-392 was the first of her type to enter Cherbourg after it was taken and made 55 crossings of the English Channel to bring men and equipment to the continent. On one of these trips, she had Ernie Pyle as a passenger and he wrote several articles about her.

She returned to Norfolk in May 1945, was converted to an ordnance installation ship, and was sent to Pearl Harbor in August. Arriving too late for the war in the Pacific, she returned to the U.S. and was decommissioned in April 1946. In October 1947 LST-392 was sold, and she was later scrapped at Philadelphia.

LST-393
1942

LST-393 and LST-394 were also built together on an inclined shipway while the first six of their type were under construction in Shipway 11. The keels for these two LSTs were laid on July 27, 1942, and both were launched on November 11. LST-393 was sponsored by Miss Lucy J. Sorenson and, after a quick fitting out, was commissioned under the command of Lt. John H. Halifax, USNR, on December 11.

LST-393 followed her sisters to the Mediterranean and earned three battle stars at Sicily, Salerno, and Normandy. She returned to the U.S. and was decommissioned in March 1946 but, unlike most of her type, was destined for a long career.

In March 1948 LST-393 was sold to Sand Products Corp. of Detroit and was converted for merchant service and renamed HIGHWAY 16. She served her new owner for almost 30 years in general cargo service on the Great Lakes, then was laid up in 1976. She remained idle into the mid-1980s.

LST-394
1942

LST-394 brought the number of LSTs built at Newport News to an even dozen. She was constructed on the same inclined shipway as LST-393 and was christened by Miss Dorothy L. Comstock on November 11, 1942.

LST-394 was commissioned on December 15 and soon sailed to the war in Europe. She won two battle stars in the invasions of Sicily and southern France in July 1943 and August and September 1944, then was transferred to Britain in December 1944.

LST-394 served out the war with the Royal Navy, then was returned to the U.S. Navy in May 1946. She was then laid up for over a year before being sold in December 1947 and subsequently scrapped at Norfolk.

LST-395
1942

LST-395 was the first of the second group of six LSTs built together in submerged Shipway 11 in 1942. The keels for all six of these ships were laid down on September 28, the same day that the first six LSTs were floated out. Prefabrication and series production enabled completion of these LSTs for launch on November 23, and LST-395 was christened by Miss Audrey J. Terry on that date.

LST-395 was placed in commission less than a month later on December 19 with Lt. A.C. Forber, USNR, commanding. The new ship was only the second Newport News-built LST to be sent to the Pacific war, and she earned six battle stars and the Navy Unit Commendation there. LST-395 participated in operations at New Georgia and Cape Torokina in 1943 and at Hollandia and Western New Guinea in 1944. In 1945 she engaged in landings on Mindanao in April and at Balikpapan in June and July.

She remained in the Far East on occupation duty until October 1945, then returned to the U.S. for decommissioning in April 1946. In September 1947 LST-395 was sold and she was later scrapped at Baltimore.

LST-396
1942

LST-396 was the only Newport News-built LST to be lost in World War II. Her keel was laid down with five others in Shipway 11 on September 28, 1942, and she was launched with them on November 23 after christening by Miss Ann H. Callis.

LST-396 was placed in commission exactly a month later under the command of Lt. E.W. White and soon left for the Pacific. She and her crew won one battle star and participated in the Solomons campaign from March to August 1943. LST-396 served as a hospital evacuation ship at Guadalcanal and this helped her win the Navy Unit Commendation for service in the Solomons.

On the night of August 18, 1943, she was near New Georgia carrying a dangerous cargo of gasoline and ammunition when she was rocked by an accidental explosion and was set on fire. LST-396 later sank and was struck from the Navy list on September 3, 1943.

LST-397
1942

LST-397 was nicknamed "Lucky Lady" because of the many close calls which she had during the war in the Pacific. She was in the second group of six LSTs, laid down in Shipway 11 on September 28, 1942, and launched on November 23. LST-397 was sponsored by Miss Gretchen L. White and was commissioned on December 28.

LST-397 saw more action than any of her Newport News-built sisters, earning seven battle stars and the Navy Unit Commendation for her World War II service. She was active in the Solomons campaign and at Cape Torokina in 1943, then participated in operations at Hollandia, Western New Guinea, and Leyte in 1944. In 1945 she saw action at Lingayen Gulf in January and at Mindanao Island in March.

LST-397 stayed in the Far East on occupation duty after the war, then returned to the U.S. to be decommissioned in April 1946. In September of the next year the tired veteran LST was sold, and she was later scrapped at Baltimore.

LST-398
1942

Sixteenth in the series of LSTs built at Newport News in 1942 was LST-398, which was sponsored by Miss Mary Sherwood Giese and was floated out on November 23 of that year. The LST was placed in commission on January 2, 1943, and soon thereafter sailed to the Pacific war.

She was active with her sisters in operations in the Solomons and at New Georgia and Cape Torokina in 1943, then participated in the taking of Guam in 1944. She won four battle stars and the Navy Unit Commendation for her service and remained on duty with occupation forces after the war.

LST-398 left the Far East in February 1946 and returned home to be decommissioned late in that month. In March 1948 she was sold, and she was subsequently scrapped at Seattle.

LST-399
1942

LST-399 saw more action in World War II and enjoyed a longer career than most of her sisters. She was christened by Miss Valerie Macpherson on November 23, 1942, and was commissioned on January 4, 1943.

LST-399 earned five battle stars and was awarded the Navy Unit Commendation for her service in the war in the Pacific. She was active in the Solomons at New Georgia and at Treasury Island in 1943, then fought at Guam in 1944. In 1945 she moved with the fleet on Guam and Iwo Jima. After the Japanese surrender in September 1945, LST-399 remained on occupation duty in the Far East.

She returned home in December 1945 and was decommissioned, but instead of being sold for scrap was placed in service with the Military Sealift Command as USNS LST-399. She served with MSC from March 1952 until she was laid up in Suisun Bay in 1974. Six years later she again entered naval service as a support ship for the Pacific Missile Range and was classified as IX-511.

LST-400
1942

Newport News' last World War II LST was christened by Miss Judith Flaxington on November 23, 1942, and was commissioned on January 7, 1943. Although the shipyard was the next-to-last of 15 builders to begin construction of LSTs, it had been the first to deliver a completed ship to the Navy and LST-400 was the 45th commissioned.

LST-400 was active in the European war and earned battle stars at Sicily in July 1943 and at Normandy in June 1944. She was the only one of her Newport News sisters to remain in commission after the war, and was renamed BRADLEY COUNTY in July 1955.

In September 1958 LST-400 was transferred to Taiwan and was renamed CHUNG SUO (LST-217). She remained active with the Navy of Taiwan into the mid-1980s.

YORK COUNTY
1957

YORK COUNTY

Hull No: 516
Navy No: LST-1175
Launched: March 5, 1957
Commissioned: November 8, 1957
Dimensions: 442 x 64 x 38.17 ft
Displacement: 8,320 tons
Armament: 3 Twin 3″ Guns
Machinery: 6 Geared Diesels, Twin Screw
Horsepower/Speed: 14,400/17.5 knots
Fate: In Commission

On June 1, 1955, Newport News was awarded contracts for the construction of two LSTs of modern design. These LSTs were considerably larger than the 18 ships built at the shipyard in 1942, and they featured a high standard of habitablity for their crews. Capable of landing 600 troops and 20 amphibious vehicles ashore, they were the last LSTs built with the traditional bow door arrangement.

The keel for the first of these ships, later named YORK COUNTY (LST-1175) after counties in five states, was laid down on Shipway 7 on June 4, 1956. YORK COUNTY was sponsored on March 5, 1957, by Mrs. William C. France, widow of Capt. France, USN, who died in action off Okinawa in 1945.

YORK COUNTY completed her trials in October and was commissioned on November 8 under the command of LCdr. Warren M. Schafer, USNR. The new LST joined Amphibious Force, Atlantic Fleet, and served on the East Coast, in the Caribbean, and in the Mediterranean until she was decommissioned in July 1972.

On that same date she was transferred to the Italian Navy and was renamed CAORLE (L-9891). The LST remained in active service in the Mediterranean into the mid-1980s.

GRAHAM COUNTY
1957

GRAHAM COUNTY

Hull No: 517
Navy No: LST-1176
Launched: September 19, 1957
Commissioned: April 17, 1958
Dimensions: 442 x 64 x 38.17 ft
Displacement: 8,344 tons
Armament: 3 Twin 3″ Guns
Machinery: 4 Geared Diesels, Twin Screw
Horsepower/Speed: 14,400/17.5 knots
Fate: Scrapped, 1977

The second LST built at Newport News in the 1950s was GRAHAM COUNTY (LST-1176), named for counties in three states. This ship was laid down on Shipway 5 on February 4, 1957, and was launched on September 19 of the same year. Mrs. R.O. Davis, wife of retired VAdm. Davis, former Commander, Amphibious Force Atlantic, served as sponsor for GRAHAM COUNTY.

The new LST was commissioned and placed under the command of LCdr. Gordon H. McCrea on April 17, 1958.

Except for the fact that she was fitted with four engines instead of six, GRAHAM COUNTY was identical to YORK COUNTY and other ships of the DE SOTO COUNTY class. Like her sister, she also served with Amphibious Force, Atlantic Fleet, in the Caribbean and Mediterranean for all of her Navy career.

In 1972 she was converted to a gunboat support ship and was redesignated AGP-1176. Fitted with repair shops and provided with a supply of spare parts, GRAHAM COUNTY spent the next five years in the Mediterranean at Naples in support of Navy patrol gunboats in her area. The requirement for this support was terminated in 1976, and the former LST underwent deactivation at Naples during the first quarter of 1977, then was decommissioned and towed to Boston. Her years of active duty over, GRAHAM COUNTY was laid up briefly, then was sold and scrapped.

SHADWELL *Continued from page 349*

the 1950s, then in 1956 began a series of deployments with the Sixth Fleet in the Mediterranean.

After this second career SHADWELL was again decommissioned, in September 1970, and was placed in the James River Reserve Fleet. She remained there until 1985 when she was transferred to the Naval Research Laboratory for use as a fire test ship based at Mobile, AL.

CATAMOUNT *Continued from page 350*

During the remainder of the 1950s and into the 1960s CATAMOUNT served the Pacific Fleet on a number of special missions.

In 1957 she was in Arctic waters resupplying DEW Line bases, then in 1960 she provided relief to earthquake-devastated Chile. CATAMOUNT was active in the Pacific until she was decommissioned at Bremerton in April 1970.

She lay in reserve for almost six years until she was sold to Max Rouse & Sons and was converted for merchant service. Renamed WARESHIP TWO, she continued her long career into the 1980s as a supply ship with Amoco Drilling Services of Panama. In 1983 she was sold to Hycom International of Singapore, and was subsequently scrapped in Taiwan.

CHARLESTON
1968

CHARLESTON

Hull No: 583
Navy No: LKA-113
Launched: December 2, 1967
Commissioned: December 14, 1968
Dimensions: 580 x 82 x 48 ft
Displacement: 18,568 tons
Armament: 4 Twin 3″ Guns
Machinery: Geared Turbines, 2 Boilers
Horsepower/Speed: 22,000/20 knots
Fate: In Commission

In June 1965 Newport News won a contract for the construction of four attack cargo ships (AKA) for the Navy which, with a fifth ship ordered in August 1966, became the CHARLESTON (AKA-113) class. These ships were later designated as amphibious cargo ships (LKA) and were capable of carrying a "main battery" of nine medium landing craft (LCM) and equipment for amphibious operations. They were the first Navy ships with fully automated machinery and were provided with two Newport News Heavy Lift 78-ton booms as well as ten other booms, and helicopter pads.

The keel for CHARLESTON was laid on December 5, 1966, and she was launched on December 2, 1967, after christening by Mrs. John S. Thatch. CHARLESTON, later nicknamed "Chuck," was commissioned on December 14, 1968, under the command of Capt. Walter F. Zartman.

After shakedown in the Caribbean and PSA at Norfolk Naval Shipyard, the new LKA engaged in local and Caribbean operations until she sailed in February 1971 on a round-the-world cruise with units of the Seventh Fleet. On this trip she delivered supplies to build a base at Diego Garcia in the Indian Ocean.

In 1972 she made the first of many deployments to the Mediterranean, and in June 1976 she assisted in the evacuation of civilians from Lebanon. CHARLESTON alternated local and Caribbean operations with frequent deployments to Europe and the Mediterranean during the 1970s.

She was overhauled at New York in 1982 and rejoined the fleet for Caribbean and Central American operations in 1983, then participated in Exercise Teamwork 84 in Norwegian waters in March 1984. She participated in Exercise Solid Shield with MOUNT WHITNEY and 48 other ships in 1985 and in September of that year was moored at Norfolk awaiting her next assignment.

DURHAM
1969

DURHAM

Hull No: 584
Navy No: LKA-114
Launched: March 29,1968
Commissioned: May 24, 1969
Dimensions: 580 x 82 x 48 ft
Displacement: 18,426 tons
Armament: 4 Twin 3″ Guns
Machinery: Geared Turbines, 2 Boilers
Horsepower/Speed: 22,000/20 knots
Fate: In Commission

The second of the CHARLESTON-class attack cargo ships built at Newport News was DURHAM (LKA-114), which was laid down on July 10, 1967. DURHAM was christened by Mrs. Alton A. Lennon, wife of Rep. Lennon of North Carolina, on March 29, 1968. Sen. Sam Ervin was the principal speaker at the ceremony in which DURHAM was commissioned and placed under the command of Capt. John D. Stensrud on May 24, 1969.

After her PSA in mid-1969, the new LKA sailed for her homeport of Long Beach, and after experiencing boiler problems enroute, arrived for duty in the Pacific. DURHAM made a number of deployments to the Vietnam area, first to carry equipment and supplies and later to aid in the evacuation of Vietnamese refugees. She made regular deployments to the Far East during the 1970s, and when not overseas she engaged in local operations off southern California and along the West Coast.

DURHAM was transferred to the Naval Reserve with CHARLESTON in the fall of 1979, then was returned to the active fleet in October 1982. She resumed her former routine of local operations and Far East deployments in 1983, carrying out her mission in support of amphibious forces. She remained active with the Pacific Fleet into the mid-1980s.

MOBILE
1969

MOBILE

Hull No: 585
Navy No: LKA-115
Launched: October 12, 1968
Commissioned: September 20, 1969
Dimensions: 580 x 82 x 48 ft
Displacement: 18,392 tons
Armament: 4 Twin 3″ Guns
Machinery: Geared Turbines, 2 Boilers
Horsepower/Speed: 22,000/20 knots
Fate: In Commission

The shipyard's third LKA, later named MOBILE, was laid down with DURHAM on July 10, 1967. MOBILE was launched on October 12, 1968, and was sponsored by Mrs. John J. Sparkman, wife of the senator from Alabama.

MOBILE underwent trials in July 1969 and was commissioned on September 20 under the command of Capt. Samuel Lorenz, Jr. The new MOBILE visited her namesake city in December enroute to her homeport of San Diego.

In May 1970 she made the first of many deployments to the Far East, and in 1972 on her third such deployment, she became the first of her class to receive the Combat Action Ribbon for action in Vietnam. In 1975 MOBILE evacuated over 1,200 refugees from Vietnam and she also helped escort 26 former Vietnamese Navy ships to the Philippines.

MOBILE was in Alaskan waters in 1976 to help that state celebrate the Bicentennial, and in 1980 she made a six-month deployment to the Far East and Indian Ocean, which included a visit to Kenya.

She returned to San Diego in June 1980 and in September was transferred to the Naval Reserve and was moved to Long Beach. MOBILE served with the Reserve Force for three years, then returned to the active fleet in September 1983.

At the end of 1983, she and her crew were in port preparing for their first Far East deployment in over three years. She departed San Diego with PhibRon 3 on May 30, 1984, for exercises in the western Pacific, then returned home again on the following December 6 to prepare for exercises in 1985.

ST. LOUIS
1969

ST. LOUIS

Hull No: 586
Navy No: LKA-116
Launched: January 4, 1969
Commissioned: November 22, 1969
Dimensions: 580 x 82 x 48 ft
Displacement: 18,431 tons
Armament: 4 Twin 3″ Guns
Machinery: Geared Turbines, 2 Boilers
Horsepower/Speed: 22,000/20 knots
Fate: In Commission

Last of the four attack cargo ships ordered on June 11, 1965, ST. LOUIS (LKA-116) was laid down on April 25, 1967. Rep. Leonor K. Sullivan of Missouri served as sponsor and christened ST. LOUIS on January 4, 1969. The new LKA was commissioned at Norfolk Naval Shipyard on November 22, 1969, and was placed under the command of Capt. John W. Klinefelter.

Assigned to the Pacific Fleet, ST. LOUIS sailed for Long Beach in February 1970. After training in local waters, she made her first deployment to the Far East and Vietnam, which lasted from August 1970 to March 1971. ST. LOUIS made almost annual deployments to the western Pacific during the 1970s and in 1981 included the Indian Ocean and Kenya on her itinerary. Unlike her sisters, she was not transferred to the Reserve Force but remained with the active fleet in the early 1980s.

ST. LOUIS underwent overhaul at San Diego from November 1981 to July 1982, then engaged in shakedown and local operations out of San Diego. She continued until July 1983, operated off the coast of Washington during the summer, then returned to San Diego. In September 1983 she and her crew sailed to Sasebo for service with the Seventh Fleet.

She returned to San Diego on March 7, 1984, then left again for the western Pacific on the following October 18 and remained at sea at year's end. Based at Sasebo as part of the Navy's Overseas Family Residency Program, she and her crew made the Far East their permanent homeport in 1985.

EL PASO
1970

EL PASO

Hull No: 591
Navy No: LKA-117
Launched: May 11, 1969
Commissioned: January 17, 1970
Dimensions: 580 x 82 x 48 ft
Displacement: 18,443 tons
Armament: 4 Twin 3″ Guns
Machinery: Geared Turbines, 2 Boilers
Horsepower/Speed: 22,000/20 knots
Fate: In Commission

On August 22, 1966, a fifth and last CHARLESTON-class amphibious cargo ship was ordered by the Navy. These were the first specially-designed ships of their type, since the 112 which preceded them had all been converted merchant vessels.

The keel for the fifth ship, later named EL PASO (LKA-117), was laid on February 5, 1968, and she was launched on May 11, 1969. EL PASO was sponsored by Mrs. John G. Tower, wife of the senator from Texas.

After eight months of outfitting and trials, EL PASO was placed in commission on January 17, 1970, under the command of Capt. Otto D. Tiderman. The new LKA was asssigned to the Atlantic Fleet with homeport at Norfolk and spent her first few months in shakedown in the Caribbean and off the Virginia Capes.

EL PASO had her PSA at Norfolk Naval Shipyard from June to August. Then in September she loaded troops and equipment at Morehead City for her first deployment to the Mediterranean. She made many more such deployments during the 1970s, then in 1980-1981 made a six-month cruise which carried her to Northern Europe, the Mediterranean, and the Indian Ocean. In March 1981 EL PASO was transferred to the Naval Reserve but her homeport remained at Norfolk.

She was returned to the active fleet in October 1982. Then in May 1983 she deployed to Lebanon with Marines, vehicles, and equipment for the international peacekeeping force there. After the tragic bombing of Marine headquarters on October 23, EL PASO played a vital role in providing medical equipment, supplies, and personnel to aid victims of the disaster.

She returned to Norfolk in December, completing a 213-day deployment in which she spent only 14 days in port. After a brief rest, she was again on the move and participated in Exercise Teamwork 84 in Norway in March 1984. She remained active with the Atlantic Fleet into the mid-1980s.

MOUNT WHITNEY
1971

MOUNT WHITNEY

Hull No: 592
Navy No: LCC-20
Launched: January 8, 1970
Commissioned: January 16, 1971
Dimensions: 620 x 108 x 70 ft
Displacement: 17,100 tons
Armament: 2 Sea Sparrow, 2 Twin 3" Guns
Machinery: Geared Turbines, 2 Boilers
Horsepower/Speed: 22,000/23 knots
Fate: In Commission

On August 22, 1966, along with the contract for EL PASO, Newport News was awarded a contract for an amphibious command ship later named MOUNT WHITNEY (LCC-20). Second of two BLUE RIDGE-class ships which were the first of their type designed and built as such, MOUNT WHITNEY was equipped with sophisticated electronic communications equipment to enable her to serve as a fast mobile headquarters for amphibious operations.

MOUNT WHITNEY, named for the 14,495-ft peak in the Sierra Nevada range in California, was laid down on January 8, 1969, and was launched exactly a year later. Mrs. William I. Martin, wife of the Deputy Commander, Atlantic Fleet, served as sponsor on a bitterly cold and snowy launch day.

MOUNT WHITNEY underwent trials in December 1970 and was commissioned on January 16, 1971, under the command of Capt. Orlie G. Baird. Homeported at Norfolk, the new LCC became flagship of the Commander, Second Fleet.

After shakedown in the Caribbean, MOUNT WHITNEY returned to Newport News for her PSA, then made her first deployment to the Mediterranean in August. In 1972 she joined NATO forces in northern European waters. Then in 1976 she participated in the Bicentennial Naval Review in New York harbor.

In 1980 MOUNT WHITNEY was a key unit in NATO operations in northern European waters, which involved over 60,000 personnel from eight countries, 116 ships, and 400 aircraft.

She continued to make overseas deployments into the 1980s, and in 1983 she was in Central American waters with CORAL SEA and her battle group.

At year's end MOUNT WHITNEY and her crew of 40 officers and 1,242 enlisted men were at Norfolk preparing for Exercise Teamwork 84. She led a 14-ship amphibious fleet to a landing in Norway in March, then was in Boston in June with JOHN F. KENNEDY for the "Spirit of Massachussets" festival. In 1985 she led Exercise Solid Shield which involved 50 ships and 43,000 men in amphibious operations.

AUXILIARY SHIPS
PROTEUS
1913

PROTEUS

Hull No: 154
Navy No: AC-9
Launched: September 14, 1912
Commissioned: July 9, 1913
Dimensions: 521.58 x 62 x 39.5 ft
Armament: 4 4" Guns
Displacement: 19,000 tons
Machinery: Triple Expansion Engines,
    3 Boilers, Twin Screw
Horsepower/Speed: 6,700/14 knots
Fate: War Loss, 1941

naval ship, PROTEUS was armed with four 4", 50-caliber guns and had a large crew of 181 men.

The new ship, with its tall funnel and unique booms and rigging, made four coal runs to Vera Cruz from Norfolk and four to the Philippines before the end of 1917. Late in 1917 she made a trip to Rio de Janeiro. She served on the East Coast for the first half of 1918, then went to Britain, returned, then spent six months in European waters.

She returned to Norfolk in August 1919, and for the next three years she cruised from there to the Caribbean. She delivered fuel and stores to Pearl Harbor and Peru on two trips in 1920 and 1921. Re-entering Caribbean service, she made her last run in April 1923.

After brief duty along the East Coast, she was decommissioned on March 25, 1924. She remained on the Navy list until stricken on December 5, 1940. PROTEUS was sold to Saguenay Terminals, Ltd. of Ottawa on March 8, 1941, and was placed in the bauxite trade between St. Thomas, V.I., and Portland, ME. On November 23, 1941, PROTEUS was reported missing, presumably torpedoed and lost in the North Atlantic with all hands.

PROTEUS and NEREUS were the only naval colliers ever built at Newport News, and they shared similar careers and ultimate fates. PROTEUS was christened by Miss Lucy Day Martin and was commissioned on July 9, 1913, under Master Robert J. Easton, Naval Auxiliary Service. The new collier was a valuable addition to the fleet with her 11,800 ton coal-carrying ability and modern (for 1913) coal handling equipment, which could unload 145 tons per hour. As a

NEREUS
1913

NEREUS

Hull No: 155
Navy No: AC-10
Launched: April 26, 1913
Commissioned: September 10, 1913
Dimensions: 521.58 x 62 x 39.5 ft
Armament: 4 4″ Guns
Displacement: 19,000 tons
Machinery: Triple Expansion Engines,
    3 Boilers, Twin Screw
Horsepower/Speed: 6,700/14 knots
Fate: War Loss, 1941

Identical to PROTEUS, NEREUS was christened by Miss Anne Seymour Jones on April 26, 1913, and was placed in commission on September 10, 1913. NEREUS was placed into service with the Atlantic Fleet carrying coal from East Coast ports to bases and ships in the Caribbean. She was assigned to the Naval Overseas Transportation Service in 1918, and throughout the First World War she supplied ships and bases for the war effort.

She was placed back in Atlantic Fleet service until she was decommissioned on June 30, 1922. She lay at Norfolk for many years until struck from the Navy List on December 5, 1940. On February 27, 1941, NEREUS was sold to the Aluminum Co. of Canada and took up the bauxite trade.

On December 10, 1941, she presumably sank after being torpedoed by a German U-Boat and joined her sister PROTEUS at the bottom of the Atlantic with all hands.

HUNLEY
1962

HUNLEY

Hull No: 550
Navy No: AS-31
Launched: September 28, 1961
Commissioned: June 16, 1962
Dimensions: 599 x 83 x 54 ft
Armament: 2 5" Guns
Displacement: 18,300 tons
Machinery: Diesel-Electric
Horsepower/Speed: 15,000/18 knots
Fate: In Commission

Named for Confederate submarine pioneer H.L. Hunley, HUNLEY was the first submarine tender designed and built to service the ballistic missile submarine fleet. She was launched by Mrs. J. Palmer Gaillard, Jr. on September 28, 1961, and was commissioned on June 16, 1962, with Capt. Douglas N. Syverson commanding. She featured accommodations for about 1,400 of her crew and submarine crew, was provided with 52 shops for repair and overhauls, and was built with a 32-ton revolving crane.

HUNLEY operated along the East Coast during 1962, then relieved tender PROTEUS as tender to Submarine Squadron 14 at Holy Loch, Scotland. In 1964 she was converted for handling the new A3 Polaris missile.

HUNLEY returned to the United States in 1966 and took up station at Charleston in 1967. In the early 1970s her crane was replaced with two amidships cranes, and she continued in fleet service at Holy Loch, with occasional return trips to the U.S. for overhaul, into the mid-1980s.

COAST GUARD CUTTERS
SENECA
1908

SENECA

Hull No: 85
Owner: U.S. Coast Guard
Launched: May 18, 1908
Commissioned: November 6, 1908
Dimensions: 204 x 34 x 25.75 ft
Armament: None
Displacement: 1,575 tons
Machinery: Triple Expansion Engine,
    2 Boilers
Horsepower/Speed: 1,500/12.52 knots
Fate: Scrapped, 1950

SENECA, the first of seven cutters built at Newport News, was christened by Miss Edith Hepburn on May 18, 1908, and was placed in commission with the Revenue Service on November 6 of that year. Named for a tribe of Indians of western New York, the new cutter had a sleek white hull topped by a tall stack and two masts with sailing gear.

The first assignment of an otherwise exciting career for SENECA was as a "derelict destroyer" removing wrecks along the Atlantic Coast. During this service until 1913, she also participated in many colorful ceremonies and sporting events.

In March 1913 she was the first cutter assigned to the International Ice Patrol out of Halifax, Nova Scotia. She remained in this service and performed other duties for the remainder of each year until the outbreak of war in 1917. She joined the Navy in that year, was armed with four 3″ guns, and was assigned to anti-submarine patrol in the warm waters around Key West.

In the autumn of 1917 she was reassigned to overseas duty, was refitted, and began convoy escort duty and rescued 80 men from the torpedoed British ship COWSLIP. Later in the year, she possibly sank two submarines and rescued 27 men from the torpedoed steamer QUEEN. SENECA gallantly went to the rescue of the sinking WELLINGTON in September 1918 and lost 11 of her own men in the attempt. Both the survivors and those who perished were decorated for this episode.

In 1919 SENECA resumed Coast Guard service and continued with ice patrol, assistance at sporting events, and pursuit of rum runners along the East Coast.

(Continued on page 368)

ACUSHNET
1908

ACUSHNET

Hull No: 88
Owner: U.S. Coast Guard
Launched: May 16, 1908
Commissioned: November 6, 1908
Dimensions: 152 x 29 x 16.33 ft
Armament: None
Displacement: 770 tons
Machinery: Triple Expansion Engine,
    2 Boilers
Horsepower/Speed: 1,000/11.36 knots
Fate: Scrapped, 1946

ACUSHNET was the smallest of the cutters built at Newport News, and she had the most unremarkable career of the seven. She was christened by Miss Aloyse Duff on May 16, 1908, and was delivered about a week after SENECA.

She took up patrol around Buzzard's Bay, Nantucket Shoals, and adjacent waters late in 1908 and served until 1917 without incident. On April 6 of that year, she was transferred to the Navy and spent the war in towing, salvage, and convoy escort duty between New York and Halifax. She served briefly at New London, then was returned to the Coast Guard late in 1919. She continued in routine patrol duty, assisting at regattas, and in assistance to vessels in distress until she was decommissioned on January 31, 1936.

She was transferred back to the Navy and was commissioned as AT-63 on September 1, 1936, at Norfolk. Except for one voyage to Panama in 1944, she served as a tug assigned to the Fifth Naval District at Norfolk until late 1945.

ACUSHNET was decommissioned on December 14, 1945, and about a year later, she was transferred to the U.S. Maritime Commission for sale and scrapping.

MIAMI
1912

MIAMI

Hull No: 152
Owner: U.S. Coast Guard
Launched: February 10, 1912
Commissioned: August 19, 1912
Dimensions: 190 x 32.5 x 17.5 ft
Armament: 3 6-pdr Guns
Displacement: 1,046 tons
Machinery: Triple Expansion Engine,
    2 Boilers
Horsepower/Speed: 1,000/13 knots
Fate: War Loss, 1918

Launched by Miss Barnes Richardson on February 10, 1912, MIAMI was to have the shortest career and most violent end of any Newport News-built cutter. She was the first of two identical cutters launched that day, and UNALGA followed her down the ways. The new cutters were of moderate size and had larger more enclosed superstructures than the two previously built at the yard.

After successful trials, MIAMI was commissioned on August 19, 1912, and soon thereafter was sent for service at Key West. Almost immediately the new cutter was recalled to New York and sent to relieve SENECA on ice patrol. She alternated service between Halifax, New York, Key West, and Tampa over the next few years.

She spent some time in the Azores with the International Derelict Patrol, and in February 1916 she was renamed TAMPA. With her new name she continued in alternating ice patrol and service in warm waters on a seasonal basis until temporarily transferred to the Navy on April 6, 1917. She traded her three 6-pounders for four 3″ guns and a pair of machine guns and sailed in convoy for Gibraltar on September 29, arriving on October 27. She was assigned to convoy patrol between Gibraltar and England and steamed more than 3,500 miles per month.

Crossing the Bristol Channel on September 26, 1918, after safely escorting her convoy from Gibraltar, she was attacked by the submerged German submarine UB-91. A single torpedo found its mark, and TAMPA went down quickly with all her 115 crew and 16 passengers.

SENECA *Continued from page 366*

She was placed out of commission for less than a year in 1927, then was recommissioned and stationed at New York. In 1932 she was reassigned to San Juan, P.R.; then in 1934 she moved to Mobile, AL. She was selected for decommissioning in 1936, but not before she rescued several vessels stranded in the ice during a big freeze along the Virginia and Maryland coasts.

After this last battle with the ice, the old cutter was decommissioned on March 21, 1936, then sold to the Boston Iron and Metal Co. of Baltimore. SENECA was owned for a few months by the Texas Refrigeration Steamship Line but when they went bankrupt,

Boston Iron and Metal bought her back at auction.

Having been repaired and overhauled, she returned to Coast Guard service in 1941. In 1942 she was turned over to the state of Pennsylvania for use in training merchant and naval cadets from the Maritime Academies of the states of Pennsylvania, Massachusetts, and New York. Renamed KEYSTONE STATE, she stayed in that service through 1948. Returned to the Maritime Commission, she was laid up until she was sold and scrapped at Baltimore in 1950.

UNALGA
1912

UNALGA

Hull No: 153
Owner: U.S. Coast Guard
Launched: February 10, 1912
Commissioned: May 23, 1912
Dimensions: 190 x 32.5 x 17.5 ft
Armament: 3 6-pdr Guns
Displacement: 1,046 tons
Machinery: Triple Expansion Engine,
   2 Boilers
Horsepower/Speed: 1,000/13 knots
Fate: Scrapped, 1946

UNALGA, the fourth cutter built at Newport News and sister to MIAMI, was launched by Miss Elizabeth Hilles on February 10, 1912, shortly after MIAMI. Commissioned at Arundel Cove, MD, on May 23, UNALGA left Norfolk on September 26 for service with the Bering Sea Fleet in Alaska.

The most widely traveled of the Newport News-built cutters, she sailed east from Norfolk and passed Gibraltar and Mediterranean ports, stopping at Port Said. She stayed there for six weeks, ready to protect American interests during the general unrest in the area, but departed to transit the Suez Canal when

things settled down.

She continued her voyage, stopping at Far East Ports and at Honolulu, then arrived at Port Townsend, WA, on March 22, 1913. She was temporarily transferred to the Navy in 1917 and remained in Alaskan waters, ready for enemy action which never came.

After the Armistice, UNALGA remained in Alaska with the Bering Sea Patrol and served there through the twenties. During her long career in northern waters, the cutter was asked to enforce treaties dealing with sealing, to carry mail and supplies to fishermen and natives in remote areas, and to perform many additional duties not normally required of a cutter.

Early in 1930 she left these waters and returned to the East Coast, was out of commission for a few months, then was recommissioned and stationed at Key West and later at San Juan.

During World War II she served the Tenth Naval District from San Juan and, equipped with anti-submarine devices, constantly patrolled the shipping lanes for enemy raiders. Her war service was uneventful, and in 1945 she was reassigned to the Fifth Naval District at Norfolk. The old cutter was decommissioned on October 10, 1945, and sold for scrap on July 19, 1946.

OSSIPEE
1915

OSSIPEE

Hull No: 183
Owner: U.S. Coast Guard
Launched: May 1, 1915
Commissioned: July 28, 1915
Dimensions: 165.5 x 32 x 20.75 ft
Armament: 2 6-pdr Guns
Displacement: 909 tons
Machinery: Triple Expansion Engine,
   2 Boilers
Horsepower/Speed: 1,000/12 knots
Fate: Scrapped, 1948

Launched shortly after sister cutter TALLAPOO-SA, OSSIPEE was christened by Miss Sallie Flemming McAdoo on May 1, 1915. Second only to ACUSHNET in size among cutters built at Newport News, these were the first cutters delivered to the new Coast Guard which replaced the U.S. Revenue Service in 1915.

OSSIPEE was designed for service on the North Atlantic Coast and took up station in New England waters after commissioning on July 28, 1915. After two years of uneventful service, OSSIPEE was transferred to the Navy and outfitted for war service. She resumed patrol in the Nantucket area until ordered to Gibraltar, arriving on August 30, 1917, where she was placed in convoy danger zone escort. Later in the year she was assigned to ocean escort duty and assisted in the escort of 596 merchant ships, only five of which were lost to enemy action.

In August 1919 OSSIPEE returned to Coast Guard service at Portland, ME, and in the following years participated in the Ice Patrol and in war against the rum-runners. The cutter continued patrol and icebreaking duties in New England waters until 1935, then was transferred to Sault Ste. Marie on the Great Lakes in 1936.

During World War II, she again joined the Navy and spent the war on patrol duty out of Cleveland and made many training cruises.

Late in the war, she took up towing duties for the Navy, and when declared surplus, she was sold to Harold H. Neff of East Cleveland on September 18, 1946. Several accounts indicate that she was placed in commercial towing service, although official records do not indicate this. She was sold for scrap to Luria Bros. of Cleveland in November 1948 and was later broken up.

TALLAPOOSA
1915

TALLAPOOSA

Hull No: 184
Owner: U.S. Coast Guard
Launched: May 1, 1915
Commissioned: August 12, 1915
Dimensions: 165.5 x 32 x 20.75 ft
Armament: 2 6-pdr Guns
Displacement: 912 tons
Machinery: Triple Expansion Engine,
  2 Boilers
Horsepower/Speed: 1,000/12 knots
Fate: In Service

TALLAPOOSA was launched from the outboard end of the same shipway one hour before her sister OSSIPEE. She was christened by Miss Mabel Hartwell and after outfitting and trials was placed in commission on August 17, 1915. Both of the new cutters were designed for service in ice and had steel hulls and oil-fired boilers and steam engines.

TALLAPOOSA was to enjoy the longest career of any of the cutters built at Newport News. Her first homeport was at Mobile where she made search and rescue patrols and participated in regattas and celebrations.

From April 6, 1917, to August 28, 1919, the cutter was temporarily transferred to the Navy. She was sent to Halifax, Nova Scotia, where she performed anti-submarine patrol and search and rescue duty in the icy waters, once being caught in a sub-zero snow storm and almost crushed by ice.

In March 1920 she returned to her old homeport of Mobile where she uneventfully resumed her former service. In January 1929 her permanent station was moved to Key West.

Her warm-water days were numbered; however, after extensive repairs and alterations, she was sent to her new homeport of Juneau, AK, where she arrived on February 6, 1931. TALLAPOOSA served in these waters on Bering Sea Patrol, Halibut Patrol, and Seal Patrol until August 1937 when she was reassigned to permanent station at Savannah. She was rearmed, repaired, and altered in 1940 and 1942 and served in the Sixth Naval District during World War II where she engaged in convoy and antisubmarine work.

Very active during the war years, she was decommissioned on November 18, 1945. On July 22, 1946, TALLAPOOSA was sold to the Caribbean Fruit and Steamship Co., who converted her for cargo service. It is believed that she continued in service into the 1980s under the Honduran flag and the name SANTA MARIA.

NORTHLAND
1927

NORTHLAND

Hull No: 318
Owner: U.S. Coast Guard
Launched: February 5, 1927
Commissioned: May 7, 1927
Dimensions: 216.58 x 39 x 24.75 ft
Armament: 2 6-pdr, 1 1-pdr Guns
Displacement: 2,023 tons
Machinery: Diesel-Electric
Horsepower/Speed: 1,000/11 knots
Fate: Scrapped, 1962

NORTHLAND was the last cutter built by Newport News and she was the first ship built there in which welding was extensively used, accounting for 20 percent of her hull. She was specifically strengthened for service in ice and had her forefoot cut away to above the waterline to assist in icebreaking. She was built with full sailing rig for use if her propeller was disabled by ice, but her rig was removed in 1936. She had diesel electric propulsion, which had become the standard for cutters in the 1920s.

NORTHLAND was christened by Clara Prentis Billard on February 5, 1927, and was placed in commission on May 7 of that year.

During the 1930s she was homeported alternately at San Francisco, Oakland, and Seattle and served primarily on Bering Sea Patrol. In June 1939 she was transferred to Boston and began outfitting for the second Byrd Antarctic Expedition. War came to Europe, however, and she was withdrawn from the expedition. She was outfitted for special duty in Greenland to gather information which was later used by the Greenland Patrol in cooperative defense of the Western Hemisphere.

During the war years, NORTHLAND served with other cutters in the waters around Greenland, and she made the first naval capture of the war when she took the sealer BUSKOE, intent on gathering information for the Nazis, in October 1941. NORTHLAND received two battle stars for her service in World War II.

She remained on weather patrol duty after the war, until she was decommissioned on March 27, 1946. On January 3, 1947, she was presumably sold for scrap to the Weston Trading Co., but she was eventually taken across the Atlantic to France by a crew of Haganah men and American Jewish volunteers. She was renamed JEWISH STATE and was used in transporting Jews from Bulgaria to Palestine in the famous exodus episode.

In May 1948 she was renamed EILAT and became the first and only ship of the Israeli Navy. She became a training ship and served in that duty until 1955 when she was renamed MATZPEN and served as a barracks or depot ship. The veteran cutter was decommissioned and broken up for scrap in 1962.

APPENDICES

REFERENCES

PERIODICALS

Daily Press/The Times-Herald
Exxon Marine/Esso Marine News
Fairplay
Marine Engineering/Log
The Mariner
Maritime Reporter and Engineering News
Masthead
Nautical Gazette
Navy Times
The New York Times
Newsweek
Proceedings of the Marine Safety Council
Shipyard Bulletin
Surveyor
Steamboat Bill
Underway
U.S. Naval Institute Proceedings
The Virginian-Pilot/Ledger Star
Yachting

BOOKS

Balison, Howard J. *Newport News Ships: Their History in Two World Wars.* Newport News: The Mariners' Museum, 1954.

Blair, Clay, Jr. *Silent Victory: The U.S. Submarine War Against Japan.* New York: Bantam Books, 1975.

Braynard, Frank O. *The Big Ship: The Story of the S.S. United States.* Newport News: The Mariners' Museum, 1981.

———. *Lives of the Liners.* New York: Cornell Maritime Press, 1947.

Brown, Alexander Crosby. *The Good Ships of Newport News.* Cambridge, MD: Tidewater Publishers, 1976.

Cairis, Nicholas T. *Passenger Liners of the World Since 1893.* New York: Bonanza Books, 1979.

Charles, Roland W. *Troopships of World War II.* Washington, D.C.: The Army Transportation Association, 1947.

Compton-Hall, Richard. *Submarine Boats: The Beginnings of Underwater Warfare.* New York: Arco Publications, 1984.

Cram, W. Bartlett. *Picture History of New England Passenger Vessels.* Hampden Highlands, ME: Burntcoat Corp., 1980.

Dulin, Robert O., Jr. and Garzke, William H., Jr. *Battleships: United States Battleships in World War II.* Annapolis: Institute Press, 1976.

Evans, Cerinda W. *Collis Potter Huntington.* Newport News: The Mariners' Museum, 1954.

Friedman, Norman. *U.S. Destroyers: An Illustrated Design History.* Annapolis: Naval Institute Press, 1982.

———. *U.S. Carriers: An Illustrated Design History.* Annapolis: Naval Institute Press, 1983.

Gardiner, Robert, ed. *All the World's Fighting Ships 1906-1921.* Annapolis: Naval Institute Press, 1985.

Lake, Simon. *The Submarine in War and Peace.* Philadelphia: J. B. Lippincott Co., 1918.

Lake Torpedo Boat Co. *The Submarine Versus the Submersible.* Bridgeport, CT, 1906.

Lang, Steven and Spectre, Peter H. *On the Hawser: A Tugboat Album.* Camden, ME: Down East Books, 1980.

McKee, Fraser. *The Armed Yachts of Canada.* Ontario: Boston Mills Press, 1983.

Moisiev, S.P. *List of the Russian Navy, 1861-1917.* Moscow, 1948.

Morison, Samuel Eliot. *The Two Ocean War.* Boston: Little, Brown, and Co., 1963.

Morison, Samuel L. and Rowe, John S. *Warships of the U.S. Navy.* London: Jane's Publishing Company Limited, 1983.

Moore, Arthur R. *A Careless Word...A Needless Sinking.* Kings Point, NY: The American Merchant Marine Museum, 1984.

Morris, James M. *Our Maritime Heritage: Maritime Development and Their Impact on American Life.* Washington, D.C.: University Press of America, 1979.

Mostert, Noel. *Supership.* New York: Alfred A. Knopf, 1974.

Navy Department, Naval History Division. *Dictionary of American Naval Fighting Ships.* Washington, D.C., 1959-1981.

Newport News Shipbuilding & Dry Dock Co. *Three Generations of Shipbuilding.* Newport News, 1961.

Polmar, Norman. *Ships and Aircraft of the U.S. Fleet,* 13th Edition. New York: Naval Institute Press, 1984.

Polmar, Norman and Allen, Thomas B. *Rickover: Controversy and Genius.* New York: Simon and Schuster, 1982.

Scheina, Robert L. *U.S. Coast Guard Cutters and Craft of World War II.* Annapolis: Naval Institute Press, 1982.

Smith, Edward O. *History of the Newport News Shipbuilding and Dry Dock Co. 1880-1934.* Newport News: NNS & DD Co., 1939.

Smith, Eugene W. *Passenger Ships of the World: Past and Present.* Boston: George H. Dean Co., 1978.

Standard Oil Co. (New Jersey). *Ships of the Esso Fleet in World War II.* New York, 1946.

Stanton, Samuel Ward. *American Steam Vessels.* New York: Smith and Stanton, 1895.

Stindt, Fred A. *Matson's Century of Ships.* Kelseyville, CA: F.A. Stindt, 1982.

White, James T. & Co. *The National Cyclopaedia of American Biography.* New York, 1966.

Willoughby, Malcolm F. *Rum War at Sea.* Washington, D.C.: Treasury Department, United States Coast Guard, 1964.

Worden, William L. *Cargoes: Matson's First Century in the Pacific.* Honolulu: University Press of Hawaii, 1981.

ARTICLES

Blandford, Thomas R. "CHEROKEE and HENRY R. MALLORY Tried in Vain." *Steamboat Bill,* No. 154 (Summer 1980).

———. "The Clyde Line, 1844-1944." *Steamboat Bill,* No. 131 (Fall 1974).

———. "Shawnee—Clyde Line's Last Flagship." *Steamboat Bill,* No. 147 (Fall 1978).

Blank, John S. III. "The Great White Fleet." *Ships & Sailing* (May 1952).

Brown, Alexander Crosby. "A Record of Newport News Ships in Naval Service in the Spanish-American War." *Shipyard Bulletin,* Vol. XII. No. 9 (March-April 1948).

Eisele, Peter T. "How to Build a Cruise Ship—AMERICA Style." *Steamboat Bill,* No. 147 (Fall 1978).

Fox, William A. "EL TORO." *Steamboat Bill,* No. 163 (Fall 1982).

———. "JOSEPH HENRY at 75." *Steamboat Bill,* No. 169 (September 1984).

Gatewood, William. "Construction of a Fireproof Excursion Steamer." *Transactions,* S.N.A.M.E., 1906.

Kassell, B.L. "Russia's Submarine Development." *Journal,* A.S.N.E., Vol. 63 (November 1951).

Long, C.L., Stevens, J.L. Jr., and Tompkins, J.T. "Modern High-Speed Tankers." *Transactions,* S.N.A.M.E., 1960.

de Luce, Hollinshead and Budd, W.I.H. "The Design of a Class of 28,000-ton Tankers." *Transactions,* S.N.A.M.E., 1950.

Mason, George C. "What Becomes of Our Merchant Ships?" *Shipyard Bulletin,* Vol. XII, No. 8 (January-February 1948).

———. "What Becomes of Our Naval Ships?" *Shipyard Bulletin,* Vol. XII, No. 12 (September-October 1948).

McAllister, Charles A. "Two New Revenue Cutters for Special Purposes." *Transactions,* S.N.A.M.E., 1907.

Norton, Harold F. and Nichols, John F. "The United States Liner AMERICA." *Transactions,* S.N.A.M.E., 1940.

Wilson, Graham T. "The Hoboken Ferries." *Steamboat Bill,* No. 150 (Summer 1979).

MISCELLANEOUS

American Bureau of Shipping, *Record* and *Supplements.*

Eldredge, Elwin M., Collection in the Mariners' Museum.

Fox, William A., "DOROTHY: Hull No. One Comes Home," paper presented to the Hampton Roads Section of S.N.A.M.E. on April 9, 1976.

Jane's Publications, *Jane's Fighting Ships.*

Lloyd's of London, *Lloyd's Confidential Index* and *Lloyd's Weekly Casualty Reports.*

Lloyd's Register of Shipping, *Lloyd's Register, Supplements, Appendices,* and *Wreck Returns*

Naval Historical Foundation, "United States Naval Hospital Ships," Washington, D.C., 1973.

Navy Department, Naval History Division, Ships Histories Branch, Historial Ship Record File.

Newell, William T., "The Chesapeake & Ohio Railway Company's Floating Equipment—Here and There," typescript of an illustrated talk given to the Fall meeting of S.S.H.S.A. at the Mariners' Museum on October 30, 1954.

Newport News Shipbuilding and Dry Dock Co., launching programs.

Newport News Shipbuilding and Dry Dock Co., "Particulars of Ships Built at NNS & DD," unpublished listing, 1891-

Newport News Shipbuilding and Dry Dock Co., "Plans of Typical Vessels," 1936.

Smith, Edward O., "List of Vessels Launched and Their Sponsors," Newport News Shipbuilding and Dry Dock Co., 1946.

Society of Naval Architects and Marine Engineers, *Transactions* and *Historical Transactions*.

U.S. Coast Guard, *Merchant Vessels of the United States*.

U.S. Coast Guard, monographs on cutter histories.

U.S. Coast Guard, merchant vessel official documents in the National Archives.

U.S. Maritime Administration, vessel data sheets, listings, and reserve fleet records.

HULL LIST

HULL	NAME	OWNER	DELIVERED	FATE
		PASSENGER SHIPS		
15	LA GRANDE DUCHESSE	Plant Investment Co.	4-9-99	War Loss, 1918
16	CREOLE	Cromwell S.S. Co.	12-5-96	Scrapped, 1930
28	COMUS	Cromwell S.S. Co.	4-28-00	Scrapped, 1934
29	PROTEUS	Cromwell S.S. Co.	6-6-00	Collided, 1918
31	KOREA	Pacific Mail S.S. Co.	6-17-02	Scrapped, 1934
32	SIBERIA	Pacific Mail S.S. Co.	11-19-02	Scrapped, 1934
42	MONROE	Old Dominion S.S. Co.	4-3-03	Collided, 1914
65	BRAZOS	N.Y.& Texas S.S. Co.	11-6-07	Scrapped, 1934
81	LURLINE	Matson Nav. Co.	3-18-08	Scrapped, 1953
121	WILHELMINA	Matson Nav. Co.	12-7-09	War Loss, 1940
125	BEAR	Union Pacific R.R. Co.	1-23-10	Stranded, 1916
126	BEAVER	Union Pacific R.R. Co.	2-13-10	Scrapped, 1952
127	CITY OF MONTGOMERY	Ocean S.S. Co.	5-25-10	Scrapped, 1947
128	CITY OF ST. LOUIS	Ocean S.S. Co.	6-15-10	Scrapped, 1946
136	MADISON	Old Dominion S.S. Co.	1-31-11	Scrapped, 1947
157	LENAPE	Clyde S.S. Co.	1-18-13	Burned, 1925
166	MATSONIA	Matson Nav. Co.	11-6-13	Scrapped, 1957
168	MANOA	Matson Nav. Co.	12-13-13	Rep. Ship, 1967
193	HENRY R. MALLORY	Mallory S.S. Co.	10-21-16	War Loss, 1943
256	GOLDEN STATE	Emergency Fleet Corp.	2-1-21	War Loss, 1942
257	SILVER STATE	Emergency Fleet Corp.	5-16-21	Scrapped, 1948
266	CITY OF CHATTANOOGA	Ocean S.S. Co.	9-28-23	Scrapped, 1948
267	CITY OF BIRMINGHAM	Ocean S.S. Co.	11-3-23	War Loss, 1942
274	CHEROKEE	Clyde S.S. Co.	6-17-25	War Loss, 1942
275	SEMINOLE	Clyde S.S. Co.	8-19-25	Scrapped, 1952
276	GEORGE WASHINGTON	Old Dominion Line	11-16-24	Scrapped, 1955
277	ROBERT E. LEE	Old Dominion Line	1-17-25	War Loss, 1942
280	COAMO	N.Y. & Porto Rico Co.	12-22-25	War Loss, 1942
287	MOHAWK	Clyde S.S. Co.	2-1-26	Collided, 1935
288	CHATHAM	Mer. & Miners Tr. Co.	5-17-26	War Loss, 1942
289	DORCHESTER	Mer. & Miners Tr. Co.	7-17-26	War Loss, 1943
290	FAIRFAX	Mer. & Miners Tr. Co.	9-4-26	Scrapped, 1957
306	IROQUOIS	Clyde S.S. Co.	4-18-27	Scrapped, 1981
307	SHAWNEE	Clyde S.S. Co.	7-14-27	Burned, 1949
315	CALIFORNIA	Inter. Merc. Marine	1-13-28	Scrapped, 1964
317	ALGONQUIN	Clyde S.S. Co.	12-10-26	Scrapped, 1956
319	CARACAS	Red "D" Line	8-27-27	Scrapped, 1961
326	VIRGINIA	Inter. Merc. Marine	11-26-28	Scrapped, 1964
329	PENNSYLVANIA	Inter. Merc. Marine	10-10-29	Scrapped, 1964
337	MORRO CASTLE	Ward Line	8-15-30	Burned, 1934
338	ORIENTE	Ward Line	11-21-30	Scrapped, 1957
339	PRESIDENT HOOVER	Dollar Line	7-11-31	Stranded, 1937
340	PRESIDENT COOLIDGE	Dollar Line	10-1-31	War Loss, 1942
342	FLORIDA	P. & O.S.S. Co.	5-20-31	Scrapped, 1969
344	TALAMANCA	United Fruit Co.	12-12-31	Scrapped, 1965
345	SEGOVIA	United Fruit Co.	—	Burned, 1931
346	CHIRIQUI	United Fruit Co.	3-18-32	Scrapped, 1971
347	COLOMBIA	Colombian Mail Corp.	11-17-32	Scrapped, 1967
348	HAITI	Colombian Mail Corp.	12-15-32	Scrapped, 1968
350	SAINT JOHN	Eastern S.S. Lines	4-22-32	Scrapped, 1959
351	ACADIA	Eastern S.S. Lines	6-7-32	Scrapped, 1955
354	PETEN (ex-SEGOVIA)	United Fruit Co.	2-24-33	Scrapped, 1969
369	AMERICA	U.S. Lines	7-2-40	Laid Up, 1982
379	PRESIDENT JACKSON	Amer. President Lines	10-25-40	Scrapped, 1973

HULL	NAME	OWNER	DELIVERED	FATE
380	PRESIDENT MONROE	Amer. President Lines	12-19-40	Scrapped, 1970
381	PRESIDENT HAYES	Amer. President Lines	2-20-41	Scrapped, 1975
382	PRESIDENT GARFIELD	Amer. President Lines	3-26-41	Scrapped, 1973
383	PRESIDENT ADAMS	Amer. President Lines	11-19-41	Scrapped, 1973
384	PRESIDENT VAN BUREN	Amer. President Lines	9-11-41	War Loss, 1942
386	PRESIDENT POLK	Amer. President Lines	11-6-41	Scrapped, 1970
488	UNITED STATES	U.S. Lines	6-20-52	Laid Up, 1969
521	SANTA ROSA	Grace Line Inc.	6-12-58	Laid Up, 1975
522	SANTA PAULA	Grace Line Inc.	10-9-58	Hotel, 1978

CARGO SHIPS

HULL	NAME	OWNER	DELIVERED	FATE
3	EL SUD	Pacific Improvement Co.	7-27-92	Foundered, 1900
4	EL NORTE	Pacific Improvement Co.	9-15-92	Stranded, 1908
5	EL RIO	Pacific Improvement Co.	2-9-93	Scrapped, 1922
6	EL CID	Pacific Improvement Co.	8-24-93	Scrapped, 1933
22	EL SUD	Southern Pacific Co.	7-26-99	Scrapped, 1935
23	EL NORTE	Southern Pacific Co.	9-13-99	Scrapped, 1934
24	EL RIO	Southern Pacific Co.	10-19-99	Collided, 1942
27	EL CID	Southern Pacific Co.	12-16-99	Scrapped, 1934
34	EL VALLE	Southern Pacific Co.	6-5-01	Scrapped, 1951
35	EL DIA	Southern Pacific Co.	9-15-01	Scrapped, 1953
36	EL SIGLO	Southern Pacific Co.	11-30-01	Scrapped, 1934
37	EL ALBA	Southern Pacific Co.	1-28-02	Scrapped, 1934
117	JEAN	A.H. Bull & Co.	8-2-09	Scrapped, 1954
130	EL SOL	Southern Pacific Co.	8-20-10	Collided, 1927
131	EL MUNDO	Southern Pacific Co.	9-25-10	Scrapped, 1947
132	EL ORIENTE	Southern Pacific Co.	10-24-10	Scrapped, 1947
133	EL OCCIDENTE	Southern Pacific Co.	12-2-10	War Loss, 1942
135	RUTH	A.H. Bull & Co.	8-8-10	Scrapped, 1933
142	COROZAL	N.Y. & Porto Rico Co.	2-19-11	Scrapped, 1958
143	MONTOSO	N.Y. & Porto Rico Co.	3-5-11	Scrapped, 1953
145	ISABELA	N.Y. & Porto Rico Co.	8-25-11	War Loss, 1942
146	HILTON	A.H. Bull & Co.	7-8-11	Scrapped, 1951
156	EVELYN	A.H. Bull & Co.	6-11-12	Scrapped, 1946
158	CAROLYN	A.H. Bull & Co.	7-20-12	War Loss, 1942
161	PETER CROWELL	Crowell & Thurlow Co.	12-21-12	Scrapped, 1939
163	LORENZO	N.Y. & Porto Rico Co.	2-19-13	War Loss, 1918
169	LEWIS K. THURLOW	Crowell & Thurlow Co.	11-14-13	Scrapped, 1951
175	NECHES	Mallory S.S. Co.	8-20-14	Collided, 1918
176	MEDINA	Mallory S.S. Co.	9-29-14	In Service
188	MARIANA	N.Y. & Porto Rico Co.	7-3-15	War Loss, 1942
190	EDGAR F. LUCKENBACH	Luckenbach S.S. Co.	5-10-16	Collided, 1939
198	WILLIAM A. McKENNEY	Crowell & Thurlow Co.	11-29-16	War Loss, 1942
199	FELIX TAUSSIG	Crowell & Thurlow Co.	2-14-17	Scrapped, 1954
200	MUNDELTA	Munson S.S. Co.	4-18-17	War Loss, 1944
203	EL ALMIRANTE	Southern Pacific Co.	8-2-17	Foundered, 1943
204	EL CAPITAN	Southern Pacific Co.	9-20-17	War Loss, 1942
206	MUNINDIES	Munson S.S. Co.	12-7-17	War Loss, 1939
207	MUNAIRES	Munson S.S. Co.	1-12-18	War Loss, 1942
212	AGWIDALE	Atl. Gulf & W.I. Co.	11-16-18	Scrapped, 1960
213	AGWISTAR	Atl. Gulf & W.I. Co.	2-17-19	Scrapped, 1953
357	ANGELINA	A.H. Bull & Co.	4-25-34	War Loss, 1942
358	MANUELA	A.H. Bull & Co.	5-30-34	War Loss, 1942
373	NIGHTINGALE	W.R. Grace & Co.	10-30-39	Scrapped, 1973
374	STAG HOUND	W.R. Grace & Co.	12-4-39	Scrapped, 1974
375	SANTA ANA	W.R. Grace & Co.	2-15-40	Scrapped, 1968
376	SANTA TERESA	W.R. Grace & Co.	3-27-40	Scrapped, 1969
387	HAWAIIAN PLANTER	Matson Nav. Co.	5-15-41	Scrapped, 1980
388	HAWAIIAN PACKER	Matson Nav. Co.	6-16-41	Scrapped, 1984
389	IRENEE DU PONT	Int. Freighting Corp.	8-1-41	War Loss, 1943
458	PARISMINA	United Fruit Co.	1-16-47	Scrapped, 1977
459	HEREDIA	United Fruit Co.	3-19-47	Scrapped, 1977
460	METAPAN	United Fruit Co.	5-7-47	Scrapped, 1977
490	OLD DOMINION MARINER	Maritime Administration	10-8-52	Scrapped, 1986
491	TAR HEEL MARINER	Maritime Administration	11-28-52	Scrapped, 1980
492	VOLUNTEER MARINER	Maritime Administration	8-14-53	Scrapped, 1980
493	PALMETTO MARINER	Maritime Administration	12-11-53	Scrapped, 1974
494	CRACKER STATE MARINER	Maritime Administration	5-29-54	Laid Up, 1978
551	CALIFORNIA	States Steamship Co.	1-18-62	Laid Up, 1979
552	OREGON	States Steamship Co.	4-19-62	Laid Up, 1985
553	WASHINGTON	States Steamship Co.	6-26-62	Laid Up, 1985
554	HAWAII	States Steamship Co.	8-16-62	Laid Up, 1985
556	PIONEER MOON	U.S. Lines	8-21-62	Laid Up, 1981
557	AMERICAN CHALLENGER	U.S. Lines	10-23-62	Laid Up, 1982
558	AMERICAN CHARGER	U.S. Lines	12-18-62	Laid Up, 1981

HULL	NAME	OWNER	DELIVERED	FATE
559	AMERICAN CHAMPION	U.S. Lines	3-8-63	Laid Up, 1983
560	AMERICAN CHIEFTAIN	U.S. Lines	4-24-63	Laid Up, 1983
583	ALASKAN MAIL	American Mail Line	10-29-68	In Service
588	INDIAN MAIL	American Mail Line	12-31-68	In Service
589	KOREAN MAIL	American Mail Line	4-25-69	In Service
590	HONG KONG MAIL	American Mail Line	7-25-69	In Service
593	AMERICAN MAIL	American Mail Line	10-22-69	In Service

TANKERS

HULL	NAME	OWNER	DELIVERED	FATE
44	W.S. PORTER	Associated Oil Co.	11-1-06	War Loss, 1944
64	SUN	Sun Co.	4-8-07	War Loss, 1943
82	TEXAS	Texas Co.	7-18-08	Stranded, 1927
129	J.A. CHANSLOR	Associated Oil Co.	3-24-10	Stranded, 1919
141	WM. F. HERRIN	Associated Oil Co.	3-20-11	Scrapped, 1950
162	ILLINOIS	Texas Co.	5-17-13	War Loss, 1917
167	TOPILA	East Coast Oil Co.	7-22-13	Scrapped, 1950
170	JOHN D. ARCHBOLD	Standard Oil Co.	3-17-14	War Loss, 1917
177	JOHN D. ROCKEFELLER	Standard Oil Co.	9-11-14	Scrapped, 1954
186	CHARLES PRATT	Standard Oil Co. of NJ	3-18-16	War Loss, 1940
187	H.H. ROGERS	Standard Oil Co. of NJ	5-25-16	War Loss, 1943
191	ANTWERPEN	Standard Oil Co. of NJ	8-24-16	War Loss, 1916
196	WM. G. WARDEN	Standard Oil Co. of NJ	2-2-17	Scrapped, 1947
197	F.Q. BARSTOW	Standard Oil Co. of NJ	4-12-17	Scrapped, 1946
201	O.B. JENNINGS	Standard Oil Co. of NJ	10-31-17	War Loss, 1918
202	TORRES	Southern Pacific Co.	6-28-17	Scrapped, 1950
205	J.C. DONNELL	Atlantic Refining Co.	1-21-18	Scrapped, 1947
208	H.M. FLAGLER	Standard Oil of NJ	7-17-18	Scrapped, 1949
209	F.D. ASCHE	Standard Oil of NJ	12-10-18	Scrapped, 1959
248	PATOKA	U.S. Shipping Board	9-3-19	Scrapped, 1948
249	RAMAPO	U.S. Shipping Board	10-22-19	Scrapped, 1953
250	RAPIDAN	U.S. Shipping Board	11-26-19	Scrapped, 1947
251	SALINAS	U.S. Shipping Board	5-13-20	Scrapped, 1960
252	SAPELO	U.S. Shipping Board	1-30-20	Scrapped, 1946
253	SEPULGA	U.S. Shipping Board	5-27-20	Scrapped, 1946
254	TIPPECANOE	U.S. Shipping Board	8-4-20	Scrapped, 1946
255	TRINITY	U.S. Shipping Board	9-4-20	Scrapped, 1954
259	AGWISTONE	Atl. Gulf & W.I. Co.	7-26-22	Scrapped, 1949
260	AGWISMITH	Atl. Gulf & W.I. Co.	7-26-22	Scrapped, 1954
261	JOHN D. ARCHBOLD	Standard Oil of NJ	9-24-21	Scrapped, 1962
262	WM. ROCKEFELLER	Standard Oil of NJ	11-9-21	War Loss, 1942
273	J.H. SENIOR	Standard Oil of NJ	2-23-24	Scrapped, 1973
367	ESSO DELIVERY NO. 11	Standard Oil of NJ	2-8-38	Scrapped, 1953
370	ESSO RICHMOND	Standard Oil of NJ	4-20-40	Scrapped, 1970
371	ESSO RALEIGH	Standard Oil of NJ	6-21-40	Scrapped, 1975
372	ESSO COLUMBIA	Standard Oil of NJ	4-28-41	Scrapped, 1970
475	ESSO SUEZ	Esso Shipping Co.	4-1-49	Scrapped, 1984
476	ESSO MONTEVIDEO	Esso Shipping Co.	5-26-49	Scrapped, 1976
477	ESSO CRISTOBAL	Esso Shipping Co.	7-15-49	Scrapped, 1972
478	ESSO STOCKHOLM	Esso Shipping Co.	8-26-49	Scrapped, 1978
479	ATLANTIC EMPEROR	Atlantic Marine Co.	10-1-49	Scrapped, 1972
480	ESSO GENOVA	Esso Shipping Co.	11-11-49	Scrapped, 1976
481	ESSO LIMA	Esso Shipping Co.	12-21-49	Scrapped, 1984
482	ESSO BERMUDA	Esso Shipping Co.	1-27-50	Scrapped, 1976
483	ESSO HAVANA	Esso Shipping Co.	3-3-50	In Service
484	ESSO NEW YORK	Esso Shipping Co.	4-14-50	Drillship, 1975
485	ESSO SANTOS	Esso Shipping Co.	5-19-50	Scrapped, 1972
495	NORTH DAKOTA	Texas Co.	3-6-53	Scrapped, 1984
496	NEW YORK	Texas Co.	7-31-53	In Service
497	CONNECTICUT	Texas Co.	11-6-53	In Service
498	CALIFORNIA	Texas Co.	2-5-54	In Service
499	ESSO NEWARK	Esso Shipping Co.	8-19-52	Scrapped, 1984
500	ESSO CHESTER	Esso Shipping Co.	10-10-52	Scrapped, 1984
501	ESSO BANGOR	Esso Shipping Co.	1-16-53	Scrapped, 1984
502	ESSO GLOUCESTER	Esso Shipping Co.	5-1-53	Scrapped, 1977
503	ESSO HUNTINGTON	Esso Shipping Co.	10-9-53	Scrapped, 1984
504	ESSO FLORENCE	Esso Shipping Co.	1-15-54	Laid Up, 1982
508	FLYING A NEW YORK	Tide Water Associated Oil	3-26-54	In Service
509	FLYING A DELAWARE	Tide Water Associated Oil	7-2-54	Scrapped, 1984
510	W. ALTON JONES	Grand Bassa Tankers	6-15-54	Drillship, 1976
511	STATUE OF LIBERTY	Grand Bassa Tankers	8-16-54	Scrapped, 1983
512	CRADLE OF LIBERTY	Grand Bassa Tankers	10-15-54	In Service
513	LIBERTY BELL	Grand Bassa Tankers	12-15-54	Scrapped, 1977
515	FLORIDA	Texas Co.	7-14-56	In Service
519	ESSO GETTYSBURG	Esso Shipping Co.	3-1-57	In Service
520	ESSO WASHINGTON	Esso Shipping Co.	5-17-57	In Service

HULL	NAME	OWNER	DELIVERED	FATE
527	ESSO JAMESTOWN	Esso Shipping Co.	12-20-57	In Service
528	ESSO LEXINGTON	Esso Shipping Co.	4-25-58	In Service
529	ARIETTA S. LIVANOS	Ocean Tanker Line Ltd.	6-30-58	Scrapped, 1979
530	G.S. LIVANOS	Ocean Tanker Line Ltd.	8-27-58	Scrapped, 1984
531	SANSINENA	Barracuda Tanker Corp.	10-24-58	Exploded, 1976
532	TORREY CANYON	Barracuda Tanker Corp.	1-9-58	Stranded, 1967
533	LAKE PALOURDE	Barracuda Tanker Corp.	5-25-59	Scrapped, 1984
535	THETIS	Rye Marine Corporation	9-15-59	In Service
536	ACHILLES	Newport Tankers Corp.	6-7-60	In Service
537	NATIONAL DEFENDER	National Transport Corp.	10-23-59	In Service
540	ESSO BALTIMORE	Esso Standard Division	7-15-60	In Service
541	ESSO BOSTON	Esso Standard Division	11-22-60	In Service
564	ATLANTIC PRESTIGE	Atlantic Refining Co.	11-27-62	In Service
573	ESSO HOUSTON	Humble Oil & Ref. Co.	12-11-64	In Service
576	ESSO NEW ORLEANS	Humble Oil & Ref. Co.	4-9-65	In Service
608	EL PASO SOUTHERN	El Paso LNG Co.	5-31-78	Laid Up, 1980
609	EL PASO ARZEW	El Paso LNG Co.	12-8-78	Laid Up, 1980
610	EL PASO HOWARD BOYD	El Paso LNG Co.	6-29-79	Laid Up, 1980
613	U.S.T. ATLANTIC	Connecticut National Bank	3-7-79	Laid Up, 1981
614	U.S.T. PACIFIC	Connecticut National Bank	12-7-79	Laid Up, 1981

LUMBER CARRIERS & COLLIERS

HULL	NAME	OWNER	DELIVERED	FATE
43	FRANCIS H. LEGGETT	Hammond Lumber Co.	4-21-03	Foundered, 1914
79	GEORGE W. FENWICK	Hammond Lumber Co.	1-28-08	War Loss, 1942
80	NANN SMITH	C.A. Smith Timber Co.	12-12-07	War Loss, 1917
159	ADELINE SMITH	C.A. Smith Timber Co.	11-27-12	Scrapped, 1949
182	EDWARD PIERCE	Crowell & Thurlow Co.	11-6-14	Scrapped, 1949
189	WALTER D. NOYES	Crowell & Thurlow Co.	7-29-15	Scrapped, 1951
192	STEPHEN R. JONES	Crowell & Thurlow Co.	11-11-15	Stranded, 1942

FERRIES

HULL	NAME	OWNER	DELIVERED	FATE
47	SCRANTON	Hoboken Ferry Co.	1-31-05	Sank, 1968
48	ELMIRA	Hoboken Ferry Co.	2-24-05	Scrapped, 1983
49	BINGHAMTON	Hoboken Ferry Co.	3-25-05	Rest. Boat, 1975
50	SCANDINAVIA	Hoboken Ferry Co.	4-24-05	Scrapped, 1967
62	ITHACA	D.L. & W.R.R. Co.	9-9-06	Burned, 1946

TUGBOATS

HULL	NAME	OWNER	DELIVERED	FATE
1	DOROTHY	James Sheffield	4-30-91	Restored, 1976
2	EL TORO	Pacific Improvement Co.	5-20-91	Scrapped, 1982
12	JOHN H. ESTILL	Savannah Pilots Assn.	11-25-94	Scrapped, 1952
13	ALBERT F. DEWEY	Albert F. Dewey	4-15-95	Unknown
17	SOMMERS N. SMITH	Pilots' Benev. Assn.	9-14-96	Scrapped, 1937
30	EL AMIGO	Southern Pacific Co.	9-9-99	Scrapped, 1950
83	CORNING	D.L. & W.R.R. Co.	3-18-08	Laid Up, 1985
84	BATH	D.L. & W.R.R. Co.	4-9-08	In Service
118	JOHN TWOHY, JR.	Twohy Tow Boat Co.	5-15-09	Scrapped, 1970
294	P.R.R. NO. 18	Pennsylvania R.R. Co.	11-11-25	Scrapped, 1970
295	P.R.R. NO. 26	Pennsylvania R.R. Co.	11-19-25	Sunk, 1982
313	P.R.R. NO. 15	Pennsylvania R.R. Co.	5-30-26	Scrapped, 1972
314	P.R.R. NO. 20	Pennsylvania R.R. Co.	5-30-26	Scrapped, 1976
327	W.J. HARAHAN	Chesapeake & Ohio Ry.	4-26-28	In Service
356	HUNTINGTON	N.N.S. & D.D. Co.	11-18-33	In Service
365	GEORGE W. STEVENS	Chesapeake & Ohio Ry.	10-14-37	In Service
366	F.M. WHITAKER	Chesapeake & Ohio Ry.	10-29-37	In Service
467	R.J. BOWMAN	Chesapeake & Ohio Ry.	7-2-48	Sank, 1981
468	A.T. LOWMASTER	Chesapeake & Ohio Ry.	6-25-48	In Service

YACHTS

HULL	NAME	OWNER	DELIVERED	FATE
263	DOLPHIN	Mortimer L. Schiff	6-2-22	Stranded, 1960
26	OHIO	E.W. Scripps	11-16-22	Stranded, 1953
281	NENEMOOSHA	Alfred I. DuPont	2-15-25	Unknown
293	PAWNEE	Harry P. Bingham	1-15-26	In Service
303	SAVARONA	Richard M. Cadwalader	10-1-26	Sunk, 1968
304	ARCADIA	Galen L. Stone	9-1-26	Scrapped, 1969
305	JOSEPHINE	E.S. Burke, Jr.	6-19-26	Scrapped, 1952
308	ARAS	Hugh J. Chisholm	6-11-26	Sank, 1930
316	ROBADOR	Robert Law, Jr.	8-17-26	Scrapped, 1956
328	VIKING	George F. Baker, Jr.	4-27-29	Collided, 1944

HULL	NAME	OWNER	DELIVERED	FATE

BAY & RIVER STEAMERS

HULL	NAME	OWNER	DELIVERED	FATE
14	NEWPORT NEWS	Norf. & Wash'n. St. Co.	6-15-95	Burned, 1924
20	MARGARET	Plant Investment Co.	10-14-96	Sank, 1924
61	JAMESTOWN	Norf. & Wash'n. St. Co.	6-20-06	Converted, 1930
107	SOUTHLAND	Norf. & Wash'n. St. Co.	2-15-09	Scrapped, 1955
150	CAROLINA	Albemarle St. Nav. Co.	11-4-11	Scrapped, 1974
151	VIRGINIA	Albemarle St. Nav. Co.	11-18-11	Foundered, 1942
325	YORKTOWN	Chesapeake S.S. Co.	5-17-28	War Loss, 1942

DREDGES & A CABLE SHIP

HULL	NAME	OWNER	DELIVERED	FATE
75	CAYO PIEDRA	Amer. Locomotive Co.	4-3-07	Unknown
87	CLATSOP	U.S. War Dept.	9-2-08	Scrapped, 1961
282	NORFOLK	A.G. & P. Co.	6-1-25	Unknown
292	RAYMOND	U.S. War Dept.	9-5-26	Scrapped, 1980
299		R.B. Knox	9-4-25	Unknown
114	JOSEPH HENRY	U.S. War Dept.	3-31-09	Laid Up, 1983

CONVERSIONS & RECONDITIONINGS

HULL	NAME	OWNER	DELIVERED	FATE
172	CAROLINA	N.Y. & Porto Rico Co.	3-1-14	War Loss, 1918
195	STANDARD	Standard Oil of NJ	2-18-86	Scrapped, 1954
264	LEVIATHAN	U.S. Lines	5-16-23	Scrapped, 1938
272	REPUBLIC	U.S. Lines	4-11-24	Scrapped, 1952
322	AMERICA	U.S. Lines	3-3-28	Scrapped, 1957
330	PRESIDENT JOHNSON	Dollar Line	1-19-29	Scrapped, 1952
331	CITY OF ELWOOD	U.S. Shipping Board	6-12-29	Scrapped, 1946
332	WARD	U.S. Shipping Board	8-1-29	Scrapped, 1949
333	PRESIDENT HARRISON	Dollar Line	4-29-29	War Loss, 1944
334	PRESIDENT GARFIELD	Dollar Line	7-13-29	Scrapped, 1948
341	PRESIDENT FILLMORE	Dollar Line	1-11-30	Scrapped, 1947
343	JACONA	New. Eng. Pub. Ser. Co.	11-7-30	In Service
377	URUGUAY	Maritime Commission	9-2-38	Scrapped, 1964
461	AMERICA	Maritime Commission	10-31-46	Laid Up, 1981
462	ARTILLERO	Dodero Navigation	12-16-47	Stranded, 1967
463	CORACERO	Dodero Navigation	1-12-48	Scrapped, 1973
464	LANCERO	Dodero Navigation	2-9-48	Scrapped, 1973
465	CORRIENTES	Rio De La Plata, S.A.	1-19-49	Scrapped, 1964
466	GENERAL S.B. BUCKNER	U.S. Army	2-12-48	Laid Up, 1970
469	GENERAL E.D. PATRICK	U.S. Army	4-29-48	Laid Up, 1968
470	GENERAL D.I. SULTAN	U.S. Army	6-24-48	Laid Up, 1968
471	GENERAL H.J. GAFFEY	U.S. Army	8-19-48	Barracks, 1978
472	SALTA	Rio De La Plata, S.A.	4-4-49	Scrapped, 1966
473	GENERAL W.O. DARBY	U.S. Army	10-14-48	Barracks, 1981
474	CARPENTER	USN DDK-825	12-15-49	In Commission
487	ANKARA	Turkish Govt.	4-12-49	Scrapped, 1981
489	LAKE CHAMPLAIN	USN CV-39	9-19-52	Scrapped, 1972
505	RANDOLPH	USN CV-15	7-1-53	Scrapped, 1975
507	INTREPID	USN CV-11	6-18-54	Museum, 1982
518	JOHN SERGEANT	Maritime Administration	9-26-56	Scrapped, 1974
523	MATSONIA	Matson Navigation Co.	5-10-57	In Service

AIRCRAFT CARRIERS

HULL	NAME	OWNER	DELIVERED	FATE
353	RANGER	USN CV-4	6-4-34	Scrapped, 1947
359	YORKTOWN	USN CV-5	9-30-37	War Loss, 1942
360	ENTERPRISE	USN CV-6	5-12-38	Scrapped, 1958
385	HORNET	USN CV-8	10-20-41	War Loss, 1942
392	ESSEX	USN CV-9	12-31-42	Scrapped, 1975
393	YORKTOWN	USN CV-10	4-15-43	Museum, 1975
394	INTREPID	USN CV-11	8-16-43	Museum, 1982
395	HORNET	USN CV-12	11-29-43	Laid Up, 1970
396	FRANKLIN	USN CV-13	1-31-44	Scrapped, 1966
397	TICONDEROGA	USN CV-14	5-8-44	Scrapped, 1974
398	RANDOLPH	USN CV-15	10-9-44	Scrapped, 1975
410	BOXER	USN CV-21	4-16-45	Scrapped, 1971
439	MIDWAY	USN CVB-41	9-10-45	In Commission
440	CORAL SEA	USN CVB-43	10-1-47	In Commission
446	LEYTE	USN CV-32	4-11-46	Scrapped, 1971
506	FORRESTAL	USN CVA-59	10-1-55	In Commission
514	RANGER	USN CVA-61	8-10-57	In Commission
546	ENTERPRISE	USN CVAN-65	11-25-61	In Commission
561	AMERICA	USN CVA-66	1-23-65	In Commission
577	JOHN F. KENNEDY	USN CVA-67	9-7-68	In Commission

HULL	NAME	OWNER	COMMISSIONED	FATE
594	NIMITZ	USN CVAN-68	5-3-75	In Commission
599	DWIGHT D. EISENHOWER	USN CVN-69	10-18-77	In Commission
611	CARL VINSON	USN CVN-70	3-13-82	In Commission
624	THEODORE ROOSEVELT	USN CVN-71	Fall-86	Under Construction
630	ABRAHAM LINCOLN	USN CVN-72	12- -89	Under Construction
631	GEORGE WASHINGTON	USN CVN-73	12- -91	Under Construction

BATTLESHIPS

HULL	NAME	OWNER	COMMISSIONED	FATE
18	KEARSARGE	USN BB-5	2-20-00	Scrapped, 1955
19	KENTUCKY	USN BB-6	5-15-00	Scrapped, 1924
21	ILLINOIS	USN BB-7	9-16-01	Scrapped, 1956
25	MISSOURI	USN BB-11	12-1-03	Scrapped, 1922
40	VIRGINIA	USN BB-13	5-7-06	Sunk, 1923
45	LOUISIANA	USN BB-19	6-2-06	Scrapped, 1923
46	MINNESOTA	USN BB-22	3-9-07	Scrapped, 1924
86	DELAWARE	USN BB-26	4-4-10	Scrapped, 1924
147	TEXAS	USN BB-35	3-12-14	Memorial, 1948
171	PENNSYLVANIA	USN BB-38	6-12-16	Sunk, 1948
185	MISSISSIPPI	USN BB-41	12-18-17	Scrapped, 1956
210	MARYLAND	USN BB-46	7-21-21	Scrapped, 1959
211	WEST VIRGINIA	USN BB-48	12-1-23	Scrapped, 1959
378	INDIANA	USN BB-58	4-30-42	Scrapped, 1962

CRUISERS

HULL	NAME	OWNER	COMMISSIONED	FATE
38	WEST VIRGINIA	USN ACR-5	2-23-05	Scrapped, 1930
39	MARYLAND	USN ACR-8	4-18-05	Scrapped, 1930
41	CHARLESTON	USN C-22	10-17-05	Scrapped, 1930
57	NORTH CAROLINA	USN ACR-12	5-7-08	Scrapped, 1930
58	MONTANA	USN ACR-13	7-21-08	Scrapped, 1935
323	HOUSTON	USN CA-30	6-17-30	War Loss, 1942
324	AUGUSTA	USN CA-31	1-30-31	Scrapped, 1959
361	BOISE	USN CL-47	8-12-38	Scrapped, 1981
362	ST. LOUIS	USN CL-49	5-19-39	Sank, 1980
390	BIRMINGHAM	USN CL-62	1-29-43	Scrapped, 1959
391	MOBILE	USN CL-63	3-24-43	Scrapped, 1960
399	BILOXI	USN CL-80	8-31-43	Scrapped, 1961
400	HOUSTON	USN CL-81	12-20-43	Scrapped, 1959
408	AMSTERDAM	USN CL-101	1-8-45	Scrapped, 1971
409	PORTSMOUTH	USN CL-102	6-25-45	Scrapped, 1971
411	VICKSBURG	USN CL-86	6-12-44	Scrapped, 1964
412	DULUTH	USN CL-87	9-18-44	Scrapped, 1960
456	NEWPORT NEWS	USN CA-148	1-29-49	Stricken, 1978
595	CALIFORNIA	USN DLGN-36	2-16-74	In Commission
596	SOUTH CAROLINA	USN DLGN-37	1-25-75	In Commission
601	VIRGINIA	USN CGN-38	9-11-76	In Commission
606	TEXAS	USN CGN-39	9-10-77	In Commission
607	MISSISSIPPI	USN CGN-40	8-5-78	In Commission
612	ARKANSAS	USN CGN-41	10-18-80	In Commission

SUBMARINES

HULL	NAME	OWNER	COMMISSIONED	FATE
51		Lake Torpedo	10-17-04	Stricken, 1913
52		Lake Torpedo	10-17-04	Stricken, 1913
53	SIMON LAKE X	Lake Torpedo	2-23-05	Stricken, 1913
54		Lake Torpedo	1-2-05	Stricken, 1913
55		Lake Torpedo	1-2-05	Stricken, 1913
56	LAKE	Lake Torpedo	6-25-06	Stricken, 1913
119	SEAL	Lake Torpedo	7-29-11	Sunk, 1921
120	TUNA	Lake Torpedo	5-15-12	Sank, 1919
545	SHARK	USN SSN-591	2-9-61	In Commission
547	ROBERT E. LEE	USN SSBN-601	9-16-60	Laid Up, 1983
548	SAM HOUSTON	USN SSBN-609	3-6-62	In Commission
549	JOHN MARSHALL	USN SSBN-611	5-21-62	In Commission
555	THOMAS JEFFERSON	USN SSBN-618	1-4-63	Laid Up, 1985
562	JAMES MONROE	USN SSBN-622	12-7-63	In Commission
563	HENRY CLAY	USN SSBN-625	2-20-64	In Commission
565	JAMES MADISON	USN SSBN-627	7-28-64	In Commission
566	JOHN C. CALHOUN	USN SSBN-630	9-15-64	In Commission
567	VON STEUBEN	USN SSBN-632	9-30-64	In Commission
568	SAM RAYBURN	USN SSBN-635	12-2-64	In Commission
569	SIMON BOLIVAR	USN SSBN-641	10-29-65	In Commission
570	LEWIS AND CLARK	USN SSBN-644	12-22-65	In Commission
571	QUEENFISH	USN SSN-651	12-6-66	In Commission

HULL	NAME	OWNER	COMMISSIONED	FATE
572	RAY	USN SSN-653	4-12-67	In Commission
574	GEORGE C. MARSHALL	USN SSBN-654	4-29-66	In Commission
575	GEORGE WASHINGTON CARVER	USN SSBN-656	6-15-66	In Commission
578	LAPON	USN SSN-661	12-14-67	In Commission
579	HAMMERHEAD	USN SSN-663	6-28-68	In Commission
580	SEA DEVIL	USN SSN-664	1-30-69	In Commission
581	SPADEFISH	USN SSN-668	8-14-69	In Commission
582	FINBACK	USN SSN-670	2-4-70	In Commission
597	L. MENDEL RIVERS	USN SSN-686	2-1-75	In Commission
598	RICHARD B. RUSSELL	USN SSN-687	8-16-75	In Commission
600	LOS ANGELES	USN SSN-688	11-13-76	In Commission
602	BATON ROUGE	USN SSN-689	6-25-77	In Commission
603	MEMPHIS	USN SSN-691	12-17-77	In Commission
604	CINCINNATI	USN SSN-693	5-26-78	In Commission
605	BIRMINGHAM	USN SSN-695	12-16-78	In Commission
616	SAN FRANCISCO	USN SSN-711	4-24-81	In Commission
617	ATLANTA	USN SSN-712	3-6-82	In Commission
618	HOUSTON	USN SSN-713	9-25-82	In Commission
619	NORFOLK	USN SSN-714	5-21-83	In Commission
620	BUFFALO	USN SSN-715	11-5-83	In Commission
621	SALT LAKE CITY	USN SSN-716	5-12-84	In Commission
622	OLYMPIA	USN SSN-717	11-17-84	In Commission
623	HONOLULU	USN SSN-718	7-6-85	In Commission
625	CHICAGO	USN SSN-721	-86	Under Construction
626	KEY WEST	USN SSN-722	-86	Under Construction
627	OKLAHOMA CITY	USN SSN-723	-87	Under Construction
628	NEWPORT NEWS	USN SSN-750	-87	Under Construction
629		USN SSN-753	-88	Under Construction
632		USN SSN-756	-89	Under Construction
633		USN SSN-758	-89	Under Construction
634		USN SSN-759	-90	Under Construction
635		USN SSN-760		Under Construction

DESTROYERS

HULL	NAME	OWNER	COMMISSIONED	FATE
115	ROE	USN DD-24	9-17-10	Scrapped, 1934
116	TERRY	USN DD-25	10-18-10	Scrapped, 1934
134	MONAGHAN	USN DD-32	6-21-11	Scrapped, 1934
144	FANNING	USN DD-37	6-21-12	Scrapped, 1934
217	LAMBERTON	USN DD-119	8-22-18	Scrapped, 1947
218	RADFORD	USN DD-120	9-30-18	Sunk, 1936
219	MONTGOMERY	USN DD-121	7-26-18	Scrapped, 1946
220	BREESE	USN DD-122	10-23-18	Scrapped, 1946
221	GAMBLE	USN DD-123	11-29-18	War Loss, 1945
222	RAMSAY	USN DD-124	2-15-19	Scrapped, 1946
223	HOPEWELL	USN DD-181	3-22-19	War Loss, 1941
224	THOMAS	USN DD-182	4-25-19	Scrapped, 1949
225	HARADEN	USN DD-183	6-7-19	Scrapped, 1945
226	ABBOT	USN DD-184	7-19-19	Scrapped, 1945
227	BAGLEY	USN DD-185	8-27-19	Scrapped, 1945
228	CLEMSON	USN DD-186	12-29-19	Scrapped, 1946
229	DAHLGREN	USN DD-187	1-6-20	Scrapped, 1946
230	GOLDSBOROUGH	USN DD-188	1-26-20	Scrapped, 1946
231	SEMMES	USN DD-189	2-21-20	Scrapped, 1947
232	SATTERLEE	USN DD-190	12-23-19	War Loss, 1942
233	MASON	USN DD-191	2-28-20	War Loss, 1941
234	GRAHAM	USN DD-192	3-13-20	Scrapped, 1922
235	ABEL P. UPSHUR	USN DD-193	11-23-20	Scrapped, 1945
236	HUNT	USN DD-194	9-30-20	Scrapped, 1945
237	WELBORN C. WOOD	USN DD-195	1-14-21	Scrapped, 1947
238	GEORGE E. BADGER	USN DD-196	7-28-20	Scrapped, 1946
239	BRANCH	USN DD-197	7-26-20	War Loss, 1943
240	HERNDON	USN DD-198	9-14-20	War Loss, 1945
241	DALLAS	USN DD-199	10-29-20	Scrapped, 1945
363	MUSTIN	USN DD-413	9-15-39	Sunk, 1948
364	RUSSELL	USN DD-414	11-3-39	Scrapped, 1947

GUNBOATS & A MONITOR

HULL	NAME	OWNER	COMMISSIONED	FATE
7	NASHVILLE	USN PG-7	8-19-97	Scrapped, 1957
8	WILMINGTON	USN PG-8	5-13-97	Sunk, 1947
9	HELENA	USN PG-9	7-8-97	Scrapped, 1934
26	ARKANSAS	USN BM-7	10-28-02	Scrapped, 1922

HULL	NAME	OWNER	DELIVERED	FATE

AMPHIBIOUS SHIPS

HULL	NAME	OWNER	DELIVERED	FATE
401	EASTWAY	USN LSD-9	9-14-43	Scrapped, 1972
402	HIGHWAY	USN LSD-10	10-19-43	Scrapped, 1960
403	NORTHWAY	USN LSD-11	2-15-44	Scrapped, 1975
404	OCEANWAY	USN LSD-12	3-29-44	Sunk, 1969
405	CASA GRANDE	USN LSD-13	6-5-44	Laid Up, 1970
406	RUSHMORE	USN LSD-14	7-3-44	Laid Up, 1971
407	SHADWELL	USN LSD-15	7-24-44	Test Ship, 1985
448	CABILDO	USN LSD-16	3-15-45	Sunk, 1984
449	CATAMOUNT	USN LSD-17	4-9-45	Scrapped, 1983
450	COLONIAL	USN LSD-18	5-15-45	Laid Up, 1970
451	COMSTOCK	USN LSD-19	7-2-45	Scrapped, 1985
413	LST-383	USN	10-27-42	Scrapped, 1951
414	LST-384	USN	11-2-42	Scrapped, 1948
415	LST-385	USN	11-6-42	Unknown
416	LST-386	USN	11-10-42	Scrapped, 1950
417	LST-387	USN	11-17-42	Scrapped, 1947
418	LST-388	USN	11-20-42	Scrapped, 1948
419	LST-389	USN	11-24-42	In Commission
420	LST-390	USN	11-28-42	Scrapped, 1948
421	LST-391	USN	12-3-42	In Commission
422	LST-392	USN	12-7-42	Scrapped, 1947
423	LST-393	USN	12-11-42	Laid Up, 1976
424	LST-394	USN	12-15-42	Scrapped, 1947
425	LST-395	USN	12-19-42	Scrapped, 1947
426	LST-396	USN	12-23-42	War Loss, 1943
427	LST-397	USN	12-28-42	Scrapped, 1947
428	LST-398	USN	1-2-43	Scrapped, 1948
429	LST-399	USN	1-4-43	In Service
430	LST-400	USN	1-7-43	In Commission
516	YORK COUNTY	USN LST-1175	11-8-57	In Commission
517	GRAHAM COUNTY	USN LST-1176	4-17-58	Scrapped, 1977
583	CHARLESTON	USN LKA-113	12-14-68	In Commission
584	DURHAM	USN LKA-114	5-24-69	In Commission
585	MOBILE	USN LKA-115	9-20-69	In Commission
586	ST. LOUIS	USN LKA-116	11-22-69	In Commission
591	EL PASO	USN LKA-117	1-17-70	In Commission
592	MOUNT WHITNEY	USN LCC-20	11-16-71	In Commission

AUXILIARY SHIPS

HULL	NAME	OWNER	DELIVERED	FATE
154	PROTEUS	USN AC-9	7-9-13	War Loss, 1941
155	NEREUS	USN AC-10	9-10-13	War Loss, 1941
550	HUNLEY	USN AS-31	6-16-62	In Commission

COAST GUARD CUTTERS

HULL	NAME	OWNER	DELIVERED	FATE
85	SENECA	U.S. Coast Guard No. 17	11-6-08	Scrapped, 1950
88	ACUSHNET	U.S. Coast Guard No. 18	11-6-08	Scrapped, 1946
152	MIAMI	U.S. Coast Guard	8-19-12	War Loss, 1918
153	UNALGA	U.S. Coast Guard	5-23-12	Scrapped, 1946
183	OSSIPEE	U.S. Coast Guard	7-28-15	Scrapped, 1948
184	TALLAPOOSA	U.S. Coast Guard WPG-52	8-12-15	In Service
318	NORTHLAND	U.S. Coast Guard WPG-49	5-7-27	Scrapped, 1962

SHIP NAME INDEX